THE ORIGINS OF *BEOWULF*

The Origins of *Beowulf*

From Vergil to Wiglaf

RICHARD NORTH

OXFORD
UNIVERSITY PRESS

OXFORD

UNIVERSITY PRESS

Great Clarendon Street, Oxford OX2 6DP

Oxford University Press is a department of the University of Oxford.
It furthers the University's objective of excellence in research, scholarship,
and education by publishing worldwide in

Oxford New York

Auckland Cape Town Dar es Salaam Hong Kong Karachi
Kuala Lumpur Madrid Melbourne Mexico City Nairobi
New Delhi Shanghai Taipei Toronto

With offices in

Argentina Austria Brazil Chile Czech Republic France Greece
Guatemala Hungary Italy Japan Poland Portugal Singapore
South Korea Switzerland Thailand Turkey Ukraine Vietnam

Oxford is a registered trade mark of Oxford University Press
in the UK and in certain other countries

Published in the United States
by Oxford University Press Inc., New York

British Library Cataloguing in Publication Data

Data available

Library of Congress Cataloging in Publication Data

Data available

Typeset by SPI Publisher Services, Pondicherry, India.
Printed in Great Britain
on acid-free paper by
Biddles Ltd., King's Lynn, Norfolk

ISBN 978–0–19–920661–2

1 3 5 7 9 10 8 6 4 2

For Miriam and Alexander
and in memory of
Patrick Wormald

Preface

> The Kingdom of God is to be sought above all earthly gains, for Paul the
> Apostle is witness that 'what is seen is transient, but what is not seen lives for
> ever'. What does it serve a man to gain the whole world if his soul should
> suffer harm?
>
> Wiglaf, king of Mercia, 836

This book suggests that *Beowulf* was composed in the winter of 826–7 by
Eanmund, abbot of the minster of Breedon on the Hill in north-west Leicestershire, not only as a requiem for King Beornwulf of Mercia who was killed in
battle earlier that year, but also as a work of recommendation for Wiglaf, an
ealdorman who was plotting to succeed him.

If I sketch out my view of how *Beowulf* was composed, the story goes
something like this. The poet had seen a few changes by the time he wrote
Beowulf. Forty years earlier, when he was a child, his country was rising, jubilant
under King Offa (757–96), but there was a purge of princes in Offa's last years.
After the heady days of having Cenwulf as a new king (796–821), Mercia fell into
such wrangling and torpor that under King Beornwulf (823–6) she slid into
economic decline. In 826 memories of Offa were positive, despite his murder of
the king of East Anglia more than thirty years earlier; those of Cenwulf were
bitter, because he and his family robbed the Church of land; on Beornwulf's
death in East Anglia, few Mercians had any hope for the future unless this was in
the West Saxons ruling for them. In Mercia the true line of kings was broken.

The good news in 826 was that the Franks had baptized the king of Denmark.
Here at last was a chance of the Danes staying at home, rather than coming here
to sack one minster after another. Not that Breedon had missed (or would miss)
the Vikings. In 809 an early band of them sold an important captive there, a
papal envoy, back to the king of Northumbria. Hosting the deal was the abbot,
Wigmund (*c*.792–814 × 816). Both Priest Abbot Wigmund and the monk
Eanmund had grown up with verse on Danish kings. Back in the days of
Unwona, bishop of Leicester (*c*.785–*c*.800), Wigmund had heard the performance of a great poem on Ingeld, king of the Heathobards, and his wedding to a
Danish princess in Norway. There had been complaints, but if Ingeld was a
damned heathen, still he was the ancestor of Ealdorman Æthelmund of the
Hwicce. Wigmund passed the poem on to Eanmund. When Wigmund died, the
monks elected Eanmund to the abbacy (814 × 816–848), although he had gone
further with heathens than Unwona ever did: at the meeting of 809, Eanmund
had questioned the Danes about their gods; and in 826, when the news arrived
confirming the baptism, Eanmund hoped that more heathens could be saved.

Like most of the clergy about him, however, he doubted King Beornwulf could be, for he had coveted earthly more than heavenly rewards.

That summer, after Beornwulf's death, Mercia lay open to infighting and attack. With Ludeca, Beornwulf's cousin, holding power (826–7), Eanmund put his hopes in the old abbot's nephew. Ealdorman Wiglaf was close to their community. Indeed he named his son after Wigmund when he died. To win support in the south-west he had recently married the boy to Cenwulf's niece. But Wiglaf was a stranger there, he would still have to persuade Beornwulf's people that he and not Ludeca was the dead king's choice to succeed. That would be hard for neither Cenwulf nor Beornwulf had honoured Wiglaf's family. Nonetheless, Wiglaf came to Eanmund before the summer was out. Could he compose a memorial to Beornwulf, one to herald Wiglaf as his long-lost kinsman and heir? Something in the style of old Wigmund's lays. Could Eanmund use one of these to mourn Beornwulf as a king of old? Yet also to tell the Mercians that it was Wiglaf who had the blood to succeed him.

Eanmund took up an old theme about King Hrothulf's bearlike champion, changing it so as to let the monster-slayer become a king. 'Beowulf' had to be royal by the time he went to Sweden to help King Eadgils in battle against Onela, otherwise the poem would fail. This meant forgetting Beowulf's service with King Hrothulf; better, it meant bringing him to Denmark earlier, in the days of King Hrothgar. How else to raise Beowulf to his own kingship, if not by measuring him against Ingeld, Hrothgar's son-in-law? It was a rivalry he could base on a big one in the *Aeneid*. King Hrothgar he would model on Wulfred, the old archbishop who had been Cenwulf's enemy and was now Wiglaf's friend. He put Beowulf in a royal family, one he made up for Hygelac in Geatland.

With his triumphant return from Denmark begins Beowulf's own political career. So, too, the royal allegory leading into Wiglaf's hoped-for reign: first Offa of Angeln, then Hygelac, then Beowulf, then Wiglaf. King Offa had always been linked with his namesake. Few, therefore, would fail to grasp the manner in which Eanmund made Hygelac match the asset-stripping Cenwulf point for point. In due course after Hygelac's sudden death, as after Cenwulf's, the kingdom would pass to Beowulf. The poet could then retell the battle against Onela with Eadgils as a renegade and Beowulf as his backer. Later King Beowulf would have to die far away from Hrothulf. The East Anglian disaster was still too fresh for Beowulf to be seen dying in battle with his army. Yet what of the drab cause, Beornwulf's need of money? Eanmund gave Beowulf Sigemund's part with the dragon along with the cursed hoard. He would let this gold give Beowulf his choice for heaven or hell.

By now the abbot's friends were asking for Beowulf's young comrade, so far missing. Enter a son of Weohstan, the Swedish prince from whom the old abbot used to claim descent. He should have Wiglaf's name and a blood tie to Beowulf. The name of their family would also remind Mercians of young Wigmund and his claim to rule. With Beowulf dead, Wiglaf would arrange for the funeral, deliver an epitaph of unwitting Christian efficacy, then disappear, perhaps to Britain. For the Geats Wiglaf is a lost opportunity; for the Mercians, a new king. And the poet? Everyone would hear that Eanmund's poem, like his sword, was at Wiglaf's service.

Everything in this sketch is in some way argued below. Of course, not all of it can be true and I know that some will continue to treat this story as a fantasy even after finishing my book. It would be a shame, however, if such readers did not offer a case for *Beowulf*'s origins that works better than mine. I would welcome this development as constructive. The problem is that little can be proved in Anglo-Saxon literature or history. Consequently I must build my case on a few facts and a string of incremental suppositions. Although I am hardly alone in the need to trust likelihood rather than fact, I invite serious critics to turn their attention to the premiss which grounds one sequence in another, Beowulf–Wiglaf in Beornwulf–Wiglaf; then to the correlations that follow: between the murder of a suitor by 'Thryth' and Cynethryth's alleged martyrdom of St Æthelberht of East Anglia; between the Offas; and between nine motifs to do with Hygelac and Beowulf and nine episodes in the reigns of Cenwulf and Beornwulf in Mercian history. Here are some twelve parallels which must be explained as coincidences if my case is to fail. That may happen, for coincidences are not unknown in Anglo-Saxon studies. One case in point is two abbots named Eanmund of Bre(e)don. Another thing worth noting here, however, is my integration of the passage on Offa into *Beowulf*'s main purpose, for I argue that the poet presents Offa as the first in a line of three, soon to be four, great Mercian kings. Offa is the signal for his allegory to start. I also give reasons to believe that the poet innovated with each treatise, poem, legend, or myth which he took as his source. Essential to my case is his style, not only the eclectic reading, baroque creativity, and flashes of brilliant sardonic humour, but also the gathering gloom of his concentration on Beowulf's soul. My aim is not to record these and other elements for themselves, but to use them to find out when, how, where, and by whom the poem was composed.

In the writing of this book I owe debts of various sorts to many people over a period of twenty years. First and foremost, I talked about *Beowulf* with Patrick Wormald off and on for ten years on a few all too brief occasions before his death. His gentle advocacy of the Beornwulf–Wiglaf premiss decided the course of my book. Further back, I owe longer-standing debts to teachers, fellow students, friends, and colleagues. Ursula Dronke taught me that the poet could innovate; Ray Page, to study the cruces. Michael Lapidge introduced me to Donald Bullough's article on Ingeld and both he and Andy Orchard straightened me out in other ways. Orchard's great knowledge of *Beowulf* led me down many productive avenues of research. Each in his own field, James Graham-Campbell, Éamonn Ó Carragáin, and Alan Thacker pointed me in what I believe to be the right direction. I am grateful to my student Dong-Ill Lee for illuminating to me Beowulf's youth and sense of honour; to Rolf Bremmer, Sally Burch, David

Dumville, John Hines, Nick Howe, and Bryan Wyly, for their wise words here and there; and to Simon Keynes for sending me materials including a copy of his Brixworth lecture on the Councils of *Clofesho*. My thanks go also to Heather O'Donoghue, Jane Roberts, Clive Tolley, and Susan Irvine, who, when the project got going, read drafts of various chapters and offered much useful advice. Other friends and colleagues, also in University College London, including Timothy McFarland, Henry Woudhuysen, Paul Davis, and the librarian John Allen, helped me out in other ways. I am grateful to my wife, Inma Ridao, and to my children, for putting up with this and to my parents John and Marion North, for helping me with the maps and giving more general support. I could never have finished this without Andrew McNeillie and Tom Perridge, from Oxford University Press. For his warm welcome and their help with the cover photograph I wish to thank the Reverend John Dawson of St Mary's and St Hardulph's at Breedon on the Hill, and Mr Glyn Barnett of the same parish. I am also grateful to Richard Jewell for a copy of his 1986 article and permission to use one of his drawings and I acknowledge the Conway Library, Courtauld Institute, for the use of three photographs. Last but not least, I am indebted to the libraries of Bloomsbury, particularly to the staff of the Institute for Historical Research in Senate House, London, for providing—so may they always—a true haven of scholarship and research.

R. N.

Contents

List of Illustrations   xiii
List of Figures   xiv
Abbreviations   xv

1. Introduction: Beowulf and Wiglaf   1
2. Dynastic Innovation in *Beowulf*   36
3. Vergil and the Monastery in *Beowulf*   66
4. Ingeld's Rival: Beowulf and Aeneas   100
5. 'Quid Hinieldus?' Bishop Unwona and Friends   132
6. *Beowulf* and the Library at Breedon on the Hill   157
7. The King's Soul: Danish Mythology in *Beowulf*   194
8. 'Thryth' and the Reign of Offa   225
9. Hygelac and Beowulf: Cenwulf and Beornwulf   254
10. King Wiglaf and *Eanmundes laf*   297

Bibliography   333
Index   347

List of Illustrations

1. Mercia in the eighth and early ninth centuries — 149

2. East Mercia and north Francia in the eighth and early ninth centuries — 158

3. Reconstruction of the broad friezes in Breedon (after R. H. I. Jewell) — 162

4. Relief panel (St Mary), Breedon on the Hill. The Conway Library, Courtauld Institute of Art — 179

5. Relief panel (Angel: St Michael?), Breedon on the Hill. The Conway Library, Courtauld Institute of Art — 189

6. Relief panel (St Michael), Fletton. The Conway Library, Courtauld Institute of Art — 190

List of Figures

1. Progress of Bishop Unwona (785–*c*.800)   140
2. Unwona's priest abbots (*c*.792–803)   145
3. Wigmund, his successor, and their minster (803–823)   152
4. Hierarchy of Breedon and Bredon (816–836)   153
5. Kindred of Priest Abbot Wigmund (in *c*.792–803)   244
6. Elevation of Beornnoth (798–808)   259
7. Cenwulf's crisis: the emergence of Beornwulf (809–816)   269
8. Elevation of Beornwulf (816–825)   279
9. Wiglaf's kindred takes power (825–848)   303
10. A life in politics: Abbot Eanmund of Breedon (814–848)   325

Abbreviations

ab	archbishop
ABäG	*Amsterdamer Beiträge zur älteren Germanistik*
Abn	Abingdon
Aen.	*Aeneid*
Akv	*Atlakviða*
ANQ	*American Notes and Queries*
Archiv	*Archiv für das Studium der neueren Sprachen und Literaturen*
ASC	*The Anglo-Saxon Chronicle*
A	ed. Bately
C	ed. O'Brien O'Keeffe
D	ed. Cubbin
ASE	*Anglo-Saxon England*
BCS	Birch, *Cartularium Saxonicum*
ben	beneficiary
Beo	*Beowulf*
BGdSL	*Beiträge zur Geschichte der deutschen Sprache und Literatur*
bp	bishop
C	AM 748 II 4to (Stofnun Arna Magnússonar, Reykjavík)
CCC	Christ Church, Canterbury
CCSL	Corpus Christianorum Series Latina
chc	church council
Chel	Chelsea
Clof	*Clofesho*
Croy	Croydon
CSASE	Cambridge Studies in Anglo-Saxon England
Dan	Danish
DB	The Domesday Book
Dream	*The Dream of the Rood*
EA-SE	*Encyclopedia of Anglo-Saxon England*, ed. Lapidge *et al.*
Eccles.	Ecclesiastes

EETS	Early English Text Society
EHD	*English Historical Documents*, ed. Whitelock
EHR	*English Historical Review*
el	*electus*
El	*Elene*
EME	*Early Medieval Europe*
ep	*episcopus*
EPNS	English Place-Name Society
ES	*English Studies*
EStn	*Englische Studien*
Flat	*Flateyjarbók*, ed. Unger; cited by volume and page number
f.r.	*filius regis* ('king's son')
Gen.	Genesis
Gen	*Genesis* (A, B)
Glast	Glastonbury
Got	Gothic
Grím	*Grímnismál*
Guth	*Guthlac*
Gylf	*Gylfaginning*, ed. Faulkes
Hamð	*Hamðismál*
HE	Bede's *Historia ecclesiastica gentis Anglorum*
HHund	*Helgakviða Hundingsbana* (I, II)
HSJ	*Haskins Society Journal*
Hym	*Hymiskviða*
Hynd	*Hyndluljóð*
ÍF	Íslenzk Fornrit
JEGP	*Journal of English and Germanic Philology*
Lat	Latin
Ldn	London
LSE	*Leeds Studies in English*
Macc.	Maccabees
Maldon	*The Battle of Maldon*
Malm	Malmesbury

ME	Middle English
MGH	Monumenta Germaniae Historica
Antiq.	Antiquitates
Auct. Antiq.	Auctores Antiquissimi
SRG	Scriptores Rerum Germanicarum
SRLI	Scriptores Rerum Langobardicarum et Italicarum, Saeculorum VI–IX
SRM	Scriptores Rerum Merovingicarum
SS	Scriptores
MLQ	*Modern Language Quarterly*
MLR	*Modern Language Review*
Neophil	*Neophilologus*
NS	New Series
OE	Old English
OIce	Old Icelandic
OS	Ordnance Survey
os	old series
p'	*p[?-incerna]* ('servant')
pat	*patricius*
pb	*presbyter*
PBA	*Proceedings of the British Academy*
Pet	Peterborough
pin	*pincerna* ('servant')
PL	Patrologia Latina
PL	*Paradise Lost*
PMLA	*Proceedings of the Modern Language Association*
pre	*prefectus*
pri	*princeps*
R	GkS 2367 4to (Stofnun Arna Magnússonar, Reykjavík)
Rept	Repton
RES	*Review of English Studies*
Roch	Rochester
S	Sawyer
s.a.	*sub anno*
Saga-Book	*Saga-Book of the Viking Society* (formerly *Club*)
Skj	*Den norsk-islandske Skjaldedigtning*, ed. Finnur Jónsson
SP	*Studies in Philology*

ss	supplementary series
StAC	St Augustine's, Canterbury
StAlb	St Albans
T	University Library Utrecht MS No. 1374
Tam	Tamworth
TOE	*A Microfiche Concordance to Old English*, ed. Venezky
TRHS	*Transactions of the Royal Historical Society*
U	University Library Uppsala DG 11
Vaf	*Vafþrúðnismál*
Vsp	*Vǫluspá*
Wald	*Waldhere* (I, II)
Wan	*The Wanderer*
Werb.wic	*Werburgingwic*
Wid	*Widsith*
Win	Winchester
Winch	Winchcombe
Wor	Worcester
WS	West Saxon

1

Introduction: Beowulf and Wiglaf

A young man towards the end of *Beowulf*, Wiglaf, helps King Beowulf slay a dragon, stays near him until he dies, and delivers his epitaph to the Geats. In Anglo-Saxon history, an ealdorman named Wiglaf became king of Mercia in 827 about a year after King Beornwulf was killed in battle in East Anglia. This book will see how far Beornwulf goes with *Beowulf*, the king with the poem. I shall try out an old hypothesis which holds that Wiglaf of Mercia not only commissioned this poem as Beornwulf's allegorical requiem, but presented himself as the dead king's successor. To this end, as the self-styled offshoot of Swedish kings, Wiglaf would have had himself cast as his ancestor. By themselves, the names 'Beornwulf' and 'Wiglaf' and the sequence of these kings in almost contiguous reigns (823–6 and 827–39) have long begged the question of a link with the like-named heroes of *Beowulf*. Is this likeness coincidence or design? Whichever it is, the case for Wiglaf's patronage has barely begun. Theories about *Beowulf*'s origins, with a few exceptions, have housed the poem variously in Northumbria or Wessex or East Anglia in the early eighth century, in Offa's reign in Mercia in the late eighth century (757–96), Æthelstan's in Wessex in the tenth (924–39), or Cnut's in the eleventh (1016–35). This book speaks for an origin in Mercia in the first third of the ninth century. The premiss is that the sequence Beowulf–Wiglaf in *Beowulf* reflects one between Kings Beornwulf and Wiglaf of Mercia.

PROBLEM AND METHOD

Before he joins battle in aid of Beowulf, Wiglaf is introduced towards the end of Fitt (section) XXXV of *Beowulf* and named on line 2602 at the head of Fitt XXXVI. After Beowulf, hero of this poem, Wiglaf stands in the foreground for longer than anyone else except perhaps King Hrothgar of the Danes. His entry into *Beowulf* is formalized: the poet gives him a lineage on both sides, implicating him in Beowulf's family before we know his name (lines 2600–1). Later he is called Beowulf's *mæg* ('kinsman', line 2675) and both are said to be 'Wægmundings' (lines 2813–14). He is placed at the head of each of the next four fitts in this poem (XXXVII–XL); and he orders Beowulf's obsequies, delivering his epitaph before the funeral takes place (lines 3077–109, 3114–25). Altogether Wiglaf shares the limelight with Beowulf for the last 580 lines of *Beowulf*, a fifth of the poem.

The problems with Wiglaf are both literary and historical. For a start, there is no longer the interest in *Beowulf*'s Scandinavian analogues, or even a knowledge of how to read them, with which to see how far, if at all, the poet changed his legend about Beowulf in order to introduce Wiglaf towards the end of the hero's life. In any case the reigns of Beornwulf and Wiglaf are among the most obscure in Anglo-Saxon history. The scant knowledge of this period reflects Mercia's decline and the beginning of the Viking Age in the mid- to late ninth century. Both George Bond, then after him Patrick Wormald, suggested on the strength of these names that *Beowulf* was composed at a time in the ninth century in the era of Beornwulf and Wiglaf.[1] Yet their idea won no followers in the Toronto symposium of 1980, the last major forum devoted exclusively to the dating of *Beowulf*. Here Beornwulf was cited only in passing in the opening survey of critical heritage.[2] Later Sam Newton aimed to dispose of the Beornwulf–Wiglaf sequence by suggesting that it was *Beowulf* that inspired these royal Mercian names, whilst he argued that the poem came from East Anglia in the early eighth century.[3] Otherwise it is perhaps due to a broader distaste for allegorical approaches to *Beowulf* that Kings Beornwulf and Wiglaf have been left to one side.

My book is going to leave no stone for either of these men unturned. The method is literary-historical, one which proceeds outwards from the *Beowulf*-text into comparisons with literary, historical, or archaeological record. The present chapter continues with a summary of what is known about the poem's manuscript, dialect, and metre: one which attempts to show that *Beowulf* survives in a late copy whose West Saxon standard obscures its earlier status as a metrically disciplined Mercian work. I also lay the foundations for the arguments of my later chapters which concern Vergil and the use of Scandinavian legends. Namely I aim to test and vindicate the idea that the poet of *Beowulf* enlarged on his Germanic narrative with motifs from Vergil's *Aeneid*; then to test and refute the idea that he took his tales of Scandinavian heroes directly from the Danes. Although I will propose Danes as living informants for the Norse mythology which we find in three major places in *Beowulf*, in this chapter I put forward the Frisians, not the Danes, as mediators of *Beowulf*'s (much older) Scylding tradition.

In Chapter 2, I weigh up Norse analogues as indications of what the heroic sources of *Beowulf* were like. The aim is to consider ways in which it is likely the poet changes his version of Scylding history. On the basis of comparative analyses I conclude that the poet puts Beowulf in Denmark a generation early in order to

---

[1] Bond, 'Links between *Beowulf* and Mercian History', 481–93, esp. 489–91 (with *Beowulf* composed in two stages: the first half in Beornwulf's reign; the second, after Wiglaf's restoration in 830 or 831). Wormald, 'The Age of Offa and Alcuin', 128. *Beornwulf* is variously spelt *Bernwulf*, *Bernulf*, *Bernulph(us)*.

[2] C. Chase, 'Opinions on the Date of *Beowulf*, 1815–1980', in Chase (ed.), *The Dating of Beowulf*, 3–8, at 5.

[3] Newton, *The Origins of Beowulf*, 71.

separate him from Hrothulf, changes his career so as to make him king of Geatland, with a new death in the dragon's fire, then only towards the end brings up his traditional lieutenant, calling him by a name ('Wiglaf') for which he appears to have had no legendary source. These changes look consistent with the Mercian Wiglaf's patronage and a date of composition between Beornwulf's death in 826 and Wiglaf's in *c*.839.

In Chapter 3, my aim is to assess *Beowulf*'s Latinate background. What emerge are some familiar and more recondite works from the Bible, patristic commentary, vernacular and Latin versions of the *Visio s. Pauli*, fabulous literature, and Books I, III, and VI of Vergil's *Aeneid*. I take the character of this range of works as confirmation that *Beowulf* was written in a monastery. The Vergilian theme continues in Chapter 4, in which I claim that Hrothgar and Wealhtheow are patterned after Latinus and Amata in Books VII and XI of the *Aeneid*. The effect of all this, a characterization of Beowulf as Ingeld's rival on the basis of Aeneas with Turnus, is here explained as the poet's competitive engagement with a work on Ingeld which he took as his source. This suggestion leads to another, in Chapter 5, that the now-lost monument on Ingeld in question was none other than the performance on 'Hinieldus' to which Alcuin broadly refers in a letter of 797. If 'Speratus', the addressee, is identified with Bishop Unwona of Leicester, we can follow this putative Ingeld-poem to the poet of *Beowulf* through the bishop's entourage. Out of Unwona's friends and former pupils, the name of a certain Priest Abbot Wigmund commends him as the most likely purveyor. On the assumption that Wigmund's name is related to the importance of Wiglaf's role in *Beowulf*, I attempt to trace him to a minster, one identifiable with Breedon on the Hill, in north-west Leicestershire.

In Chapter 6, I present this minster as the community in which a former pupil of Wigmund, in 826 × *c*.839, could have composed *Beowulf*. First I consider Breedon's Frankish connections and documentary and art-historical record to see how far these accord with the likely Latinate sources of *Beowulf*. On this perforce tenuous basis it can be argued that some nine of the books which could have influenced *Beowulf* were housed in the Breedon library. In Chapter 7, I attempt to show how the poet's knowledge of Norse mythology, in three vital areas, could have come about through his contact with Danish visitors to Mercia in 809. The *Beowulf*-poet's concern for the spiritual welfare of heathens is here presented as topical, the reflection of Frankish preparations to baptize King Heriold of the Danes: a ceremony which took place near Mainz in 826. Chapter 8 begins work on historical contexts, arguing that 'Thryth' and the Offa-digression in *Beowulf* allude to Offa's execution of St Æthelberht of East Anglia in 794. It can be shown that Offa is not interpolated into *Beowulf*, as some believe, but is placed there deliberately as the first in a sequence of great kings. This sequence continues with Hygelac and Beowulf before leading suggestively to Wiglaf at the end. As I go on to argue, in Chapter 9, an allegorical reading of the first three kings may be made with reference to the great kings of Mercia before Wiglaf, respectively Offa

(757–96), Cenwulf (796–821), and Beornwulf (823–6). Chapter 10 proposes a date for *Beowulf,* together with a hypothesis about the poem's transmission to Wessex. I conclude that the poem was composed in order to secure the Mercian throne for its patron, Wiglaf, by performing a requiem for King Beornwulf in the aftermath of his death in battle in 826. My final suggestion is that the poet of *Beowulf* signs his work aurally shortly after introducing Wiglaf at the head of Fitt XXXVI.

MANUSCRIPT, DIALECT, METRE

Three preliminaries in any study of *Beowulf*'s date and provenance are the poem's manuscript, dialect, and metre. Scholars have handled these subjects so fully that the scope of this monograph precludes more than citing the best results.[4] *Beowulf* is uniquely preserved in the Nowell Codex, which was bound together with the preceding Southwick Codex, in BL, Cotton Vitellius A.XV (s. x/xi). This manuscript narrowly survived destruction in the Cotton Library fire of 1731. Although much of its text was singed on outer margins, two brief excerpts of *Beowulf* had been printed in 1705 (lines 1–19 and 53–73); and in 1787–9 two copies of the poem (Thorkelin A and B) were made after the fire, before more serious damage set in.[5] These copyings allowed for the restoration of some 2,000 lost letters before the manuscript was rebound in 1845.[6] In the Nowell Codex, *Beowulf* follows *The Passion of St Christopher, The Wonders of the East*, and the Old English *Letter of Alexander to Aristotle*; and is followed by the poem *Judith*. It has been suggested that the compiler of the Nowell Codex, taking monsters as his theme at the outset of the eleventh century, ordered a copying from two exemplars, one containing probably *Judith, The Passion of St Christopher*, and *The Wonders of the East*, the second the *Letter* and *Beowulf*.[7] Boyle's suggestion, that the fitt divisions in *Beowulf* were inherited from the copy-text and numbered one fitt too late by the first copyist, is to be preferred probably because it takes account of human error.[8]

The Nowell Codex was copied by two scribes, named A and B, with B taking over from A at the beginning of the third line on fo. 172^v, on *Beo* 1939 (after

---

[4] There is a concise account in Newton, *The Origins of Beowulf,* 1–9.

[5] At the behest of the Icelander Grímur Jónsson Thorkelin: 'Thorkelin A' (by a scribe in 1787); and 'Thorkelin B' (by Thorkelin himself in 1789). See K. Kiernan, *The Thorkelin Transcripts of Beowulf,* Anglistica 25 (Copenhagen, 1986), 144.

[6] Orchard, *Companion,* 12–23, esp. 19.

[7] *Beowulf* is found on fos. 129^r to 198^v. As to the other works: *The Passion of St Christopher,* fos. 93[94]^r to 97[98]^r (incomplete at the beginning); *The Wonders of the East,* fos. 97[98]^r to 103[106]^v; *The Letter of Alexander to Aristotle,* fos. 104[107]^r to 128[131]^v; *Beowulf,* fos. 129[132]^r to 198[201]^v; *Judith,* fos. 199[202]^r to 206[209]^v (incomplete at the end). Foliation in square brackets is the so-called 'new' foliation of 1884 (of Kemp Malone), which has not superseded the old (used here).

[8] 'The Nowell Codex and the Poem of *Beowulf*', 30–1.

scyran, with *moste*); Scribe B continued copying till the end of *Judith*, a poem whose position in the exemplar, probably before *St Christopher*, would have been changed here so as to follow *Beowulf* at the end of the new codex.[9] Scribe B also corrects the text of Scribe A in a series of interventions. Characterizing these as revisions of poetic substance, Kevin Kiernan has argued that Scribe B composed the final draft of *Beowulf* as an autograph in the reign of King Cnut (1016–35).[10] In his view the poem represents one older work which Scribe B joined to another with a bridge-piece of his own ('Beowulf's Homecoming', lines 1888–2199).[11] His case for a composite *Beowulf* relies on his argument that fo. 179^r is an autograph page, rather than one on the top of a quire which had been left (out to the weather) for Scribe A to correct; and Kiernan asks other scholars to believe in the ability of Scribe B to perform an intelligent scrutiny of the earlier scribe's poem.[12] This belief has not been widely accepted, but nonetheless, Kiernan's work has revitalized the study of the *Beowulf* manuscript in several ways.[13] One of these has been to encourage an increased scrutiny of the codicology and palaeography of the Nowell Codex within Cotton Vitellius A.XV. Consequently it has been restated that Scribe B wrote in a hand of the late tenth century, Scribe A in one of the early eleventh; that combinations of two or more scribes occur in other millennial manuscripts besides this one, with the second scribe copying in a supervisory role; and that not only a high number of garbled spellings, but also some likely textual lacunae in *Beowulf*, ones indeed greater than previously thought, show that the scribes were probably copying from an exemplar which was itself defective.[14] The poem, then, was composed some time before the manuscript, with its fitt divisions and numeration also older than Vitellius A.XV.[15] An abundance of corrections in a problematic text, one with textual lacunae, points to a difficulty in understanding this poem. In the light of these uncertainties between scribes *c*.1000, the text of *Beowulf* shows signs of antiquity. Michael Lapidge accordingly proposes that *Beowulf* preserves a range of archaic scribal forms which point to a date of first copying before *c*.750.[16] It has been demonstrated, however, that the same forms occur in later Anglo-Saxon manuscripts, including the Arundel Psalter, which is dated to the ninth century by its

[9] P. J. Lucas, 'The Place of *Judith* in the *Beowulf*-Manuscript', *RES* 41 (1990), 463–78, esp. 473–4.

[10] Kiernan, *Beowulf and the Beowulf Manuscript*, 18–23 and 191–270.

[11] Ibid. 249–58.

[12] Ibid. 219–43. *Contra*, Boyle, 'The Nowell Codex and the Poem of *Beowulf*', 24–6. J. Gerritsen, 'Have with You to Lexington! The *Beowulf* Manuscript and *Beowulf*', in J. Lachlan MacKenzie, and R. Todd (eds.), *In Other Words: Transcultural Studies in Philology, Translation and Lexicography Presented to Hans Heinrich Meier* (Dordrecht, 1989), 15–34, esp. 25–31.

[13] Orchard, *Companion*, 43–56.

[14] D. N. Dumville, '*Beowulf* Come Lately: Some Notes on the Palaeography of the Nowell Codex', *Archiv*, 225 (1988), 49–63, esp. 50–5. Orchard, *Companion*, 22.

[15] Boyle, 'The Nowell Codex and the Poem of *Beowulf*', 30–1.

[16] 'The Archetype of *Beowulf*', 5–41. Orchard, *Companion*, 39–54.

use of the *Gallicanum* version of the Psalms.[17] From this point of view, between the two dating extremes, a date for *Beowulf* in the first half of the ninth century can still be ruled in on palaeographical grounds.

The problem with dating by manuscript lies in eliminating alternatives; success in this matter looks no more likely than it did before Kiernan's time. If we turn to the related questions of *Beowulf*'s metre and dialect, we find much valuable work commensurate in energy and talent with that of Kiernan and others on the manuscript. Orchard's conclusions about poetic formulae and effects are the latest in a body of skilled research.[18] Yet the problem of alternatives remains. For example, the authors of a meticulous joint study of *Beowulf*'s language declared that they 'could not call any date in the Old English period impossible, on linguistic grounds'.[19] Whereas Thomas Cable scanned twenty-two Old English poems to create a metrical typology, by which he then dated *Beowulf* to the ninth century, R. D. Fulk puts the date of *Beowulf*, if this is a Mercian work, before *c.*725; if a Northumbrian, before *c.*825.[20] According to 'Kaluza's Law', words with long inflexional endings were placed differently from words with short ones, before the time when these long endings became short and both categories of word attained equal metrical value; in Mercia the time of this change is datable to a generation before *c.*750, in Northumbria before *c.*850.[21] There is no doubt that the poet of *Beowulf* observes this metrical law with startling regularity. *Beowulf* for this reason may be as old as Fulk has said it is. On the other hand, the metre of *Beowulf* may reflect a dialect with an older morphology, in which case Fulk's evidence would show that the poet of *Beowulf*, if he composed in a region of Mercia closer to Northumbria, could have worked later than *c.*750. To a greater extent, we know of a similar effect from regional variance in three poets of the late fourteenth century, the *Gawain*-poet, Langland, and Chaucer, whose dialects recall different eras because the poets respectively come from around Cheshire, Malvern, and London. Although the Old English poetic tradition was more uniform over a longer period, each Anglo-Saxon poet had his own metrical grammar (rules of verse composition) and it is accepted that these would have been related to dialect.[22] The difficulty arises with the dialect of the *Beowulf* manuscript, which is composite in being made up of late West Saxon with Mercian and Northumbrian elements and with an

---

[17] E. G. Stanley, 'Paleographical and Textual Deep Waters: <a> for <u> and <u> for <a>, <d> for <ð> and <ð> for <d> in Old English', *ANQ* NS 15 (2002), 64–72, esp. 66.

[18] Orchard, *Companion*, 57–91.

[19] A. Cameron, A. Crandell Amos, and G. Wite, with the assistance of S. Butler and A. diPaolo Healey, 'A Reconsideration of the Language of *Beowulf*', in Chase (ed.), *The Dating of Beowulf*, 33–75, esp. 37.

[20] T. Cable, 'Metrical Style as Evidence for the Date of *Beowulf*', in Chase (ed.), *The Dating of Beowulf*, 77–82. Fulk, *A History of Old English Meter*, 385–90 (§§ 413–19).

[21] Fulk, *A History of Old English Meter*, 153–68.

[22] Kendall, *The Metrical Grammar of Beowulf*, 10.

admixture of Kentish forms.[23] Klaeber proposed that *Beowulf* was composed in a form of Anglian, but the Anglian features may be attributed to the general use of this dialect as a poetic *koine*.[24] Even Kiernan, though he discounts any long transmission for the poem, regards the Mercian element in its language as sufficiently strong for the poet to have been a Mercian who wrote in an accented West Saxon standard.[25] Recently, it appears that the Midlands are gaining ground over other parts of England as the region to which it is thought the poet's dialect belonged.[26] The weakness, if any, in Fulk's argument about *Beowulf*'s date is that the Mercian charter evidence on which he bases his argument (in the retention of m. gen. sg. *-aes* over *-es*, for example) derives from the south-west Midlands, as nearly all surviving Mercian charters do. On the other hand, if the Mercian language of the *Beowulf*-poet was more northern in form, from the northern Midlands, the date of this poem would be more in line with Fulk's Northumbrian model, with its latest date of composition in *c*.825.

Calvin B. Kendall has made a metrically based profile of the *Beowulf*-poet. In his view, which is based on metrical-syntactical style, the poet grew up with formulaic poetry, having heard hundreds of boastful recitations in an aristocratic setting: 'his genius manifested itself in early adolescence; he was not a late bloomer, like Cædmon'.[27] Having entered a monastery, he 'became acquainted with Vergil's *Aeneid* and Prudentius's *Psychomachia* and gained an appreciation of the possibilities of extended epic narrative'. The abbot allowed him to recite the exploits of heroes at mealtimes; 'he could turn a story familiar to them from childhood into a meditation on the dilemmas of human conduct and the universal dependence of pagans and Christians on God.' Today most readers of *Beowulf* would follow this profile some of the way. In the following chapters I shall support nearly all of it with literary evidence which suggests the poet's use of heroic, Classical, and biblical sources, his monastic background, and his place as an observer of Mercian politics from the late 780s to the late 820s.

BEOWULF AND THE *AENEID*

Kendall is more controversial than he appears in suggesting that the poet of *Beowulf* knew the *Aeneid*: many would reject this as wishful thinking.[28] Initially

---

[23] Anglian forms in Fulk, *A History of Old English Meter*, 317 (§ 354), 318–25 (§ 355, esp. 321), 330–1 (§ 361), and 390–2 (§ 420). For a more open-ended view, Stanley, *In the Foreground*, 155–63, esp. 156–8.

[24] *Beowulf*, ed. Klaeber, pp. lxxxviii–xcv. K. Sisam, 'Dialect Origins of the Earlier Old English Verse', in *Studies*, 119–39, esp. 138.

[25] Kiernan, *Beowulf and the Beowulf Manuscript*, 37–59, esp. 49.

[26] Newton, *The Origins of Beowulf*, 10–17. R. E. Bjork and A. Obermeier, 'Date, Provenance, Author, Audiences', in Bjork and Niles (eds.), *Beowulf Handbook*, 13–34, esp. 25–6.

[27] Kendall, *The Metrical Grammar of Beowulf*, 2–6, esp. 4.

[28] Andersson, 'Sources and Analogues' 139–41, esp. 140. Orchard, *Companion*, 132–3.

the idea seemed plausible, until Klaeber set out his parallels, which proved too many and vague.[29] Today it is the number more than the vagueness of these parallels that causes disquiet, for together they give an impression of loose odds and ends. In vain did Thomas Burns Haber try to make them more specific.[30] A word or phrase in *Beowulf*, however, such as the many he provides as matches for expressions in Vergil's *Aeneid*, could never sustain the case for an important influence from one great work to the other.[31] With a more conceptual approach, Alois Brandl took twelve epic features of the *Aeneid* and searched *Beowulf* for their reflexes.[32] When this method failed, also because the parallels were too diffuse, a riposte was delivered by Alain Renoir, who highlighted differences between two scenes whose resemblance had been thought strong, the Classical Underworld in *Aen.* VI and Grendel's Mere in *Beo* 1357–76.[33] Theodore Andersson has revived the claim for Vergil's influence on the *Beowulf*-poet, by showing a common approach to scenic techniques, but since then, for other reasons, more scholars publicly doubt any connection between this poet and Vergil.[34]

Jack Niles appears to seal the discussion by making a test case for phrasal borrowings, one which fails, out of the dislocated parallel *conticuere omnes* ('all fell quiet', *Aen.* II. 1), for *swigedon ealle* ('all fell quiet', *Beo* 1639). He treats the similarity between the Danish *scop* in Heorot and Vergil's minstrel Iopas in *Aen.* I, both singing of creation, as a coincidence; and presents a list of epic features in

---

[29] Klaeber, 'Aeneis und Beowulf', 40–8 and 339–59. The borrowing from Vergil is disputed in H. Chadwick, *The Heroic Age* (Cambridge, 1912), 73–4; but thereafter treated as obvious in Chambers, *Beowulf*, 329–31.

[30] Haber, *A Comparative Study*. The groundwork is careful (I: introduction; II: the early Anglo-Saxon knowledge of Vergil; III: non-Germanic influence in *Beowulf*), the classification sensible (IV: broad similarities between *Beowulf* and the *Aeneid*; V: parallels in phraseology; VI: parallels in motif and sentiment), but there is no attempt to rank the parallels in order of plausibility.

[31] For example: 'swigedon ealle', in *Beo* 1639 (the Danes fall silent) and 'conticuere omnes' in *Aen.* II. 1 (the Tyrians); 'stige nearwe, enge anpaðas' in *Beo* 1409–10 (Hrothgar's trail to the Mere) and 'tenuis semita, angustae fauces' in *Aen.* XI. 524–5 (of Turnus' planned ambush); 'wordes ord breosthord þurhbræc' in *Beo* 2791–2 (the dying Beowulf speaks) and 'rumpit hanc pectore vocem' in *Aen.* III. 246 (the Harpy Queen curses Aeneas). The first parallel, in particular, has been undermined in Niles, *Beowulf*, 75–6 and 78; and in Orchard, *Companion*, 133.

[32] Brandl, 'Beowulf-Epos und Aeneis', 166–71.

[33] Renoir, 'Originality, Influence, Imitation: Two Medieval Phases', in F. Jost (ed.), *Actes du IVe Congrès de l'Association Internationale de Littérature Comparée, Fribourg 1964: Proceedings of the IVth Congress of the International Comparative Literature Association* (The Hague, 1966), 737–46; 'The Terror of the Dark Waters', 151–7. See Haber, *A Comparative Study*, 94–6.

[34] *Early Epic Scenery: Homer, Virgil, and the Medieval Legacy* (Ithaca, NY, 1976). For a focus, instead, on Vergil's Latin imitators as sources for the poet of *Beowulf*, see: J. A. Nist, '*Beowulf* and the Classical Epics', *College English*, 24 (1963), 257–62, esp. 258; and R. J. Schrader, 'Beowulf's Obsequies and the Roman Epic', *Comparative Literature*, 24 (1972), 237–59, esp. 238–42. For a belief in the overriding difference of *Beowulf* (as an inferior poem), see B. Trnka, 'The *Beowulf* Poem and Virgil's *Aeneid*', *Poetica: An International Journal of Linguistic-Literary Studies*, 12 (1981), 150–6, esp. 154: 'its unity as a single epic almost disappears and is sustained only by the person of Beowulf himself.'

the *Aeneid*, all of which, in his view, *Beowulf* fails to match.[35] The claim is that *Beowulf* has no: (i) invocations of a muse; (ii) epic catalogues; (iii) great deliberative assemblies; (iv) epic similes; (v) dreams or portents; (vi) reference to the heroes of ancient mythology. Some of these failings are arguable. Hrothgar's and Hygelac's halls might qualify for (iii), Beowulf's prediction about Ingeld and the Geatish Messenger's about the Geats for (v), or Scyld Scefing and 'Beow', Hama, Heremod, Sigemund, Herebeald, and Hæthcyn for (vi). Yet these are features which might equally be attributed to *Beowulf*'s place in an antique Anglo-Saxon tradition. Respectively, they do not come close enough to the Trojan, Tyrian, or Latin multitudes, the variegated prophecies strewn across Books I–VI of the *Aeneid*, or Vergil's habitual allusions through names, epithets, or digressions to a rich Greek mythology in Roman form.

Niles, who supports an anti-Latinate folklore model for *Beowulf*'s poetic style, has rightly asked for more rigour in the presentation of Vergilian parallels, particularly for 'thematic parallels accompanied by verbal similarities, especially if the two passages in question seem to lock into a wider context'.[36] This requirement matches the third of Christine Rauer's three definitions of a source (as against an analogue): 'demonstrable antecedence, a shared literary and historical context, and parallel phraseology or imagery cogent enough to make an argument for direct influence plausible'.[37] Rauer's first two conditions are easily fulfilled in the case of the *Aeneid* and *Beowulf*. Where the third is concerned, however, we need to go deeper into the question of parallels by asking how the poet of *Beowulf* could have set out to imitate the *Aeneid*.

In this enquiry a cross-reference to the English Renaissance might help us, first with respect to Ben Jonson's depiction of bad and good categories of poetic imitation in his *Timber: Or, Discoveries* (after 1623). Jonson holds that, to imitate the Classical poets, including Vergil, an English poet must be able to 'convert' their riches to his own use:

Not, as a Creature, that swallowes, what it takes in, crude raw, or indigested; but, that feedes with an Appetite, and hath a Stomacke to concoct, divide, and turne all into nourishment. Not, to imitate servilely, as *Horace* saith, and catch at vices, for vertue: but, to draw forth out of the best, and choisest flowers, with the Bee, and turne all into Honey.[38]

By looking for the Anglo-Saxon Vergil, perhaps we are placing the poet of *Beowulf* in Jonson's category of servile imitation. At least it could be said that looking for verbal parallels is not the best approach, given that if the English poet

[35] Niles, *Beowulf*, 76–8. See Andersson, 'Sources and Analogues', 141: 'a telling list'.
[36] Niles, *Beowulf*, 66–95, esp. 76; cf. 163–76 ('Barbaric style').
[37] Rauer, *Beowulf and the Dragon*, 20.
[38] Quoted and discussed in R. S. Peterson, *Imitation and Praise in the Poems of Ben Jonson* (New Haven 1981), 6; cf. 23, in which it is 'the transformation and assimilation of gathered knowledge which constitute the imitation'.

had been able to move freely across the *Aeneid*, so could his similarly educated audience: their common facility in Latin would have obviated the need for minutely exact verbal transpositions into the vernacular, of the kind for which so many *Beowulf*-scholars have been searching up to now.

With *Beowulf*, a vernacular poem in a predominantly Latin literary culture, it is narrative motifs which provide the better opportunity for novelty; and here a comparison with John Milton could help us. Renoir, who briefly cites the imagery of *Paradise Lost* in his essay on Grendel's Mere and Avernus, does not take the comparison further.[39] But Milton borrowed from Vergil: not only did he imitate Vergil's words, for example by adapting the sibyl's warning to Aeneas of a hard ascent from Avernus (*Aen.* VI. 126–9) into Satan's expression of the difficulty of leaving hell (*PL* II. 432–3), and Milton's own misgivings about the same (*PL* III. 20–1); but he also converted narrative motifs. Indeed, through his stated ambition 'to soar Above th' Aonian mount' (*PL* I. 14–15), it becomes obvious that he built his epic form on Classical and poet-Classical Latin works which include the *Aeneid*. Milton's debt to Vergil and the two Homeric poems is a fact which, as one commentator puts it, 'hardly needs any demonstration'.[40] Sceptics, therefore, about Vergil's influence on *Beowulf* may gain from a discussion of his influence on *Paradise Lost*.

A study of the narrative influence can start with the scene in the *Aeneid* where Dido joins Aeneas in a cave. Vergil decribes this as a marriage of sorts with a thunderstorm, Earth opening the ceremony with Juno, High Heaven bearing witness, and nymphs wailing from mountain-tops (*Aen.* IV. 160–72):

> ille dies primus leti primusque malorum
> causa fuit; (*Aen.* IV. 169–70)

[That day was the first cause of death and the first of ill fortune;]

Milton adapts this Dionysian scene in order to lend tragedy to the bare biblical story of the eating of the forbidden fruit (Gen. 3: 6). When Eve eats, in his words:

> Earth felt the wound, and nature from her seat
> Sighing through all her works gave signs of woe. (*PL* IX. 782–3)[41]

Later, when Adam eats the fruit:

> Earth trembled from her entrails, as again
> In pangs, and nature gave a second groan,
> Sky loured and muttering thunder, some sad drops
> Wept at completing of the mortal sin
> Original. (*PL* IX. 1000–4)

---

[39] Milton is cited second-hand through Sergei Eisenstein, in Renoir, 'The Terror of the Dark Waters', 154.

[40] So Blessington, *Paradise Lost and the Classical Epic*, 100. Condee, *Structure in Milton's Poetry*, 4–20.

[41] All Milton's text from *Paradise Lost*, ed. A. Fowler (Harlow, 1968).

Milton develops the scene that follows, Adam's love play with Eve, from the same passage in *Aen.* IV.[42] Two more episodes show that he borrows also to enlarge existing narrative with scenes for which the Bible or his biblical commentaries gave him no authority. In the *Aeneid*, when Venus tearfully questions Jupiter about the fate of Aeneas, now in danger from Juno, Jupiter calms her with a prophecy of Aeneas' part in Rome's imperial future (*Aen.* I. 223–96). Milton transforms the scene so that God the Father, having seen Satan fly out of hell towards Eden, invites Jesus the Son, in whose face 'Divine compassion visibly appeared', to elicit from him a discourse on the destiny of man (*PL* III. 56–415, esp. 141). Thirdly, in Vergil's poem, Jupiter commands Mercury to remind Aeneas that his destiny lies in Italy, whereupon Mercury flies down to Carthage, circling the snowy sides of Mount Atlas (*Aen.* IV. 246–51). In Milton's poem, the Father tells Raphael to warn Adam of Satan's threat to Paradise, whereupon the archangel sets off on his own heavenly descent (*PL* V. 238–75). When Raphael alights in Paradise, Milton draws attention to the *Aeneid* by comparing him to 'Maia's son' (*PL* V. 285), an epithet which renders one of Vergil's for Mercury (*Maia genitum*, in *Aen.* I. 297).[43] What Milton does in each case is to recast an episode from the *Aeneid*.

It may be presumed that Vergil in his own day did likewise, for many scenes which Milton found in the *Aeneid* themselves appear to be borrowed from the *Iliad* or *Odyssey.* Jupiter's words to Venus, cited above, enlarge on Zeus' encouragement to Athene at the beginning of the *Odyssey*, Book I; and Jupiter's dispatch of Mercury to free Aeneas from Dido is probably based on the opening scene of *Odyssey*, Book V, in which Zeus sends Hermes to stimulate the departure of Odysseus, slave of Calypso.[44] Why Vergil should borrow in this way from 'Homer', or Milton from Vergil, among many others, is best explained in terms of the opportunities which each poet found in the work of his great predecessor. In borrowing his older rival's stories, each man cast them into something new.[45] This is particularly a light in which to see the poet of *Beowulf*. He is at ease with his own narrative tradition, unlike Milton and Vergil, each of whom set out to create an epic form in a language which, as he understood it, did not effectively have this; this is clear in his proem's use of a traditional poetic form (*we . . . gefrunon*, lines 1–2), one which he idealizes as inherently true (*word oþer . . . soðe gebunden*, lines 870–1).[46] Yet there is no reason why at the same

---

[42] Blessington, *Paradise Lost and the Classical Epic*, 62–3.

[43] Ibid. 26.

[44] Blessington suggests (ibid. 25–6), that the latter scene is derived from Zeus' dispatch of Hermes to Troy in *Iliad* XXIII. 333–470.

[45] C. Burrow, *Epic Romance: Homer to Milton* (Oxford, 1993), 5: 'The rebellions of these great figures against their predecessors are not patriarchal gigantomachies, as a poet-hero struggles for mastery over a Great Name from the past. They are revolutions of discourse.'

[46] On the poet's 'appeal to a supposed common knowledge of famed past events', see Orchard, *Companion*, 60.

time the poet of *Beowulf*, like Jonson's 'Bee', could not have drawn out and transformed the 'choisest flowers' of Vergil's *Aeneid*.

So, for example, there is an echo of Dido's palace when the Danish minstrel first sings of Creation upon the building of Heorot:

>   þær wæs hearpan sweg
> swutol sang scopes.   Sægde se þe cuþe
> frumsceaft fira   feorran reccan,
> cwæð þæt se ælmihtiga   eorðan worhte
> wlitebeorhtne wang   swa wæter bebugeð,
> gesette sigehreþig   sunnan ond monan
> leoman to leohte   landbuendum
> ond gefrætwade   foldan sceatas
> leomum ond leafum,   lif eac gesceop
> cynna gehwylcum   þara ðe cwice hwyrfaþ. (*Beo* 89–98)

[A melody of the lyre was there, the minstrel's clear song. He spoke, who knew how to relate from long ago the first creation of men, said that the Almighty made the earth, a plain dazzling bright as far as the water moves, that, exulting in his victory, he appointed sun's and moon's gleams as light for land-dwellers and adorned earth's surfaces with branches and leaves, and also created life for all living things that move.]

A case has long been made here for a debt to the *Aeneid*.[47] When Dido's assembly prepares to hear of Aeneas' wanderings, the Trojans drain their cups and listen:

>   cithara crinitus Iopas
> personat aurata, docuit quem maximus Atlas.
> hic canit errantem lunam solisque labores,
> unde hominum genus et pecudes, unde imber et ignes,
> Arcturum pluuiasque Hyadas geminosque Triones,
> quid tantum Oceano properent se tingere soles
> hiberni, uel quae tardis mora noctibus obstet. (*Aen.* I. 740–6)

[Long-haired Iopas, whom most mighty Atlas taught, resounds with his golden cithara. He sings of the wandering moon and the labours of the sun, of whence come mankind and the beasts, whence rainclouds and flames, of Arcturus, the rainy Pleiades and the Two Bears, of why the suns of winter should hasten so much to plunge into Ocean, or of the procrastination that slows down winter's sluggish nights.]

It has also been suggested that this passage underlies Raphael's planetary discourse to Adam in *PL* VI. 618–27.[48] Common to the relevant scenes in *Beowulf* and the *Aeneid* is the theme of a minstrel reciting a poem on the sun, moon, and creation in a newly built hall.

---

[47] Klaeber, 'Aeneis und Beowulf', 343. Brandl, 'Beowulf-Epos und Aeneis', 167. Haber, *A Comparative Study*, 132: 'the most noteworthy parallel'.
[48] Blessington, *Paradise Lost and the Classical Epic*, 34–5.

Niles, however, arguing against a connection, says that 'the main correspondence remains inexact' because Iopas's song 'breathes a spirit of scientific rationalism that reflects Virgil's interest in the natural philosophy of Lucretius and that is foreign to the Anglo-Saxon poet's simpler piety'.[49] From this statement it follows that the poet of *Beowulf* could not have borrowed from the *Aeneid* without retaining the ideology of this poem. That is to say, he must be classified as Jonson's 'Creature, that swallowes, what it takes in, crude, raw, or indigested'. Few would have such a low opinion of Milton, expecting to find, say, Rome at the centre of the Father's discourse on predestination in Book III of *Paradise Lost*. Yet it is the absence of a fidelity of this kind which appears to justify Niles in ruling out an influence from Vergil to *Beowulf*. He calls *Beowulf*'s Danish minstrelsy a 'hymn', regards Cædmon's *Hymn* (also about creation but sung in a cow-byre) as closer to *Beowulf*, and he describes the *Beowulf*-poet's aim as the creation of an implicit threefold analogy between the men who created Heorot, God who created the world, and the singer who creates songs. Creative as this theory is, it overlooks the resemblances between one text and another. Iopas's song could be called a hymn, for Dido introduces it with a libation and prayer to Jupiter, Bacchus, and Juno. There is also a wider resemblance of theme. By now Venus has conspired with Juno to keep Aeneas in Carthage. She switches her son Cupid for the boy Ascanius. Cupid, in the shape of Aeneas' young son, then *reginam petit* ('seeks out the queen', *Aen.* I. 717). He does so in order to destroy her, turning her mind towards Aeneas so that by the end of his tale about Troy and the voyage to Italy, she has fallen in love. When Dido and Aeneas, therefore, applaud Iopas's song about the planets some thirty lines later in *Aen.* I. 747, they do so without knowing their future, or the extent to which the same planets will combine to change them. A similar lack of foreknowledge is highlighted in *Beowulf*, lines 86–98, the Danes being unaware of Grendel. In *Beowulf*'s case, however, the pathos is heightened, for the Danes know nothing of Christianity either.

This kind of literary borrowing, the transformation of old narrative into new, differs from imitating Roman epics as a mechanical endeavour. The poet of *Beowulf*, to feed on the *Aeneid* in this way, was not obliged to replicate any epic features such as the six which Niles has made the test of borrowing from Vergil.[50] Perhaps he could do better. As I hope to show with other examples, he appears to recast some episodes from the *Aeneid* as the narrative need arises, using Vergil's work probably in combination with others and at least as one source among many.[51] In this book I shall present three such uses of Vergil in Chapter 3 and a fourth in Chapter 4. None of these passages in *Beowulf* should have to translate Vergil into Old English in order to qualify as literary adaptations.

---

[49] Niles, *Beowulf*, 74–9, esp. 76–7.   [50] Ibid. 78–9.
[51] Orchard, *Companion*, 98–168.

Rather, they can be seen as enhancements of existing Germanic or biblical narrative or as the poet's creation of new scenes which his Germanic or biblical legends did not authorize.

Historically, there is no objection to treating Vergil as the leading Latin poetic model of the eighth and ninth centuries. Alcuin cites Vergil's place in the library in his poem on the saints of York and shows that Vergil was a staple in the school in York when he begs a friend living there *comprehendere plectra Maronis* ('to comprehend the poems of Vergil').[52] The *Vita Alcuini*, his biography, claims, perhaps with some exaggeration, that Alcuin loved Vergil as a youth, but learned to prefer the Psalms; although his poems object to Vergil on moral grounds, as false, he knew that no other poet provided such competition for biblical verse or such a standard for poets to follow.[53] In a letter to Charlemagne (August, 799), Alcuin quotes Vergil alongside St Augustine and Matthew's Gospel without the slightest difficulty, urging the emperor *parcere subiectis et debellare superbos* ('to spare the vanquished and battle down the proud') in the words of Anchises to his son down in Avernus, the Underworld, in *Aen.* VI. 853.[54] At the end of the same year Alcuin again identifies Charlemagne with Aeneas, when he tells the king's daughter that he had heard of Charlemagne's arrival from *Fama per multorum ora volitans* ('the rumour flying through many mouths from one person to another'): thus he modifies Vergil's expression for the swift passage of Faunus' oracle that Aeneas would arrive (to marry Lavinia) in *Aen.* VII. 104 (*late volitans iam Fama*).[55] Alcuin makes many references to Vergil, always in awe of his power, always aware that Vergil composed *mendacia* ('falsehoods' or 'fictions').[56] Perhaps it is of more interest that Alcuin, in a letter to Charlemagne, calls the poet *Vergilius vester* ('Your Vergil').[57] Einhard, the emperor's biographer, says that Charlemagne ordered the transcription of *barbara et antiquissima carmina quibus veterum regum actus et bella canebantur* ('barbarian [or: "heathen"] and most ancient songs in which the deeds and wars of old kings were sung'). Here, as the *Waltharius* would later testify, is a case in which Vergil was compatible with an interest in heroic Germanic poetry.[58]

---

[52] Lapidge, *The Anglo-Saxon Library*, 231 (no. 30). Orchard, 'Wish You Were Here', 42–3 (*Carmen* LIX. 11). Dümmler (ed.), *Poetae Latini aevi Carolini*, i. 273.

[53] Bolton, *Alcuin and Beowulf*, 47–52, esp. 47–8 (see *Carmina* XVIII.19–20 and LXXVIII.6). Suspect to Bullough, in 'Charlemagne's "Men of God" ', 137.

[54] Bolton, *Alcuin and Beowulf*, 48–9. *Epistolae*, ed. Dümmler, ii. 294 (no. 178: with *De civitate Dei*, I. vi and Matt. 5: 7).

[55] *Epistolae*, ed. Dümmler, ii. 266 (no. 164).

[56] Bolton, *Alcuin and Beowulf*, 48. *Epistolae*, ed. Dümmler, ii. 475 (no. 309: to Gundrada, Charlemagne's sister, in 801–4); cf. 39 (no. 13: to Abbot Ricbod of Triers, c.791–2), 290 (no. 175: to Abbot Adalhard of Corbie, 799), 359 (no. 215: to pupils setting off to Rome, 799).

[57] Ibid., ii. 233 (no. 145, spring 798).

[58] *Einhardi Vita Karoli Magni*, ed. G. H. Pertz and G. Waitz, rev. O. Holder-Egger, 6th edn., MGH, SRG, sep. edn., 25 (Hanover, 1947), 33 (ch. 29). On the *Waltharius*, a Germanic tale in Latin with Vergilian quotations from the ninth or tenth century, see U. Dronke and P. Dronke,

Alcuin himself supervised the copying of a rare commentary on Vergil when he was abbot of St Martin's at Tours.[59] He congratulated his rival, Theodulf of Orléans, on becoming archbishop in 801 with Turnus' words to Aeneas in *Aen.* XII. 932, *utere sorte tua* ('make the most of your good fortune'), spoken when Aeneas is about to finish him off at the end of the *Aeneid*.[60] Alcuin's younger contemporaries used Vergil with the same expectation of common knowledge. Vergil's picture of the rising Carthage in *Aen.* I, the new city to which the song of Iopas belongs, forms the basis of passages on the building of two Carolingian palaces: Charlemagne's in Aachen, in *Karolus Magnus et Leo Papa*, probably of Einhard (*c*.800); and the Ingelheim of Louis the Pious, in the *In honorem Hludovico Pii* of Ermoldus Nigellus (*c*.827 × 830).[61] Ermoldus borrows from all over the *Aeneid*, for instance modelling Louis on Aeneas in the hunting scene in *Aen.* IV, where Vergil likens the Trojan to Apollo.[62] Louis's father Charlemagne had already received the same style from Alcuin. In Chapters 3–4 of this book I shall suggest that the poet of *Beowulf* styles his hero, too, on Aeneas. This identification may be seen to have a political dimension, if we keep the premiss that *Beowulf* was composed in Ermoldus' time partly in reflection of King Beornwulf of Mercia (d. 826). But that can wait for a later chapter. What remains here is to introduce the Germanic material from which the story of *Beowulf* is derived.

HEROIC SOURCES AND ANALOGUES

The heroic sources of *Beowulf* belonged to a western Germanic tradition which will be considered in greater detail in Chapters 2, 4, and 8. Unlike *Beowulf*'s presumed Latinate sources, some of which are identifiable, the outlines of any Germanic legends that informed this poem must be deduced from comparison with analogues. These are of two types, Anglo-Saxon and Scandinavian: *The Finnsburh Fragment* and *Widsith*, on one hand; and on the other, the Skjǫldung-dynasty as represented largely in the thirteenth-century histories of medieval Denmark, Norway, and Iceland.

Barbara et antiquissima carmina (Barcelona, 1977), 27–79. On the fusion, see N. Voorwinden, 'Latin Words, Germanic Thoughts — Germanic Words, Latin Thoughts: The Merging of Two Traditions', in R. North and T. Hofstra (eds.), *Latin Culture and Medieval Germanic Europe*, Germania Latina I (Groningen, 1992), 113–28.

[59] Bullough, 'Charlemagne's "Men of God" ', 142.

[60] *Epistolae*, ed. Dümmler. ii. 369 (no. 225).

[61] Godman, *Poetry of the Carolingian Renaissance*, 24–5 (Einhard), 46–7 (Ermoldus), 202–3 (no. 25: *Karolus Magnus et Leo Papa*, lines 97–136) and 250–5 (no. 37: *In honorem Hludovici Pii*, lines 521–34). See also below in my Chapter 3.

[62] Ibid. 47 (for example, *Aen.* I. 187 (line 521), I. 502 (line 534), IV. 156–8 (line 519), V. 430 (line 509), etc.) and 256–7.

Beowulf is about kings. The hero Beowulf becomes one and some believe that Wiglaf succeeds him. If Grendel and the other monsters in this poem take up much of the foreground, it is also true that nearly a third of *Beowulf* reveals a Danish dynastic background against which the great deeds of our hero must be measured. The poet makes clear in his opening lines that his tale is but one among many that start with the kings of Denmark:

> HWÆT WE GARDEna   in geardagum
> þeodcyninga   þrym gefrunon,
> hu ða æþelingas   ellen fremedon. (*Beo* 1–3)[63]

[Listen. We have heard of the glory of the nation-kings of the Spear-Danes in days of yore, how those princelings carried out deeds of courage.]

Namely this poet presents Danish royal history as the foundation of heroic narrative. Effectively, he reveals an expectation in his audience that no tale of Beowulf, Ingeld, Hnæf, or any other Scandinavian heroes can be told without a footing in the Scyldings. For its own part, *Beowulf* opens with Scyld Scefing and descends unhurriedly through the generations until the poet stops with Hrothgar, his building of Heorot, and the first encounter with Grendel. The modern title of this poem reflects an observation that most of it concerns the Geatish hero Beowulf. The importance of analogues in finding the poet's lost background in widely known Scylding poems is demonstrated by the fact that Beowulf, for all his later predominance, is neither introduced until line 194 nor named until line 343.

There are two other Old English poems which treat of Danish heroes: the so-called *Finnsburh Fragment*, which survives in a partial transcription made before 1705, from a manuscript which has since been lost; and another analogue, named *Widsith*, a rambling digest of older themes and poems preserved in fos. 84ᵛ to 87ʳ of the Exeter Book, which was compiled in *c.*1000. The value of the *Fragment* is that it tells the first half of the tale about the 'Half-Danes' in Frisia, the second of which is told in *Beo* 1066–159.[64] But this tale is not contemporary with the Scyldings in *Beowulf*. In this regard there is more to say about *Widsith*, whose narrator persona, 'Widsith' ('widely travelled'), lists the names of all the kings and tribes through which he has passed. Most scholars assume that this poem comes from Mercia, whether of the ninth or tenth century.[65] Widsith alludes to the Scyldings after a passage on King Offa of Angeln (lines 35–44; see my Chapter 8). In lines 45–9 Hrothwulf and Hrothgar are presented as uncle and nephew, both driving off King Ingeld's *wicinga cynn* ('tribe of pirates', line 47; see my Chapter 4). This story is known also in *Beowulf*, while *Widsith*'s reference to

---

[63] OE *ða* as in *Beowulf*, ed. Mitchell and Robinson, 288 (*s.v. se*).

[64] North, 'Tribal Loyalties', 15–16. *Finnsburh: Fragment and Episode*, ed. D. K. Fry (London, 1974). *Beowulf*, ed. Mitchell and Robinson, 212–15 (with translation).

[65] *The Exeter Book*, ed. G. P. Krapp and E. v. K. Dobbie, ASPR III (New York, 1936), pp. xliii–xlv; Chambers, *Beowulf*, 206–11.

Hrothgar's family appears to have a verbal affinity with the language of *Beo* 1162–5. Elsewhere, however, the poet of *Widsith* does not connect Scyld with Sceaf, as does the poet of *Beowulf* with the formulation *Scyld Scefing* in his prologue (*Beo* 4). In *Widsith*, *Sceafa* is a king of the Longobards (*Wid* 32), whereas in *Beowulf* a certain *Scef* is the inferred father of Scyld, to whom the Danish Scyldings trace their line in *Beo* 4–52. Nor does the poet of *Widsith* appear to know either of Hygelac, king of the Geats, who are named without their ruler (*Wid* 58). Nor is there a King Beowulf himself, who might have been expected to fill a place in *Widsith* had the poet known the poem now bearing his name. These omissions and differences imply that the poet of *Widsith* did not know *Beowulf*, but that the poet of *Beowulf* probably knew a work on Ingeld and the Scyldings which was known to the compiler of *Widsith*. In Chapter 5 I shall suggest that this was the work to which Alcuin refers in his denunciation of 'Hinieldus' in the context of *carmina* that were performed in the court of 'Speratus' in 797.

Unlike *Widsith*, *Beowulf*'s Norse analogues are a little out of fashion. Their loss of prestige in modern times has made *Beowulf* look more unusual than it is.[66] The content of these analogues may be divided into monsters and heroes. Both types of theme have been considered exhaustively, the former more lately.[67] The greater challenge, however, lies in reconsidering *Beowulf*'s Scylding kings and their retainers. Many have named counterparts in what R. W. Chambers called the *disiecta membra* of Danish and Old Norse historiography.[68] This diverse material includes four or five thirteenth-century Scandinavian prose works about the 'Skjǫldungar', that is, about the Scyldings in their native setting: *Skjǫldunga saga* of c.1200, Snorri's *Ynglinga saga* and *Skáldskaparmál* of c.1220, a now-lost version of *Hrólfs saga kraka* in the same period, and the extant *Hrólfs saga kraka* and the ballad *Bjarkarímur* of c.1400, if not also the fragmentary *Bjarkamál* which appears to paraphrase a lost work from the tenth century. *Skjǫldunga saga* represents a learned, *Hrólfs saga* an originally learned then popular tradition, about the Scylding kings.[69] Also the works of Sven Aggesen and Saxo Grammaticus and other Danish chronicles and histories from the eleventh and twelfth centuries throw light on both the Danes' use of Icelandic sources and the relics of their own legends about the earliest kings of Denmark. There are other derivative texts in the vernacular, such as *Hyndluljóð*, a poetic catalogue of the fourteenth century, which preserves older material on the Scandinavian kings.[70] Chambers vindicated the use of these works in throwing light on *Beowulf*, against Axel Olrik, who

---

[66] *Beowulf and its Analogues*, trans. Garmonsway and Simpson, with notes by Ellis Davidson. For the idea that *Beowulf* was a literary one-off, see C. R. Davis, *Beowulf and the Demise of Germanic Legend in England* (New York, 1996), 65–87.

[67] Orchard, *Pride and Prodigies*, 140–68; *Companion*, 123–9 and 132–7. Rauer, *Beowulf and the Dragon*, 9–51.

[68] Chambers, *Beowulf*, 427.

[69] Jakob, 'Icelandic Traditions of the Scyldings', 48–52 and 55–7.

[70] A. Ya. Gurevich, 'Hyndluljóð', in Pulsiano and Wolf (eds.), *Medieval Scandinavia*, 309.

sought to rule them out.[71] Olrik's objection lay in the relatively late dates of these works, which allow that none could have influenced *Beowulf* in their present form.

Perhaps because these works are analogues, not sources, less was done with them after the publication of *Beowulf and its Analogues* (1968). Larry D. Benson dismisses most of the Norse material when he calls *Beowulf* a free adaptation of 'brief lays'.[72] His complaint is that the poem's critics 'have reconstructed the earliest versions of the Bjarki story on the basis of its most modern versions'.[73] Benson thus treats *Hrólfs saga* as overrated, omits reference to *Skjǫldunga saga*, and claims that the Norse analogues of Hrothgar and the Danes have no bearing on *Beowulf*. He states that the poet's true source was 'the tale in *Grettis saga*', one derived from 'a kernel of tradition' involving a hero who slays two monsters, one of each sex.[74] As analogues go, there is no doubt that the Icelandic *Grettis saga*, a sprawling family saga of the late fourteenth century, is easier to compare with *Beowulf*, in that rootless monsters, not royal dynasties, are involved. Beowulf's fights with the Grendels resemble two or three of the strong-man Grettir: first with Glámr, a Swedish living dead, in Þórhallsstaðir (chs. 32–5); later with a troll-wife; and then with a giant behind a waterfall by Sandhaugar in Iceland (chs. 64–6). These parallels were first noted more than a century ago.[75] Yet kings are more complex than monsters. Benson, for example, mistrusts *Beowulf*'s Norse Skjǫldung-analogues because their narratives differ: Bǫðvarr takes service with King Hrólfr whereas Beowulf deals with Hrothgar, an older kinsman of Hrothulf, counterpart of Hrólfr. Though this disparity is more revealing than harmful, it seems to have stopped the great *Analogues* book in its tracks.[76] When Andersson later discussed Saxo's *Gesta Danorum* and *Hrólfs saga*, he dismissed their relevance to the poem.[77] Generally he appears to take his lead from Benson without going too far into Danish dynastic legend, beyond endorsing the monster-slaying type-scene which is known from *Grettis saga*.[78]

Recently, however, even *Grettis saga* has lost its glamour. The existence of Benson's 'ecotype' has been challenged. In 1998, not long after Andersson's discussion in the *Beowulf Handbook*, Magnús Fjalldal reclassified the episodes from this saga, the fights in Þórhallsstaðir and Sandhaugar, not as related analogues but as scenes with no more than a coincidental likeness to those with

---

[71] Chambers, *Beowulf*, 54–86. A. Olrik, *Danmarks Heltedigtning*, i: *Rolf Krake og den ældre Skjoldungrække* (Copenhagen, 1903), 135–6.

[72] Benson, 'The Originality of *Beowulf*', 12.

[73] Ibid. 15.

[74] Ibid. 19 and 23–4.

[75] *Sturlunga saga Including the Islendinga Saga of Lawman Sturla Thordsson and Other Works*, ed. Gudbrand Vigfusson, vol. i (Oxford, 1878), p. xlix. *Corpus poeticum boreale: The Poetry of the Old Northern Tongue*, ed. Gudbrand Vigfusson and F. York Powell, vol. ii (Oxford, 1883), 502.

[76] Witness the passing reference to Skjǫldungar in Orchard, *Companion*, 245.

[77] Andersson, 'Sources and Analogues', 125–48, esp. 132–3.

[78] Ibid. 134: '*Grettis saga*, and by extension *Beowulf*, belong to a Norse "ecotype" in which a hero enters a cave and kills two giants, usually of different sexes.'

Grendel and his Mother in *Beowulf*.[79] Predictably, his case falls down over
Grettir's fights in Sandhaugar in chs. 64–6, in which the form of the unique
word *heptisax* bears such an indelible resemblance to that of the unique word
hæftmece in the scene with Grendel's Mother. Little can be done with this
likeness but to treat it as proof of a textual relationship between *Beowulf* and
Grettis saga. If due to an influence from England to Iceland, the type of
relationship suggested between *Beowulf* and *Grettis saga* appears to differ from
the connection between the poem and the Bjarki analogues which this raucous
saga has displaced. In general, however, *Grettis saga* is losing its importance in
Beowulf studies. In their edition of the poem (in 'key documents'), Bruce
Mitchell and Fred C. Robinson include no more than Simpson's translation of
Grettis saga, chs. 64–6, Grettir's fight with the troll-wife and giant: with nothing
on Glámr, Grendel's counterpart.[80] Andy Orchard wrote a big chapter on *Grettis
saga* in 1994, but his title, 'Grettir and Grendel Again', acknowledges a growing
fatigue. In his *Critical Companion* of 2003, *Grettis saga* yields up pride of place as
an analogue to a number of minor Icelandic *fornaldarsögur* ('sagas of ancient
times').[81] With all this long goodbye to the comparative use of Saxo, *Hrólfs saga*,
Skjǫldunga saga, and finally *Grettis saga*, it could be said that today's readers of
Beowulf are losing their incentive to read the Norse analogues which matter.

These developments belie the fact that the Norse Skjǫldung-analogues contain
enough detail for a plausible outline of the *Beowulf*-poet's 'Danish' material to be
drawn on the basis of whatever narrative they have in common. Unravelling their
relationships is complex, but it is still obvious that these analogues descend from
one tradition. Perhaps, as was once accepted without challenge, this is what we
could call 'North Sea Germanic', a body of legends that came to England in the
Age of Migrations; perhaps, as many now believe, these legends reached the poet
directly from Danes of the Viking Age. Below I shall steer a middle course,
pleading that Frisians, not Danes, brought tales of the Scyldings to England.
Before we study the poet's Scylding legends in the following chapter, let us look at
their means of transmission.

SONGS ON SHIPS: THE FRISIANS

A combination of two lines in *Beowulf* reveals the poet's belief that sailors can
pass stories, as poems, from one shore to another: he says that after a few years
Grendel's raids on Heorot become *ylda bearnum undyrne cuð gyddum geomore*

[79] *The Long Arm of Coincidence: The Frustrated Connection between 'Beowulf' and 'Grettis saga'*
(Toronto, 1998), 39–44 and 49–66.
[80] *Beowulf*, ed. Mitchell and Robinson, 218–32, esp. 218.
[81] Including *Hrómundar saga Gripssonar, Egils saga einhenda ok Ásmundar berserkjabana*, and
Ǫrvar-Odds saga. Orchard, *Companion*, 123–8.

('openly put forth to the sons of men, sadly in songs', lines 150–1); and when Beowulf says that the business with Grendel became *undyrne cuð* to him in his own land, he adds that it is what *secgað sæliðend* ('seafarers say', lines 410–11).

Throughout the Anglo-Saxon period, even in the Viking Age, most North Sea sailors were Frisian traders. Frisians have never been taken seriously as mediators of legends in *Beowulf*, but the poem has two stories about them: the lay of Finnsburh, recited to Hrothgar's court while the Danes celebrate their deliverance from Grendel; and Hygelac's last raid. First, in *Beowulf*'s 'Finnsburh episode' (lines 1063–160), the poet's allusive narrative is compressed to the point of obscurity: an indication that he was dealing with a longer established poem. Elsewhere the story appears to have been told in the full version of *The Finnsburh Fragment*.[82] *Widsith* also appears to know it, giving the Frisians as subjects of Finn Folcwalding on line 27, after the *Ytum* ('Jutes', *Wid* 26) and before the *Sædenum* ('Sea-Danes', *Wid* 28). For his own part the poet of *Beowulf* focuses on Hengest, probably a Jute, as the instrument of Danish vengeance on Finn. As Hengest was known as the first Germanic invader of Kent, it is plausible that his source-poem came from Canterbury. The place of Finn Folcwalding in a genealogy in *Historia Brittonum* (*c*.829) suggests that a poem on the Frisians was known in Kent by this time.[83] But the poet also reveals a closer knowledge of Frisia, through its old cults and landscape. The crux *icge gold* (line 1107) describes the gold on which, with MS *að wæs geæfned* ('the oath was performed', line 1107), the Frisian king makes the former combatants swear. Christopher Ball's suggestion that MS *icge* should be read as *incge* fits nicely with '?**ngz inguz ngz**', a runic legend on an antler found in the terp at Wijnaldum, in west Friesland.[84] Possibly this inscription dates from the seventh or eighth centuries.[85] The poet of *Beowulf* associates the stem of 'Ingui' or 'Ing' not only with the Frisians (in lines 1089, 111–12, 1155, and 1142), but also with the Danes (*Ingwine* on lines 1044 and 1319) and Geats (Beowulf's *incge laf* on line 2577).[86] This vision of an ancient cult extending for the length of the north Germanic seaboard is fully in keeping with the idea that the stories about Denmark and beyond were mediated by Frisians. In addition, the poet knows of *Fryslond* ('Friesland') as *hamas ond heaburh* ('homes and high-fortresses', lines 1126–7). This

---

[82] For a reconstruction, see North, 'Tribal Loyalties'; *Heathen Gods*, 65–70. For other interpretations, see Chambers, *Beowulf*, 245–89; Tolkien *Finn and Hengest*, ed. Bliss.

[83] *Nennius et l'Historia Brittonum*, ed. Lot, 171–2 (ch. 31): 'Finn, Fodepald, Geta, qui fuit, ut aiunt, filius Dei.' The Finn son of Godewulf in the Lindsey and West Saxon genealogies appears to be of a different origin. See Sisam, 'Anglo-Saxon Royal Genealogies', 311; Dumville, 'The Anglian Collection', 31, 34, and 37; Bremmer, 'Frisians in Anglo-Saxon England', 76.

[84] C. Ball, 'Incge Beow. 2577', *Anglia*, 78 (1960), 403–10, at 409–10. North, 'Tribal Loyalties', 32–8, at 33; *Heathen Gods*, 70–2. T. Looijenga, 'Runes around the North Sea and on the Continent: AD 150–700: Texts & Contexts', Ph.D. thesis, University of Groningen, 1997, 193 (no. 22: *Wijnaldum A*): '**z ng z u ng i z ng**'.

[85] J. Zijlstra, 'Onderzoek Wijnaldum: Supplement "Finns Fibula" ', *Friese Bodemvondsten*, 2 (Leeuwaarden, 1991), 1–30.

[86] Ibid. 70–7.

is an accurate description of Frisian *terpen*, built-up mounds which are known to have covered the Frisian areas from the fifth to the thirteenth centuries, when coastal dykes allowed the Frisians to drain the tidal flats in which they lived.[87]

This poet's second Frisian foray is Hygelac's last raid, a story to which he alludes four times. One version of this story was familiar to the author of *Liber monstrorum*, an insular treatise on monsters which is dated to *c*.650 × *c*.750. The author of the *Liber* says that Hygelac's bones *in Rheni fluminis insula, ubi in Oceanum prorumpit, reseruata sunt, et de longinquo uenientibus pro miraculo ostenduntur* ('are preserved on an island in the river Rhine, where it breaks into the Ocean, and they are shown as a wonder to travellers from afar').[88] So it looks as if this author got his story from pilgrims who stopped in Dorestad on their way back from Rome.[89] Theirs could be called the import of an Anglo-Frisian tale of Hygelac's death. Moreover, like the poet of *Beowulf*, the author of the *Liber* refers to 'Huncglacus' or 'Higlacus' as a king of the *Getae* ('Geats'). Hygelac's namesake is given as a Dane in the two Frankish sources which relate his last raid in Frisia, as a Swedish king in Snorri Sturluson's *Ynglinga saga*. A literary version of Hygelac's story was almost certainly known to the poet of *Beowulf* from the later Frankish source, a copy of *Liber historiae Francorum* that may have reached England as early as the 730s.[90] The near certainty that this was one of *Beowulf*'s sources gives the poem a *terminus a quo* of *c*.727.[91]

There again, the Geatishness of Hygelac in the *Liber monstrorum* shows even more clearly than the *incge*-term that the poet of *Beowulf* got a vernacular version of Hygelac's tale from a network linking England with Frisia. Bremmer doubts whether it is necessary to assume Frisian middlemen for this and other heroic material in Old English poems, saying that the Gothic tales in *Deor*, for example, are unlikely to have arrived via Gothic embassies.[92] Yet the trade between England and Scandinavia from the sixth to the eighth centuries was mostly in Frisian hands.[93] The Frisians started from their *terpen* near tidal creeks and streams in the late sixth century. From *c*.650 onwards they began to settle at beach-markets including Dorestad, already the site of a mint.[94] According to the *Vita Vulframni*, there were Frisian monks at Saint-Wandrille in Normandy, from which Gervold, abbot of this house in 787–807, travelled to Mercia as the go-between of Kings

---

[87] H. Halbertsma, *Terpen tussen Vlie en Eems*, 2 vols., i: *Atlas*, ii: *Text* (Groningen, 1963), ii. 159–207.

[88] Orchard, *Pride and Prodigies*, 258–9 (I. 2).

[89] The sources of *Waldere* and related Nibelung material in *Widsith* and *Beowulf* may have reached England from Bavaria, through returning pilgrims. See *Waldere*, ed. F. Norman (London, 1933), 7–13 and 18–34, at 28.

[90] Goffart, 'Datable Anachronisms in *Beowulf*', 84–7, at 87 n. 24.

[91] Rauer, *Beowulf and the Dragon*, 21.

[92] Bremmer, 'Frisians in Anglo-Saxon England', 75–6.

[93] Hines, *The Scandinavian Character of Anglian England*; 'The Scandinavian Character of Anglian England: An Update', 323–6. Näsman, 'Vendel Period Glass from Eketorp II', 83–8.

[94] D. Ellmers, 'The Frisian Monopoly of Coastal Transport in the 6th–8th Centuries AD', in McGrail (ed.), *Maritime Celts*, 91–2.

Offa and Charlemagne.[95] The Frisians also moved into towns. Bede has a story of a Frisian merchant in London in 679 (*HE* IV. 22).[96] There were Frisians in Ipswich and in *Hamwih*, near Southampton (see Ill. 2).[97] According to the *Vita s. Liudgeri* (*c*.840) there was also a colony in York.[98] One such foreigner might be taken as the husband of the *Frysan wife* ('the Frisian's wife') who welcomes him home from the sea in *Maxims I* (lines 23–9, at 25).[99]

Frisian merchants settled also in Paris, Mainz, Worms, Cologne, Hedeby in Denmark, and Birka in Sweden.[100] Their range may be better understood from a reference nearly a century earlier in 747/8, in an anonymous letter which duns the recipient for some garments he had vowed to send from Frisia.[101] Given the plenitude of wool in England at this time, these *vestimenta* were probably silks from Persia which the Frisians bought in Birka from merchants who had reached the Baltic from the Black Sea.[102] It was from Utrecht in Frisia that Willibrord sailed to Denmark, probably Ribe in south-west Jutland, in the early eighth century.[103] In his *Vita s. Willibrordi*, Alcuin says that Willibrord, having failed to convert cruel King Ongendus, baptized thirty Danish youths *ne aliquod propter pericula longissimi navigii vel ex insidiis ferocissimorum terrae illius habitatorum damnum pateretur in illis* ('lest any damnation should befall them, whether on account of the dangers of this longest of sea-voyages or through ambushes from the most savage inhabitants of this land').[104] Willibrord's pastoral concern may have belied an interest in acquiring helpers for God's work in Frisia. He may have bought them, for excavations in Ribe have turned up at least thirty Anglo-Frisian *sceattas*, silver coins which were struck in Frisia in *c*.720 × 750.[105] Many other *sceattas* and other coins have been found on the islands nearby, but Ribe was probably the biggest Danish market, with lively connections west to Dorestad, Domburg on Walcheren, and Quentovic (Étaples) on the river Canche.[106] These

---

[95] Levison, *England and the Continent in the Eighth Century*, 56 n. 2. *Gesta abbatum Fontanellensium*, ed. Loewenfeld, 46 (ch. 16).

[96] Bremmer, 'Frisians in Anglo-Saxon England', 72–6.

[97] Ibid. 55. C. Scull, 'Urban Centres in Pre-Viking England', in J. Hines (ed.), *The Anglo-Saxons from the Migration Period to the Eighth Century: An Ethnographic Perspective* (Woodbridge, 1997), 269–310, at 272–8.

[98] *Vita s. Liudgeri*, ed. Pertz, 406–8 (I. 10–12).

[99] Quoted in Bremmer, 'Frisians in Anglo-Saxon England', 74–5.

[100] Halbertsma, 'Frieslands Oudheid', 484–5. See further S. Lebecq, *Marchands et navigateurs frisons du Haut Moyen Âge*, 2 vols. (Lille, 1983).

[101] 'Quare non transmisisti vestimenta, quae debuisti mittere de Fraesarum provincia?' *The Letters of Saint Boniface*, trans. Emerton, 119–20, at 119 (LXIII [79]).

[102] Halbertsma, 'Frieslands Oudheid', 489–90. On the eastern textiles in Cenwulf's Mercia, see my Chapter 6.

[103] Bencard and Jørgensen, 'Excavation and Stratigraphy', 147–8; Bendixen, 'Sceattas and Other Coin Finds', 77.

[104] *Passiones vitaeque sanctorum*, ed. Krusch and Levison, 81–141, esp. 124 (ch. 9). *EHD*, 775–7, at 756 (no. 157). Halbertsma, 'Frieslands Oudheid', 49 and 540–4.

[105] Halbertsma, 'Frieslands Oudheid', 540. Bendixen, 'Sceattas and Other Coin Finds', 64–77, at 71–5.

[106] Bencard and Jørgensen, 'Excavation and Stratigraphy', 145–8.

and other later coins, some of which were struck in Denmark in imitation of Carolingian types, bear witness to a Frisian–Danish trade.[107] Not only these coins, but also Swedish finds of English glassware, confirm that Frisians ran the networks concerned.[108] They were active in a zone which starts in England, moves to the mouth of the Rhine, extends over the north Frisian seaboard into Zealand, and from there goes either north to Hadeland in south-east Norway, or east into Skåne ending in the archipelago of Swedish Uppland.[109] *Beowulf* has stories for all these areas.

As to the medium of literary transmission, the Frisian language was the North Sea lingua franca from *c.*680 to *c.*780, even if it is uncertain what 'Frisian' was.[110] The eighth-century Frisians were different from the *Fresii* or *Fresones* contemporary with the Romans, and in the eighth to tenth centuries it seems that these terms, just like OE *Fresan*, could be used as a synonym for long-range traders in general.[111] It is possible that the language of *Fresia citerior*, centred in Domburg on Walcheren, was really Frankish by another name.[112] Alcuin names a merchant in Dorestad, presumably a Frisian, *niger Hrotberct* ('black Hrothberht'), in his poem on a trip down the Rhine in the 780s; this name appears to be Frankish in that it is identical with the name of the abbot of Fontanelle in 779.[113] In some short texts it is hard to see much difference between Old Frankish on one hand, and Old English and the oldest Old Frisian on the other.[114] This common intelligibility is especially important for my Chapters 6–7, in which I suggest the poet embellished his tale of Hygelac's death in Frisia with details from Carolingian Francia. From the Rhineland perspective, the Frisians can be regarded as maritime Franks.

The Frisians had their own poetry. They had a poet named Bernlef, who lived at *Helewirt* (Holwyrde) near Delfzijl by the river Ems in the 780s (see Ill. 2). The

[107] Bendixen, 'Sceattas and Other Coin Finds', 78–9.

[108] Näsman, 'Vendel Period Glass from Eketorp II', 88–93; 'Om fjärrhandel i Sydskandinaviens yngre järnålder', 109–13. Gerrets, 'The Anglo-Frisian Relationship from an Archaeological Point of View', 126–8.

[109] Halbertsma, 'Frieslands Oudheid', 488–9. A skipper might accomplish 82 miles a day under sail, about half of that with oars, whereas the best result on land per day is about 15 miles: M. O. H. Carver, 'Pre-Viking Traffic in the North Sea', in McGrail (ed.), *Maritime Celts*, 117–25, at 120 (fig. 15.3).

[110] J. J. van Weringh, 'The Heliand and Bernlef', *Michigan Germanic Studies*, 12 (1986), 21–33, at 24. Hofstra accepts the likelihood, whilst not knowing of proof, in 'Ier-Aldfrysk neist Aldingelsk en Aldsaksysk', 45–6.

[111] Ermoldus equates these ideas, with the phrase *Frisones atque marini* ('traders and seafarers') in a poem in honour of Pepin, son of Louis the Pious (*c.*830). See *Poetae Latini aevi Carolini*, ed. Dümmler, I. 83. See Lebecq, 'On the Use of the Word "Frisian" ', 87. L. Whitbread, 'The Frisian Sailor Passage in the Old English Gnomic Verses', *RES* 22 (1946), 215–19.

[112] Lebecq, 'On the Use of the Word "Frisian" ', 86–7.

[113] Ibid. 87. *Poetae Latini aevi Carolini*, ed. Dümmler, i. 221 (*Alcuini carmina* IV). Halbertsma, 'Frieslands Oudheid', 486 n. 551.

[114] Hofstra, 'Ier-Aldfrysk neist Aldingelsk en Aldsaksysk', 44. See further H. F. Nielsen, 'Ante-Old Frisian: A Review', *NOWELE* 24 (1994), 91–136.

missionary Liudger cured him of blindness, according to his *Vita*, which adds that Bernlef *antiquorum actus regumque certamina bene noverat psallendo promere* ('well knew how to recite the deeds of ancient men and the battles of kings with songs at the lyre').[115] It seems likely that at least some of this material dealt with Hrothgar's family not far away in Denmark. There was a scribe in Corvey in Saxony in the 820s, *Hrodgar(i)us*, presumably named after the Scylding king.[116] It thus seems almost certain that Bernlef in Frisia knew of the Scyldings some sixty years before Alcuin complained about their son-in-law 'Hinieldus' in a letter in 797.[117] Alcuin, Liudger's teacher, leaves no word of Bernlef, but he hints at the singing of Frisian songs. In his *Carmen* LIX, he portrays the North Sea as *pelagi aequora magni* ('an expanse of mighty ocean', line 8), a perilous distance for any letter to travel. Then, asking a former pupil in York to visit him in Francia, Alcuin recommends that he improve his Latin verses with Vergil:

> Moenibus Euboricae habitans tu sacra inventus,
> Fas idcirco, reor, comprehendere plectra Maronis,
> Somnigeras subito te nunc excire camenas,
> Carminibusque sacris naves implere Fresonum,
> Talia namque placent vestro quia munera patri (lines 10–14)

[For you, sacred youth, dwelling inside the walls of York, it is now proper to comprehend the poems of Vergil, to jolt your sleepy verses suddenly awake and to fill Frisian ships with sacred songs, seeing how pleased your father is by such gifts.][118]

Here we might see Frisian ships as importers of profane poems; much as the *sæliðend* to whom Beowulf refers. Alcuin's lines tell us how some ultimately Danish legends about Scandinavian heroes could end up in England before, and for some time into, the Viking Age, in the vernacular verse of monks who had been trained to read Vergil: just the circumstances in which *Beowulf* may have arisen.

DANISH INFLUENCE ON *BEOWULF?*

The above arguments steer a course between two widely divergent views. One of these, as we have seen, regards the sixth century as the period in which all *Beowulf*'s legends crossed to Britain. The other points out that there were people in England from the mid-ninth to the late eleventh centuries, Danes and

---

[115] *Vita s. Liudgeri*, ed. Pertz, 412 (II.1).
[116] Bischoff, 'Hadoard und die Klassikerhandschriften aus Corbie', 60 n. 34.
[117] *Epistolae*, ed. Dümmler, ii. 183 (no. 124).
[118] Text from Orchard, 'Wish You Were Here', 42–3. See also *Poetae Latini aevi Carolini*, ed. Dümmler, i. 273.

Norwegians, who might have helped create the poem.[119] There are many scholars of *Beowulf* who variously look to these people as the means of transmission.

For scholars of this party, the problem is that the violence of the Viking Age does not tally with *Beowulf*'s praise for Hrothgar's people as being often *an wig gearwe* ('ready for war', line 1247) and *þeod tilu* ('a fine nation', line 1250). As Dorothy Whitelock observed, these plaudits would be odd in a country that was suffering from Danish pillage.[120] R. I. Page and others show that Danish settlers apparently blended into Anglo-Saxon society soon after the initial attacks.[121] Yet Page was dealing firstly with King Æthelstan and his tenth-century successors, secondly mainly with Anglo-Danish relations of Alfred's time. Perhaps through the dearth of evidence, he says little about Danes in the early raids from about 835 to Alfred's early wars with them in the 870s. Even if the size of the ninth-century Viking companies was below that of one's impression of them in the *Chronicle*, as Page argues, the outcome of Danish campaigning speaks for itself.[122] Alfred, referring to the east side of England in his preface to the translation of *Cura pastoralis* in *c.*890, speaks of the monasteries all burned, before he enlarges on the decay of monastic learning that had set in earlier. Alfred, as Wormald says, 'can hardly have thought that the burning itself was the work of idle monks'.[123] In the 'Danelaw' where the Viking armies took land in the late 870s, some minsters may have eked out a continuity.[124] Nonetheless, the episcopal lists of every diocese bar York and Lindisfarne were interrupted for decades, from Lindisfarne St Cuthbert's relics went into peregrination to Ireland, and the bishoprics of Hexham, Leicester, and southern East Anglia disappeared.[125] Consequently no books survive from middle, eastern, or northern England in Offa's time through which his reign (757–96) will ever be understood to the same degree as Charlemagne's. In the light of these upheavals, *Beowulf* would have to be read as anti-clerical if it was written near Mercia in the Viking Age.

Today, notwithstanding, *Beowulf*'s tales of Scandinavia are thought to show an acquaintance with Danes living in England; suggested dates bring the poem into the tenth century. It has been noted, above all, that Scyld Scefing of the opening fitt has a namesake, Scyldwa son of Sceaf, in the

---

[119] Stenton, *Anglo-Saxon England*, 239–70, 319–51, 356–63, 374–432, 502–25, 588–91.

[120] Whitelock, *The Audience of Beowulf*, 25.

[121] Page, 'The Audience of *Beowulf* and the Vikings', 113–22. Jacobs, 'Anglo-Danish Relations, Poetic Archaism, and the Date of *Beowulf*', 23–43. Murray, '*Beowulf*, the Danish Invasions, and Royal Genealogy', 109–10. Frank, 'Skaldic Verse and the Date of *Beowulf*', 123.

[122] Page, 'The Audience of *Beowulf* and the Vikings', 120. P. H. Sawyer, *The Age of the Vikings*, 2nd edn. (London, 1971), 202–3. K. Cameron, *The Significance of English Place-Names* (London, 1976), 18.

[123] Campbell (ed.), *The Anglo-Saxons*, 147–8, at 148. Lapidge (*The Anglo-Saxon Library*, 45–6) points out that west Mercia probably lay untouched.

[124] Blair, *The Church in Anglo-Saxon Society*, 292–5 and 315–23.

[125] Abrams, 'The Conversion of the Danelaw', 32–5. See Wormald, in Campbell (ed.), *The Anglo-Saxons*, 147: 'medieval bishoprics were durable institutions, which seldom, if ever, disappeared because of mere "decay".'

Anglo-Saxon Chronicle (*s.a.* 855).[126] Accordingly, since it was the West Saxons who conquered, converted, and absorbed the Vikings from Alfred's reign (871–99) to those of his grandsons Æthelstan, Edmund, and Eadred (924–54), *Beowulf* has been taken for a courtly work of this period in which the Danes, now having a destiny in common with their West Saxon rulers, might applaud an attempt with 'Scyld' in an Alfredian *Beowulf* to suggest that their kings shared an ancestor as well. To this we can add a recent demonstration, through place names, that Anglian and Danish dialects in the ninth and tenth centuries were mutually intelligible.[127]

If we look further into Scyld Scefing, we see that from line 4 of *Beowulf* onwards, he is given as the founder of Hrothgar's line, his people as the *Scyldingas*. The royal genealogy of the West Saxons in the *Anglo-Saxon Chronicle* under the year 855 contains a long list of names based on *Sceaf(a)–Scyldwa* (or *Sceldwea)–Beaw*, with Sceaf(a) given as a son of Noah born to the biblical patriarch in the Ark.[128] This list seems expanded from *Scef–Scyld–Beo*, a sequence extant in a Latin translation of the *Chronicle* which was made by the West Saxon nobleman Æthelweard in 975 × 983. Æthelweard's vernacular version of the *Chronicle* is lost, but he takes Æthelwulf's lineage back no further than Scef.[129] As Audrey Meaney points out, Æthelweard could claim descent from Æthelwulf and he is not likely to have discarded a set of ancestors older than Scef if he had known of one; his source is thus taken to be the common archetype of the *Chronicle*, written before 892.[130] The genealogy in this archetype must have been written earlier, however, before Æthelwulf's death in 858, because Æthelweard's Latin refers to this king in the present tense as if he were living.[131] The year in which Scef and the other names appear, 855, suits Æthelwulf's dynastic aims, in that his journey to Rome at this time concluded with his marriage to Judith, daughter of Charles the Bald of the western Franks.[132] The extension from Sceaf(a) through his father Noah back to Adam, which was devised in 892 or after, appears to be the work of Alfred or one of his bishops.[133] In this way it

---

[126] Meaney, 'Scyld Scefing Again', 13–22. Murray, '*Beowulf*, the Danish Invasions, and Royal Genealogy', 103–5.

[127] Townend, *Language and History*, esp. 43–87.

[128] Orchard, *Companion*, 100–1.

[129] Sisam, 'Anglo-Saxon Royal Genealogies', 297–8 and 307–22. The full sequence is *Sceaf(a)–Bedwig–Hwala–Hrathra–Itermon–Heremod–Scyldwa–Beaw* (BC); in the other versions Hrathra and Bedwig are missing (ADEF).

[130] Meaney, 'Scyld Scefing Again', 13. Newton, *The Origins of Beowulf*, 54–76, at 71–5.

[131] *Chronicle of Æthelweard*, ed. and trans. Campbell, 33 (translation mine): *de cuius prosapia ordinem trahit Æðulf rex* ('from whose stock King Æthelwulf takes his line'). See North, *Heathen Gods*, 183–4. This tense escapes not only Meaney ('Scyld Scefing Again', 13), but also Newton (*The Origins of Beowulf*, 73) and Orchard (*Companion*, 101).

[132] Kirby, *Earliest English Kings*, 198–201. On Æthelwulf's possible use of 'Geat' at this time, see North, *Heathen Gods*, 160–71. J. L. Nelson, *Charles the Bald* (London, 1992), 182: 'Charles as his father-in-law (though probably a younger man) could assume the senior position in an extended family of kings.'

[133] For arguments that this part of *Beowulf* derives from this genealogy in the Chronicle, see: Meaney, 'Scyld Scefing Again', 13–22; cf. Murray, '*Beowulf*, the Danish Invasions, and Royal

appears to be Æthelwulf who quarried the prologue of *Beowulf* for ancestors, rather than the reverse; and in *c.*855, some time before the Danes could lend their ancestors to West Saxons.

The dating of *Beowulf* in the Viking Age has long received sociological underpinning. With the West Saxons of Alfred's time or a few decades later, it has been argued that *Beowulf*'s Danish concerns, particularly the Scylding prologue to the poem, are evidence of the desire for cohesion between West Saxon royals and their new Danish subject-allies.[134] The Danish names in Æthelwulf's genealogy, Heremod as well as Sceaf, Scyld, and Beaw, are treated as proof of Alfred's need to strengthen his position in the Danelaw.[135] The Danes in Mercia and E. Anglia, it is thought, would become better neighbours to Wessex once they knew that King Alfred was really a Dane. In Roberta Frank's words, 'the new genealogy reflected a new social reality'.[136] In another study she claims that 'the *Beowulf* poet anchors the West Saxon *imperium* in a brilliant North Germanic antiquity', and that Scyld's opening the poem 'fits nicely with the efforts of Alfred and his successors to promote an Anglo-Danish brotherhood, to see Dane and Anglo-Saxon as equal partners in a united kingdom'.[137]

This case is eloquently made, but it can be shown that neither Alfred nor his successors wanted a social equality with the Danes. It is true that Alfred made a treaty with Guthrum and stood sponsor for his baptism in 879 and for Hæsten's son probably in 894.[138] Asser, Alfred's biographer, says that he saw a monk, *unum paganicae gentis edoctum* ('one of heathen race being instructed'), in Athelney, presumably a Dane; also that there were *pagani* ('heathens'), presumably Danes, at the West Saxon court along with other foreigners.[139] From an interpolation in the Alfredian translation of Orosius' *Historia adversus paganos*, it seems that at some time in the 880s one of these was Ohthere (i.e. Óttarr), a skipper from Hálogaland in Norway, who calls Alfred his *hlaford* ('lord').[140] However, religion was an issue. Alfred brought Guthrum to the font in order to ensure his fealty to Christian symbols, having learned his lesson in Chippenham in 878–9, when the Danes, breaking their oaths, surprised him on Twelfth Night.

Genealogy', 103–5. For arguments in favour of the reverse, that the genealogy was plundered from *Beowulf,* see: North, *Heathen Gods,* 182–96, at 188–91; cf. Tolley, '*Beowulf*'s Scyld Scefing Episode', 8–12.

[134] Frank, 'Skaldic Verse and the Date of *Beowulf*', 127–9; 'The *Beowulf*-Poet's Sense of History', 110. Murray, '*Beowulf,* the Danish Invasions, and Royal Genealogy', 110–11. Niles, 'Reconceiving *Beowulf*', 126–7.

[135] Frank, 'Skaldic Verse and the Date of *Beowulf*', 129. Murray, '*Beowulf,* the Danish Invasions, and Royal Genealogy', 105.

[136] Frank, 'Skaldic Verse and the Date of *Beowulf*', 128.

[137] 'The *Beowulf*-Poet's Sense of History', 110.

[138] *ASC* A, *s.a.* 878 [879] (pp. 50–1) and 894 [893] (pp. 58–9). *The Anglo-Saxon Chronicle,* trans. and ed. Swanton, 76–7 and 84–6.

[139] *Asser's Life of King Alfred,* ed. Stevenson, 60 (ch. 76) and 81 (ch. 94).

[140] *The Old English Orosius,* ed. J. Bately, EETS ss 6 (1980), 15–16. *Alfred the Great,* trans. Keynes and Lapidge, 228–30.

Alfred's new expediency with Guthrum hardly makes it more likely that he ordered a set of Danish ancestors for his father in the *Chronicle* for the year 855. Any notion that he did would ask us to believe that Alfred endorsed a record of his descent from Scyldwa in the 890s in order to become one with the people who tried to take his kingdom four times (in the early 870s, in 878–9, in 885, and in 892–6). Doubtless Alfred respected the Danes, but the idea that he grafted his ancestry on to theirs, as 'an efficient means of promoting ethnic unity', carries this admiration too far.[141] The West-Saxonness of 'Æthelstan', the baptismal name which Alfred chose for Guthrum in 879, shows that Alfred did not want his new friend to remain Danish.[142] Eirenic readings of *Beowulf* in relation to Alfred's policy towards Guthrum seem thus misplaced. Perhaps they owe something to ideals of integration in the twentieth century. Where the ninth is concerned, as Page shows, the Danes were seen as religious aliens.[143]

In this regard, the Danes adapted to English life by becoming Christian, while partly retaining their own laws.[144] But first, as heathens in the 'Danelaw', the Danes let the Church infrastructure fall into ruin while they ruled the eastern Midlands, East Anglia, and Yorkshire for some forty years;[145] later the West Saxons brought the surviving minsters more into the secular world.[146] The Danes held the boroughs of Leicester, Lincoln, Nottingham, Stamford, and Derby from 877 to 917 (Lincoln until 920), when Edward the Elder and his sister Æthelflæd overran them with a joint West Saxon and Mercian force.[147] Although little about these petty earldoms is known, Levin Schücking proposed that *Beowulf* was composed in one of them in *c*.900 by a Mercian poet for the education of a Danish prince.[148] In general, the poet's praise of the Scyldings seemed to him to fit, for who but a Danish audience could have wished to know about Scyld Scefing, Hrothgar, and Hrothulf? Yet there is no evidence that the Mercian Danes of this time were Christians like the poet of *Beowulf*.[149] Even if he composed his work for Danish converts later, say in the 920s, it is worth asking what they would have thought of his view of their ancestors in lines 175–88. Besides this, the poet ends his work with Geats or Wægmundings, not with the Danes, whom he leaves behind in line 1887 at the end of Fitt XXVI. For these reasons Schücking's idea lacks the force it would

[141] Niles, 'Reconceiving *Beowulf*', 115.

[142] *ASC* A, *s.a.* 890 (p. 54). *The Anglo-Saxon Chronicle*, trans. and ed. Swanton, 82–3. Niles, 'Reconceiving *Beowulf*', 115.

[143] 'The Audience of *Beowulf* and the Vikings', 117–22.

[144] Hart, *The Danelaw*, 145–8, 177–80, and 281–8.

[145] Abrams, 'The Conversion of the Danelaw', 35–7. On problems with the term 'Danelaw', see K. Holman, 'Defining the Danelaw', in Graham-Campbell, Hall, Jesch, and Parsons (eds.), *Vikings and the Danelaw*, 1–11.

[146] Blair, *The Church in Anglo-Saxon Society*, 323–38.

[147] Hart, *The Danelaw*, 3–24, at 16–20.

[148] L. Schücking, 'Wann entstand der Beowulf? Glossen, Zweifel, und Fragen', *BGdSL* 42 (1917), 347–410; 'Die Beowulfdatierung: Eine Replik', *BGdSL* 47 (1923), 293–311.

[149] Abrams, 'The Conversion of the Danelaw', 35–40.

have if the Danes were not portrayed as idolaters or were the subject of an encomium in *Beowulf*'s closing fitts.[150]

Schücking's study was useful, however, in airing a new idea of co-operation between a Christian poet and his Danish overlords. As Niles argues, Anglo-Danish harmony is more plausible in the reign of Æthelstan (925–39), Alfred's grandson.[151] Æthelstan succeeded in consolidating his father Edward's West Saxon and his aunt Æthelflæd's Mercian gains and extending these into Cumbria, while in 937 his forces defeated an Irish–Norse–Scottish alliance in the Battle of *Brunanburh*, probably at Bromborough on the Wirral. It has been shown that Æthelstan was strongly affiliated with Scandinavian subjects of various kinds. He had a European policy and provided for young foreign nobles in his court, at least one of whom, Hákon *Aðalsteinsfóstri* ('Æthelstan's fosterson') Haraldsson, may have been Norwegian; six out of thirteen earls attending him in Colchester in 931 were probably Danish; and the thirteenth-century Icelandic tradition preserved in *Egils saga*, chs. 50–5, that Egill and his brother Þórólfr fought for 'Aðalsteinn' in Vinheiðr, appears prima facie to descend from a story of Icelanders fighting for Æthelstan at *Brunanburh* in 937.[152] For reasons of this kind, particularly to do with his fostering of young Hákon, Æthelstan's reign has seemed right for the social-aristocratic milieu of *Beowulf*, a poem in which an interest in Denmark could have nestled with West Frankish embassies and a renaissance of Latin learning.[153]

To help this view there is a present-day illusion of stability in Æthelstan's England with which the earlier 'Heptarchy' is unfavourably compared. It has been claimed that *Beowulf* aims for a tenth-century national concord with a narrative in which regional rivalries of the sixth- to eighth-century kind 'are scarcely discernible'.[154] Yet one only need think of a few altercations in *Beowulf* to question this idea.[155] Others believe that the poet imitated Danish skaldic verse, despite the formal difference between *Bogenstil* lines on the Old English

---

[150] These points are not addressed in those who follow Schücking's idea, in either N. F. Blake, 'The Dating of Old English Poetry', in B. S. Lee (ed.), *An English Miscellany Presented to W. S. Mackie* (New York, 1977), 14–27; or Jacobs, 'Anglo-Danish Relations, Poetic Archaism, and the Date of *Beowulf*', 23–43.

[151] Niles, *Beowulf*, 104–7.

[152] *Egils saga Skalla-Grímssonar*, ed. Sigurður Nordal, 127–48. Page, 'The Audience of *Beowulf* and the Vikings', 113–17. Murray, '*Beowulf*, the Danish Invasions, and Royal Genealogy', 109–110. A stanza and refrain from Egill's *Aðalsteinsdrápa*, quoted in *Egils saga*, is nowadays taken to be a genuine survival from Egill's works, datable to 937: Jesch, 'Skaldic Verse in Scandinavian England', 317; Townend, *Language and History*, 152–3.

[153] Goffart, 'Datable Anachronisms in *Beowulf*', 96–100. See also Niles, 'Reconceiving *Beowulf*', 131. Stenton, *Anglo-Saxon England*, 343–62, at 349 and 360. *Agrip af Nóregskonunga Sögum*, ed. Bjarni, 7–10 (*Agrip*, chs. 5–6) and 74–95 (*Fagrskinna*, chs. 6–13). On the poetic consequences, see North, *Heathen Gods*, 118–24.

[154] Niles, 'Reconceiving *Beowulf*', 130.

[155] Heathobards versus Danes (lines 83–5), Danes versus Geats (lines 1856–7), Half-Danes versus Frisians (lines 1068–159), Geats versus Swedes (lines 2476–8), a Wægmunding versus Geats (lines 2612–16).

side, and stanzas on the Norse.[156] Roberta Frank has written widely on this and
other cases of suggested Anglo-Scandinavian poetic relationships.[157] A corpus of
Norse poems produced in England has since been established, showing that the
opportunity for skaldic contacts existed at West Saxon, Mercian, or Norse courts
in England during the Viking Age.[158] Yet Frank's best linguistic parallels for
Beowulf come from Eddic poems.[159] Her evidence for Norse skaldic influence
comes from particularly the 'Geatish' part of this poem, where six postponed
demonstratives (for example, *grundwong þone*, line 2588), a funeral genre resem-
bling the Norse *erfidrápa* ('memorial lay'), and a common Germanic vocabulary
for heroic hall activities are held up to show that nothing in her 'information
extracted from skaldic verse was found incompatible with a date for *Beowulf* in the
late ninth century or the first half of the tenth century'.[160] If that is so, it is partly
because of common patterns and type-scenes in Germanic verse, partly because
Frank does not go into differences between skaldic and Old English poetry.

One illustration of these will suffice. *Ragnarsdrápa* is Snorri's name for a work
whose verses he scatters though *Skáldskaparmál* (as numbered in the quotation
below). This occasional poem is datable to *c.*850 × *c.*870, the maturity of
Ragnarr *loðbrók* ('hairy breeches'), legendary father of the Vikings who first
invaded England. Snorri attributes the poem to Bragi Boddason *inn gamli* ('the
old').[161] *Ragnarsdrápa*, then, is a useful companion piece to *Beowulf*. It is not
only the oldest skaldic poem surviving, but one allegedly dedicated to a Viking
with British relatives and composed before the period in which many have dated
Beowulf. *Ragnarsdrápa* is composed in a form of *dróttkvætt* ('court metre'), and
reputedly describes the panels on a shield which Ragnarr gave to Bragi.[162] It is
believed that Bragi's verses on Þórr's fishing trip were a part of this poem. Let us
see Þórr as he prepares to fight the World Serpent, Miðgarðsormr:[163]

---

[156] Skaldic verse is occasional, usually in the complex *dróttkvætt* metre, with attribution to a
named author. See R. Frank, *Old Norse Court Poetry: The Dróttkvætt Stanza* (Ithaca, NY, 1978),
55–70. See also J. Turville-Petre, 'The Metre of Icelandic Court Poetry', *Saga-Book*, 17/4 (1969),
326–51, at 345. On OE metre and line-types, see Stanley, *In the Foreground*, 110–14.

[157] Frank, 'Skaldic Verse and the Date of *Beowulf*'; 'Did Anglo-Saxon Audiences have a Skaldic
Tooth?', *Scandinavian Studies*, 59 (1987), 338–55; 'Anglo-Scandinavian Poetic Relations', *ANQ* ns
3 (1990), 74–9.

[158] Jesch, 'Skaldic Verse in Scandinavian England', 314–18.

[159] Verse from the *Poetic Edda* is anonymous, pre-balladic, stanzaic, but still more like Old
English verse than is skaldic. See J. Harris, 'Eddic Poetry', in C. J. Clover and J. Lindow (eds.), *Old
Norse-Icelandic Literature: A Critical Guide*, Islandica 45 (Ithaca, NY, 1985), 68–156. The pairing of
Sigmundr and Hermóðr in *Hynd* 2, like that of Sigemund and Heremod in *Beo* 874–915; Helgi's
parting words in *HHund* II. 49, *mál er mér at ríða* ('it's time for me to ride'), which resemble the
Danish coastguard's in *Beo* 316, *mæl is me to feran*, of similar meaning; Beowulf accuses Unferth of
fratricide in *Beo* 587, as does Guðmundr to Sinfjǫtli in *HHund* I. 36. See Frank, 'Skaldic Verse and
the Date of *Beowulf*', 131–3.

[160] Frank, 'Skaldic Verse and the Date of *Beowulf*', 134–7, at 137.

[161] *Gylf*, 7. *Skáldskaparmál*, ed. Faulkes, i. 50–1 (vv. 154–8).

[162] Turville-Petre, *Scaldic Poetry*, pp. xxi–xxiii and 1–6.

[163] *Skáldskaparmál*, ed. Faulkes, i. 14–16 (text), 160 (note to v. 24), 164–5. *Skj* A I, 1–4. Above,
'verse' refers to citation in *Skáldskaparmál*. Turville-Petre, *Scaldic Poetry*, 5–6 (his text).

Vaðr lá Viðris arfa   vilgi slakr er rakðisk,
á Eynæfis ǫndri,   Jǫrmungandr at sandi. (verse 42)

. . . .

Hamri fórsk í hœgri   hǫnd þar er allra landa
œgir Ǫflugbarða   endiseiðs of kendi. (verse 48)

. . . .

Ok borðróins barða   brautar hringr inn ljóti
á haussprengi Hrungnis   harðgeðr neðan starði. (verse 51)

[The fishing line of the heir of Viðrir [: of Óðinn's son: Þórr] lay by no means slack on the
sand, when Jǫrmungandr [: Universal ?Magic, the World Serpent] unwound himself on
the snow-shoe of Eynæfir [: sea-king's snowshoe: ?boat]. . . . Strong-Beard's terrifier [giant's
terrifier: Þórr], when he felt the boundary-coalfish of all lands [: World Serpent], got his
hammer into the right hand. . . . And the ugly encircling ring of the road of the beaked
prow which is rowed from the gunwale [: ring of the boat's road: World Serpent] stared
from below with harsh spirit at the skull-splitter of Hrungnir.]

The order of these stanzas is unknown, but the above sequence follows the
story as it can be judged from *Hymiskviða*. These stanzas of Bragi's might be
set alongside the scene in which Beowulf meets his own *wyrm* ('serpent', *Beo*
2287):

Biorn under beorge   bordrand onswaf
wið ðam gryregieste   Geata dryhten;
ða wæs hringbogan   heorte gefysed
sæcce to seceanne.   Sweord ær gebræd
god guðcyning   gomele lafe
ecgum ungleaw;   æghwæðrum wæs
bealohycgendra   broga fram oðrum. (*Beo* 2559–65)

[The warrior beneath the mound, lord of Geats, swung his shield-face towards that
terrible stranger; then was the heart of the coiled bow made keen to seek battle. First
the good king of battle drew his sword, the ancient heirloom very sharp in its edges;[164] in
each opponent intending to do harm there was a terror of the other.]

What parallels arise between *Beo* 2559–65 and *Ragnarsdrápa* seem due to a
common type-scene: Beowulf's dragon is called *hringboga*, a unique compound
which echoes the World Serpent's coil in Bragi's *hringr* in v. 51 above; and each
poet dwells on the serpent's mental state (*heorte gefysed* and *harðgeðr*), with
Beowulf's given as well; each poet focuses on the hero's seizing of his weapon.

On the other hand, Bragi's verses differ from the *Beowulf* lines in being
ornamental, teasing the brain with kennings which draw in unrelated figures
and scenes: Óðinn (*Viðrir*), a sea-king (*Eynæfir*), giants (*Ǫflugbarði, Hrungnir*),
and winter snow (with *ǫndurr*). The effect is one of a compressed riddle which
buries its meaning in misleading perspectives. This style, as an invitation to

---

[164] See *Beowulf*, ed. Wrenn and Bolton, 282–3 ('ungleaw').

mental agility, is typical of *dróttkvætt* verse and of other skaldic poetry in general; it may be humorous; it is certainly driven by metre. As a poetic form, however, it exceeds the misdirections of the *Beowulf* poet, who avoids alien tangents and above, in his lines with Beowulf and the dragon, narrows the focus to mental states: those of duellists in a fight to the death. In this way there is no small gap in technique between Bragi and the poet of *Beowulf*. In the unlikely event that the English poet could have understood Bragi's kennings or those of other skalds, he seems to have left this style of poetry alone. If we are going to think of Danish influence on *Beowulf*, we must look at the idea of Danish influence in another way. Later in this book, in Chapter 7, I shall indeed argue that the Danish Þórr–Serpent myth, told as a story or even as an 'Eddic' ballad, is one of the means by which the poet of *Beowulf* innovates in the manner of Beowulf's death.[165] In Bragi's poem Þórr wants to kill the Serpent; in other Norse poems Þórr dies fighting the World Serpent in Ragnarǫk, in a scene which Dronke believes influenced Beowulf's casting in his final role.[166] But there is no evidence that skaldic poetry, essentially a cryptic form, could have been this or any other Norse myth's means of transmission.

The broader objection to a Danish context for *Beowulf* in the early tenth century is that the Danish gentry of England were West Saxon underlings, their dynastic roots unclear, their Christianity not yet certified. *Beowulf* deals with Danish heathens and leaves it understood that the hero of the poem, a Geat, is heathen too, just like the Swedes. Worse still, from the Christian point of view, the poet of *Beowulf* stands advocate for his heathens from beginning to end. He states their ignorance rather than knowledge of supernatural powers, on Scyld's funeral in lines 50–2, on Hrothgar's view of Grendel's Mother's sword-hilt in lines 1687–93, and on Beowulf's breach of an old barrow-spell in 3066–73. He omits Hrothgar's name in the devil-worship in lines 175–83, while turning his ire on present-day Christians, not past heathens, as people who may thrust their souls into hell-fire in lines 183–6. He goes as far as allowing his benighted heroes a faith in one god: as with Hrothgar, in lines 381–2, 478–9, 930–1; and Beowulf, in lines 967, 977–9, 1658, 2329–32.[167] Moreover, although Beowulf is cremated on a pyre at the end of the poem, the poet does not treat him as hell-bound, but leaves the question of Judgement carefully open in lines 2819–20; and his imagery looks favourably upon this question on line 3155b: *Heofon rece (s[w]ealg)* ('Heaven swallowed the smoke').[168]

This degree of latitude is an obfuscation, as if the poet shrank from the truth of the heathen condition as something too awful to contemplate. With this kind of compassion he looks unlike Alfred in his approach to the Classical pagan gods in

---

[165] Orchard, *Companion*, 119–23.
[166] Dronke, '*Beowulf* and Ragnarǫk', 313–16.
[167] There are other examples. See North, *Heathen Gods*, 173–81.
[168] *Beowulf*, ed. Zupitza, 144 n. 4 (*sealg* from Thorkelin A and B).

the 880s translation of Boethius' *De consolatione Philosophiae*. Alfred has been seen as tolerant, for he tells pagan Roman stories in order to moralize them, 'something Alcuin never managed to do'; without flinching, for example, Alfred renders Boethius' 'Fabricius' as the heathen 'Weland'.[169] But it is worth adding that he retells Circe's story without keeping Ulysses' patron, the Odinic 'Mercurius'.[170] It is not clear whether Alfred's grandson was more tolerant towards his heathens fifty years later. Frank alludes to the aristocratic interest in heroic tales which endured in Europe in the ninth and tenth centuries.[171] But heathen heroes are one thing, heathen rites another. Anyone who thinks that Alfred or Æthelstan liked to hear stories of idolaters in their reigns must justify *Beowulf*'s pagan sympathy against the English Benedictine reform, which took root in the 890s.[172]

By the time of Æthelstan's death in 939 the Danes in the Five Boroughs had become Christian.[173] When Olaf Guthfrithson, the Norwegian king of York, conquered the east Midlands one year later, he probably had to renew the Danes' acquaintance with heathen laws. Their liberation in 942 by the young King Edmund, Æthelstan's half-brother, is hailed in a poem in the *Anglo-Saxon Chronicle* (AD), *On the Capture of the Five Boroughs*:[174]

> Dæne wæran ær
> under Norðmannum,   nyde gebegde
> on hæþenra   hæfteclommum
> lange þrage,   oþ hie alysde eft
> for his weorþscipe   wiggendra hleo
> afera Eadweardes,   Eadmund cyning. (lines 8–13)

[earlier the Danes were under Northmen, subjected by force in heathens' captive fetters, for a long time, until, for the sake of his honour, the protector of warriors, Edward's son, King Edmund, ransomed them again.]

There is an ambitious type-scene in these lines. To judge by the language of *The Dream of the Rood* (*he us onlysde*, 'he redeemed us', line 147), Edmund's encomiast styles his master's invasion of the Danelaw as the Harrowing of Hell. This poet shows the townsmen glad to abandon Norwegian laws, so close to their old sinful ways, but nonetheless he calls them *Dæne* ('Danes', line 8). He keeps them foreign, even while he proclaims their Christianity and eagerness to be English. Despite noting their true faith, Edmund's poet does not see the Danes as equals.

As the Danes settled in, however, attitudes changed, perhaps enough to allow the composition of *Beowulf*. From the 940s to the late 980s, England was ruled

---

[169] Frank, 'The *Beowulf*-Poet's Sense of History', 105.
[170] *King Alfred's Old English Boethius*, ed. Sedgefield, 46 and 165. North, 'Boethius and the Mercenary', 95–6.
[171] Frank, 'The *Beowulf*-Poet's Sense of History', 105–7.
[172] Gretsch, *Intellectual Foundations of the English Benedictine Reform*, 230–51, esp. 245–50.
[173] Abrams, 'The Conversion of the Danelaw', 39.
[174] *ASC* A, *s.a.* 942 (p. 73). *ASC* D, *s.a.* 942 (p. 43).

well enough for the ecclesiastical culture to bloom, for monastic reforms to be implemented, challenged, and reaffirmed, and for a West Saxon standard to grow up in prose. During this period, the Danes assimilated vigorously into English public life. Among their descendants were men such as Oskytel, archbishop of York (956–71), his kinsman Oda, bishop of Ramsbury (from 927) and archibishop of Canterbury (941–58), and Oda's nephew, Bishop (St) Oswald (d. 992), who played an important role in the Benedictine reform.[175] The Danelaw regions were governed locally by a gentry of Anglo-Danish descent.[176] By this time a descendant of Alfred, Ealdorman Æthelweard in *c*.975 × 983, knew enough to change the names *Woden* and *Bældæg* into the Norse forms *Vuothen* and *Balder*.[177] His friend the homilist Ælfric, abbot of Eynsham (*c*.1005–*c*.1010), discusses heathen gods as a threat with an accurate knowledge of Norse names in his *De falsis diis* of 990–2 and his *Life of St Martin* in 992–8.[178] So does Archbishop Wulfstan *c*.1000 in his own *De falsis deis*, based on that of Ælfric.[179] By then some Danes were naturalizing, but the enduring vitality of their gods makes it unlikely that *Beowulf*, a work which admires heathen Danes, was composed at this time. For if *Beowulf* was a work of the tenth or eleventh century, its poet's Christianity was unorthodox. Again, it is not easy to see how Cnut, 'a strong, internationally honoured Christian king', could have tolerated the scene of Danish devil-worship such a short way into *Beowulf* (in lines 175–88).[180]

To sum up, not one of the Viking Age contexts so far given for the origin of *Beowulf* fits with the poem. This is not to underrate the reason for proposing them. These various proposals at least acknowledge, rather than disregard, the waves of Danish and Norwegian settlement in England over three centuries. There is no denying that the impact of Danish settlers on English society seems more relevant now to the question of *Beowulf*'s sources than the sixth-century model which, according to Frank and others, is the sole alternative, 'a distant folk memory imported by the Anglo-Saxons from their continental homeland'.[181] Yet Whitelock's caveat remains unshaken. The sympathy accorded to Danish heathens in *Beowulf* would flout the memory of the widespread damage their offspring inflicted on English ecclesiastical property and life. That is why we must treat the Frisians, at the dawn of the Viking Age, as the best model for the transmission of Scylding legends in *Beowulf*.

---

[175] Jacobs, 'Anglo-Danish Relations, Poetic Archaism, and the Date of *Beowulf*', 23–43.

[176] Hall, 'Anglo-Scandinavian Urban Development in the East Midlands', 143–55.

[177] *Chronicle of Æthelweard*, ed. and trans. Campbell, 33 (cf. 7, 9, 17, and 25). Townend, *Language and History*, 122–7.

[178] *Homilies of Ælfric*, ed. Pope, ii. 683–5 (*Þor*: lines 122–5, *Oðon*: 133–5 and 141–4, *Fricg*: 176–7). *Ælfric's Lives of Saints: Being a Set of Sermons on Saints' Days Formerly Observed by the English Church*, ed. W. W. Skeat, EETS os 94 and 114 (2 vols.) (Oxford, 1890 and 1900, repr. (1 vol.) 1966), ii. 265 (*Oðon*: line 715). Townend, *Language and History*, 133–8, esp. 135.

[179] *The Homilies of Wulfstan*, ed. Bethurum, 223 (XII) and 336–8 (note).

[180] Kiernan, *Beowulf and the Beowulf Manuscript*, 21–63, at 23; see also his 'The Eleventh-Century Origin of *Beowulf* and the *Beowulf* Manuscript', 10.

[181] Frank, 'Skaldic Verse and the Date of *Beowulf*', 124.

CONCLUSION

In this chapter I have argued that *Beowulf* owes some debt to Vergil's *Aeneid* and that the poet derived his material about the Scyldings and related kings from a lively Franco-Frisian trade. Later this argument will encompass a connection between the poet and Carolingian Francia, but it cannot be used to consider the Frisians as sources for myths which belong in the heathen domain. In Chapter 7, I shall suggest that *Beowulf* uses three Norse myths of heathen currency which the poet can have heard from no one but the Danes themselves. The heroic-mythological divide resulting from this classification of *Beowulf*'s Germanic sources may at first be held up as an anomaly in my attempt to date *Beowulf* before, rather than during, the Viking Age. However, I shall also suggest, in Chapter 7, a set of circumstances in which the poet could have met Danish Vikings for himself, as early as 809. For his heroic source-material, to be considered in Chapters 2–4 and 8, no direct Danish influence was necessary. *Beowulf* starts with Danish kings, but its tales are not Danish enough to represent a work commissioned either in the Danelaw or for Cnut. Its tale of heroism and monarchic decay is too divisive to plead for social cohesion at the end of Alfred's reign. Set outside England, the tale seems ill chosen to plead the values of Æthelstan's *imperium*, nor is the poem safe enough doctrinally to have sprung from the English Benedictine reform. First and foremost, *Beowulf*'s opening focus on Scyld seems to have been imitated, not inspired, by the dynastic pretensions of King Æthelwulf in *c*.855. This is the *terminus ad quem*, whereas, as we have seen, the *Liber historiae Francorum* gives *c*.727 as *Beowulf*'s *terminus a quo*. For now, in other words, *Beowulf* is datable to the period *c*.727 × *c*.855.

2
Dynastic Innovation in *Beowulf*

It is the differences between *Beowulf* and its Norse analogues that give the latter their value, for thereby we can discern the poet's manipulation of Scylding legend. In this chapter I shall start with his creation of Scyld Scefing, then focus on Hygelac, whose role as Beowulf's uncle appears to be made up without basis in tradition. The transposition of Beowulf from Hrothulf's to Hrothgar's court, so that the hero comes to Denmark a generation earlier than it seems the traditional stories allowed, is the third manner in which the poet entitles Beowulf to a royal career. His fourth innovation is consequently to make Beowulf a king in the Geatish half of the poem. This status is never accorded to Beowulf's monster-slaying counterpart, Bǫðvarr bjarki, in any of the diverse Old Norse analogues. Fifth and last, when the poet introduces Beowulf's companion in his traditional role, he delays his entrance until near the end of Beowulf's life, and, by calling him 'Wiglaf', gives him a name without precedent.

VERGIL AND SCYLD SCEFING

Sources for 'Scyld Scefing' appear to be at least three: a legendary heroic tradition, likely to be of ultimately Danish origin, to do with the *Scyldingas*, from which the poet created the eponym 'Scyld'; a literary precedent for linking the Longobards with Scandinavia, whereby 'Sceaf(a)' could be made into the ancient king of 'Scedelond' or 'Scedenig'; and a piece of Anglian monastic folklore to do with 'sheaf' and 'shield', which enabled the poet to make Sceaf into Scyld's father. An overall authority for this confection might have been provided by Vergil's genealogy for King Latinus in Book VII of his *Aeneid*.

First, it might seem that Scyld had always existed independently of *Scylding*, the tribal name. This is because he has a counterpart in the Norse analogues named 'Skjǫldr' or 'Scioldus'. Snorri Sturluson cites Skjǫldr in his *Edda* and *Heimskringla* in the 1220s and 1230s; and Scioldus is found in the works of Sven Aggesen and Saxo Grammaticus. All three historians derived their name from 'Skjǫldr' at the head of royal Danish genealogies in the first version of *Skjǫldunga saga*, in *c.*1190–1200. Bishop Páll Jónsson of Skálholt (ruled 1195–1211), presumed by some to have written *Skjǫldunga saga*, may have learned of Skjǫldung traditions in

Lincoln in 1175–80, from tales preserved in the former Danelaw.[1] But it is believed that *Skjǫldunga saga* was based on the *Langfeðgatal* (*c*.1120s), a royal genealogy traceable to Páll's great-grandfather, Sæmundr Sigfússon of the Oddaverjar. The twenty-seven generations in the oldest version of *Langfeðgatal* start with 'Skjǫldr'. It is thought that Sæmundr put this genealogy together as a Danish royal lineage for his son, Loptr, whose wife-to-be in *c*.1120, Þóra, claimed to be a daughter of King Magnús berfœttr of Norway (d. 1103).[2] Through Sæmundr, therefore, 'Skjǫldr' can be traced back to the late eleventh century.

Cognate with OE *Scyldingas* is the name *skjǫldungar* in Icelandic skaldic poetry of the late tenth and early to late eleventh centuries.[3] Although this term connotes 'kings' in general, not Danes in particular, a Danish reference emerges in its association with King Cnut in a verse in 1014.[4] Sighvatr Þórðarson alludes to a 'Skjǫldr' in his *Knútsdrápa*, a memorial poem of 1038, in which he calls Cnut *hlíf-Skjǫldr Danakonunga* ('protecting-Skjǫldr [i.e. "shield"] of the kings of the Danes').[5] This could be a revival of an older meaning in the *skjǫldung*-term, which itself can be traced back to the mid-tenth century if we assume that the name *Scaldingi*, in the anonymous *Historia de sancto Cuthberto*, reflects a form such as **Skeldingar*.[6] On the other hand, the *Chronicon Lethrense* makes no mention of Skiold, nor is there evidence that Danish or Norwegian skalds knew of a separate 'Skjǫldr' before their contact with England.[7] For these reasons it is equally plausible to suggest that Sighvatr and other skalds made up the Skjǫldr-eponym on the authority of *Scyldwa* or *Sceldwea* in the *Anglo-Saxon Chronicle*. Since it seems likely that the *Chronicle*'s Scyldwa, in turn, was borrowed from Scyld Scefing, it might have been the poet of *Beowulf* who created the name Scyld or Scyldwa out of OE *Scylding*. At the end of the enquiry there is not enough evidence to decide whether this was the case or whether Scyld was known from a popular tradition.

'Sceaf', the name of Scyld's father, intrudes alliteratively on the poet's H-sequence of Danish kings at the start of *Beowulf*: [Heremod]–Scyld Scefing–Beowulf–Healfdene–the brothers Heorogar, Hrothgar, and Halga. The poet makes it clear that Scyld Scefing does not arrive in Denmark until after

---

[1] *Danakonunga Sögur*, ed. Bjarni, pp. xvi–xvii. Bjarni, 'The Icelandic Sources of Saxo Grammaticus', 89.

[2] *Danakonunga Sögur*, ed. Bjarni, pp. lii–lvi. Bjarni, 'The Icelandic Sources of Saxo Grammaticus', 88. For the text, *Íslendingabók – Landnámabók*, ed. Jakob, p. xxiii.

[3] *Skáldskaparmál*, ed. Faulkes, 120 (v. 457: *Þulur*).

[4] *Skj* B I, 205 (Þórðr Kolbeinsson). Frank, 'Skaldic Verse and the Date of *Beowulf*', 125–7, at 126.

[5] *Skj* B I. 234.

[6] *Symeonis monachi Opera omnia*, ed. Arnold, i. 196–214, at 200 and 202. For the date, see E. Craster, 'The Patrimony of St. Cuthbert', *EHR* 69 (1954), 177–99. *Scaldingi*, which pre-dates i-mutation to *skjǫldr*, appears to reflect a ninth-century form **skealdur* (< **skeldur*): *Asser's Life of King Alfred*, ed. Stevenson, 218 n. 1; Frank, 'Skaldic Verse and the Date of *Beowulf*', 127 n. 17. In *Hyndluljóð*, a poem preserved in the fourteenth-century *Flateyjarbók*, it is said that 'Hálfdan the Older [was] the highest of the Skjǫldungs' (*Hálfdan fyrri hæstr Scioldunga*, st. 14).

[7] *Scriptores minores historiae Danicae*, ed. Gertz, i. 43–4.

Heremod (lines 14–15). Sceaf not Heremod is thus the progenitor of Hrothgar's kindred in *Beowulf.* It is also clear that Scyld Scefing is a composite figure. To the extent that *Widsith* knows of a certain King 'Sceafa' of the Longobards (line 32), it seems that Sceaf(a) figured in a different royal genealogy before the composition of *Beowulf.* The Longobards' own tradition in the *Origo gentis*, a work of the mid-seventh century, makes no mention of Sceaf(a), although it traces their ancestors (the Winnili and other tribes) back to *insula qui dicitur Scadanan* ('an island which is called Scadanan', ch. 1).[8] This name bears a certain resemblance to *Scedenig* (*Beo* 1686), the land to which Scyld Scefing comes in a boat in *Beowulf.* Other literary names for 'Scandinavia' are the Lombardic *Scadinavia* in the late eighth-century *Historia Langobardorum* of Paul the Deacon, and Got *Scandzia* in the mid-sixth-century *Getica* of (Cassiodorus and) Jordanes.[9] Like *Scadanan*, these forms resemble *Scedenig* in *Beowulf*: more closely, too, than either *Sconeg*, which is the name for the same area in the late ninth-century Alfredian translation of Orosius' *Historia adversus paganos*; or *Scani*, in Æthelweard's *Chronicon* of the late tenth century.[10] Eric Stanley believes that the forms *Scedenig* and *Sconeg* could have coexisted.[11] That would mean that the poet of *Beowulf* archaized a late ninth-century place name. On the other hand, Roberta Frank suggests that *Sconeg* is the native English form, older than *Scedenig* which she takes to be a Norse loan.[12] The early dates, however, of the above Latin sources make her view implausible. There is more reason to suppose that *Scedenig* in *Beowulf* was an Old English name used with knowledge of *Scadanan* in the Lombardic *Origo gentis* or *Scadinavia* in Paul's *Historia.* The source which gave Skåne its antiquity was rather a literary authority than a legendary heroic poem.

The poet of *Beowulf* needed a precedent for making Sceaf(a) the father of Scyld, given the fact that these two figures are not found related in any other source. A pattern for this precedent can be found in a half-heathen ritual with which the abbot of Abingdon is said to have resolved a land dispute with the men of Oxfordshire in the first third of the tenth century.[13] According to this oft-cited story, written in the thirteenth-century *Chronicon de Abingdon* but with signs of an Anglo-Saxon origin, the monks placed a sheaf of corn in a round shield and a lit wax taper over the sheaf, then pushed the shield out into the river Thames.[14] Each time the shield zigzagged downstream to right and left, it indicated

---

[8] *Historia Langobardorum*, ed. Waitz, 48.

[9] *Romana et Getica*, ed. T. Mommsen, MGH, Auctores Antiquissimi 5, 2 vols. (Berlin, 1882), 56–8, at 56 (ch. 3). *Historia Langobardorum*, ed. Waitz, 53 (ch. 1).

[10] *The Old English Orosius*, ed. J. Bately, EETS ss 6 (1980), 16. 24 (I. i). *Chronicle of Æthelweard*, ed. and trans. Campbell, 33.

[11] Stanley, 'The Date of *Beowulf*: Some Doubts and No Conclusions', 207: 'We can date *Sconeg* philologically. . . . We cannot date the obsolescence of *Scedenig*.'

[12] Frank, 'Skaldic Verse and the Date of *Beowulf*', 125–6 n. 8.

[13] *Chronicon monasterii de Abingdon*, ed. Stevenson, i. 88–9.

[14] An Anglo-Saxon tale, because of the rounded shield and the eleventh-century spelling of *Gifteleia* (Iffley): see North, *Heathen Gods*, 189–91. This text is aired in Sisam, 'Anglo-Saxon Royal Genealogies', 343.

the possessions of the monastery of Abingdon. This tale appears to show the inanimate aspect of Scyld Scefing as the instrument of God's favour for the Danes. The ritual aspect of Scyld's funeral in the opening lines of *Beowulf* suggests that the poet linked Scyld with Sceaf and Beow because he knew that the shield, sheaf, and barley were linked in Anglian folklore.[15]

If it is thought that folklore is a humble source for the genealogy of mighty Danish *þeodcyningas* (line 2), it is possible that the poet took his authority from Vergil. There is a literary precedent in Book VII of the *Aeneid*, in which Vergil, as he prepares to embark on the second half of his epic, builds the ancestry of Latinus, a forefather of Rome, straight out of Italian folklore:

> Rex arua Latinus et urbes
> iam senior longa placidas in pace regebat.
> hunc Fauno et nympha genitum Laurente Marica
> accipimus; Fauno Picus pater, isque parentem
> te, Saturne, refert, tu sanguinis ultimus auctor. (*Aen.* VII. 45–9)[16]

[King Latinus, now grown old, was ruling his ploughed lands and settled towns through a long period of peace. We have learned that he was begotten by Faunus on a nymph, Marica of the Laurentines. The father of Faunus had been Picus, and he claims you for sire, O Saturn: you are furthest back the founder of his blood.]

Vergil, the new Roman patriot, grafts a Trojan ancestor on to the stem of a homely race of gods. He prefers this type of genealogy to one based on the mightier gods of the Greeks. The father of Latinus is *Faunus*, a woodland deity; Faunus' father is *Picus*, 'beak', whose traditional woodpecker shape Vergil presents as the outcome of Circe's witchcraft in *Aen.* VII. 187–91; and Picus' father is Saturn, an even bigger Italian parvenu. The meanings of *faunus* and *picus* were clear enough to Anglo-Saxon monks educated in Latin.[17] Vergil's aggrandizement of these terms could give a licence to the poet of *Beowulf*, if he read Vergil, to combine Beow, Scyld, and Sceaf at the outset of his 'epic'. By following Vergil he would dignify his own folklore, while avoiding the direct involvement of a true heathen progenitor, such as that contained in the stem of *Ingwine* (lines 1044 and 1319).[18]

HYGELAC AND HIS ANALOGUES

Hygelac is Beowulf's uncle, brother of Hrethel's only daughter whom the old king gave to Ecgtheow (lines 373–5). When he comes to grief in a raid on Frisia,

---

[15] So Chambers, *Beowulf*, 68–86, 81–2.

[16] Text from *Vergili Opera*, ed. Mynors.

[17] See my *Heathen Gods*, 172–203, at 182–91. On the Anglo-Saxon knowledge of Lat *faunus*, the half-human wood-dweller, see the *Liber monstrorum*, in *Pride and Prodigies*, ed. Orchard, 260 (I.); of Lat *picus*, the woodpecker, see *Épinal-Erfurt Glossary*, ed. Pheifer, 43 (808: Épinal, Erfurt 'fina *uel* higrae') and 114 (note on *higrae* as sign of a confusion with Lat *pica*, 'jay').

[18] 'Ingui' or 'Ing': North, *Heathen Gods*, 188–91. Tolley, '*Beowulf*'s Scyld Scefing Episode', 8–12.

the poet alludes to his death four times, using a different perspective with each reference. There are many repetitions in *Beowulf*, but not to the extent of this one, which Michael Lapidge calls the 'most puzzling of all'.[19] Perhaps, however, Hygelac's death is repeated so often because it shows a moral choice. The poet's first use of this leitmotif arises in a sudden leap into the future which he makes in lines 1197–214, after the first speech of Wealhtheow. This queen, having implied that Hrothgar should give Beowulf portable wealth rather than a kingdom, appears to arrange for Beowulf to receive, in the poet's words, *healsbeaga mæst þara þe ic on foldan gefrægen hæbbe* ('the greatest necklace of which I have heard tell on earth', lines 1195–6). The reason for this ring's renown becomes clearer. The poet compares it with the *Brosinga mene* which was stolen from the Gothic emperor Eormanric by a certain Hama, who then *geceas ecne ræd* ('chose eternal reward', line 1201).[20] After this brief allusion, the poet shows the later history of Beowulf's Danish necklace:

> Þone hring hæfde   Higelac Geata
> nefa Swertinges   nyhstan siðe
> siðþan he under segne   sinc ealgode,
> wælreaf werede;   hyne wyrd fornam
> syþðan he for wlenco   wean ahsode
> fæhðe to Frysum.   He þa frætwe wæg
> eorclan stanes   ofer yða ful
> rice þeoden;   he under rande gecranc.
> Gehwearf þa in Francna fæþm   feorh cyninges,
> breostgewædu   ond se beah somod;
> wyrsan wigfrecan   wæl reafedon
> æfter guðsceare,   Geata leode
> hreawic heoldon.   Heal swege onfeng. (*Beo* 1202–14)

[Hygelac of the Geats had that ring, Swerting's nephew, on his last expedition, when he guarded his treasure beneath a banner, defended spoil of the slain; fate seized him when through pride he asked for woe, a feud with Frisia. He, a powerful chieftain, carried that adornment of the precious stone over the cup of the waves; he perished beneath a targe. Passed then into the bosom of the Franks the king's life, his breast-covering, and the necklace, all of them together; lower-ranking war-braves plundered the slain after the war-squadron, the princes of the Geats kept possession of a settlement of dead bodies. The hall received the applause.]

Through this brilliant contrast between present and future, the poet suggests that the necklace, and behind that, the pursuit of wealth in general, leads Hygelac to pay the ultimate price.

---

[19] '*Beowulf* and Perception', 70.

[20] The emendation 'Br*e*osinga' brings this apparently tribal term closer to the form of Freyja's necklace, the *Brísinga men*. See H. Damico, '*Sörlaþáttr* and the Hama Episode in *Beowulf*', *SS* 5 (1983), 222–35. *Pace* my earlier reading: on *fealh* as 'concealed', see North, *Heathen Gods*, 196–8; as 'endured', see Orchard, *Companion*, 114–16, at 114 n. 84.

Hygelac's death is mentioned again briefly as the poet leaps fifty years into Beowulf's future on lines 2200–1. Then, while alluding to Beowulf's glory in Heorot in the context of his decision to fight the fire-dragon, the narrator comments on Hygelac's raid after the event (lines 2354–66): it was not the smallest of battles when Hygelac, heir to King Hrethel of the Geats, was slain in Friesland; Beowulf got away, swimming back home carrying thirty corslets and apparently the sole survivor:

> Nealles Hetware   hremge þorfton
> feðewiges þe him foran ongean
> linde bæron;   lyt eft becwom
> fram þam hildfrecan   hames niosan. (*Beo* 2363–6)

[Not at all did the Hetware have any need to exult over the pitched battle, those who carried their linden shields before them; none among those battle-braves came back to find their home.]

Beowulf swims back to Geatland, where Hygd, not trusting in her son to succeed, offers Beowulf the throne. Beowulf, however, prefers to act as regent, so the poet moves out of Hygelac's story into that of the Swedish wars. The poet's fourth allusion to the Frisian raid concerns Beowulf's destruction of Dæghrefn, the warrior who killed Hygelac. This he delivers in his own words in the course of surveying his achievements. Beowulf says that Hygelac trusted him and so never had to hire foreign mercenaries, *wyrsan wigfrecan* ('lower-ranking war-braves', line 2496: the phrase repeats the poet's term for Hygelac's victors in line 1212). Beowulf repaid Hygelac by crushing his Frankish killer to death.

    The poet's fifth and last allusion to the Frisian raid comes as part of a speech which an unnamed Geatish messenger delivers to the Geats after Beowulf's death (lines 2913–20).[21] When this calamity becomes known, he says, the surrounding tribes will rush in, Franks and Frisians as well:

> 'Wæs sio wroht scepen
> heard wið Hugas   syððan Higelac cwom
> faran flotherge   on Fresna land
> þær hyne Hetware   hilde genægdon,
> elne geeodon   mid ofermægene
> þæt se byrnwiga   bugan sceolde,
> feoll on feðan;   nalles frætwe geaf
> ealdor dugoðe.   Us wæs a syððan
> Meroingas   milts ungyfeðe.' (*Beo* 2913–21)

['That strife with the Hugas shaped up harsh when Hygelac came sailing with his fleet-raiders into the Frisians' land, where the Hetware laid him low in battle, bravely brought it about with an overwhelming force that this mailed warrior should yield, that he fell

---

[21] These are not Wiglaf's words, as stated in Lapidge, '*Beowulf* and Perception', 71. See *Beo* 2906–10.

among the foot-troop; not at all did the leader live to give his company treasure. To us ever since the Merovingian's generosity has been denied.']

Here we learn that Hygelac's enemies had the advantage of bigger numbers. If we refrain from treating some names as full synonyms of others, we have a picture of three or four battle-groups: Hetware from the lower Rhine valley; Frisians from the coast; 'lower-ranking war-braves', whose origin is not specified; and 'Hugas'.[22] The Frankish army is thus portrayed as a well-organized imperial force, against whom Hygelac *for wlenco wean ahsode* ('through pride asked for woe', line 1206). Almost by itself (*gehwearf,* line 1210), the great necklace finds its way to a man equal to it, the Merovingian emperor. Yet when Hygelac is destroyed, so is the flower of his nation.

In all this the poet appears to turn a familiar tale into a moral judgement on Hygelac. His sources appear to fall into two groups: Frankish Latin chronicles; and heroic poems which leave traces in Latin and Germanic vernacular references. The analogues for Hygelac's death are six in number; in the case of the second, it is almost certain that we have a source. The first analogue occurs surprisingly early, *c.*575 in the *Historiae* of Bishop Gregory of Tours. In this work, in an aside to the main action, the politics of the Merovingian court, Gregory reports an attack by *Dani* ('Danes') on the coast of Gaul in a context which dates this incident very roughly to *c.*525. This account confirms that 'Chlochilaichus', Beowulf's 'Hygelac', was a man who lived in history.[23] Second, Gregory's report was used in *c.*726 by the anonymous author of the *Liber historiae Francorum.* In the passage concerned:

In illo tempore Dani cum rege suo nomine Chochilaico cum navale hoste per alto mare Gallias appetent, Theuderico paygo Attoarios vel alios devastantes atque captivantes, plenas naves de captivis alto mare intrantes, rex eorum ad litus maris resedens. Quod cum Theuderico nuntiatum fuisset, Theudobertum, filium suum, cum magno exercitu in illis partibus dirigens. Qui consequens eos, pugnavit cum eis cede magna atque prostravit, regem eorum interficit, preda tullit et in terra sua restituit.[24]

[The Danes with their king, whose name was Chochilaicus, then attacked Gaul with a naval army from across the high sea, devastating a region belonging to Theuderic, [namely] that of the Attoarii and other tribes, and taking captives, embarking on to their ships full of captives and [ready] for the high sea, with their king remaining on the seashore. When this was announced to Theuderic, he sent his son Theudebert to these parts with a great army, who, pursuing them, fought them with great slaughter and laid them low, killed their king, seized their booty, and restored it to his own land.]

The *Attoarii* are an anachronism upon which two allusions to the *Hetware* in *Beowulf* appear to be based (lines 2363 and 2916). Hetware are also cited early in *Widsith,* their king being 'Hun' (*Hun Hætwerum,* line 33). As we have seen,

---

22 To be discussed in Chapter 6.
23 *Gregorii libri historiarum,* ed. Krusch and Levison, 99 (III. 3).
24 *Liber historiae Francorum,* ed. B. Krusch, MGH, SRM 2 (Hanover, 1888), 274–5 (ch. 19).

Widsith was probably assembled without knowledge of *Beowulf*. Its allusion to *Hetware* does not impair the near certainty that the poet of *Beowulf* used Hygelac's story in the *Liber* as one of his sources.[25]

That the poet of *Beowulf* used other sources for Hygelac is clear in this king's status as a Geat, for both Bishop Gregory and the author of the *Liber* refer to Chochilaicus as a Dane. A clue as to what one of these other sources may have been is provided by the first entry in the *Liber monstrorum*, an Insular Latin work of *c*.650 × *c*.750:[26]

Et fiunt monstra mirae magnitudinis, ut rex Higlacus,[27] qui imperauit Getis et a Francis occisus est, quem equus a duodecimo aetatis anno portare non potuit. Cuius ossa in Rheni fluminis insula, ubi in Oceanum prorumpit, reseruata sunt, et de longinquo uenientibus pro miraculo ostenduntur.

[And there are monsters of an amazing size, like King Hygelac, who ruled the Geats and was killed by the Franks, whom no horse could carry from the age of twelve. His bones are preserved on an island in the river Rhine, where it breaks into the Ocean, and they are shown as a wonder to travellers from afar.]

In its own brief way this entry tells us that by the early eighth century, Hygelac had been honoured with a life-story in three parts (childhood, reign in Geatland, death in Frisia), both in England and on the Frisian island in which Rhineland travellers heard of him. The variant spellings of 'Higlacus' in this passage show that these stories were passed about in Frisian or Old English.[28] One of these was a source for the poet of *Beowulf*, to judge by the fact that he calls Hygelac a king of the Geats. Given the Rhineland provenance of the version in *Liber monstrorum*, this source might be called 'Anglo-Frisian'. Its nexus with Bishop Gregory's source, if any, was probably a story in northern Francia in the mid-sixth century.

The remaining three analogues for Hygelac come from Scandinavia from around the turn of the thirteenth century. Two of these tales, one of 'Hugleikr' by Snorri and another of 'Huglecus' by Saxo, are closely related and concern the death of the Hygelac-figure in battle. Snorri tells us of Hugleikr in his *Ynglinga saga*, written in the 1220s.[29] Hugleikr, son of King Álfr of Sweden, *var engi hermaðr, ok sat hann at lǫndum í kyrrsæti* ('was no man of war and ruled his lands in peace', ch. 22). Worse still, he keeps *sinni alls konar leikara, harpara ok gígjara*

[25] See Goffart, 'Datable Anachronisms in *Beowulf*', 85–7. This influence is discounted by Whitelock, in *The Audience of Beowulf*, 41 ('possible…but not very likely'); and not considered by Chambers, in *Beowulf*.

[26] Text and translation in Orchard, *Pride and Prodigies*, 258–9 (I. 2).

[27] *Var.* huncgacus *corr. in* huncglacus, huncglagus, huiglaucus.

[28] Michael Lapidge uses the monosyllabic forms of the prefixes in 'Higlacus' and 'Hylac' (*Beo* 1530) to suggest that a West Saxon dialect, such as that spoken by Aldhelm in and around Malmesbury, was also the language of the poet of *Beowulf*. See his '"Beowulf", Aldhelm, the "Liber monstrorum" and Wessex', 176–9.

[29] *Heimskringla I*, ed. Bjarni, 42–3 (*Ynglinga saga*, ch. 22).

ok fiðlara ('an entourage with all kinds of players, harpers, strummers, and fiddlers'), with witches and other magicians as well. Two brothers appear, pirates named Haki and Hagbarðr, each with his retinue. Before long Haki sails to Sweden to lay waste to Hugleikr's kingdom. Hugleikr is feeble, but his fighting strength is boosted by the arrival of another set of brothers, Svipdagr and Geigaðr, *ágætir menn báðir ok inir mestu kappar* ('both excellent men and the greatest champions'). King Haki's twelve champions include Starkaðr the Old, but Snorri says that Haki is also a great champion himself. The outcome is not in doubt. Hugleikr's army is wiped out, while Haki *gekk . . . inn í skjaldborg at Hugleiki konungi ok drap hann þar ok sonu hans tvá* ('fought his way into King Hugleikr's shield-fortification and killed him there with his two sons').

Saxo appears to use the same material in his story of Huglecus (or Hugletus), a king of Ireland. His tale is a digression within a longer account of Starcatherus, the old champion who has lately joined the army of King Haco of Denmark. Together, these warriors decide to win glory for Danish arms by invading Ireland: an easy task given Huglecus' indolence. Saxo transforms this foible into greed and in his version even a gift from this king, a handsome pair of shoes, arrives minus the laces which Huglecus has removed. For all this meanness, Huglecus is unrestrained in the money he lavishes on mimes and jugglers and shares their decadence.[30] He pays two princes, Gegathus and Suipdagerus, to defend him. When battle is joined and Huglecus' mimes take to their heels, Gegathus wounds both Haco and Starcatherus: *unde postmodum in quodam carmine non alias tristiorem sibi plagam incidisse perhibuit* ('whereof later, in a certain song, Starcatherus asserted that he had never at any other time encountered a graver blow'); *victo occisoque Hugleco* ('with Huglecus defeated and slain'), Starcatherus flogs any of the king's mimes he captures. The size of Huglecus' wealth is made known when the Danes scatter his treasure all over Dublin. So great is it *ut minor partitionis cura cunctis exsisteret* ('that the less care there was in how it was shared out to all men present'). This analogue resembles the Franks' pillage of Hygelac's dead army.

With his focus on Starcatherus, Saxo shows that his source may have been an Icelandic *páttr* on Starkaðr such as we have in *Gautreks saga* (ch. 7: a work datable to *c*.1265).[31] Snorri, however, pulls Starkaðr back in order to dwell on Haki as a usurper of the Uppsala throne, whose history he relates on the basis of the *Ynglingatal* of Þjóðólfr of Hvinir (*c*.890). As the extant poem has nothing on Hugleikr, it seems clear that Snorri has added him in along with Haki and Starkaðr. His other main source was a version of *Skjǫldunga saga*, which contains stories of Hugleikr's father and uncle Alfus (Álfr) and Yngvo (Yngvi) of Sweden, one generation before Hugleikr.[32]

---

[30] *Gesta Danorum*, ed. Olrik and Ræder, 154–5 (VI. v. 11–13). See *Beowulf and its Analogues*, trans. Garmonsway, Simpson, and Ellis Davidson, 114–15.

[31] Skovgaard-Petersen, *Da Tidernes Herre var nær*, 137–68, at 160–3.

[32] *Danakonunga Sögur*, ed. Bjarni, pp. xlii–xliii, at xliii, and 72–4.

Saxo moreover refers to an earlier Huglecus, son of Dan, the son of Uffo son of Wermundus: *Post hunc regnat Huglecus, qui Hømothum et Høgrimum Suetiæ tyrannos maritimo fertur oppressisse conflictu* ('After this there reigns Huglecus, who is said to have defeated Hømothus and Høgrimus, despots of Sweden, in a sea-battle').[33] Once again, there is a battle with sea-raiders; this time, however, 'Huglecus' is a Dane who takes on two kings of the Swedes at sea, probably off their coast. This scrap might be overlooked, were it not that it reveals a Danish tradition analogous to Hygelac's invasion of Sweden and defeat of Ongentheow in *Beo* 2941–98.

Overall, the earliest retrievable Icelandic source for Hugleikr's death would appear to be the *quoddam carmen* ('certain song') which Saxo attributes to Starcatherus, but which he does not quote.[34] This was probably an eleventh- or twelfth-century Norwegian poem similar to a verse which is presented as Starkaðr's work in *Gautreks saga* (the *Víkarsbálkr*, ch. 7).[35] As Snorri gives it, Hugleikr's death inside a *skjaldborg* ('shield-fortification') may derive from this *carmen*. Moreover, his death-scene resembles that in *Beowulf*, in which Hygelac *under rande gecranc* ('perished beneath a targe', line 1209) after defending his treasure. The force of this half-line in *Beowulf* is not its encapsulation, but its position: as the first of the poet's four references to the end of his life, Hygelac's death *under rande* sums up his story.

In this way, *Beowulf*'s sources for Hygelac can be put into two groups. First, the poet appears to have read about Hygelac in Latin, either in the *Liber historiae Francorum*, which may have circulated in England from as early as 727 onwards, or in a quotation from this. Second, he seems to have known about Hygelac the Geat from a heroic legend of Anglo-Frisian transmission. With their emphasis on Hugleikr's greed and folly, the Norse analogues throw light on the content of the latter tradition. Altogether these sources tell us two things. One is that Hygelac was celebrated as the king who lost everything in pursuit of wealth. The other is that he was not connected with either Beowulf or Hrothgar. The poet of *Beowulf* has integrated Beowulf into Hygelac's story in a way that cannot have been precedented.

A NEW STORY FOR BEOWULF

In Scandinavia Beowulf was known as Hrothulf's man. In all Norse ana- logues that have survived, Bjarki or Bǫðvarr (bjarki) fights for King Hrólfr kraki of Denmark, along with Hjalti, a reformed weakling who becomes his

---

[33] *Gesta Danorum*, ed. Olrik and Ræder, 101 (IV. vii).
[34] Ibid. 154 (VI. v. 12).
[35] *Fornaldarsögur Norðurlanda*, ed. Guðni and Bjarni, iii. 1–41 (esp. 12–29). Discussed in *Saxo Grammaticus*, trans. Fisher and ed. Ellis Davidson, ii. 126 n. 1.

constant companion. Both die fighting for Hrólfr when Earl Hjǫrvarðr, Hrólfr's brother-in-law, and Skuld, Hrólfr's half-sister, attack the king's hall in Lejre. This narrative differs from that of *Beowulf*, in which Beowulf does not interact with Hrothulf, becomes king of his own homeland, and dies in battle against a fire-dragon.[36] The differences allow us to see how the poet of *Beowulf* has renovated the hero of his work.

Exit Hrothulf, enter Hygelac

In *Beowulf*, it is King Hrothgar, not his nephew Hrothulf, who welcomes the hero into the Danish court (lines 456–90). Given Bǫðvarr's friendship with Hrólfr in the Norse analogues, it might be thought that *Beowulf* has an older story unknown to the poets of the oldest tradition from which the Old Norse-Icelandic tales of the Skjǫldungar were derived;[37] or known to them but later changed in favour of a bond between Bjarki and the charismatic Hrólfr. As Hrólfr became more famous than Hróarr in Scandinavia, so Bjarki's adventures might have been shifted to his court.

Yet there is a story in *Beowulf* which shows that the Norse analogues carry the older tradition. Towards the time of the dragon-fight the poet relates some Geatish history in which Beowulf, some time after becoming king, supports a Swedish exile named Eadgils in a winter campaign against King Onela of Sweden (lines 2391–6). There is a reference to a counterpart of Eadgils in *Bjarkamál*, which describes Hrólfr's fighters as *Aðils sinnar* ('[former] companions of Aðils'). This epithet, an allusion to Hrólfr's acquisition of these men in Uppsala, reveals that Hrólfr and Aðils were commonly regarded as contemporaries.[38] In *Skjǫldunga saga*, Snorri's *Edda*, and Arngrímr's translation, King Hrólfr sends Bǫðvarr bjarki to fight as a champion for King Aðils of Uppsala against King Áli of Uppland in Norway.[39] Beowulf's support of Eadgils against Onela must be a story from the same tradition. However, whereas Beowulf intervenes as a king's foot-soldier in Scandinavia, he acts as a king in *Beowulf* without connection with Hrothulf. It is therefore clear that the English poet has severed a bond between Beowulf and Hrothulf in order to make Beowulf into the necessary assisting king.[40]

There is no such promotion of Bjarki in the Norse analogues, although Hrólfr's offer of a kinswoman in all five of them might give this hero a landed

[36] Summarized in Chambers, *Beowulf*, 54–61.

[37] Malone, *The Literary History of Hamlet*, 80–1, at 81: 'the authority of the English poem here cannot be challenged'. Newton, *The Origins of Beowulf*, 23–5.

[38] *Heimskringla II*, ed. Bjarni, 361 (*Óláfs saga helga*, ch. 208). In *Ynglingatal* 19, þjóðólfr calls Aðils 'the foe of Áli' (*Ála dolgr*): *Heimskringla I*, ed. Bjarni, 59 (*Ynglinga saga*, ch. 29).

[39] North, 'Saxo and the Swedish Wars in *Beowulf*', 180–1.

[40] Unless implicitly in the Geatish Messenger's summary of Beowulf's career (*Beo* 3003–7), as argued in North, 'Saxo and the Swedish Wars in *Beowulf*', 185–6. Beowulf's absence in Heardred's reign has been noted but not explained. See Lawrence, *Beowulf and Epic Tradition*, 102. Chambers, *Beowulf*, 12. A. Bonjour, 'Beowulf and Heardred', *ES* 32 (1951), 194–5.

status equivalent to Beowulf's initial 7,000 hides (*Beo* 2195).[41] Yet the hero of *Beowulf* wins his estates from Hygelac, a Geatish king. To test the antiquity of Beowulf's relationship with the Geats, we must look more closely at the fullest account of Bǫðvarr's life, which is given in *Hrólfs saga kraka*. Here Bǫðvarr is said to be the son of a prince named Bjǫrn, son of a certain King Sigurðr of Uppdalir (ch. 17). Bjǫrn rejects the advances of his stepmother Hvít, who then bewitches him so that he haunts the boundaries of his father's kingdom as a bear by day, a man by night (ch. 19). Bjǫrn's true-love is a peasant woman named Bera; after Hvít tricks her into eating Bjǫrn's cooked bear's flesh, Bera gives birth to three sons, *Elg*-('elk')-Fróði, Þórir *hundsfótr* ('hound's foot'), and Bǫðvarr (ch. 20). Fróði is an elk below the navel, Þórir has dog's feet from the instep down, while Bǫðvarr is outwardly a man and inwardly, it turns out, a bear. After killing Hvít in revenge for his father, Bǫðvarr goes looking for his brothers; when he arrives in Gautaland, where his brother Þórir has become king, the local people mistake him for Þórir and put him to bed with the queen; but Þórir turns up and so Bǫðvarr, having declined his brother's offer to rule half the Gautish kingdom, moves on to Denmark (ch. 23). This is the only association between Bǫðvarr and the Gautar in the Norse analogues; it suggests an older Icelandic source in which Bǫðvarr was said to take service with them. On the other hand, we have seen that no Bǫðvarr appears in the story of Hugleikr in his reign or in his last raid. In this light, it seems that Beowulf's strongest family tie, his relationship with Hygelac, has been fabricated. The severing of Beowulf's bond with King Hrothulf of Denmark appears to allow the poet of *Beowulf* to use Hygelac in a similar role.

There are further likely inventions in Hygelac's family. No one may be found in the analogues answering to Hygd, Hygelac's allegorically apposite wife in *Beo* 1926–31, 2172–6, and 2369–72; nor any son such as Heardred for whom Beowulf acts as regent in lines 2202–6. Hygelac's tragic brothers Herebeald and Hæthcyn, who rule before him in lines 2432–83, seem to have been imported into the Geatish royal family (Herebeald with an alliterative prefix) from a Danish myth of common ancestry with the tale of gods Baldr and Hǫðr in Old Norse mythology.[42] In the same episode the poet portrays Hrethel as king of Geatland.[43] Hrethel is Beowulf's favourite grandfather, looking after the 7-year-old with the same care as his sons (*Beo* 2428–34), and, with his name cited twelve times in *Beowulf*, his stature there is considerable.[44] Yet his name is unattested in *Widsith* or elsewhere and has no counterpart in Old Norse analogues. 'Hreðel' (gen. *Hreðles, Hrædlan*) indeed can be interpreted as 'little Goth', a back-formation from the first element of *Hreðgotas* ('Hreth-Goths',

---

[41] *Danakonunga Sögur*, ed. Bjarni, 28. *Gesta Danorum*, ed. Olrik and Ræder, 51 (II. vi. 11), 55 (II. vii. 10), and 60 (II. vii. 25–6). *Hrólfs saga*, ed. Slay, 86. *Hrólfs Saga Kraka*, ed. Finnur, 161 (cf. p. 74).

[42] Orchard, *Companion*, 116–19.

[43] North, *Pagan Words*, 60–2; *Heathen Gods*, 198–202, at 199.

[44] *Beo* 374, 454, 1485, 1847, 1923, 2191, 2358, 2430, 2474, 2995, 2960, 2992.

Wid 57, *El* 20).[45] With Hrethel, in other words, the poet of *Beowulf* carves a royal name out of a prefix for a tribe close to the Geats. The suspicion one gains from all these manoeuvres is that the poet knew little more of the Geats than that they lived between Denmark and Sweden, that Hygelac was their king, and that Beowulf stayed there once before moving on. Otherwise the Geatish dynasty in *Beowulf* is artificial and Beowulf's birth into it is the poet's first means of making him a king.

Beowulf's name

The name *Bjarki* appears to mean 'little bear' (**bjarn-ki*); in *Hrólfs saga*, Bǫðvarr's father was transformed into a bear, while 'bear' is the meaning of both his name and that of Bera, Bǫðvarr's mother; also in *Hrólfs saga*, Bǫðvarr fights Hjǫrvarðr's army with his body in a trance, in such a way that *biǫrn einn mikill fór fyrir Hr(olfz) kongz mǫnnum, og jafnan þar næst sem kongurinn er* ('a big bear advances before King Hrólfr's men, and always nearest to where the king was', ch. 33). The etymology of Beowulf's name (*beo-wulf,* 'wolf of bees') indicates also that he was formerly conceived as a 'bear'.[46] This homely conclusion is opposed by Andy Orchard, who acknowledges Beowulf's bearlike qualities (his mighty strength, death-hug of Dæghrefn, three times cited swimming endurance), but glosses OE *beowulf* as 'Beow-wulf, "the wolf of (the god) Beow"' on the basis of a comparison with OIce *Þórólfr* ('the wolf of the god Þórr').[47] Yet the *Þór*-prefix can be found in more than one third of Old Norse names, whereas there are no *Beow*-prefixes in other Anglo-Saxon personal names.

Bjarki's first feat for King Hrólfr is to kill a monster. Saxo, moving Biarco into Rolvo's narrative only before the end of this king's career, nonetheless says that he killed a *silvestris fera* ('wild creature from the woods'), an *ursum quippe eximiæ magnitudinis obvium sibi inter dumeta* ('a bear of enormous size which he met in a thicket'); Biarco also forces his comrade Hialto to drink from this monster's blood in order to increase his power.[48] It appears that the author of *Skjǫldunga saga* does not include this story, but it is told in *Hrólfs saga*, in which Bǫðvarr kills *dijr eitt... mykid ok ögurligt* ('a big frightful beast'), *ed mesta trǫll* ('the biggest demon', ch. 23), with wings on its back; giving the credit to Hjalti, whom he has already transformed from the coward Hǫttr by forcing him to drink its invigorating blood; in *Bjarkarímur* the creature is called *ylgrin* ('the she-wolf', IV. 60), but Hjalti drinks her blood just the same.[49] Hilda Ellis Davidson believes

---

[45] Cognate with OIce *(h)reiðgotar,* the guardians of Skinfaxi the sun-horse in *Vaf* 12).

[46] W. W. Skeat, 'On the Signification of the Monster Grendel in the Poem of *Beowulf*; with a Discussion of Lines 2076–2100', *Journal of Philology,* 15 (1886), 120–31. Supported in Chambers, *Beowulf,* 365–81; discussed with other interpretations in Stanley, ' "A Very Land-Fish" ', 88–9.

[47] *Companion,* 120–1 n. 117.

[48] *Gesta Danorum,* ed. Olrik and Ræder, 51 (II. vi. 11); see *Saxo Grammaticus,* trans. Fisher, i. 55.

[49] *Hrólfs saga,* ed. Slay, 79. *Hrólfs Saga Kraka,* ed. Finnur, 139 (cf. p. 68).

that Bjarki's earliest monstrous opponent was a bear, but Beowulf cites the binding of five giants and slaying of *niceras* ('sea-monsters') in his *curriculum vitae* (*Beo* 419–24), and tells Unferth that he killed nine *niceras* and other monsters, probably including whales, while he swam in the sea away from Breca (lines 549–79).[50]

In England in this way, Beowulf's reputation seems to have been founded on combats with monsters before the poet made use of him in *Beowulf.* Bjarki's wild opponents in the Norse analogues show that Beowulf's combat with Grendel and other monsters, including Grendel's Mother (whom the poet calls *seo brimwylf,* 'that she-wolf of the sea', lines 1506 and 1599), was probably integral to his role.[51] In this context Beowulf is also described as *beadwe heard* ('battle-hardened') in *Beo* 1539, reminiscent of *Bǫðvarr,* as he begins to grapple with Grendel's Mother.[52] This epithet may be as old as Beowulf's name, retained here for his role in a traditional scene: Bjarki in the Scandinavian analogues is also known as *Bǫðvarr* bjarki; in *Skjǫldunga saga,* apparently just as *Bǫðvarr* ('Bodvarus'). The development of the last name is clear in Saxo's adaptation of *Bjarkamál,* in which Biarco claims that *belligeri cepi cognomen* ('I took the nickname of "warlike"') from slaying Agner.[53] This line is thought to refer to an earlier form of his Norse name as *bǫðvar-Bjarki* ('Bjarki of battle (*bǫð*)'), which became *Bǫðvarr* bjarki and then *Bǫðvarr,* all before *c.*1200, when *Skjǫldunga saga* was written.

The diffusion of *Bjarkamál*

The oldest source for Bjarki is the fragmentary *Bjarkamál in fornu* ('the old lay of Bjarki'). This poem, thought to date from the tenth century, is a glorification of King Hrólfr's last stand.[54] When King Hjǫrvarðr prepares to storm the hall in Lejre, Bjarki's friend Hjalti wakes up the Danish guard, calling each of Hrólfr's twelve champions by name. After drinking toasts the king and his men set out to meet Hjǫrvarðr's attack. Bǫðvarr stays behind (or leaves his body behind while his bear-spirit fights outside) and Hjalti reproaches him until he answers by vindicating his past achievements, sortying with Hjalti, and remarking on the battle as it takes place.

Bjarkamál survives in fragments: two stanzas, apparently from the beginning, which Snorri quotes in *Óláfs saga helga* (ch. 208), both in the Separate version

---

[50] *Saxo Grammaticus,* trans. Fisher, ii. 45–6 n. 51.

[51] Berendsohn (*Zur Vorgeschichte des 'Beowulf',* 218) compares the invulnerability of monsters here: of the Lejre winged troll in *Hrólfs saga,* ch. 23 (ÁÁ *þad bijta ecki vopn,* in *Hrólfs saga,* ed. Slay, 78) with that of Grendel's Mother in *Beo* 1523 (*se beadoleoma bitan nolde*).

[52] *Saxo Grammaticus,* trans. Fisher, ii. 49 (n. 69). *Danakonunga Sögur,* ed. Bjarni, 27 n. 33.

[53] *Gesta Danorum,* ed. Olrik and Ræder, 58 (II. vii. 19).

[54] See *Skáldskaparmál,* ed. Faulkes, i. 188–9. Argued to be little older than Snorri, in K. von See, 'Hastings, Stiklastaðir und Langemarck: Zum Überlieferung vom Vortrag heroischer Lieder auf dem Schlachtfeld', *Germanisch-romanische Monatschrift,* 57 (NS. 26) (1976), 1–13.

and that contained in *Heimskringla*, with which he says the poet Þormóðr roused the troops of King Óláfr before the Battle of Stiklastaðir (in 1030);[55] three verses on *gulls heiti* ('synonyms for gold') which Snorri also attributes to this poem in *Skáldskaparmál*, but which had probably been interpolated;[56] a Latin adaptation written by Saxo apparently in imitation of the sack of Troy in *Aeneid* II in his *Gesta Danorum* (Book II);[57] and the prose description of Hjalti's speech and Bǫðvarr's reply towards the end of *Hrólfs saga* (ch. 33), which appears to rely on a prose paraphrase of the complete poem.[58] In Saxo's ponderous hexameters, Hialto makes his and Biarco's devotion to King Rolvo clear:[59]

> 'At nos, qui regem voto meliore veremur,
> iungamus cuneos stabiles tutisque phalangem
> ordinibus mensi, qua rex præcepit, eamus,
> qui natum Bøki Røricum stravit avari
> implicuitque virum leto virtute carentem.'

['But we, who worship the king with keener devotion, let us close in firm ranks, measuring out the phalanx in sure battle lines, let us march as bidden by the king who at one time cut down Røricus the son of Bøk the miser, and wrapped in death the man who lacked manliness.']

Biarco in this poem also calls himself *Rolvonis generum* ('Rolvo's brother-in-law') and says that Rolvo gave him *bissenas gentes* ('twelve vassals', estates). Biarco finally declares that he will die at Rolvo's head, Hialto at his feet.[60]

Saxo calls his version of *Bjarkamál* an *exhortationum series* ('set of admonitory speeches').[61] This term indicates that both Hjalti and Bjarki had speaking parts in *Bjarkamál*; and it resembles another name for the poem in *Óláfs saga helga*, in which Snorri says that Óláfr's men, after they have risen, call *Bjarkamál* the *Húskarlahvǫt* ('the housecarls' incitement').[62] Since King Rolvo's housecarls are performing rather than hearing the incitement, it seems that the name *Húskarlahvǫt* is older than Snorri, who reinterpreted its origin because he lacked Bjarki's part in the poem. The association between Hrólfr and Bjarki in Scandinavia is also confimed in other works which did not rely on *Bjarkamál* for all their information on King Hrólfr: in Arngrímr's translation of *Skjǫldunga saga*, where 'Bodvarus', a Norwegian, is said to be Rolfo's other *pugilem celeberrimum* ('most famous champion', ch. 12; the first one is the Swede Witserchus); in Saxo's

---

[55] *Heimskringla II*, ed. Bjarni, 361 (*Óláfs saga helga*, ch. 208).

[56] *Skáldskaparmál*, ed. Faulkes, i. 60–1 (vv. 188–90).

[57] *Gesta Danorum*, ed. Olrik and Ræder, 53–61 (II. vii. 4–28); see *Saxo Grammaticus*, trans. Fisher and ed. Ellis Davidson, i. 56–63 and ii. 47–50 (commentary).

[58] *Hrólfs saga*, ed. Slay, 98–100.

[59] *Gesta Danorum*, ed. Olrik and Ræder, 56 (II. vii. 13) and 58 (II. vii. 17); see *Saxo Grammaticus*, trans. Fisher, i. 59 and 60.

[60] *Gesta Danorum*, ed. Olrik and Ræder, 60–1 (II. vii. 28).

[61] Ibid. 61 (II. viii. 1).

[62] *Heimskringla II*, ed. Bjarni, 362.

prose, based on this lost saga and possibly also a certain *Bjarka þáttr*,[63] in which Biarco first appears in the wedding between Agner and Ruta, Rolvo's sister and later Biarco's wife; in the prose *Edda*, where Snorri lists Bǫðvarr bjarki as the first of King Hrólfr's champions; in the late *Hrólfs saga kraka* (ch. 23), where Hrólfr is drawn to Bǫðvarr in a witty exchange; and in *Bjarkarímur*, where Hrólfur likewise welcomes Bjarki as a substitute for the man Bjarki has killed with a bone (IV. 56).[64]

Hrothulf's men get transfers

Hrólfr's champions are called *Aðils sinnar* in *Bjarkamál* in order to show the strength of their loyalty to Hrólfr, to whom they all transfer while he visits King Aðils's court in Uppsala. In the extant *Bjarkamál* two of Hrólfr's men are named as Hár *enn harðgreipi* ('the hard-gripper') and Hrólfr *skjótandi* ('the shooter').[65] Hrólfr's men are unnamed in Saxo's adaptation of *Bjarkamál*, but for Biarco and Hialto, whereas the list of twelve names in *Hrólfs saga* gives reason to believe that this saga's author had a paraphrase of the whole of *Bjarkamál* before him.[66] According to *Skjǫldunga saga*, Hrólfr has a bodyguard of twelve: Witserchus, Bodvarus, and ten others who go with him constantly (ch. 12). Snorri, using a version of this saga, gives more names: not only Bǫðvarr bjarki, Hjalti *hugprúði* ('the proud of heart'), and Hvítserkr *hvati* ('the keen'), but also Vǫttr ('glove'), Véseti, the brothers Svipdagr and Beiguðr.[67] In *Hrólfs saga*, the king's men are Hrómundr *harði* ('the hard') and Hrólfr *skjóthendi* ('quick-handed'), Svipdagr, Hvítserkr and Beigaðr, Haklangr, Harðrefill, Haki *inn frækni* ('the bold'), Vǫttr *hinn mikilaflaði* ('the arrogant'), Starólfr, and lastly Hjalti *hinn hugprúði* ('the proud of heart', formerly Hǫttr, ch. 24) and Bǫðvarr himself.[68]

It is interesting to see four of the same figures in *Beowulf*. One of them is Hondscio, the Geat whom Beowulf allows Grendel to eat alive before he grapples with the monster in Heorot (lines 740–5 and 2076–80). The meaning of Hondscio's name, 'glove' ('hand-shoe'), is identical with that of 'Vǫttr', one of Hrólfr's champions above. In *Ynglingatal*, a Norwegian poem probably of *c*.890, Vǫttr is one of the Danish king Fróði's two *eylands jarlar* ('earls of the island'; the other is Fasti), who kill King Óttarr Egilsson of Sweden in Zealand: this reference authenticates the tradition preserved in Oddi that Vǫttr was a Danish king's retainer, albeit of one two generations before Hrólfr.[69] Hondscio is eaten by

---

[63] Bjarni, *Um Skjöldungasögu*, 61–2.
[64] *Danakonunga Sögur*, ed. Bjarni, 27. *Gesta Danorum*, ed. Olrik and Ræder, 50–1 (II. vi. 9). *Skáldskaparmál*, ed. Faulkes, 58 (ch. 44). *Hrólfs saga*, ed. Slay, 76–7. *Hrólfs Saga Kraka*, ed. Finnur, 139 (cf. p. 67).
[65] *Heimskringla II*, ed. Bjarni, 361 (*Óláfs saga helga*, ch. 208).
[66] *Gesta Danorum*, ed. Olrik and Ræder, 60–1 (II. vii. 28).
[67] *Skáldskaparmál*, ed. Faulkes, i. 58 (ch. 44).
[68] *Hrólfs saga*, ed. Slay, 85. See *Hrólfs Saga Kraka*, ed. Finnur, 74.
[69] *Heimskringla I*, ed. Bjarni, 53–5, at 54–5 (*Ynglinga saga*, ch. 27).

Grendel. Beowulf remembers him without sentiment, perhaps because Hondscio could have been thought to invite his death by falling asleep at his post; indeed, with the words *glof hangode* ('the bag (/glove) hung' i.e. out of Grendel's mouth), line 2085), it is possible that Beowulf puns on his name to his uncle for sardonic effect, although his description of Hondscio's death is flattering, more so than the poet's.[70] In *Beowulf* Hondscio is not in Danish service: he is part of that *sibbegedriht* ('band of kinsmen', line 729) of fourteen Geats which Beowulf hand-picks before sailing to Denmark (lines 205–7). Vǫttr's role in the analogues may show that the poet of *Beowulf* has moved Hondscio out of Hrothulf's retinue into Beowulf's.

Secondly, the name Hrothmund, son of Hrothgar, which is analogous with Hrómundr, suggests that the poet of *Beowulf* gave Hrethric a new brother with the name of a fighter from Hrothulf's retinue.[71] Thirdly, Beowulf's flyting with Unferth, soon after his arrival in Heorot, flares up because Unferth would not allow any other man to be called more famous than he (lines 499–505). This rivalry resembles the initial contest between Bǫðvarr and one of Hrólfr's men and his later scuffles with Hrólfr's other champions in *Hrólfs saga* (chs. 23–4). Lastly, *Hjalti*, the new sobriquet for Hǫttr in *Hrólfs saga*, is a name formed on Hrólfr's sword *Gullinhjalti* ('golden-hilt'), which Hǫttr asks the king to give him so that he can slay the winged demon in a public demonstration arranged by Bǫðvarr (ch. 23). It cannot be a coincidence in *Beowulf* that the hilt which Beowulf takes out of Grendel's Mother's lair, and which is given into Hrothgar's hand, is called *gylden hilt* ('a golden hilt') by the poet on line 1677. In both cases a golden hilt is produced after a monster is slain, although, unlike the case in the Norse analogues, there is no younger companion at this moment in *Beowulf* to whom the name 'hilt' can be given. Not until Wiglaf intervenes at the end of the story do we meet the 'Hjalti' of Beowulf's tale.

Beowulf dies in a new fire

With the dragon the poet makes his greatest change to Beowulf's career. Having detached him from Hrothulf's company, he cannot arrange for Beowulf to die for this king in Denmark. Rolfo dies when his hall is attacked and burned down by Hiørvardus, in Arngrímr's translation of *Skjǫldunga saga* (ch. 12); just like Rolvo with Earl Hiarwarthus in *Gesta Danorum*; and Hrólfr with Hjǫrvarðr in *Hrólfs saga* (chs. 33–4; the story in *Bjarkarímur* does not go so far). That the poet of *Beowulf* knows of Hrothulf's death by a sneak attack is clear from his reference to Heoroweard when Beowulf gives his treasures to Hygelac on his return from Denmark. Having declared that Hygelac is the only chief kinsman he has

---

[70] Lee, 'Character from Archetype', 192–6. For a comparison with Skrýmir's glove in *Gylfaginning*, see Orchard, *Companion*, 122 and 222–3.
[71] Pace Newton, *The Origins of Beowulf*, 127–31.

(lines 2150–1), Beowulf has Hrothgar's panoply brought before the king, saying that Hrothgar gave him this armour with the words that King Heorogar of the Scyldings had it for a long while:

'no ðy ær suna sinum   syllan wolde
hwatum Heorowearde,   þeah he him hold wære,
breostgewædu.   Bruc ealles well.' (*Beo* 2160–2)

['Not any the sooner for that did he wish to give his breast-garment to the keen Heoroweard, his own son, though this man was loyal to him. Make good use of all of it.']

If Heorogar did not pass on his armour to Heoroweard, it is unlikely that he could bequeath him his kingdom. Although we never see Heoroweard, his father was the eldest of three brothers: perhaps, for that reason, he has a better claim to rule Denmark than either Hrethric, Hrothgar's son, or the stronger Hrothulf to whom the kingdom passes. Once again, there is no way of knowing whether it is the poet of *Beowulf* who creates Heoroweard's blood-kinship with Hrothulf, for in the analogues, Hjǫrvarðr is only the brother-in-law of Hrólfr through his half-sister Skuld. To Hygelac with this precious gear, which was denied to Heoroweard, go four of the eight stallions Beowulf received in Heorot. Heoroweard's treacherous attack on Hrothulf is probably what the poet of *Beowulf* means by *facenstafas* ('criminal acts'), by which he has already characterized the Scyldings of the future (line 1018). With this forewarning of Hrothulf's death, the poet shows us the end of the Scyldings not long before he begins to focus on the Geats. It becomes clear that the poet's greatest innovation is to reserve Beowulf for the dragon's fire.[72]

Beowulf's dragon-fight is in the foreground for the last third of the poem (*Beo* 2200–3182). A slave on the run from his master, wishing to be reconciled, steals a precious cup from an ancient barrow-hoard and brings it home. However, a dragon has lived there for three hundred years (line 2278). This beast wakes up to the man's smell and the loss of one item from its massive hoard, and flies out to burn the local country. Beowulf is now fifty years older. He hears that his hall has burned down; after some dark thoughts (lines 2327–32), he has an iron shield made in readiness for vengeance. The poet says that this will be the last battle for both Beowulf and the dragon (lines 2341–4). Remembering past glories with Grendel, his prowess in Hygelac's last raid, and later his victory against King Onela of Sweden (lines 2349–96), Beowulf sets off to kill the dragon with a company of eleven, plus the slave now acting as a guide. Beowulf knows that his time is near, gloomily sits on a headland, and gives a long record of past achievements, the first in this last third of the poem (lines 2426–509). Thereafter a short formal vow (lines 2511–15) and an order to his guard to wait are preludes to the action, in which the dragon sets Beowulf alight and all but one of his men

---

[72] Berendsohn also notes the originality of the *Beowulf*-'adapter' here, in *Zur Vorgeschichte des 'Beowulf'*, 226: 'Wie früher dargestellt, sehe ich den Tod Beowulfs im Drachenkampf als planvolle Umgestaltung des englischen Bearbeiters an.'

desert him. Wiglaf, the last man standing, remembers his vow to Beowulf and delivers an exhortation to his fleeing companions (lines 2633–60), before telling Beowulf that he is coming to join him (lines 2663–8). After they kill the dragon, there are other speeches, in which Beowulf praises Wiglaf, thanks God for the treasure while ordering his own barrow, and declares their bond of kinship before dying (lines 2729–51, 2794–808, 2813–16). But it is the earlier speeches which are of interest here, for both Beowulf's record of achievement and Wiglaf's exhortation appear to be based on a version of *Bjarkamál*.

In *Beowulf* the hero's death is partly due to injury, partly to fire; more problematically, a fire is also raging in Bjarki's final moments. In *Hrólfs saga kraka*, Hjalti returns to drag Bǫðvarr from his chamber, threatening to burn down the hall unless he comes out (ch. 33). Bǫðvarr answers him with a speech which appears to paraphrase a passage from *Bjarkamál*.[73] From Saxo's version we can see that Rolvo's hall is on fire, when Biarco tells Hialto that *nemo magis clausis refugit penetralibus uri | cumque sua rogus esse domo* ('No one has been more loath to burn in barred chambers and become a pyre in his own home'); and perhaps Biarco's earlier words to a servant, to stoke up the fire in his quarters, may be taken as Saxo's mistranslation of an understatement whereby Biarco encourages the attackers to increase their efforts.[74] Biarco's words to Hialto on the firing of Hrólfr's hall resemble the attack on Hálfr's hall in *Hálfs saga ok Hálfsrekka*, in a scene which is thought to be written in imitation of *Bjarkamál*.[75] Hjalti's threat in *Hrólfs saga*, to burn Bjarki inside, may be treated as an adaptation of this common motif, one which helps the author to highlight Hjalti's bafflement at Bjarki's withdrawal. When Wiglaf speaks in *Beowulf*, Beowulf is already on fire: *geseah his mondryhten under heregriman hat prowian* ('he saw his man and lord enduring hot agony beneath his war mask', lines 2604–5).

There is a string of six or seven correspondences between Beowulf's avowed list of achievements and what is known of Bjarki's in *Bjarkamál*.[76] Before he joins battle with the dragon, Beowulf starts by stressing his long experience of war:

> 'Fela ic on giogoðe   guðræsa genæs
> orleghwila;   ic þæt eal gemon.' (*Beo* 2426–7)

['Many are the battle-charges, the periods of warfare, that I survived in my youth; I will recall all of it.']

His grandfather Hrethel took him from Ecgtheow when he was 7. On this note Beowulf leads into a long preamble of a tale: Hrethel's sons Herebeald and Hæthcyn, the death of the first at the hands of the second, Hrethel's own

[73] *Hrólfs saga*, ed. Slay, 118–19. See *Hrólfs Saga Kraka*, ed. Finnur, 101–2.
[74] *Gesta Danorum*, ed. Olrik and Ræder, 58 (ii. vii. 17); 53–4 (ii. vii. 5).
[75] *Saxo Grammaticus*, trans. Fisher, ii. 47 n. 58. A. Olrik, *The Heroic Legends of Denmark*, trans. L. M. Hollander (New York, 1919), 171.
[76] The broad likeness between *Bjarkamál* and Beowulf's long monologue is already noted in Berendsohn, *Zur Vorgeschichte des 'Beowulf'*, 221–7, at 223–6.

grief-stricken death and Hæthcyn's untimely end in battle against Ongentheow, along with the implicit rise of Hygelac who gave the young Beowulf his chance:

> 'Ic him þa maðmas   þe he me sealde
> geald at guðe,   swa me gifeðe wæs,
> leohtan sweorde;   he me lond forgeaf
> eard eðelwyn.   Næs him ænig þearf
> þæt he to Gifðum   oððe to Gar-Denum
> oððe in Swiorice   secean þurfe
> wyrsan wigfrecan,   weorðe cypan:
> simle ic him on feðan   beforan wolde
> ana on orde   ond swa to aldre sceall
> sæcce fremman   þenden þis sweord þolað
> þæt mec ær ond sið   oft gelæste
> syððan ic for dugeðum   Dæghrefne wearð
> to handbonan,   Huga cempan.' (*Beo* 2490–502)

['I repaid him in battle for the treasures he gave me, as it was granted for me to do so, with a gleaming sword; he gave me lands, a homeland, and the joy of inheriting an estate. For him there was no need to look for lower-ranking war-braves among the Gifthas or the Spear-Danes or in the kingdom of the Swedes, to buy them at their price: constantly I would go ahead of him in the foot-troop, alone on point, and just so evermore I shall pursue combats for as long as this sword endures, the sword which then and now has always obeyed me, since that time when before the hosts I became the slayer of Dæghrefn, champion of the Hugas, with my own arms.']

In *Hrólfs saga*, Bjarki first replies to Hjalti by vindicating his experience:

Þä eg var vngur flyda eg huǫrki elld nie jarn, enn elld hef eg sialldan reynt, enn järna gang hef eg stundum þolad, og fyrir huǫrugu geingid hingad til, og skalltu ad sǫnnu seigia, ad eg vil fulluel beriast.

['when I was young, I fled neither fire nor iron, and while I have seldom been put to the test by fire, once in a while I have suffered the passage of steel and up to now I have gone down before neither, and to tell the truth you will have to say that I want to fight at my best.']

That is to say, Bǫðvarr claims to have survived many battles from the time of his youth. He continues:

og jafnann hefur Hr(olfur) k(ongur) kallad mig kappa fyrir sijnum mǫnnum. ÁÁ eg honum og margt ad launa, fyrst mægd, og xij bv er hann gaf mier, þar med marga dijrgripe.

['and King Hrólfr has always called me a champion in front of his men; I have a lot of other things to repay him, first my kinship with him by marriage and the twelve farms he gave me, and many other precious possessions as well.']

He thus claims to have been royally rewarded for leading the king's battle line, with gifts which go beyond requirements. He continues and the author takes over in indirect speech:

Eg drap Agnar berserk og eij sidur kong, og er þad verk haft j minnum. Telur nu vpp fyrir honum mǫrg störvirki, er hann hafdi vnnid, og bana madur ordid margra manna, og bad hann so til ætla, ad hann mundi öhræddur til bardaga ganga.

['I killed Agnarr the berserk, a king no less, and that deed is well remembered'—and now Bǫðvarr recounts to Hjalti the many great deeds he has done, how he became the slayer of many men, and so asked him to recognize that he would go into battle unafraid.]

So Bjarki gives us the same five elements as Beowulf does, in almost the same order: a military youth; his survival in battle; priority over the king's other warriors; the king's gifts of land and treasure; and his killing of an enemy champion for the king.[77]

In addition, Saxo includes two more elements from *Bjarkamál* which the author of *Hrólfs saga* seems to have left out. First, Biarco says that gave him twelve estates, *licet insula memet | ediderit strictæque habeam natalia terræ* ('although an island produced me and I have a narrow piece of land for my birthplace').[78] His island origin seems in keeping with the folktale in *Hrólfs saga* (ch. 20) in which Bera gives birth to Bjarki and his brothers some way off from human settlements, in a cave; but Bjarki makes no mention of his birth in his reply to Hjalti. Biarco's reminiscence of childhood, however, matches with Beowulf's starting point *syfanwintre* ('of seven winters', line 2428). Second, Biarco cites 'Snyrtir', a famous Teuton sword with which he killed Agner; Beowulf twice alludes to his *leohtan sweorde* ('gleaming sword') even as part of the combat in which we know he crushed Dæghrefn to death with his bare arms. These two elements may be added to the five which Beowulf's speech has in common with Bjarki's in *Hrólfs saga* (ch. 33).

Lastly, we may consider Wiglaf's initial exhortation in the context of *Bjarkamál*. Wiglaf thus rouses the king's men to stay and protect Beowulf against the dragon:

> 'Nu is se dæg cumen
> þæt ure mandryhten   mægenes behofað
> godra guðrinca;   wutun gongan to,
> helpan hildfruman   þenden hyt sy
> gledegesa grim.' (*Beo* 2646–50)

['Now is the day come that our man and lord has need of the strength of good fighting men; let us go in, help the battle-chief for as long as the grim fiery terror may last.']

There is similar language in *Bjarkamál*, which contained words also of Hjalti, on whom Wiglaf is based. The surviving vernacular stanzas of this poem are worth quoting in full, from *Óláfs saga helga* (ch. 208) in which the poet Þormóðr is charged with rousing the king's men (also to a last stand) in Stiklastaðir:[79]

---

[77] Berendsohn, *Zur Vorgeschichte des 'Beowulf'*, 224.
[78] *Gesta Danorum*, ed. Olrik and Ræder, 58 (II. vii. 17).
[79] *Heimskringla II*, ed. Bjarni, 361.

Dagr es upp kominn,   dynja hana fjaðrar,
mál es vílmǫgum   at vinna erfiði.
Vaki æ ok vaki   vina hǫfuð,
allir enir œztu   Aðils of sinnar.

Hár enn harðgreipi,   Hrólfr skjótandi,
ættum góðir menn,   þeirs ekki flyja,
vekka yðr at víni   né at vífs rúnum,
heldr vekk yðr at hǫrðum   Hildar leiki.

['Day has come up, the cocks shake their feathers, it is time for serving-men to carry out their tasks. Let the main man of the friends [: King Hrólfr] wake for all time, and let them wake, all the best companions of Aðils. Hár ('Hoary') the hard-gripper, Hrólfr the shooter, men of good family who do not flee, I do not wake you to wine nor to the mysteries of a woman, rather I wake you into the hard play of Hildr [: battle].]

Wiglaf's initial words also resemble Hildegyth's in *Waldere*, in which she exhorts Waldere to battle against Guthere and Hagena: *[Nu] is se dæg cumen þæt ðu scealt aninga oðer twega* ('[Now] the day is come that you alone must do one of two things', *Wald* I. 8–9).[80] This first half-line is thus a topos. But it can also be said that three of Wiglaf's expressions in *Beowulf* (*is se dæg cumen*; *godra guðrinca*; *hildfruman*) come close enough, both in form and sequence, to three of Hjalti's (*dagr es upp kominn*; *ættum góðir menn*; *Hildar leikr*). On this evidence, it seems that the English poet models the boastful part of Beowulf's speeches and the exhortation of Wiglaf's on a version of *Bjarkamál in fornu* which was even older than the tenth century. This parallel may be added to the seven correspondences already noted between Beowulf's speech of record and the paraphrases of *Bjarkamál* in *Hrólfs saga* and Saxo's *Gesta*. These correspondences are so many, and in so similar an order, that they may be explained as a case of influence from a truly old version of *Bjarkamál* to *Beowulf*.

Summary

The poet of *Beowulf* appears to have changed his sources concerning 'Beowulf' the monster-slayer. Beowulf retains the monstrous aspect of his supernatural background, but takes service briefly with Hrothgar, not permanently with Hrothulf. He gains the honour of birth into the Geatish royal family and an uncle to whom the intensity of his older friendship with Hrothulf is transferred. Beowulf even becomes a king. Although he retains his supporting role in the war with Onela, he does so as Eadgils' royal backer, not as Hrothulf's champion on loan; some of Hrothulf' retinue is redeployed in *Beowulf* and Beowulf meets his death not in Hrothulf's burning hall, but in the dragon's fire, although even here the evidence suggests that the poet has fashioned Beowulf's and Wiglaf's valedictory speeches out of a version of *Bjarkamál*.

[80] *Beowulf*, ed. Mitchell and Robinson, 208–9.

WIGLAF AND INVENTION

Hjalti's English counterpart seems to be Wiglaf, who delivers speeches of *Bjarkamál*-style exhortation (*Beo* 2633–60, 2663–8) and rebuke (lines 2864–91). Yet Wiglaf is not like Hjalti for long: whatever his nationality, he is not a Dane; he is not where we would expect him to be, in Hrothgar's hall; above all, the names differ. Wiglaf's name links him alliteratively with the Wægmundings, a kindred which is also Beowulf's. An implication of Wiglaf's kinship with Beowulf, at the close of Fitt XXXV, is the first thing we hear about him. When Beowulf burns and his new bodyguard runs to the woods, one of them chooses to stay:

XXXVI   Wiglaf wæs haten,   Weoxstanes sunu,
         leoflic lindwiga,   leod Scylfinga,
         mæg Ælfheres;   geseah his mondryhten
         under heregriman   hat þrowian.
         Gemunde ða ða are,   þe he him ær forgeaf,
         wicstede weligne   Wægmundinga,
         folcrihta gehwylc,   swa his fæder ahte. (*Beo* 2602–9)

[Wiglaf he was called, son of Weohstan, admirable shield-warrior, prince of the Scylfings, kinsman of Ælfhere; he saw his man and lord enduring hot agony beneath his war mask. Then it was that he remembered the favours which Beowulf had formerly given him, a wealthy dwelling-place of the Wægmundings, each and every tribal entitlement just as his father had had.]

Wiglaf has here received his father's life-estate from Beowulf without difficulty: what this means, we shall see in Chapter 10.[81] Wiglaf is not called a Geat but a Wægmunding, so he is related to Beowulf through Ecgtheow, Beowulf's father. On the other hand, the poet says he is a Swede as well, *leod Scylfinga* ('prince of the Scylfings', line 2604). 'Ælfhere' is unknown, unless we treat him as Waldere's father (*Wald* I. 11; II. 18). But it is more likely that Ælfhere is another Swede, proof of Wiglaf's claim to be related to the Scylfing royal house, for there is an Álfr (whom Snorri names also Elfsi), son of Alrekr, among the early kings of Uppsala in *Ynglingatal*;[82] and if the expression *mæg Ælfheres* is used like *mæg Higelaces* (on lines 407–8, 736–7, 758, 813, 914, and onwards), we would expect him to be Wiglaf's mother's brother. Wiglaf can thus be placed as a Swede on his mother's side, a Wægmunding on his father's.

Whereas Wiglaf is not matched by a named Norse analogue (Saxo's *Wiggo* is his form for OIce *Vǫggr*), Weohstan does find a counterpart in Icelandic recollections

---

[81] Farrell, '*Beowulf*, Swedes and Geats', 242–3. Bond ('Links between *Beowulf* and Mercian History', 484) sees in *wicstede* an allusion to *Wicbold*, the name for King Wiglaf's vill in his charter of 831 (S 188 (BCS 400), Wychbold in north Worcestershire).

[82] *Heimskringla I*, ed. Bjarni, 40–2, at 42 (*Ynglinga saga*, ch. 21).

of Sweden in the heroic age.[83] *Alsvinnsmál* is a poem probably of the twelfth
century preserved in three manuscripts of *Snorra Edda* (RTC, but not U). This is
a collection of *hesta heiti* ('synonyms for horses') with a reference to Áli and Aðils
in the battle of Lake Vänern:

> Vésteinn Vali,   enn Vifill Stúfi,
> Meinþjófr Mói   enn Morginn Vakri,
> Áli Hrafni,   til íss riðu
> en annarr austr   und Aðilsi,
> grár hvarfaði,   ge[i]ri undaðr.[84]

[Vésteinn on Falcon, and Vifill on Stub, Meinþjófr on Heath and Morginn on Waker, Áli
on Raven, they rode to the ice, and another [horse] east under Aðils, grey it wandered,
wounded with a spear.]

The plural of *riðu* suggests that the first part of this list is coherent and that
Vésteinn is named as a champion of King Áli of Uppland, in the same winter
battle which is said, in *Beo* 2391–6, to take place between Onela and Beowulf's
protégé Eadgils. Yet the poet makes no reference to Weohstan in this winter
campaign, giving him the role, instead, of killing Eanmund, Eadgils' brother, in
the same Swedish incursion (lines 2612–19) that leads to Beowulf's revenge-
attack on Onela.

Eanmund's Norse analogue is Aun, father of Egill, in *Ynglingatal* 16–17,
whose name corresponds with the prefix of Eanmund's name (*Ean* < *Æan* <
Aun). Besides growing to an immense age, Aun is famous for two defeats: one
from a certain King Hálfdan of Denmark, who drove Aun into Väster-Götland,
ruled Uppsala in his place, and died there twenty years later; and the other from
one Áli *inn frœkni* ('the bold'), who likewise drove Aun into exile in Väster-
Götland, also for twenty years. In the first story, Aun may be connected to
'Eymundr' (a counterpart of [On]ela on *Beo* 62) whose marriage with the
daughter of the Danish Hálfdan is celebrated in *Hynd* 15. However, it is not
Eymundr who resembles Eanmund entering Geatland on the run from his uncle
Onela in *Beowulf* 2380, but rather the Aun of the second story, on the run from
Áli. If this Áli was ever identical with Áli of Uppland, it is possible that Vésteinn
fought in this battle too, and correspondingly, that Weohstan's role in the pursuit
of Eanmund was not fabricated by the poet of *Beowulf*. And yet in *Ynglingatal*
Aun is said to die of decrepit old age. So Weohstan's killing of Eanmund appears
to be an innovation of the poet of *Beowulf*. Later Weohstan is allowed to keep
Eanmund's panoply *fela missera* ('for many six-months', line 2620) until Wiglaf
can carry out heroic deeds like his father before him. Weohstan *geaf him ða mid
Geatum guðgewæda* ('then gave him the battle-raiment among the Geats', line

[83] The 'narratological good sense' of *wig-laf* as 'he who is left when the strife is over' is praised in
Stanley, ' "A Very Land-Fish" ', 87. The problem is lines 2999–3003, the strife about to start.
[84] *Skáldskaparmál*, ed. Faulkes, i. 89 (v. 329) and 211 (note).

2623) along with other wealth, when he departed this life *frod on forðweg* ('wise and experienced on the way hence', line 2625). In this case, it appears that the poet arranges for Weohstan to kill Eanmund so that Eanmund's sword may pass to Wiglaf.

This narrative in *Beowulf* is compressed as much as that of the 'Finnsburh episode', as if the poet were telescoping material from a longer poem on Eadgils' battle with Onela. A number of things may be deduced: Eadgils's vengeance does not follow on immediately from Eanmund's death; when Beowulf's army destroys Onela, Weohstan is too old to fight; Wiglaf is born in Sweden to a Swedish mother; before Eadgils can find them, the aged Weohstan takes his son from Sweden back to Geatland, his land of origin. Some reconstruction of this kind is necessary; this one is borne out by the Geatish jurisdiction over Weohstan's estate when Beowulf hands it on to Wiglaf in lines 2602–9. Of Vésteinn, no more survives in Norse records than his association with Áli the enemy of Aðils. As far as we can deduce the change to his story in *Beowulf*, Weohstan is withdrawn from the Eadgils–Onela battle and moved to Geatland, all so that his son may stand with Beowulf.

Although it is not clear who the Wægmundings are, what they are is important. Beowulf in his last words names them as a kindred common to himself and the young Wiglaf (*Beo* 2813–16). These people live within Geatish territory, but are distinct from the Geats, as Wiglaf later points out to the cowards with the phrase *eowrum cynne* ('your race', line 2885). The only Norse cognate of OE *Wægmundingas* is clear in the name *Vǫggr* (deriving from a *wa*-stem **wagw-*), identical with the prefix *Wæg*.[85] 'Vǫggr' makes friends with King Hrólfr in *Skjǫldunga saga* (both in Snorri's excerpt in *Skáldskaparmál* and as 'Woggerus', in Arngrímur's Latin translation), in Saxo's *Gesta Danorum* (as 'Viggo'), in *Hrólfs saga kraka* and in *Bjarkarímur*. In *Skjǫldunga saga*, upon which all the other versions seem to be based, Vǫggr is a man of no means and little account who charms the king by naming him *kraki*, his nickname from then on ('pole-ladder').[86] King Hrólfr rewards him with a golden ring. When Vǫggr praises the ring, promising one day to avenge him, Hrólfr declares: *Litlu verðr Vǫggr feginn* ('pleased with little is "Vǫggr"').[87] This exchange was probably modelled by the author of *Skjǫldunga saga* on one between St Constantius and a peasant in the *Dialogues* of Gregory the Great.[88] In its heroic context, however, Hrólfr's conversation with Vǫggr takes place early in the king's career before his trip to

---

[85] E. V. Gordon, *An Introduction to Old Norse*, 2nd edn., rev. A. R. Taylor (Oxford, 1957), 284–5 (§ 82).

[86] Arngrímur confused this with Dan *kraghe* ('crow'). *Danakonunga Sögur*, ed. Bjarni, 26 n. 30 (ch. 12).

[87] *Skáldskaparmál*, ed. Faulkes, i. 58 (ch. 44). *Danakonunga Sögur*, ed. Bjarni, 26 (ch. 12); see 43. There is possibly a pun here on OIce *vagga* ('cradle'), by which Hrólfr also means 'the child is pleased with little'.

[88] *Danakonunga Sögur*, ed. Bjarni, pp. lx–lxi and nn. 31–2. On the wider influence of Gregory's *Dialogues* in Iceland, see G. Turville-Petre, *Origins of Icelandic Literature* (Oxford, 1953), 135–7.

Uppsala. Vǫggr is otherwise renowned for avengeing Hrólfr six hours after his death.[89] In *Hrólfs saga*, however, when Vǫggr makes his vow, he is said to be a servant of Queen Yrsa and helps King Hrólfr survive King Aðils in Uppsala (ch. 28).[90] In this tradition, Vǫggr is a younger contemporary of Bǫðvarr bjarki, who speaks with him in the king's council of war.

These versions descend in part from *Skjǫldunga saga*, in which, as we have seen, Vǫggr's vow appears to be embellished with a patristic text. The *Chronicon Lethrense*, which might be treated as a control in this matter, reports that Rolf's killer Hiarwart ruled for six hours, but that he was then killed by Aco, son of Hamund: another name for the pirate Haki Hámundarson.[91] All that might be Germanic in Vǫggr's surviving tale, therefore, is his creation of a famous nick-name for King Hrólfr. Nor is there is any reason to treat Vǫggr or Viggo as Hrólfr's retainer, given his absence in the roll-call of king's champions in the prose paraphrase of *Bjarkamál* that survives in *Hrólfs saga kraka* (ch. 32). Vǫggr turns up early in *Skjǫldunga saga* probably because the author wished to give Hrólfr his cognomen near the start. In this case, it seems likely that the fuller treatment of Vǫggr in *Hrólfs saga* (ch. 28) is truer to his older legend than his role in the other versions. Doubtless in twelfth-century Iceland, before then more widely in Scandinavia, Vǫggr was known as a Swedish retainer of Queen Yrsa who disliked his master Aðils and gave help to King Hrólfr.

In this way the Wægmundings might be regarded as Swedish in origin, yet as living in (western) Geatland. Wiglaf's lineage is thus complex: Swedish on his mother's side, at least if we distinguish Scylfings from Wægmundings; yet also Swedish by origin on Weohstan's side; while he keeps a separate identity as a 'Wægmunding'. Ecgtheow, who is Beowulf's link to the Wægmundings, was taken to be a Swede by Edith Wardale, probably correctly.[92] His people are probably to be understood as the Swedes; at least on his father's side, given the formal likeness of *Ecg-þeow* with *Ongen-þeow* and less closely with the other Swedish names. On the other hand, given that Ecgtheow's people have to be treated as Wægmundings as well, with whom they do not alliterate, the conclusion is that Beowulf was a Wægmunding through Ecgtheow's mother.

There is no sense in refining the connection between Beowulf and Wiglaf further. Norman Eliason has suggested that Wiglaf is Beowulf's sister's son; through a sister whom the poet neither names nor cites (unless she is the woman at Beowulf's funeral).[93] As Eliason admits, however, the poet leaves

---

[89] *Danakonunga Sögur*, ed. Bjarni, 37. *Gesta Danorum*, ed. Olrik and Ræder, 51–2 (ii. vi. 12); see *Saxo Grammaticus*, trans. Fisher, i. 55. *Hrólfs Saga Kraka*, ed. Finnur, 112–13 (*Bjarkarímur* I. 9–17).

[90] *Hrólfs saga*, ed. Slay, 98–100 and 124. See *Hrólfs Saga Kraka*, ed. Finnur, 84–7 and 106–7.

[91] *Scriptores minores historiae Danicae*, ed. Gertz, i. 52 (*Chronicon Lethrense*, ch. 8).

[92] E. E. Wardale, '*Beowulf*: The Nationality of Ecgþeow', *MLR* 24 (1929), 322. The smaller grouping is overlooked in R. P. M. Lehmann, 'Ecgþeow the Wægmunding: Swede or Geat?', *English Language Notes*, 31/3 (1994), 1–5.

[93] Eliason, 'Beowulf, Wiglaf and the Wægmundings', 101–5, at 104: 'the existence of Beowulf's sister is . . . a logical necessity.'

this relationship vague.[94] Witness his celebration of Beowulf and Wiglaf, as together they close with the dragon:

> XXXVII   Ða ic æt þearfe [gefrægn]   þeodcyninges
> andlongne eorl   ellen cyðan,
> cræft ond cenðu,   swa him gecynde wæs. (*Beo* 2694–6)

[Then, I have heard, in the great king's hour of need did his upright nobleman make known his courage, his strength and bravery, as was fitting for the kin they had in common.]

If Beowulf is related to Wiglaf through his paternal grandmother, it looks as if their kinship has been made deliberately tenuous. Why the poet might wish to emphasize this kinship and yet leave it remote, I shall attempt to answer in the conclusion to this book.

For now, two things are explained by Beowulf's being a quarter Swedish on his father's side: Onela's withdrawal to Sweden leaving Beowulf as the next king of Geatland; and Beowulf's apparent sorrow at having to kill Onela in revenge for Heardred, his cousin on the mother's side. As regards Weohstan and his long stay abroad with Onela, the poet uses him to let us know Wiglaf's status at home in Geatland. Weohstan's home was there; yet he fights the Geats from the Swedish vanguard when Onela crosses the border after his rebel nephews Eanmund and Eadgils; Heardred is killed in the same action. Beowulf for these reasons might have cause to kill Weohstan and exile Wiglaf. But Beowulf allows Weohstan back to his home in Geatland and later confirms the same land rights in favour of Wiglaf. In the narrative context, one can see an understatement in Beowulf's claim that *me witan ne ðearf waldend fira morðorbealo maga* ('the Ruler of Men will have no need to blame me for the violent murder of kinsmen', lines 2741–2). So Beowulf ends up putting his mother's kin second to his father's, Heardred second to Weohstan. This occurs in spite of his great friendship with Hygelac, Heardred's father: all the more reason to ask why Beowulf rewards Wiglaf rather than punishes him.

Probably Beowulf does so in order to right an old wrong. Why did Weohstan leave the Geats to take service in Sweden while Hygelac was king? We must turn back a generation to the first Swedish war, in step with the Geatish Messenger whose disclosures enable an audience to understand Hygelac as never before. Hygelac's brothers die before him: Herebeald, accidentally at the hands of Hæthcyn, who himself dies in battle against Ongentheow. Hæthcyn had unwisely, *for onmedlan*, the poet says ('through arrogance', line 2926), seized Ongentheow's queen, possibly for ransom. Ongentheow destroys him, lays siege to the Geatish survivors around Ravens' Wood, and promises them death in the morning. Hygelac marches to their rescue towards the end of this fitt. With his entry into history placed here, Hygelac appears to be *se goda* in several ways:

---

[94] Eliason, 'Beowulf, Wiglaf and the Wægmundings', 101–5, at 104: 'the existence of Beowulf's sister is . . . a logical necessity.' 98–9.

the brightness of his sunlit entry into the battle; his promise of relief to the Geats in Ravens' Wood; and as we see in the next fitt, his victory and the generosity which follows. The *goda* epithet, connoting capable leadership, is also used of Hrothgar (line 355) and widely of Beowulf (lines 205, 384, 675, 758, 1190, 1518, 2327).

In Fitt XLI, Hygelac is called *se goda* again (line 2949), as if to help an audience regain the thread, when the new Geatish leader pursues Ongentheow back to his fortress in Sweden. Having heard of Hygelac's skill in warfare, Ongentheow pulls back; like an animal at bay it can be presumed, *beah eft þonan eald under eorðweall* ('he retreated back from there, old, under an earth-wall', lines 2956–7). The scale of the Geatish invasion is shown in the poet's panoramic image of Hygelac's *segn* ('banners', line 2958) moving across Swedish holy ground, *freoðowong þone* ('that ritually hallowed field', line 2959), after Ongentheow:[95]

> 'Þær wearð Ongenðiow   ecgum sweord*a*,
> blondenfexa   on bid wrecen,
> þæt se þeodcyning   ðafian sceolde
> Eafores anne dom.' (*Beo* 2961–4a)

[There Ongentheow, the grey-haired man, was driven into a corner with swordblades, so that the great king was obliged to consent to the one and only judgement of Eofor.]

Herein lies the story behind the epithet *bonan Ongenþeoes* ('slayer of Ongen-theow', line 1968) which the poet bestows on Hygelac shortly before we meet him for the very first time. Over lines 2964–81 Ongentheow is slain at enormous risk by two of Hygelac's men, the brothers Eofor ('boar') and Wulf ('wolf'), both apparently sons of Wonred ('ill counsel'). While Ongentheow tries to finish off the prostrate Wulf, Eofor splits the Swede's *entiscne helm* ('giant-made helmet') with an *ealdsweord eotonisc* ('ancient sword of giants' line 2979) and strikes down his life (*wæs in feorh dropen*, line 2981). Reserving these 'works of giants' epithets for his description of Ongentheow's last stand, the poet wishes to present this combat as unparalleled in its ferocity either then or since. But with the bestial names of Hygelac's two assassins, it is also clear that the fight has been stylized as a hunt, but with the hunter brought down by his prey. This is the readiest meaning to be taken from the analogous Norse scene, in which King Egill of Uppsala, Ongentheow's counterpart, is pierced by the tusk or horn of a wild beast.[96] The Norse variant may show that the poet of Beowulf personified Hygelac's cham-pions from wild animals (*eofor* and *wulf*) in order to turn an accident into a battle.

---

[95] On Lat *pax et quies* (Tacitus' *Germania*, ch. 40), *pax et prosperitas* (Rimbert's *Vita s. Anskarii*, ch. 26), and separately OIce *ár ok friðr* as typical of east Scandinavian paganism, see North, *Heathen Gods*, 44–5, 73, 75–6, 306–7. On MS *hige lace* and *segn* in *Beo* 2958–9, see A. Green, 'An Episode in Ongentheow's Fall (*Beowulf* ll. 2957–2960)', *MLR* 12 (1917), 340–3.
[96] *Heimskringla I*, ed. Bjarni, 52–3 (*Ynglinga saga*, ch. 26).

As we have seen, Weohstan's is a name out of tradition. Yet here the poet of *Beowulf* gives him an elaborate new identity. It seems that he keeps Weohstan in his role as a champion of King Áli of (Swedish) Uppland, possibly also as the pursuer of Eanmund into exile; but the poet adapts this tradition so as to let Eadgils accompany Eanmund into exile, on one hand, and let Weohstan kill Eanmund there on the other. The poet also seems to shape a new past for Weohstan in which he retains his Swedish origins, but has always lived in Geatland. When Hygelac defeats the Swedes and in particular old Ongentheow, the poet shows a mad surfeit of generosity in Hygelac's endowment of Eofor and Wulf in the hypermetric *Beo* 2995–6. The implication is that Weohstan joins up with Onela because Hygelac has taken his lands to give to Eofor and Wulf. Weohstan probably has this motive to be seen fighting the Geats when Hygelac's son is slain in the action against Eanmund and Eadgils. Hence the passage of Eanmund's sword and armour into Wiglaf's hands, where the poet gazes on them in lines 2610–25, not long after we first meet Wiglaf. In these lines Eanmund's sword becomes a symbol of Wiglaf's obligation to a kinsman, a physical token of gratitude for Beowulf's restoration of land.

CONCLUSION

A study of *Beowulf*'s Norse analogues with reference to Bǫðvarr bjarki reveals innovations in this poem whose number grows towards the end. Hrothgar, not Hrothulf, is presented as the Danish king who makes Beowulf his thegn. The interaction of Beowulf with his court allows the poet both to present Beowulf as a prince and to distance him from Hrothulf, which he must do if Beowulf is to get a kingship of his own. From this manipulation of legends, it seems clear that the aim of making Beowulf a king was fundamental. In order to smooth Beowulf's path to kingship, the poet goes another step further than his Scylding sources allow. He integrates Hygelac the Geat into Beowulf's story in order to give Beowulf a royal birth, as Hygelac's sister's son, in a dynasty which appears invented. Beowulf thus grows up to fight for Hygelac, to receive land and honours from him, and to avenge his death on the Frankish champion who kills Hygelac in the Frisian raid. The last is a notorious incident in which no analogue gives Beowulf a place. Yet the poet of *Beowulf* puts Beowulf in this battle in order to present him as Hygelac's most suitable heir.

Hereafter the poet lets his innovations reign. He can have had no authority for Beowulf's accession to Heardred's throne, nor any for Beowulf's death in battle against a fire-dragon in Geatland, nor any for Beowulf's kinship with the Wægmundings whose other survivor Wiglaf tries to save his life. Where the W-names are concerned, only Weohstan, Wiglaf's father, appears to have had a basis in what we can surmise as the poet's sources. His kindred, the *Wægmundingas*, seem to get their name from a certain *Wægmund*, a counterpart of (the Swedish) *Vǫggr* whose presumed English name **Wǣg* has been extended with a suffix. For Wiglaf's name the poet seems to have had no heroic source at all. He models Wiglaf's role on that of Hjalti, Beowulf's friend of tradition, while moving him from Denmark to Geatland with a new part to play as Beowulf's executor. In short, the Old Norse analogues of *Beowulf* tell us that the poet innovated by crowning Beowulf king and giving him a kinsman named Wiglaf. These changes bring the poem particularly close to the memory of King Beornwulf of Mercia, for either it is a coincidence, or *Beowulf* was composed for the Wiglaf who became king of Mercia in 827 (–*c.*839) about a year after Beornwulf died in battle. This conclusion puts the date of *Beowulf* in the period 826 × 839.

3

Vergil and the Monastery in *Beowulf*

There is more than one trace of a monastery in *Beowulf*. Almost certainly we have the use in this poem of (part of) the *Liber historiae Francorum*, a learned work from Francia; and in the last chapter I argued that the passage on Scyld Scefing in the 'Prologue' is a confection of legendary heroic verse, Latin historiography, and superstitious ritual. Such sources as these would fit with a monastic community. There is also the poet's sounding of a bell for the hours. While the Geats wait for Beowulf to surface from Grendel's Mere, the Danes decide to leave. The poet says, as if thinking of Christ's words 'Why hast Thou forsaken me?' (Matt. 27: 46, Mark 15: 34), that the time is *non dæges* ('the nones of the day' (3 p.m.), line 1600). 'Prime' or the *hora prima*, six o'clock in the morning, may also be the basic meaning of his expression *ymb antid* for the 'appropriate hour' at which Beowulf's ship sights Denmark on the second day of sailing from Geatland (line 219). 'Nones' and 'Prime' denote times for liturgical offices. Yet another trace of a monastic background is the conjunction *ac* in Hygelac's speech to the returning Beowulf, in lines 1987–98. This scene appears to be an invention, for there is no surviving analogue which associates Hygelac with Beowulf; and in this speech, in the words *Ac ðu Hroðgare wean ... gebettest* (lines 1990–1), we have a conjunction which resembles a Latin interrogative particle such as *num* ('surely').[1]

Furthermore, the poet's asides betray an ecclesiastical world-view. He remarks that much must be suffered of both good and bad by the man *se þe longe her on ðyssum windagum worolde bruceð* ('who long makes trial of the world here in these days of strife', lines 1061–2). He refers to the child of Hildeburh, when living, as her *mæste ... worolde wynne* ('greatest joy of the world', line 1080). As if knowing that some men claim to avoid aesthetic pleasure, he says that Hrothgar's gold-inlaid tapestries shone with things wondrous to behold *secga gehwylcum þara þe on swylc starað* ('for each man who stares at such a thing', line 996). He adds that death is not easy to flee for the man who must seek the prepared place where his body *swefeþ æfter symle* ('will sleep when the banquet is over', line 1008). Above all, he exclaims that it is a *wundur* ('wonder', line 3062) to see where a courageous warrior may reach his end *þonne leng ne mæg mon mid his [ma]gum meduseld buan* ('when he, a man, can no longer inhabit the mead-building with

---

[1] Fulk, *A History of Old English Meter*, 324–5 (§ 355). Fulk likewise attributes the term *non* to a monastery.

his kinsmen', lines 3064–5). These are instances of 'the authenticating voice'.[2] The divide which they claim between poet and laity is one between the monastery and the world.

These monastic tendencies within *Beowulf* invite us to go back into the poem for more. While the indications of one particular minster over others as a place of origin for *Beowulf* will be considered in a later chapter, here we may look for general evidence of monastic learning. By and large the poet conceals his Latin sources, but the influence of these, when detected, gives an impression of books. This chapter attempts to throw light on the mixture of Latin with Germanic elements in *Beowulf.* It is accepted that the Anglo-Saxon clergy listened to heroic aristocratic themes, at least for the first two-thirds of their history.[3] In the following sections I shall argue that the poet borrowed from Old and New Testaments, patristic commentaries and saints' lives, fabulous literature based on the Classics, Vergil's *Aeneid*, and vernacular homilies. Chiefly I shall suggest that he imitated these variegated works in order to lend the character of Beowulf, his hero, the attributes of young David, Samson, Jesus, St Michael, Hercules, Alexander, and Aeneas.

BIBLICAL AND DEVOTIONAL SOURCES
FOR THE MONSTERS

So far we have deduced from Beowulf's names and Norse analogues that the slaying of monsters was his archetypally Germanic role. Yet it also appears that the poet constructed Grendel, Grendel's Mother, and the dragon with the help of sources which reached him in Latin. It is hard to define what these were, given the poet's lack of erudite display.[4] Yet his reticence does not extend to Genesis, for he says that Grendel is descended from Cain (lines 105–7). The biblical context for this relationship is introduced early: first in the association with Satan, whose defeat lurks behind God's creation of the world in line 94; then by name in the context of Cain's fratricide of Abel in lines 107–8; and later with regard to his descendant Grendel's Mother on line 1261. Genesis is thus an early port of call, but this book could not provide the poet with the authority for connecting Grendel with Cain: that would appear to be uncanonical, derived from early medieval Judaism.[5] According to the First Book of Enoch, a sprawling near-anthology of tales starting with Cain's son Enoch, the fallen angels begot giants on Cain's female descendants. For the poet of *Beowulf* these two categories

[2] Greenfield, 'The Authenticating Voice in *Beowulf*', 57–60.

[3] Wormald, 'Bede, *Beowulf*, and the Conversion of the Anglo-Saxon Aristocracy', 38–58, esp. 51–4.

[4] Rauer, *Beowulf and the Dragon*, 20–3.

[5] R. E. Kaske, '*Beowulf* and the Book of Enoch', *Speculum*, 46 (1971), 421–31. Mellinkoff, 'Cain's Monstrous Progeny: Part I'.

appear to be represented respectively in Grendel's unknown father and his Mother. When Hrothgar says that no one knows the identity of Grendel's father (lines 1355–7), the poet plays upon his ignorance in contrast to what we may assume is the biblical knowledge of his audience. In probably *c*.900, an extract of the Book of Enoch travelled from Brittany to Worcester in BL, Royal 5. E. xiii, fos. 79ᵛ–80ʳ; whether or not this manuscript influenced *Beowulf*, it has been argued that the poet knew of the Jewish Cain legend either from 1 Enoch or out of quotations in other uncanonical works.[6] Grendel's father is unnamed, but appears to be a devil; and Grendel's later association with the devil, in Hrothgar's term *ealdgewinna* (line 1776), which unwittingly renders *antiquus hostis* ('ancient enemy'), may show him to be born from the union specified in 1 Enoch 7: 2–6.[7] In this light, Grendel's Mother, as *merewif mihtig* ('a mighty sea-wife', line 1519), recalls the 'female monster named Leviathan' whom the angels cast down to dwell 'in the abysses of the ocean over the fountain of the waters' in 1 Enoch 60: 7–10; Grendel, the other *mearcstapa* ('boundary roamer', line 1348), resembles Leviathan's former companion Behemoth, consigned to 'the dry land of the wilderness'.[8]

Cain is also to be inferred in the story of Noah's flood inscribed on the hilt which Beowulf brings back from the lair of Grendel's Mother. As Ruth Mellinkoff has shown, 1 Enoch identified the sinners of Noah's time with giants and traced these from Cain.[9] In *Beowulf*, Hrothgar launches into his panegyric on Beowulf's fame after studying the hilt of Grendel's Mother's sword. He finds a story about the Lord's destruction of *giganta cyn* ('the race of giants', line 1690). A Latin source, such as Gen. 6: 4, for this scene is evident from the poet's use of the Latinized Greek word *gigantas*, as earlier in Cain's story on line 113. On the metal of the hilt is also a runic inscription revealing for whom the sword was made. That the name on the hilt is Cain's becomes plausible if we take the poet to have used Cassian's *Conlationes*, a work which was known to Bede and others and was a staple of Anglo-Saxon libraries.[10] Both this work and another by Cassian, the *Institutae*, refer to the the codes and virtues of monastic life.[11] According to the *Conlationes*, Cham, Noah's evil son, preserved his black magic from the flood by writing, before he took ship on the Ark, *scelestas artes ac profana commenta diversorum metallorum lamminis, quae scilicet aquarum conrumpi inundatione non passent, et durissimis lapidibus insculpsit* ('these wicked arts and profane commentaries on sheets of various metals and on the hardest rocks, which

---

[6] Mellinkoff, 'Cain's Monstrous Progeny: Part I', 160–2. Lapidge, *The Anglo-Saxon Library*, 170 (no. 43).

[7] Mellinkoff, 'Cain's Monstrous Progeny: Part I', 148–9.

[8] Ibid. 152.

[9] Ibid. 155–7.

[10] S. Lake, 'Knowledge of the Writings of John Cassian', *ASE* 32 (2003), 27–41. Lapidge, *The Anglo-Saxon Library*, 127.

[11] *De coenobiorum institutis libri duodecim et vigintiquatuor collationes*, PL XLIX (1846).

would not be harmed by the surge of waters').[12] The Irish *Reference Bible*, which twice borrows this story from Cassian, does not cite the metals on which Cham writes his spells, but only the stone.[13] In the manuscripts of this work, as Orchard and others have shown, Cham is frequently confused with Cain, just as by Scribe A of the *Beowulf* manuscript, whose form *cames* on line 107 was corrected by Scribe B to *caines*.[14] Cain is probably the owner of the inscribed hilt of Grendel's Mother's sword. With this artefact the poet of *Beowulf* seems to look back to the beginnings of Cain's feud with man, forwards to Hama's *Brosinga mene* on line 1200, and then beyond: to the association of treasure with ancient evil in Beowulf's viewing of a cup from the dragon's hoard in lines 2403–5; and to the dire effects of his tampering with this hoard in lines 3065–75.

These are the wider-reaching implications in *Beowulf* of the story of Cain. As a visible grafting of Danish history on the stem of Gen. 4 and other works from and associated with the Bible, the poet adds moral layers with his use of biblical and patristic material. The Noah legend, for example, helps to explain why the bits of human flesh, when Grendel eats them, become *synsnædum* ('sinful morsels', line 743): doctrinally as well as legally wrong.[15] 1 Enoch says that the giants descended from Cain became cannibals and began 'to devour one another's flesh, and drink the blood' (7: 2–6).[16] The prohibition against drinking blood in Gen. 9: 4 was well known to Anglo-Saxon commentators, including Bede in his *Libri IV in principium Genesis*.[17] Knowledge of this legend would have given him an authority for a cannibalistic image of Grendel, one which is not supported in Norse mythology whose giants do not eat human flesh. As Orchard has suggested, the poet could then embellish his Enochian image of Grendel with the story of the persecutor Nicanor whose head and right hand are cut off by Judas Maccabaeus to be hung up over Jerusalem (1 Macc. 8: 47). The longer version of Nicanor's tale concludes with the display of the arm on the temple, and his head at the top of the castle in Jerusalem as *manifestum signum auxilii Dei* ('a clear and manifest sign of God's aid', 2 Macc. 15: 35). As Orchard points out, this phrase and the scene behind it recall the nailing of Grendel's hand, arm, and shoulder under Heorot's gable as *tacen sweotol* ('a clear token', line 833) of Beowulf's victory.[18]

---

[12] *Iohannis Cassiani Conlationes*, ed. M. Petschenig, Corpus Scriptorum Ecclesiasticorum Latinorum 13.2 (Vienna, 1886), 239–40 (*Conlatio* VIII. xxi. 7). Text and translation in Orchard, *Companion*, 140.

[13] Orchard, *Pride and Prodigies*, 72–5. J. E. Cross, 'Towards the Identification of Old English Literary Ideas: Old Workings and New Seams', in P. E. Szarmach (ed.), *Sources of Anglo-Saxon Culture*, Studies in Medieval Culture 20 (Kalamazoo, Mich., 1989), 77–101, esp. 92–3 and 99–100.

[14] Orchard, *Pride and Prodigies*, 69–70.

[15] F. C. Robinson, 'Lexicography and Criticism: A Caveat', in *Philological Essays: Studies in Old and Middle English Literature in Honour of Herbert Dean Meritt* (The Hague, 1970), 99–110, esp. 102–3.

[16] Mellinkoff, 'Cain's Monstrous Progeny: Part I', 148–9.

[17] Orchard, *Companion*, 141.

[18] Rob Getz, cited ibid. 146–7.

The dragon in *Beowulf* also represents a fusion of Germanic with Latin sources. There is one poem or more on the dragon-fight of Sigemund, son of Wæls and the kinsman and companion of Fitela; and saints' lives, in which, as Rauer has shown, a saint confounds and defeats a dragon with his prayers.[19] The new episode thus created for the end of *Beowulf*, as we have seen in the previous chapter, appears to overlay the end of Beowulf's career as it would have run on analogy with his last stand in *Bjarkamál*. Sigemund, first, is the subject of an allusion in *Beo* 875–97. In his early outlaw days, with Fitela alongside him, he performs feats which no one but he and his nephew know (lines 876–81); this part of his story, full of incest and lycanthropy, the poet seems to have suppressed on grounds of taste.[20] But his greatest exploit Sigemund carried out alone, killing a dragon, *hordes hyrde . . . under harne stan* ('a hoard-guardian under a grey rock', lines 887). This is an older version of the story of Sigurðr *Fáfnisbani* ('slayer of Fáfnir'), as preserved in the probably eleventh-century *Fáfnismál* and the thirteenth-century *Vǫlsunga saga*, one created at a time before the dragon-slaying was transferred to Sigurðr from his father Sigmundr.[21] In close context, the aim of the Danish poet is to compare one monster-slayer with a great predecessor; later, Beowulf's solitary approach to the Geatish dragon may show that he takes this story to heart. Yet the poet's interest in Sigemund is probably a sign that he borrowed the dragon from this hero's legends also. In both stories within *Beowulf*, Sigemund's and Beowulf's, the hero proceeds alone against a dragon by a stone structure in which there is a treasure hoard. The poet's portrait of Sigemund has been recognized as morally ambiguous.[22] Through a curse, Fáfnir's treasure brings down destruction on all who own it. In *Beowulf* we learn that the Geatish dragon's hoard is cursed as well, *galdre bewunden* ('encircled with a spell', lines 3051–7, at 3052).

Sigemund aside, however, it has been shown that Beowulf's dragon-fight, his treasure hunting apart, is more deeply indebted to saints' lives. To date, all possible hagiographical analogues for this defining part of *Beowulf* have received their fullest discussion from Christine Rauer.[23] Those Latin analogues which offer the most parallels with Beowulf's dragon are the first and second *Vitae* (I, II) of St Samson of Dol, a sixth-century Welsh saint who is said to have fought four dragons in the process of migrating to Brittany from Wales and Cornwall; and item 55 of the *Homiliary of Saint-Père*, a story derived from Revelation in which the dragon is defeated by St Michael the Archangel.[24] The *Vita I. S. Samsonis* has

---

[19] Rauer, *Beowulf and the Dragon*, 41–2 and 116–24.

[20] See North, 'Metre and Meaning in *Wulf and Eadwacer*', 40–6.

[21] First suggested by G. Neckel, 'Sigmunds Drachenkampf', *Edda*, 13 (1920), 122–40 and 204–9. Followed by T. D. Hill, 'The Confession of Beowulf and the Structure of *Vǫlsunga saga*', in R. T. Farrell (ed.), *The Vikings* (London, 1982), 165–75.

[22] M. S. Griffith, 'Some Difficulties in *Beowulf*, lines 874–902: Sigemund Reconsidered', *ASE* 24 (1995), 11–41, esp. 20. Orchard, *Companion*, 108–110.

[23] Rauer, *Beowulf and the Dragon*, 77.

[24] Ibid. 80–124.

been dated variously, but probably dates to a time in the eighth century; the *Vita II S. Samsonsis*, which survives in fewer copies, seems to have been written partly on the basis of the *Vita I*, no earlier than the mid-ninth century.[25] Together these works present parallels with *Beowulf*'s dragon-fight for which the Germanic analogues offer no matching detail.[26]

It is unlikely to be a coincidence that the story of Beowulf's last hours may be read out of this profusion of motifs from St Samson's *Vitae* I and II. The *Vita II S. Samsonis*, in particular, contains what Rauer calls 'an extraordinary constellation of parallels'.[27] If this Life were the only possible source for *Beowulf*'s dragon-fight, its mid-ninth-century date would make the tenth century the likeliest time for the composition of *Beowulf*, for Rauer shows that there is abundant evidence for a royal West Saxon connection with Brittany from Alfredian times, and an English knowledge of St Samson of Dol, throughout the tenth century.[28] Yet many of the same motifs are found in other saints' lives from which the author of the *Vita II S. Samsonis* could have borrowed them.[29] Rauer further notes three motifs which appear to come from the other source, the homily on St Michael's dragon-fight in item 55 of the *Homiliary of Saint-Père*.[30] Of these motifs, the first, the dragon's fire-breath (lines 2522–3, 2556–7, 2582), is more clearly paralleled in the *Saint-Père* homily than in *Vitae Samsonis* or elsewhere; and two more, the cutting up of the dragon and its disposal over the edge of a cliff, seem to occur only in *Beowulf* and the *Saint-Père*.[31] Some version of the latter, then, may be treated a source for the poet of *Beowulf*. Whatever the provenance, saints' lives and homilies were commonly written in monasteries. On this account it seems likely that the poet of *Beowulf* lived in a monastery himself.

This initial survey of *Beowulf*'s monsters shows that the poet had read not only from Genesis, but also from less canonical works of the Old Testament, such as 1 Enoch and Maccabees, together with commentaries including the *Conlationes* of the monastic author John Cassian, plus some hagiographical literature probably including the Lives of either St Samson or St Michael or both. This is not quite the 'thin trickle' of scriptural and patristic sources which has been attributed to the author of *Beowulf*.[32] The following enquiry allows for the inclusion of more.

---

[25] Ibid. 90–3.

[26] Ibid. 62, 65–72, and 75–85: (i) the dragon's arrival as the greatest threat to a surrounding country; (ii) his devastation of the land; (iii) his place in a secluded mountain by the sea from which smoke and fire can be seen to rise; (iv) the hero's guided journey to the dragon's cave; (v) his friends' attempts to dissuade him, (vi) their common procession to the cave; (vii) their terror; (viii) the loyalty of one companion above all the others; (ix) their role as witnesses to the hero's speech and to his fight; (x) their waiting on the mountain; (xi) the hero's old age; (xii) the dragon's sniffing; (xiii) the summoning of the dragon from his cave; and (xiv) the sending of a messenger when the fight is over.

[27] Ibid. 113.   [28] Ibid. 95–104.   [29] Ibid. 94.   [30] Ibid. 118.

[31] Ibid. 120–1.   [32] Andersson, 'Sources and Analogues', 142.

SOME BIBLICAL TYPOLOGY IN *BEOWULF*

The influence of St Augustine's theology has been claimed in several ways, not least in themes of ideal kingship,[33] *caritas* versus *cupiditas*,[34] *sapientia* and *fortitudo*,[35] and the operation of grace for non-Christians.[36] Aside from these claims for the poet's use of Augustine, the most prolix contribution to *Beowulf*'s list of claimed Christian sources is that of Andy Orchard, who starts by laying out twelve parallels between Beowulf's fight with Grendel and David's with Goliath in 1 Samuel.[37] Orchard suggests that 1 Samuel, if the poet used it here, was 'perhaps heard rather than read'.[38] To these parallels he adds one between Samson (of the tribe of Dan, Judges 13–14) and Beowulf: Samson kills a lion with his bare hands, then kills thirty Ashkelites and returns home with their garments as spoils (Judges 14: 9); Beowulf, having killed Dæghrefn the Frankish champion with his bare hands (*Beo* 2501–2), swims back to Geatland with the war-gear of thirty Frankish warriors on his shoulders (lines 2361–8).[39] Furthermore, the story of David gives reason to suppose that 1 Sam. 17 furnished the poet with his type-scenes for Beowulf's arrival, speeches to Hrothgar, Unferth, and Wealhtheow, preparation for meeting Grendel, and later his beheading of Grendel with the magical sword.

David was identified as an antetype of Christ, as may be seen, for example, in Blickling Homily III.[40] St Matthew's Gospel tells us that Christ was descended

---

[33] L. L. Schücking, 'The Ideal of Kingship in *Beowulf*', in Nicholson (ed.), *An Anthology*, 35–49. First printed as 'Das Königsideal im *Beowulf*', *Bulletin of the Modern Humanities Research Association*, 3 (1929), 143–54. C. R. Dahlberg, *The Literature of Unlikeness* (Hanover, NH, 1988).

[34] D. W. Robertson, Jr., 'The Doctrine of Charity in Mediaeval Literary Gardens: A Topical Approach through Symbolism and Allegory', in Nicholson (ed.), *An Anthology*, 165–88. First printed in *Speculum*, 26 (1951), 24–49. B. F. Huppé, *The Hero in the Earthly City: A Reading of Beowulf*, Medieval and Renaissance Texts and Studies 33 (Binghamton, NY, 1984).

[35] Kaske, '*Sapientia et Fortitudo*', 269–310. M. E. Goldsmith, *The Mode and Meaning of Beowulf* (London, 1970).

[36] M. P. Hamilton, 'The Religious Principle in *Beowulf*', in Nicholson (ed.), *An Anthology*, 105–35. First printed in *PMLA* 61 (1946), 309–30.

[37] Orchard, *Companion*, 144–6, esp. 146.

[38] Ibid. 142. King Saul suffers the ravages of Goliath, a giant, in the course of his war against the Philistines (1 Sam. 17: 3 and 23). Once held to be of little worth (1 Sam. 16: 11 and 17: 15), the promising youth David appears (1 Sam. 16: 12 and 20). Saul offers a reward for Goliath's killing (1 Sam. 17: 25). When David's capability is challenged (by his brother, Eliab: 1 Sam. 17: 28 and 33), he recounts his experience in fighting savage beasts (1 Sam. 17: 35–7) and presents himself as heaven-sent (accepted by Saul: 1 Sam. 17: 37). Before the battle David removes his armour and weapons (because he has not tried them: 1 Sam. 17: 39), boasts of victory with God's help (1 Sam. 17: 46), and takes Goliath on alone and without a sword (1 Sam. 17: 39, 42, and 50). With Goliath dead he cuts off the head with the giant's sword (1 Sam. 17: 51) and returns to Saul with both (1 Sam. 17: 54).

[39] S. H. Horowitz, 'Beowulf, Samson, David and Christ', *Studies in Medieval Culture*, 12 (1978), 17–23.

[40] *The Blickling Homilies*, ed. and trans. Kelly, 20–1: *Wel geheowede Dauid þæt, þa he wolde wiþ Goliaþ feohtan* ('David effectively devised his duel with Goliath') . . . *Swa Crist oferswiþde þæt deofol* ('Christ similarly overcame the devil'). See Orchard, *Companion*, 145.

from David by twice fourteen generations (Matt. 1: 17). In this light it may be no surprise to see some moments of typology in *Beowulf* in which Hrothgar is rendered intuitive or prophetic and the hero momentarily Christlike. After Beowulf's victory over Grendel, Hrothgar declares that Beowulf's mother may justly say that *hyre Ealdmetod este wære bearngebyrdo* ('the Ancient Lord of Destiny showed favour to her in the birth of her child', lines 945–6). This language suggests the beatification of Mary as the Mother of God, in the words of a woman from the crowd in Luke 11: 27: *Beatus venter qui te portavit et ubera quae suxisti* ('Blessed the womb which bore you and the breasts which suckled you').[41] When Beowulf, secondly, after dealing with Grendel's Mother, returns victorious with Grendel's head, Hrothgar looks at the hilt of their sword, praises Beowulf's superior birth, then comments on his present and potential fame:

> 'Blæd is aræred
> geond widwegas,   wine min Beowulf,
> ðin ofer þeoda gehwylce.' (*Beo* 1703–5)

['Fame is raised up on roads through distant regions, my friend Beowulf, your fame over each and every nation.']

These words appear to recapture the priest Simeon's premonition of the young Jesus in the Temple in Luke 2: 30–2:

> 'Quod parasti ante faciem omnium populorum:
> Lumen ad revelationem gentium, Et gloriam plebis tuae Israel.'

['For you have appeared before the face of all the peoples: as a light of revelation to the nations, and as the glory of your people Israel.']

Beowulf's use of this passage, if it occurred, would style Hrothgar as a prophet and Beowulf as the growing Christ. A third loan from the Gospels may be found in the Danes' departure from Grendel's Mere at *non dæges* (line 1600), when they sight their idea of Beowulf's blood on the surface. The context might recall the *hora nona* ('ninth hour') of the Crucifixion when Jesus asks God why is he forsaken shortly before dying and resurrecting (Matt. 27: 46 and Mark 15: 34). More of a type-scene, perhaps, is the poet's fourth apparent borrowing, a picture of Beowulf's last feelings before his battle with the dragon:

> Gesæt ða on næsse   niðheard cyning
> þenden hælo abead   heorðgeneatum
> goldwine Geata.   Him wæs geomor sefa
> wæfre ond wælfus,   wyrd ungemete neah. (*Beo* 2417–20)

[Then, the battle-hardened king sat down on a headland, gold-friend of the Geats, while offering his hearth companion good omen. His feelings were sad, restless, and eager for death, fate immeasurably near.]

---

41 Supported in *Beowulf*, ed. Klaeber, 166–7; opposed by Orchard, *Companion*, 147.

At this moment his portrait would appear to be based on that of Jesus in Gethsemane, who tells his disciples *Sedete hic donec vadam illuc, et orem* ('sit while I go over there to pray', Matt. 26: 36) and taking Peter with him, and two sons of Zebedee, says *Tristis est anima mea usque ad mortem: sustinete hic, et vigilate mecum* ('Sad is my heart in expectation of my death: stop here and stay awake with me', Matt. 26: 38).[42] Two other Gospels share details of this scene (Mark 14: 32–42 and Luke 22: 39–46). A fifth apparent borrowing is the general typology of Christ's arrest in Gethsemane. Like Jesus before the final battle, Beowulf has twelve followers, of whom one is an informer, ten defect, and one (Wiglaf) remains to show courage.[43] Although this motif is already claimed as part of hagiographical dragon-fights, it has to be said that the authors of these themselves looked for typology in the Gospels.[44] In John 18: 10, but not in the other Gospels, the model for Wiglaf's characterization at this moment is named as Simon Peter, physically the bravest of all Christ's disciples and founder of his Church.

Together with the poet's historical foundation in Genesis and 1 Enoch and with his reading of hagiography, these instances of biblical typology might be used to show that the poet of *Beowulf* borrowed motifs from 1 Samuel, Judges, and the Gospels in order to style Hrothgar, Beowulf, and Wiglaf in the noblest possible light. They are heathens, after all; their hereafter is hell. It is perhaps a desire to plead against the potential damnation of all three heroes that led the poet to risk styling, if he did, Hrothgar as Simeon, Beowulf as both David and Jesus, and Wiglaf as Simon Peter, Jesus' apostolic successor.

THE *EPISTOLA ALEXANDRI* AND *LIBER MONSTRORUM*

There are some passages in *Beowulf* which show borrowing from fabulous as well as devotional sources. Ultimately, in Chapter 6, I shall use these to help place *Beowulf* in a particular minster. The question of the relation of the *Epistola Alexandri* to *Beowulf* has already been defined in one way by Orchard's persuasive use of parallels to suggest that the Anglo-Saxon author of the Old English *Alexander's Letter to Aristotle*, a text found immediately before *Beowulf* in the same manuscript, used *Beowulf* to build a translation for the relevant passages from the *Epistola*.[45] It seems that the compiler of the Nowell Codex intended his readers to consider the vernacular *Alexander's Letter* and *Beowulf* together,

---

[42] Supported in Rauer, *Beowulf and the Dragon*, 78, and Orchard, *Companion*, 148.

[43] Argued in *Beowulf*, ed. Klaeber, 217; opposed by Orchard, *Companion*, 148–9; and W. Whallon, *Formula, Character, and Context: Studies in Homeric, Old English, and Old Testament Poetry* (Washington, DC, 1969), 136–7.

[44] In the *Vita S. Magni*, by Otloh of Emmeram, and the *Miracula S. Maglorii*: see Rauer, *Beowulf and the Dragon*, 68.

[45] Orchard, *Companion*, 25–39, esp. 33–6.

perhaps because these works were traditionally associated.[46] But there is also a likelihood that, earlier still, the poet of *Beowulf* borrowed from the Latin *Epistola*. This is to be seen in three motifs. The first of these concerns sea-monsters: both as *niceras* ('water-monsters', line 422) which Beowulf cites to Hrothgar as part of his monster-killing record at the outset of his stay in Heorot; and as the *merefixa mod* ('anger of sea-fishes', line 549) which he describes in his flyting with Unferth, in the story of his swimming match with Breca:

'Me to grunde teah
fah feondscaða,   fæste hæfde
grim on grape;   hwæþre me gyfeþe wearð
þæt ic aglæcan   orde geræhte
hildebille;   heaþoræs fornam
mihtig meredeor   þurh mine hand.' (*Beo* 553–8)

['An evil attacking fiend dragged me to the bottom, the savage one held me fast in his grip; and yet it was ordained for me that I should strike the monster with the point of my battle-blade; a war-charge seized the powerful sea-beast through my hand.']

Beowulf goes on to say (in a new fitt, no. IX, lines 559–69) that these *manfor-dædlan* ('criminals and destroyers', line 563) could not enjoy *ðære fylle* ('that feast', line 562), for he served death to them in their would-be banquet down on the sea-floor, so clearing the sea-lanes of monsters for all time. There are no waterborne feats with monsters in the analogous Norse tales of Bǫðvarr bjarki, albeit their references to monsters are limited. Instead, the most apt surviving analogue for this passage in *Beowulf* is from the *Epistola*'s account of Alexander's expedition to India. In this story, presented as episodes in an epistolary journal dedicated to Aristotle, his former tutor, Alexander first mentions water-monsters when he finds a river. Having marched his men along the banks for some days, Alexander loses some of them to hippopotami when he sends a few swimmers across:

Maiores elefantorum corporibus hipopotami inter profundos aquarum emersi apparuer-unt gurgites raptosque in uorticem crudeli poena uiros flentibus nobis adsumpserunt. Iratus tum ego ducibus qui nos in insidias deducebant, iubeo ex his .CL. in flumen mitti. Quibus propulsis natantibusque inuicti hipotami rursum dignos iusta poena affecere; sed maiorum decuplato numero beluarum quam prius affuit. Ad spem inde contingentis cibi ubi cum apparerent, ueluti formicae per flumen efferuere. Et *ne qua noctu* cum aquarum prodigiis bel*l*a gereremus, iussi dato signo bucino ad iter militem aptari. Quid enim manere in talui sitientibus proderat loco?[47]

[Hippopotami greater than elephants in bodily size appeared emerging from among the deep watery abysses and in cruel punishment took with them into the whirlpool the men whom they had caught, while we wept. Angry then with the guides who had led us into

<hr/>

[46] Ibid. 38–9.
[47] Orchard, *Pride and Prodigies*, 209 (§ 15) : for *nequati octu*, read Group II *ne qua noctu*. On *in uerticem* ('into their mouths') as a variant reading for *in uorticem*, see Orchard, *Companion*, 31–2.

the trap, I gave orders for 150 of them to be dispatched into the river. On these men who, driven forward, were swimming the unvanquished hippopotami enacted a just punishment to account for the worthy men; but in a tenfold number of even bigger beasts than had been there before. Thereupon in hope of finding food wherever they appeared, like ants they burst forth all over the river. And lest we wage war with these marvels of the waters in any manner by night, I ordered the army to be made ready for the march with a trumpet on the given signal. What use was it for thirsty men to stay in such a place?]

This scene from the *Epistola* could also be presented as a source for the *wundra . . . fela* ('host of marvels', *Beo* 1509) who strike Beowulf's mail-coat with their tusks as he swims down to Grendel's Mother's lair (lines 1501–12).[48] If the differences between *Beowulf* and this section of the *Epistola* are considerable (in the numbers of dead and in that Beowulf makes the monster, not himself, the victim in a sea rather than on a river), the parallels are more numerous: the dragging of men down into the depths; the description of human victims as a monster's meal; legal notions of the horror as either a 'crime' (*man-*) or 'a cruel punishment' (*crudeli poena*); and the question of making war on these creatures (*bella gereremus*; *heaþoræs*); by night (*noctu*; *nipende niht* ('darkening night'), *Beo* 547).[49]

A second parallel in motifs between *Beowulf* and the *Epistola* occurs in the imagery of Grendel's Mere. Orchard notes a general similarity between this, with trees and overhanging cliffs, and the undrinkable river found earlier by Alexander, *cuius ripas pedum sexagenum arundo uestiebat, pinorum abietumque robora uincens grossitudine* ('the banks of which were covered by reeds sixty feet high, surpassing in their girth the trunks of pines or silver-firs').[50] As well as including the pines and firs in his version of the scene, the author of the Old English *Letter of Alexander* appears to have embellished the Latin with the description of the Mere in *Beowulf*, to which, as we shall see, the language of the end of Blickling Homily XVI is also related.[51] On closer inspection, the Mere is found to have serpents who normally, the poet says, threaten ships at sea, but which now scatter upon the Danish-Geatish arrival:

> Hie on weg hruron
> bitere ond gebolgne;   bearhtm ongeaton,
> guðhorn galan.   Sumne Geata leod
> of flanbogan   feores getwæfde
> yðgewinnes   þæt him on aldre stod
> herestræl hearda;   he on holme wæs
> sundes þe sænra   ðe hyne swylt fornam.
> Hræþe wearð on yðum   mid eoferspreotum
> heorohocyhtum   hearde genearwod,
> niða genæged   ond on næs togen,
> wundorlic wægbora;   weras sceawedon
> gryrelicne gist. (*Beo* 1430–41)

[48] Orchard, *Companion*, 33.   [49] *Epistola Alexandri*, ed. Boer, 14 (lines 1–2).
[50] Orchard, *Companion*, 30 (*Epistola*, § 12).   [51] Ibid. 30.

[They rushed away biting and swollen up with rage; they heard the blast, the singing of the battle-horn. One of them striving against the wave a Geatish warrior with bow and arrow deprived of his life, in that the hard war-shaft stood fast in its vitals; he was the slower in swimming for being seized by dying. Swiftly on the waves he was harshly captured with savagely hooked boar-spears, violently attacked and dragged on to the headland, a wondrous wave-roamer; the men beheld a terrible stranger.]

Later in the *Epistola*, a confrontation takes place with a more tragic outcome for Alexander's men:

Palus erat sicca et canna habundans. Per quam cum transitum tempteremus, belua noui generis prosiluit serrato tergo, duo capita habens, alterum lunae simile, hippopotamo pectore, corcodrilli gerens alterum simillimum duris munitum dentibus, quod caput duos milites repentino occidit ictu. Quam ferreis uix umquam comminuimus malleis, quam hastis non ualebamus transfigere. Ammirati diu nouitatem eius.[52]

[There was a marsh, dried up and abundant in reeds, through which, when we tried to make a crossing, a new kind of monster issued forth with a notched back and two heads, one of them like the moon, with the belly of a hippopotamus, and having another head fortified with hard teeth most like those of a crocodile. This head slew two soldiers in a sudden snap. This [monster], which we scarcely even threatened with iron hammers, we were not able to pierce with spears. We gazed at the novelty of it for a long time.]

If a borrowing from here into *Beowulf* was made, it appears to have been an adaptation in which the Alexandrine party, the Geats, kill their water-monster with ease. The *Epistola Alexandri* was popular: there are some sixty-seven manuscripts, divided into four groups (of which the second is probably closest to the text used by the author of *Liber monstrorum*).[53] Variant readings abound: for example, one of the beast's heads is *leaneae simile* ('like that of a lioness') in the first group, but *lunae simile* in the second and third ('like the moon').[54] *Beowulf* differs considerably from this passage in having a monster probably with one head, not with two; a monster who slays no one, but is himself pierced by one of the Geatish soldiers' missiles and then drawn in with barbed hunting spears; the Geats do not bring hammers. However, the text in the third group of *Epistola*-manuscripts omits the phrase *duo capita habens*: in their version the beast has one head. The relevant part of the oldest member of this group, Leiden Vos. Lat. Q.20, which contains other material on Alexander in Books III–X of Curtius' Histories, is dated to *c*.830 in Tours, formerly ruled by Alcuin; so it is possible that the 'one-headed crocodile' exemplar of the *Epistola* reached Francia from the British isles, where the poet of *Beowulf* may have read the same version of the *Epistola*.[55] The parallels would then be clearer: with a one-headed beast swimming in a similar water-hole, attacked by spears (*hastis*; *eoferspreotum*), and the

---

[52] Orchard, *Pride and Prodigies*, 127 and 214 (§ 27: Group II *hastis* for *hostis*).

[53] *Epistola Alexandri*, ed. Boer, pp. vi–xxi (description of MSS), xxxii (four-group stemma).

[54] Ibid. 29. Orchard, *Pride and Prodigies*, 127.

[55] *Epistola Alexandri*, ed. Boer, pp. iv, xii, xxvii and 29 n. (line 3). *Texts and Transmission*, ed. Reynolds, 148.

object of men's wondering gaze (*ammirati eius nouitatem*; *wundorlic, weras sceawedon*). The battle-horn (*guðhorn*) is paralleled in the trumpet (*bucino*) which Alexander orders to be blown at the end of his army's earlier encounter with hippopotami.[56]

A third parallel has been noted between *Beowulf* and the *Epistola*: between Beowulf giving orders for his tomb in lines 2802–8:

> 'Hatað heaðomære   hlæw gewyrcean
> beorhtne æfter bæle   æt brimes nosan;
> se scel to gemyndum   minum leodum
> heah hlifian   on Hronesnæsse
> þæt hit sæliðend   syððan hatan
> Biowulfes biorh,   ða ðe brentingas
> ofer floda genipu   feorran drifað' (*Beo* 2802–8)

['Command those famed in war to build a mound, a bright one after the pyre, at the promontory of the flood, which shall as a memorial to my people tower up high on Whale's Ness, so that seafarers may henceforth call it "Beowulf's barrow", as their tall prows drive from far and wide across the sea's mists.'];

and Alexander's recounting of similar commands to Aristotle, his former tutor:

Atque in ultima India ultra Liberi et Herculis trophea, quae centum erant, ego quinque mea aurea altiora denis pedibus statui imperaui, quae miraculo futura sunt, carissime praeceptor, posteris saeculis non paruo. Nouum perpetuumque statuimus uirtutibus monimentum inuidendum, ut immortalitas esset perpetua et nobis opinio et animi industriae, optime Aristotles, indicium.

[And in the farthest reaches of India, beyond the monuments of Bacchus and Hercules, which were a hundred feet, I ordered my five golden trophies to be set up, ten feet taller, to be no small wonder, dearest teacher, to coming generations. We have set up to be gazed upon a new and permanent monument to courage, so that there might be for us immortality and esteem forever, and a sign, finest Aristotle, of the exertion of the spirit.][57]

The author of *Liber monstrorum* often uses the *Epistola Alexandri* as a source; in that the *Epistola*'s Alexander refers to Hercules as his model, it is possible that the poet of *Beowulf* informed his own lines with a combination of both sources, the *Liber*'s Hercules and the *Epistola*'s Alexander.[58] He appears to represent both the image of Hercules' seaside monument in the *Liber* and Alexander's command for a memorial in the *Epistola*. As ever, however, the *Beowulf*-poet makes a change. Just as the author of the Old English *Letter of Alexander*, as Orchard shows, turns Alexander's pride into egocentricity, the hero of *Beowulf* looks morally superior to Alexander.[59] If the poet did model Beowulf on the *Epistola*'s Alexander, the pride is made less obvious. Beowulf, more concerned that the

---

[56] Orchard, *Pride and Prodigies*, 209 (§ 15).
[57] Orchard, *Companion*, 37 (*Epistola*, § 41: with omission of 'to be envied' for *inuidendum*).
[58] Ibid. 37–8.
[59] Orchard, *Pride and Prodigies*, 134–6.

treasure should go to his people, wants them to build his mound as a landmark for fog-bound sailors. The fact that the Geatish followers, as Fred Robinson has observed, later go beyond requirements in building the mound, is not an arrogance to be laid at Beowulf's door.[60] In this way, and also in the ways in which Beowulf and the Geats get the better of water-monsters such as those that always slaughter Alexander's men, the English poet appears willing to exceed Alexander's glories in the *Epistola Alexandri*.

In the *Liber monstrorum*, Orchard has drawn attention to three parallels other than the Hygelac-entry at the start. In the first, when Grendel's Mother has killed Hrothgar's counsellor, Beowulf declares that she will not escape him anywhere, *ne on foldan fæpm ne on fyrgenholt ne on gyfenes grund, ga þær he[o] wille* ('either in earth's embrace, or in mountain woods, or on the ground-bed of ocean, go where she will!', lines 1393–4). The opening sentence of the preface to *Liber monstrorum* describes monsters as living only *in abditis mundi partibus per deserta et Oceani insulas et in ultimorum montium latebris* ('in the hidden parts of the world, throughout the deserts and islands of the Ocean, and in the recesses of the farthest mountains').[61] A second parallel concerns the giant-made sword with which Beowulf slays Grendel's Mother. Despite its size and antiquity, the blade of this sword melts in her blood:

> sweord ær gemealt,
> forbarn brodenmæl;   wæs se blod to þæs hat
> ættren ellorgæst,   se þær inne swealt. (*Beo* 1615–17)

[by now the sword had melted, the patterned blade was burned up; that blood, the posionous alien spirit who died in there, was too hot for it.]

Beowulf's own words echo this description when he reports on the fight to Hygelac later in the poem (lines 1666–8). The only passage which bears a resemblance is found in *Liber monstrorum*:

Bestia autem illa inter omnes beluas dirissima fertur, in qua tantam ueneni copiam adfirmant ut eam sibi leones quamuis inualidioris feram corporis, timeeant, et tantam uim eius uenenum habere arbitrantur, ut eo licet ferri acies intincta liquescat. (II. 23)

[But that beast [a two-headed monster from India] is said to be amongst the fiercest of all brutes, in which they assert that there is such a quantity of venom that lions fear it although it is an animal of weaker body, and they reckon that its poison has such strength, that the cutting edge even of iron, dipped in it, melts.][62]

Orchard's third parallel consists of Beowulf's funeral rites, which the hero dictates to Wiglaf in lines 2802–8: a bright burial mound over the pyre on a headland by the sea, which shall act *to gemyndum* ('as a memorial', line 2804) to

---

[60] F. C. Robinson, *The Tomb of Beowulf and Other Essays on Old English* (Oxford, 1993), 3–19, esp. 17.
[61] Orchard, *Pride and Prodigies*, 110–11 and 254–5.
[62] Ibid. 111–12 and 300–1.

the seafarers who call it *Biowulfes biorh* ('Beowulf's barrow', line 2807). In lines 3156–62 these wishes are enacted, in the crowning image of the poem, in the *beadurofes becn* ('beacon of the battle-brave', line 3160). With 'the construction of sea-side monuments to the courage of a celebrated monster-slayer', as Orchard points out, there is a parallel in a passage in the *Liber monstrorum* (I. 12) on Hercules, who is said to have erected pillars as a spectacle for the human race, and constructed trophies as a memorial for posterity.[63] Alexander, too, in the *Epistola Alexandri*, after hearing a prophecy of his own death, gives orders for a memorial structure to exceed those of Hercules.[64] It might be said that there is little else in *Beowulf* to show that the poet borrowed from *Liber monstrorum*.[65] On the other hand, the progression from a humanoid monster (Grendel), to a beast (his Mother), to a serpent (the dragon), has been cited as shadowing the tripartite structure of *Liber monstrorum*.[66] Moreover, this poet's interest in pagans and monsters is clear in at least four major debts to Vergil, the *Liber*'s most significant source.

VERGIL RECAST: BOOKS I, III, AND VI OF THE *AENEID*

A suggested adaptation in *Beowulf* of three episodes from the *Aeneid* will be discussed here. My discussion of a fourth, from Books VII and XI, will be held back for the following chapter.

Heorot and Carthage (*Aen.* I)

The Vergilian dimension to Heorot becomes clearer the more we study the presentation of Hrothgar's tale in Germanic analogues. Hrothgar reaches his zenith in building Heorot, not only in *Beowulf*, but also in the *Chronicon Lethrense*. This book is anonymous, datable to *c.*1170, and local to Roskilde in Zealand. In it the first king of Denmark is given as Dan, son of King Ypper of Uppsala; Dan is the father of Ro (OIce *Hróarr*, OE *Hroþgar*), father of the brothers Helgi and Haldan.[67] Ypper gives Dan the rule of four islands: Sjælland (Zealand), Møn, Falster, and Låland. Dan builds 'Lethra' (Lejre) on Zealand, rules for three years, and with Dannia, his queen, has a son named Ro. When Dan dies, Ro buries him in a mound at Lethra and sets about moving the people

---

[63] Orchard, *Pride and Prodigies*, 264–7.

[64] Ibid. 37; Orchard, *Pride and Prodigies*, 222–3 (§ 41).

[65] For a claim that he did, see L. Whitbread, 'The *Liber Monstrorum* and *Beowulf*', *Mediaeval Studies*, 36 (1974), 434–71. Orchard further compares this sword-melting with the sword of Turnus, which shatters like ice against Aeneas' armour, in *Aen.* XII. 740–1: *Companion*, 135–6.

[66] N. Chadwick, 'The Monsters and Beowulf', in P. Clemoes (ed.), *The Anglo-Saxons: Studies in Some Aspects of their History and Culture Presented to Bruce Dickins* (London, 1959), 171–203, esp. 172–93.

[67] *Scriptores minores historiae Danicae*, ed. Gertz, i. 43–7 (*Chronicon Lethrense*, chs. 1–3).

of Høkæbiærgh, an older town in the middle of Zealand, to a new place on the shores of Isefjord:

et circa fontem pulcherrimum domos disponere. Edificauit ibi Ro ciuitatem honestam, cui nomen imposuit partitiuum post se et fontem, partem capiens fontis partemque sui, Roskildis Danice uocans; que hoc nomine uocabitur in eternum. Vixit autem Ro rex ita pacifice, ut nullus ei aciem opponeret; nec ipse usquam expedicionem direxit.[68]

[and he ordered houses to be set up there around a most beautiful well-spring. There Ro built a fine town, on which he bestowed a name assigned in memory of himself and the well-spring, part for the well-spring and part for his own name, calling it 'Roskilde' in Danish; a name by which it will be known for all time. And now King Ro lived in such peace that no one put up a blade against him; neither did he command any expedition abroad.]

His wife gives birth to two sons, Helgi and Haldan. When Ro dies, he is laid in a mound in Lethra and Helgi takes the rule of Danish lands, Haldan that of Danish waters. Saxo lived at the court of Bishop Absalon of Roskilde (1158–92), but all he says of Roskilde is that *a Roe Roskildia condita memoratur* ('it is commemorated in its foundation by Roe').[69] Sven Aggesen makes no mention of Ro at all. In neither case was the history of Roskilde important to men more closely associated with Lund. As Saxo acknowledges, however, *Roskilde* means 'Ro's spring' (OIce *Hróars kelda*). There are two possibilities: either this name was created in Zealand in the early twelfth century to rationalize a like-sounding place name whose meaning had become obscure; or the town was so named because there was a legend in which a king named Ro did live there. Whichever is the case, it seems that the author of the *Chronicon Lethrense* knew a local Zealand tale which was not shaped by such foreign sources as those works from England and Iceland upon which Sven and Saxo more ambitiously drew.

'Dan', the name of Ro's father, was probably coined for the first time in *c*.1070 by William of Jumièges in his *Gesta Normannorum ducum* (chs. 6–8); Sæmundr, from whom Danish historians took the name in the early twelfth century, may have borrowed this learned eponym in the 1070s while he studied in France, presumably in Paris.[70] The author of *Chronicon Lethrense* seems to have borrowed Dan's name from William or Sæmundr, but his work is essentially a local history. To the unnamed Lejre cleric who wrote this brief work, Ro's fame as the founder of his regional capital was such that he is there presented as the son of Dan in Haldan's traditional place, with Haldan now filling Ro's role as Helgi's brother.[71] Despite this variance, this part of the *Chronicon Lethrense* is a true analogue of *Beowulf*, for it represents a Zealand tradition without clear sign of

---

[68] Ibid. 46–7 (*Chronicon Lethrense*, ch. 3).

[69] *Gesta Danorum*, ed. Olrik and Ræder, 47 (ii. v. 2).

[70] *Works of Sven Aggesen*, trans. and comm. Christiansen, 112–13 n. 47.

[71] The association between King Ro and Roskilde is doubted in Chambers, *Beowulf*, 14–16. The view of Garmonsway, Simpson, and Ellis Davidson, in *Beowulf and its Analogues*, 125 (IID 3), is that 'This text incorrectly makes Haldanus the son of Ro (Hroðgar).'

influence from England. In the twelfth century it seems that the Zealanders used Ro's memory to glorify an expanding market town on Isefjord. Ro's story, preserved in this way, allows us to fathom four features as original to the source for the Hrothgar legend on which the English poet relied: Hrothgar builds a great settlement; he lives there for for a long while in peace; this is near a spring; he dies of old age.

It is interesting to note that the poet of *Beowulf* has barely told us the names of Healfdene's children on lines 61–2, before he prepares us for Heorot by announcing Hrothgar's *heresped* ('success in expeditions', line 64), the growth of his retinue, and his new idea:

> Him on mod bearn
> þæt healreced   hatan wolde
> medoærn micel   men gewyrcean
> (þone yldo bearn   æfre gefrunon!) (*Beo* 67–70)

[It ran into his mind that he wanted to order men to construct a hall-building, a great mead-house—the sons of men have always heard of him!][72]

In these lines we have a Germanic type-scene with a king who becomes famous (*þone æfre gefrunon*) for showing presence of mind (*mod*) in, with, or for a mead-house (*medoærn*). This is also known in *Atlakviða*, probably of the late tenth century, just before Gunnarr tells the people of his plan to visit King Atli of the Huns:

> qvaddi þá Gunnarr,   sem konungr skyldi,
> mærr, í miðranni,   af móði stórum: (*Akv* 9/5–8)

[then Gunnar declared, as a king should, famous in the mead-house, with great heart.][73]

Yet the hall-building scene and its aftermath in *Beowulf* do not match the context of *Atlakviða*. Rather they look like the poet's recasting of an episode from Vergil's *Aeneid*. Hrothgar also plans an infrastructure:

> ond þær on innan   eall gedælan
> geongum ond ealdum   swylc him God sealde
> buton folcscare   ond feorum gumena. (*Beo* 71–3)

[and there inside that place he would share out whatever God had granted him to young men and old, all but the inalienable lands of his people and the lives of men.]

Put together, lines 67–73 of *Beowulf* recall Dido's founding of Carthage, buildings together with laws:

---

[72] As in A. Bammesberger, 'Five *Beowulf* Notes', in Korhammer, Reichl, and Sauer (eds.), *Words, Texts and Manuscripts*, 239–55, at 254–5. For a different reading ('of which the sons of men should hear for all time'), see *Beowulf*, ed. Mitchell and Robinson, 50, n. line 70.

[73] See also North, *Pagan Words*, 67–8.

instant ardentes Tyrii: pars ducere muros
molirique arcem et manibus subuoluere saxa,
pars optare locum tecto et concludere sulco;
iura magistratusque legunt sanctumque senatum. (*Aen.* I. 423–6)

[Ardent they strove, the men of Tyre: some, to lay down walls and build an arch and roll up the stones with their hands, others to choose a place for a house and mark it with a furrow; laws they establish, and magistrates, and the sacred senate.]

Hrothgar's plans concern the founding of a state in which he, too, respects a public interest, even while reserving his kindred's land to himself and his heirs. Wealhtheow later reminds him to do the same when it becomes likely that he will reward Beowulf, a foreigner, with the entire Danish kingdom (lines 1178–80). Moreover, the influence of this scene from the *Aeneid* appears to go further, in *Beowulf*'s *chiaroscuro* prediction of Heorot's end as implicit within its glorious beginning:

Sele hlifade
heah ond horngeap,   heaðowylma bad
laðan liges;   ne wæs hit lenge þa gen
þæt se ecghete   aþumsweorum
æfter wælniðe   wæcnan scolde. (*Beo* 81–5)

[The hall towered, high and horn-gabled, awaited the hostile flame of battle-surges; nor was it then yet at hand that sword-hate should awake after murderous enmity between father- and son-in-law.]

This anticipates the attack by Ingeld on Hrothgar, his father-in-law, through which Heorot burns down. Hereby the poet establishes the theme of Freawaru's marriage, which remains important in the poem until Beowulf's report to his uncle back home in Geatland. Yet if the *Beowulf*-poet's foreknowledge of Heorot also highlights the Danes' ignorance of the fate that awaits them, the same might be said of Vergil's intimation of the Carthaginian doom through the unwitting irony of Aeneas, its first cause:

'o fortunati, quorum iam moenia surgunt!'
Aeneas ait et fastigia suspicit urbis. (*Aen.* I. 437–8)

['How fortunate they are, whose city walls are rising now!' said Aeneas surveying the gables of the town.]

The *Beowulf*-poet's own foreboding, about Ingeld, immediately extends to the Danish songs inside the new hall which innocently arouse the attention of a closer enemy outside (lines 86–9). The term for Grendel, as *se ellengæst* suffering in the dark outside ('the alien spirit', line 86), has already identified him with God's hell-bound adversary Satan. With the element *sige* on line 94 the poet thus emphasizes God's 'victory' over Satan before the creation of man. In the above lines we see the Danes hailing this creation. As they are heathens, however, it has to be said they know nothing of the war in heaven which caused it, nor anything of the devil's influence lingering on through Grendel.

The pathos of this ignorance suggests a third Vergilian comparison, one which I have noted in Chapter 1, between this scene in *Beowulf* and a song about the universe in Queen Dido's hall in *Aen.* I. 740–6. When the Trojans listen to Dido's minstrel Iopas, he tells them of the creation of moon, sun, mankind and beasts, rain-clouds and flames, constellations and seasonal movement of the planets. This passage has justly been compared to the song in *Beowulf*, lines 89–98, in which another poet sings of sun, moon, and creation within a festive hall.[74] The pathos in both cases is in man's lack of foreknowledge: that of Dido and Aeneas in *Aen.* I, on one hand; that of the Danes in *Beo* 89–98, on the other. Had the Danes been Christian, moreover, they would have known enough to guard against Grendel, the spiritual (and perhaps incarnate) heir of Satan. In short, the poet of *Beowulf* seems to build up Heorot on the model of Carthage.

Grendel and the Cyclops (*Aen.* III)

If Grendel's ferocity is the terror against which Beowulf's courage is measured, it is worth noting that none of the Norse analogues, with monsters aplenty, contain instances of cannibalism; not even in the story of Glámr, Grettir's undead opponent in Þórhallstaðir (*Grettis saga*, chs. 32–5), whom it is probably safest to classify as the reflex of Grendel in part of an Icelandic tradition inherited from *Beowulf*.[75] With Grendel the poet of *Beowulf* is unique in his descriptive skill and emotive power. He develops the image of this predator slowly, as Cain's monstrous descendant (lines 102–14), Heorot's sudden attacker (lines 120–5), Hrothgar's reported nemesis (lines 149–52 and 274–7), Heorot's new night-time ruler (lines 166–9), invincible enemy (lines 480–7) and humbler of all the Danes (lines 595–601). During this time the detail of Grendel's appearance and atrocities is a mystery which the poet keeps hidden, reserving it for his encounter with Beowulf in Fitts XI–XII (lines 710–824). At first his descent from Cain is reiterated in that, as he approaches Heorot not for the first time, Grendel (in one sense) *Godes yrre bær* ('bore the wrath of God', line 711); and as he comes up to Heorot itself, he is *dreamum bedæled* ('deprived of joys', line 721). He bursts open the doors and steps into the mouth of the building:

> Raþe æfter þon
> on fagne flor   feond treddode,
> eode yrremod;   him of eagum stod
> ligge gelicost   leoht unfæger. (*Beo* 724–7)

[74] F. Klaeber, 'Aeneis und Beowulf', *Archiv*, 126 (1911), 40–8 and 339–59, esp. 343.

[75] For the 'English hypothesis', see A. Liberman, 'Beowulf-Grettir', in B. Brogyanyi and T. Krömmelbein (eds.), *Germanic Dialects: Linguistic and Philological Investigations* (Amsterdam, 1986), 353–401, esp. 355.

[Swiftly after that the fiend stepped on the stained floor, walked with heart full of rage; from his eyes there stood an unbeautiful light, most like a flame.]

His spirits lift with *wistfylle wen* ('the expectation of a lavish feast', line 734) when he sees a new band of warriors, all apparently asleep. Calmly Beowulf looks on in order to see how Grendel will proceed. The monster does not keep him waiting:

> ac he gefeng hraðe   forman siðe
> slæpendne rinc,   slat unwearnum,
> bat banlocan,   blod edrum dranc,
> synsnædum swealh,   sona hæfde
> unlyfigendes   eal gefeormod,
> fet ond folma. (*Beo* 740–5)

[but he swiftly seized as his first enterprise a warrior who was asleep, ripped him open countless times, bit the bone-locks, drank blood from the arteries, swallowed sinful morsels, straightaway had used up the provender of all the dead man, down to his feet and hands.]

The victim's name is later given as 'Hondscio' (line 2076). The poet's earlier conceit, of Grendel as Heorot's ruler, is expressed here through the words *wistfyll* and *gefeormod*, which portray Grendel's habits as the banqueting rights of a king on *feorm* ('itineration').[76] The final touch, an eating of feet and hands, has been connected to 2 Kings 9: 35, in which the dogs who devour Jezebel's dead body refrain from these extremities.[77] Beowulf waits for Grendel to come within range, grips him and holds on, while Grendel tries to escape, seeking *deofla gedræg* ('company of devils', line 756). While the hall withstands the shock of their contest, the Danes cower outside:

> Norð-Denum stod
> atelic egesa   anra gehwylcum
> þara þe of wealle   wop gehyrdon,
> gryreleoð galan   godes andsacan
> sigeleasne sang,   sar wanigean
> helle hæfton. (*Beo* 783–8)

[The North-Danes were struck with a terrible fear, each one of those who heard the weeping from the rampart, heard God's adversary keening a poem of horror, a song without victory, hell's captive lamenting his pain.]

These lines convey a foretaste of the damnation to which Grendel, Cain's descendant, was always predestined: a dimension which the poet of *Beowulf* is unlikely to have found in his Germanic sources, even if, as seems probable, he based this passage on a tale of Beowulf's fight with a monster. Nor do the tales of

---

[76] See T. Charles-Edwards, 'Early Medieval Kingships in the British Isles', in Bassett (ed.), *The Origins of Anglo-Saxon Kingdoms*, 28–39, esp. 28–33.
[77] Orchard, *Companion*, 141.

Bǫðvarr bjarki tell of this hero's encounter with monsters within a hall, but always outside it. The hall-location would appear to belong to the poet of *Beowulf.*

If we try to trace this element to Latin sources, we might see that Grendel's fight with Beowulf resembles yet another passage from the *Aeneid.* In Book III, just before Aeneas winds up his story before Dido and her company, he says that his ships put in for water below Mount Etna in Sicily. Here he encounters a Greek named Achaemenides, whom Odysseus abandoned when his party scrambled to safety from the Cyclops, a one-eyed man-eating giant in a cave. The Cyclops has eaten most of the Greeks in this place, *domus sanie dapibusque cruentis, intus opaca, ingens* ('a house with blood and gory banquets, dark within, huge', *Aen.* III. 618–19). The scene was unspeakable:

> 'uisceribus miserorum et sanguine uescitur atro.
> uidi egomet duo de numero cum corpora nostro
> prensa manu magna medio resupinus in antro
> frangeret ad saxum, sanieque aspersa natarent
> limina; uidi atro cum membra fluentia tabo
> manderet et tepidi tremerent sub dentibus artus—' (*Aen.* III. 622–7)

['he fed up on the guts and black blood of those wretched men. I myself saw two of our number when he picked up their bodies with his great hand, reclining in the middle of the cave, and smashed them on a rock, while the bespattered threshold flooded with gore; I saw their organs flowing with black matter as he chewed them and their limbs still warm quivering in his teeth—']

Having washed his guests down with wine, Cyclops falls into a stupor. Odysseus organizes an escape for the survivors:

> 'et telo lumen terebramus acuto
> ingens quod torua solum sub fronte latebat,
> Argolici clipei aut Phoebeae lampadis instar.' (*Aen.* III. 635–7)

['and with a pointed shaft we pierced that huge single light which lurked beneath his frightful brow and was like a shield-disk from Argos or the lamp of Phoebus.']

Achaemenides now tells Aeneas to put to sea immediately, warning him of a hundred other *haec habitant ad litora . . . infandi Cyclopes et altis montibus errant* ('unspeakable Cyclops-monsters dwelling on these shorelines and wandering in the high mountains', *Aen.* III. 643–4).[78] They ship out just in time, with the blind Cyclops listening for the sound of oars in their wake. When he hears them row out of range:

> clamorem immensum tollit, quo pontus et omnes
> intremuere undae, penitusque exterrita tellus
> Italiae curuisque immugiit Aetna cauernis. (*Aen.* III. 672–4)

---

[78] This line was used by Aldhelm in his *Enigmata* LIII. 6.

[he raised a boundless roar at which the sea and all the waves trembled, and far inland the land of Italy was affrighted and Etna rumbled in her vaulted caverns.]

The aetiological bent of these lines, whereby Vergil accounts for volcanic action in southern Italy, should not blind us to the use which the poet of *Beowulf* seems to have made of this part of the *Aeneid*. There are obvious differences, including *Beowulf*'s admixture of biblical sources, but also a number of parallels. Grendel is a giant (*eoten*, line 761/*immensus*, *Aen*. III. 632). His atrocity is a banquet in a dark hall (*reced*, *wistfyll*, *gefeormod*; *domus*, *dapibus*). His eyes produce a light (*leoht*; *lumen*) like a flame (*ligge gelicost*; *lampadis Phoebae instar*). He consumes human flesh and blood (*blod*, *synsnædum*; *uisceribus*, *sanguine uescitur*). There is a quiet witness to his consumption of the witness's companion(s) (Beowulf/ Achaemenides). Other monsters keep company with Grendel in the marshes and moors outside (*deofla gedræg*, *fenhopu*; *ad litora ... infandi Cyclopes et altis montibus errant*). Grendel's howling frightens not only the Danes in the immediate neighbourhood, but also the Danes who live in the north: north of Zealand, if not the sea, is south-east Norway in which historically the Danes were rulers.[79] There is even the possibility of an eighth parallel, by which Grendel's sleeping victim (*slæpendne rinc*) might be a misreading of Cyclops himself reclining (*resupinus*) as he devours two Greek sailors. In the case of Grendel's *leoht unfæger*, Orchard has suggested that the poet of *Beowulf* may have used a motif of flaming eyes which recurs in the *Liber monstrorum*, particularly in the monstrous men whose *oculi sicut lucerna lucent* ('eyes shine like torches', I. 36).[80] Yet otherwise it appears to be Vergil's Cyclops on whom the poet builds a type-scene for Grendel. These parallels with *Aen*. III could be treated as seven coincidences, or as the use of a second Vergilian episode in *Beowulf*.

Grendel's Mere, Avernus, and hell (*Aen*. VI)

Grendel's Mere represents another feature common to Hrothgar and Ro in the *Chronicon Lethrense*. In the twelfth-century Zealand legend Ro builds around a pool of water which is known as *fons pulcherrimus* ('a most beautiful spring').[81] Yet the historical evidence for such places suggests that if there was an old link between King Ro and his spring, it took the form of rituals that were anything but beautiful. Wells were popular sites of superstition. They are recorded in Gaul in the fourth century; in the late sixth century, in his story of St Hilarius of Poitou, Gregory of Tours says that peasants left offerings of food by the edge of *stagna* ('pools').[82] In England there were similar customs until the end of the

---

[79] Roesdahl, *The Vikings*, 73. Maund, ' "A Turmoil of Warring Princes" ', 33–4.
[80] Orchard, *Pride and Prodigies*, 111 (cf. *Liber monstrorum* I. 28, III. 2, III. 7, III. 10).
[81] *Scriptores minores historiae Danicae*, ed. Gertz, i. 46–7 (ch. 3).
[82] *Gregorii episcopi Turonensis miracula et opera minora*, ed. B. Krusch, Scriptores Rerum Merovingicarum, MGH 1.2 (Hanover, 1885), 294–370, at 299–300 (*Liber in gloria confessorum*).

Anglo-Saxon period. As late as the eleventh century, Wulfstan included *wæterwyllas* ('wells with flowing water', i.e. 'springs'), in the list of idolatrous acts in *hæðenscype* ('heathendom'), in the law-code which he wrote for King Cnut (1016–35).[83] There are about fifteen *wylle*-suffixed English place-names which testify to associated superstitious or religious beliefs.[84] English fens were associated with hell and its demons, particularly the Crowland fens in the *Vita sancti Guthlaci* written by Felix in near the middle of the eighth century, and in the Old English *Guthlac* poems, the Guthlac homily in the late tenth-century *Vercelli Book* and the Guthlac entry in the *Old English Martyrology*.[85] The Icelanders had their own accounts of heathen worship at springs and bogs; and in Jutland and elsewhere the heathen Danes are known to have filled bogs with victims and treasures from the fourth century onwards.[86] Doubtless this was the character of the spring in Zealand long before its legend was cleaned up in the *Chronicon Lethrense*.

With 'Grendel's Mere' in *Beowulf* the poet appears to refer to a similar heathen place. That this mere is also a spring may be seen in the mingling of rising waves (*Þonon yðgeblond up astigeð*, line 1373). But it is a long time coming in *Beowulf*, where the poet first says that a *fen* ('fen', line 104) is part of the moorland wilderness in which Grendel, Heorot's inveterate attacker, dwells. Later, however, after Grendel's fatal injury at the hands of Beowulf, we learn that he had to flee *under fenhleoðu* ('beneath the fenland-hillsides', line 820).[87] Finally, the next morning, before the young Danes ride out after Grendel's blood-trail, we learn:

> hu he werigmod   on weg þanon
> niða ofercumen   on nicera mere
> fæge ond geflymed   feorhlastas bær.
> Ðær wæs on blode   brim weallende,
> atol yða geswing   eal gemenged
> haton heolfre   heorodreore weol;
> deaðfæge deog   siððan dreama leas
> in fenfreoðo   feorh alegde
> hæþene sawle;   þær him hel onfeng. (*Beo* 844–52)

[how, weary of heart, overcome by hostilities, he made blood-tracks out of that place, doomed to die and put to flight, into a monsters' mere. There the surface of the water was welling up with blood, a terrible turmoil of waves welled up all mingled with burning hot gore, with the blood of battle; death-doomed he dived, when bereft of joys he laid down his life's blood, his heathen soul, in the fen-sanctuary; there hell received him.]

---

[83] *Die Gesetze der Angelsachsen*, ed. and comm. Liebermann, i. 312–13 (Cnut's Laws, § 5).

[84] Gelling, *Place-Names in the Landscape*, 31–2.

[85] Roberts, 'Hagiography and Literature', 72–4.

[86] Ólafur Briem, *Heiðinn Siður á Íslandi* (Reykjavík, 1945), 71–90, at 75–6. P. V. Glob, *The Bog People: Iron Age Man Preserved*, trans. R. Bruce-Mitford (London, 1971), 39–44 and 61–74.

[87] A compound which shows the emotional, rather than visual, effects for which the poet strives: see Shippey, *Beowulf*, 46.

By slow degrees, in this way, the poet reveals a fen or bog near Heorot which the Danes seem to know as a *freoðo*, a heathen 'sanctuary', and which the poet calls 'hell' itself.

At first sight it might be thought there is no prior connection in *Beowulf* between this place and Hrothgar. The poet removes Hrothgar from the worst heathen taints, separating his lineage from that of the Ingwine by interpolating 'Scyld' (lines 4–46), whilst he attributes the devil-worship to Danish counsellors in general (lines 175–83) in order to distinguish the old king from them as a virtuous king.[88] On the other hand, when Hrothgar speaks of Grendel's Mere, he knows where to find it: *Nis þæt feor heonon milgemearces þæt se mere standeð* ('It is not far from this place, in a measure of miles, that the lake stands', lines 1361–2). He describes the Mere (a bottomless pool overhung by a frozen forest, with nocturnal eruptions of fire) with the familiarity of an observer. Indeed he leads them all there the next day. His knowledge is unexplained in the context of men's ignorance of supernatural comings and goings (lines 162–3), but it is anticipated, in that both young and old Danish thegns have ridden there the day before (lines 840–52). Having revealed Hrothgar's knowledge to us slowly, the poet then displays it unequivocally in the king's image of the *heorot hornum trum* ('hart strong in his antlers'), who chooses to die rather than hide in the waters. The link between Hrothgar and the heathen fen is his name for the new mead-house: Hrothgar *scop him Heort naman* ('fashioned "Hart" as a name for it', line 78). Elsewhere, on the basis of Freyr's use of the *hjartarhorn* ('stag's horn') in *Gylfaginning*, I have suggested that *heorot* whose antlers adorn Hrothgar's hall-gables (line 82) may be seen as a token of his friendship with 'Ingui', the devil worshipped by his people.[89] Given Hrothgar's formal leadership over the *Ingwine* (on lines 1044 and 1319), this connection seems likely. But what lines 1361–72 immediately imply is that Hrothgar knows of the haunted Mere because he passed it while hunting. Unlike Ro's connection with the 'spring' by which the oldest extant Danish tradition names this hall, Hrothgar's encounter with the Mere is given as a matter of chance, not of custodianship. For the poet, this may go some way to exonerating him.

So, in the vagueness of the link between Hrothgar and the Mere, it is likely that the poet departed from a tendency in his sources to make their connection obvious. If King Hrothgar, like Ro, was guardian of this spring we are not going to hear about it in *Beowulf.* Yet there is reason to believe that the poet still had this relationship in mind when he presented a scene which we might call 'Hrothgar's approach to the Mere'. First it seems more likely that Hrothulf, not Hrothgar, was associated with a tale of monsters attacking his hall: Saxo and the authors of *Hrólfs saga* and *Bjarkarímur* associate their monsters with Rolvo or Hrólfr.[90] In

---

[88] Irving, *Rereading Beowulf,* 53–4. North, *Heathen Gods,* 174–81 and 202–3.

[89] North, *Heathen Gods,* 51, 64–5. *Gylf,* 31 (ch. 36).

[90] *Gesta Danorum,* ed. Olrik and Ræder, 51 (II. vi. 11); see *Saxo Grammaticus,* trans. Fisher, i. 55. *Hrólfs saga,* ed. Slay, 79. *Hrólfs Saga Kraka,* ed. Finnur, 139 (cf. p. 68).

all this it looks as if the poet of *Beowulf* has transported Beowulf's opponents to Hrothgar's court along with Beowulf himself. Thus a spring associated with Hrothgar appears to have become useful as the place from which Hrothgar's new monsters come. Yet the poet was probably on his own, working without Germanic sources, when writing 'Hrothgar's approach to the Mere'. To do this on the basis of precedent he seems to have recast another episode from Vergil's *Aeneid*, while Christianizing the imagery with vivid borrowings from a description of hell in a vernacular homily based on the *Visio s. Pauli.*[91]

The scene with Aeneas and the sibyl of Cumae seems to have provided the poet of *Beowulf* with an authority for Hrothgar's new type-scene, one which it seems unlikely the Scylding legends gave him. In *Beowulf* there is the hero descending into a hellish lake with Hrunting, a trustworthy sword; in *Aen.* VI, Aeneas stepping after the sibyl into Avernus also with drawn sword in hand. In this book Aeneas must find a way into the Underworld in order to question Anchises, his dead father, about a future for the Trojans in Italy. Aeneas thus begs help from *Phoebi Triuiaeque sacerdos* ('a priestess of Apollo and Diana of the Cross-roads', *Aen.* VI. 35), of the temple in Cumae near to which the entrance to 'Avernus' is found. The priestess describes the place. Then, after an intermission in which Aeneas buries Misenus and sacrifices to the gods in the manner prescribed, she leads Aeneas on into the cave-mouth entrance herself. Some scholars have already detected parallels between *Beowulf* and this passage from the *Aeneid*, but none have seen fit to consider the context of each passage as an episode, or why the English poet should wish to borrow from Vergil here. Common to both great poets is a narrative outline in which a speaker, in some way the guardian of an entrance to the Underworld, describes its scenery before leading a young hero there in person.

At first it is true that there seems to be nothing in common between Hrothgar and the sibyl of Cumae. Not only a man and king, Hrothgar is also more involved in the story in that Æschere, his best friend, has been snatched by Grendel's Mother (lines 1323–33). Nor does Beowulf have a motive for visiting Grendel's Mere other than to track down this attacker on behalf of Hrothgar. In this way the relationship between guide and hero is different in each case. Yet when the old king predicts that Beowulf will become king of Geatland (lines 1707–9 and 1845–53), this comes to pass (lines 2207–8). Hrothgar's warning to Beowulf not to heed pride (lines 1758–68) might also be taken as a premonition of the young man's future. When we review Beowulf's decision to fight the dragon alone (lines 2532–5) for treasure (lines 2535–7) in the light of this warning, it is hard to sustain the claim that there are no portents in *Beowulf*, except in the most literal-minded way.[92] The poet here seems inclined to give Hrothgar a premonitory grasp of Beowulf's character whereby his long speech

---

[91] Magennis, *Images of Community in Old English Poetry,* 134–8.
[92] This is one of several arguments againt the poet's use of Vergil, in Niles, *Beowulf,* 78 (v).

indirectly works as a prophecy: just the kind of utterance for which Aeneas first applies to the sibyl of Cumae in *Aen.* VI. 56–76 and which she grants him in VI. 83–97.

Hrothgar for a moment thus resembles the priestess.[93] His desire for Beowulf to avenge Æschere by entering Grendel's Mere might then be taken as a recasting of the sibyl's insistence on Aeneas' rites for Misenus before his entry into Avernus in the *Aeneid* (I. 149–55). The Danes find Æschere after finding out his death:

> Denum eallum wæs
> winum Scyldinga   weorce on mode
> to geþolianne,   ðegne monegum
> oncyð eorla gehwæm   syðþan Æscheres
> on þæm holmclife   hafelan metton. (*Beo* 1417–21)

[to all the Danes, [and] to the friends of the Scyldings, there was distress to suffer in their hearts, grief for many a thegn, for each and every man, when on the sea-cliff they encountered Æschere's head.]

The manner and location of this discovery bear a resemblance to the way Misenus is found after the sybil's notice of his death. Misenus, having dared the gods to compete with him on the trumpet, is *exceptum* ('caught up') by Triton, who:

> inter saxa uirum spumosa immerserat unda.
> ergo omnes magno circum clamore fremebant,
> praecipue pius Aeneas. (*Aen.* VI. 174–6)

[among the rocks had enveloped the man in the foaming surf. Thus did all of them groan with a great cry of sorrow as they stood about him, chiefly Aeneas the dutiful.]

Then Hrothgar tells Beowulf of the place from which Grendel's Mother came. Having pictured the two monsters as reported to him by local peasants, Hrothgar describes their homeland, including the pool itself:

> 'Hie dygel lond
> warigeað wulfhleoþu   windige næssas
> frecne fengelad   ðær fyrgenstream
> under næssa genipu   niþer gewiteð
> flod under foldan.   Nis þæt feor heonon
> milgemearces   þæt se mere standeð;
> ofer þæm hongiað   hrimde bearwas,
> wudu wyrtum fæst   wæter oferhelmað.
> Þær mæg nihta gehwæm   niðwundor seon
> fyr on flode.   No þæs frod leofað
> gumena bearna   þæt þone grund wite.' (*Beo* 1357–67)

---

[93] If the gender transfer is seen as problematic, note that Condee (*Structure in Milton's Poetry*, 149–50) shows an echo of the words of the hero Nisus in *Aen.* IX. 427–30 in Eve's speech in Milton's *PL* X. 914–16 and 927–36.

['They inhabit a secret land, wolf-slopes, windy bluffs, savage fenland roads, where the mountain stream passes down beneath the mists of headlands, a river beneath the earth. It is not far from my place, in a measure of miles, that the lake stands; above it there hang frost-rimed groves, a wood made fast by its roots overshadows the water. There each night a fearful wonder may be seen, fire on the flood. No man lives of the sons of men so wise that he may know the bottom.']

Hrothgar goes on to tell of the stag who prefers death from the hounds to the prospect of hiding in these waters, then adds that this pool is not a pleasant place:

> 'Þonon yðgeblond   up astigeð
> won to wolcnum   þonne wind styreþ
> lað gewidru   oð þæt lyft drysmaþ,
> roderas reotað.' (*Beo* 1373–6)

['From there a mingling of waves rises up, dark towards the clouds, when stirred by wind, a hostile storm, until the sky grows gloomy, the heavens weep.']

The Vergilian frame of Hrothgar's speech is apparent in several ways. To Aeneas, in Book VI of the *Aeneid*, the priestess of Cumae remarks that with the correct rites of sacrifice it is easy to descend into Avernus:

> 'noctes atque dies patet atri ianua Ditis;
> sed reuocare gradum superasque euadere ad auras,
> hoc opus, hic labor est. pauci, quos aequus amauit
> Iuppiter aut ardens euexit ad aethera uirtus,
> dis geniti potuere. tenent media omnia siluae,
> Cocytusque sinu labens circumuenit atro.' (*Aen.* VI. 127–32)

['By night and day the doors of black Dis [: Pluto] lie open; but to recall one's steps and to escape to the upper air, that is an undertaking, here lies the work. A few, whom fair-minded Jupiter has loved or fiery courage lifted up to the ether, men begotten of gods, have been able to do this. Woods hold all the ground between, and with black curves the turgid river Cocytus winds around.']

The fire on the water is contained in Vergil's naming of the burning river 'Phlegethon' (*Aen.* I. 265), but the *flumen igneum* ('river of fire') is also part of hell in the Latin text of *Visio s. Pauli*.[94] Vergil's influence has long been suggested in this part of *Beowulf*.[95] There are three or four motifs in common: the night-time vista (*nihta gehwæm*; *noctes*), the failure of mortals to come back alive (*no þæs frod leofað gumena bearna*; *pauci . . . dis geniti potuere*), the troubled black waters (*yðgeblond . . . won to wolcnum*; *Cocytusque sinu labens . . . atro*), even the suggestion of (albeit different) divine attitudes to the place (*roderas reotað*; *aequus . . . Iuppiter*). These are common features from which suggest that Hrothgar's speech is outlined on that of Vergil's sibyl.

   94 Wright, *The Irish Tradition*, 134–5.
   95 Haber, *A Comparative Study*, 92–6. Orchard, *Pride and Prodigies*, 44. *Pace* Renoir, 'The Terror of the Dark Waters', 153–7.

Beowulf's renewed vow arouses a positive response from Hrothgar, who then leads him to Grendel's Mere:

> Ahleop ða se gomela,   gode þancode
> mihtigan drihtne   þæs se man gespræc.
> Þa wæs Hroðgare   hors gebæted
> wicg wundenfeax.   Wisa fengel
> geatolic gende.   Gumfeþa stop
> lindhæbbendra. (*Beo* 1397–1402)

[The old man leapt up, thanked God, the mighty Lord, for what the man had spoken. Then a horse was bridled for Hrothgar, a charger with twisted locks. The wise lord proceeded in splendour. There marched a troop of men bearing linden-wood shields.]

Hrothgar's prayer resembles the sudden manner in which Vergil's sibyl reacts to the earth's resounding reply to Aeneas' sacrifice, proof that the gods will allow them both to enter:

> tantum effata furens antro se immisit aperto;
> ille ducem haud timidis uadentem passibus aequat. (*Aen.* VI. 262–3)

[Having pronounced so much, she cast herself in wildness into the open cave; with no fearful steps Aeneas keeps pace with the leader as she moves.]

The differences are in Hrothgar's horse and foot-soldiers, but his sudden uplift and speed towards the Mere recapture the motion of the sibyl. Thirdly, the Danes see monsters around the lake:

> Gesawon ða æfter wætere   wyrmcynnes fela
> sellice sædracan   sund cunnian,
> swylce on næshleoðum   nicras licgean
> ða on undernmæl   oft bewitigað
> sorhfulne sið   on seglrade,
> wyrmas ond wildeor. (*Beo* 1425–30)

[Then they saw along the water's edge many kinds of serpent, marvellous sea-dragons testing the strait, likewise those water-monsters lying on the slopes of the headland which in the morning time often undertake a journey filled with sorrow for the sail-road, as well as serpents and wild beasts.]

The complication of this sea-imagery in what was hitherto described a land-locked lake has long been noted.[96] This imagery makes better sense if we compare it with some of the apparitions at the gates of Orcus in the *Aeneid*:

> multaque praeterea uariarum monstra ferarum,
> Centauri in foribus stabulant Scyllaeque biformes
> et centumgeminus Briareus ac belua Lernae
> horridum stridens (*Aen.* VI. 285–8)

---

[96] *Beowulf*, ed. Klaeber, 182.

[and many other monstrous shapes of different beasts, Centaurs abide in the doorway and twin-formed Scyllas and the hundred-armed Briareus and the Lernaean hydra hissing horribly.]

The focus in *Beowulf*, moreover, on the daily routine of sea-monsters molesting ships gives an impression of the poet's acquaintance with the Scylla in the *Liber monstrorum*, who *monstrum nautis inimicissimum in eo freto quod Italiam et Siciliam interluit* ('has been the monster most hostile to sailors in that channel which washes between Italy and Sicily', I. 14).[97] So far, with imagery apparently based on fabulous poetry and prose as well as the Bible, it seems likely that the poet of *Beowulf* drew upon this range of Latin literature. Let us now see his use of the Christian vernacular.

HOMILETIC INFLUENCE FROM THE VERNACULAR

It has long been mooted that the poet of *Beowulf* was influenced by vernacular writing.[98] Not only has it been suggested that *Genesis A* was known to the *Beowulf*-poet, but the style of discourse on Danish devil-worship in lines 178–88, together with the exclamation on the mystery of death in lines 3064–5, resembles the prose of some Old English homilies.[99] In some vernacular form, in particular, the originally fourth-century *Visio s. Pauli* appears to have influenced the imagery of *Beowulf*. In England this was treated as an uncanonical work, repudiated by both Aldhelm and Ælfric.[100] Yet the poet of *Beowulf* seems to have used it for Hrothgar's account of Grendel's Mere and for his own description of the place as having *nicorhusa fela* ('many homes to monsters', line 1411) and mountain trees leaning *ofer harne stan* ('over the hoary grey rock', line 1415) above dark waters which *under stod* ('stood beneath', line 1416). These lines appear to capture the description of hell in the *Visio s. Pauli* as appended to a homily on the Feast of St Michael, in Homily XVI of the tenth-century *Blickling Homilies*.[101] Here, at the end of an account of Michael's protection of a church on Monte Gargano in Apulia on the border with Campania, the homilist cites St Paul, who was looking towards the northern parts of the earth:

[97] Orchard, *Pride and Prodigies*, 266–7. These lines from *Beowulf* may also show knowledge of Aldhelm's marine metaphors at the beginning and end of the prose *De virginitate*, or of the *Epistola Alexandri*. See Orchard, *Pride and Prodigies*, 45–7 (*Letter*) and 96–7 (Aldhelm).

[98] M. Goldsmith, *The Mode and Meaning of Beowulf* (London, 1970).

[99] F. Klaeber, 'Die *Ältere Genesis* und der *Beowulf*', *Estn*, 42 (1910), 321–38. Orchard, *Companion*, 167 and 151–3.

[100] A. DiPaolo Healey, 'Visio s. Pauli', in Biggs, Hill, and Szarmach (eds.), *Sources of Anglo-Saxon Literary Culture*, 66–7.

[101] *The Blickling Homilies*, ed. and trans. Kelly, 144–5. Also (numbered erroneously as XVII) in *The Blickling Homilies of the Tenth Century*, ed. and trans. R. Morris, EETS os 73 (London, 1880), pp. vi–vii and 208–9. *Beowulf*, ed. Klaeber, 182–3. *Beowulf*, ed. Wrenn and Bolton, 152–3.

þær ealle wætero niðergewítað, ond he þær geseah ofer ðæm wætere sumne harne stan, ond wæron norð of þæm stane awexene swiðe hrimige bearwas. Ond ðær wæron þystrogenipo, ond under þæm stane wæs niccra eardung ond wearga. Ond he geseah þæt on ðæm clife hangodan on ðæm ísigean bearwum manige swearte saula be heora handum gebundne. Ond þa fynd þara on nicra onlicnesse heora gripende wæron, swa swa grædig wulf. Ond þæt wæter wæs sweart under þæm clife neoðan.[102]

[from where all waters pass down, he saw above the water a hoary stone, and north of the stone the woods had grown very frosty. Dark mists existed there, and under the stone was the dwelling place of monsters and abominable creatures. He saw many black souls with their hands bound hanging on the cliff of these icy woods. The devils in the likeness of monsters were seizing them like greedy wolves. The water under the cliff beneath was black.]

The likeness between the two works is striking: we see waters which pass down beneath the earth (*niðergewítað / niþer gewiteð*); and a grey rock (*har stan*) is surmounted by frosty groves (*hrimge / hrimde bearwas*) which loom over dark mists (*þystrogenipo / næssa genipu*) and monsters' lairs (*niccra eardung / nicorhusa fela*). The *Visio s. Pauli* has fiery trees whereas in both the homily and *Beowulf* the trees are icy. A more general point of resemblance, as Orchard observes, is one between the rare doublet *geweox ond gewridode* ('increased and flourished'), which describes cattle herds at the start of the homily, and Hrothgar's comment on pride at the start of Fitt XX[V], that this vice *weaxeð ond wridað* ('grows and flourishes', *Beo* 1741).[103]

In the face of these parallels, scholars have argued either that the homily was based on *Beowulf* or that this part of *Beowulf* was adapted from the homily.[104] Winning ground at present is a third view, that both authors rely on the same source. Peter Clemoes suggests that this was 'a vernacular "literary", scenic, description of hell, which belonged to a quasi-Latin, quasi-vernacular, tradition known to them alike'.[105] As he observes, the 'visionary mode' was popular in many literary forms in the early centuries of Anglo-Saxon England.[106] Charles Wright, in his discussion of the two versions of *Visio s. Pauli*, shows that hell in the Blickling homily is described not only on the basis of the *Visio*, but also on that of two separate scenes in the redactions that were conflated in the homilist's source (the fiery trees and the beast-filled river). The recently discovered 'Redaction XI', in a manuscript of Irish provenance, shows that these scenes had already been combined in a Latin text 'at least a century' before Blickling Homily XVI

[102] Text and translation from Kelly, *The Blickling Homilies*, 144–5.

[103] Ibid. 136–7. As noted in Orchard, *Companion*, 30.

[104] For the first view, C. Brown, '*Beowulf* and the *Blickling Homilies* and Some Textual Notes', *PMLA* 53 (1938), 905–16; acknowledged by R. J. Kelly, in his *The Blickling Homilies*, 191–2. For the second view, R. I. Collins, 'Blickling Homily XVI and the Dating of *Beowulf*', in W.-D. Bald and H. Weinstock (eds.), *Medieval Studies Conference, Aachen, 1983*, Bamberger Beiträge zur Englischen Sprachwissenschaft 15 (Frankfurt, 1984), 61–9.

[105] Clemoes, *Interactions of Thought and Language*, 25.

[106] Discussed in Sims-Williams, *Religion and Literature*, 243–72.

was written.[107] Wright goes on to argue that a vernacular version of this text was known to both the Blickling homilist and the poet of *Beowulf*.[108] This argument allows a date for *Beowulf*'s composition in 826 × 839.

What other Latin or Latin-based sources the poet of *Beowulf* may have used particularly with Grendel's Mere, and in what form he may have found them, are matters for even greater conjecture than the Vergilian narrative parallels which I have given above. A thematic relationship of some kind may be observed between *Aen.* VII and the now-lost source for the Blickling homily, sufficient for the poet of *Beowulf*, if he did so, to have integrated them with each other and within his own work. He appears to use Vergil to establish an authority for new narrative motifs and type-scenes; and he appears to know the source of the Blickling homily, in that he adds such scenic details as to encourage the belief that Grendel's Mere is hell or a place like it. Nor is it so far-fetched that he recast the sibyl as King Hrothgar, if we consider the role of guardianship of a gateway to the Underworld which was likely to be common to the king's heathen prototype and the Cumae priestess even as a Christian reader of Vergil would have understood her. The fact that, as a sibyl, she is also a visionary of divine worlds could also have recommended her to a poet whose view of hell depended on a *Visio* ascribed to St Paul.

It is in Hrothgar's central speech in *Beowulf* (lines 1700–84), otherwise known as his 'sermon'), that the remaining area of homiletic influence in *Beowulf* has been found. Beowulf walks back from the Mere, sets down Grendel's head, and proclaims his victory. Then he gives Hrothgar the hilt from the sword which achieved this. Hrothgar *maðelode, hylt sceawode* ('made a speech, looked at the hilt', line 1687); Orchard suggest that the rhyme here emphasizes 'the connection between what Hrothgar says and what he sees'.[109] In his speech Hrothgar thanks Beowulf partly in hypermetric lines (lines 1700–9), warns him about Heremod (lines 1709–24), generalizes this exemplum with a statement on human folly and pride (lines 1724–68), and finishes with a note on himself (lines 1769–84). The third part of this contains Augustinian theological motives through which some call Hrothgar's speech a 'sermon'.[110] Hrothgar remarks that *wundor is to secganne* ('it is a wonder to say', line 1724) how God deals out wisdom, land, and rank to all men; sometimes he brings a man such joy, wealth, and power *þæt he his selfa ne mæg his unsnyttrum ende geþencean* ('that the man himself, in his lack of wisdom, cannot imagine an end to it', lines 1733–4); he lives on in good fortune with neither *adl ne yldo* ('disease nor old age', line 1736) nor *inwitsorh* ('sorrow of conscience', line 1736) afflicting him, while all the world turns to his will: he knows of nothing worse:

[107] Wright, *The Irish Tradition*, 106–36, esp. 120–4.

[108] Ibid. 133–5. Followed by Jack, in his *Beowulf: A Student Edition*, 110, Magennis, *Images of Community in Old English Poetry*, 135, and Orchard, *Companion*, 158.

[109] Orchard, *Companion*, 159 n. 143.

[110] Kaske, '*Sapientia et Fortitudo*', 279–85. *Beowulf*, ed. Klaeber, 190. Whitelock, *The Audience of Beowulf*, 8. Stanley, *In the Foreground*, 240: 'The densest concentration in *Beowulf* of pious thoughts.'

XX[V]   'Oð þæt him on innan   oferhygda dæl
        weaxeð ond wridað,   þonne se weard swefeð,
        sawele hyrde;   bið se slæp to fæst,
        bisgum gebunden,   bona swiðe neah,
        se þe of flanbogan   fyrenum sceoteð.
        Þonne bið on hreþre   under helm drepen
        biteran stræle   —him bebeorgan ne con—
        wom wundorbebodum   wergan gastes;
        þinceð him to lytel   þæt he lange heold,
        gytsað gromhydig,   nalles on gylp seleð
        fætte beagas   ond he þa forðgesceaft
        forgyteð ond forgymeð   þæs þe him ær god sealde,
        wuldres waldend,   weorðmynda dæl.' (*Beo* 1740–52)

['And then[111] a measure of prideful thoughts grows and flourishes within him, when the keeper sleeps, the guardian of the soul; that sleep is too sound, bound with cares, the slayer very close, who shoots wickedly from a fiery bow. Then beneath his armour is he struck in his heart with a bitter arrow, with the crooked miraculous commands of the accursed spirit—he knows not how to protect himself! It seems too little to him, what he has long held, angry at heart he grows greedy, not at all nobly does he give plated rings, and then forgets and neglects the world to come, the portion of worldly honours which God, the Ruler of Glory, had once given him.']

Against this image of a rake's progress, Hrothgar now urges Beowulf—as if he were like the pagan Judas after baptism in *Elene* (*he þæt betere geceas*, line 1038)— to choose *þæt selre, ece rædas* ('the better part, eternal rewards', *Beo* 1759–60), not to heed *oferhyda* ('prideful thoughts', line 1760). The glory of Beowulf's strength, he says, will last only for a while:

                    'eft sona bið
        þæt þec adl oððe ecg   eafoþes twæfeð
        oððe fyres feng   oððe flodes wylm
        oððe gripe meces   oððe gares fliht
        oððe atol yldo,   oððe eagena bearhtm
        forsiteð ond forsworceð;   semninga bið
        þæt ðec, dryhtguma,   dead oferswyðeð.' (*Beo* 1762–8)

['Soon it will happen that disease or the blade will separate you from your strength, or the fire's grip or the flood's surge or the sword's bite or the spear's flight or terrible old age, or the brightness of your eyes will fail and grow dim; in the end it shall happen that death, man of the retinue, will overpower you.']

The homiletic train of this passage has been demonstrated.[112] There are three examples of an alliterating pair of finite verbs (*weaxað ond wridað*, line 1741; *forgyteð ond forgymeð*, line 1751; *forsiteð ond forsworceð*, line 1767); and the poet

---

111 *Beowulf*, ed. Mitchell and Robinson, 105, n. to lines 1739b–1741a.
112 Clemoes, *Interactions of Thought and Language*, 42–6.

links alliterating noun-pairs together seven times with polysyndeton (*oððe*, lines 1763–6); and in Hrothgar's motif of the soul's guardian defending a man's soul from the devil's arrow, the same guardian who, in the Mercian Vercelli Homily IV, *wyle us forstandan æt þam awyrgden diofle, þe of þære stylenan helle cymð mid his scearpum strælum us mit to sciotianne* ('will defend us against the accursed devil, who comes from the steel hell with his sharp arrows to shoot us with').[113] The source appears to be Ephesians 6: 10–20, in which St Paul enjoins converts to take on God's armour and *scutum fidei, in quo possitis omnia tela nequissimi ignea extinguere* ('the shield of faith with which you will be able to quench all the flaming arrows of the evil one', 6: 16).[114] Orchard notes that Aldhelm, in his *Carmen de virginitate*, plays on a similar motif in his portrait of Pride (*Superbia*), who *probos propriis prosternere telis|nititur* ('strives to lay low the virtuous with her own shafts', lines 2708–9).[115] Yet Orchard considers the poet of *Beowulf* to be alluding to the 'flaming arrows' of Ephesians 6, given that his devil shoots *of flanbogan fyrenum* (line 1744), with a play on two senses of the term *fyren*: 'crime' or 'sin', and 'fiery'.[116]

It is fair to say that the richly various meanings in Hrothgar's sword-hilt speech (lines 1700–84) converge on the death of its dedicatee fifty years later, when at an advanced age, in lines 2529–37, Beowulf tells his guard he will face the dragon alone *gold gegangan* (in order to 'get gold', line 2536). Here we stand at the end of a moral trail which starts with the poet's first mention of Cain (lines 105–7), leads on to Hama's *Brosinga mene* and the necklace on Hygelac's breast (lines 1197–211), and continues with the Cain-inscribed hilt in Hrothgar's hands (lines 1687–98), before showing us the stolen cup in Beowulf's (lines 2404–5). In all this, the question following Beowulf's death must be whether or not he is saved. As we shall see further in Chapter 7, the unknowable answer depends on the force of Beowulf's interest in *hæðen gold* ('heathen gold', line 2276), especially in the light of the curse which, so the poet says, has bound it since it was laid in the ground (lines 3051–7 and 3069–75).

CONCLUSION

The poet of *Beowulf* seems to have imitated a wide range of Latin sources, both to make Beowulf's adventures more exciting and to moralize the story leading up to

[113] *The Vercelli Homilies*, ed. D. G. Scragg, EETS, os 300 (London, 1991), 104. On the Mercian origin of Homilies XV–XVIII, see D. G. Scragg, 'The Compilation of the Vercelli Book', *ASE* 2 (1973), 189–207, esp. 202–5.

[114] Discussed in: M. Atherton, 'The Figure of the Archer in *Beowulf* and the Anglo-Saxon Psalter', *Neophil*, 77 (1993), 653–7; Wright, *The Irish Tradition*, 260–1; and Orchard, *Companion*, 160–1. Cf. Psalm 90: 4–6.

[115] Orchard, *Pride and Prodigies*, 103.

[116] Orchard, *Companion*, 161. On the same imagery in the *Psychomachia* of Prudentius, widely read in Anglo-Saxon England, see also Orchard, *The Poetic Art of Aldhelm*, 170–8. On Hrothgar's *sawele hyrde* (line 1742) and St Michael, see further in Chapter 6.

his death. The last would amount to the spiritual salvage of heathens, an ultimately theological use of Latin and Latin-based material. This poet probably read other Latin books as well. Of those which have been guessed at in this chapter, the foremost are verses from the Old and New Testaments: Genesis, 1 Enoch, 1 Samuel, Judges, Psalms, Maccabees; and St Mark or St Matthew, St Luke, St John, and St Paul's Letter to the Ephesians 6. One item of patristic commentary, seemingly familiar to the poet, comes from the *Conlationes* of the monastic author John Cassian. For the dragon-fight, in line with Rauer's observations, it seems likely that the poet knew of one or both *Vitae s. Samsonis*; in addition, a text analogous to, or identical with, St Michael's dragon-fight in item 55 in the *Homiliary of Saint-Père*. For his description of the haunted Mere, he appears to have known a vernacular version of the *Visio s. Pauli*, if not also a Latin version of the same, and perhaps another homily on St Michael such as that which precedes the vernacular *Visio s. Pauli* in Blickling Homily XVI. It can be argued that the poet read both the *Epistola Alexandri ad Aristotelem*, a popular work of a fourth-century date, and the *Liber monstrorum*, an Insular text from a circle associated with Bishop Aldhelm of Sherborne in the early eighth century. Last but not least, there are three or four scenes in *Beowulf* which appear to have been cast on the basis of episodes set respectively in Vergil's *Aeneid* I, III, and VI. In an interesting splicing of sources, Beowulf thus appears to be characterized (*i.a.*) with the aid of Samson, young David, Jesus, St Michael, and Aeneas. In the next chapter, I shall argue that the poet made further use of the *Aeneid*, from Books VII and XI, in order to authorize his juxtaposition of Beowulf with Freawaru and Ingeld. For now, it seems fair to say that *Beowulf* is richly hybrid, an Old English work composed by a monk with an interest in Latin, Greek, Hebrew, and Germanic.

4

Ingeld's Rival: Beowulf and Aeneas

In Chapter 2, I have sought to establish that the poet of *Beowulf* innovated with Germanic legend, transforming his Beowulf-archetype by detaching him from Hrothulf's retinue, placing him in Hrothgar's court a generation earlier, and making him both Hygelac's sister's son and a king. In Chapter 3, I have suggested that the poet used a variety of ecclesiastical, fabulous, and homiletic sources, as well as *Aeneid* Books I, III, and VI, in order to flesh out Beowulf's character in his new role. The aim of this chapter is to pursue the implications of Beowulf's novel interaction with Hrothgar. I shall begin with the poet's early signals that Beowulf will become a king, by considering Beowulf's growing prestige in Denmark and Hrothgar's offer to cherish him as a son. From here I progress to the relevance of Ingeld to Beowulf's career. I shall consider Norse analogues to suggest the likely shape of the Ingeld legend which was known to the poet of *Beowulf*. The case I will make is that Hrothgar decides to marry Beowulf to his daughter Freawaru, against his older plan to marry her to Ingeld; but that Queen Wealhtheow, burying this impulse, keeps Beowulf from their daughter. When her marriage with Ingeld fails, just as Beowulf predicts it will in lines 2021–69, the Heathobards will attack Heorot and burn it down. The poet's creation of rivalry in the bridal quest between Beowulf and Ingeld is the political aspect of Beowulf's new place in Hrothgar's, not Hrothulf's, reign. I argue that the poet authenticates this rivalry by characterizing Wealhtheow with Hrothgar just here on the basis of Amata with Latinus in Vergil's *Aeneid*, Books VII and XI, as if Beowulf were Aeneas and Ingeld were Turnus. I conclude that this brief but inventive concentration on Beowulf as Ingeld's rival betokens an 'anxiety of influence': the poet's rivalry with a major English poet before him.

In Chapters 5–7, I shall argue that Ingeld leads us to the minster in which *Beowulf* was written. By a long process of incremental supposition, in Chapter 5, I will suggest that *Beowulf*'s source-poem on Ingeld was the subject of Alcuin's famous complaint about 'Hinieldus' together with a *citharista* ('harper') and *carmina* ('songs') at the court of 'Speratus' in 797. Identifying the latter with Unwona, bishop of Leicester, I posit a transmission of this presumed Ingeld *carmen* to the poet of *Beowulf* through a pupil of Unwona's named Priest Abbot Wigmund. I go on to argue that in 797 Wigmund was abbot of the minster of Breedon on the Hill, some 20 miles north of Leicester, and that *Beowulf* was later conceived and composed with reference to the presumed Ingeld *carmen* in this minster. Chapter 6 seeks to strengthen this conjecture by matching what can be deduced about the contents of Breedon's library with those Latin sources of *Beowulf* which I have attempted to discern in Chapter 3. In Chapter 7, having delved into the poet's use of a specifically Danish mythology, I make a case for Danish contacts with Breedon in 809, less than twenty years before the period in which, in Chapter 2, I have argued *Beowulf* was written.

Pushed as it is beyond all previous limits, at least this theory about *Beowulf*'s origins begins with an attempt to to fathom the poet's intentions. It is one thing that the poet of *Beowulf* appear to innovate by bringing Beowulf to Hrothgar. But why does he choose to dwell on the story of Hrothgar's son-in-law? To find out, we can start with Hrothgar's changing view of Beowulf as he begins to prove himself, in younger Danish eyes, a worthier ruler of Denmark than Hrothgar himself.

'NIW SIB': THE RIGHT TO FREAWARU

At the beginning, it is only when Beowulf has proved himself against Unferth (*Beo* 530–606) that Hrothgar *geoce gelyfde* ('believed in the aid', line 608) which Beowulf offers. In indirect speech this belief is then reiterated by Wealhtheow *wisfæst wordum* ('profoundly wise in [her] words', line 626). Having greeted Beowulf, she thanks God for the fruition of her desire *þæt heo on ænigne eorl gelyfde fyrena frofre* ('that she might believe in any nobleman for succour against [their] evils', lines 627–8). In direct speech Hrothgar then gives expression to his belief in Beowulf by saying:

> 'Næfre ic ænegum men   ær alyfde,
> siþðan ic hond ond rond   hebban mihte,
> ðryþærn Dena   buton þe nu ða.' (*Beo* 655–7)

['Never before, since I have been able to lift arm and shield, have I believed in entrusting the mighty house of the Danes to any man now except to you.'][1]

By the same token, it is likely that Hrothgar means he had had no faith in those (drunken) Danes who perished in the hall in earlier attempts to defend it (lines 480–8).[2] Beowulf's stock has risen in his eyes. That night, fighting for survival against Grendel in Heorot, Beowulf fulfils his vow and drives the monster mortally wounded back to his lair. Riding back from the Mere to which they have followed Grendel's blood-trail, the Danes think of their visitor in a new light:

[1] Irving (*Rereading Beowulf*, 52) points out that Hrothgar would be within his rights to ban Beowulf's entry into the hall.
[2] Irving (ibid. 40) sees drinking as the prime instigator of these suicide missions.

> Ðær wæs Beowulfes
> mærðo mæned;   monig oft gecwæð
> þætte suð ne norð   be sæm tweonum
> ofer eormengrund   oþer nænig
> under swegles begong   selra nære
> rondhæbbendra,   rices wyrðra. (*Beo* 856–61)

[In that place Beowulf's exploit was proclaimed; many a man often said that neither south nor north between the seas or across the earth's vast terrain, beneath the sun's compass was there any other shield-bearing warrior better, nor worthier of a kingdom.]

This is their first thought; the second, which the poet supplies, delineates Beowulf's new status yet more clearly:

> Ne hie huru winedrihten   wiht ne logon,
> glædne Hroðgar,   ac þæt wæs god cyning. (*Beo* 862–3)

[Nor, indeed, did they lie about their friend and lord in any way, about gracious Hrothgar, for he was a good king.]

The question raised by these lines is whether or not Beowulf would be a better king than Hrothgar.[3]

The poet returns to this question after appearing to outline the end of Beowulf's career through a figure from an even older history: Sigemund the dragon-slayer, whose tale a Danish thegn relates to the company riding back from the Mere (lines 875–900). Our poet, not this one, then contrasts Sigemund with Heremod, whose initial promise was forgotten when he became the greatest tyrant the Danes had ever seen:

> he his leodum wearð,
> eallum æþellingum   to aldorceare.
> Swylce oft bemearn   ærran mælum
> swiðferhþes sið   snotor ceorl monig,
> se þe him bealwa to   bote gelyfde,
> þæt þæt ðeodnes bearn   geþeon scolde,
> fæderæþelum onfon,   folc gehealdan,
> hord ond hleoburh,   hæleþa rice,
> eðel Scyldinga.   He þær eallum wearð,
> mæg Higelaces,   manna cynne,
> freondum gefægra;   hine fyren onwod. (*Beo* 905–15)

[he became to his people, to all men of noble family, a life-endangering worry. Likewise did many a wise churl for the times past often lament the career of the strong-hearted

---

[3] Irving (ibid. 50–1) does not relate this comment, which he calls 'a careful aside', to the preceding passage in which Beowulf's abilities are praised, but more conservatively claims that the poet 'is quite sensitive to the potential tension inherent in any open comparison of Hrothgar and Beowulf'. However, when he compares them as kings (ibid. 59–62), Irving himself makes a less sensitive case for preferring Beowulf's abilities to Hrothgar's.

man, having believed as a cure for their evils that this king's son would thrive, receive his father's noble rank, guard his nation, hoard, and citadel, the kingdom of heroes, the Scyldings' inherited land. Beowulf in that place, to everyone, the tribe of men, friends, became more beloved; crime passed into Heremod.]

With the word *gelyfde*, given to the churl on line 909, the poet makes capital of the theme of trust which we have seen used three times with Beowulf (in lines 608, 627, and 655). So the true comparison is between Heremod and Beowulf; in lines 913–15, the poet goes on to make this explicit. He does so after first presenting the whole Danish hierarchy, with princes alongside churls, as well as the due process of Danish kingship. And so back to the ride from the Mere. But with his emphasis on Heremod in the meantime, the poet has transformed an initial Scylding wonder at Beowulf's kingly prowess into their clear desire that he should be their next king.

Fitt XIII closes with an image of how this can happen. First Hrothgar welcomes Beowulf, with Wealhtheow and all her ladies in a troop behind him, having left a *brydbur* ('bridal bower'). If Beowulf is to become Hrothgar's heir, the Danish bloodline requires that this comes about by marriage. Hrothgar's words to the returning hero in Fitt XIV amount to his adopting Beowulf as a new son-in-law:

> 'Nu ic Beowulf þec
> secg betsta   me for sunu wylle
> freogan on ferhþe;   heald forð tela
> niwe sibbe.   Ne bið þe [n]ænigra gad
> worolde wilna,   þe ic geweald hæbbe.' (*Beo* 946–50)

['Now Beowulf, best of men, I wish to love you in my heart as a son. From this time forth, as is right, keep a new kinship. Nor will you want for anything in the world which you desire and which is mine to command.']

Mitchell and Robinson call the words *niwe sibbe* a 'new relationship' and state that this 'does not constitute literal adoption but was merely a king's way of affirming a close alliance and firm bond of fealty'.[4] Irving, without probing the wider context, calls this offer 'impulsive', the culmination of his love for Beowulf.[5] Yet the force of Wealhtheow's later intervention is at odds with this generality. The earnest of Hrothgar's intention here is borne out in her retort to Hrothgar later the same day, in hall after the recital of the Danish Finnsburh epic. At first she hands Hrothgar the ceremonial cup, and all is well, with her family at peace with itself and its retainers. She bids Hrothgar take the cup and be generous to the Geats in words and also with the gifts which he has in his keeping *nean ond feorran* ('from far and near', line 1174). Then she changes tack:

---

[4] *Beowulf*, ed. Mitchell and Robinson, 79.
[5] Irving, *Rereading Beowulf*, 55 and 61.

> 'Me man sægde,   þæt þu ðe for sunu wolde
> hereri[n]c habban.   Heorot is gefælsod,
> beahsele beorhta;   bruc þenden þu mote
> manigra medo,   ond þinum magum læf
> folc ond rice,   þonne ðu forð scyle,
> metodsceaft seon.' (*Beo* 1175–80)

['It has been said to me that you would have the raiding warrior as your son. Heorot is cleansed, the bright ring-hall; use, while you may, the rewards of the many, and leave your people and kingdom to your kinsmen when you must go hence to see the Lord's creation.']

So her point becomes known. By claiming that Hrothgar did not tell her of his plan to make Beowulf his heir, Wealhtheow opposes Hrothgar in public, even rebuking him for the announcement of a 'new kinship' with Beowulf.[6] To some formal extent this kinship is now visible, for climactically at the end of this fitt (XVII) the poet tells us that Beowulf sits between Hrethric and Hrothmund, the two sons of Wealhtheow and Hrothgar (lines 1190–1). This is as if Beowulf is already Hrothgar's son: he remembers this scene in lines 2011–13. In her own words, however, Wealhtheow distinguishes between the material things which a king may bestow as rewards to many different men (*manigra medo*, line 1178) and the Danish nation and kingdom which are entrusted to Hrothgar until his death on behalf of their blood-kindred (*þinum magum* i.e. his *mægð*), line 1178). There are other worries in Wealhtheow's speech, to do with her sons, but in this part of it she suggests that Hrothgar bury any idea of making Beowulf his successor.[7] She openly rejects Beowulf in order to support Hrothulf instead:

> 'Ic minne can
> glædne Hroþulf,   þæt he þa geogoðe wile
> arum healdan,   gyf þu ær þonne he,
> wine Scildinga,   worold oflætest;
> wene ic þæt he mid gode   gyldan wille
> uncran eaferan,   gif he þæt eal gemon
> hwæt wit to willan   ond to worðmyndum
> umborwesendum ær   arna gefremedon.' (*Beo* 1180–7)

---

[6] Dong-Ill Lee, however, suggests ('Character from Archetype', 168) that the indirectness of *me man sægde* is a sign of Wealhtheow's politeness.

[7] As Overing points out (*Language, Sign, and Gender in Beowulf*, 88–101, at 96), Wealhtheow 'attempts to undo her husband's past words by a kind of poetic admonition or embarrassment. Her exhortation to the king to do what is proper calls attention to his previous impropriety: his excessively generous offer to adopt Beowulf as his son when he already had two of his own.... She seeks to negate her husband's promise.' Similarly persuasive ideas of a hard-headed Wealhtheow are presented in C. Cramer, 'The Voice of Beowulf', *Germanic Notes*, 8 (1977), 40–4, at 43 (Wealhtheow's use of five imperatives); J. Chance, *Woman as Hero in Old English Literature* (Syracuse, NY, 1986); and Damico, in *Beowulf's Wealhtheow and the Valkyrie Tradition*. Irving (*Rereading Beowulf*, 74) credits Wealhtheow with 'the insight that her ageing husband seems to lack', but otherwise sees her as 'pathetic', judging hers to be a plaintive role.

['I know my Hrothulf is well-disposed, that he will keep these youths in his favour, if you, O friend of the Scyldings, depart the world sooner than he; I expect it is with advantage that he will repay our heirs, if he remembers everything the two of us performed for him before, for his pleasure and honour, while he was a child.']

Her expectation of support from Hrothulf, in return, is clear in the publicity of her declaration. It is also clear in the fact that she reinterprets the *are* ('favours', line 1187) shown to Hrothulf by herself and Hrothgar as an advance payment for the same *are* (line 1182) which her nephew will soon have to show his cousins Hrethric and Hrothmund.[8] If she holds any fear that Hrothulf will kill them rather than share power, this cannot be the primary meaning of her words.[9]

It is clear as well from Beowulf's report to Hygelac that he considers Wealhtheow to have been the prime mover of Freawaru's betrothal to Ingeld. Beowulf's term for the queen in retrospect, *friðusibb folca* ('treaty-pledge of the nations', line 2107), appears pointed enough to suggest that the queen, not the king, has driven this match as an attempt to heal an old feud between Danes and Heathobards.[10] In the next fitt, no. XVIII, Wealhtheow shows her appreciation of Beowulf in another way. The poet briefly flashes forward so as to show Wealhtheow's great necklace, which she gives to Beowulf, being stripped off Hygelac's body on the beach in Frisia. Then back into the narrative present, with the applause echoing in Heorot. Wealhtheow makes a speech to Beowulf, calling him *hyse* ('young man', line 1217), and urging him to commute this necklace in any way he sees fit (*'bruc þisses beages... þisses hrægles neot... geþeoh telaˊ*, lines 1216–18).[11] Then she begs a favour:

> 'cen þec mid cræfte,   ond þyssum cnyhtum wes
> lara liðe;   ic þe þæs lean geman.
> Hafast þu gefered,   þæt ðe feor ond neah
> ealne wideferhþ   weras ehtigað,
> egne swa side   swa sæ bebugeð
> windgeard, weallas.   Wes, þenden þu lifige,
> æþeling, eadig!   Ic þe an tela
> sincgestreona.   Beo þu suna minum
> dædum gedefe,   dreamhealdende!
> Her is æghwylc eorl   oþrum getrywe,
> modes milde,   mandrihtne hold;
> þegnas sindon geþwære,   þeod ealgearo,
> druncne dryhtguman   doð swa ic bidde.' (*Beo* 1219–31)

   [8] Lee, 'Character from Archetype', 172–4.

   [9] For pathos but no brains in Wealhtheow's speech, see Shippey, *Beowulf*, 33: 'no-one can mistake its tone of fear.'

   [10] On the generality of *friðusibb* and related terms, see Sklute, '*Freoðuwebbe* in Old English Poetry', 204–10, at 208; F. Battaglia, '*Sib* in *Beowulf*', *In Geardagum*, 20 (1999), 27–47. Irving (*Rereading Beowulf*, 61) treats the Ingeld-match as Hrothgar's, not Wealhtheow's, failure of judgement.

   [11] The poet in *Widsith* commutes treasures for (his deceased father's) land; see *Wid* 88–96, discussed in Campbell, 'The Sale of Land and the Economics of Power', 32–4.

['Declare yourself with skill, and be kind in giving instruction to these boys; for this, I will remember a reward for you. You have brought it to pass that far and wide men will respect you for ever and always, just as far as the sea, the wind-enclosure, surrounds coast-walls. Be, for as long as you live, a prince of good fortune! I will grant you treasure as is right. You be gracious to my son in your deeds, O joyful one! In this place each noble is true to the other, generous of heart, loyal to his man and master; thegns are in harmony, the nation is absolutely prepared, having drunk their fill the men of the retinue do as I ask them.']

Ealgearo for what? This speech, too, is public, for the poet has already told us that Wealhtheow *fore þæm werede spræc* ('spoke before the host', line 1215). So we must regard as secondary any inference of pathos, that the queen is asking Beowulf to save her sons from Hrothulf, in spite of Beowulf's last words to Hrothgar inviting his son Hrethric to visit the Geats (lines 1836–9).[12] On the face of it, Wealhtheow uses her speech to give notice of Hrothgar's death or decline and Hrothulf's imminent rise to power; also, with the words *lara liðe*, to keep Beowulf in his place: like a *lareow* or tutor to her sons, sitting at their side, but at arm's length from her daughter. Depending on whether her word *æþeling* on line 1225 is a nominative complement to the imperative *wes* on the line before, rather than a vocative, Wealhtheow could further be exhorting Beowulf to be a happy subject for the rest of his life. He is royal only through his mother. The editor's comma after *æþeling* on this line of Wealhtheow's speech seems unnecessary. Hrothulf, given that the poet has linked him with Hrothgar in the phrase *æghwylc oðrum trywe* on line 1165, is probably to be seen as the intended referent of her identical words on line 1228. That is to say, Wealhtheow tells Beowulf that Hrothulf's place after Hrothgar is secure and that all other retainers will support him because she, who pours for everyone in Heorot, has fixed it.[13]

So the company turns in, and before long Grendel's Mother surprises them, murdering Æschere in exchange for her son. Beowulf, led once more to Grendel's Mere, arms himself there for a second battle with a monster. Before he dives, however, he reminds Hrothgar, perhaps with a touch of sarcasm, to think of *hwæt wit geo spræcon* ('what the two of us spoke of earlier', line 1476), *þæt þu me a wære forðgewitenum on fæder stæle* ('that you would always stand for me in the role of a father, should I depart this life', lines 1478–9).[14] To be a father in this life, is what Hrothgar's words had promised. It does not bode well for his new kinship with Beowulf that Hrothgar and his men leave the scene, believing him dead, when the first blood rises to the top of Grendel's Mere (lines 1600–5). His faith in Beowulf fails to match his earlier words, with *gelyfan*, on line 655 (cf. lines 608

[12] As inferred by Sklute, '*Freoðuwebbe* in Old English Poetry', 207–8; but discounted by Irving, *Rereading Beowulf*, 43.
[13] See Irving, *Rereading Beowulf*, 61: 'she moves instinctively away from him [Hrothgar] toward where the real power lies'; and Damico, *Beowulf's Wealhtheow and the Valkyrie Tradition*, 6: 'the queen states unambiguously that the warriors in the hall pay her homage and obedience.'
[14] On Beowulf's more youthful emotions, see Lee, 'Character from Archetype', 97–104.

and 627). When Beowulf returns to Heorot with Grendel's head and the giants' sword, Hrothgar alludes no further to their earlier exchange.

Yet the matter of the king's promise remains. The giant-made sword-hilt is passed to Hrothgar, proof of Beowulf's victory. When he delivers his central speech (lines 1700–84), we might expect him to confirm his earlier promise of kinship. At least it might be said that Beowulf expects to hear more on this theme. Indeed Hrothgar starts off encouragingly, stating that Beowulf was *geboren betera* ('born better', line 1703). By this he appears to mean that Beowulf's achievements have made up for the maternal source of his royal blood. He reaffirms Beowulf's new glory, reiterates the pledge of yesterday, but then delivers it only in symbolic form:

> 'Blæd is aræred
> geond widwegas,   wine min Beowulf,
> ðin ofer þeoda gehwylce.   Eal þu hit geþyldum healdest,
> mægen mid modes snyttrum.   Ic sceal mine gelæstan
> freoðe,[15] swa wit furðum spræcon.   Ðu scealt to frofre weorþan
> eal langtwidig   leodum þinum,
> hæleðum to helpe.' (*Beo* 1703–9)

['Fame is raised up on roads through distant regions, my friend Beowulf, your fame over each and every nation. All this power you are keeping with patience, with wisdom of mind. I shall fulfil my agreement, just as the two of us spoke earlier. You shall become a comfort, all long-lasting, to your people, an aid to men.']

As we have seen, these words recall Simeon's verses to Jesus in the Temple in Luke 2: 30–2. They might at first characterize Hrothgar benevolently in a holy light.[16] Yet Hrothgar is sly in his apparent awareness, through the idea of *geþyld* ('patience', line 1705), of what must be his idea of Beowulf's impatience to seal the friendship promised him the day before.[17] These lines of Hrothgar's are also meant to be emphatic within *Beowulf* as a whole, in that the length of three of them is extended beyond the norm of four stressed syllables to six (the other two cases of extended hypermetrics are lines 1163–8 and 2995–6).[18] Thus there is an anticlimax in the poet's sudden return to a line of four syllables on line 1708. If Beowulf was hoping for a statement of his inauguration as the next solace, *frofor*, to the Danes (like 'Beowulf' in lines 13–14), Hrothgar is putting him off. Hrothgar avoids the material promise in the words *niwe sibbe* (line 949),

---

[15] *Beowulf*, ed. Zupitza, 78–9, esp. 78 n. 20: 'I think the MS. has *freoðe*, not *freode*; although the left half of the cross stroke in *ð* has entirely faded, yet the place where it was is discernible, and the right half of it is left.' Read as *freode* (i.e. 'friendship') by Thorkelin: *Beowulf*, 4th edn. ed. Wrenn and Bolton, 163.

[16] Irving, *Rereading Beowulf*, 54.

[17] Mitchell and Robinson (*Beowulf*, 104) translate *geþyldum* as 'with equanimity', arguing that 'Hrothgar seems to be praising Beowulf for not letting his fame and greatness go to his head.'

[18] Michael Lapidge dismisses lines 2995–6, but apparently not the other groups, as an interpolation, in 'The Archetype of *Beowulf*', 37–8.

to join Beowulf to his family. Instead, his following speech is couched in the language of parental wisdom, a father advising his son.[19] For Beowulf not a political, but a spiritual kinship is now on offer. Although it may not be to Hrothgar's credit why he does this, his speech exceeds his earlier offer by granting Beowulf a spiritual reward, the wisdom of seeking the *ece rædas* ('eternal rewards', line 1760) by which we must judge Beowulf when he becomes king of Geatland; also a heap of treasures. Whether or not on the latter account, Beowulf is said to be *glædmod* when the speech ends ('minded to be gracious', line 1785).[20]

On leaving Heorot, Beowulf proffers his uncle's army to help Hrothgar in any hour of need (lines 1830–5). Here he appears to be anticipating an attack on Heorot such as that which is delivered in the event by Ingeld and the Heathobards, as the poet has told us (lines 81–5; cf. *Wid* 45–9). The poet's sense of this peril may be read in his otherwise odd image of the *hrefn blaca* ('shining black raven'), a bird of battle, singing at dawn *bliðheort* ('with joyful heart', lines 1801–2) to the sleeping troops of Heorot.[21] Beowulf prepares to leave. He claims that Hrothgar has treated the Geats well, but his words go further. There is a hint that Hrothgar could have given more:

'Gif ic þonne on eorþan   owihte mæg
þinre modlufan   maran tilian,
gumena dryhten,   ðonne ic gyt dyde,
guðgeweorca,   ic beo gearo sona.' (*Beo* 1822–5)

['If, then, there is any way on earth that I can gain a greater love of your heart than I have now done, O lord of men, with deeds of battle, I will be ready immediately.']

There is a taint of sarcasm in his speech, for his promise to be *gearo* echoes Wealhtheow's remark that the Danes are *ealgearo* on line 1230, but only in order to emphasize, through the thousands of new Geatish allies (line 1829) and their forest of spears (line 1834), that once more Denmark will lie helpless before an aggressor. From his ensuing offer to host Hrethric it may also be clear that Beowulf can foresee the later risk to him and his brother posed by Hrothulf, their cousin and rival.

All this asks why Beowulf should need to claim *modlufe mare* from Hrothgar in the first place. Surely Beowulf gained all his love by cleansing Heorot of monsters. And what form would this love take? So far as we can find any meaning

[19] E. Tuttle Hansen, 'Hrothgar's "Sermon" in *Beowulf* as Parental Wisdom', *ASE* 10 (1982), 53–67.
[20] In Irving's view (*Rereading Beowulf*, 64), Hrothgar's sermon has little to offer because it is 'bleakly dominated by the simple fear of death'.
[21] Just as oddly, no one seems to have noted the connection between this raven and Ingeld's attack. Not even Lapidge ('*Beowulf* and Perception', 67), who confines himself to an attribution of vague import: 'the raven was chosen because of its sinister associations with death and carnage, teasing the audience (as it were) with the anticipation of yet another slaughter-attack, and then dispelling the tension by allowing the raven, improbably, to announce the light of day.' S. H. Horowitz compares this bird with Noah's raven, in 'The Ravens in *Beowulf*', *JEGP* 80 (1981), 502–11.

in *mare*'s comparative form, Hrothgar's 'greater love of heart' would mean access to his daughter. Hrothgar probably catches Beowulf's drift, for his reply, with its elegant vision of Beowulf as Hygelac's successor, makes it publicly clear that he will not be Hrothgar's:

> 'Wen ic talige,
> gif þæt gegangeð,   þæt ðe gar nymeð,
> hild heorugrimme   Hreþles eaferan,
> adl oþðe iren   ealdor ðinne,
> folces hyrde,   ond þu þin feorh hafast,
> þæt þe Sæ-Geatas   selran næbben
> to geceosenne   cyning ænigne,
> hordweard hæleþa,   gyf þu healdan wylt
> maga rice.' (*Beo* 1845–53)

['I expect, if it turns out that spear, sword-fierce battle, sickness, or iron blade takes off Hrethel's offspring, your chieftain, the guardian of his people, and you have your life, that Geats of the Seas may not have any better man than you to elect as their king, as a keeper of their heroes' hoard, if you wish to hold your kinsmen's kingdom.']

So Beowulf has his answer. Hrothgar's speech is both gracious, a little condescending, and finally slighting: with *Sæ-Geatas* ('Geats of the Seas'), he may imply a lack of landed territory; for the Danes are never compounded with OE *sæ-* in any of their names in this poem. Yet Hrothgar's words are also politically opportune. They echo those of Wealhtheow (*maga rice*, on lines 1178–9), which pointedly bar Beowulf from an alliance with Danish kindred. Instead, Beowulf may take a more public pleasure in opening a new trade network between Denmark and Geatland (lines 1855–65). In the context of the *niw sib* Hrothgar promised earlier, his term for this network, *sib gemæne* ('a common relationship', 1857), represents a shift of meaning. At its least offensive, Hrothgar's reuse of *sib* tells Beowulf that 'trade' is the closest kinship with Denmark he can expect.

If Hrothgar's parting speech is evasive, more characteristic of the 'empty formulas and patches' with which Irving characterizes him, the spiritual value of his earlier speech on pride rings true.[22] The kinship which he promised Beowulf nearly a thousand lines earlier, having left the *brydbur* presumably after speaking with Freawaru (lines 920–49), has not come to pass. The question of who marries Freawaru has been a leitmotif for even longer, ever since the poet's allusion to the Heathobards on lines 81–5; the climax is reached in Beowulf's initial report to Hygelac in lines 2016–69; *Widsith* tells us that Hrothulf takes joint command when Ingeld attacks, while the Norse analogues imply that later he kills one if not both of his cousins, Hrothgar's sons (see below); and the poet's allusions to Heoroweard on line 2161 and to kindred betrayal in lines 2166–9

---

[22] Irving, *Rereading Beowulf*, 60.

predict the undoing of King Hrothulf (as Hrólfr is undone by Hjǫrvarðr) as an even remoter consequence of Freawaru's marriage. For the first two-thirds of *Beowulf*, in this way, it appears that the poet has chosen to present Beowulf as Ingeld's rival.

BEOWULF'S PREDICTION ABOUT INGELD

Although Beowulf never meets Ingeld, the poet throws the two men into juxtaposition when he lets Beowulf predict the outcome of Ingeld's marriage with Freawaru in lines 2021–69. It is puzzling that Beowulf here should present such a fully formed vision of Freawaru's wedding plans, not as a by-product or embellishment, but as the prelude of his report for Hygelac when he comes home. This is a speech above all critical of Hrothgar's wisdom. Just when we expect to hear of Beowulf's glory with the Grendels, the young man diverts us for forty-eight lines with a prediction about Hrothgar's daughter. If Freawaru in *Beowulf* is no more than how she first seems, a name in an allusion of little relevance to the hero of this poem, then the length of Beowulf's speech must be taken as a sign of the poet's loss of control. Yet this is far from being the case. The poet alludes to Ingeld, Freawaru's destined husband, early with a *chiaroscuro* image of Heorot, newly built and *horngeap* ('horn-gabled', line 82) while it awaits the flames of battle:

> ne wæs hit lenge þa gen
> þæt se ecghete   aþumsweorum
> æfter wælniðe   wæcnan scolde. (*Beo* 83–5)

[nor was it then yet at hand that sword-hate should awake after murderous enmity between father- and son-in-law]

As we have seen in the foregoing chapter, the poet times his premonition as if he had borrowed it from Aeneas' innocent remark on Carthage (*Aen.* I. 437–8). In the lines from *Beowulf*, the words *wælnið* ('murderous enmity') and *wæcnan* ('awake') on line 85 resemble compounds which the poet later uses to tell the story: Ingeld's bride will anger his people, the Heathobards, on whom the Danes inflicted a defeat; one of the Heathobards will *wigbealu weccean* ('rouse the evil of war', line 2046) with another, the son of a man whom the Danes killed; after a fight at the bridal feast Ingeld will grow to feel *wælniðas* (line 2065) towards his Danish in-laws; we know that these feelings will lead to his attack on Hrothgar. The term *wælnið wera* ('murderous enmity of men', line 3000) later occurs among the Geatish Messenger's words for the wars which his people may expect after Beowulf's death. Nonetheless, it is striking that the word *wælnið* appears twice to describe Ingeld in *Beowulf*; and the compound '*heaðo*wylmas' ('battle-surges') on line 82 might further recall the '*Heaðo*-Beardan' who burn Heorot down. In this way the story of Ingeld is far from being *Beowulf*'s occasional embellishment. Rather, as we have seen in the frequency of the poet's asides, it is the leitmotif of Beowulf's three days in Denmark.

Formally, at least, Ingeld is the subject of a prediction which Beowulf makes to his uncle about the chances of a planned Danish–Heathobard alliance. Once Hygelac has finished chiding Beowulf for helping Hrothgar against his tearful entreaties (lines 1987–98), the hero replies with an account of his welcome in Heorot (line 2000), of his success on the mission against Grendel (lines 2005–9), and of his status in the court of Hrothgar, who gave him a seat next to his own sons (line 2013). The Danish host rejoiced, Beowulf says, nor did he ever see greater festivity under heaven's vault (lines 2013–16); at times the queen crossed the floor to show young warriors favour, giving one or other a bracelet before returning to her seat (lines 2016–19). After Wealhtheow comes her daughter:

> 'Hwilum for duguðe   dohtor Hroðgares
> eorlum on ende   ealuwæge bær
> þa ic Freaware   fletsittende
> nemnan hyrde   þær hio nægled sinc
> hæleðum sealde.' (*Beo* 2020–4)

['At times before the tried men's troop Hrothgar's daughter carried an ale-cup for the warriors to use in turn, she whom I heard called Freawaru by men sitting on the benches, where she gave each hero a studded vessel.']

It is worth noting that Hrothgar, although he honours Beowulf in the seating arrangement, has told him neither his daughter's name nor her future. Beowulf by implication has had to find these things out for himself. He goes on:

> 'Sio gehaten is,
> geong goldhroden,   gladum suna Frodan;
> hafað þæs geworden   wine Scyldinga,
> rices hyrde,   ond þæt ræd talað
> þæt he mid ðy wife   wælfæhða dæl
> sæcca gesette.   Oft seldan hwær
> æfter leodhryre   lytle hwile
> bongar bugeð   þeah seo bryd duge.' (*Beo* 2024–31)[23]

['She is promised, young and gold-adorned, to the gracious son of Froda; concerning that man it has occurred to the lord and friend of the Scyldings, their kingdom's keeper, and he counts it a profitable plan, that with this woman he may settle a share of deadly feuds, of conflicts. Often it is the case that anywhere after a nation's defeat the death-spear is seldom lowered even for a little while, though the bride may do.']

It turns out that Beowulf believes Hrothgar is wrong to hope that Freawaru's marriage to Ingeld will end the feuding which, as we discover, has long set the Heathobards against the Danes. Ingeld's avowed benevolence sits uneasily with

---

[23] On the use of *dugan* ('to avail') with female potential, see North, 'Metre and Meaning in *Wulf and Eadwacer*', 38 (cf. 44).

this use of a patronymic to describe him, for Froda, his father, was killed by the people now offering Freawaru. It is clear, as Beowulf shows in lines 2029–31, that the Heathobards will need more than a Danish bride to forget their *leodhryre* ('nation's defeat', line 2030). As Freawaru comes in, Ingeld will join his people in their dawning recognition of the various weapons and treasures on her retinue:

> 'Mæg þæs þonne ofþyncan   ðeod*ne* [MS -en] Heaðo-Beardna
> ond þegna gehwam   þara leoda
> þonne he mid fæmnan   on flett gæð:
> dryhtbearn Dena   duguða biwenede,
> on him gladiað   gomelra lafe,
> heard ond hringmæl   Heaða-Bear[d]na gestreon
> þenden hie ðam wæpnum   wealdan moston.' (*Beo* 2032–8)

['It can seem to go too far to the lord of the Heathobards, and to each of the thegns of those princes, when he walks on to the floor with his bride: [to see] the sons of the Danish host lavishly entertained, on them gleam ancestors' heirlooms, the strong and ring-patterned treasures which had belonged to the Heathobards while they might wield their weapons'.]

The last line, in particular, adapts a formula which occurs elsewhere, notably in *Maldon* (*c*.991–) 14–15, 95, and especially 83 (*þa hwile þe hi wæpna wealdan moston*).[24] Since the formula in these instances describes a doomed army, it may do so in *Beowulf* as well; and with this phrase it appears that the Heathobards commemorate their past defeat in battle against the Danes. Here Fitt XXIX ends and a new one, an unmarked XXX, begins. The use of *oð ðæt* ('and then') as an adverbial phrase on line 2029 following, at the head of Fitt XXX, is paralleled in line 1740 in which the words *oð þæt* initiate Fitt XX[V]: in both cases the new fitt marks a turning point.

> [XXX]   'Oð ðæt hie forlæddan   to ðam lindplegan
> swæse gesiðas   ond hyra sylfra feorh.' (*Beo* 2039–40)

['And then they led their dear companions and their own life-blood to destruction in the play of shields']

History will repeat itself, Beowulf predicts, for the Heathobards will go back to war with the Danes:

> 'Þonne cwið æt beore   se ðe beah gesyhð,
> eald æscwiga   se ðe eall geman
> garcwealm gumena   —him bið grim sefa—
> onginneð geomormod   geongum cempan
> þurh hreðra gehygd   higes cunnian,
> wigbealu weccean   ond þæt word acwyð:
> "Meaht ðu, min wine,   mece gecnawan

---

[24] The phrase *wealdan motan* occurs also in *Beo* 442, 2574, 2827, and 2984.

þone þin fæder   to gefeohte bær
under heregriman   hindeman siðe,
dyre iren,   þær hyne Dene slogon,
weoldon wælstowe,   syððan Wiðergyld læg,
æfter hæleþa hryre   hwate Scyldungas?
Nu her þara banena   byre nathwylces
frætwum hremig   on flet gæð,
morðres gylpeð   ond þone maþðum byreð
þone þe ðu mid rihte   rædan sceoldest."' (*Beo* 2041–56)

['Then at the beer-drinking an old spear-fighter will speak, who sees a precious ornament, who remembers all that lance-killing of men (his disposition is fierce), with sad mind he begins to explore the courage of a young champion through the thoughts of his heart, to rouse the evil of war, and he will say these words: "Can you, my friend, recognize that sword, an expensive blade, which your father was carrying, while he wore his war-mask for the last time, to the fight where the Danes slew him, where they took possession of the killing-ground once Withergyld lay dead, fierce Scyldings after the fall of heroes? Now in this place the boy of one or other of those killers, exulting in his trappings, walks on to the floor, boasts of the murder and bears the treasure which you by right should have in your power."']

Asking him to look at his father's sword, now strapped to the son of the Dane who killed him, the old spearman begins to work on the young Heathobard's sense of grievance. Withergyld is probably to be seen as the boy's father: the name is also found in *Wid* 124, but without an attribution to a tribe; in the form *wiþer-gield*, it is possible that the poet of *Beowulf* has invented this name, or Beowulf himself is meant to, as 'Recompense', an (otherwise unattested) allegory for the to and fro of a feud.[25] The second element *-gield* in any case resembles a suffix *-geld* in *Ingeld*, the name of the Heathobards' king. Beowulf predicts that the old spear-fighter will continue to sow discord:

'Manað swa ond myndgað   mæla gehwylce
sarum wordum   oð ðæt sæl cymeð
þæt se fæmnan þegn   fore fæder dædum
æfter billes bite   blodfag swefeð
ealdres scyldig;   him se oðer þonan
losað lifigende,   con him land geare.' (*Beo* 2057–62)

['Thus he will urge and remind at each opportunity with grievous words until a time will come when, having forfeited his life for the deeds of his father, the bride's thegn sleeps bloodstained after the bite of a blade. From that place the other one escapes alive, he knows the country well.']

The second *oð ðæt*, a conjunction at line 2058, refines the meaning of the first one, which is used as an adverb at the beginning of Fitt [XXX] on line 2039. It is inevitable, Beowulf says, that the old feud will lead to a new one. The killer will

[25] See *Beowulf*, ed. Klaeber, 195 (n. to line 2051b).

have the advantage of home ground; Ingeld, the duty of finishing what his people have started:

> 'Þonne bioð gebrocene   on ba healfe
> aðsweord eorla;   syððan Ingelde
> weallað wælniðas   ond him wiflufan
> æfter cearwælmum   colran weorðað.
> Þy ic Heaðo-Bear[d]na   hyldo ne telge,
> dryhtsibbe dæl   Denum unfæcne,
> freondscipe fæstne.' (*Beo* 2063–9)

['Then will be broken on both sides the oath-pledges of noblemen; thereafter in Ingeld murderous enmities will surge and in him, after waves of grief, the love of his wife will cool. For this reason I do not reckon the loyalty of the Heathobards, their part in a military alliance with Danes, to be free of deceit, their pact of friendship firm.']

This is the first and only reference to Ingeld in *Beowulf* by name; in that it occurs within the same clause as *wælniðas*, it seems likely that this passage is intended to provide the link to the image of Heorot in flames in lines 81–5. The person on whom this transformation depends is the unnamed *eald æscwiga*, whose counterpart in the Norse analogues, Starkaðr Stórvirksson, is a giant's grandson, mercenary, friend of Óðinn, and enemy of Þórr. This figure is crucial to nearly all surviving stories of Ingeld's marriage.[26]

Beowulf's meaning is clear, his prediction later borne out by events. It may be assumed that the audience of *Beowulf* knows the outcome: Heathobards will fight Danes. In terms of its plausibility, this premonition of snowballing violence shows Beowulf to be a fine judge of Hygelac's interests, which lie in knowing the strengths and weaknesses of his neighbours. Yet the cause of Beowulf's vehemence lies elsewhere, in that he not only begins but also closes this prediction with reference to Freawaru. Beowulf's interest in Freawaru is consistent with the reward his archetype can expect in five Scandinavian analogues of his tale in which Bǫðvarr bjarki gets a royal Danish bride. In the surviving abstract of *Skjǫldunga saga* (ch. 12), Rolfo Krage has two daughters, Driva and Skur; he marries the first off to a Swede named Witserchus, the second to 'Bodvarus', the Norwegian praised above all others for his courage: *illi filiam Scuram elocavit* ('on him be bestowed his daughter Scura').[27] In Saxo's *Gesta Danorum*, Rolvo sends Biarco to destroy Agnarus (son of Ingellus) who is about to get married to Ruta, Rolvo's sister; Biarco takes on Agnarus and then all his court, slaying them all; then Biarco and Hialto, his comrade, kill an enormous bear:

---

[26] See further below. On the development of the Starkaðr-figure, see Skovgaard-Petersen, *Da Tidernes Herre var nær*, 136–78. Elsewhere I suggest that the same figure re-emerges as the 'anhaga' in *The Wanderer*: 'Boethius and the Mercenary', 75–80. Whether or not by chance, there are two other correspondences between *Beowulf* and *The Wanderer* in the phrases *hreðra gehygd* (only in *Beo* 2045 and *Wan* 72) and *ond þæt word acwyð* (*Beo* 2046 and *Wan* 91 (with *þas* for *þæt*)).

[27] *Danakonunga Sögur*, ed. Bjarni, 28.

His facinorum virtutibus clarissimas optimatum familiaritates adeptus etiam regi percarus evasit, sororem eius Rutam uxorem ascivit victique sponsam victoriæ præmium habuit.[28]

[By such deeds of courage Biarco made distinguished friendships among the nobility and even became a firm favourite of the king, who gave him his sister Ruta for a wife, the betrothed of the late victim [Agnarus], as a prize of victory.]

In Saxo's translation of the (mostly lost) *Bjarkamál*, Hialto asks Ruta for Biarco's whereabouts in the defence of Lejre against Hiarwarthus, Rolvo's brother-in-law; and Ruta also gives aid to Biarco towards the end.[29] In *Hrólfs saga kraka*, Böðvarr attempts anything asked of him and wins so much honour with King Hrólfr that *hann eignadist hanz einka döttur Drifu* ('he married his only daughter Drífa', ch. 24).[30] Lastly, in the *Bjarkarímur*, probably of the fifteenth century, it is said that *stillir gaf honum stórbú tólf og stolta dóttur sína* (the 'monarch' Hrólfur gave Bjarki 'twelve great farmsteads and his proud daughter', VIII. 12); whether this is Drífa or Skúr (both announced as Hrólfur's daughters in V. 28), we do not know.[31] On the basis of a comparison with these Bjarki-analogues, it may be deduced that the poet of *Beowulf* worked with a 'Beowulf'-story in which Hrothulf gave Beowulf a Scylding princess.

In *Beowulf*, however, the same champion does not get the royal bride whom we discover to have been in the Danish court all along. For one thing, we have seen (in Chapter 2) that the poet of *Beowulf* has probably moved his hero away from Hrothulf backwards in time into Hrothgar's service. Hrothgar's context contains the legend of Ingeld, to which Beowulf must react. What the poet had to work with here may be seen from the following suggested outline of Ingeld's story, as this was before its diverse adaptations in some of *Beowulf*'s analogues.

INGELD IN *WIDSITH* AND SCANDINAVIAN ANALOGUES

There is a brief yet climactic reference to Ingeld in *Widsith*, with Ingeld cited for raiding Denmark in the vanguard of a Heathobard attack:

> Hroþwulf ond Hroðgar   heoldon lengest
> sibbe ætsomne   suhtorfædran,
> siþþan hy forwræcon   wicinga cynn
> ond Ingeldes   ord forbigdan,
> forheowan æt Heorote   Heaðobeardna þrym. (*Wid* 45–9)

[Hrothwulf and Hrothgar, uncle and nephew, had kept their family united for the longest time when they drove off a tribe of pirates (*or*: men from Vík), crushed Ingeld's front line, and at Heorot cut down the glory of the Heathobards.]

---

[28] *Gesta Danorum*, ed. Olrik and Ræder, 51 (II. vi. 11). *Saxo Grammaticus*, trans. Fisher, i. 55.
[29] *Gesta Danorum*, ed. Olrik and Ræder, 55 (II. vii. 10) and 60 (II. vii. 25–6).
[30] *Hrólfs saga*, ed. Slay, 86; see *Hrólfs Saga Kraka*, ed. Finnur, 74. Earlier (ed. Slay, 48; ed. Finnur, 44) it is said that Hrólfr had two daughters, Skúr as well as Drífa.
[31] *Hrólfs Saga Kraka*, ed. Finnur, 161.

Mitchell and Robinson take *forwræcon* as a pluperfect, with the line meaning 'when they had driven away', but Ingeld's raid can hardly mark the beginning of a long period in which Hrothulf rules jointly with his uncle.[32] I take these lines to hail a long-lasting association between Hrothgar and Hrothulf which is ended by Ingeld's raid. Independently of *Beowulf*, these lines from *Widsith* tell us of an Anglo-Saxon legend in which Ingeld attacked Hrothgar and Hrothwulf in Heorot. This story would appear to be a sequel to the story of Ingeld's marriage. In *Beowulf* Ingeld's raid also triggers the end of Hrothgar's reign. Later in the poem, the poet refers to future Danish *fácenstafas* ('criminal acts') in *Beo* 1018–19 and gives hints of Unferth's treachery to come in *Beo* 1162–8 (the first and longest hypermetric sequence in *Beowulf*). These references fall on either side of the Finnsburh episode (1068–1159), whose story of feud and betrayal, given the poet's prefiguration of Wealhtheow in Hildeburh, anticipates such events in Heorot.[33] But the poet of *Beowulf* makes it clear that Hrothgar lives into a peaceful old age (lines 1885–7). In the imagined background, therefore, it seems Hrothulf kills his cousins after he succeeds their father as sole king of Denmark.

The relationship, if any, between *Widsith* and *Beowulf* is considered in my first chapter, in which I suggest that the poet of *Widsith* shows no knowledge of *Beowulf*, whereas it is possible that the poet of *Beowulf* consulted either *Widsith* or a work from which *Widsith* was derived. In respect of the *Beowulf*-poet's source-material on Ingeld, no other vernacular work survives with which to get an impression of its contents. Only the Scandinavian analogues may tell us the shape of Ingeld's story in the poet's source.

At first glance Ingeld's Norse analogues appear quite dissimilar. The chief difference between them and the English sources is tribal affiliation. In *Widsith*, and in *Beowulf*, Ingeld is a Heathobard and his wife's kinsmen are Danes, whereas his counterpart in the two extant Norse analogues is a Dane, his wife's family either Swedes or Germans. A related figure in the Helgi Lays, Hǫðbroddr, is probably a Norwegian; whereas in Saxo's *Gesta Danorum* Hothbroddus is a Swede. There are other problems. Snorri Sturluson, an Icelander with Norwegian affiliations, makes no allusion to the Ingjaldr-story, either in his *Edda* or elsewhere, despite knowing *Skjǫldunga saga* in which the story of 'Ingjaldr' was told. Nor is there is a single allusion to Ingjaldr in the extant works of the skaldic and Eddic poets of Iceland and Norway.[34] Even among the Danes themselves, with the exception of Saxo who knew some Icelandic literature, it seems that

---

[32] *Beowulf*, ed. Mitchell and Robinson, 199. This meaning is also given in *Beowulf and its Analogues*, trans. and ed. Garmonsway, Simpson, and Ellis Davidson, 127–8 (II E.1).

[33] See Tolkien, *Finn and Hengest*, ed. Bliss; *Finnsburh: Fragment and Episode*, ed. D. K. Fry (London, 1974); North, *Heathen Gods*, 64–70; A. H. Olsen, 'Gender Roles', in Bjork and Niles (eds.), *Beowulf Handbook*, 311–24, esp. 316–17.

[34] See *Gylfaginning*, ed. Faulkes, 169; *Skáldskaparmál*, ed. Faulkes, ii. 483–4; *Háttatal*, ed. Faulkes, 160.

'Ingell' was then taken as irrelevant to royal Danish history: Sven Aggesen omits him from his work, as do the compilers of the *Chronica Roskildense* and *Lethrense* from theirs.

Our first two analogues are *Skjǫldunga saga* and the older *Langfeðgatal*. As already shown, *Skjǫldunga saga* is thought to have been written in Iceland at the beginning of the thirteenth century.[35] Its author knew some tales about Danish kings which were no longer available to the anonymous authors of the *Chronica Roskildense* and *Lethrense* of *c*.1160–80, or to Sven Aggesen in *c*.1185.[36] Of the Danish historians, only Saxo includes a version of the Ingeld-legend in his *Gesta Danorum* shortly before the end of the twelfth century. In his search for this story from old Danish history, Saxo relied partly on a version of *Skjǫldunga saga*, whose own author, among his varied sources, made use of a genealogy named the *Langfeðgatal* ('list of forefathers'). Bjarni Guðnason has suggested that this genealogy, which both Saxo and Sven consulted separately, was put together before 1133 by the priest Sæmundr *inn fróði* ('the learned') Sigfússon.[37] Sæmundr numbered his family's generations probably on the model of either *Háleygjatal* (composed in Trøndelag by Eyvindr skáldaspillir in *c*.985) or the older *Ynglingatal* (by Þjóðólfr of Hvinir, in Grenland, *c*.890), or of both poems.[38] These poems were probably part of Sæmundr's material, useful compendia of kings' names respectively from Sweden and Norway. It is worth noting, however, that there never seems to have been a similar poem in honour of the Skjǫldungar of Denmark. The impulse to compile a *Skjǫldunga saga* and other Scandinavian histories came after Sæmundr's death, ultimately from the *Gesta regum Brittanniae* of Geoffrey of Monmouth (*c*.1135).[39] The leading source for *Skjǫldunga saga* was the lineage which probably Sæmundr compiled.[40] In this lineage, in eleventh place, is Fróði *frækni* ('the bold'), father of Ingjaldr *Starkaðarfóstri* ('Starkaðr's foster-son'), in twelfth. So in the twelfth century Ingjaldr Fróðason was held to be a Dane.

Sæmundr established a school in Oddi at which later generations of Icelanders learned some Latin and also the native lore of genealogies, laws, and skaldic and Eddic poems.[41] Snorri Sturluson grew up there in 1183–97; probably in the 1220s,

[35] My text is from *Danakonunga Sögur*, ed. Bjarni, 1–38. This supersedes the edition in *Arngrimae Jonae Opera Latine conscripta*, ed. Jón Helgason, Bibliotheca Arnamagnæana 9 (Copenhagen, 1950), 331–456.
[36] *Danakonunga Sögur*, ed. Bjarni, pp. lii–lxx. Jakob, 'Icelandic Traditions of the Scyldings', 49. *Works of Sven Aggesen*, trans. and comm. Christiansen, 18–23.
[37] *Flat*, I. 4. See Bjarni, *Um Skjöldungasögu*, 150–80. On Sæmundr, see D. Edwards Whaley, 'Sæmundr Sigfússon inn fróði', in Pulsiano and Wolf (eds.), *Medieval Scandinavia*, 636–7.
[38] *Danakonunga Sögur*, ed. Bjarni, pp. lii–lvi.
[39] *Danakonunga Sögur*, ed. Bjarni, p. lxi. On an Icelandic translation of this work, *Breta sǫgur*, see J. Louis-Jensen, 'Breta sǫgur', in Pulsiano and Wolf (eds.), *Medieval Scandinavia*, 57–8.
[40] *Danakonunga Sögur*, ed. Bjarni, pp. liv–lv.
[41] [E. O.] G. Turville-Petre, *Origins of Icelandic Literature* (Oxford, 1953; repr. w. corrections 1967), 220–2.

he wrote his *Ynglinga saga* on the model of *Skjǫldunga saga*.[42] During this time Snorri also drew the tale of Hrólfr kraki in *Skáldskaparmál*, in his prose *Edda*, from *Skjǫldunga saga*.[43] An early saga of Hrólfr which Snorri also used, and from which the fourteenth-century *Hrólfs saga kraka* and fifteenth-century ballad *Bjarkarímur* are derived, was itself probably influenced by *Skjǫldunga saga* (although no Ingjaldr is cited either by Snorri or in *Hrólfs saga* or in *Bjarkarímur*).[44] *Skjǫldunga saga* was probably written at Oddi in the first decade of the thirteenth century, possibly with the aid of Bishop Páll of Skálholt (pallium 1195–1211), who was the son of Jón Loptsson of the Oddaverjar and could himself claim descent from Skjǫldr in line with the *Langfeðgatal*.[45]

The Icelandic text of *Skjǫldunga saga* was destroyed in the Copenhagen Royal Library fire of 1728. Six vellum leaves, written *c.*1300, survive from another codex (the 'Sögubrot') and contain nothing of relevance to Ingjaldr.[46] Otherwise this saga must be read through a Latin translation or adaptation which had fortunately been made in 1596 by the Icelandic antiquarian Arngrímur Jóns-son.[47] Arngrímur's tale of Ingjaldr, or 'Ingialldus', is found in chapters 9–10 of his *Rerum Danicarum fragmenta*. In chapter 9 we start with the father of Ingialldus: King Frodo (IV) of the Danes, half-brother of King Alo of Sweden. Frodo is urged by his earls to have Alo killed, lest he attack Denmark; to this end he sends Starcardus (i.e. Starkaðr Stórvirksson), a warrior recently returned from south-eastern Europe, to take service with Alo and kill him. Starcardus stabs Alo in his bath. Stricken by remorse, however, he leaves Denmark for Sweden and is absent when Iorundus, the new king of Sweden, assassinates King Frodo one night as he performs a heathen sacrifice. Iorundus does this with the help of one of his earls, Svertingus, whose daughter is married to Ingialldus. Svertingus and Ingialldus then agree on a settlement for the death of the latter's father. In this story it is Halfdanus, Ingialldus' brother, who avenges their father Frodo (by slaying Svertingus' twelve sons).[48] Starcardus, having returned from Sweden, persuades Ingialldus to repudiate the daughter of Svertingus. Ingialldus bestows a third of his kingdom on Halfdanus, but then kills his brother in order to rule Denmark alone. Yet Ingialldus marries Halfdanus' widow. Many years later he is killed by Roas and Helgo, sons of Halfdanus.[49] In this version, it is clear that

[42] *Heimskringla I*, ed. Bjarni, pp. xlix–xliv. Sigurður Nordal, *Snorri Sturluson*, 2nd edn. (Rey-kjavik, 1973), 12–13, 23–8, and 49–53.

[43] *Skáldskaparmál*, ed. Faulkes, i. 51–60, at 58–9 (chs. 43–4); see *Danakonunga Sögur*, ed. Bjarni, 43–5 (chs. 54–5).

[44] *Fornaldarsögur Norðurlanda*, ed. Guðni and Bjarni, ii. 1–93; *Hrólfs saga*, ed. Slay; *Hrólfs Saga Kraka*, ed. Finnur; see *Danakonunga Sögur*, ed. Bjarni, p. xx.

[45] *Danakonunga Sögur*, ed. Bjarni, pp. xv–xvii and lxix–lxx.

[46] Ibid. 46–71.

[47] Ibid., pp. xix–xxvii; K. Wolf, 'Skjǫldunga saga', in Pulsiano and Wolf (eds.), *Medieval Scandinavia*, 597–8.

[48] *Danakonunga Sögur*, ed. Bjarni, 21–2. *Beowulf and its Analogues*, trans. and ed. Garmonsway, Simpson, and Ellis Davidson, 128–9 (IIE 4) and 242 (VB 5).

[49] *Danakonunga Sögur*, ed. Bjarni, 22–3.

Hrothgar's and Ingeld's counterparts are both contemporaries and enemies. Here, and presumably in *Skjǫldunga saga*, Ingialldus casts off his wife but refrains from avenging his father on her brothers; that task falls to Halfdanus, on whom the rest of his story dwells. But Starcardus does prompt Ingialldus to end his marriage with Svertingus' daughter. In the *Langfeðgatal*, Ingjaldr's byname *Starkaðarfóstri* ('Starkaðr's foster-son') shows that in Scandinavia his connection with Starkaðr was at least as old as the eleventh century.[50] Just as old would be Ingjaldr's rejection of the queen at the prompting of Starkaðr.

Let us consider Saxo's version of the Ingeld-legend in his *Gesta Danorum*. Ingellus, in Book VI of this work, is at first portrayed as a glutton. After his father Frotho's death by the swords of the Saxon Svertingus and his sons, he readily yields to their offer of their sister's hand in marriage, an attempt to atone for this murder.[51] There begins a course of Ingellus' degeneracy with his new German brothers-in-law. Starcatherus, hearing that he has fallen into depravity with former enemies, races back to Denmark. Dressed as a charcoal-burner, he enters King Ingellus' hall and goes to the high seat where he used to sit in the days of Frotho. Ingellus is out, and his queen, not knowing the filthy newcomer, tries to eject him. There is a scene in which Starcatherus almost wrecks the building. Then Ingellus returns, recognizes his old foster-father, and orders the queen to serve him. She does, but without mollifying Starcatherus. During the feast with the sons of Svertingus that follows, he complains that Ingellus has changed the austerity of his Danish forebears for the gourmand ways of Saxon enemies. In stanza after stanza Starcatherus berates Ingellus for befriending the Germans and for eating and drinking like them to excess. After a while he comes to his main theme:[52]

> 'Ære quis sumpto toleraret umquam
> funus amissi redimi parentis
> aut loco patris peteret necati
>   munus ab hoste?
>
> 'Qui valens heres subolesque fausta
> talibus iunctum latus applicaret,
> ut viri nervos vacuaret omnes
>   pactio turpis?
>
> 'Unde, cum regnum tituli canuntur
> et ducum vates memorant triumphos,
> pallio vultum pudibundus abdo
>   pectore tristi.'

---

[50] Ibid., pp. lii–lv, at lv. On the antiquity of the Starkaðr-legend, which seems to have reached Scandinavia from sixth-century Ostrogothic Italy, see Skovgaard-Petersen, *Da Tidernes Herre var nær*, 163–6.

[51] *Gesta Danorum*, ed. Olrik and Ræder, 162. For the whole story in translation: *Saxo Grammaticus*, trans. Fisher, i. 75–95. On Saxo's patriotic intent, see I. Skovgaard-Petersen, 'Saxo, Historia of the Patria', *MScan*, 2 (1969), 54–77; and Friis-Jensen, 'Saxo Grammaticus' Study of the Roman Historiographers', 61–81.

[52] *Gesta Danorum*, ed. Olrik and Ræder, 175–6 (vi. ix. 12–13, at 13); trans. Fisher (*Saxo Grammaticus*, i. 191–2).

['What man would ever permit the killing of his parent to be bought off by taking bribes, ask from a foe payment to atone for a murdered father? Would any sturdy, prosperous successor have let such creatures jostle his side, or would have allowed this despicable bargain to drain all his manly vigour? Thus, when the glories of kings are sung and generals' triumphs are hymned by the poets, I shroud my blushing face in my mantle, sick at heart.']

Saxo modelled this long verse sequence on Horace's *Satires*, in order to lend his adaptation of the (probably Icelandic) original a Roman moral of patriotism.[53] Of interest in the above-cited stanzas is Starcatherus' mention of the *pactio* ('bargain') that Ingellus' marriage with the German princess represents. In due course the sons of Svertingus will see one of their own blood take the throne of Denmark, Starcatherus says. The trappings of this marriage are an incitement to revenge:[54]

> Dum gravem gemmis nitidamque cultu
> aureo gaudes celebrare nuptam,
> nos dolor probro sociatus urit,
>   turpia questos.

['While you delight to honour a bride weighed down with jewels, clad in glittering gold, I am scorched with vexation and shame, lamenting the degradation.']

Ingellus is stung by this tirade and rises up and slaughters his brothers-in-law, breaking their treaty. Starcatherus gleefully returns to hexameters, his usual style:

> 'nam damna moræ probitate rependis,
> torporem animi redimis virtute potenti.'[55]

['Your courage makes reparation for the harm of delay and a strong fortitude redeems your flaccidity.']

In the lines of this poem, with which Saxo closes his Book VI, Starcatherus praises his foster-son, counsels him to expose the Germans' bodies in a field, and tells Ingellus to flee his bride before she bears him a wolf-cub to hurt its own father. There is no aftermath to this tale in Saxo's *Gesta*, although Starcatherus' adventures continue separately there as far as Book VIII. It is clear that one of Saxo's aims in telling this story was to collude with the anti-German nationalism of his day.[56] On the other hand, his old retainer's tirade has much in common with that of the *eald æscwiga* in *Beowulf.* Ingellus carries out his own revenge, just

---

[53] K. Friis-Jensen, 'The Lay of Ingellus and its Classical Models', in K. Friis-Jensen (ed.), *Saxo Grammaticus: A Medieval Author between Norse and Latin Culture* (Copenhagen, 1981), 71–6.

[54] *Gesta Danorum*, ed. Olrik and Ræder, 177 (VI. ix. 16); *Saxo Grammaticus*, trans. Fisher, i. 193.

[55] *Gesta Danorum*, ed. Olrik and Ræder, 178–9 (VI. ix. 19); *Saxo Grammaticus*, trans. Fisher, i. 194.

[56] E. Christiansen, 'Saxo Grammaticus', in Pulsiano and Wolf (eds.), *Medieval Scandinavia*, 566–9, at 568; see his *Works of Sven Aggesen*, 21.

as Ingeld is probably at the head of the *ord* ('vanguard') which attacks the Danes in *Wid* 48.

As noted, the main difference between Anglo-Saxon and Norse versions of Ingeld is his tribe: Ingeld's people are Heathobards, whereas Ingjaldr is a Dane. To find out if the latter was always the case, we can turn to Ingjaldr's story as this is presented in the tales of *Hǫðbroddr* ('battle-spike'). This name has the same form as OE *Heapobeard* ('battle-?beard'). The Norseman who bears it, the savage son of Granmarr, is a figure in *Helgakviða Hundingsbana* I and II, both poems probably of a Norwegian origin in the eleventh century;[57] and as Hothbroddus, son of Earl Regnerus of Sweden, he is also mentioned in Saxo's late twelfth-century *Gesta*. It seems that Hǫðbroddr's tale and Ingjaldr's are branches off the same stem: not only by the common forms of the Heathobard-name, but also in some shared narrative elements. In the Helgi Lays, Hǫðbroddr is presented as the unwanted suitor of a valkyrie named Sigrún, one whom she wants the hero Helgi Sigmundarson to kill (*HHund* I. 18–19; II. 16). Helgi gathers his fleet and puts to sea, making for Frekasteinn; the coast watchman is Guðmundr, Hǫðbroddr's brother, with whom Sinfjǫtli the half-brother of Helgi embarks on an abusive flyting before the battle starts (*HHund* I. 32–46; II. 19–24). The battle ends in defeat and death for Hǫðbroddr (*HHund* I. 53–6); in the second Helgi Lay, for him and also for Sigrún's father and brothers, who fight on his side (*HHund* II. 25–9). In the latter Lay, in particular, Starkaðr is said to be Granmarr's third son and thus Hǫðbroddr's brother (before st. 14); Helgi tells Sigrún about Starkaðr's death when he meets her after the battle:

> 'Enn at Styrkleifom   Starcaðr konungr,
> enn at Hlébiǫrgom   Hrollaugs synir;
> þann sá ec gylfa   grimmúðgastan,
> er barðiz bolr,   var á brot hǫfuð.' (*HHund* II. 27)

['What's more, King Starkaðr [fell] at Styrkleifar, and Hrollaugr's sons at Hlébjǫrg; in him I saw a most fierce-hearted prince, whose trunk fought on when his head was off.']

In Saxo's *Gesta Danorum*, Hothbroddus is a king of Sweden; he conquers lands in the east and then begets two sons. *Nec Orientis victoria contentus*, Saxo says, *Daniam petit eiusque regem Roe tribus proeliis provocatum occidit.*[58] Roe, Saxo's 'Hrothgar', is Helgo's brother and Rolvo's uncle. Having slain Roe, Hothbroddus, the Ingeld-figure, occupies Denmark. Helgo (by now the slayer of Hundingus) is at sea when he hears of Roe's death; coming home, he locks up his son Rolvo in Lejre in order to protect him, then slays the Swedish

---

[57] An eleventh-century Norwegian origin for these poems is argued in A. Holtsmark, 'Kattar sonr', *Saga-Book*, 16 (1963), 144–55.

[58] 'Not content with his victory over the East, he attacked Denmark, challenged Roe, its king, in three battles and slew him.' *Gesta Danorum*, ed. Olrik and Ræder, 48 (II. v. 5). See *Beowulf and its Analogues*, trans. and ed. Garmonsway, Simpson, and Ellis Davidson, 129 and 146–7.

governors. This is how, in Danish terms, *Beowulf*'s 'Halga' (Hrothgar's brother) comes to destroy 'Ingeld':

Ipsum quoque Hothbroddum cum omnibus copiis navali pugna delevit nec solum fratris, sed etiam patriæ iniuriam plenis ultionis armis pensavit. Quo evenit, ut, cui nuper ob Hundingi cædem agnomen incesserat, nunc Hothbrodi strages cognomentum inferret.[59]

[Helgo also destroyed Hothbroddus himself, and all his forces, in a sea-battle. Nor when he carried out vengeance with full might did he think only of his brother's wrongs, but also those of his homeland. From this it happened that he who had lately gained a nickname for the killing of Hundingus now bore a surname for the slaughter of Hothbroddus.]

Saxo takes further pleasure in the humiliations Helgo inflicts on the Swedes, before relating Helgo's decision to retire from Denmark and die in the east. Once again, it seems that Saxo's aim is to glorify the Danes at the expense of their modern neighbours. But in that Hothbroddus attacks the Danish kings Roe, Helgo, and implicitly Rolvo, it is also clear that Saxo preserves a version of Hothbroddus' story closer to that in *Widsith* and *Beowulf*; this version seems to be older than that in the Norwegian Helgi Lays, whose poets have made Helgi into the second son of Sigmundr the Vǫlsung, even while they keep his enmity with Hǫðbroddr (and Starkaðr) in the form of a pitched battle which now takes place in Hǫðbroddr's, not Helgi's, country. Whereas Saxo has no tale connecting Hothbroddus to Helgo and Roe by marriage, the Helgi Lays make Hǫðbroddr into the undesired suitor of a woman whom Helgi must rescue.

It is not hard to deduce in this case how Ingjaldr is related to Hǫðbroddr. This is shown by both *Widsith* (line 48) and *Beowulf* (lines 2032 and 2067), which give the name of Ingeld's tribe as *Heaðobeardan*. One generation before Ingellus, Helgo is said to kill Hothbroddus in revenge for the death of Roe whom Hothbroddus killed when he invaded Denmark. This Hothbroddus does on his third attempt. The fact that Hothbroddus challenges Roe three times, according to Saxo, shows that this story was in more than one version by the time Saxo alluded to it. By the eleventh century one of these had travelled to Norway, where 'Hǫðbroddr' was integrated into the fable of Sigmundr the Vǫlsung. Here, in the two Lays of Helgi Sigmundarson, Hǫðbroddr works as an enemy of the Vǫlsungar, with whom the Danish Helgi has now been identified. Starkaðr, however, remains at the original Heathobard's side and indeed in *HHund* II. 13–14 (prose insert) has now become Hǫðbroddr's brother. Hǫðbroddr's marriage is a detail preserved in the Helgi Lays, but with a Vǫlsung flourish: Sigrún the daughter of Hǫgni is betrothed to Hǫðbroddr, but wishes Helgi (the grandson of Vǫlsungr) to rescue her instead. It is possible that Saxo knew this version of the Hothbrodd-tale in addition to his own, for there were Norwegians in the retinue of his patron, Archbishop Absalon of Lund (pallium

---

[59] *Gesta Danorum*, ed. Olrik and Ræder, 48 (II. v. 6); cf. 63 (III. ii. 1).

1178–1201), who arrived in the Danish kingdom in the 1180s as exiles from King Sverrir (reigned 1177–1202).[60]

The diversity in these Scandinavian tales of Ingjaldr and Hǫðbroddr is instructive. The further back we posit a shared outline for these two analogues, the more Ingjaldr's tale resembles that of Hǫðbroddr. At some point still earlier this was the same story, one in which Ingjaldr was not a Dane but rather a 'Heathobard' from *Haðaland* in Norway.[61] In Denmark in the Viking Age, therefore, it is likely that the Danish name cognate with OIce *Hǫðbroddr* was not a personal but a tribal name, one which belonged to *Ingell*. This Ingell was probably made into a Dane when his father Frothi was confused or deliberately blended with Frothi, the father of Halfdan (the father of Helgi and Roe). Whoever naturalized him as a Dane in this way (probably Sæmundr) made Starkaðr, Ingjaldr's traditional foster-father, into a Danish ally. It is certain that 'Ingeld' (along with 'Starkaðr') was known to both poetic cultures, in England and Scandinavia; and that the tale of his repudiation of a bride, followed by his war against her family, was told in Denmark because the bride's kinsmen were Danish kings: namely Roe and his nephew Rolvo, our Hrothgar and Hroth(w)ulf.

What these correspondences show is that the Ingeld-episode in *Beowulf* and the earliest Danish version of the Ingeld-legend have more in common than might be assumed from a superficial comparison of narratives in *Beowulf*, *Skjǫldunga saga*, and *Gesta Danorum*. Neither in England nor in Denmark would it have been possible to tell of Ingeld without a section on Hrothgar and related Danish kings, consistent with the theme of *Gar-Dena þeodcyninga þrym* ('the glory of the nation-kings of the Spear-Danes') which the poet of *Beowulf* handles in his opening two lines. Yet this does not mean conversely that any tale of Hrothgar brought with it one of Ingeld. The poet who composed *Beowulf*'s source-poem on Ingeld would have chosen the Danish kings as his theme, only to branch off it with the tale of a foreign interloper. This is also the style of the poet of *Beowulf*, whose hero, a Geat, has business in Denmark lasting no more than three days.

In short, the poet of *Beowulf* did not need Ingeld to tell a story of Hrothgar. Since it would be possible to remove all traces of Ingeld from *Beowulf* without altering the narrative of the foreground, it appears that the poet retains him for a purpose. By presenting Ingeld through the thoughts of Beowulf, a new addition to Hrothgar's tale, the poet juxtaposes them so that Ingeld becomes the young king against whom Beowulf, with sharp prescience, defines himself. The poet namely lets Beowulf draw attention to Freawaru's marriage with Ingeld as if he had hoped to win her. The tradition, as we have seen it, does not put Beowulf in Freawaru's time, let alone allow their marriage to take place; nonetheless, our

---

[60] *Works of Sven Aggesen*, trans. and comm. Christiansen, 23 and 82 (n. 58).
[61] Skovgaard-Petersen, *Da Tidernes Herre var nær*, 166–7.

poet spends some time, particularly with Wealhtheow, intimating why it does not. In the rest of this chapter I shall suggest that the poet's model for his new plot in Heorot is Aeneas' bridal quest in Vergil's *Aeneid*, Books VII and XI: particularly his rivalry with Turnus of the Rutuli.

VERGIL RECAST: BOOKS VII AND XI OF THE *AENEID*

So far I have made the case for Vergilian influence on *Beowulf* in my first chapter, strengthening this with parallels in Chapters 2–3 (*Aen.* I, III, and VI). Here we can consider one more. In its politics the initial Danish scene in *Beowulf* resembles the premiss of Vergil's story in the second half of the *Aeneid*. As the Trojans arrive in Latium with their fleet, having taken part in many adventures from Asia Minor through Carthage, it becomes clear that their leader, Aeneas, is destined to vie with King Turnus of the Rutuli for the hand of Lavinia, the only daughter and heir of Latinus and Queen Amata. The Italian lineage of Latinus is first given, consonant with Roman superiority over Greeks. Latinus' offspring is described:

> filius huic fato diuum prolesque uirilis
> nulla fuit, primaque oriens erepta iuuenta est.
> sola domum et tantas seruabat filia sedes
> iam matura uiro, iam plenis nubilis annis.
> multi iam magno e Latio totaque petebant
> Ausonia; petit ante alios pulcherrimus omnis
> Turnus, auis atauisque potens, quem regia coniunx
> adiungi generum miro properabat amore;
> sed uariis portenta deum terroribus obstant. (*Aen.* VII. 50–8)[62]

[To Latinus divine fate decreed no son or male heir, for the one who was born to him was snatched away in first youth. A single daughter served that house in so great a role, a girl now full in her years and ripe for marriage with a man. Many were now the men who sought her from broad Latium, from all Ausonia, but before all the others, the most handsome man to seek her is Turnus, powerful in grandfathers and ancestors, a man whom [Amata] the royal consort, with wondrous love, was hastening to unite to her family as a son; but in the way, with manifold terrors, stand portents of the gods.]

In these lines Vergil sets out the greater theme of the *Aeneid*.[63] Aeneas' interlude with Dido in Carthage (I and IV), his stories of wanderings after the sack of Troy (II–III), and his trips to Sicily (V) and the Underworld in Cumae (VI), are but the prelude to this theme.

Between Hrothgar and Latinus, on one hand, and between Wealhtheow and Amata on the other, there is an initial likeness in outline: like the royal couple of

---

[62] Text from *Vergili Opera*, ed. Mynors.
[63] See his words in *Aen.* VII. 44–5: *maior rerum mihi nascitur ordo, maius opus moueo* ('for me there springs a higher rank of subject, I set in motion a greater work').

the Laurentines, Hrothgar and Wealhtheow have a daughter whom they intend to marry to a king from a nearby land; their wedding plans are also disturbed by the arrival of a stranger; in each case it is the queen who holds to the original plan. There the resemblance ends: Latinus submits to Jupiter's purpose in continuing to promote Aeneas as his new son-in-law, despite Amata's wild candidacy of Turnus of the Rutuli; whereas in *Beowulf*, as we have seen, Hrothgar obeys Wealhtheow, letting the Ingeld-marriage go ahead. Before this narrative twist, however, the strength of the likeness holds. In this it appears that the poet of *Beowulf* adapts the culminating theme of the *Aeneid* in order to authenticate Beowulf's interaction with Hrothgar, as that of a future king.

The first details to emerge as parallels are the bridal chamber and the predestined son-in-law which the bride's father believes he must accept. In *Beowulf*, Hrothgar comes *of brydbure* (line 921) in order to see Grendel's arm now nailed up beneath the gable, and to thank God and Beowulf for this miracle (lines 928–31). No one had ever thought, he says, that Grendel could be defeated (lines 932–9). Now a *scealc* ('soldier', line 939), *þurh drihtnes miht* ('through the Lord's might', line 940), has carried out a deed beyond the ingenuity of any of them.[64] Then Hrothgar makes an announcement:

> 'Hwæt, þæt secgan mæg
> efne swa hwylc mægþa,   swa ðone magan cende
> æfter gumcynnum,   gyf heo gyt lyfað,
> þæt hyre Ealdmetod   este wære
> bearngebyrdo.   Nu ic Beowulf þec
> secg betsta   me for sunu wylle
> freogan on ferhþe;   heald forð tela
> niwe sibbe.   Ne bið þe [n]ænigra gad
> worolde wilna,   þe ic geweald hæbbe.' (*Beo* 942–50)

['Listen, she may say, if she still lives, whichsoever maiden brought forth this young boy of human race, that the Ancient Lord of Destiny showed favour to her in the birth of her child. Now Beowulf, best of men, I wish to love you in my heart as a son. From this time forth, as is right, keep a new kinship. Nor will you want for anything in the world which you desire and which is mine to command.']

The wordplay in these lines (*mæg . . . mægþa . . . magan*; *cende . . . -cynnum*) is a courtly contrivance.[65] Hrothgar's claimed ignorance of Beowulf's mother's name is another expression of courtesy: it is clear from his words to Wulfgar that he knows Beowulf is the son of Hrethel's only daughter, a Geatish princess (lines 374–5). So it is also clear, as Irving has pointed out, that Hrothgar's desire is to supplant the Geatish parent by taking Beowulf as a son.[66] For Hrothgar, so he

---

[64] Irving (*Rereading Beowulf*, 57) regards this statement as Hrothgar's means of saving face for his earlier inactivity.

[65] As noted in Orchard, *Companion*, 147.

[66] Irving, *Rereading Beowulf*, 55.

says in lines 381–4, believes that Beowulf is a man divinely sent.[67] The language of his *Ealdmetod*-formulation above is so suggestive of Mary and the Incarnation, particularly as this is presented in Luke 11: 27, that his words would blaspheme were he not an ignorant heathen.[68] The poet seems to have used the Marian motif to frame Hrothgar's belief in destiny in the strongest terms. As we have seen, the poet has prepared us in the previous fitt for the idea that Beowulf might become Hrothgar's successor (lines 856–915).

Like Latinus with Aeneas, Hrothgar believes that Beowulf's coming was ordained; in the same way he may wish to take him as a son-in-law. In the *Aeneid* Latinus and Amata are surprised by omens which a soothsayer interprets as unfavourable to the planned wedding between Lavinia and Turnus. For confirmation, Latinus consults his dead father Faunus in a grove:

> subita ex alto uox reddita luco est:
> 'ne pete conubiis natam sociare Latinis,
> o mea progenies, thalamis neu crede paratis;
> externi uenient generi, qui sanguine nostrum
> nomen in astra ferant, quorumque a stirpe nepotes
> omnia sub pedibus, qua sol utrumque recurrens
> aspicit Oceanum, uertique regique uidebunt.' (*Aen.* VII. 95–101)

[Suddenly there came back a voice from the height of the grove: 'Do not seek to bind your daughter in a Latin alliance, O offspring of mine, nor have faith in the bridal chamber already prepared. Men from abroad will come here to be your sons by marriage, men whose blood will carry our name to the stars, whose grandchildren by the same line will see all things at their feet for their transformation and control as far as the revolving sun looks down on east and west.']

Later Aeneas' emissaries arrive and Latinus thinks to himself that Faunus' prophecy must now be coming true:

> et ueteris Fauni uoluit sub pectore sortem:
> hunc illum fatis externa ab sede profectum
> portendi generum paribusque in regna uocari
> auspiciis, huic progeniem uirtute futuram
> egregiam et totum quae uiribus occupet orbem. (*Aen.* VII. 254–8)

[And within his breast he turned over the oracle of old Faunus. This is the man, he thought, who the fates foretold would come from a foreign citadel to be my son-in-law, would be called to reign here with equal authority, the man whose heirs will be brilliant in valour and take possession, through their strength, of all the world]

---

[67]   Niles, *Beowulf,* 252: 'Hrothgar takes Beowulf to be an agent of God, and neither implicitly nor explicitly does the poet contradict this judgment.'

[68]   Klaeber draws attention to this blessing on Mary in Luke, in *Beowulf,* 166–7. This parallel is discounted in *Beowulf,* ed. Wrenn and Bolton, 135; and by Orchard, *Companion,* 147–8. But see my Ch. 3.

Secondly, if we study Wealhtheow, we see the political aspect of this queen in the train with which she follows Hrothgar out of the bridal bower, just before his offer to make Beowulf their new son:

>   swylce self cyning
> of brydbure   beahhorda weard
> tryddode tirfæst   getrume micle
> cystum gecyþed   ond his cwen mid him
> medostigge mæt   mægþa hose. (*Beo* 920–4)

[likewise the king himself, keeper of the ring-hoards, stepped glorious out of the bridal bower with a great troop in excellent display, and his queen with him measured out the mead-path with a retinue of maidens.]

This image appears to owe something to Vergil's description of Amata, Latinus' queen, as she makes ready to pray for Turnus, her favourite, in a planned duel against Aeneas:

>   nec non ad templum summasque ad Palladis arces
>   subuehitur magna matrum regina caterua
>   dona ferens, iuxtaque comes Lauinia uirgo,
>   causa mali tanti, oculos deiecta decoros.
>   succedunt matres et templum ture uaporant
>   et maestas alto fundunt de limine uoces:
>   'armipotens, praeses belli, Tritonia uirgo,
>   frange manu telum Phrygii praedonis, et ipsum
>   pronum sterne solo portisque effunde sub altis.' (*Aen.* XI. 477–85)

[The queen, too, was borne in her carriage with a great company of mothers to the shrine and highest places of Pallas, herself bearing gifts, and close beside her Lavinia the maid: she, the cause of so much suffering, kept her eyes downcast. The mothers enter and shroud all that shrine with incense and raise their sad voices from the high portal in prayer: 'O power in arms, protectress in war, virgin, Tritonia, shatter in thy hand the spearhaft of the Phrygian corsair! Scatter him headlong to earth, let him lie dead below our high gates.']

Amata's hostility to Aeneas has been engendered by Juno, who sends a Fury to plant hostility not only in her breast but also in that of Turnus.

Wealhtheow, thanking Beowulf indirectly while she addresses Hrothgar in lines 1169–87, calls the Geat a *hereri[n]c* ('raiding warrior', line 1176). Hers is a context where the denotation of OE *here* ('plunder', 'raiding'), normally neutral, becomes negative. It could be said that *hererinc* is an ungrateful way to thank a man who has delivered the Danes from a true predator. This term resembles the word *praedo* ('rover') with which Amata twice refers disparagingly to Aeneas: once, as above in her curse in *Aen.* XI. 484; and earlier, when she contests the choice of Aeneas as a son-in-law with her husband King Latinus:

>   'exsulibusne datur ducenda Lauinia Teucris,
>   o genitor, nec te miseret nataeque tuique?

nec matris miseret, quam primo Aquilone relinquet
perfidus alta petens abducta uirgine praedo?
at non sic Phrygius penetrat Lacedaemona pastor,
Ledaeamque Helenam Troianas uexit ad urbes?
quid tua sancta fides? quid cura antiqua tuorum
et consanguineo totiens data dextera Turno?
si gener externa petitur de gente Latinis,
idque sedet, Faunique premunt te iussa parentis,
omnem equidem sceptris terram quae libera nostris
dissidet externam reor et sic dicere diuos.' (*Aen.* VII. 359–70)

['Is Lavinia to be given in marriage to Trojan exiles, by you her father, or have you no pity for your daughter or for yourself? Do you not pity her mother, a woman to be left alone at the first North Wind by a rover who abducted the high-born maid he was looking for? Is that not how the Phrygian shepherd [: Paris] entered Sparta and carried off Helen to the city of Troy? What of your sacred word, the long-lasting care you have shown to your people, your right hand so often given to our blood-relative Turnus? If a son-in-law of foreign blood is found for the Latins, and this holds, and the commands of Faunus, your father, push you on, then I believe that each land that remains free from our authority is a foreign country: this is what the gods were saying.']

Wealhtheow expresses no such sentiments as these. Yet this speech of Amata's is one which we could attribute to Wealhtheow as the background to her rejection of Beowulf as a 'son' or son-in-law. The crucial verbal parallel is *praedo* ('rover', *Aen.* VII. 362). Is Amata's the state of mind which the poet wished to give Wealhtheow, along with the regiment of women? If it is thought that Amata's bacchic wildness in her speech above is not to be found in Wealhtheow, it is interesting that Gillian Overing, without reference to Amata, defines Wealhtheow as 'a formidable hysteric'.[69] In the *Aeneid*, Amata's second, if not her first, use of *praedo* against Aeneas looks like the poet's model for *hereri[n]c*, Wealhtheow's word for Beowulf (line 1176). Until this moment Wealhtheow's speech to Hrothgar is derogatory, for in it she does not refer to Beowulf at all, unless he be understood in the plural *Geatas* used twice in lines 1171 and 1173.

Perhaps an unswerving allegiance to Ingeld is what an audience of *Beowulf* would expect of Wealhtheow. She says nothing about Ingeld, and later Beowulf tells Hygelac that the match between Ingeld, and Freawaru is Hrothgar's idea (lines 2026–9). Yet Beowulf's reminiscence of Wealhtheow, as *friðusibb folca* ('treaty-pledge of the nations', line 2107), suggests that she, not Hrothgar, was behind this match. We have been alerted to its disastrous outcome as early as in lines 81–5. Later, when Beowulf has put paid to Unferth in lines 530–606, the poet says that Wealhtheow emerges; but she serves Beowulf last:

> Ymbeode þa   ides Helminga
> duguþe ond geogoþe   dæl æghwylcne,

⁶⁹ Overing, *Language, Sign, and Gender in Beowulf,* 90–101, at 91.

sincfato sealde, oþþæt sæl alamp
þæt hio Beowulfe, beaghroden cwen
mode geþungen, medoful ætbær. (*Beo* 620–4)

[The lady of the Helmings then walked about each part of the divisions of tried troops and untried, gave out treasure vessels, until the moment arrived when she, the necklace-laden queen, distinguished in mind, bore the mead-cup to Beowulf.]

Whether this is protocol or a snub, there is no doubt that Wealhtheow, like Lady Macbeth, believes in 'an order of going'. The force of this sequence in Heorot, however, remains unclear. Perhaps there is some significance in Wealhtheow's epithet *ides Helminga*: 'Helm' is the name of the Wulfings' king in *Wid* 29; so Wealhtheow would seem to be a Wulfing or Wylfing princess. Sam Newton has pointed all this out;[70] but not its corollary, that the queen might be slow to welcome Beowulf because his father, Ecgtheow, killed Heatholaf *mid Wilfingum* ('among the Wylfings', line 461; see 470–2): one of her own people.

Now, however, the queen thanks God for the arrival of a man in whom she can trust, later liking Beowulf's words when he makes the vow to which her mead-cup formally prompts him. She makes no comment when Hrothgar makes his promise, but in the big party afterwards, it could be said that the lay of Finnsburh begins to express her message. This tale from Frisia could serve as a warning to the Danes not to share power: Finn dies in his own home after he kills his brother-in-law Hnæf; the presumption may be that he killed Hnæf because he suspected him of treachery.[71] Let Hrothulf take note, should Beowulf move into Heorot. It is after this lay that Wealhtheow makes her opposition to a kinship with Beowulf publicly known.

So Freawaru's wedding with Ingeld is set to go ahead, after all; Hrothgar's *modlufe mare* ('greater love of heart'; cf. line 1823) will not be granted to Beowulf. Yet Hrothgar seems to harbour a regret despite his evasive speech of thanks and farewell (lines 1841–65). The poet of *Beowulf* allows us to glimpse something of Hrothgar's shame as he embraces the departing Geat. Now that they will never meet again (lines 1873–6), his love for Beowulf is too strong to hide:

Wæs him se man to þon leof
þæt he þone breostwylm forberan ne mehte
ac him on hreþre hygebendum fæst
æfter deorum men dyrne langað
beorn wið blode. (*Beo* 1876–80)

[That man was so beloved of him that he could not restrain the breast-surge, but within his bosom, fastened within the bonds of his mind, a secret longing for the dear (or: daring) man burned against his blood.]

Vergil shows us Latinus turning over Faunus' oracle, that his daughter must marry Aeneas, within his breast (*uoluit sub pectore sortem*, *Aen.* VII. 254). The

---

[70] Newton, *The Origins of Beowulf*, 122–4.   [71] North, 'Tribal Loyalties', 13–43.

situations are different, with Hrothgar saying goodbye to Beowulf and Latinus welcoming Aeneas' envoys. In each case, however, with *on hreþre* and *sub pectore*, the poet lets us enter the mind of an aged ineffectual king. Again, it is as if Vergil's words could serve as a gloss to the unexpressed thoughts of a person in *Beowulf*: to Wealhtheow in her inferrable dislike of Beowulf as a future son-in-law; and here, to Hrothgar in the better judgement which his wife has made him suppress. It is hard to see what else Hrothgar's *langað* ('longing') could be, one that has to be repressed as *dyrne* ('secret'), unless this is to cherish Beowulf as a son. This is what he promised, but the fact that this longing now *beorn wið blode* ('burned against his blood') shows his decision not to let Beowulf partake of his blood, by marrying Freawaru.

So Hrothgar goes back on his promise, shifting *sunu*'s meaning from the political to the symbolic. The poet leaves us in no doubt about his weakness, as Irving illustrates.[72] Hrothgar is the *wigfruma* ('war-leader') who hurries out at sunset because he *wolde... Wealhþeo secan cwen to gebeddan* ('wanted to seek Wealhtheow, the queen, as his bedfellow', lines 664–5). The word *wigfruma* is inappropriate, as if the poet chides the old king for uxoriousness. The closing lines of Fitt XXVI leave a sardonic impression of Hrothgar's wisdom when the poet gives his own verdict, if not also that of Beowulf and his friends:

> Þa wæs on gange   gifu Hroðgares
> oft geæhted;   þæt was an cyning
> æghwæs orleahtre   oþ þæt hine yldo benam
> mægenes wynnum   se þe oft manegum scod. (*Beo* 1884–7)

[Then, on the trail back, was Hrothgar's gift-giving often studied and praised; that was a king blameless in every way, until old age, who has often harmed many a man, deprived him of the joys of his strength.]

With old age having weakened Hrothgar's powers, it appears that Wealhtheow has overruled his desire to give their daughter to Beowulf.[73] By juxtaposing Beowulf with Ingeld on the basis of Aeneas and Turnus in Vergil's *Aeneid*, Books VII and XI, the poet creates a rivalry which makes Beowulf fit to be king.

CONCLUSION

The prospect of Ingeld's marriage with Freawaru accounts for most of the tension in the background of Beowulf's exploits in Denmark. No sooner is Heorot built than our poet draws attention to its immolation in Ingeld's raid (lines 81–5).

---

[72] Irving, *Rereading Beowulf*, 60–2.

[73] As Irving says (ibid. 60–1), the lines 1162–231 are 'one telling instance of his lightness of heft, his strange invisibility ... where his wife Wealhtheow takes over political functions the king should properly be carrying out for himself. Both his passivity and his lack of contact with his social environment were never better illustrated.'

Grendel soon begins to disrupt Heorot for twelve years, until driven out by Beowulf. The reward for this hero at first promises to be glorious: in Danish hearts, the admiration which would make him their next king (lines 856–915); in Hrothgar's words, a *niw sib* that will confirm Beowulf in this role, as the king's *sunu* in lines 942–9. But then Wealhtheow intervenes with a speech, particularly in lines 1173–80, in which she publicly buries the idea. To Beowulf instead, sitting between her sons (lines 1188–91), she grants the lesser honour of *lar*, being the boys' adviser (line 1220). Later, when Beowulf makes ready to dive into Grendel's Mere in search of Grendel's Mother, he reminds Hrothgar that he promised to be a father to him (*on fæder stæle*, line 1479). But now Beowulf ironically asks Hrothgar to be his executor instead. On returning alive, Beowulf delivers a supernatural sword-hilt into the hands of Hrothgar, whose thanksgiving begins in hypermetric form with the promised fulfilment of his *freoðe* ('treaty, agreement', line 1707; or 'friendship', if we read *freode*). But almost in the same breath Hrothgar shifts his parental undertaking from the dynastic to the symbolic (lines 1707–84). In the morning when Beowulf asks if he can achieve the greater love of Hrothgar's heart (*modlufan maran*, line 1823), Hrothgar ignores the young man's offer to return to Heorot with an army should the Danes be attacked. He allows, instead, that Beowulf may become the next king of the Geats. When they part, Hrothgar weeps with *dyrne langað* ('a secret longing', line 1879) for whose secrecy no explanation seems more viable than the supposition that Hrothgar's true wish is to make Beowulf into his son-in-law. All this, I suggest, explains why Beowulf makes Freawaru's marriage the theme in the first part of his report to Hygelac (in lines 2000–68). Hereby he predicts what Wealhtheow wants to avoid, the vengeance of Ingeld; and a little later the poet alludes to Heoroweard, whose own attack on Denmark will cause the death of Hrothulf (lines 2160–2 and 2165–71). Within his first 2,200 lines, in this way, the poet of *Beowulf* accounts for an era in Danish history which was no doubt familiar to his audience (to judge from lines 1–3). Yet, in a novelty which may have been hard to accomplish, he interposes Beowulf. To help himself with the rivalry in this new plot, I suggest that he makes use of Aeneas and Turnus in Vergil's *Aeneid*. From the creation of a new rivalry between Beowulf and Ingeld it may be assumed that the poet of *Beowulf* thought himself no less a rival to the poet on Ingeld whose work he took as his source.

5
'Quid Hinieldus?' Bishop Unwona and Friends

This and the following two chapters now lead us up tenuous paths to the minster of Breedon on the Hill, north-west Leicestershire, in the first half of the ninth century. The paths are tenuous because of the dearth of evidence, my conclusion therefore lacking in proof. Nonetheless, my aim is to enter into the argument for *Beowulf*'s knowledge of Kings Offa in Chapter 8, Cenwulf and Beornwulf in Chapter 9, and Wiglaf in Chapter 10, at least forearmed with the hypothesis that *Beowulf* was composed in Breedon. In the previous chapter I have prepared the way for this case by suggesting that the poet of *Beowulf* makes Ingeld the glass through which he regards Beowulf and Hrothgar in his first 2,200 lines. That is to say, by making Ingeld and Beowulf not only contemporaries, but also rivals for Hrothgar's daughter, the poet appears to challenge the authority of a famous work on Ingeld which he took as his source. In the present chapter I shall identify this source with a *carmen* on 'Hinieldus' which was performed at the court of one 'Speratus', a correspondent of Alcuin's, in 797.

'QUID HINIELDUS CUM CHRISTO?'

Two letters survive from Alcuin to Speratus. The shorter (no. 285) is dated by Ernst Dümmler to *c.*793 × 803, because he takes Speratus to be Abbot Higbald of Lindisfarne.[1] The longer letter (no. 124), which refers to Hinieldus, is datable to 797 because here Alcuin also refers to Ecgfrith, son of Offa, as the king who had died not long before: Ecgfrith is known to have died in 796. In this letter, at the peak of a long passage on pastoral sloth, Alcuin exhorts Speratus to reform his spiritual life:

Verba Dei legantur in sacerdotali convivio. Ibi decet lectorem audiri, non citharistam: sermones patrum, non carmina gentilium. Quid Hinieldus cum Christo? Angusta est domus: utrosque tenere non poterit. Non vult rex celestis cum paganis et perditis nominetenus regibus communionem habere; quia rex ille aeternus regnat in caelis, ille paganus perditus plangit in inferno.[2]

---

[1] *Epistolae*, ed. Dümmler, ii. 443 and 181. On this, see Bullough, 'What has Ingeld to do with Lindisfarne?', 105–15.

[2] *Epistolae*, ed. Dümmler ii. 183. My translation is adapted from Bullough, 'What has Ingeld to do with Lindisfarne?', 124.

[Let God's word be read at the episcopal dinner table. There it is fitting for a reader to be heard, not a harper: sermons of the Fathers, not the songs of heathens. What has Hinieldus to do with Christ? The house is narrow: it will not be able to hold them both. The Heavenly King will have no communion with so-called kings who are pagan and damned; for the One King rules in Heaven, while the other, a pagan, is damned and wails in hell.]

Hereafter Alcuin questions the morals of Speratus' friends and pupils and berates him about the governance of his house.

It is worth following the detail of the text against drinking which Alcuin cites from Isaiah 5: 22 just before his denunciation of 'Hinieldus' in Speratus' court. After connecting drinking with corrupted legal judgements (5: 23), Isaiah predicts the arrival of raiders (5: 24) who will destroy the people of Israel at God's command. The Lord will whistle up the nations who will come swiftly with all speed (5: 26), well armed and with arrows sharp and bows bent (5: 27–8), their chariots like a tornado (5: 29) and their roar like the sea (5: 30): 'and behold, there is the darkness of suffering and the light is overshadowed in the calamity they bring'.[3] Isaiah 5: 30 goes on to warn of a swift barbarian invasion *sicut sonitus maris* ('like the roaring of the sea'). For *nationibus* (the 'nations', 5: 26), we might read 'Scandinavians'. The Vikings had been on Alcuin's mind since their raids on Lindisfarne on 8 June 793 and on Jarrow the following year.[4] In 793 Alcuin invoked the Chaldean attack on Judaea, from Jeremiah 52, in his consolation of Abbot Higbald for the ruin of Lindisfarne.[5] In letters to King Æthelred and his thegns and also probably to Archbishop Æthelheard of Canterbury, Alcuin makes further allusion to Lindisfarne and to other unspecified Viking raids.[6] In his letter to Speratus of 797, therefore, Alcuin appears to have chosen his text partly through its proximity to a warning to expect invaders.

Not only is the context of Isaiah 5: 22 apposite for Alcuin's time. In addition, it mimics Ingeld's raid on Heorot. The presence of one narrative incident in the work on 'Hinieldus' may be deduced from this immediate biblical context. The poet of *Widsith* shows us how Ingeld could be celebrated as a raider. Hrothgar and Hrothwulf, he says, had kept their kindred united for the longest time:

> siþþan hy forwræcon   wicinga cynn
> ond Ingeldes   ord forbigdan,
> forheowan æt Heorote   Heaðobeardna þrym. (*Wid* 47–9)

---

[3] I quote the Vulgate Bible from *Biblia Sacra iuxta Vulgatam Clementinam*, ed. A. Colunga and L. Turrado, Biblioteca de Autores Cristianos 14, 7th edn. (Madrid, 1985). My quotations from this edition will only approximate to the biblical books and quotations which Alcuin used, for it is not possible to know what these were. On Alcuin's bibles, see Marsden, *The Text of the Old Testament*, 18–29 and 222–35.

[4] *ASC* (E), pp. 55–7 (*s.a.* 793, 794 (E)).

[5] In two letters: *Epistolae*, ed. Dümmler, ii. 58–9 (no. 21: after 8 June 793); and 65 (no. 24: ?794). The 'north' as the provenance of enemies of the chosen race is a commonplace. See further Page, 'The Audience of *Beowulf* and the Vikings', 118, and Townend, *Language and History*, 174–6.

[6] *Epistolae*, ed. Dümmler, ii. 42–4 (no. 16), 49–52 (no. 18), 71–2 (no. 30), 193 (no. 130).

[when they drove off a tribe of pirates (*or:* men from Vík), crushed Ingeld's front line and at Heorot cut down the glory of the Heathobards.]

If we put these vernacular lines alongside Alcuin's suggestions with Isaiah 5, it looks as if he, too, conceives of Hinieldus as a *wicing*.[7] Alcuin's context appears to mean that the present Viking havoc should convince Speratus of the folly of consorting with Hinieldus.

Whitney Bolton claims that Alcuin's complaint about Hinieldus tells us 'little beyond the fact that stories, apparently poems, about Ingeld were known or known of in Alcuin's day'.[8] Yet we can note that Alcuin refers first to a *citharista* ('harper'), secondly to *carmina* ('songs'). In the light of this sequence, it seems likely that Alcuin means the performance of lays in Speratus' court. A little earlier in the same letter, Alcuin adapts Ps. 39: 5 on hope in the Lord. Here we might assume that Speratus knew, without being told, that the preceding verse begins: *Et immisit in os meum canticum novum, Carmen nostro Deo* ('And he has put into my mouth a new song, a song of praise to our God', Ps. 39: 4). Earlier still, when Alcuin advises Speratus to give alms to the needy, he says that paupers should eat at his table better *quam istriones vel luxoriosos quoslibet* ('than actors or any kind of rioters').[9] Given that actors perform speeches rather than third-person narrative, the context makes dramatic poetry likely. Fourthly, as Bolton shows, Alcuin's Latin style mimics the alliteration of Anglian verse as we know it from the vernacular canon.[10] In the Hinieldus passage Alcuin's clauses are short, his antitheses well balanced. As if to emphasize the contrast between good and bad, Alcuin alliterates the words '*l*egantur' with '*l*ectorem' on one hand, '*c*onvivio' with '*c*itharistam' and '*c*armina' on the other; then rounds off his point more emotionally with '*p*aganis et *p*erditis', followed by '*p*aganus *p*erditus *p*langit'. This alliteration captures the technique of an eighth-century Mercian poem.

Alcuin's complaint about Hinieldus tells us something about the content of the relevant *carmen*. When he says that the King of Heaven will not take communion with so-called kings who are at present damned in hell, it is clear that he believes an attempt had been made to exonerate Hinieldus of his paganism.[11] As his question demonstrates, Alcuin rejects this course. If such was attempted in the heroic poem he condemns, this work was a cut above *Widsith* or *The Finnsburh Fragment*. Indeed, by attempting to exonerate heathens, Speratus' lost poem on Ingeld would resemble *Beowulf*, where, as we have seen, a certain Christian typology presents Hrothgar, Beowulf, and Wiglaf respectively as Simeon, Jesus, and Peter. In *Beowulf* also there are some more outspoken attempts to grant

---

[7] A man from the *Vík*, not far from '*Haða*-land' upon which the '*Heatho*-bards' take their name. See also C. Fell, 'Old English *Wicing*: A Question of Semantics', *PBA* 72 (1987), 295–316.

[8] Bolton, *Alcuin and Beowulf*, 102.

[9] *Epistolae*, ed. Dümmler, ii. 183.

[10] Bolton, *Alcuin and Beowulf*, 55–71, at 57–9.

[11] His wording recalls St Paul's expression for the demon Belial in 2 Cor. 6: 15–16.

communion to the damned. In one, the poet says that Hama *geceas ecne ræd* ('chose an eternal reward', line 1201), perhaps by donating the treasure that he stole from Eormanric. Hama's refuge in *þære byrhtan byrig* ('that bright city', line 1199), either Rome or Ravenna, from the wiles of this Gothic king is the poem's first allusion to a heathen eligible for grace. In the second, Hrothgar urges Beowulf in his sword-hilt speech to think more of the spiritual life, commanding him as follows: *þe þæt selre geceos, ece rædas* ('choose for yourself the better part, eternal rewards', lines 1759–60). In the third example, Beowulf says that Hrethel *godes leoht geceas* when he died ('chose God's light', line 2469).[12] If it is objected that the poet of *Beowulf* does not treat Ingeld as seriously as these other heathens, it is worth adding that the tale of Freawaru's wedding, at least as Beowulf predicts it, differs from the Norse analogues in blaming the first violence not on Ingeld, but on one of his men; less louchely than in Saxo, Ingeld's coolness to his wife results from others' broken oaths (lines 2057–69, esp. 2063–6; cf. Chapter 4). So we know that this story can allow for sympathy with Hinieldus or Ingeld.

Hama, Hrothgar (in prospect), and Hrethel are three obvious cases in which Alcuin might have held the poet of *Beowulf* equally to account. From the terms of Alcuin's denunciation of Speratus' court it seems that the intellectual ambition which is clear in these regions of *Beowulf* had a match in the work on Hinieldus. At least there is no other historical record of a poem on Ingeld in England at this time, whereas it seems unlikely that *Widsith*, as we have it now, provided the material to which Alcuin's word *carmina* refers. On the other hand, we have seen from the Norse material that any tale of Ingjaldr was also one of Hróarr, Hrólfr, and the Danish princess. In other words, the lost work on 'Hinieldus', which we can infer to be a poem, would have had the same Danish backdrop as the first two-thirds of *Beowulf*. In this regard, the fact that both works, and no others extant, attempt to exonerate ancient heathens strengthens the possibility that Speratus' poem, if poem it was, was famous in its day, known to the compiler of *Widsith* and a formative influence on *Beowulf*.

BISHOP SPERATUS, HIS FRIENDS AND PUPILS

Looking for agents of this transmission, we see that both Alcuin's extant letters to Speratus throw light on his friends and pupils. In Alcuin's view these men were either going to tell the world of Speratus' pastoral corruption or more likely they would themselves succumb to it. His portrait of Speratus is not flattering in either letter and I shall address this before moving on to the man's associates. Donald Bullough believes that the shorter of the two letters (no. 285, without Hinieldus)

---

[12] North, *Heathen Gods*, 173–81 and 196–8, 200–1; *Pagan Words*, 59–62; 'The Pagan Inheritance of Egill's *Sonatorrek*', 152–3.

'could be either earlier or later in date' than the first (no. 124).[13] However, it can be deduced from comparing Alcuin's address to the bishop in each case that letter no. 285 probably pre-dates no. 124. In no. 124, Alcuin sends *sanctissimo fratri et filio carissimo Sperato episcopo humilis pater Albinus salutem* ('to the most holy brother and most dear son Bishop Speratus, from the humble father Albinus, greetings'); in no. 285, this is *dilectissimo patri Sperato episcopo fidelis amicus Alchvinus salutem* ('to the most beloved father Bishop Speratus, from Alhwine, a loyal friend, greetings'). The fact that in both cases Speratus is addressed first, shows him to be of higher rank. However, with Speratus as *pater* and Alcuin as *fidelis amicus* in no. 285, and with Alcuin as *pater* and Speratus as *frater* in no. 124, a change in Alcuin's status seems to have arisen. This is best identified with his promotion to abbot of St Martin's at Tours in 796, when Alcuin's rank could have approached that of Speratus.[14] On this basis I will treat Alcuin's shorter letter to Speratus (no. 285) as the earlier of the two.

The opening lines of this letter complain about the growing rarity of letters from Speratus.[15] Despite accusing him of *oblivio* ('forgetfulness'), Alcuin recalls Speratus' hospitality. A former warmth between these two men is claimed by Alcuin's appeal to Speratus' *dulcedinem* ('sweetness').[16] His main business is to urge Speratus to think of his duties *ubi maneas, ubi statuta sit dignitas tua* ('where you reside, where your rank is established'). With an allusion to 2 Tim. 4: 2, Speratus is encouraged to think of his pupils as well as the laymen in his flock. If we choose to look further at the context, St Paul throws light on what Alcuin took to be his friend's surroundings:

3. Erit enim tempus, cum sanam doctrinam non sustinebunt, sed ad sua desideria coacervabunt sibi magistros, prurientes auribus, 4. et a veritate quidem auditum avertent, ad fabulas autem convertentur. (2 Tim. 4: 3–4)

[3. For there will be a time when people will not stand sound teaching, but will heap together schoolmasters for themselves and to their own desires, their ears itching [to hear more]; 4. they will even stop their ears to the truth and moreover they will turn to fables.]

From this background it appears that Speratus is entrusted with the teaching of pupils whom he has now helped corrupt with *fabulae*. This reading is consistent with Alcuin's allusion to *carmina* in the longer letter.

Alcuin alludes to Speratus' associates as clergy, fellow servants of God, when he adapts Christ's parable in Luke 12: 35 about a lord coming back from a wedding feast. He requests that Unwona should keep *irreprehensibiles socios* ('companions beyond reproach'), namely *tales iuvenes apud te, qui semper discant, et magis*

---

[13] Bullough, 'What has Ingeld to do with Lindisfarne?', 102.

[14] *Epistolae*, ed. Dümmler, ii. 146 (no. 101: Alcuin to Offa, 796).

[15] Ibid. 443–4, at 443 (no. 285).

[16] Ibid. 443. Taken to be a sign of his exile, in Orchard, 'Wish You Were Here', 42. But Alcuin uses the word *dulcedo* similarly in other letters. See *Epistolae*, ed. Dümmler, ii. 82–3, at 83 (no. 39: to an unknown friend, *c*.793–5); 148–9, at 148 (no. 102: to Æthelburh, 796).

gaudeant discere quam inebriari ('young men around you who always learn and take greater pleasure in learning than in becoming intoxicated'); it is in their context that he asks Speratus *non saeculi sectari pompas* ('not to chase the pomp and ceremony of the age').[17] Alcuin is vague about whether it is the bishop or his associates who are lowering the tone of Mercian social events. But these expressions make it clearer that he thinks the bishop's pupils have a role to play in his secular diversions. He relates the parable from Luke 12: 36–40: not Speratus' servants, but he himself must sit in readiness for the lord to come home, for the Son of Man will not come at an expected hour. Luke 12: 35 is one of Alcuin's favourite verses to bishops, another reason to trust Donald Bullough's conclusion that Speratus is a bishop.[18] Alcuin refers to this parable also in an open letter to the bishops of Britain, written shortly after 18 April 796;[19] and again in a letter to an archbishop (name unknown), referring to good Christians as men who must daily carry *lucernas ardentes bonorum operum* ('the lit lamps of good works').[20] But in neither of these epistles does Alcuin make such use of this verse as in his shorter letter to Speratus.

As we have seen, Alcuin's other letter, probably the second, is datable to 797. In polished style Alcuin starts with a eulogy on Speratus as Alcuin's friend.[21] There is a routine allusion to the distance and the length of time since they have met. Then Alcuin begins with a few injunctions to preach more often. The tone of his letter becomes querulous, with a quotation from Isaiah 58. The larger context is God's appeal to the Israelites (*domus Iacob*, 58: 1) to fast, to feed the hungry, and to keep the sabbath.[22] Speratus' congregation will be caught unawares if the camp is open to attack, or if the watchman sleeps, or *si pastor in silvestribus luxoriae dumis latitat* ('if the shepherd lies hidden in the wooded thickets of riotousness'). More to the point, the sheep will not find pasture *si ductor vagabundis per foveas vestigiis errat* ('if their leader wanders into pitfalls with his vagabond trails').[23] Alcuin's reference to a straying nun in another letter as an *ovicula* ('little lamb') makes it clear that his image of sheep here refers to the young male clergy.[24] Negligence, sloth, extravagance, and secular diversions, if we believe this Lycidean commentary, appear to be the hallmarks of Speratus' office. Once more, however, Alcuin draws attention to the involvement of his friend's pupils.

---

[17] *Epistolae*, ed. Dümmler, ii. 444.

[18] Bullough, 'What has Ingeld to do with Lindisfarne?', 105–15.

[19] *Epistolae*, ed. Dümmler, ii. 150–1 (no. 104).

[20] Ibid. 446–7 (no. 288).

[21] Ibid. 103. Alcuin modelled this on the letters of St Jerome, which he had been reading at Tours.

[22] For a hypothesis that Anglian kings of the early eighth century identified themselves as new Israelites, descendants of a Germanic Jacob, see North, *Heathen Gods*, 114–17.

[23] *Epistolae*, ed. Dümmler, ii. 182. Bullough ('What has Ingeld to do with Lindisfarne?', 123) translates *foveas* as 'snares'.

[24] Alcuin to Abbot Wulfheard (probably of Dunwich, East Anglia), *c*.789 × 796. *Epistolae*, ed. Dümmler, ii. 113–14 (no. 70): *Inveni oviculam istam per negligentiae precipitia errantem* ('I discovered this little lamb wandering through the pitfalls of negligence').

Between these remarks on lost sheep and his later discourse on a father and his sons, Alcuin alludes to Offa's failure to settle the succession on his son Ecgfrith, as a sign of the futility of man's endeavours when set against the judgement of God: *sed, ut rerum eventus demonstrabat, exemit* ('however, as the outcome of these affairs demonstrated, he perished').[25] Now Alcuin repeats advice on the good priestly life, alluding to actors and rioters. The *istriones* whom Alcuin mentions here count as his first allusion to a performance in Speratus' court. In Jerome's expression, repeated by Alcuin here, the bishop is urged to avoid the company of determined drinkers *quasi infernam foveam devita* ('as you would the pit of hell'). Although drunkenness is one of Alcuin's favourite themes, his allusion to actors grounds the complaint in reality.[26] Here he adapts Ps. 39: 5 on hope in the Lord, in which David declares that blessed is the man who hopes in the Lord *Et non respexit in vanitates et insanias falsas* ('and has not looked back upon vanities and false attacks of madness').[27] Alcuin then turns to Isaiah 5: 22 in order to denounce drunkards, with a larger scriptural context that, as we have seen, both warns Speratus of barbarian invaders and leads the way to Hinieldus. After alluding to this heathen king in hell, Alcuin turns specifically to the bishop's associates:

Voces legentium audire in domibus tuis, non ridentium turbam in plateis. Clericorum tales habeas socios, ex quorum conversatione tua laudetur auctoritas. Filius sapiens gloria est patris, et econtra filius stultus ignominia est magistri. Quomodo, dicente apostolo, curam ecclesiae poterit habere qui suam domum nescit regere?[28]

[It is proper to hear readers' voices in your household, not a crowd of merry-makers in the corridors. From the clergy you should have such companions as those from whose conversation your authority may be praised. A wise son is his father's glory, whereas a foolish son is his master's disgrace. As the Apostle [St Paul] says, how can a man have care of a church who knows not how to rule his own household?]

Alcuin's first sentence is adapted from one in a letter to Abbot Higbald of Lindisfarne in 793: *Audiantur in domibus vestris legentes, non ludentes in platea* ('let readers be heard in your household, not men playing in the corridor').[29] The difference is that in Speratus' case Alcuin describes a school: one in which Speratus is a paternal *magister* ('master') and in which each one of his *socii*

---

[25] *Epistolae*, ed. Dümmler, ii. 182 (no. 124). Bullough ('What has Ingeld to do with Lindisfarne?', 110 n. 58 and 123) shows that *exentit* is the form in all MSS, while translating the first sentence as 'You well know how the illustrious king prepared for his son to inherit the kingdom, as he thought: but as events showed, he took it from him'.

[26] *Epistolae*, ed. Dümmler, ii. 81 (no. 38), 83 (no. 40), 88 (no. 43), 117 (no. 74), 132 (no. 88), and 168 (no. 114).

[27] It appears from a story in the *Vita s. Gregorii Magni* (704 × 714) that Paulinus taught this verse to Anglian heathens in York while he catechized King Edwin of Deira in 627. In *Vita sancti Gregorii Magni: The Earliest Life of Gregory the Great*, ed. B. Colgrave (Lawrence, Kan., 1968), p. 97 (ch. 15).

[28] *Epistolae*, ed. Dümmler, ii. 183. The biblical reference is to 1 Tim. 3: 5. Alcuin's first sentence is adapted from one in a letter to Abbot Higbald of Lindisfarne in 793 (ibid. 59, no. 21): *Audiantur in domibus vestris legentes, non ludentes in platea* ('let readers be heard in your household, not men playing in the corridor').

[29] *Epistolae*, ed. Dümmler, ii. 59 (no. 21).

clericorum ('companions from the clergy') is a *filius* ('son'). The word *stultus* implies an interest in new fashions: in a letter to a Mercian patrician in *c.*797, probably Brorda, Alcuin bewails a post-Offan restoration, alluding in particular to the seeker after new fashions in dress and feasting *qui stultior est omnibus* ('who is more foolish than everyone').[30] In his letter to Speratus around then, it is this term, above all, that defines the style of the bishop's pupils whom we presume the *carmen* on Hinieldus has corrupted. If it was one *filius* among these who transmitted the Ingeld-poem to the poet of *Beowulf*, there is no doubt that Alcuin would have seen him as more *stultus* than *sapiens*.

BISHOP UNWONA, HIS FRIENDS AND PUPILS

Bullough has argued that Speratus was a bishop, and that his name is Alcuin's *nom de plume* for Bishop Unwona of Leicester.[31] As Speratus' name can mean 'hoped for', it has become conventional to identify this *bon viveur* with another correspondent of Alcuin's, Abbot '*Hig*-bald' of Lindisfarne, by confusing OE *hyge* ('mind') with *hyht* ('hope'). On the other hand, the suffix of 'Unwona' or 'Unwana', intensified by the *un*-prefix, resembles OE *wen* ('expectation'). 'Speratus' can be read as the Latin calque of a Germanic name, one among several created by Alcuin for his friends in England back home.[32] The charters show that Bishop Unwona was close to the heart of Mercian ecclesiastical and secular power. They also show that after Lichfield, in the late eighth and early ninth centuries, Leicester was the most important diocese in Mercia.[33] Enjoying this status, Unwona was a member of important councils and a frequent guest at high-level social events from 785 to *c.*800, across the reigns of Offa, Ecgfrith, and Cenwulf (Fig. 1). In the adjoining table I have selected witnesses at representative church councils (excluding the Council of the Legates).[34] This evidence reveals that it took Unwona some five years to climb to a steady position of fourth or

[30] *Epistolae*, ed. Dümmler, ii. 178–80 (no. 122); *EHD*, 786–8 (no. 202: 'Osbert'). Thacker, 'Some Terms for Noblemen', 218–19; Kirby, *Earliest English Kings*, 177; Bullough, 'What has Ingeld to do with Lindisfarne?', 118–19; Keynes, 'Councils of *Clofesho*', 42 n. 180. Brorda attests charters usually as the first non-royal lay witness from 764 to 799: initially without title; then, from the 770s, with the titles *princeps*, *dux*, *praefectus*, and *patricius*. See Keynes, *Atlas of Attestations*, tables X and XVII.

[31] Bullough, 'What has Ingeld to do with Lindisfarne?', 105–8 (on *convivium*), 108–9 (on *sacerdotalis*), and 118–21.

[32] M. Garrison, 'The Social World of Alcuin: Nicknames at York and at the Carolingian Court', in L. A. J. R. Houwen and A. A. MacDonald (eds.), *Alcuin of York: Scholar at the Carolingian Court*, Germania Latina III (Groningen, 1998), 59–79, esp. 61–4 and 69.

[33] Keynes, 'Councils of *Clofesho*', 24–5.

[34] Ibid., table I ('Attestations of bishops at church councils, 747–845'); see also Keynes, *Atlas of Attestations*, tables VIII and XIII. Dioceses: Iænberht, Æthelheard (Canterbury); Heardred, Ælfhun, Tidfrith (Dunwich); Alhheard (Elmham); Ceolmund, Utel (Hereford); Unwona (Leicester); Hygeberht, Aldwulf (Lichfield); Ceolwulf, Eadwulf (Lindsey); Cœnwalh, Heathoberht (London); Wærmund (Rochester); Wiohthun (Selsey); Æthelmod, Denefrith, Wigberht (Sherborne); Cyneberht (Winchester), Heathured, Deneberht (Worcester).

	123	128	1430	136	139	132	150	153	155	106
S:	123	128	1430	136	139	132	150	153	155	106
BCS:	247	254	256	267	274	265	281	289	293	201
Archive:	CCC	CCC	Wor	StAlb	Wor	CCC	StAlb	CCC	CCC	CCC
Place of issue:	Chel	Chel	Chel	Chel	*Clof*	Ldn	Chel	[ ]	Tam	Chel
Year:	785	788	789	793	?794	'790'	796	798	799	*c*.800
Iænberht	1	1	1							
Æthelheard				2	2	1	1	1	2	1
Heardred	4	4	4							
Ælfhun				7	12	7	4			
Tidfrith								11	8	11
Alhheard	9	10	[7]	6	11	6		9	5	10
Ceolmund		11	8	5	8	5				
Utel								8	7	4
Unwona	8	7	5	4	5	3	2	4	3	2
Hygeberht	2	2 *ep*	2 ab	1 ab	1 ab			2 ab	1 ab	
Aldwulf										3
Ceolwulf	3	[3]	3	3	3	2				
Eadwulf								7	9	5
Cœnwalh				12	9					
Heathoberht								6	11	7
Wærmund	10	8	11	13	10	10				
Wiohthun				15	13	[cited]	3	10	10	?'abbas'
Æthelmod	5	5	9							
Denefrith				11	7	9				
Wigberht	[bp Sherborne]									9
Cyneberht	6	6	10	[10]	6	8		5	4	8
Heathured	7	9	6	9	4	4		3	6	
Deneberht										6

Figure 1. Progress of Bishop Unwona (785–*c*.800)

Source: Keynes, *Atlas of Attestations*, VIII, XIII.

fifth bishop in Mercia and southern England, which he then held from *c*.789 to *c*.794; from then until his death in *c*.800, he enjoyed the status which he held at the time of Alcuin's letters to 'Speratus'.[35]

The year 785, around the time Unwona was appointed as bishop of Leicester after Eadberht (760s–780s), was a watershed. In this year King Offa was preparing for the creation of a new metropolitan see in Lichfield as a means of overseeing the coronation of his son Ecgfrith as his successor.[36] As Alcuin says to Speratus, most probably to Unwona, in 797: *Scis optime, quanta intentione rex ille clarissmo filio suo praeparavit, ut arbitratur, regnum heredi* ('You, best of men, know with what great aim that king prepared, so it is believed, the kingdom for his most illustrious son as heir').[37] This sentence presents Speratus as a man close to the heart of power, Offa's trusted enforcer. The most likely time for Alcuin to have met Unwona was at the Southumbrian Council of the Legates in 786, about a year after the bishop's appointment. At the time this council was believed to be the first attended by papal envoys since the coming of Augustine (in 597).[38] A record of their visit survives in a report of the Northumbrian council which was drafted by Bishop George of Ostia. This report includes George's brief mention of a second Mercian council, chaired by Offa, in which the proceedings were read out in Latin and English.[39] Alcuin would have met Unwona here after accompanying George south from York, *en route* to join Charlemagne's itinerant court circle.[40] Alcuin's later nickname for a leading bishop, probably the Mercian Unwona, in his letters is a sign that their relationship was comparable with those later existing between Alcuin and Charlemagne's other courtiers in Aachen.[41] If Unwona had entertained Alcuin in Leicester, the *germanitas quam habuimus inter nos praesentia corporali* ('brotherhood which we shared between us in physical presence') to which Alcuin refers in his shorter, possibly earlier, letter to Speratus would describe a working relationship.[42]

Bishop Unwona of Leicester witnessed the Mercian Legatine council in fourth place. Before him, the list of bishops shows Archbishop Iænberht of Canterbury in first place, Bishops Hygeberht of Lichfield in second, and Ceolwulf of Lindsey in third.[43] The abbots who witnessed were ordered in the same way as their

---

[35] On Unwona's rankings, see Bullough, 'What has Ingeld to do with Lindisfarne?', 121.

[36] Brooks, *Early History of the Church of Canterbury*, 117–23. Kirby, *Earliest English Kings*, 173.

[37] *Epistolae*, ed. Dümmler, ii. 182 (no. 124).

[38] Ibid. 19–29 (no. 3); in extract, *EHD*, 836–40 (no. 19). Theodore in 667 and John the Archchanter in 679 were also papal envoys.

[39] Kirby, *Earliest English Kings*, 169–71. See BCS 250, translated in *EHD*, 836–40, at 838 (no. 191).

[40] Bullough, 'Charlemagne's "Men of God" ', 138.

[41] On these nicknames, see McKitterick, *The Frankish Kingdoms under the Carolingians*, 160–2; and Orchard, 'Wish You Were Here', 34–6.

[42] *Epistolae*, ed. Dümmler, ii. 443 (no. 285).

[43] Keynes, 'Councils of *Clofesho*', table I ('Attestations of bishops at church councils, 747–845'); *Atlas of Attestations*, table VIII. After Unwona come Alhheard of Elmham (5), Eadberht of London (6), Cyneberht of Winchester (7), Heardred of Dunwich (8), Esne of Hereford (9), Tota of Selsey (10), Wærmund of Rochester (11), Æthelmod of Sherborne (12), and Heathured of Worcester (13).

bishops.[44] They were likewise men of promise: Abbot Æthelheard of Louth in Lindsey (1) was later consecrated archbishop of Canterbury on 21 July 793; Abbot Utel (4), though he disappears from the charter record as an abbot in 795, was consecrated bishop of Hereford in the south-west Midlands in the reign of Cenwulf in c.798.[45] Abbot Botwine (3) ruled the minster of *Medeshamstede* near Peterborough. He and an Abbot Alhmund ruled minsters in Unwona's Middle Anglian diocese of Leicester, which was large and wealthy.[46]

Alhmund was prominent from 786 to 805, as one of four *presbyteres abbates* ('priest abbots'), a title which means that Unwona appointed them: the others were named Beonna (who succeeded Botwine to *Medeshamstede* in 787/8),[47] Forthred, and Wigmund. Already in 786, therefore, in the Council of the Legates, the configuration of dioceses and minsters around Unwona shows that he was close to Offa and may have owed his appointment to this king. Offa was looking for ecclesiastical allies for his creation of the new Lichfield archdiocese. To do this, he had to split the ecclesiastical province of Canterbury, for which he had taken pains to secure not only the pope's but Charlemagne's approval.[48] In spite of the imperial sanction, in particular, the papal report of the 786 Council of the Legates contains nothing related to Lichfield. Later Pope Leo III (795–816) claimed to have known nothing of the bitterness which Offa's scheme caused in Canterbury.[49] Yet 787 was a year of turmoil for the Anglo-Saxon Church, as an entry in the *Anglo-Saxon Chronicle* (A) testifies:

785 [787]. Her wæs geflit fullic senoþ æt Cealchyþe, 7 Iænbryht ærcebisc. forlet sumne dæl his bisc.domes, 7 from Offan kyninge Hygebryht wæs gecoren, 7 Ecgferþ to cyninge gehalgod.[50]

[In this year there was a contentious council at Chelsea, and Archbishop Iænberht lost a part of his diocese, and Hygeberht was elected [archbishop] by King Offa, and Ecgfrith consecrated king]

The division of the Canterbury archdiocese caused much rancour, not only here but also further afield, in Mercia, and for years afterwards. The strength of Unwona's position after 787 may tell us that he helped to enforce the Lichfield regime.[51] To

---

[44] Keynes, 'Councils of *Clofesho*', 47 and table II ('Attestations of abbots at church councils, 747–845'); *Atlas of Attestations*, table IX.

[45] Keynes, 'Councils of *Clofesho*', 46–7. Kirby, *Earliest English Kings*, 172.

[46] Keynes, 'Councils of *Clofesho*', 30–48.

[47] Ibid. 46–7. Kirby, *Earliest English Kings*, 172.

[48] McKitterick, *The Frankish Kingdoms under the Carolingians*, 64–70. See also J. L. Nelson, *Politics and Ritual in Early Medieval Europe* (London, 1986), 319 n. 4. McKitterick, *The Frankish Kingdoms under the Carolingians*, 68–9. On Charlemagne's interest, see ibid. 59. Wormald, 'The Age of Offa and Alcuin', 101–6.

[49] *Epistolae*, ed. Dümmler, ii. 187–9, at 187 (no. 127): 'Offa suis litteris testatus est, ut in id omnium vestrum una voluntas et unanima esset petitio.' See *EHD*, 861–2 (no. 205).

[50] *ASC*, 53–4.

[51] Bullough ('What has Ingeld to do with Lindisfarne?', 120) suggests, however, that 'distrust of, or even antagonism towards, the incumbent of Lichfield is presumably a factor' in Alcuin's acquaintance with Unwona.

this it may be worth adding the legend in the *Vitae duorum Offarum* that Unwona was an associate of Bishop Humbertus (i.e. Archbishop Hygeberht) of Lichfield, who, like Unwona perhaps, *magnæ facilitatis vir fuit, literaturæ et prudentiæ sæcularis* ('was a man of great ability, in both literature and knowledge of the world').[52]

If it was Unwona, therefore, who commissioned a now-lost poem on Hinieldus which the poet of *Beowulf* could have used as his source in *c*.826 × *c*.839, it is reasonable to suppose that this poem was transmitted to the poet of *Beowulf* by one of the bishop's former pupils. The most suitable candidates for Unwona's pupils and fellow revellers are the 'priest abbots' of his diocese. Priest abbots of the late eighth and early ninth centuries differed from ordinary abbots in being both ordained as priests and set over minsters as abbots by their bishop.[53] This means that Unwona knew and appointed Priest Abbots Alhmund (a witness from 786 to 805), Beonna of *Medeshamstede* (late 780s to *c*.805), Forthred (789 to 803), and Wigmund (*c*.792 to 814). Keynes shows that they had a special identity as a group.[54]

There is no evidence for the name of the insider who would have known enough to tell Alcuin that a poem on Hinieldus was performed in the bishop's court. On the other hand, in the 790s Alcuin wrote an open letter to be shown to acquaintances in minsters across Europe by one 'Fordradus'. This man appears to have been a priest on pilgrimage. With his usual flourishes, Alcuin commends *hunc presbyterem Fordradum nomine diligentissime* ('this priest, Forthred by name, most diligently').[55] The one known namesake who fits the chronology is Priest Abbot Forthred in the court of Bishop Unwona.[56] There is a record of a Forthred's death *s.a.* 805 in the Parker manuscript of the *Anglo-Saxon Chronicle*.[57] This shows that Priest Abbot Forthred, if the same man, became highly regarded by the West Saxons: unusual for a Mercian abbot, unless he visited their courts.

In this way it seems likely that Alcuin's phrase *filius stultus* typifies one of Unwona's other colleagues. This could be Alhmund, Beonna, Wigmund, or someone else. The name of this man, if one is intended, cannot be known, but Alcuin's assumption of Speratus' interest in Ingeld's salvation shows that the poet of the offending work was a member of the clergy. From the parallels between *Beowulf* and the *Aeneid* which I have discussed earlier in Chapters 2–4, it seems clear that the poet of *Beowulf*, also, was educated in a monastery. If we choose his source from one of the known names around Unwona, Wigmund's fits best of all.

---

[52] *Vitae duorum Offarum*, ed. Wats, 22.

[53] Keynes, 'Councils of *Clofesho*', 46. See Brooks, *Early History of the Church of Canterbury*, 163; Sims-Williams, *Religion and Literature*, 156, 170–1, and 357.

[54] Keynes, 'Councils of *Clofesho*', 26–7; *Atlas of Attestations*, tables IX and XV, at BCS 312 (*s.a.* 803, *Clofesho*).

[55] *Epistolae*, ed. Dümmler, ii. 37–8, at 38 (no. 12).

[56] There is an Abbot Forthred, uncle of King Æthelred of Northumbria, whom Alcuin would probably have known; but he flourished in the 750s, was an abbot, not a priest, and would have been too old. See Kirby, *Earliest English Kings*, 150.

[57] CCCC 173, from Winchester. Unless, perhaps, he had met Ecgberht on his way to Rome. See ibid. 176–7. *ASC*, 58 (*s.a.* 805): '7 Forþred abbud forþferde'.

PRIEST ABBOT WIGMUND

The name *Wigmund* recommends itself in that a certain *Wægmund* is to be inferred as Beowulf's ancestor: on his father's side, Beowulf hails from the *Wægmundingas* whose number also includes *Weohstan* (*Weoxstan*, *Wihstan*) and his son *Wiglaf* in the last 580 lines of *Beowulf*. If the poem was finished in the period 826–*c*.839, as I have suggested in Chapter 2, it is unlikely that Wigmund composed it, for by then he had been dead for at least ten years. The name 'Wigmund', however, does provide the best connection between the poet of *Beowulf* and Unwona's circle. That is, the name 'Wiglaf the Wægmund-ing' in the poem fits with that of a priest abbot, thus almost certainly a former pupil and latter-day drinking companion, of a bishop whom Bullough identifies with the 'Speratus' whom Alcuin in 797 blames for the performance of a poem which was arguably *Beowulf*'s major source.

As the charters show (Fig. 2), Priest Abbot Wigmund was probably kin to the laymen Wigberht, Wigferth, and Wigheard. After Wigmund's day, in Cenwulf's reign, the position of this family drifted downwards (Fig. 8). The ranking of Wigheard, in particular, sinks after his last witness above and then erratically rises and dips through the years leading up to 816;[58] he seems to be replaced by a kinsman named Wighelm in 817, whose second and last witness is in 823.[59] It seems likely that Wiglaf, who became king of Mercia in 827, was a younger member of this family.[60] His son was named Wigmund, like Unwona's priest abbot of a generation earlier; he and his grandson St Wigstan Wigmunding show that this family kept its identity through the leaner years of Cenwulf's reign.

In his own day Bishop Unwona of Leicester seems to have appointed Wig-mund as a priest abbot in his diocese in *c*.792, the date of his first likely extant witness.[61] That is to say, Wigmund was probably associated with Unwona as a pupil in the late 780s, the time when Unwona's star was rising with Offa's. Wigmund continued to witness charters until *c*.814. As noted earlier, Keynes has shown that he was one of the four priest abbots in the diocese whose 'special identity as a group' is made clear in Archbishop Æthelheard's decree at *Clofesho* in 803 and who were probably, therefore, of special status in the diocese at least ten years earlier.[62] An impression of Wigmund's relationships with other powerful

---

[58] He is 6 *dux* in 804 (S 1187/BCS 313), 9 *dux* twice in 805 (S 40, 161/BCS 322, 321), 5 *dux* in 809 (S 164/BCS 328, at which another layman named Wigheard attended at no. 11), 8 *dux* in 812 (S 170/BCS 340: here the other Wigheard is no. 12), oddly 2 *dux* in 816 (S 180/BCS 357) and 10 *dux* the same year, his last witness (S 179/BCS 356).

[59] At no. 9 (S 186/BCS 370); then, after a gap in the charter evidence, at no. 12 in 823 (S 187/BCS 373).

[60] For the finding of this and other Mercian kindreds by name-prefixes, see Yorke, *Kings and Kingdoms*, 120; Keynes, 'Mercia and Wessex in the Ninth Century', 314–19.

[61] If he is not the same as the Wigmund who witnessed as second abbot in S 118 (BCS 235) in 780.

[62] Keynes, 'Councils of *Clofesho*', 26–7, at 26, and table II ('Attestations of abbots at church councils, 747–845').

S:	138	139	149	150	151	153	155	106	1260	
BCS:	264	274	279	281	280	289	293	201	308	312
Archive:	StAlb	Wor	Malm	StAlb	StAlb	CCC	CCC	CCC	Wor	CCC
Place of issue:	?Barford	*Clof*	[chc?]	Chel	Chel	[*?Clof*]	Tam	Chel	*Clof*	*Clof*
Year:	*c*.792	?794	796	796	796	798	799	*c*.800	*c*.800	803
KINGS										
Offa	+	+								
Ecgfrith			+	+	+					
Cenwulf						+	+	+	+	+
BISHOPS										
Hygeberht	1 ab	1 ab				2 ab	1 ab			
Unwona	4	5		2	2	4	3	2		
Werenberht									3	
PRIEST ABBOTS										
Alhmund	1	1				1	1			1 Lei
Beonna	2	2		1	1	2	2	2		2 Lei
Forthred	4			2	2	4	3	?3		3 Lei
Wigmund	3	3				3	4			4 Lei
LAYMEN										
Brorda (1)	1 *pat*	1		1 *pre*	1 *dux*	1 *dux*	1 *pri*	1 *pri*		
Æthelmund	6 *d*	5		2 *pre*			5 *dux*	3 *dux*	2	
Wigberht	5 *dux*	6 *dux*			2 *dux*	.*dux*	4 *dux*	4 *dux*		
Wigferth				6						
Wigheard									6 *p'*	

Figure 2. Unwona's priest abbots (*c*.792–803)

Source: Keynes, *Atlas of Attestations*, VIII–X, XIII, XV, XVII.

Mercians in this period may be found in a select list of ecclesiastical and secular witness rankings in charters from *c*.792, when Wigmund first appears, to *c*.803, the council at which the Lichfield archdiocese was abolished and at which dioceses were attributed to men's names.[63]

---

[63] Keynes, *Atlas of Attestations*, tables VIII, IX, X, and XIII, XV, XVII.

These charters do not show the full range, and many of the names in these
tables are absent from other charters which there is not space to include.
However, a few patterns emerge which will be of interest to any discussion of
Unwona and his priest abbots. One pattern is that the group of four to which
Wigmund belongs keeps its identity and fairly well its hierarchy across three
reigns, over more than ten years, even after Unwona's death. Wigmund and
Forthred switch positions a couple of times, as if they were of permanently
comparable status: in this light of this association it is worth returning to the
speculation that Alcuin's informant about the Hinieldus incident may have been
Forthred. Here it is interesting to note that Wigmund convened with groups
which included Bishop Unwona and Ealdorman Æthelmund of the Hwicce, son
of Ingeld, the other two Leicestershire priest abbots Beonna and Alhmund
(and, of course, many other men).[64]

Also evident from Keynes's tables is the dogged rise of the same Ealdorman
Æthelmund. Bullough believes that Speratus commissioned the poem on Hinieldus as a compliment to the namesake who was Æthelmund's deceased father.[65]
This idea can be supported with a reading of Alcuin's letter which Bullough does
not himself make. In his aforesaid complaint to Speratus Alcuin denigrates
Hinieldus and other heathens as *nominetenus reges* ('so-called kings').[66] His
snobbery here tells us that Speratus and his crowd regarded Ingeld as a king
who lived in history. Why else would they want him at the Lord's banquet in
heaven? If the bishop's offending communion with Ingeld speaks of his interest in
Ingeld's place in a royal genealogy, then Bullough's suggestion works. Genealogy
is an interest which Sam Newton rightly finds in *Beowulf*, whether in honour of
Hrothmund, forebear of East Anglian kings, Offa of Angeln in *Beo* 1944–62, or
anyone else.[67] As he shows, royal lineage is a focus in the story of the martyrdom
of St Æthelberht in the twelfth-century Hereford *Passio*, in which it is said that
King Æthelberht, to pass the time on his fateful road to Offa, asked his poets
to recite *carmina regio* ('songs in royal style') and then heard two men
perform *carmina de regis eiusdem regia prosapia* ('songs about the royal lineage
of the same king').[68] Alcuin's letter to Speratus could thus refer indirectly to a
connection between Unwona in north-eastern and Ealdorman Æthelmund in
south-western Mercia.

Research into Æthelmund shows him to have been a new man, first in the
service of the sub-kings of the Hwicce and then granted their old royal lands by

[64] S 139 (BCS 274).
[65] Bullough, 'What has Ingeld to do with Lindisfarne?', 122 n. 100.
[66] Ibid. 124. Bullough, perhaps thinking of *Widsith*, takes *nominetenus regibus* to mean 'kings listed
by name'. Yet Alcuin himself uses the adverb *nominetenus* with the meaning 'so-called' in two instances:
in a letter to Priest Eanwulf (*Epistolae*, ed. Dümmler, ii. 441–2, at 442 (no. 283): *plurimi sunt
nominetenus doctores, sed pauci charitati officio*); and in his diatribe against a Spanish adoptionist (*Contra
Elipandum*, PL XCVI, *extraneam nominetenus tantum in illo* [scil. *Christo*] *generositatem affirmans*).
[67] Newton, *The Origins of Beowulf*, 77–131, at 95–104.
[68] Ibid. 63–4. James, 'Two Lives of St Ethelbert', 238.

Offa in south-west Mercia at about this time.[69] The charters in Fig. 2 are a selection, but not even all of those extant could represent all the meetings that took place between Offa, his court, and his bishops in the 780s and 790s. In just four charters, however, we can see that Æthelmund met Unwona at *Clofesho* in *c*.794, in one place undisclosed in 798, in Tamworth in 799, and in Chelsea in *c*.800, Unwona's last extant witness.[70] Priest Abbot Wigmund was present at all of these meetings but the last, along with Alhmund; Forthred missed the meeting in *Clofesho* in *c*.794 but was there at the others, in Tamworth, the place undisclosed, and Chelsea; Beonna was there at all four. It is noteworthy that the separate positions of Unwona and Æthelmund during these six years were roughly comparable: both seem to have been men on the rise, both apparently artistic patrons;[71] and any political alliance between them, one which would underpin any performance of the work on 'Hinieldus' for the ealdorman's father, is possible within the frame of their frequent meetings at which the bishop's entourage also attended.

To sum up, these names and their twofold coincidence with those of the Wægmundings in the last fifth of *Beowulf* make it tempting to believe that Priest Abbot Wigmund transmitted the famous work on 'Hinieldus' to the poet of *Beowulf*. From the end of the eighth century, a poem of Theodulf of Orléans shows how easily (Latin) poems could be passed from hand to hand among members of a court.[72] By the same token the strongest possibility is that the work now known as *Beowulf* was composed in Wigmund's minster.

WIGMUND'S MINSTER: BREEDON ON THE HILL?

Offa's Mercian territory covered a large area, including at least fourteen monastic foundations in the late eighth century in the eastern Midlands alone.[73] The scarcity of charters from here is proof of the havoc wrought about a century later by the Danes, who occupied the urban centres of the 'Five Boroughs' of the southern Danelaw.[74] In north-east England during this period the episcopal lists of every diocese except York and Lindisfarne were interrupted for decades; Leicester was one of three that disappeared.[75] With the absence of all but scraps of information from Offa's late reign, it has so far proved impossible to connect

[69] Wormald, 'The Age of Offa and Alcuin', 123. Sims-Williams, *Religion and Literature*, 123–6.
[70] S 139, 153, 155, and 106 (resp. BCS 274, 289, 293, 201).
[71] For Unwona, if he is Speratus, there is the poem on Hinieldus; on Æthelmund's and his son Æthelric's patronage of the eighth-century church in Deerhurst (Gloucs.), see Wormald, 'The Age of Offa and Alcuin', 123–4, and fig. 116.
[72] Godman, *Poetry of the Carolingian Renaissance*, 151 (*Ad Carolum regem*).
[73] Keynes, 'Councils of *Clofesho*', 30–58 (Castor, Peakirk, Thorney, *Medeshamstede*, Breedon on the Hill, Repton, Oundle, Brigstock, Ely, St Albans, Wing, Buckingham, Brixworth, Charlbury).
[74] Hart, *The Danelaw*, 7–19, at 17–19.
[75] Wormald, 'The Ninth Century', 147.

Unwona's priest abbots to minsters in his diocese in all but one or two cases. Beonna is known to have succeeded Abbot Botwine of *Medeshamstede* in the late 780s; and Alhmund is perhaps identifiable as the man of this name who held land to the south-west of the minster in Wing (Bucks.), according to S 138 (BCS 264), a charter of *c.*792.[76] The names of Forthred's and Wigmund's minsters are unknown.

Notwithstanding this lack of knowledge, some place names and charters point to one place more than others as the site of Wigmund's minster. The first clue, one of three, arises in place names in the north of Unwona's likely diocese which have the personal name *Wigmund* attached to them: Wymeswold (Leics.) and Wymondham (Leics., formerly Rutland). The name 'Wymeswold' derives from *Wigmundes wald* ('Wigmund's part of the district called *Wold*'; DB *Wimundes- wald*).[77] The same Wigmund's stamp on the area is visible, moreover, in the name *Wymundesdisch* or *Wimundesche Dysch* ('Wigmund's ditch'), which was recorded for this village in a grant of land to Garendon Abbey in the early thirteenth century.[78] Wymeswold lies at 240 ft above sea level, in wold country hemmed in by hills to north, east, and south and with a vale opening up towards the west. The name 'Wymondham' derives from *Wigmundes ham* ('Wigmund's ?home'); there is one village by this name in Norfolk, in East Anglia, and one about 20 miles east-north-east of Leicester and 15 miles east of Wymeswold. The eastern Wymondham falls outside the likely bounds of Unwona's diocese.[79] The western Wymondham (DB *Wimvndesham*), situated near a three-way border between Rutland, Leicestershire, and Lincolnshire, would be within Unwona's area but lies some way distant from any sites of former minsters, at 20 miles to the north-west of Peakirk, the nearest of them.[80] Wymeswold, on the other hand, is found 20 miles north of Leicester off the Fosse Way and some 13 miles due east of one of the most distinguished monasteries in Mercia, Breedon on the Hill.[81] In the eighth and ninth centuries this monastic site would have been visible for miles around. Today the minster has gone, but the church at Breedon can still be seen perched on its limestone outcrop by anyone walking a mile out of Wymeswold west towards the river Soar.

As the poet of *Beowulf* says of Heorot, sighted by Beowulf on his road to Hrothgar:

Guman onetton,
sigon ætsomne   oþþæt hy sæl timbred

[76] Keynes, 'Councils of *Clofesho*', 36 and 47.

[77] Gelling, *Place-Names in the Landscape*, 226–7. Ekwall, *Oxford Dictionary of Place-Names, s.v.* 'Wymeswold' (p. 541).

[78] S. P. Potter, *A History of Wymeswold* (London, 1915), 46–7; cf. 1–3.

[79] See also Gelling, *Place-Names in the Landscape*, 212–13, for *Wimundestreu* ('Wigmund's tree') in Herefordshire. OE Wigmund may survive also in 'Wymington', Bedfordshire (DB *Wimentone*, possibly from *Wigmundes tun*): Ekwall, *Oxford Dictionary of Place-Names, s.v.* 'Wymington' (p. 541).

[80] *The Place-Names of Leicestershire, Part II*, ed. B. Cox, EPNS 78 (Nottingham, 2002), 286.

[81] On this and other roads, see Hill, *Atlas of Anglo-Saxon England*, 116 (no. 199).

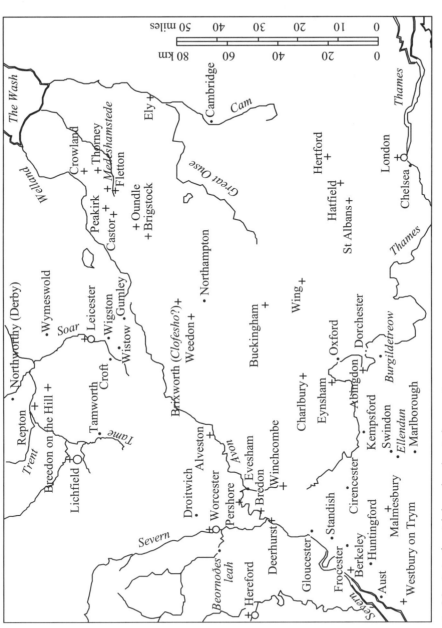

1. Mercia in the eighth and early ninth centuries

geatolic ond goldfah   ongyton meahton;
þæt wæs foremærost   foldbuendum
receda under roderum   onþam se rica bad:
lixte se leoma   ofer landa fela. (*Beo* 306–11)

[Men hastened, marched down the road together until they could make out the timbered hall, splendid and adorned with gold; to those who dwelt in that country, that building in which the mighty one waited was the most famous beneath the skies: the gleam shone over many lands.]

The church at Breedon is dedicated to SS Mary and Hardulph.[82] This place, close to the site of the old minster, lies west of the Soar, not far south of the river Trent, and about 8 miles east-south-east of Repton (Derbys.) which is also on the Trent's southern bank.[83] Repton was the site of a royal Mercian mausoleum in the eighth and ninth centuries, with an eighth-century church, distinguished for the architecture of its crypt.[84] In this crypt King Æthelbald is said to have been buried after his assassination in 756; so was King Wiglaf, after his death *c*.840; and also, eventually, St Wigstan, Wiglaf's grandson, after his murder by a cousin in *c*.849.[85] Kirby has suggested that Wiglaf and Wigstan were related to Æthelbald;[86] the fact that they all were interred in Repton would probably indicate that a kindred with *Wig*-prefixes had an interest in the lands of the surrounding country. St Wigstan was murdered in *c*.849: the site of his martyrdom has been identified as either Wistanstow (Shrops.) or Wistow (Leics.), with preference for the latter.[87] Wistow lies 7 miles south of Leicester and possibly shows this as another area in the same region in which the *Wig*-kindred owned lands. In this connection it is interesting that a certain Wigferth is attested as the fourth priest of Lichfield in the Council of *Clofesho* in 803 (BCS 312). In addition, there was a Wigfrith who worked as the secretary of Bishop Hædda whose name is preserved in Felix's *Vita s. Guthlaci*, written in the first half of the eighth century.[88] Wigfrith and Hædda are here said to have visited St Guthlac in Crowland;[89] probably this would have been in the early 690s, when Hædda, abbot of Breedon on the Hill

---

[82] See B. C. J. Williams, *The Story of St. Mary and St. Hardulph Church: A Cradle of our Faith* (Nottingham, 1996).

[83] OS, Landranger Series 128, 129.

[84] D. Parsons, 'The Mercian Church: Archaeology and Topography', in Brown and Farr (eds.), *Mercia* 51–68, at 63–4. M. Biddle and B. Kjølbye-Biddle, 'The Repton Stone', *ASE* 14 (1985), 233–92, at 233–6. Bond ('Links between Beowulf and Mercian History', 484 n. 17) considers *Beowulf*'s toponyms *Hrefneswudu*, *Hreosnaburh*, and *Hronesnæs* (lines 2935 (cf. 2925); 2477; and 2805, 3136) to be chosen as alliteratively reminiscent of *Hreopedun* (*Hrypandun*).

[85] Thacker, 'Kings, Saints, and Monasteries', 12–14. Rollason, 'The Search for Saint Wigstan', 7–12; 'The Cults of Murdered Royal Saints', 5–6.

[86] Kirby, *Earliest English Kings*, 191.

[87] D. J. Bott, 'The Murder of St. Wistan', *Transactions of the Leicestershire Archaeological Society*, 29 (1953), 30–41, esp. 39–40. *Chronicon abbatiae de Evesham*, ed. Macray, 325–37, esp. 329.

[88] Roberts, 'Hagiography and Literature', 70–1 and 75.

[89] *Felix's Life of St Guthlac*, ed. and trans. B. Colgrave (Cambridge, 1956), 142–4.

and bishop of Lichfield, had been appointed bishop of Leicester also.[90] Wigfrith had lived in Ireland, according to Felix, but his is not an Irish name; and it seems likely that Hædda had employed him as a native of the east Midlands. The *Ars grammatica* of Tatwine, a priest who lived in Breedon before becoming archbishop of Canterbury in 731 (see Chapter 6), has a number of sources in common with the anonymous, but Irish, *Ad Cuimnanum*. This leads Vivien Law to ask whether or not the Breedon library, where she assumes Tatwine wrote his grammar, 'derived its grammatical holdings from wandering Irish teachers'.[91] It has been suggested that this Tatwine is identical with the man of that name who guides Hædda to Guthlac in Crowland in Felix's *Vita Guthlaci*.[92] The chronology fits, given that a mature man before 714 (when Guthlac died) would be old enough to become archbishop of Canterbury in 731. If the two Tatwines are one, then Wigfrith likewise was perhaps linked to Breedon. At least a localization of Wigstan, Wiglaf, Wigferth, and Wigfrith in the Trent valley is a second piece of evidence with a bearing on where Priest Abbot Wigmund, apparently a member of the same kindred, might have ruled his family minster. If we turn back to a map, Breedon can be found on a line one-third of the way from Repton to Wymeswold.

The third clue is found in Mercian charters issued from *c*.786 to *c*.848. Priest Abbot Wigmund's name and ranking is clear from a number of these, most of which are shown in the adjoining table (Fig. 3). If we look for the man who appears in Wigmund's ranking after Wigmund disappears, taking him to be abbot of the same house, we can see whether or not he can be matched with a minster. The potential weakness of this approach is that a new man with a different minster may have come into Wigmund's signatory place. On the other hand, if the archive is the same, and the name that takes Wigmund's ranking is not found in previous charters, we can suppose that this man was appointed abbot of Wigmund's minster not long after Wigmund died. The charters allow us to deduce the name of Wigmund's successor, especially the major attestations for Mercian abbots, in church councils, from 803 to 823.[93]

As Keynes reminds us, charters must be treated cautiously, for gaps may be assumed even when all attestations are assembled.[94] Yet some observations may be made. The first is that generally the priest abbots of Middle Anglia lost their Offa-derived precedence over abbots from Canterbury after 805, for by this time the Lichfield archdiocese had been defunct for two years. Thus Wilheard, an

---

[90] Keynes, 'Councils of *Clofesho*', 33–40, at 39 n. 166.

[91] Law, 'The Study of Latin Grammar in Eighth-Century Southumbria', 67.

[92] Tom Chivers, '*Beowulf* and Mercia: A Re-evaluation', extended essay for the BA submitted to Heather O'Donoghue in the University of Oxford. Chivers associates *Beowulf* with Breedon (among other possibilities) through the parallels between the fenland descriptions in *Guthlac* A and Grendel's Mere.

[93] Keynes, 'Councils of *Clofesho*', table II; see Keynes, *Atlas of Attestations*, table XV (2).

[94] Keynes, *Atlas of Attestations*, preface.

S:			40	161	41	173	180	187
BCS:	312	310	322	321	318	343	357	373
Archive:	CCC	CCC	CCC	Wor	CCC	Wor	CCC	
Place of issue:	*Clof*	*Clof*	*Aclea*	*Aclea*		[chc]	[chc]	*Werburgingwic*
Year:	803	803	805	805	805x7	814	816	823
Alhmund	1Leic	1	1					
Beonna	2Leic	2	2		2			
Forthred	3Leic	3	[deceased]					
Wigmund	4Leic	4			1	2		
Wernoth		3	3					
Dud(em)an		4	2					
Feologeld	2Cant	5	1					2
Wilheard						1	1...	
Rethhun						3[then bishop of Leicester		
Piot						4	*pb*	*pb*
Tidbald						5		
Wulfheard						6		
Cuthwulf						7		
Eanmund							2	1...
Wihtred							3	
Tilberht							4	
Biornhelm								3
Æthelheah	1Cant							

Figure 3. Wigmund, his successor, and their minster (803–823)

Source: Keynes, *Atlas of Attestations*, XV.

abbot of Canterbury (for he succeeds Feologeld), witnesses as first abbot in 814 (S 173), with Wigmund as second.[95] Wilheard is the key to unlocking the identity of Wigmund's successor, for he witnessed as first abbot in four surviving charters: two in Fig. 3;[96] two outside it.[97] When Wilheard is thus first abbot in S 180, in 816, Wigmund's second-place ranking falls to Eanmund. The archive of both relevant charters, S 173 and S 180, is the same, Worcester, so the question of the same minster being ranked differently between regions does not arise. After

[95] Wilheard or *P*ilheard? See Brooks, *Early History of the Church of Canterbury*, 142–3.
[96] S 173 (BCS 343), *s.a.* 814; S 180 (BCS 357), *s.a.* 816.
[97] S 179 (BCS 356), *s.a.* 816; S 182 (BCS 359), *s.a.* 817.

	180	187	1434	1433	1436	1437	190
S:	180	187	1434	1433	1436	1437	190
BCS:	357	373	378	379	384	386	416
Archive:	Wor	CCC	CCC	Wor	CCC	Wor	Wor
Place of issue:	[chc]	*Werb.wic*	*Clof*	*Clof*	*Clof*	*Clof*	Croft (Leics.)
Year:	816	823	824	824	825	825	836
Wernoth			4				
Feologeld		2					
Wilheard	1						
Piot	pb	pb			[cited]	[cited]	
Cuthwulf			1	2	1	4	
Eanmund	2	1	2	1	3	2	1 . . .
Wihtred	3			3	6	3	2
Tilberht	4						
Biornhelm		3					3
Eanmund			3		4	5 . . .	
Wilferth				4	2		

Figure 4. Hierarchy of Breedon and Bredon (816–836)

Source: Keynes, *Atlas of Attestations*, XV–XVI.

816 Eanmund's subsequent rankings are consistent in that they hover between 1 and 2, and once 3, in the 820s and 830s. In this way, it looks as if the years 814–16 saw Eanmund succeed to the position of Wigmund over the same house.

It is difficult, but not impossible, to identify the house over which this Eanmund was appointed. The difficulty is that later on, in the charters of the 820s and 830s, there are two abbots named Eanmund. One is the man who is here likely to succeed Wigmund; the other, styled 'priest abbot', attests here in only three surviving charters, all in *Clofesho*, one in 824 and two in 825. The fuller picture emerges in the charters from church councils 816–36 (Fig. 4).[98]

With the Eanmunds a typically bizarre complication arises in that each abbot ruled a minster named Bre(e)don. In 841, King Berhtwulf of Mercia gave a privilege either to Abbot Eanmund of Bredon in Worcestershire or to Abbot Eanmund of Breedon in Leicestershire (S 193). This charter, issued at Tamworth, with Eanmund as the first abbot, and preserved in the Worcester archive, is usually taken to be in favour of Abbot Eanmund of Bredon in

---

[98] Keynes, 'Councils of *Clofesho*', table II; see Keynes, *Atlas of Attestations*, table XVI (1) (*c*.830–*c*.920).

Worcestershire.[99] Yet not everyone has agreed with this, given the charter's association with Tamworth, which is closer to Breedon.[100] It is conceivable that S 193 ended up in the Worcester archive because it was appropriated from the defunct Leicester diocese after 971 when the sees of Worcester and York were held in plurality.[101] It is also worth noting that S 193 quotes a line from Aldhelm's *In basilica beatae Mariae semper virginis* (*c*.685).[102] Aldhelm's context, a passage on Gabriel and the Annunciation, identifies S 193 with Breedon, for Breedon by this time was dedicated to St Mary and contains a panel with an angel which it is possible to interpret as the Archangel Gabriel. However, the dedication of the church at Bredon at this time is unknown.[103]

In S 197, issued in 848 at Repton, with Eanmund as the first abbot, Berhtwulf granted immunities to Abbot Eanmund of Breedon in Leicestershire. It seems likely that the Eanmund who seems to follow Wigmund as second abbot after Wilheard in 816 (S 180) would have been the Breedon abbot in Wigmund's Leicester diocese. When Wilheard was absent in 823, Eanmund signed in first place, the Kentish Feologeld second (S 187). This ranking suggests that the first of the two Eanmunds was appointed abbot in *c*.816 in one of the prestigious houses of the Leicester diocese, rather than of Worcester; for the Kentish Feologeld, in his earlier period of attestation in 803–5, yields precedence to the Middle Anglian Alhmund and Beonna despite being of the archdiocese of Canterbury which regained its primacy over Lichfield in *c*.803. So, in all, we may take the eastern Eanmund to be Wigmund's successor. He is not a priest abbot like Wigmund or indeed the Worcestershire Eanmund; but Bishop Unwona (785–*c*.800) was dead by 824 and his 'group of four' was dissolved by then also. Listed solely as *abbas*, the eastern Eanmund seems to have been elected by his peers.

In the three Mercian charters for 824–5 to which both Eanmunds are witness (S 1434, 1436, and 1437; all of the reign of King Beornwulf), the bishop of Leicester (Rethhun, signing third) comes above that of Worcester (Heahberht, signing fourth, fifth, and fourth respectively).[104] Given that neither of these bishops was head of an archdiocese such as Canterbury, or Lichfield (786–*c*.803), we have grounds for taking the episcopal hierarchy in these charters to be

[99] Keynes, 'Councils of *Clofesho*', 20 n. 171, and 47.

[100] Sims-Williams, *Religion and Literature*, 137 n. 103. *Charters of Abingdon Abbey, Part I*, ed. Kelly, 56–7.

[101] On Worcester's administration of Danelaw territories, see Blair, *The Church in Anglo-Saxon Society*, 313. Cf. S 749 (BCS 1283): King Edgar, probably in *c*.972, of lands belonging to Breedon, to Bishop Æthelwold of Winchester (archive Burton on Trent). Keynes (*Atlas of Attestations*, LV (4)) takes this grant to refer to Breedon in Leicestershire. This grant shows how widely the possessions of the former Leicester diocese could be parcelled out at this time.

[102] 'Qui Solymis quondam dives regnavit in arvis', in *Aldhelmi Opera*, ed. Ehwald, 13 (*In basilica beatae Mariae semper virginis*, line 19) and 423 (Poem *De virginibus*, line 1697).

[103] T. Bridges, *Churches of Worcestershire* (Logaston, 2000), 46–8. This church is dedicated to St Giles, a rededication which probably took place in the eleventh or twelfth century; see Arnold-Forster, *Church Dedications*, ii. 46–51.

[104] Keynes, 'Councils of *Clofesho*', tables I and II.

reflected in that of the lesser Mercian clergy. In this case, the second Eanmund (witness 824–5) is later identifiable with the abbot in Bredon, near Worcester; the first, with the abbot of Breedon on the Hill, to whom Berhtwulf granted immunities in 848 (S 197). *Venerabilis*, the traditional epithet reserved for Eanmund in the 848 charter, would be consistent with the age of a man who had become abbot in *c*.816, more than thirty years earlier.

Breedon was a prestigious minster in the eighth and ninth centuries.[105] This minster most probably lay within the Leicester diocese at this time. Michelle Brown holds that Breedon's diocese was Lichfield, noting some parallels between the famous Breedon sculptures and some manuscript illumination in books of the Tiberius Group, most notably the Book of Cerne, whose compilation she places in or near Lichfield.[106] Yet Breedon's sculptures also show similarities to patterns in illuminations in manuscripts and other artistic media in a variety of places, some of these in the eastern Midlands.[107] In one case, four beasts on one of the broad friezes in the church at Breedon have a parallel in a Mercian bone girdle-end found in Leicester.[108] Although Breedon was close to Lichfield and no doubt under its influence through Lichfield's role as the Mercian arch-diocese from 786 to *c*.803, its diocesan focus was Leicester. Keynes seems to have little difficulty in treating Breedon as a minster of the Leicester diocese in company with *Medeshamstede* from where it was founded; in his view the association between them 'was perhaps the main axis in a Middle Anglian monastic "empire" which appears to have taken shape in the late seventh century, and which seems to have endured well into the ninth'.[109]

CONCLUSION

Alcuin alludes to a poem on Ingeld, 'Hinieldus', which was heard in the court of an acquaintance named 'Speratus', probably Bishop Unwona, in Leicester in 797. The outline of Unwona's career gives reason to suppose that he was a man who rose to power in step with Offa's interests. His anonymous poet probably featured Ingeld's attack on Heorot, yet may have had an interest in the salvation of Ingeld as the ancestor of one man present, possibly Ealdorman Æthelmund son of Ingeld of the Hwicce. The attempt to grant communion to ancient heathens is visible in Alcuin's complaint about this performance and in *Beowulf* but in no other extant work in Old English literature. On these grounds I suggest that the now-lost 'Hinieldus' was *Beowulf*'s source. From what Alcuin assumes about his

---

[105] For a comprehensive account, see ibid. 37–40.
[106] Brown, *The Book of Cerne*, 76–7 and 119.
[107] For a clear introduction, see Cramp, 'Schools of Mercian Sculpture', 191–233. The latest study of the Breedon sculptures is in Jewell, 'Classicism of Southumbrian Sculpture'.
[108] Jewell, 'The Anglo-Saxon Friezes at Breedon-on-the-Hill', 105.
[109] Keynes, 'Councils of *Clofesho*', 37–40, at 40.

friend's drunken *socii clericorum* and the *filius stultus*, it appears that he took some of them to be with Speratus when the offending work was performed. Having posited an influence from the Hinieldus-poem to *Beowulf*, I focus on these associates, Unwona's priest abbots, as the most plausible means of transmission. The name of one of them, Wigmund (*c.*792–814 × 816), is closely identifiable with names of the Wægmunding kindred in the last 580 lines of *Beowulf*. On the assumption, therefore, that Wigmund's kindred had a presiding interest in the composition of *Beowulf*, in which Wiglaf shares the limelight for the last 580 lines, I suggest that it was Priest Abbot Wigmund who took the poem on Hinieldus to his minster. This place I identify with Breedon on the Hill. In the following two chapters I shall give reasons to suppose that the minster at Breedon was also where Wigmund passed down the 'Hinieldus' to the future poet of *Beowulf*.

6

Beowulf and the Library at Breedon on the Hill

This chapter aims to show that *Beowulf*, some time in 826 × 839, was written more plausibly at Breedon than in any other house in Bishop Unwona's diocese. Below I shall see what evidence, if any, survives in the site and documentary record of Breedon which might correspond with the works which I presume to have been among *Beowulf*'s sources. There are various reasons for believing that some nine of these, eight in Latin and one in the vernacular, lay in the Breedon library.

THE LIBRARY AT BREEDON ON THE HILL

No manuscript from Breedon has ever been identified.[1] On the other hand, the book in the right hand of the Virgin Mary, in a panel carved in *c*.820–30, probably tells us that reading was an important activity in the minster which housed her.[2] When the Virgin was carved, Breedon was an old and prestigious monastery within the diocese of Leicester.[3] If we believe the Peterborough version of the *Anglo-Saxon Chronicle* (E), *s.a.* 675, it was founded through a grant by King Æthelred of Mercia (ruled 675–704) of lands which included Breedon, to the monastery of St Peter's at *Medeshamstede* near Peterborough.[4] There is also a charter of 675 × 690 which records a grant by 'Friduricus princeps' to St Peter's at *Medeshamstede* of 20 *manentes* ('hides') at *Briudun*.[5] Two more charters confirm this minster as Breedon's mother house, with Hædda, a priest at *Medeshamstede*, as

---

[1] Lapidge, *The Anglo-Saxon Library*, 44.

[2] Jewell, 'Classicism of Southumbrian Sculpture', 262. Cramp, 'Schools of Mercian Sculpture', 210 (fig. 58a). See my Ill. 4 on p. 179.

[3] The following is based largely on Dornier, 'Breedon on the Hill', 155–68, and on Keynes, 'Councils of *Clofesho*', 37–43.

[4] *ASC* E, *s.a.* 675. See *The Anglo-Saxon Chronicle*, trans. Swanton, 35–7, at 37 (the other lands, after Breedon, are *Hrepingas*, Cadney [?, for *Cadenan ac*], Swineshead, *Heanbyrig*, Louth, Shifnal, Costesford, Stratford, Wattlesborough, the Lizard, *Æthelhuniglond*, Bardney). Dornier, 'Breedon on the Hill', 157.

[5] Dornier, 'Breedon on the Hill', 157 (S 1803/BCS 841). The charter's reference to Æthelred (succeeded 675) and Bishop Seaxwulf (died *c*.690) sets limits for the date, whether or not this charter is trustworthy.

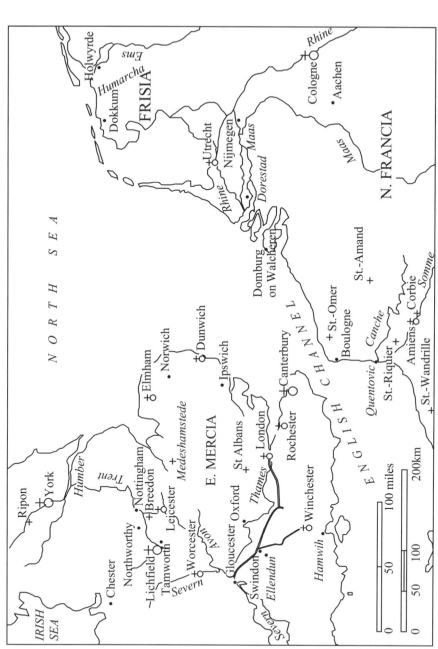

2. East Mercia and north Francia in the eighth and early ninth centuries

first abbot.[6] In one of these (S 1805), Friduricus granted the new abbot 31 *manentes* at *Hrepingas*, a place which is thought to be Repton (Derbys.).[7] In Dornier's view, this is how the monastery at Repton was founded.[8] Hædda, whom the monks of *Medeshamstede* elected abbot of Breedon, is thought to be the same as the Hædda who became bishop of Lichfield on Seaxwulf's death in *c.*690 and later took over the Leicester diocese after Bishop Wilfrid's ejection in 706.[9] Hædda's connection with St Guthlac in Crowland, north of *Medeshamstede* (see Ill. 1 and Chapter 5), may be set alongside certain parallels which Dorothy Whitelock noted between terms for Grendel in *Beowulf* and those for the fenland demons in *Vita Guthlaci*, composed by Felix for King Ælfwald of East Anglia probably in the 730s: *semen Cain* ('Cain's seed') with *Caines cynne* (line 107); and *antiquus hostis prolis humanae* ('ancient enemy of the human race') with *feond mancynnes* (line 164) and *ealdgewinna* (line 1776).[10] If the poet of *Beowulf* borrowed from Felix, as some scholars believe, then his text of the *Vita Guthlaci* may have come either from *Medeshamstede*, nearest to Crowland, or (as is more likely) from Repton; as the daughter of one and the mother of the other, Breedon is better connected with Felix's work than most other minsters in Mercia.[11] From Hædda's time onwards, the young foundation at Breedon could be said to have gained royal friends from the region and to have moved swiftly to the centre of a constellation of wealthy churches and houses with lands not only in Mercia but also in areas controlled by the West Saxons.[12] Some archaeological finds testify to the wealth and international connections that Breedon enjoyed in Offa's reign (757–96).[13]

6 Ibid. 157–8 (S 1805/BCS 842 and S 1804/BCS 843). Keynes, 'Councils of *Clofesho*', 37–9 and n. 160.
   7 Rippingale (Lincs.) is also suggested, although this lies at a greater distance from Breedon. Stenton ('Medehamstede and its Colonies', 185 n. 3) leaves *Hrepingas* unidentified; Swanton (*The Anglo-Saxon Chronicle*, 37) treats it as Rippingale. Repton, however, is accepted by A. Rumble, '"Hrepingas" Reconsidered', in Dornier (ed.), *Mercian Studies*, 169–72; and by Dornier, 'Breedon on the Hill', 158; and cautiously by Keynes, 'Councils of *Clofesho*', 38 n. 163.
   8 Dornier, 'Breedon on the Hill', 158. ; the claim by Hugh Candidus, the twelfth-century monk of Peterborough, that *ad Repingas* was a colony of *Medeshamstede* is doubted by Keynes, in 'Councils of *Clofesho*', 38–9 n. 163.
   9 Keynes, 'Councils of *Clofesho*', 39.
   10 Whitelock, *The Audience of Beowulf*, 80–1. *Felix's Life of St Guthlac*, ed. and trans. B. Colgrave (Cambridge, 1956), 94–5 and 106–7. Accepted tentatively by Niles, *Beowulf*, 89; and less so, by Newton, *The Origins of Beowulf*, 142–3.
   11 On Repton as the impetus for Felix's *Vita Guthlaci*, see Roberts, 'Hagiography and Literature', 70. This *Vita* was probably the third of three saints' lives held in Anglo-Saxon Peterborough, according to Oxford, Bodleian Library, Bodley 163, fos. 250–1 (s. xi/xii): Lapidge, *The Anglo-Saxon Library*, 143–5 (INV(i)f.16).
   12 Keynes, 'Councils of *Clofesho*', 42–3.
   13 There is not only money (a *sceatta*, plus a (lost) coin of Cenwulf's reign (796–821) and a bronze stylus for manuscript illuminations, but also imports of Carolingian and Irish metalwork (a ribbed bow brooch with circular punched terminals, from northern France in the seventh or eighth century; a bronze book-clasp or buckle-plate with cloisons of red, yellow, and blue enamel, from the eighth century), and Carolingian pottery (a well-fired black jug with flanged rim and strap handle, from eighth- or ninth-century northern France). See Dornier, 'Breedon on the Hill', 162–6, at 163. On Mercian wealth, see Wormald, 'The Age of Offa and Alcuin', 101–31.

Bede says that Archbishop Tatwine of Canterbury (731–4), before he was consecrated, was a priest of *Briudun* in the province of Mercia.[14] This was probably not the Worcestershire 'Bredon', which in Bede's time lay under the *Hwicce*.[15] Bede knew Tatwine to be a scholar in sacred texts; an *Ars grammatica* is ascribed to him in four manuscripts and forty Latin *Aenigmata* ('riddles') to him in two.[16] The former work shows his 'heavy but intelligent use' of at least five late Classical and post-Classical Latin authors including Donatus and Isidore of Seville; and his *Aenigmata* are influenced by those of Aldhelm.[17] As we have seen in the foregoing chapter, the quotation of a line from Aldhelm in S 193, probably a Breedon charter of 841, may show that Aldhelm's *Carmina*, and probably his poetic (if not his prose) *De laudibus virginitatis*, were also at Breedon.[18] In his grammar, Tatwine quotes snatches from Vergil which he inherits from earlier grammarians, but his riddles allude to Books VI and XI of the *Aeneid*.[19] Tatwine's riddles reveal something else of the Breedon library in which he composed them; no. 3, in particular, on the four types of meaning (historical, spiritual, moral, and allegorical), would have had little meaning unless it were supported by patristic commentaries and theological works.[20]

So wealthy was Breedon that it became a lodge for passing ecclesiastical and royal envoys. In S 197, a grant issued in 848 to Abbot Eanmund at *Breodune*, King Berhtwulf of the Mercians and Humberht *princeps* of the *Tonseti* grant Eanmund immunities to be observed henceforth by Humberht's people, the *principes* of the *Tonseti* (i.e. the *Tomsæte* (*l-an*), by Tamworth and the river Tame.[21] According to the charter, Eanmund was no longer required to feed passing officials, although it was still his duty to give food and shelter to envoys from overseas or from either Northumbria or Wessex.[22] Humberht's role may have been that of a permanent royal official, who held his tribal lands in fief from

---

[14] *HE* V. 23 (pp. 557–8). The *Anglo-Saxon Chronicle* (E) dates his ordination to 731 (*ASC*, I. 45: *Breodune*).

[15] Dornier, 'Breedon on the Hill', 158. Keynes, 'Councils of *Clofesho*', 39.

[16] Law, *The Insular Latin Grammarians*, 64–7.

[17] Lapidge, *The Anglo-Saxon Library*, 43–4, esp. 43. Law, 'The Study of Latin Grammar in Eighth-Century Southumbria', 61–2.

[18] 'Qui Solymis quondam dives regnavit in arvis', in *Aldhelmi Opera*, ed. Ehwald, 13 (*In basilica beatae Mariae semper virginis*, line 19) and 423 (Poem *De virginibus*, line 1697). On the placing of S 193 in Breedon (Leics.) rather than in Bredon (Worcs.), see the previous chapter.

[19] *Tatuini Opera*, ed. de Marco, 184 (XVII, *De sciuro*, 'On the squirrel': line 2, *Aen*. XI. 532; line 4, *Aen*. VI. 451); cf. 181 (XIV, *De caritate*, 'On charity': line 5, *Georgics* IV.101). Lapidge, *The Anglo-Saxon Library*, 44: 'the writings of Tatwine imply access to a decent working library.' Praise indeed, given the limitations of Tatwine's time, according to Lapidge, *The Anglo-Saxon Library*, 130–1.

[20] *Tatuini Opera*, ed. de Marco, 170.

[21] S 197 (CS 454). Keynes, 'Councils of *Clofesho*', 39–40. Dornier, 'Breedon on the Hill', 158–9. On the *Tomsæte*, see M. Gelling, *The West Midlands in the Early Middle Ages* (Leicester, 1992), 146–53. Hill, *Atlas of Anglo-Saxon England*, 80 (no. 141).

[22] In exchange, Eanmund was to give lands to Berhtwulf at *Stanlega* (Stanley, Derbys.) and *Bellanforde* (unidentified), and portable treasure to Humberht. See C. R. Hart, *The Early Charters of Northern England and the North Midlands* (Leicester, 1975), 68.

Mercian kings.[23] Although Breedon was probably part of the Leicester diocese as a daughter foundation of *Medeshamstede*, it enjoyed a political affiliation with Tamworth in the diocese of Lichfield (see Ill. 1).[24]

For the first three-quarters of the ninth century it seems likely that Breedon kept its wealth. Then, around the time the Danish army left Nottingham and descended on Repton further up the Trent in 874/5, it must be assumed that the library in Breedon disappeared. In Repton the Danes dug a trench through the graveyards, demolished the western end of Wiglaf's royal mausoleum, turned the eastern end into a burial chamber, the church into a gatehouse, and crosses and dressed stone blocks into rubble for a cairn.[25] The scattered disposition of the carvings at St Mary's and St Hardulph's shows more likely than not that the Danes redecorated Breedon in a similar way. The fact that Breedon's land holdings were later accredited to Peterborough, based on its mother foundation, may show that the abbot transferred the deeds before the Danes arrived. It is possible that some life continued in Breedon after the Vikings settled in Leicestershire, but in due course the famous minster was reduced to a church.[26] Breedon is cited as an *ecclesia* in the first extant charter that refers to it after the first Viking Age, one of *c*.972.[27] This is the late Saxon foundation by which the church at Breedon is now known. Many of the carvings now on the inside walls are sophisticated relics of the monastery which once housed them; now gone, this lay to the north of the church. Richard Jewell divides the carvings into a narrow frieze (*c*.6.5 inches high), a broad frieze (8.5 inches high), and relief-carved figure panels of various sizes.[28] These sculptures, once painted, resemble friezes in Fletton and Peterborough, all of them blending styles from Hibernian and Anglian Britain with motifs from Carolingian France, Byzantine Italy, Egypt, Syria, and Persia.[29]

In general the Breedon stone-carvers show sylvan hunting scenes, with mounted and running spearmen, hounds, falcons, and various beasts all inhabiting vinescroll tendrils and trees. Jewell judges the broad frieze to have been carved in the last years of the eighth century, the narrow in the first decade of the ninth; he reconstructs a plan of the broad frieze in two bands running up either side of the exterior wall of the nave of Breedon's original church, whereas he suggests that 'the narrow frieze blocks were originally laid in courses at the top of interior walls, supporting vaulting (as in the Visigothic and Greek churches), or a wooden roof'.[30]

[23] Keynes, 'Councils of *Clofesho*', 40.

[24] *Pace* Dornier, 'Breedon on the Hill', 159.

[25] Biddle and Kjølbye-Biddle, 'Repton and the "Great Heathen Army", 873–4', 84–5. For a dissenting view, see Welch, 'The Archaeology of Mercia', 156.

[26] Dornier, 'Breedon on the Hill', 159–60.

[27] S 749 (BCS 1283). For a grant of 13 hides by King Edgar ((957–) 959–75) to the *ecclesia* at *Breodone*: Dornier, 'Breedon on the Hill', 159.

[28] Jewell, 'The Anglo-Saxon Friezes at Breedon on the Hill', 95–100 and 100–12; 'Classicism of Southumbrian Sculpture'.

[29] Cramp, 'Schools of Mercian Sculpture', 194–218; R. N. Bailey, 'The Early Christian Church in Leicester and its Region', Vaughan Paper No. 25 (Leicester, 1980), 1–25, at 18–20.

[30] Jewell, 'The Anglo-Saxon Friezes at Breedon on the Hill', 99–100 and 109–10.

Blocks

						U
INTERLACE	FIGHTING BEASTS	KEY PATTERN	PAIRED HOUNDS	FRET	PAIRED PEACOCKS	PELTA	INHABITED SCROLL (12 VOLUTES)

Panels

?South wall, length 8.875m (35cm conjectural)

Blocks

U						
	INHABITED SCROLL 8 VOLUTES	LOOPED INTERLACE	HORSEMEN	TRUMPET PATTERN	HERALDIC LIONS	INTERLACE	GRAPE PICKERS 2 FALCONS	COCKERELS ETC.

Panels

?North wall, length 8.875m (193cm conjectural)

3. Reconstruction of the broad friezes in Breedon (after R. H. I. Jewell)

A Middle Eastern origin for Breedon's vinescrolls and exotic birds and beasts has been traced to a revival of interest in Persian and Coptic motifs in eastern Europe, particularly in the aftermath of Charlemagne's victory over the Avars in 796.[31] From Charlemagne in this year Offa received an Avar hatchet, a sword, and two silk mantles from Syria. Doubtless there were then other eastern spoils heading to Mercian minsters as well. Even before Offa died later that year, Mercia began to grow more prosperous, for the surviving sculpture of the Midlands, an Anglian fusion of diverse influences from abroad, bears witness at this time to the import, through Charlemagne's Francia, of artistic styles from the Middle East and Byzantine Italy.[32]

This increased prosperity is consistent with the mix of sources which we find in two charters, Breedon's S 193 and 197. The proems of both of them are insular, written in a flamboyant Aldhelmian style.[33] As we have seen, S 193 quotes from Aldhelm's poem on a church dedicated to St Mary, from a context which refers to the Song of Songs; this charter also alludes to Solomon as the poet of the Psalms.[34] S 197, of 848, indulges in a poetic description of the natural world:

Qui monarchiam mundi tocius ac celsitudinem celorum abditamque profunditatem turgentis oceani in altis et in imis. omnia cum suo majestatis imperio. Qui in primordio mundi creavit. et nunc in ævum gubernat et regit summus pater omnipotens Deus.

[Who in the beginning created the world and now by the command of his greatness steers and governs for eternity the one rule of all this world, the loftiness of the heavens and the hidden depths of the surging ocean, and all things both high and low, the Highest Father, Almighty God.]

'A thorough knowledge' of Aldhelm's *Carmen de virginitate* and *Enigmata* is also found in Tatwine's works.[35] Yet the language of both Breedon charters above is erudite in other ways. This is clear not only in the more familiar quotations from St Paul (S 193: 1 Cor. 7: 31), Old Testament wisdom (S 197: Eccles. 3: 24), the Psalms (S 197: 39: 6), but also in Graecisms (S 193: *sophista, katolectico versu*; S 197 *agyae sophiæ, monarchiam*), one word from Persian (S 197: *gaza*, 'treasure'), another from Hebrew (S 197: *Zabaoth*), together with patristic flourishes (St Paul, in S 193: *janitor caelestis bibliothece*, 'heaven's librarian'; *vas electionis*, 'prophet of grace') and other Graecisms typical of John Cassian's *Institutae* (S 197: *phylargiriam et gastrimargiam*, 'greed and gluttony').[36] This baroque

---

[31] Cramp, 'Schools of Mercian Sculpture', 205–6.

[32] Hodges, *The Anglo-Saxon Achievement*, 126–32. Cramp, 'Schools of Mercian Sculpture', 191–233. Wormald, 'The Age of Offa and Alcuin', 101–31.

[33] On this in Aldhelm's prose works, see M. Lapidge, 'Aldhelm', in *EA-SE*, 25–7, esp. 26.

[34] *Aldhelmi Opera*, ed. Ehwald, 13 (*In basilica beatae Mariae semper virginis*, line 19: 'Qui Solymis quondam dives regnavit in arvis'); and 423 (Poem *De virginibus*, line 1697).

[35] Orchard, *The Poetic Art of Aldhelm*, 242–3.

[36] Souter, *Glossary of Later Latin*, s.v. 'catalecticus', 'gastrimargia', 'gaza', '(h)agios', 'philargyria', 'sabaoth', 'sophista', 'the(n)saurizo'. *De Coenobium institutis libri duodecim*, PL XLIX (1846), chs. V (*De spiritu gastrimargiae*) and VII (*De spiritu philargyriae*).

style is similar to that in other charters; indeed, in two ways S 197 seems to have a more ambitious version of a proem drawn up in Worcester in 802.[37] The vocabulary in both S 193 and 197 is in keeping with Breedon as a house filled with biblical, apocryphal, fabulous, Classical, and homiletic books, just as it was with Middle Eastern, Classical, and Insular styles of stone sculpture. Much of this speaks of a lively connection between Breedon and courts of the Carolingian empire.

BEOWULF, THE *LIBER HISTORIAE FRANCORUM* AND CAROLINGIAN FRANCIA

Evidence of a Frankish connection in *Beowulf* is plain to see when we compare this poem with the *Liber historiae Francorum*.[38] The author of the Frankish work, a Neustrian (between the rivers Seine and Loire), not only introduces the *Attoarii* (Beowulf's *Hetware*) but omits the offshore battle and expands Theuderic's force into *magno exercitu* ('a great army'). As Walter Goffart has shown, these changes match features of Hygelac's raid in *Beowulf*, in which there is no naval action, Hygelac and his men are defeated *mid ofermægene* ('by an overwhelming force', line 2917), and the *Hetware* arrive as a contingent in the Frankish army (lines 2363, 2916).[39] In 715 Saxon pirates raided Hettergouw between the lower Rhine and Maas (or Meuse; see Ill. 2).[40] Goffart seems right to attribute the 'Attoarii' in the *Liber* to a Frankish memory of this raid; and the Hetware and the other two details in *Beowulf* to the English poet's use of the *Liber* as a source.[41]

Besides this presumed Carolingian source, four details with which the poet of *Beowulf* describes Hygelac's raid might be described as topical of Francia in the late eighth to early ninth centuries. The first of these is the name *Dæghrefn*, that of Hygelac's killer whom Beowulf crushes to death. With this name the poet of *Beowulf* recalls not only the Merovingian kings Dagobert I (623–39), II (676–9), and III (711–15), but also some Carolingian names from the late eighth and early ninth centuries: *Daga-* or *Taga*-were popular Frankish prefixes and a certain

---

[37] BCS 307 (Bishop Deneberht to Eanswith, of land and appurtenances at Hereford): 'generatio generationem sequitur, quia alii transeuus et alii adveniunt' (Eccles. 1); 'sepe possessiones in varios deveniunt 'heredes'. modo optatissimi. modo exosissimi dominatores illorum percipiunt hereditatem'. Compare respectively with S 197 (BCS 454): '"Generatio" inquid "venit et generatio vadit"'; 'proh dolor incertis heredibus. interdum optatis. interdum exosis relinquitur'.

[38] *Liber historiae Francorum*, ed. B. Krusch, MGH, SRM 2 (Hanover, 1888), 274–5 (ch. 19). See my Chapter 2.

[39] 'Datable Anachronisms in *Beowulf*', 87.

[40] Halbertsma, 'Frieslands Oudheid', 104–5.

[41] Goffart, 'Datable Anachronisms in *Beowulf*', 84–7, at 85. Supported by Rauer, *Beowulf and the Dragon*, 21.

'Daigramnus' inscribed his name in the Confraternity Book of Augsburg (Swabia) in the eighth century; a 'Dagaramnus' was inscribed in that of Schwarzach (Baden-Württemberg) in 825/6.[42] These foundations lay to east and west of Alemannia, a region run since the 730s by families from Alsace, whence the name *Dagaramnus* may have come.[43]

Dæghrefn is *Huga cempa* ('champion of the Hugas', *Beo* 2502); and the Geatish Messenger says the Hugas became the Geats' enemy once Hygelac invaded Frisia (lines 2913–15). The Hugas might be Franks, given that Dæghrefn's name makes him look Merovingian, like Dagobert, but it might not follow that Dæghrefn's employers were Franks also. In Cynewulf's *Elene*, by emendation, the *Hugas* (MS *Hunas*, already cited on *El* 20) march alongside the *fyrdhwate Francan* ('Franks keen for campaigning', *El* 21) united with other barbarians against the Emperor Constantine.[44] On the strength of this emended reference the Hugas might be a tribe (such as the Alemans) who were later identified with Franks in the Carolingian empire. The *Chauci* from Tacitus' *Germania* have been invoked as the *Hugas'* first-century ancestors, but as Goffart shows, they are too ancient to be considered here.[45] A better clue is provided by the *Quedlinburg Annals* of *c*.1000–30. The author of this work says that Theoderic, the illegitimate son of King Clovis by a Gothic mother, was called 'Hugh', that is 'Hug-Theodoric' (Hug-Dietrich), *quia olim omnes Franci Hugones vocabantur a suo quondam duce Hugone* ('because, formerly, all the Franks used to be called Hughs after a certain duke of theirs named Hugh').[46] This passage contains two etymologies: *Hug*-from *Hugones*, and *Hugones* from *Hugo*. Goffart discredits the former etymology but mimics the latter in a theory of his own.[47] As he well shows, the name 'Hugh' was popular among Frankish nobility in the ninth and tenth centuries.[48] In his view, *Beowulf*'s name *Hugas* echoes an (unattested) sobriquet for the Neustrians, who would have called themselves *Hugas* or similar after their duke, Hugh the Great, in the first half of the tenth century (ruled 923–56); *Beowulf* would thus have been written in his time, perhaps during the reign of King Æthelstan (*c*.924–939), whose sister was married to Hugh in 926.[49] Yet Goffart, for all the flaws he shows up in the chronology of the *Quedlinburg Annals*, cannot prove that the name *Hug-Theoderic* was not formed

[42] Noted by Goffart, 'Datable Anachronisms in *Beowulf*', 87 n. 22. *Libri confraternitatum Sancti Galli, Augiensis, Fabariensis*, ed. P. Piper, MGH, Antiq. 2, 6 vols. (Berlin, 1884), ii. 208 and 215; other *Daga*-names, for example: Dagabrant (ii. 179), Dagabreht (ii. 464), Daganolt (ii. 467), Dagabertus (ii. 58, 59), Dagoaldus (i. 181, 191), Dagolfus (ii. 25), Dagomarus (ii. 259), Daguinus (i. 26).
[43] Reuter, *Germany in the Early Middle Ages*, 58–60.
[44] *Cynewulf's 'Elene'*, ed. P. O. E. Gradon, rev. M. J. Swanton (Exeter, 1996), 26.
[45] Goffart, 'Datable Anachronisms in *Beowulf*', 83 nn. 2 and 4, and 90–1 n. 41; *pace* R. Derolez, 'Cross-Channel Language Ties', *ASE* 5 (1974), 1–14, at 5 n. 2.
[46] *Annales Quedlinburgenses*, ed. G. H. Pertz, MGH, SS 3 (Hanover, 1889), 31.
[47] Goffart, 'Datable Anachronisms in *Beowulf*', 90–9, at 90–4 (see below).
[48] Ibid. 94–7.
[49] Ibid. 96–100, at 98–9.

before these *Annals*, for it is clearly a name which aims to distinguish a Merovingian Theoderic from Theoderic the Ostrogoth (ruled 493–526). In this light it seems likely that both the *Hug*-prefix and OE *Hugas* denoted 'Franks'.

This conclusion is supported by a place name recorded in the first half of the ninth century. The name of today's place Humsterland (see Ill. 2), near Oldehove on the Groningen coast, takes its first syllable from *Humarcha* (*Hugumarchi*, or *Hugmerchi*). This toponym is preserved both in the *Vita s. Liudgeri*, written *c*.840, and in the *Vita Willehadi*, written in Echternach in 843 × 855.[50] Liudger, a Frisian missionary, passed through *Humarcha* in the early 780s; Willehad followed him there in *c*.786/7. At this time the name *Humarcha* denoted a larger area, the coastline and islands between the mouths of the rivers Lauwers and Hunze.[51] As is clear from its variants, the name *Humarcha* is derived from **Hugumarkja*: '*Hugumarkja*-tribal name *Hugas* + *marko* = frontier, border region.'[52] 'It remains to be shown', says Goffart, 'that the toponym must refer to a tribe rather than to a magnate named Hugh.'[53] Yet as he shows, the Hugh-name gained legitimacy among Frankish nobles only in the early ninth century; the name *Humarcha* is older. The wider region has place names, Fransum, Engelum (north of Leeuwarden), and Saaksum (north of Groningen), which have been explained as names for settlements of 'Franks', 'Angles', and 'Saxons' in this zone as a whole;[54] Saaksum is closest to Humsterland; it has been suggested that *Hugas* in *Humarcha* is a term of the same category for the Frankish military who overran this district after the murder of St Boniface further west near Dokkum in 754.[55] Although *Humarcha* is far from the Rhine, Hygelac's traditional point of entry into Frankish lands, its name gives out the *Hugas* as Frankish defenders of Christendom.

The poet of *Beowulf* appears to make at least two more topical references to the Carolingian army over the same period. One is in the phrase *wyrsan wigfrecan* ('lower-ranking war-braves'), an expression for Frankish soldiers looting the dead on line 1212. This phrase is found in the poet's first reference to Hygelac's Frisian raid. The poet repeats these words on line 2496, as Beowulf's term for mercenary soldiers which he says Hygelac, thanks to his nephew's valour, had no need to buy from Gifthas, Spear-Danes or Swedes. But the relevance of this phrase to the wider Frankish army seems assured. OE *wyrsa* ('worse') denotes the opposite of *selra*, *sylra*, or *betera* ('better', 'higher-ranking'), as this is used, for example: of

[50] Halbertsma, 'Frieslands Oudheid', 675. *Vita s. Liudgeri*, ed. Pertz, 410 (I. 19). *Anskarii vita S. Willehadi episcopi Bremensis*, ed. G. H. Pertz, MGH, SS 2 (Hanover, 1879), 380 (ch. 3).

[51] Halbertsma, 'Frieslands Oudheid', 682–4.

[52] M. Gysseling, *Toponymisch Woordenboek van België, Nederland, Luxemburg, Noord-Frankrijk en West-Duitsland vóór 1226* (Tongeren, 1960), s.v. 'Humsterland': 'Germ. Hugumarkja— volksnaam Hugas + marko = grens, grensstreek'; 'De oudste Friese toponymie', *Philologia Frisica anno 1969* (Grins [Groningen], 1970), 41–51, at 46.

[53] Goffart, 'Datable Anachronisms in *Beowulf*', 89 n. 35.

[54] W. de Vries, 'Humsterland', *Nomina Geographica Neerlandica*, 8 (1932), 34–6.

[55] Halbertsma, 'Frieslands Oudheid', 683.

Welund's rank or wealth in comparison with Nithad's in *Deor* 5–6 (*nede... on syllan monn*); of Heorogar's with Hrothgar's (*Beo* 469); of Hygelac's with Beowulf's in *Beo* 2199 (*selra*). The Merovingians called the lowest-ranking soldiers *inferiores* ('lesser men'), a term which is found once in an account of a punitive raid on Brittany in *c.*590, written by Gregory of Tours; more often they were then known as *pauperes* ('poor men').[56] In the Carolingian era the term *pauperes* prospered: Charlemagne's government had a more complex hierarchy of classes and officials, and *pauperiores* ('the poorer men') is used to distinguish between *pauperes* in codes concerning the recruitment of soldiers from classes of inferior means.[57] *Beowulf*'s phrase *wyrsan wigfrecan* appears to be a calque of *pauperiores*, which is found, for example, in three of Charlemagne's capitularies for the years 807–8. In a memorandum of 807 concerning the raising of an army for campaign in western Gaul, any man who finds himself poor, that is not in possession of lands, and yet has money, must join another such four *pauperiores* ('poorer men') to raise money for the supply of a sixth for active service; two men with small plots of land must supply a third.[58] In another capitulary, probably edited in the same year, there are similar regulations for the raising of *pauperiores* from Saxon and Frisian regions for campaign in Spain and Hungary.[59] Similar guidelines for landless *liberi* ('freemen') and *pauperiores homini* ('poorer men') are issued in a code in a more general capitulary for the raising of troops promulgated early in 808.[60]

This Carolingian terminology was evidently widespread; in this case it lends *Beowulf* some imperial colour:

> wyrsan wigfrecan   wæl reafedon
> æfter guðsceare (*Beo* 1212–13)

[lower-ranking war-braves plundered the slain after the war-squadron]

Wrenn sees a m. *guðscear* here, meaning 'slaughter in battle', as do Mitchell and Robinson ('battle-carnage'), probably because Swedish incursions are later described in the phrase *eatolne inwitscear oft gefremedon* (line 2478): in this line the word *scear* is masculine (in agreement with *eatolne*, m. acc. sg. of *(e)atol*). But OE *scear* does not mean 'slaughter' or 'carnage'; it means 'ploughshare'

---

[56] *Gregorii libri historiarum*, ed. Krusch and Levison, 493 (*Historiae* X. 9). B. S. Bachrach, *Merovingian Military Organization 481–751* (Minneapolis, 1972), 125–6.

[57] Halsall, *Warfare and Society in the Barbarian West*, 89–100, esp. 95. Reuter, *Germany in the Early Middle Ages*, 21–36.

[58] *Capitularia regum Francorum*, ed. Boretius and Krause, i. 134–5 (no. 48: *Memoratorium de exercitu in gallia occidentali praeparando*, § 2). On military organization and recruitment in capitularies, see Reuter, *Germany in the Early Middle Ages*, 26–9 and 34–6.

[59] Where six poorer men may equip a seventh, in *Capitularia regum Francorum*, ed. Boretius and Krause, i. 136 (no. 49: *Capitula de causis diversis*, § 3).

[60] Ibid. i. 137 (no. 50: *Capitulare missorum de exercitu promovendo*, § 2: 'de liberis et pauperioribus hominibus').

(Lat *vomer*).[61] In this light the poet seems to mean that the Swedes 'often performed a terrible hatred-ploughing', as if the latter term were a kenning for battle, a ploughshare breaking the soil.[62] The term *guðsceare* appears to differ from this metaphor, in that with OE *guð* a term for 'battle' is straightforwardly given. In *guðsceare* we may have the use of *scearu*, a feminine noun, as a fourth reference to the Carolingian military. In f. *scearu* ('share'), the stem of dative *guðsceare* might be different from of *inwitscear*, as being a phrase which would refer to the rights of plunder (thus: 'in accordance with their share of battle'). On the other hand, this meaning of OE *æfter* is secondary although in *Beowulf* it is found in *æfter rihte* ('according to law', lines 1049, 2110).[63] If we look elsewhere, we see how the unique term *æfter guðsceare* could refer to Frankish soldiers superior to the *wyrsan wigfrecan*. The nucleus of Charlemagne's army was his bodyguard, from which a unit might be sent off as a *scara*, a fast-moving squadron.[64] From *scara* is derived the Modern German word f. *Schar* ('flock').[65] With the use of a f. *scearu* in *æfter guðsceare* (line 1213), the poet of *Beowulf*, with the meaning 'after the war-squadron', would mean that the first rights of plunder went to the *scara*.

In short, the poet of *Beowulf* appears to use the names *Dæghrefn* and *Hugas*, along with his expressions *wyrsan wigfrecan* and *æfter guðsceare*, as an authentication for his stories of Hygelac's last raid. What we get is an image of a Carolingian army consisting of three or four battle-groups: 'Hugas', in a squadron deployed from the emperor's bodyguard, with Dæghrefn, its champion, from Alemannia; Hetware from the lower Rhine valley; Frisians from the coast; and 'lower-ranking war-braves', whose origin goes unspecified as they wait while the Hugas loot the best off Hygelac and his men. It is almost certain that the poet of *Beowulf* read the *Liber historiae Francorum*; and these three or four phrases in *Beowulf* reveal a knowledge of Francia consistent with the poet's having some contact in the early ninth century with Carolingian aristocracy, both around the Rhine mouth in south-west Frisia and in the royal minsters of northern Francia. Such contacts were possible, as we see in Alcuin's friendship with Maganfrid, who was both one of Charlemagne's generals and his military treasurer.[66]

Where Breedon is concerned, it is accepted that most of the eastern features among Breedon's friezes and panels, though of Carolingian provenance rather

[61] *Ælfric's Colloquy*, ed. G. N. Garmonsway, 2nd edn. (Exeter, 1978), 20 (line 26). *Anglo-Saxon and Old English Vocabularies*, ed. Wright and Wülcker, ii. 36 (line 65: *vomer vel vomis*). OE f. *scear* means 'scissors', 'shears': ibid. ii. 36 (line 65: *forfex*); *Épinal-Erfurt Glossary*, ed. Pheifer, 22 (line 401: *forfices: sceroro*) and 86.

[62] *Beowulf*, 4th edn. ed. Wrenn and Bolton, 246. *Beowulf*, ed. Mitchell and Robinson, 266.

[63] See *Beowulf*, ed. Mitchell and Robinson, 243.

[64] Halsall, *Warfare and Society in the Barbarian West*, 54. Reuter, *Germany in the Early Middle Ages*, 26.

[65] A. Johannesson, *Altisländisches etymologisches Wörterbuch* (Bern, 1956), 836 (*s.v.* OIce *skári*, OHG *scara*).

[66] Story, *Carolingian Connections*, 103.

than origin, 'betray an ambition quite consistent with the spirit embodied in the monumental basilicas of the Carolingian age'.[67] This is in keeping with the minster's designation, in King Berhtwulf's grant of 848, as a lodge for overseas envoys, thus Carolingian and papal legates.[68] To give an example of a Frank visiting Mercia from north-west Francia, it is said that Abbot Gervold of St Wandrille (787–807), who was Charlemagne's customs officer at Quentovic at this time, *multis vicibus ipse per se iussione invictissimi regis Caroli ad praefatum regem Offam legationibus functus est* ('on many occasions worked at the command of the most invincible King Charles as an envoy to the aforesaid King Offa on official visits').[69] In the light of this background and the *Liber historiae Francorum* and the other Frankish aristocratic colour in *Beowulf*, a strong bond with Francia is something which *Beowulf* and Breedon have in common.

BEOWULF, BOETHIUS, AND CICERO; AND THE BOOKS OF CORBIE

The Frankish connection is also apparent in less obvious ways, to do with *Beowulf*'s reflections on destiny and time. The first of these occurs as Beowulf's Geats bed down in Heorot, none expecting to see his home again. Nonetheless, the poet says, the Lord had granted them *wigspeda gewiofu* ('a woven destiny of battle victories', line 697). With the fight in progress and Grendel pulling away to the door, the tide turns in favour of the Danes, to whom, with a change of metaphor, *wearð... ealuscerwen* ('a carving of good fortune was assigned', lines 767–9).[70] Later Hrothgar rewards Beowulf and the other Geats and promises an indemnity for the comrade whom Grendel killed:

> swa he hyra ma wolde
> nefne him witig god   wyrd forstode
> ond ðæs mannes mod. (*Beo* 1055–7)

[and so he would have killed more of them if the wise God, together with the man's courage, had not obstructed the event.]

With these words, as Greenfield observes, there is a shift from our assumption of Beowulf's power over his own destiny towards an acknowledgement that this lies in God's hands.[71] The poet continues:

---

[67] Hodges, *The Anglo-Saxon Achievement*, 126–32, at fig. 39 and 129.

[68] S 197 (BCS 454): 'Præcones si trans mare venirent ad regem venturi' ('envoys, if they come from overseas on their way to meet the king').

[69] *Gesta abbatum Fontanellensium*, ed. Loewenfeld, 46. *EHD*, 341 (no. 20). McKitterick, *The Frankish Kingdoms under the Carolingians*, 200–2.

[70] North, '"Wyrd" and "wearð ealuscerwen" in *Beowulf*', 74–80.

[71] Greenfield, 'The Authenticating Voice in *Beowulf*', 55–7.

> Metod eallum weold
> gumena cynnes   swa he nu git deð.
> Forþan bið andgit   æghwær selest
> ferhðes foreþanc.   Fela sceal gebidan
> leofes ond laþes   se þe longe her
> on ðyssum windagum   worolde bruceð. (*Beo* 1057–62)

[The Measurer governed all people of the human race, just as he does now. For this reason, understanding, the forethought of the mind, is the best option everywhere. Much good and evil will a man have to endure who long makes trial of the world here in these days of strife.]

On this homiletic note, the poet proceeds to report the lay of Finnsburh, its omen of Heorot's destruction, and its aftermath in the attack of Grendel's Mother. But the main flow of his thoughts is backwards. As Lapidge has shown, the nostalgia that pervades this poem is due to the poet's desire to show that 'knowledge in *Beowulf* is always a matter of retrospection and re-interpretation', unreliably dependent on 'present perceptions – recollections – of past events'.[72] The poet's qualification of human *foreþanc* is sardonic in its implication that true forethought belongs to God alone.[73]

   Towards the end of *Beowulf*, the blindness of mortal foresight informs the poet's view of the hero's death. In killing the dragon, Beowulf seeks to plunder the hoard of princes who long ago cursed such mound-breakers with an eternity in hell. Although the question of Beowulf's damnation is left open, this is no end for our hero that any apologist for heathens, or even a moral guardian such as Alcuin, could have wished:

> Wundur hwar þonne
> eorl ellenrof   ende gefere
> lifgesceafta   þonne leng ne mæg
> mon mid his magum   meduseld buan.
> Swa wæs Biowulfe   þa he biorges weard
> sohte searoniðas,   seolfa ne cuðe
> þurh hwæt his worulde gedal   weorðan sceolde. (*Beo* 3062–8)

[It is a wonder where a courageous warrior may reach the end of his predestined life when he, a man, can no longer inhabit the mead-building with his kinsmen. So it was with Beowulf, when he sought the barrow's guardian, cunning enmities, that he himself did not know by what means his departure from the world should come about.]

It has been claimed that the adverb *swa* on line 3066 looks forward to a correlative *swa* on line 3069, confirming Beowulf's damnation.[74] Yet the immediate context

---

[72] Lapidge, '*Beowulf* and Perception', 87.

[73] L. C. Gruber, 'Forethought: The New Weapon in *Beowulf*', *In Geardagum*, 12 (1991), 1–14, esp. 4.

[74] Bliss, '*Beowulf* Lines 3074–3075', 47–8. *Beowulf: A Student Edition*, ed. Jack, 203–4. For the second half of this passage, see p. 209.

of the first *swa* is retrospective, to do with the mystery of a foreknowledge reserved for God.[75] Although the poet foretells Beowulf's death as early as lines 2341–3, Beowulf says nothing to show that this outlook is also his. On the contrary, he ends his life not only in ignorance of God's plan, but unwillingly: when Beowulf's shield gives out against the dragon-fire, the poet says that it protected *life ond lice læssan hwile mærum þeodne þonne his myne sohte* ('the renowned lord's life and body for a lesser time than sought by his desire', lines 2571–2).

In all this, the poet of *Beowulf* reveals a view of time which is faithful to the conclusion of Boethius' *De consolatione Philosophiae*.[76] Above the poet calls the place of Beowulf's death *wundur* ('a wonder', line 3062) in order to prevent us from treating the hoard's discovery in *Beowulf* as a matter of random chance. The poet has told us three times already that Beowulf is destined to die in the dragon-fight that follows (lines 2341–4, 2420, and 2858). By alluding to the hoard as part of the *wundur* of Beowulf's end, the poet shows predestination in a miraculous aspect. He leaves it to Wiglaf to provide the more familiar metaphors for this process twelve lines later in his own comment on Beowulf's fate:

> 'Heold on heahgesceap;   hord ys gesceawod,
> grimme gegongen;   wæs þæt gifeðe to swið
> þe ðone þeodcyning   þyder ontyhte.' (*Beo* 3084–6)

['He held to a high destiny; the hoard has been seen, fiercely won as it was; the fate was too powerful which impelled the king of the people to that place.']

Predestined to meet it, Beowulf with his hoard is like the exemplum at the beginning of *De consolatione*, Book V. As Lady Philosophy says to Boethius (citing Aristotle's *Physica*), *casus* ('chance') is nothing more than the name people give to things which they did not intend to happen:

ut si quis colendi agri causa fodiens humum defossi auri pondus inveniat. Hoc igitur fortuito quidem creditur accidisse, verum non de nihilo est; nam proprias causas habet quarum inprovisus inopinatusque concursus casum videtur operatus.[77]

['as if a man digging in the ground, in order to till the field, were to find a mass of gold. Now although this is believed to have happened by chance, it does not come from nothing: it has its own causes, whose coming together, unforeseen and unexpected, seems to have produced a chance event.']

If the poet of *Beowulf*, through three remarks followed by Wiglaf's comment, puts us in the position of seeing Beowulf's fate as something divinely foreknown,

---

[75] Bolton, 'Boethius and a Topos in *Beowulf*', 34–5.

[76] Ibid. 35–9. Supported by Lapidge, in '*Beowulf* and Perception', 87–8. Here I am indebted to Éamonn Ó Carragáin, whose idea it is to connect the hoard in *Beowulf* with Boethius' image of buried treasure.

[77] My translation is based on *Consolation of Philosophy*, ed. and trans. Tester, 386–9 (V. Prose I).

this is not a perspective open to anyone else in the story, Beowulf included. The poet is careful to stress the others' lack of foreknowledge even in the 'prologue' of *Beowulf*, which, as everyone knows, ends by stating man's ignorance:

> Men ne cunnon
> secgan to soðe   seleræden*de*
> hæleð under heofenum   hwa þæm hlæste onfeng. (*Beo* 50–2)

[Men do not know, retainers, hall-advisers, heroes under heaven, how to say in truth who received that cargo.]

These lines could be said to introduce the 'Boethian' theme of *Beowulf*, whose circular structure (inherent in the funerals and in the pattern of Hrothgar's, then Grendel's Mother's (line 1498), then Beowulf's, unexpected test after fifty years' rule) seems contrived both to show the endless lack of *foreþanc* among the men in the story and to lend us, outside it, the divine privilege of knowing their future.[78]

The theological implication of the poet's parting lines after the first funeral in *Beowulf* is that only God can reveal the *soð* ('truth') of which man has no knowledge. The poet returns to this revelatory theme later in his first reflection on destiny (line 697). Just after announcing that God will save Beowulf's Geatish escort from Grendel through the hero's victory (lines 697–8), the poet, with his present tense, states something that we know and that Beowulf and the other heathens can only suspect:[79]

> Soð is gecyþed
> þæt mihtig god   manna cynnes
> weold [wide]ferhð. (*Beo* 700–2)

[It is a truth made manifest that mighty God has always governed mankind.]

The present tense invites another application to a present-day audience. Inevitably for Christians, any knowledge of God from which heathens are excluded is revealed through the word of God. While neither heathens nor Christians may be said to know the future, for Christians some knowledge of truth about the present world is possible from divinely inspired works such as the Bible, or patristic writing, or Christian teaching. A reading of this material amounts to the *andgit* ('understanding', line 1059) which the poet invokes at the beginning of Fitt XVI.

It is an odd coincidence that the younger manuscript of King Alfred's ninth-century translation of Boethius' *De consolatione* is divided into a preface and forty-two sections, whereas the scribes of the Nowell Codex, in the early eleventh, sectioned *Beowulf* into forty-four fitts (the 'prologue' and forty-three (mostly)

---

[78] This circularity is compatible with the 'ring composition' which Niles (*Beowulf*, 152–60, esp. 158) has shown to be widespread in *Beowulf*.

[79] On the poet's 'moral translation' of Hrothgar's faith into Old Testament monotheism, see my *Heathen Gods*, 173–81, esp. 180.

numbered fitts, with nos. XXVIIII, XXX, and XXXVIIII left unnumbered).[80] Among several possible explanations, one is that both the fitt divisions and the total number of fitts in *Beowulf* descend from the poet himself.[81] So much could he have loved the *De consolatione* that he emulated its pedagogical sectioning in a version, or commentary, of common ancestry with Alfred's text.[82]

In all his display of foreknowledge versus ignorance, one which he appears to derive from Boethius, the poet of *Beowulf* uses a vocabulary that points to a training in Ciceronian ideas about truth and perception. As well as in time, the poet is interested in the gap of understanding between his Christian audience and the heathen subjects of *Beowulf.* With the possible exception of Wiglaf, the poem's preliterate heroes, in contrast to their modern admirers including the poet himself, are seen to grope after truths they cannot hope to divine. Notwithstanding their lack of knowledge, the poet gives the best of them intellectual powers equal to those of Christians. This is clear enough from Hrothgar's intuition of eternity and one god in his speech of lines 1700–84. Nor is the poet focused solely on the gap in understanding between Christian and heathen. He is also interested in the way understanding differs between one heathen and another, for example through Beowulf's correction of Unferth's version of Breca's version of their swimming match (lines 530–606), or his brisk account of Hrothgar's speeches to Hygelac back in Geatland (lines 2105–14), or Beowulf's (lines 2501–8) and the Geatish Messenger's (lines 2913–21) versions of Hygelac's last raid to which the poet has alluded three times earlier (lines 1202–14, 2201, and 2354–66). In the volatility of this narrative progress and its animation through the differing perceptions of speakers in the story, the *Beowulf*-poet's mental orientation, as Lapidge shows, is 'philosophical and epistemological'.[83]

Lapidge's study of verbs of perception in *Beowulf* shows that among all the many words for 'intellection' which were available to Anglo-Saxon writers and poets, the usage in *Beowulf* is uniquely defined. For physical acts of apprehension the poet uses several verbs: *cunnian* ('to explore'), *(ge-) fandian* ('to search out'), *findan* ('to find'), *gemetan* ('to encounter'), *geniman* ('to grasp'), and *begietan* ('to seize'); although the last two of these elsewhere connote mental perception as well, this is not so in *Beowulf*.[84] For mental acts of apprehension the poet uses just

---

[80] A. J. Frantzen, *King Alfred* (Boston, 1986), 43–6: Oxford, Bodleian Library, Bodley 180 (first half of the twelfth century) (the older BL, Cotton Otho A.VI, of the mid-tenth century, does not have divisions). Bolton, 'Boethius and a Topos in *Beowulf*', 36 and 42 n. 24.

[81] *Beowulf*, ed. Mitchell and Robinson, 6–7. The corrections made to fitt nos. XXIIII (from XV?), XXVI (from XXVII?), XXVII (from XXVIII?), and XXVIII (from XXVIIII?) suggest that a reviser (Scribe B?) started and broke off a renumbering of the fitts correctly back to, and including, the 'prologue'. *Beowulf*, ed. Zupitza, 76–7, 82–3, 86–7, and 90–1 (cf. Fitt XX[V] on 80–1).

[82] Alfred's hand in the chapter divisions of his *Boethius* is disputed by Janet Bately, in 'Book Divisions and Chapter Headings in the Translations of the Alfredian Period', in E. Treharne and S. Rosser (eds.), *Early Medieval English Texts and Interpretations: Studies Presented to Donald G. Scragg* (Tempe, Ariz., 2002), 151–66, esp. 165–6.

[83] Lapidge, '*Beowulf* and Perception', 84–9, esp. 88.

[84] Ibid. 89–90.

two terms, *ongi(e)tan* and *onfindan*. His use of these marks him out from other poets even further. Whereas *ongi(e)tan*, with some 800 instances in the corpus as a whole, frequently denotes 'realizing' or 'understanding', in *Beowulf* it appears to mean only 'to perceive'.[85] Lapidge attributes this meaning to all but one of the of twelve instances of *ongi(e)tan* in the poem.[86] But he could have included the twelfth example, with Hrothgar urging Beowulf to learn from Heremod's failures:

> 'Đu þe lær be þon,
> gumcyste ongit.　Ic þis gid be þe
> awræc wintrum frod.' (*Beo* 1722–4)

['You teach yourself from this, take note of a man's excellence. I, made wise by winters, have composed this song about you (/for your sake).']

This context supports a meaning of 'perception' in line with the others, with Hrothgar commanding Beowulf first to reject Heremod and then to admire Hrothgar. There are two instances in *Beowulf* of the phrase *gumcystum god* ('good in the manly virtues'). One describes Hrothgar, as Hygelac will see him in his gifts when these are sent home (line 1486); the other, Beowulf's long experience as a warrior as he peers into the dragon's lair (line 2543). So it seems clear that the words *gumcyste ongit* tell the young man to 'take note' of externals, either Hrothgar's generosity or his visible old age or both. In this way it appears that the uses of *ongi(e)tan* in *Beowulf* are quite consistent. The remaining verb of perception, *onfindan*, which occurs about 100 times in the corpus, usually denotes in *Beowulf* 'the mental process of realisation and intellection'.[87] Although this word can mean 'to discover' in *Beowulf*, Lapidge notes that the poet employs it for the mental act of realization about ten times, 'more frequently than any other Anglo-Saxon author'.[88] The peculiarity of *Beowulf*, then, is that *ongi(e)tan* and *onfindan* are used in complementary senses, the former for sensory perception and the latter for acts of intellection or cognition.

---

[85] See *Beowulf*, ed. Mitchell and Robinson, 284.

[86] Lapidge, '*Beowulf* and Perception', 90–1. To take them in order: God *fyrenðearfe ongeat* ('perceived the crime-fuelled distress', line 14) of Heremod's Danish subjects; the Geats marched until *ongytan mihton* ('they could make out', line 308) Heorot; the monsters in Grendel's Mere *bearhtm ongeaton* ('heard the blast', line 1431) of a Danish horn; Hygelac, Beowulf says, can *on þæm golde ongitan* ('see' Hrothgar's generosity 'in the gold' sent back to him, line 1484); Beowulf dived for a day before *þone grundwong ongytan mehte* ('he could make out the bottom', line 1496); once below, he *ongeat* ('noticed', line 1512) that he was in a hostile hall, whereupon he *ongeat... merewif mihtig* ('caught sight of the mighty sea-wife', line 1518); on their way home, the Geats sailed until *clifu ongitan meahton* ('they could see the cliffs' of their country, line 1911); having killed the dragon, Beowulf asks *þæt ic ærwelan goldæht ongite* ('that I may see the goldhoard of ancient wealth', line 2748); in a bizarre echo of Beowulf earlier, Wiglaf descends into the vault until *þone grundwong ongitan meahte* ('he could see the bottom', line 2770); Heardred's survivors *byman gealdor ongeaton* ('made out the refrain of the trumpet' of Hygelac, line 2944).

[87] Lapidge, '*Beowulf* and Perception', 84–5 and 91–3.

[88] Ibid. 92 (*Beo* 595, 750, 809, 1497, 1522, 2269, 2300, 2713, and possibly 2219 and 2226).

As Lapidge goes on to observe, the same pattern is found in the use of the Latin words *visa* ('things seen, perceived by the senses') and *comprehensa* ('things understood by the intellect') in Cicero's treatise on perception and cognition, the *Academica priora*.[89] In this work Cicero's friend Lucullus attacks the Epicurean position on perception, in order to claim that all sense-perceptions are true; Cicero counters that we must suspend judgement as to how things are in nature because there is no external criterion with which to judge between conflicting perceptions in different people. His treatise defines true knowledge against sensory supposition, declaring the former impossible. As Lapidge points out, there is no evidence that this work or any of those from which it was partially derived were known in Anglo-Saxon England. Consequently, Lapidge believes that the poet of *Beowulf* generated his distinction between the verbs *ongi(e)tan* and *onfindan* out of a home-grown interest in narrative perception, rather than from such literary models as Cicero's *Academica priora* or from a passage on sensory perception in Lucretius' as yet unrecovered poem *De rerum natura* (IV. 478–85).[90]

It seems wrong, however, to rule out a Latin basis for the *Beowulf*-poet's strict usage, even if this is not to be found directly in Cicero. In Chapter 3 I have already attempted to show other traces of erudition in *Beowulf*. While it is true that no record survives of the *Academica priora* in Anglo-Saxon England, the Frankish monastic evidence, better preserved as it is, shows that this work probably lay in Charlemagne's palace library at Aachen; before being sent to Corbie after his death in 814, where it is known to have been copied, along with other pagan philosophical and rhetorical works, by the librarian Hadoard in *c*.850–70.[91] In his two *florilegia*, however, Hadoard treats Cicero cautiously and retouches his works with St Augustine's ideas.[92] In Francia in the early ninth century, at least outside Charlemagne's library, which acquired these texts from Italy, Cicero's philosophy was still thin on the ground.[93] Alcuin, who calls Cicero *rhetor ingens* ('the great rhetorician'), did not see him as a philosopher.[94] Even in the 860s Hadoard's interest in Cicero was exceptional.[95] Given the unease with pagan philosophy in Frankish minsters at this time, it is unlikely that any Mercians had been teaching philosophy with a copy of *Academica priora* some thirty years earlier, the period in which I suggest *Beowulf* was written.

[89] Ibid. 87 and 93–7, esp. 96.

[90] Ibid. 86–7. On Lucretius, see *Texts and Transmission*, ed. Reynolds, 218–22, esp. 220; and Orchard, *The Poetic Art of Aldhelm*, 130.

[91] Ganz, *Corbie*, 60–2. Bischoff, 'Die Hofbibliothek Karls des Grossen', 152 n. 17 and 168–9. L. D. Reynolds and N. G. Wilson, *Scribes and Scholars: A Guide to the Transmission of Greek and Latin Literature*, 3rd edn. (Oxford, 1991), 102–6, esp. 103. *Texts and Transmission*, ed. Reynolds, 124–6.

[92] Ganz, *Corbie*, 93. Bischoff, 'Hadoard und die Klassikerhandschriften aus Corbie', 52.

[93] Wallace-Hadrill, *The Frankish Church*, 348–9. Bischoff, 'Hadoard und die Klassikerhandschriften aus Corbie', 62; 'Die Hofbibliothek Karls des Grossen', 162–5.

[94] *Alcuin: The Bishops, Kings, and Saints of York*, ed. and trans. P. Godman (Oxford, 1982), 124–5 (line 1550) and 125 n. 1550.

[95] Ganz, *Corbie*, 97.

If there is still a problem, therefore, in finding a source for the *Beowulf*-poet's apparent training in cognition, an answer may be found in a work which was derived from Cicero's, the *Contra academicos*, which St Augustine wrote after studying Platonism in 386.[96] This work is predicated on the distinction between *visa* and *comprehensa* in Cicero's *Academica priora*. In three books Augustine defends the attainability of knowledge against the scepticism advanced by Cicero, whose argument he utters through 'Carneades'. Augustine asks in Book I whether wisdom consists of finding truth or of seeking it. Though believing the former, he never repudiates his premiss that seeking truth may be a worthy activity.[97] In Book II, after restating the sceptical dogma that true knowledge is impossible, Augustine develops his objections. He concludes in Book III that, with God's help (III. vi), the senses do obtain impressions which are true, from which knowledge can be derived by cognition. In the process of describing this mechanism, Augustine praises dialectic as an aid to finding truth:

Ego uero plura quam de quauis parte philosophiae. Nam primo omnes illas propositiones, quibus supra usus sum, ueras esse ista me docuit. Deinde per istam noui alia multa uera.[98]

[Indeed I have learnt more from this than from any part of philosophy. All those propositions I have used above, it was dialectic that first taught me they were true. Thence by the same means I know that many other things are true also.]

Besides Augustine's use of Ciceronian terms with which that of *ongi(e)tan* and *onfindan* is comparable, we might note a resemblance between his stress on dialectic and the *Beowulf*-poet's tendency to juxtapose people, stories, and even versions of the same incident in *Beowulf*. Hrothgar's sword-hilt speech fulfils the same conditions, in which he instructs Beowulf to choose between *bealonið* ('grievous enmity') and *þæt selre . . . ece rædas* ('the better course, eternal rewards', lines 1758–60). Hrothgar starts this speech by calling himself the man *se þe soð ond riht fremeð* ('who furthers truth and law', lines 1700–1). Through dialectic in *Beowulf*, therefore, it seems that even one heathen can equip another with the means to choose between truth and falsehood. Fitt XX[V] begins with Hrothgar's theme of *oferhygda dæl* ('a measure of prideful thoughts', line 1740), continuing with his urging Beowulf not to heed any thoughts of pride (*oferhyda ne gym*, line 1760: his fifth imperative). By the end of this central speech, therefore, we know that even Beowulf's slim hope of heavenly reward may depend on his understanding of what Hrothgar has said. Through dialectic, in the way praised by Augustine, Hrothgar's *soð* ('truth', line 1700) is something Beowulf can know, unlike the *wundur* ('wonder', line 3062) of divine foreknowledge from which he and everyone else, heathen and Christian, are excluded.[99]

---

[96] O'Daly, 'The Response to Skepticism', 159.
[97] Ibid. 161.   [98] *Contra academicos*, ed. Green, 51 (III. xiii).
[99] I shall consider the question of Beowulf's success in this 'cognition' in the next chapter.

It seems unlikely that Breedon held copies of St Augustine's *Contra academicos* or Boethius' *De consolatione* in Tatwine's time there before 731. After the first Viking Age, Bishop Æthelwold of Winchester included the *Contra academicos* in a donation to rebuild the library of the newly refounded minster of *Medeshamstede*, near Peterborough, after 963.[100] In Breedon, Tatwine seems to have heard or read of Boethius' Lady Philosophy in his first of his *Aenigmata*, where the female speaker says that she has seven wings (of *trivium* and *quadrivium*):

> Vecta per alma poli quis nunc volitare solesco,
> Abdita nunc terrae penetraris atque ima profundi.[101] (lines 2–3)

[I often fly through the blessed spheres of the world, or fathom the secrets of earth and the abysmal depths.]

In the *De consolatione*, Lady Philosophy offers to fix wings to Boethius' mind both in Book I and more particularly in her song on winged flight over the earth at the beginning of Book IV:

> 'Sunt enim pennae volucres mihi
> Quae celsa conscendant poli.' (IV. I met.)[102]

['For I have wings swift flying which can ascend to the heights of heaven.']

The generality of this likeness, however, suggests that Tatwine got this part of Boethius indirectly from a commentary or an even more derivative source. Evidence for any eighth-century acquaintance with *De consolatione* points to its circulation in Frankish minsters west and east of the Rhine from the 790s onwards, when it is thought that Alcuin brought a copy-text of this work to Aachen from one of his journeys to Italy. Until then, with the exception of Corbie, Boethius' greatest work had been avoided; Alcuin's reference to 'Boetius' in his passage on the library in York at about this time is thought to refer to Boethius' translations of Aristotle.[103] Where Alcuin alludes to the *De consolatione* in his correspondence, he probably uses the text which he acquired in Italy.[104] Before long, however, versions of the *De consolatione* were known to Bishops Moduinus of Auxerre in 820 and Jonas of Orléans in 834; it was also copied for schools in north Francia and German regions from the beginning of the ninth century onwards, in minsters such as Saint-Riquier, Nevers, Reichenau, Freising, Saint-Gall, Lorsch, and Murbach; there were also commentaries, of which one

---

[100] Lapidge, 'Surviving Booklists', 116–18 (IV. 6); *The Anglo-Saxon Library*, 55 ('a sort of start-up collection') and 134–6 (INV(i)b.5).

[101] *Tatuini Opera*, ed. de Marco and trans. von Erhardt, 168.

[102] *Consolation of Philosophy*, ed. and trans. Tester, 314–15.

[103] *Poetae Latini aevi Carolini*, ed. Dümmler, i. 204: 'Quae Victorinus scripsere Boetius atque' ('what things both Victorinus and Boethius wrote', *Versus de patribus regibus et sanctis Euboricensis ecclesiae*, line 1547). Bolton, '*Consolation of Philosophy* in Anglo-Saxon England', 34 and n. 4. Lapidge, *The Anglo-Saxon Library*, 230 (no. 16): '(some of) Boethius' logical writings'.

[104] Bullough, 'Charlemagne's "Men of God"', 140. *Epistolae*, ed. Dümmler, ii. 128 (no. 86; I. 6), 373 (no. 229; I. 4), 385 no. 240; I. 1).

from the Loire of the early ninth century (possibly from Fleury), is known to have gone to Britain (possibly Glastonbury).[105]

Francia, particularly Corbie, provides the Boethian link which may be invoked in the case of Breedon. To start with the sculptures. The friezes at Breedon contain at least four stylistic parallels with manuscript illuminations in the books of Corbie (see Ill. 2). Jewell notes that the earliest Carolingian parallels for the eastern-derived foliage in the Breedon narrow frieze is found in Corbie manuscripts such as the *c.*700 'Leningrad Basilius' and 'Jerome'. 'Heart-shaped and oval leaves' in *c.*780 manuscripts from Charlemagne's scriptorium at Aachen are found only in the same Breedon frieze.[106] The trefoil there also, though widespread in Persian-derived textiles, 'is found in the same Corbie and Court School manuscripts as the heart', as well as in the Mercian Barberini Gospels of the Tiberius Group to which the Lichfield-derived Book of Cerne belongs.[107] The vinescroll tendrils on the narrow Breedon frieze, without Anglo-Saxon parallels, can be matched with those in Frankish court-related manuscripts such as the Dagulf Psalter.[108] Jewell also notes that the drawing of an Arab horseman beside Psalm 32 in fo. 26^v of the *c.*800 Corbie Psalter closely resembles one of the mounted spearmen in the Breedon broad frieze.[109] A vintage scene on the broad frieze, moreover, suggests more Carolingian influence at Breedon, on which the cockerels, in particular, 'may have been inspired by a Court School miniature', such as the bird groups on fo. 11^r of the Harley Gospels.[110] The drapery conventions in a picture in fo. 46^r of the Corbie Psalter match those in the Breedon Virgin panel, which Jewell dates to *c.*820–30.[111] Here the Virgin's outsize hand is paralleled, not only frequently in England, but also by several figures in the Corbie Psalter.[112] This Psalter offers yet more parallels, on fos. 28^v, 46^r, and 108^v, for the facial type and curly hair of the Breedon Angel, which Jewell dates to *c.*800–10.[113] Rosemary Cramp states that it is 'impossible to say' whether these foreign motifs arrived in Breedon within manuscripts.[114] Jewell believes that the sculptors took their models from late antique ivories and eastern textiles.[115] Yet Breedon's designs

---

[105] Vatican City, BAV, Vat. Lat. 3363. Lapidge, *The Anglo-Saxon Library*, 173 (no. 77). Bolton, 'Consolation of Philosophy' in Anglo-Saxon England', 35–6.

[106] Respectively, St Petersburg State Public Library, MS Lat. Fv. I. N. 2 and Qv. I. N. 13. Jewell, 'The Anglo-Saxon Friezes at Breedon on the Hill', 97. There are, however, related volute-endings in contemporary carvings in the church in Britford (Wilts.).

[107] Ibid. Brown, *The Book of Cerne*, 172.

[108] Vienna, Österreichische Nationalbibliothek 1861, fo. 21.b. Jewell, 'The Anglo-Saxon Friezes at Breedon on the Hill', 98; 'Classicism of Southumbrian Sculpture', 249.

[109] Amiens, Bibliothèque Municipale, 3. Jewell, 'The Anglo-Saxon Friezes at Breedon on the Hill', 105 (3.c).

[110] Ibid. 109 (5.b).

[111] Jewell, 'Classicism of Southumbrian Sculpture', 254 and 262.

[112] Ibid. 254.

[113] Ibid. 258 and 262.

[114] Cramp, 'Schools of Mercian Sculpture', 194.

[115] Jewell, 'The Anglo-Saxon Friezes at Breedon on the Hill', 102; 'Classicism of Southumbrian Sculpture', 250.

4. Relief panel (St Mary), Breedon on the Hill. The Conway Library, Courtauld Institute of Art

make it certain that its monks had direct communication with ecclesiastical centres in Francia and Italy. On the way, to judge by the mounted spearmen in the Breedon broad frieze, these designs seem to have passed through Corbie; Alcuin called Corbie a *bivium* ('meeting of the ways').[116]

Alcuin again is central, a correspondent of Abbot Adalhard of Corbie whom he asks for news in five surviving letters.[117] Adalhard was Charlemagne's cousin and ruled Corbie from 780 to 814 and again (after a period of exile) from 821 to 826. Corbie's even earlier links with England are proved by its abbot Grimo's friendship with Boniface, who adapted Tatwine's *Ars grammatica*;[118] and by the discovery of a English *sceatta* in Corbie from 690 × 725.[119] Later Corbie was just as prestigious, if not more, in north-western Francia as Breedon in eastern Mercia. In 762, Corbie was integrated into a network of minsters consisting of Saint-Denis, Saint-Riquier, Saint-Germain, Saint-Cloud, and Rebais; and elevated further in 769 with a confirmation of its unique privileges by Charlemagne. The *Statutes* of Abbot Adalhard show that Corbie owned unparalleled wealth, with 350 monks, 150 prebends, and 12 poor men and a size greater than St Martin's at Tours or even Saint-Denis outside Paris.[120] In his second abbacy Adalhard endowed the project of his first, the minster of Corvey in Saxony, which thereafter played a seminal role, through Ansgar and his monks, in the mission to Scandinavia in 826.[121] In the ninth century, therefore, Corbie not only owned a library stocked from other minsters, Italy, and the Frankish court, but had opened lines of communication to Frisia, Saxony, and heathen Denmark on one hand and to England on the other. This will be mentioned again in the following chapter, in relation to the baptism of King Heriold of Denmark in 826.

Of itself, Corbie's eighth-century library does not prove that the same and related Latin works were then held in England. Lapidge, who dates *Beowulf* to the west of England before *c*.750, makes it clear that there is no evidence for these works in England at this time.[122] Yet Breedon and Corbie were comparable minsters in more than one way. Not only the wealth of both foundations, their access to royal power, and the position of each at the centre of a constellation of lesser monasteries, but also King Offa's ambition to rival Charlemagne, make it probable that the library at Breedon was later stocked so as to keep up with those of Corbie or Saint-Riquier. If the *De consolatione* and other relevant books were not at Breedon before the early impact of the Carolingian renaissance in *c*.800, the intensity of Breedon's sculptures

---

[116] *Epistolae*, ed. Dümmler, ii, no. 181. Allott, *Alcuin of York*, 151 (no. 153).

[117] Ganz, *Corbie*, 20–4. *Epistolae*, ed. Dümmler, ii. 9, 175, 176, 222, and 237.

[118] Law, *The Insular Latin Grammarians*, 66.

[119] Ganz, *Corbie*, 19.

[120] Ibid. 25–6.

[121] McKitterick, *The Frankish Kingdoms under the Carolingians*, 117–18.

[122] Lapidge, 'Surviving Booklists', 109: 'it has yet to be demonstrated that the *De consolatione Philosophiae* was known in England before the late ninth century'; *The Anglo-Saxon Library*, 127–8, esp. 127: 'not necessarily earlier than *c*.900'. See also his 'The Archetype of *Beowulf*', 5–41; '*Beowulf* and Perception', 80, 87, and 97.

shows that these and other books were probably imported soon afterwards both to Breedon and to other rich Mercian houses which matched the leading minsters of Francia. Lapidge considers the lost Anglo-Saxon library holdings as inferior to those in Francia, but we need only to consider Jewell's statement that the Breedon carvings 'constitute the largest and most important group of architectural sculptures of their date in Europe', to attribute a correspondingly impressive library to the early ninth-century minster at Breedon.[123] As regards the *Contra academicos* and the *De consolatione*, traces of which I find in *Beowulf*, we may note that both works were copied in the minsters of Corbie and Saint-Riquier, while Maurdramn was Corbie's abbot (*c.*771–*c.*783).[124] This period, moreover, was one in which Corbie's library contained copies of John Cassian's *Conlationes*, which, in Chapter 3, I have suggested was another source of *Beowulf*.[125] In short, Breedon's carvings show that this minster looked up to what Corbie had to provide. The fact, therefore, that Corbie held the *De consolatione*, *Contra academicos*, and *Conlationes* goes some way to showing that Breedon did also.

'WUNDORSIONA FELA': *BEOWULF* AND THE BREEDON SCULPTURES

Breedon's sculptures hardly illustrate *Beowulf*, although the sylvan hunting scenes on the broad friezes, supposedly greeting newcomers on the outside walls of the nave of Breedon's church (see Ill. 3), might be matched with Hrothgar's imagery of the stag-hunt in *Beo* 1368–72; or the panel fragment of the early ninth century which depicts the wine jars of the miracle at Cana, with the poet's words for festivity in Heorot, *byrelas sealdon win of wunderfatum* ('boys served wine from miraculous vessels', lines 1161–2; after the Finnsburh lay).[126] There is also an image in which the Lord is said to create earth, sun and moon:

> ond gefrætwade   foldan sceatas
> leomum ond leafum,   lif eac gesceop
> cynna gehwylcum   þara ðe cwice hwyrfaþ. (*Beo* 96–8)

[and adorned earth's surfaces with branches and leaves, and also created life for all living things that move.]

---

[123] Lapidge, *The Anglo-Saxon Library*, 58–62. Jewell, 'The Anglo-Saxon Friezes at Breedon on the Hill', 95.

[124] Ganz, *Corbie*, 138 (Paris BN Lat. 13377, incl. *De consolatione Philosophiae*) and 139 (Paris, BN Lat. 13369, incl. *Contra academicos*). *Texts and Transmission*, ed. Reynolds, 246. *Hariulf: Chronique de l'Abbaye de Saint-Riquier (Ve siècle–1104)*, ed. F. Lot, Collections de Textes pour Servir à l'Étude et à l'Enseignement de l'Histoire 17 (Paris, 1894), 90–1 (Hariulf's book inventory, *c.*831). In the same type of script, copies of *Contra academicos* lay also in Lorsch and Rheims: B. Bischoff, *Die Abtei Lorsch im Spiegel ihrer Handschriften*, 2nd edn. (Lorsch, 1989), 98 n. 42.

[125] Ganz, *Corbie*, 131 (Leningrad [St Petersburg], Lat. O v I 4) and 139 (Paris, BN Lat. 13384); see also 157 (Cassian's *Institutiones*, in Paris BN Lat. 12292).

[126] Jewell, 'Classicism of Southumbrian Sculpture', 260–1 (fig. 17.5 (a)).

The word *gefrætwade* ('adorned') is a telling metaphor, for hereby the poet seems to imagine the Lord creating leaf and branch as if making inhabited vinescroll. In this case the present tense of the living things that *hwyrfaþ* ('move') suggests the merging of past and present for an audience acquainted with depictions of animal life. A yet more particular correlation between *Beowulf* and the sculptures of Breedon may be seen through two of the poem's presumed Latin sources, the *Epistola Alexandri ad Aristotelem* and the *Liber monstrorum*. In Chapter 3 I have followed Orchard in suggesting that these books were used as sources for *Beowulf.* To argue a place for them in the library at Breedon, we can cite the likewise eastern origin of the designs in the sculptures.

The carvings in Breedon in *c*.800–10 featured animals which can be found in both the *Epistola* and the *Liber*. The broad frieze, in particular, shows a common interest with these books, for it displays real and fantastical animals whose nearest parallels come from the East, from Persia, Syria, or Byzantine Italy. These areas match with territories forever exoticized by the *Epistola* and plentifully used in the *Liber*. There are *albi leones taurorum comparandi magnitudine* in the *Epistola* ('white lions comparable to bulls in size', § 19) and in Breedon four unexplained beasts derived from eastern art 'of a leonine type' yet with heavily built bodies and spindly legs, with heads 'round and catlike, with pointed ears and hollowed sockets for eyes'.[127] There are lions and tigers in the *Epistola* (§§ 16 and 18) and *Liber* (II. 1 and 4) and five heraldic lions in the Breedon broad friezes, whose closest parallels are found in Coptic textiles of the fifth and sixth centuries;[128] in addition, there are lynxes, leopards, and panthers in the *Liber* (respectively II. 5; II. 6, II. 18, II. 30; II. 7) and some thin vinescroll on another broad frieze in Breedon inhabited by 'an addorsed pair of running quadrupeds, possibly felines'.[129] There are *nocticoraces uenere aues uulturibus similes* in the *Epistola* ('night-crows, hunting birds like vultures', § 21) and in Breedon one panel which originally contained three pairs of birds along with hounds and mounted spearmen, another panel containing cockerels with an eagle and possibly a hawk, and a third with two birds of prey matching a pair on the Hedda Stone in Peterborough Cathedral, but one more faithful to Byzantine designs.[130]

The *Liber monstrorum* has more fantastical animals than the *Epistola*. Breedon also has some ambiguous animals of this kind. Hippocentaurs, ass-centaurs, and the centaur Chiron himself in the *Liber* (respectively I. 7, I. 10, and I. 12) have a near-match in Breedon in 'a rearing centaur with outspread wings attached to its shoulders', which inhabits the thin vinescroll of a broad frieze and is probably derived from fifth- or sixth-century textiles from the Christian East.[131] The *Liber*

---

[127] In their eyes these beasts resemble the foliate-tailed bipeds on a Mercian bone girdle-end found in Leicester. See Jewell, 'The Anglo-Saxon Friezes at Breedon on the Hill', 105 (4.a).

[128] Ibid. 108 (4).

[129] Ibid. 100 (1.b).

[130] Ibid. 103 (3), 106 (4.b), and 108 (4.d).

[131] Ibid. 101–2 (1.c). Discussed in Gannon, *Iconography of Early Anglo-Saxon Coinage*, 151–3.

also refers to Circean monsters such as lions and bears, boars and wolves, *qui cetero corpore in ferarum natura manente, hominum facies habuerunt* ('who, whilst the rest of their body kept the nature of wild beasts, had human faces', I. 41); one broad frieze in Breedon contains 'a group of extraordinary monsters with long necks and semi-human faces, with deeply drilled eyes', simian in the way 'they crouch or squat on their long hind legs', one of them with a beard.[132] There are harpies *in forma uolucrum, facie tamen uirginali* in the *Liber* ('in the form of birds, with the faces of maidens', I. 44); and on the thin-vinescrolled broad frieze in Breedon a pair of 'squatting winged quadrupeds with quasi-human heads', with parallels not only in the Hoddom cross-head, West Tanfield, and Easby, but also in late antique textiles, particularly a tapestry-woven panel from Egypt, and in the Soissons Gospels, associated with the court of Charlemagne.[133]

In this way, Breedon has lions, tigers, leopards, and hunting birds in common with the *Epistola Alexandri* and a (female) centaur, half-human beasts, and harpies in common with the *Liber monstrorum*. Breedon does not include snakes, rhinoceri, crocodiles, hippopotami, elephants, or dogheads, such as are found in the *Epistola*. Yet the fact that the Breedon sculptors based their images on eastern textiles, ivories, and coins as well as Carolingian manuscript illustrations is evidence of Breedon's general interest in eastern animals and marvels. Something of the same interest appears in *Beowulf*, whose author shows himself to be aware of beautiful tapestries, in particular, when he describes the Danish feast preparations on Beowulf's first triumphant return from the Mere:

> Goldfag scinon
> web æfter wagum   wundorsiona fela
> secga gehwylcum   þara þe on swylc staraδ. (*Beo* 994–6)

[Gold-ornamented the tapestries shone along the walls, a host of wondrous sights for any of those men who stare at such things.]

The poet's claimed scorn, which reveals that others around him enjoy the sight of marvels, is part of his contemporizing 'authenticating voice'.[134] Somewhat less lachrymosely, it corresponds with Alcuin's denunciation of new Mercian fashions in 797, after Offa's death:

Nec enim priorum patrum vel in vestimentis vel in conviviis vel in moribus honestatis sufficit vestigia sequi. Sed qui stultior est omnibus, novum quid excogitans et humanae naturae ineptum et Deo odibile, hoc maxime totus paene mox populus exsequi satagit.[135]

---

[132] Jewell, 'The Anglo-Saxon Friezes at Breedon on the Hill', 105 (4.a).

[133] Ibid. 101–2 (1.c: Paris, BN Lat. 8850, fo. 6'). McKitterick, *The Carolingians and the Written Word*, 142.

[134] Greenfield, 'The Authenticating Voice in *Beowulf*', 55–8.

[135] *Epistolae*, ed. Dümmler, ii. 178–80, at 179 (no. 122: to 'Osberht', probably Brorda). My translation is based on Whitelock's, in *EHD*, 786–8 (no. 202: 'Osberht'). On the identification with Brorda, see Thacker, 'Some Terms for Noblemen', 218–19; Kirby, *Earliest English Kings*, 177; Keynes, 'Councils of *Clofesho*', 42 n. 180.

[Nor, indeed, it is now enough to follow the tracks of our fathers before us either in dress, or in feasts, or in honourable behaviour. But he who is more foolish than everyone invents something new and unsuited to human nature and hateful to God, and soon almost the whole people strives with the utmost eagerness to follow it.]

Not only Alcuin's words speak of a new taste for mythology and exotica in Mercian art just before the beginning of the ninth century.[136] All three instances, not only Alcuin's but also in *Beowulf* and Breedon, bear witness to *wundorsiona fela*. It is obvious, on one hand, that other English centres than Breedon, most no longer extant, boasted relief carvings and other artefacts, from which a knowledge of the *Epistola* and *Liber* could also be deduced as evidence for their housing the production of this poem. On the other hand, the strongest defence against these objections is the Breedon carvings themselves. The unparalleled intensity, quantity, and range of her friezes make Breedon the most plausible home for copies of the *Epistola* and *Liber*, works of which I find traces in *Beowulf.*

'SAWELE HYRDE': *BEOWULF* AND THE BREEDON ANGEL

One of the homiletic flourishes in Hrothgar's sword-hilt speech in the textual heart of *Beowulf* is his use of an epithet for St Michael apparently to denote a man's conscience guarding him from pride. First he describes a man so blessed with fame and worldly success that *inwitsorh* no longer bothers him (line 1736). Soon the man forgets that things were ever different. Then a new fitt begins:

XX[V] 'Oð þæt him on innan   oferhygda dæl
weaxeð ond wridað,   þonne se weard swefeð,
sawele hyrde;   bið se slæp to fæst,
bisgum gebunden,   bona swiðe neah,
se þe of flanbogan   fyrenum sceoteð. (*Beo* 1740–4)

['And then a measure of prideful thoughts grows and flourishes within him, when the keeper sleeps, the guardian of the soul; that sleep is too sound, bound with cares, the slayer very close, who shoots wickedly from a fiery bow.']

It seems clear that with the words *weard, sawele hyrde*, Hrothgar means the *inwitsorh* just mentioned: Conscience.[137] Yet Orchard observes that in Old English homilies phrases such as *sawele hyrde* are used to describe St Michael in his role as a guide for Christian souls.[138] The Archangel Michael does not seem to be attested in any other surviving Old English poem.[139] His presence in *Beowulf*, however, might tell us that Beowulf's soul has become the theme of

---

[136] Gannon, *Iconography of Early Anglo-Saxon Coinage*, 151–6, esp. 153.
[137] *Beowulf*, ed. Mitchell and Robinson, 105. For *sapientia* ('wisdom') in this role, see Kaske, 'Sapientia et Fortitudo', 280–1.
[138] Orchard, *Pride and Prodigies*, 51. Rauer, *Beowulf and the Dragon*, 124.
[139] He is popular in OE prose, however: see Johnson, *Saint Michael the Archangel*, 89–102.

Fitt XX[V], just over halfway through the poem. If Hrothgar refers to St Michael, hitting a mark of Christian theology without knowing it, he is far from having, in Irving's words, a 'sacerdotal air of pseudo-Christian sententiousness'.[140]

Earlier in the poem, it is also clear that the poet seems to have based both Hrothgar's and his own descriptions of Grendel's Mere on a vernacular adaptation of the *Visio s. Pauli*, such as that which concludes Blickling Homily XVI, a text for Michaelmas (29 September).[141] That an earlier version of this homily as a whole was known to the poet of *Beowulf*, however, might be seen in its opening story of the magnate Garganus. This man gives his name to the hill Monte Gargano in Apulia in south-west Italy, after losing his life there in an attempt to shoot a stray bull with a poisoned arrow. After the local bishop orders observances, St Michael appears with a revelation: *Wite þu eac þæt se mon se þær mid his agenum stræle ofsceoten wæs, þa þæt wæs mid minum willan gedon* ('Know also concerning the man who was shot with his own arrow that that was done by my will').[142] The motif differs from Hrothgar's, in that the arrow is another's which the Michael-figure lets through by sleeping on his watch. On the other hand, as Orchard notes, the phrase *geweox ond gewridode*, with which the Blickling homilist describes how Garganus' herds 'grew and flourished' just before his death, resembles the way in which Hrothgar says a man's pride *weaxeð ond wridað* at the start of Fitt XX[V] of *Beowulf* on line 1741.[143] Garganus becomes angry that the bull *swa ofermodlice ferde* ('wandered so arrogantly'), but the story is really about his pride growing in pace with the herd. It seems likely, therefore, that the poet based the growing pride and arrows of Hrothgar's sword-hilt speech on the language of a homily on St Michael which has an ancestor in common with the whole of Blickling Homily XVI.[144]

As we have seen in Chapter 3, it is thought that the two *Vitae Samsonis* influenced the poet of *Beowulf* in his story of Beowulf's fight with the dragon. Yet Christine Rauer, who demonstrates this, also shows his use of St Michael in three motifs in the same narrative at the end of his poem. Individually these motifs are hagiographical commonplaces too, but in this 'precise constellation' they are found only in item 55 of the *Homiliary of Saint-Père*.[145] The first, the dragon's fire-breath (lines 2522–3, 2556–7, 2582), is more clearly matched by the *flatus flamiuomus* ('fire-spitting breath') of the *Saint-Père* homily on

[140] Irving, *Rereading Beowulf*, 54.
[141] Wright, *The Irish Tradition*, 132–6.
[142] *The Blickling Homilies*, ed. and trans. Kelly, 138–9.
[143] Ibid. 136–7. Orchard, *Companion*, 30.
[144] A version of the 'De apparitione Sancti Michaelis', from which Blickling XVI is derived, was used in Anglo-Saxon homiliaries and legendaries in the early to mid-ninth century: J. E. Cross, 'An Unrecorded Tradition of St. Michael in Old English Texts', *Notes & Queries*, NS 28 (1981), 12 n. 4; and was known as early as the second half of the eighth century: G. Otranto, 'Per una metodologia della ricerca storico-agiografica, il santuario micaelico del Gargano tra Bizantini e Longobardi', *Vetera Christianorum*, 25 (1988), 381–405, esp. 383.
[145] Rauer, *Beowulf and the Dragon*, 118–20, esp. 121.

St Michael than in the *Vitae Samsonis* or elsewhere. A combination of two more motifs, Beowulf's cutting through the dragon's middle (line 2705) and the Geats' disposal of the body in the sea (lines 3131–3), is paralleled only in the *Saint-Père*:[146]

Factum est autem silentium in caelo dum praeliaretur Michael archangelus cum dracone. Cumque fecisset uictoriam, draconem in xii partes interficiens, exaudita est uox milia milium dicentium: Salus, honor, uirtus, et imperium semper omnipotenti deo. Dec cum incolae regionis illius post haec deum glorificantes reuertissent, uix unamquamque partem huius draconis per xii iuga bouum ad mare usque trahere conantes preualuerunt ne suo fetore homines et iumenta mortificarentur.

[And there was silence in heaven while the Archangel Michael was battling against the dragon. When he had achieved victory, killing the dragon and splitting it into twelve parts, the voice of thousands and thousands of men was heard, saying: 'Salvation, honour, power and authority to the almighty God forever.' But when the people of that region [Asia] had come back afterwards, praising God, they could hardly with twelve teams of oxen drag the individual parts of that dragon to the sea when they tried—they did this so that the people and cattle might not die from its stench.][147]

Ultimately the scene in this homily is based on Rev. 12: 7. Yet there the violence of the dragon's death is lacking, just as in both *Vitae Samsonis*.[148] Whether the poet of *Beowulf* used one or both of these saints' lives, it is not these, but St Michael's dissection and his supporters' removal of the dragon, which seem to give him the authority for Beowulf's hacking the dragon to death and the Geats' shoving the body over a cliff into the sea.

In all, therefore, it is possible to find three indications of a homily upon St Michael among the varied sources of *Beowulf*. It is uncertain whether this homily was item 55 of the *Homiliary of Saint-Père*, which is the name for a collection surviving in eight manuscripts (four with item 55).[149] The date for the (lost) original form of this work, whose oldest copy survives in Cambridge, Pembroke College 25 (s. xi), is placed by James Cross at 822 or after.[150] Cross suggests that the St Michael passage in this manuscript was derived from a Carolingian version of an Irish source, although Rauer is inclined to treat this version as either Breton or northern Frankish.[151] Nonetheless, there is a broad consensus that the Old English St Michael texts were influenced in more than one way from Ireland, from where the cult of St Michael spread to Northumbria

---

[146] Rauer, *Beowulf and the Dragon*, esp. 120–1.

[147] Cited and translated ibid. 158–61, esp. 160–1 (cf. 120); and in Ruggerini, 'St Michael and the Dragon', 57.

[148] Rauer, *Beowolf and the Dragon*, 70–1 and 158–9.

[149] Ibid. 118.

[150] Cross, *Cambridge Pembroke College MS. 25*, 37–8. See, however, R. McKitterick, *The Frankish Church and the Carolingian Reforms, 789–895* (London, 1977), 106–9, esp. 107 ('written some time after 826').

[151] Cross, *Cambridge Pembroke College MS. 25*, 84–7. Rauer, *Beowulf and the Dragon*, 121–3.

and Mercia in the seventh century, at about the time the minster of Breedon was founded.[152] Of the main legendary versions of St Michael's dragon-fight, one is set on Monte Gargano, the other in Mont-Saint-Michel (Normandy); the first, represented also in Blickling Homily XVI, derives from Ireland, where it is now contained in the fifteenth-century Leabhar Breac.[153] Rauer's concluding remarks are worth quoting in full:

If one would like to concur with the theory that the Blickling homilist and the *Beowulf*-poet both drew on a lost vernacular version of the *Visio S. Pauli*, it might not be unreasonable to suggest that such material could, like Blickling Homily XVI, also have contained elements of St Michael's hagiography, including, one might suggest, the description of hell, the archangel's role as psychopomp (*sawele hyrde*), and an account of his dragon fight.[154]

If we look for St Michael in Breedon, we find a panel of an angel in the ringing chamber of the church tower, the so-called 'Breedon Angel'. Jewell, when discussing it, is cautious in suggesting that with this impressive large sculpture (36.5 × 21 inches) the sculptor 'wished to represent the Angel Gabriel of the Annunciation: a fitting subject for a church dedicated to the Virgin'.[155] It has been assumed that the Breedon minster was dedicated to Mary in its earlier history in the eighth century.[156] This idea is not supported, however, by the relative dating of the Breedon Virgin and Angel panels. Jewell dates the Angel to *c.*800–10 and the Virgin panel to *c.*820–30, having moved this back from *c.*830–40.[157] It is unclear why the Virgin should be carved at least ten years later than the Angel, if the minster was dedicated to her before the end of the eighth century. Of course she may have had another panel that went missing. But her present panel is recognized as unusual: a half-length, frontal figure, with banded drapery; veiled, but without a halo, with deeply drilled eyes; with an outsize right hand held up in blessing and the left holding a book. Her attitude here suggests that the sculptor adapted a picture of an apostle, keeping the masculine attributes while turning it into an image of the Virgin.[158] The awkwardness in iconography, together with the later date of this carving, may indicate that the Breedon minster or church was dedicated to Mary after the Angel was carved. (See Ill. 4 on p. 179.)

---

[152] Wright, *The Irish Tradition*, 262. Johnson, 'Archangel in the Margins', 64–86; *Saint Michael the Archangel*, 45–6. Ruggerini, 'St Michael and the Dragon', 23–8.

[153] Rauer, *Beowulf and the Dragon*, 118.

[154] Ibid. 124.

[155] Jewell, 'Classicism of Southumbrian Sculpture', 258 and fig. 17.4.

[156] Cramp, 'Schools of Mercian Sculpture', 210. Jewell, 'Classicism of Southumbrian Sculpture', 253. Clayton (*The Cult of the Virgin Mary*, 151–2) is more cautious about the date of Breedon's dedication to St Mary.

[157] Jewell, 'Classicism of Southumbrian Sculpture', 254; 'The Pre-Conquest Sculpture at Breedon on the Hill', 261–2.

[158] Cramp, 'Schools of Mercian Sculpture', 210. Jewell, 'Classicism of Southumbrian Sculpture', 253. Clayton, *The Cult of the Virgin Mary*, 152–3.

Jewell identifies the angel on this panel with Gabriel because it bears a close resemblance to an ivory panel of the Annunciation in the back-rest of Maximian's mid-sixth-century throne in Ravenna. Both have similar faces and sparsely feathered wings and both step forward to give the Greek blessing with the right hand raised.[159] Yet Jewell also notes that the Breedon Angel has 'an early prototype' in an image of the Archangel Michael on a Constantinopolitan ivory diptych-wing from c.520. Despite differences in drapery styles and frames, the two have 'a general typological connection'.[160] This is how the Breedon Angel resembles a portrait of St Michael in the church at Fletton, close to Breedon's mother house, *Medeshamstede* near Peterborough.[161] In style this is related to a box panel with two apostles in Breedon and another apostle panel in Castor, both of which are fragments based on early Christian sarcophagi.[162] As we have seen, Breedon remained on close terms with *Medeshamstede* and her other colonies around Peterborough.[163] The Breedon Angel is like the Fletton St Michael in that he raises one hand in salutation and holds a long staff in the other. Although the Breedon Angel holds the staff in his left hand, the Fletton St Michael in his right, each staff is the same in having not only a cruciformed head at the top end, but also a spherical terminal at the bottom (with that of Breedon now broken off).[164] In the light of Breedon's typological Michael-prototype from Constantinople and the above three points of resemblance between the Fletton and Breedon angels, it seems more likely, on balance, that the Breedon figure was carved as a depiction of Archangel Michael in his role as the protector of souls.

It is unknown when Breedon was dedicated to St Mary (and St Hardulph). Yet as we have seen, Breedon's problematic Virgin panel has been dated variously to 830–40 and 820–30; and the draftsman of a charter in favour probably of Breedon in 841 (S 193) uses a line from a Marian poem of Aldhelm's, in which he also celebrates Gabriel in the Annunciation.[165] This is evidence that the church at Breedon was (re-)dedicated to St Mary by the 830s at the latest. At this time the older Angel panel could have been reinterpreted as Gabriel, but it is worth remembering that Mary was already associated with Michael in her Assumption, as in the Latin sources for Blickling Homily XIII.[166] Carved in c.800–10, before the Mary panel, the Breedon Angel is an older conception, possibily as old as the founding of the minster itself. From the late seventh to the mid-ninth century, as many as five Anglo-Saxon pilgrims left their names

---

[159] Jewell, 'Classicism of Southumbrian Sculpture', 258.
[160] Ibid. 257.
[161] Cramp, 'Schools of Mercian Sculpture', 209 (fig. 56.b).
[162] Jewell, 'Classicism of Southumbrian Sculpture', 254–5.
[163] Keynes, 'Councils of *Clofesho*', 37–9.
[164] Ibid. 256. Cramp, 'Schools of Mercian Sculpture', 207 and 211.
[165] S 193 (BCS 434). *Aldhelmi Opera*, ed. Ehwald, 13 (*In basilica beatae Mariae semper virginis*, line 19) and 423 (Poem *De virginibus*, line 1697).
[166] Johnson, *Saint Michael the Archangel*, 76–82.

5. Relief panel (Angel: St Michael?), Breedon on the Hill. The Conway Library, Courtauld Institute of Art

6. Relief panel (St Michael), Fletton. The Conway Library, Courtauld Institute of Art

(in runes) on the walls of St Michael's grotto chapel on Monte Gargano.[167] By this time in England, many old pagan sites had been reconsecrated, in association with Celtic missionaries, into churches in honour of St Michael.[168] In this respect, the antiquity of Breedon is clear in the derivation of its first name-element from a British word for 'hill'.[169] Today not only a church derived from a monastic cell in Lichfield, but also the churches of Melbourne and Diseworth around Breedon itself, are dedicated to St Michael.[170] Was the church at Diseworth dedicated after Breedon? Edgar's grant to Bishop Æthelwold, probably of *c*.972, reveals *Digþeswyrþe* ('Diseworth') as belonging to the church *Æbreodone* ('at Breedon'), though for how long is unknown.[171] In these ways it is possible that the first patron saint of Breedon was St Michael.

The size and Carolingian features of Breedon's Angel, if this is St Michael, bear witness to the re-invigoration of his cult in the Frankish empire at the time this panel was carved, in *c*.800–10.[172] By now St Michael had been in Francia for some time. Mont-Saint-Michel had been founded in northern Francia (now Normandy) as early as the beginning of the eighth century. It was an Englishman, Cathwulf, who induced Charlemagne to celebrate St Michael and St Peter in 775, one year after his conquest of Lombardy, whose dukes had brought the cult north from their holdings in Apulia. In his *Admonitio generalis* of 789, and in other councils, Charlemagne decreed the observance of Michaelmas (29 September) across Francia; and when Charlemagne was crowned emperor in Rome in 800, the royal hymns (*laudes regiae*) sung in his honour associated him with St Michael; the archangel was also depicted on the imperial standard with the words *Patronus et Princeps Imperii Galliarum* ('Patron and Prince of the Empire of the Gauls'). At Charlemagne's command, probably between 789 and *c*.800, Alcuin composed the 'Sequentia de sancto Michaele', a hymn in which he hails the archangel as *supernorum principem civium* ('the chief citizen of heaven', 2. 2), the heavenly commander and intercessor, swinger of God's golden censer in his temple and victor over the serpent:

> Tu crudelem cum draconem forti manu straveras,
> faucibus illius animas eruisti plurimas. (5. 1–2)[173]

[You, when you scattered the fierce dragon with your strong hand, plucked many souls from his jaws.]

---

[167] Ibid. 36–7.

[168] Arnold-Forster, *Church Dedications*, i. 37–9, esp. 39: 'There is a saying that churches to S. Michael should by rights be situated on the crown of a hill, or at least on rising ground.'

[169] Gelling, *Place-Names in the Landscape*, 128–9.

[170] Blair, *The Church in Anglo-Saxon Society*, 218–19; cf. 201 (on St Michael's prompting Wilfrid to make a dedication to St Mary). Arnold-Forster, *Church Dedications*, i. 38; iii. 106 (Diseworth), 181 (Lichfield), and 199 (Melbourne).

[171] S 749 (BCS 1283).

[172] Johnson, *St Michael the Archangel*, 42–4. See also Ruggerini, 'St Michael and the Dragon', 35–6.

[173] *Poetae Latini aevi Carolini*, ed. Dümmler, i. 348–9, esp. 348 (*Alcuini Carmina* CXX).

Thus the heroic type-scene in the dragon-fight in *Beowulf* in which the hero breaks his sword at the wrong moment, in the words *wæs sio hond to strong* ('that hand was too strong', line 2684), might also prefigure St Michael against the dragon before Doomsday. Alcuin's closing invocation is matched in the beatific stance of the Breedon Angel:

> Audi nos, Michahel,
> angele summe,
> huc parum descende
> de poli sede,
> nobis ferendo opem domini
> levamen atque indulgentiae. (6. 1–6)

[Hear us, Michael, greatest angel, come down here a little from your heavenly throne, to bring us the help and solace of the mercy of the Lord.]

If the Breedon Angel, as the staff and pose both suggest, was carved as St Michael the protector and conveyor of souls, then the presence of a panel of this size and with these attributes in this minster earlier in the ninth century could have lent the poet of *Beowulf*, if he lived there, some visual confirmation of the Christian *weard, sawele hyrde* to which Hrothgar refers in his warning against pride.

CONCLUSION

This chapter gives various reasons to suppose a connection between *Beowulf* and Breedon. One is Tatwine's apparent knowledge in Breedon of Books VI and XI of the *Aeneid*, from which I have traced borrowings in *Beowulf* in Chapters 3–4. Another is the suggestion of the poet's borrowing from Felix's *Vita Guthlaci*, which was associated either with Repton or *Medeshamstede*. Two more reasons rely on hints, references, and connections with other libraries. First, *Beowulf*'s familiarity with Francia seems clear not only in the poet's near certain use of the *Liber historiae Francorum* (*c*.727), but also in some Carolingian terms for the Merovingian military in Hygelac's last raid. There are five stylistic parallels between Corbie's manuscripts, in particular, and the Breedon carvings: these parallels make it more likely that Corbie was the source of the Frankish topicality which we find in *Beowulf*. Second, there is the *Beowulf*-poet's compassion for heathens, whom he shows to be ignorant of salvation yet gifted with the facility of Christians to make moral choices. In depicting them the poet reveals a view of foreknowledge which appears to be influenced by Boethius' *De consolatione Philosophiae*; and the poet's language of perception appears to follow that of Cicero's *Academica priora*, through the medium of St Augustine's *Contra academicos*. It is known that both the *De consolatione* and Augustine's work were copied in Corbie later in the eighth century, along with John Cassian's *Conlationes*, another work traceable to *Beowulf*. From Corbie came artefacts, doubtless books, on whose styles the early ninth-century carvings in Breedon are based. A first-hand acquaintance with the great work by Boethius, at least in these circumstances, would have been relatively new to the community from which the poet of *Beowulf* came. Other reasons for comparing *Beowulf* with Breedon are based on the premiss that Breedon's surviving carvings reflect the contents of its long-lost library. The unique quantity and quality of vinescroll and animals, both real and fantastical, in the *c*.800 Breedon narrow and broad friezes bears witness to the monks' interest in the eastern exotic. This is consistent with the library's possession of at least two well-known works containing eastern animals and monsters, the *Epistola Alexandri* and the *Liber monstrorum*, whose influence may be seen in *Beowulf*. Lastly, three allusions to the hagiography of St Michael in *Beowulf* may be compared with the so-called 'Breedon Angel' of the same date as the friezes: although this figure is identified with Archangel Gabriel, its iconography appears to have been influenced by that of Archangel Michael. A text on St Michael analogous to item 55 of the *Homiliary of Saint-Père* would appear to be common to *Beowulf* and Breedon.

In these ways it is possible to associate some nine of *Beowulf*'s presumed sources with the library at Breedon on the Hill. Of course, my arguments do not constitute proof that all these books were there, partly or entirely; or that the poet of *Beowulf* used them if they were; or that other monastic libraries did not hold some or all of the same works. Nonetheless, the hypothesis that Breedon was *Beowulf*'s birthplace is now stronger than any that might link this poem with any other minsters in the diocese of Unwona, bishop of Leicester.

7

The King's Soul: Danish Mythology
in *Beowulf*

In the previous chapter we saw Beowulf endangering his already impaired hope of salvation by ordering the plunder of the dragon's hoard. The poet lets us know that this treasure has been cursed by the ancients who laid it in the ground. Indeed he presents Beowulf's act as a moral choice. With hindsight we see that 'heathen gold' was an early theme, for it is implied that Hama chooses eternal reward by giving up the Gothic *Brosinga mene* (*Beo* 1199–201), just before we see Wealhtheow presenting another great necklace to Beowulf. Later, not long before Beowulf attacks the dragon, he tells a story of Hrethel's grief for Herebeald in which the poet seems to highlight Hrethel's restrained acceptance of his son's death as a heathen's best hope (lines 2469). Finally, with Beowulf's death in the dragon-fight, the poet suggests that the treasures he sought amount to poison, the possibility of spiritual death (lines 3066–7). For each of these morally defining moments, the poet appears to draw on the unquantifiable sources of a living Danish mythology. Respectively he plays on Freyja's *Brísinga men*, Óðinn's vengeance for Baldr, and Þórr's death by the World Serpent. These are not the Scylding *res gestae* which could have reached him from a native Anglo-Saxon tradition or by a contemporary Frankish or Frisian route. Rather, as I seek to show in this chapter, their currency as a religion in the Norse homeland makes it likely that the poet of *Beowulf* got them from talking to visitors from Denmark.

Here I will plead a special case for Danish influence on *Beowulf*. Once more, the focus is on the minster at Breedon on the Hill. In the foregoing chapter I have suggested *Beowulf* was written there at least twelve years after the death of a man who influenced it, Priest Abbot Wigmund (*c*.792–*c*.814 × *c*.816). Here I deduce that the *Beowulf*-poet's interest in heathens began in Wigmund's abbacy: first planted by contacts with Danish Vikings in this part of Mercia in 809; then, after his death, cultivated by news of the Franks' patronage of rival Danish factions in the following decade; finally brought into bloom in the 820s by talk of the negotiations in Francia that led to the baptism of King Heriold of Denmark in 826.

DANISH MYTHS IN CHRISTIAN FORM

As yet we are no closer to finding out why the first audience of *Beowulf* liked to hear stories about people routinely classified as damned.[1] This question is pressing, given Page's demonstration that Anglo-Saxons saw the Danes as 'heathens' rather than as foreigners, even if he concludes that, 'in different parts of England, a variety of positions was possible', including the composition of a praise poem for Danes during the Viking Age.[2] As subjects of the poem, the Danes will always be relevant to the question of *Beowulf*'s date. Recent work has shown that in the ninth century a Dane and an Anglo-Saxon could talk intelligibly to one another each in his own language.[3] It is also clear that assimilation to the native form is the poet's aim with Danish myths, no less than I suggest it was in the recasting of episodes from Vergil's *Aeneid*. Much here depends on the strength of the Danish religion before, during, and after the Viking Age. Until the Danes converted in the last quarter of the tenth century, they presented none but a pagan aspect to those who met them in Frisia, Francia, and the British Isles. This is the force of Alcuin's interest in King Ongendus (probably of Ribe) in the (prose) *Vita Willibrordi*, which celebrates the journey to Denmark of Alcuin's kinsman Willibrord (in *c.*710) as an attempt to convert the worst pagans of all. The poet of *Beowulf*, too, though he palliates the Scyldings in lines 50–2, still treats them as damnable on line 175. For these reasons, it is intriguing to see that he knows at least three of their myths. In the following pages I shall discuss the poet's moral aim in adapting the following motifs from Scandinavian mythology: the *Brísingamen*; Baldr and Hǫðr; and Þórr with the World Serpent.

'Brosinga mene': *Brísingamen*

The poet first alludes to a non-Christian, apparently Danish, source in *Beowulf* when he uses the *Brosinga mene* to define the moral of Hygelac's ill-fated Frisian raid. This allusion starts when Wealhtheow intervenes apparently to thwart Hrothgar's offer of *niw sib*. Hereupon the poet leaps into the future in lines 1197–214, his cue being the theme of material versus spiritual wealth. Wealhtheow has just finished implying that Hrothgar should give Beowulf *manigra medo* ('rewards of the many', line 1178), rather than his kingdom; Fitt XVIII begins with the arrival of some of these lesser gifts: two arm-rings, a garment and other rings or bracelets, and last but not least:

---

[1] As Klaeber said (ed., *Beowulf*, p. cxxiii), 'the very remarkable interest taken in matters Scandinavian' is 'still calling for an adequate explanation'.

[2] 'The Audience of *Beowulf* and the Vikings', 117–22, at 122.

[3] Townend, *Language and History*, 9–41, esp. 41, and 181–5.

                                            healsbeaga mæst
            þara þe ic on foldan   gefrægen hæbbe.
            Nænigne ic under swegle   selran hyrde
            hordmaðum hæleþa   syþðan Hama ætwæg
            to *þæ*re byrhtan byrig   Brosinga mene,
            sigle ond sincfæt;   searoniðas fle*a*h
            Eormenrices,   geceas ecne ræd. (*Beo* 1195–201)

[the greatest necklace of which I have heard tell on earth. Nor have I heard of a better hoard-treasure of men beneath the sun since Hama carried off the necklace of the 'Brosings' to the bright city, the jewel and its precious setting; he fled the cunning enmities of Eormanric, chose an eternal reward.]

Mitchell and Robinson, followed by Orchard, keep MS *fealh* on line 1200, translating this word as 'endured'.[4] But OE *feolan* (preterite *fealh*) means 'to penetrate' and there is no other example of this verb used transitively with an accusative object.[5] With *fleon* ('to flee'), on the other hand, there are sufficient parallels for 'searoniðas fle*a*h': there is the slave on the run, later in *Beowulf*, who *heteswengeas fleah* ('fled the hateful lashes', line 2224); when Abraham flees into Egypt in *Genesis* A, *fleah wærfæst wean* ('firm in his undertaking, he fled woe', *Gen* 1819); there is also Lot's flight from Sodom, *he þære mægðe monwisan fleah* ('he fled the mannish ways of that nation', *Gen* 1938). The clear meaning in *Beowulf* is that Hama fled from Eormanric.

    Orchard suggests that the poet took stories of Hama and Eormanric to be well known; as he shows, this allusion is brief and 'a rich background of tradition' is clear also in the widespread references to these men and their associates in *Widsith*, *Waldere* II, and *Deor*.[6] There are two Norse analogues for Hama's theft of this necklace. One is the tale of the like-named Heimir and King Erminríkr in *Þiðreks saga af Bern*, a late thirteenth-century Norwegian translation from a Low German original.[7] In this work, the knight Heimir takes treasure from King Erminríkr which he then bequeaths to a monastery in order to become a monk. But no name is given for this treasure, whether the cognate name *Brísingamen* or anything else. For this reason, in *Beo* 1195–201, it is possible that Hama's story was well known, as its brevity would suggest, but that his association with the *Brosinga mene* was a novelty imposed by the poet of *Beowulf*.

    This splicing of stories may be seen if we add to Heimir's stolen treasure the myth of the Norse god '*Heim*dallr', along with a designation for the *Brísingamen*,

    [4] *Beowulf*, ed. Mitchell and Robinson, 88 and 258 (*s.v. feolan*). Orchard, *Companion*, 114–16, at 114 n. 84.
    [5] *A Microfiche Concordance to Old English*, ed. R. L. Venezky and A. diPaolo Healey (Newark, Del., 1980–3), *s.vv.* 'fealh', 'feolan', 'fulgon' etc.
    [6] Orchard, *Companion*, 115.
    [7] *Þiðreks saga af Bern*, ed. Guðni Jónsson, 2 vols. (Reykjavik, 1951), ii. 388–9 (ch. 288) and 579–81, at 581 (ch. 429).

as told by the Icelandic poet Úlfr Uggason in his *Húsdrápa* (*c*.995). In the larger context, which is now lost, it appears that Heimdallr, closely followed by Loki, dives into the water in an effort to win possession of the *Brísingamen*:

> Ráðgegninn bregðr ragna rein- at singasteini
> frægr við firna slœgjan Fárbauta mǫg -vári.
> Móðǫflugr ræðr mœðra mǫgr hafnýra fǫgru
> (kynni ek) áðr ok einnar átta (mærðar þáttum).[8]

[Ready with a plan, the gods' land-warmer transforms for the blessing-jewel, renowned for facing the monstrously sly kinsman of Fárbauti. Mighty in spirit, the son of eight plus one mothers—I proclaim [Óláfr] in strands of renown—is the first to get control over the dazzling sea-kidney.][9]

This complex verse survives in solitary quotation in Snorri's *Skáldskaparmál*. Over its meaning there is much disagreement, but Heimdallr's attempt to regain Freyja's *Brísingamen* seems clear, in that elsewhere in the same work, Snorri says that Loki and Heimdallr, in seal-shapes, wrestled for the possession of this jewel; in *Gylfaginning* (ch. 27), Snorri's cites a kenning for Heimdallr as *mensœkir Freyju* ('Freyja's necklace-seeker'); and Freyja is given as the owner of the *Brísingamen* in *Þrymskviða*.[10] Now that it has been shown that *Þrymskviða* may be an Anglo-Norse poem, it is possible that stories of Freyja's *Brísingamen* were told in the Danelaw, even by Danish visitors to England before the Viking Age.[11] But as there is no other allusion to this necklace in the surviving Old English literature, the existence of a myth in which Heimdallr 'seeks' Freyja's *Brísingamen* gives reason to suppose that it is the poet of *Beowulf* who has foisted this mythological necklace on Hama through the similarity of his name with '*Heim*-dallr'.

The wider Old Norse-Icelandic tradition attributes the *Brísinga men* or *girði Brísings* (Brísingr's girdle', *c*.900) to Freyja, who is at once the sister of Ingvi-freyr

---

[8] *Skáldskaparmál*, ed. Faulkes, i. 20 (v. 64 and note).

[9] On the interpretation, see (forthcoming) R. North, 'Image and Ascendancy in Úlfr's *Húsdrápa*', in A. Minnis and J. Roberts (eds.), *Word, Text, Image: Studies in Anglo-Saxon Literature and Insular Culture in Honour of Éamonn Ó Carragáin* (Turnhout, 2006).

[10] On the problems of this poem, see C. Tolley, '*Húsdrápa*', *Tijdschrift voor Skandinavistiek* (1996), 83–98. The *Brísingamen* is taken to symbolize the earth as it is created from soil lifted out of the sea: in K. Schier, 'Húsdrápa 2: Heimdall, Loki und die Meerniere', in H. Birkhan and O. Gschwantler (eds.), *Festgabe für Otto Höfler zum 75. Geburtstag* (Vienna, 1976), 577–88, esp. 583; followed by E. Marold, 'Kosmogonische Mythen in der Húsdrápa des Úlfr Uggason', in M. Dallapiazza, O. Hansen, P. Meulengracht Sørensen, and Y. S. Bonnetain (eds.), *International Scandinavian and Medieval Studies in Memory of Gerd Wolfgang Weber: Ein runder Knäuel, so rollt' es uns leicht aus den Händen*, Hesperides: Letterature e Culture Occidentali 12 (Trieste, 2000), 281–92, esp. 284. See also Schier's 'Die Húsdrápa von Úlfr Uggason und die bildliche Überlieferung altnordischer Mythen', in Guðni Kolbeinsson *et al.* (eds.), *Minnjar og Menntir. Afmælisrit helgað Kristjáni Eldjárn, 6 desember 1976* (Reykjavík, 1976), 425–43. Edith Marold treats *rein* ('land') as the object of *bregðr*, thus separate from *vári* ('defender', hap. leg.), which she links with '*rǫgna*' ('of the gods'). Marold attributes the note on the necklace in this story to Snorri alone.

[11] J. McKinnell, 'Eddic Poetry in Anglo-Scandinavian Northern England', in Graham-Campbell, Hall, Jesch, and Parsons (eds.), *Vikings and the Danelaw*, 327–44, at 334–8.

of the Vanir, the leading Norse goddess of love, and a witch with the power to revive the dead.[12] Freyja's acquisition of this necklace and its theft by Loki are the central incidents in *Sǫrlapáttr*, a short story copied into in *Flateyjarbók* in *c.*1390. Another element in this composite tale, one which seems to have been mixed in later, is Óðinn. This is namely the war-god who orders Loki to steal the necklace. Óðinn returns the *Brísingamen* to Freyja on condition that she stir up an endless battle between kings Heðinn and Hǫgni, whose fighters she must bring back to life again each night. In *Sǫrlapáttr* this battle is called the *Hjaðningavíg* ('battle of the Hjaðningar'); the same story was a subject of part of Bragi's *Ragnarsdrápa* in the ninth century.[13] It is clear that this tale is developed from an aetiology for Valhǫll, half of whose slain warriors Óðinn allows Freyja to choose in *Grím* 14.[14] For Óðinn, in this way, the *Brísingamen* is crucial in enabling him to populate a section of hell.

In this way, a comparison with some varied Norse material throws more light on Hama's choices in *Beowulf*: he flees Eormanric, a Gothic emperor of ill repute (cf. *Deor* 22–6); he becomes a Christian, for on earth the 'bright city' suggests Rome; above all, the contrast with Hama's choice of *ecne ræd* ('eternal reward') suggests that he gives away the *Brosinga mene*. The beauty of this necklace in *Beowulf* is clearly expressed, but also its paganism, in that the poet contrasts it also with *þære byrhtan byrig* on line 1199. If the *Brosinga mene* is anything like the *Brísingamen*, it casts the dismal gleam of necromancy and Óðinn's heathen eternity. It seems likely, therefore, that the poet of *Beowulf* has joined the *Brosinga mene* to Hama's story in order to link the pursuit of treasure with damnation.

This theme becomes clearer in the poet's treatment of Hygelac and Beowulf. Straight after Hama, the poet dwells four times on Hygelac's ruin, first within a passage in which *hyne wyrd fornam syþðan he for wlenco wean ahsode fæhðe to Frysum* ('fate seized him when through pride he asked for woe, a feud with Frisia', lines 1205–7). The comparison with Hama's necklace points to a quality of avarice in the glamorous Hygelac. The poet does not, as Orchard has suggested, draw a contrast between Hama's bravery and Hygelac's rashness, but one between their choices.[15] In some way Hama willingly appears to lose the Gothic necklace in exchange for God's eternity; whereas, as we have seen (ch. 5), Hygelac keeps his necklace and seeks more treasure until he dies for it under his shield.[16] A moral contrast between exaltation and ruin is made clear by a juxtaposition of two half-lines, *geceas ecne ræd* and *wean ahsode*, which turns Hygelac into an exemplum.

[12] For the second form, see *Haustlǫng*, ed. North, 6–7 (st. 9) and 40–1 (note to 9/6–7). *Þrymskviða* 13, 15, 19. *Gylf*, p. 29 (ch. 35); *Skáldskaparmál*, ed. Faulkes, i. 19, 20, 30, 32 (v. 100 = *Haustlǫng* 9).

[13] *Skáldskaparmál*, ed. Faulkes, i. 72–3 (text) and 160 (note).

[14] *Flat*, i. 275–6 (*Sǫrlapáttr*).

[15] Orchard, *Companion*, 115.

[16] On the transfer of this necklace from Hygd to Hygelac, see Lapidge, '*Beowulf* and Perception', 71 n. 29.

Herebeald and Hæthcyn: Baldr and Hǫðr

In his last long speech, Beowulf outlines his career before ending it by fighting the dragon. As we have seen in Chapter 2, this speech appears to adapt a version of the *Bjarkamál*, in which the Beowulf-figure recounts his birth, youth, and exploits before describing the present battle he is in. Almost immediately in this speech the poet interpolates the tale of Herebeald and Hæthcyn from another, mythological, source. In recent times more scholars have noted the resemblance between this pair, sons of Hrethel, and the two Norse Æsir Baldr and Hǫðr: Hæthcyn accidentally kills Herebeald, just as Hǫðr kills Baldr; the Anglo-Saxon names euhemerize the Norse ones, housing them alliteratively with the Geatish dynasty. Hrethel's lament for Herebeald refers to an elegiac genre in common with Egill's poem for his lost son Bǫðvarr, the Icelandic *Sonatorrek* (*c*.960); the Christlike passivity of Hrethel in dying, rather than avenging his son on the other brother, repudiates the violence of Óðinn's response (the fathering of Váli to avenge Baldr on Hǫðr).[17] Looking further, we see that the *gomel ceorl* ('old churl') formally recalls Óðinn in his role as a *karl* ('old man'), Baldr's grieving father, in the poem which Snorri used as his source.[18] Snorri supplies a stanza from this source as a last word to his story of Baldr's death in *Gylfaginning*:[19]

> Þǫkk mun gráta   þurrum tárum
>   Baldrs bálfarar.
> Kyks né dauðs   nautka ek karls sonar:
>   haldi Hel því er hefir.

[Þǫkk ('grace') will weep with dry tears for Baldr's funeral pyre. I have got no profit from the old man's son whether he was living or dead: let Hel keep what she has!]

Elsewhere in *Gylfaginning*, Snorri quotes the last stanza of *Skírnismál* as an epilogue to his tale of Freyr and Gerðr.[20] On analogy, it seems likely that the above stanza spoken by Þǫkk, from an otherwise unknown poem on Baldr, concluded its own poem also. If this is true, the story of Hermóðr's negotiation for Baldr's release probably made up the substance of this poem. Snorri says that Þǫkk is Loki in disguise; there is no reason to disagree with him. Snorri's understanding seems confirmed by a pun on Þǫkk's name in *Vǫluspá* (*c*.1000), after Baldr's death when one sibyl says the other has seen a *hapt* ('captive') laid out in punishment beneath *Hveralundr* ('Cauldrons' Grove'), which is *lægiarns líki Loka ápekkian* ('in the shape of malignant Loki, unmistakable', *Vsp* 34).[21] Loki's identification with this old lady appears to be old: Karl Hauck claims to have

---

[17] North, 'The Pagan Inheritance of Egill's *Sonatorrek*', 162–7; *Pagan Words* 56–62.
[18] North, *Heathen Gods*, 198–202. The resemblance is noted separately by Paul Bibire, pers. comm. to Andy Orchard, in *Companion*, 118 n. 103.
[19] *Gylf,* 48 (ch. 49).
[20] Ibid. 31 (ch. 37).
[21] *Poetic Edda II*, ed. Dronke, 16 (text), 55 (comm.), and 140 (note).

identified Loki as the same giantess on some fourth-century bracteates from northern Germany.[22] It looks as if Loki gained his special role as Hǫðr's instigator in the late days of Norse heathendom, possibly even at the hands of Snorri himself.[23] The absence of a Loki-figure in Saxo's tale of Balderus and Hotherus, and in the Icelandic source which underlay part of Saxo's tale, seems to point this way. Since there is no Loki-figure in Herebeald's story in *Beowulf*, in which Hæthcyn is solely to blame, we may assume the poet got his myth from a Danish source which was older than the Norwegian Baldr-tradition whose last days we see recorded in late tenth-century Icelandic poetry.[24] It seems that this now-lost source, like Snorri's Baldr-stanza, contained the *karl*-name for Óðinn, one which the English poet transposed into *ceorl*.

Why Beowulf should focus on Hrethel in this way is not understood. The story of Herebeald comes into view after Beowulf's notice that his grandfather adopted him when he was 7 (Ecgtheow being busy elsewhere). As noted earlier, it seems likely that Beowulf's speech is adapted from the earliest version of the theme of *Bjarkamál*, presumably handed on from Denmark. It is interesting, then, to find what appears to be some living Danish mythology interpolated (and euhemerized) into the beginning of this likely adaptation. As I have tried to show, King Hrethel's family is probably the poet's fiction: apart from Herebeald and Hæthcyn, 'Hrethel' seems invented in that his name is constructed out of a synonym for 'Goth'; and the unnamed sister, Beowulf's mother, is doubtless made up too. Only Hygelac's Geatishness finds corroboration in another text (the *Liber monstrorum*). The quantity of innovation in this part of *Beowulf* allows the poet to split Baldr's story from that of Óðinn, his mythological father, as if to insinuate that the Baldr-legend was a heathen perversion of the history of King Hrethel. Primarily, however, the poet uses this myth to formulate a new background for Beowulf within his last public address, in which the spotlight falls on his grandfather's moral choices.

Why does Beowulf reminisce at such length at the start of a speech to his men? Why, too, does the fitt end somewhere in the midst of his grandfather's tale, halfway through a simile which appears to allude to a Danish error? Orchard believes that 'Beowulf is here pondering the impotent grief and frustrated desire

---

[22] K. Hauck, *Goldbrakteaten aus Sievern: Spätantike Amulett-Bilder der 'Dania Saxonica' und die Sachsen-'Origo' bei Widukind von Corvey*, Münstersche Schriften 1 (Munich, 1970), 184–8. It is thought that the isle *Fositesland*, in Alcuin's *Vitae s. Willibrordi*, is evidence of 'Forseti', Baldr's son by Nanna. See A. Orchard, *The Cassell Dictionary of Norse Myth and Legend* (London, 1997), 46 ('Forseti'). A connection with Baldr would still need to be shown.

[23] For Snorri as the innovator in Loki's role, see E. Mogk, *Lokis Anteil an Baldrs Tode*, Suomalainen Tiedeakatemia. Academia Scientiarum Fennica 58 (Helsinki, 1925), 4–8; and J. de Vries, *The Problem of Loki*, Suomalainen Tiedeakatemia. Academia Scientiarum Fennica 110 (Helsinki, 1933), 168; and Y. Bonnetain, 'Lokis Rolle im altnordischen Mythos', unpublished MA dissertation, Frankfurt a.M., 1996, 59–64, at 61–2.

[24] North, *Heathen Gods*, 201.

for requital of two old men in a manner which surely suggests something of his own anguish in the case of the dragon.'[25] This reading gives a reason for the length of the Hrethel-passage and shows that it is not a digression. If Beowulf compares his choices with those of Hrethel and 'the old churl', otherwise known as Óðinn, it is to acknowledge that he still has the option of violent revenge. He thus makes it clear to his men that he can still kill the dragon in order to avenge the loss of his hall and the burning of Geatland.

The inclusion of the 'old churl' shows the need to avenge a son. It is true that Beowulf has not had a son (lines 2729–32). Yet the Baldr-motif serves Hrethel, not Beowulf. It is to Hrethel's soul's benefit that he refrains from the Odinic option of revenge, dying like a martyr instead. Unwittingly his grandfather's conduct equips Beowulf with an exemplum. When Beowulf says that Hrethel *godes leoht geceas* ('chose God's light', line 2469), he seems to assume that the old man died into heaven. But neither he nor Hrethel knows of heaven as Christians understand it, nor how to get there. Thus the dying Hrethel follows a Christian example without knowing Christ; Beowulf is also ignorant of the faith, even if the poet has made it clear, through the self-doubt in lines 2329–32, that he can question his own conduct. When Beowulf speaks of Hrethel, his words reveal how a heathen soul might achieve grace. A Christian audience can see that choice between heaven and hell of which both heathens know nothing; but morally, the poet's patrons are bystanders and cannot interfere. As the heathens are blind to the Christian choice, it is perhaps out of pity for them that the poet (if it is he) breaks off seemingly in the midst of his 'old churl' simile, even before the story of Hrethel's bereavement is reintroduced on line 2462, two lines into the next fitt (XXXV).

The closing image of Fitt XXXIV is of death: namely of the *ridend* ('riders') who *swefað hæleð in hoðman* ('sleep, as heroes, in the darkness', lines 2457–8), leaving the world devoid of the music that once was. Not only does this image capture the story of Baldr and other dead, closely followed by Hermóðr, riding through *døkkva dala ok djúpa* ('dark and deep valleys') towards Hel in *Gylfaginning* (and probably, given the alliteration, in Snorri's source-poem), but the English poet achieves a greater moral aim. By ending the fitt here (if he does), he leaves his audience with the thought of the destination of all subterranean horsemen who had lived without Christ.[26] In a manner of which he is unaware, Beowulf's public boast gives way to his reminiscence of Hrethel; this to an Odinic simile; and this, in turn, to Beowulf's unwitting exposure of his heathen limits. To risk a fire beside which the dragon's is hot air, Beowulf must be as

---

[25] *Companion*, 118.

[26] On some sixth-century pagan man-and-horse burials, see D. Wilson, *Anglo-Saxon Paganism* (London, 1992), 101–2 (Wanlip, Leics.; Marston St Lawrence, Northants.; Warren Hill, Suffolk; Sporle, Norfolk; Heslerton, Yorks.) and 151–3 (Lackford, Suffolk; Caistor-by-Norwich and Spong Hill, Norfolk). See North, *Heathen Gods*, 201–2 and 295–6.

attentive to right and wrong as a Christian. The poet gives him the facility for this, but not the knowledge.[27]

Beowulf and the dragon: Þórr and the World Serpent

In the last chapter, we have seen that Beowulf's dragon-fight is probably constructed along the lines of motifs from saints' lives, with a special similarity to the passage on St Michael in the *Homiliary of Saint-Père*, which could have been written as early as 822.[28] Where the final battle is concerned, however, we must consider a vernacular Danish source.[29] Beowulf's death in the dragon-fight constitutes a type-scene not found in any of the Latin saint's life analogues. As we have seen in Chapter 2, the poet appears to have changed the ending of Beowulf's life from the last stand in Hrothulf's hall by which it is likely he was known in earlier sources. Sigemund's dragon-slaying is planted as a legend in *Beowulf* more than a thousand lines earlier, apparently so as to introduce the glory of this exploit to Beowulf as a young man (lines 875–900). But neither Sigemund's tale nor the Scylding legend nor the *Homiliary* provides a motif for Beowulf's death in a fight with the dragon. For this detail the only analogue that fits comes from Old Norse myth of Ragnarǫk, which culminates with Þórr's death in combat against the Miðgarðsormr, the World Serpent, in the last battle at the end of the world. This myth, albeit one that reaches us through the Christianized *Vǫluspá* (*c*.1000), would appear to be the source of the *Beowulf*-poet's third major borrowing from a Danish source.

The heroic power of this myth is one reason the poet would need to have for using it for Beowulf's end. After Þórr's death the world sinks into chaos and the prospect for Geatland is presented (perhaps only temporarily) as similarly bleak in *Beo* 3018–30 and 3153–5.[30] Andy Orchard adds hints of more parallels to Ursula Dronke's original observations of the correspondences between Beowulf's last fight and Þórr's.[31] Both Beowulf and Þórr are associated with giant-slaying in their earlier lives. Beowulf bound five giants and *yðde eotena cyn* ('wiped out the giant tribe', line 421) as a younger man (lines 419–24); and waiting for Grendel, Beowulf *eotenweard' abead* ('he kept watch for the giant', line 668). Þórr fights giants in the east in numerous poems (for example: *Haustlǫng* 14–20, *þórsdrápa*, *Hárbarðsljóð*, *Þrymskviða*) and Snorri fairly sums him up as *dólgr ok bani jǫtna ok trǫllkvinna* ('foe and slayer of giants and troll-women').[32] It is impossible to know how much the poet of *Beowulf* supplements his hero's folktale exploits (if Grendel was one, for instance), with mythological killings which are the preserve of Þórr.

[27] Stanley, 'Hæthenra Hyht in *Beowulf*', 141.
[28] Rauer, *Beowulf and the Dragon*, 116–24, esp. 120–1.
[29] Orchard, *Companion*, 151.
[30] Niles (*Beowulf*, 193) will not treat the parallel with Ragnarǫk as valid unless it is exact.
[31] *Companion*, 119–23. Dronke, '*Beowulf* and Ragnarǫk'.
[32] *Skáldskaparmál*, ed. Faulkes, i. 15 (ch. 4).

Yet some Norse supplement there must be. A striking resemblance has already been noted between the *glof... sid ond syllic* ('wide and wonderful glove' or 'pouch', lines 2085–6) which, as Beowulf says, hangs from Grendel's belt, and the giant Skrýmir's *hanzki* ('glove') in which Þórr and his companions spend an awkward night on their way to Útgarða-Loki in *Gylfaginning*, also in the probably tenth-century *Hárbarðsljóð* (st. 26) and probably eleventh-century *Lokasenna* (st. 60).[33] The naming of Hondscio as Grendel's victim in this case, which Orchard attributes to 'the *Beowulf*-poet's tendency to etymologise names', appears rather to be an ironic splicing of two sources: Vǫttr, one of Hrólfr's bodyguard, from an ancient version of the *Bjarkamál* (see my Chapter 2), with the giant's glove in a widespread myth of Þórr.[34] The obtrusion of this parallel so early in *Beowulf* suggests that the poet was willing to style Beowulf on Þórr from the outset.

The end of Beowulf's life is like Þórr's, not only in the general situation, both males duelling with serpents, but also in the wider context. As has been shown in the last chapter, both Beowulf's sectioning of the dragon and his people's disposal of the remains seem based on St Michael's dragon-fight in a saint's life. Yet this motive also resembles Þórr's giant-killing role as *Miðgarðs véurr* ('?sanctuary-guardian of Middle Earth') when he faces the World Serpent in *Vsp* 53 (cf. *Hym* 11 and 17).[35] As we have also seen, the death of each figure brings with it the downfall of his people, Beowulf's Geats (as promised in *Beo* 3010–27) in one case, and *halir allir* ('all heroes') in the other (*Vsp* 53/7–8: see below).

Dronke lists some objections to seeing Beowulf stylized in this way. The strongest of these seems to be the lack of certainty that Þórr does kill his Serpent.[36] If we look at the Norse parallels in closer detail, we see some similarities between *Beowulf* and the language with which Bragi describes Þórr's fight with the World Serpent, apparently in *Ragnarsdrápa* (*c*.850; cf. Chapter 1). Although these common traits do not extend to skaldic diction, which seems alien to *Beowulf*, it is possible to surmise a literary borrowing from Norse to Anglo-Saxon in the type of Eddic poetry on which the skalds based their more difficult work. As I have attempted to show, Bragi's stanzas resemble the description of Beowulf's dragon (lines 2559–65) in the common type-scene. The word *hringboga*, which describes the dragon as 'coiled bow', corresponds with the coiled ring (*hringr*) in the basis for Bragi's kenning *borðróins barða brautar hringr inn ljóti* ('the ugly encircling ring of the road of the gunwale-rowed beaked prow [: ring of the boat's road: World Serpent]').[37] Each poet dwells on the serpent's mental state, with the

---

[33] *Beowulf*, ed. Klaeber, 205. E. D. Laborde, 'Grendel's Glove and his Immunity from Weapons', *MLR* 18 (1923), 202–4. S. Lerer, 'Grendel's Glove', *Journal of English Literary History*, 61 (1994), 721–51.

[34] Orchard, *Companion*, 122.

[35] On this epithet, see *Poetic Edda II*, ed. Dronke, 150 (note to 53/6).

[36] Dronke, '*Beowulf* and Ragnarǫk', 314–18, at 314 (no. 2).

[37] *Skáldskaparmál*, ed. Faulkes, i. 16 (vs. 51). The tenth-century skald Eysteinn Valdason uses a similar kenning in his poem on Þórr's fishing trip: *brattrar brautar baugr* ('necklace of the steep path [: land-encircler: World Serpent]'. See ibid. i. 15 (v. 45).

dragon's *heorte gefysed* ('heart' being 'made keen', *Beo* 2561) by Beowulf and the World Serpent *harðgeðr* ('with harsh spirit') as it stares at Þórr; and both poets focus on the hero's seizing of his weapon. Here are three likenesses which come close enough to make the two passages analogues. In this way it seems that a Danish poem or story on Þórr's exploits has influenced the poet of *Beowulf.*

From another *dróttkvætt* source, a half-stanza from Úlfr's *Húsdrápa* (*c*.995), there is another version of Hymir's fishing trip in which Þórr does slay the World Serpent:[38]

> Víðgymnir laust Vimrar   vaðs af fránum naðri
> hlusta grunn við hrǫnnum.   Hlaut innan svá minnum. (v. 56)

[The Wide-Wader of the ford of Vimur struck off into the waves the earhole's pediment from the glittering adder of the fishing line. He [Óláfr Hǫskuldsson] got it [the house] from Norway with images like this.][39]

Here Úlfr characterizes Þórr with the name 'Víðgymnir' as a giant, his enemy, rather as the poet of *Beowulf* calls both the dragon and Beowulf *aglæcan* ('monsters') before they clash for the second time on line 2592. These Icelandic verses purport to describe some mythological carvings in Hjarðarholt, western Iceland. In this context Þórr's fishing trip ends with his destruction of the World Serpent.

The duel between Þórr and the World Serpent is also the subject of a stanza in *Vǫluspá* (*c*.1000). At the battle of the end of time, Freyr fights Surtr, then Óðinn the wolf Fenrir, who swallows him whole; his son Víðarr avenges him. Finally the scene is set for Þórr:

> Þá kømr inn mæri   mǫgr Hlǫðyniar,
> gengr Óðins sonr   við *orm* vega.
> Drepr hann af móði   miðgarz véor[r]
> —muno halir allir   heimstǫð ryðia—
> gengr fet nío   Fiǫrgyniar burr
> neppr frá naðri   níðs ókvíðnom. (*Vsp* 53)

[Then comes the glorious child of Hlǫðyn, Óðinn's son strides to fight the serpent. He smites in fury, shrine-guarder of Miðgarðr – all heroes will abandon the homestead of earth – he steps nine paces, Fjǫrgyn's child, failing—leaving slain the snake that had not feared its vile act.][40]

In this stanza Þórr strikes the beast, steps back one pace for each of the nine worlds of the dead, and dies. It also appears that he steps back from the slain body of the Serpent, if we take the phrase *ganga frá* (of the Codex Regius text) as a

---

[38] *Skáldskaparmál*, ed. Faulkes, i. 17 and 165–6 (note).

[39] R. North 'Image and Ascendancy in Úlfr's *Húsdrápa*', in A. Minnis and J. Roberts (eds.), *Word, Text, Image: Studies in Anglo-Saxon Literature and Insular Culture in Honour of Éamonn Ó Carragáin* (Turnhout, 2006).

[40] Best text and translation from *Poetic Edda II*, ed. Dronke, 22. On the textual difficulties here, see ibid. 72–3 (Problem III (i) (c)), 82 (Problem V (i) (c)), and 150–1.

unique variant of *ganga af* ('to retire from a slain opponent').[41] As Orchard notes, this motif resembles Beowulf's retreat from the dying dragon to die on a seat against the wall of the barrow.[42] For the motif of Beowulf's death, therefore, it is reasonable to suppose that the poet of *Beowulf* made use of a Danish poem or story about Þórr; but one which had been Christianized, on partial analogy with St Michael, so as to postpone the Serpent's death to the end of the world.

Summary

Elsewhere I have argued that the poet of *Beowulf* describes both Hrothgar's royal status and the Frisian–Danish peace treaty in Finnsburh with reference to an ancient cult of Ingui; and that in the unique word *ealuscerwen* (*Beo* 769), in particular, he personifies the agency of *wyrd* ('fate'), in order to mark the upturn in Danish fortunes (lines 765–9).[43] The present enquiry adds to a growing consensus that the poet of *Beowulf* adapts tales connected with those of Norse mythology: Freyja's *Brísingamen*; Hǫðr's slaying of Baldr and Óðinn's vengeance; and Þórr's battle against the World Serpent.[44] Potentially these myths are among the poet's most controversial sources, for it is not easy to see how a Christian could have known of them in England. Not from native paganism, gone by the eighth century. Nor did the Anglo-Saxons, before their conversion in the seventh, have time to personify 'thunder' into any slow-witted version of Þórr such as may be imagined with the aid of *Gylfaginning* whenever the name 'Thunor' is produced. Nor could the poet have gleaned his mythology from the Frisians, Christians from the early eighth century on. There is little doubt that the Baldr-name is peculiar to Scandinavian paganism.[45] For purveyors of this and other heathen ideology, we are left with Danes before the Viking Age. That is so if we put the poem's *terminus ad quem* in or around 839 in line with my case for King Wiglaf's patronage of *Beowulf*.

'SOHTE SEARONIÐAS': THE MORAL OF BEOWULF'S DEATH

Are the heathens in *Beowulf* damned? That is not for us to know, as the poet makes clear at the end of the 'Prologue' in lines 50–2. Nonetheless, if he draws

---

[41] Ibid. 82 and 150 (note to 53/11).

[42] *Companion*, 119–20.

[43] North, *Heathen Gods*, 64–77 and 172–81; ' "Wyrd" and "weard ealuscerwen" ', 74–80.

[44] Dronke, '*Beowulf* and Ragnarǫk', 311–18. D. G. Calder, 'Setting and Ethos: The Pattern of Measure and Limit in *Beowulf*', *SP* 69 (1972), 21–37, esp. 36. Frank, 'Skaldic Verse and the Date of *Beowulf*', 132 (Baldr and Óðinn). *Beowulf: A Student Edition*, ed. Jack, 101 (*Brísingamen*). *Beowulf*, ed. Mitchell and Robinson, 134 (Baldr and Óðinn). Orchard, *Companion*, 114–23 (all three motifs). Rauer, *Beowulf and the Dragon*, 136–7 (Þórr and the World Serpent). Niles (*Beowulf*, 193) is against, albeit he believes *Beowulf* was composed partly for Anglicized tenth-century Danes.

[45] North, *Heathen Gods*, 124–31, 143–53 (Baldr); 204–13, 232–41 (OE *þunor*).

any Christian moral from their religion in *Beowulf*, this can be seen in the hero's death in the dragon's fire.

The worst aspect of this calamity is implicit in the poet's uses of the Old English cognate of a Danish form of OIce *nið* ('vile act'). In Icelandic the word *nið* is associated with sacrilege, when the poet of *Vǫluspá* (st. 53) hints that the World Serpent rejoices in killing Þórr, for it implies not only an act of hatred (comparable with OE *nið*), or sacrilege, but also the spewing of poison on Þórr that slowly kills him. Snorri makes this manner of dying clear in his précis of Þórr's end: *þá fellr hann dauðr til jarðar fyrir eitri því, er ormrinn blæss á hann* ('then he falls dead to the earth because of the poison which the serpent blows on him').[46] Úlfr himself alludes to the Serpent's *eitr* ('poison') in a stanza of *Húsdrápa*, although in this version Þórr survives:

> En stirðþinull starði   storðar leggs fyrir borði
> fróns á fólka reyni   fránleitr ok blés eitri (v. 316, also in v. 210)[47]

[But the taut rope of the wood-realm's leg, glittering-featured, stared from across the gunwale at earth-folk's adversary and blew poison.]

As Dronke says, 'poison and enmity are ancient associates'.[48] This is true of *Andreas*, where the *brandhata nið* ('brand-hot malice', line 768) of Jesus' doubters is rapidly described also as *weorm blædum fag, attor ælfæle* ('a serpent bright with blasts, all-destructive poison', lines 769–70).[49] *Vǫluspá*, in which Þórr dies from the Serpent's poison, was composed most probably more than a century after *Beowulf* and *Andreas*. However, as the poet of *Vǫluspá* makes use of older heathen poems, it is probably fair to say that the Christianized Norse myths before his time blamed Þórr's death on the *nið* of the World Serpent.

In *Beowulf* the OE word *nið* describes Beowulf's own mortal wound from the dragon. The poet first describes this monster as *niðdraca* ('a dragon of enmity', line 2273), before he introduces its role as hoard-miser, then as *niðgæst* ('demon of enmity', line 2699), just as Wiglaf helps Beowulf to kill it. With the monster dying or dead, Beowulf retreats to die against the wall of the barrow. He can understand the physical cause of his death:

> Ða sio wund ongon,
> þe him eorðdraca   ær geworhte,
> swelan ond swellan;   he þæt sona onfand
> þæt him on breostum   bealoniðe weoll
> attor on innan. (*Beo* 2711–15)

[Then the wound which the earth-dragon had just made upon him began to burn and swell; straightaway he realized that in his breast a poison was welling up with grievous enmity from within.]

---

[46] *Gylf*, 50 (ch. 51).
[47] *Skáldskaparmál*, ed. Faulkes, i. 65 (v. 210).
[48] *Poetic Edda II*, ed. Dronke, 151 (note to 53/12).
[49] *Andreas and The Fates of the Apostles*, ed. K. R. Brooks (Oxford, 1961), 25 and 88–9 (note).

It appears from Lapidge's study on perception in *Beowulf* that this passage contains the last of twelve uses of the verb *onfindan* in the poem, and that *onfindan* denotes cognition, a process of mental perception or intellection.[50] So Beowulf understands that his body is poisoned, though not that the *bealoniđ* now working inside him may kill his soul as well.

This word *bealoniđ* recalls Hrothgar's words fifty years before. In the long speech often known as his 'sermon' (lines 1700–84), Hrothgar recounts the doomed King Heremod's avarice and presents this as the conduct to avoid, creates another exemplum of a king corrupted by gold and finally urges Beowulf to look for higher rewards:

> 'Bebeorh þe þone bealoniđ,   Beowulf leofa,
> secg betsta,   ond þe þæt selre geceos,
> ece rædas,   oferhyda ne gym,
> mære cempa.   Nu is þines mægnes blæd
> ane hwile.' (*Beo* 1758–62)

['Protect yourself from that grievous enmity, my dear Beowulf, best of men, and choose for yourself the better course, eternal rewards; have no regard for prideful thoughts, renowned champion. The fame of your power is only for a little while now.']

This theme of these lines, the learning of wisdom through transience, is central to Hrothgar's speech in that his phrase *þines mægnes blæd* can be related to his opening words, *blæd is aræred . . . đin* ('fame is raised up, your fame', lines 1703–4) and *mægen mid modes snyttrum* ('power with wisdom of mind', line 1706). More widely within the poem his lines on *bealoniđ* also look back to Hama and forward to Beowulf's conduct before his fight with the dragon at the end of this poem. Hrothgar urges Beowulf to choose wisdom over avarice, saying *bebeorh bealoniđ* and *geceos . . . ece rædas*; Hama chooses the latter reward when he rejects *searoniđas* ('cunning enmities') in fleeing to the bright city (earlier in lines 1200–1). The poet thus makes Hrothgar, without knowing it, commend Hama's moral decision to Beowulf as a caveat to the great necklace which he received from Wealhtheow the day before. Beowulf's own moment of choice will lie in wait for him in the future. The poet draws attention to the coming of this moment relentlessly with four references to Hygelac's last raid. In his own lifetime Beowulf's ruined uncle is the model to avoid. Has the hero understood Hrothgar about the eternal rewards? Will he learn from Hygelac's example in time?

Perhaps not, if we study the poet's intimations of pride. Fifty years on, with his country alight and his hall in ruins, Beowulf prepares to fight the dragon alone. The poet says that this decision is due to pride: *oferhogode đa hringa fengel* ('then did the chieftain of rings become too proud', line 2345) to attack the dragon with an army. In *Beowulf* the verb *oferhycgan* occurs only here and is probably, as John

---

[50] Lapidge, '*Beowulf* and Perception', 84–93, at 92. The examples of *onfindan* are: *Beo* 595, 750, 809, 1293, 1497, 1522, 1890, [2219], [2226], 2288, 2841; 2300.

Leyerle pointed out, intended to remind us of the *oferhydas* ('prideful thoughts', line 1760) about which Hrothgar warned the hero in his youth.[51] Greenfield detaches Hrothgar's warning of *oferhydas* from Beowulf's later *oferhogode*, on the grounds that the former concerns greed, the latter tactical folly.[52] Niles clears Beowulf from *oferhygd* by comparing his deeds favourably with the failures linked with this term in *Vainglory*.[53] But it is Hrothgar talking, not the poet of *Vainglory*; and he is urging Beowulf to put *ece rædas* ('eternal rewards', line 1760) above such thoughts of pride as develop when success and physical confidence, as he illustrates (lines 1728–52), lead to complacency, which leads to greed. Later, when Beowulf stands down even his small troop on the grounds that he is stronger than they are, he tells them that it is he alone who will *gold gegangan* ('get the gold', line 2536).

With Hama, Hygelac, and Hrothgar, therefore, Beowulf's choice between heavenly and earthly reward is signalled early in the poem. Fifty years after Hrothgar warned him against *bealonið*, we see Beowulf setting off to face the dragon's version of this enmity after handling its all too glittering cause:

> hæfde þa gefrunen   hwanan sio fæhð aras
> bealonið biorna: him to bearme cwom
> maðþumfæt mære   þurh ðæs meldan hond. (*Beo* 2403–5)

[he had found out from what that feud, the grievous enmity of men, had arisen: towards his bosom came the renowned treasure cup from the hand of the informer himself.]

The informer, whom the poet counts as the thirteenth member of Beowulf's war-party (lines 2406–9), recalls Judas with Christ and eleven good disciples.[54] The word *bealonið* above is equated not only with the feud, but also with the *maðþumfæt mære* which comes close to Beowulf's bosom, as if rehearsing the flow of poison that will enter it later. This treasure might also remind us of the *sincfæt* which is part of Hama's *Brosinga mene* (line 1200).

In this deliberate way the poet uses the *Brosinga mene*, apparently importing it from the mythology of heathen Danes, to anticipate Beowulf's moral choice at the end of his life. Hama *searoniðas fleah* ('fled the cunning enmities', line 1200); not long before he dies, Beowulf says that *ne sohte searoniðas* ('I did not seek cunning enmities', line 2738); but the poet contradicts him, saying that Beowulf *sohte searoniðas* ('sought cunning enmities', line 3067).[55] Not only the poet's omniscient narration but also his Christianity gives this version the stamp of truth. Beowulf, living in an undirected age, is in no position to know of all the spiritual man-traps lying in wait; in due course the poet makes clear that the one

[51] J. Leyerle, 'Beowulf the Hero and the King', *Medium Ævum*, 34 (1965), 89–102, esp. 95.
[52] 'Beowulf and the Judgement of the Righteous', 400–1. Winning the gold cannot be as incidental to Beowulf's purpose as imagined in Niles, *Beowulf*, 244.
[53] Niles, *Beowulf*, 243.
[54] Orchard, *Companion*, 148.
[55] Greenfield, 'Beowulf and the Judgement of the Righteous', 406.

facing him is the dragon's hoard. King Beowulf, before facing the dragon, orders his men to wait while he goes in alone to get the gold (lines 2517–37, at 2536). Later, before dying, Beowulf says that he wishes to give it all to his people (lines 2797–8); he appears to instruct Wiglaf and other Geats to do this instead of him (lines 2800–1). But the poet does not say that selfless generosity was his earlier motive. Instead, with his words on *searoniðas* in the reflection on Beowulf's death in line 3066–8, the poet casts doubt on his eligibility for eternal rewards. By saying that Hama chose these rewards over the *Brosinga mene*, he implies that Hygelac lost his reward in Frisia in search of more booty such as Hygd's extraordinary necklace. As we saw, the *maðþumfæt* ('treasure cup', line 2405), which is later passed to Beowulf, may pose the same risk as the *sincfæt* which Hama rejected in favour of *ecne ræd* (lines 1200–1). So which type of wealth will King Beowulf choose? By initiating this question as early as lines 1197–201, the poet prepares us for the possibility of his hero's damnation.[56]

Having created this uncertainty over Beowulf's fate in the hereafter, the poet elaborates on his hero's ignorance. There is then a vexed passage after the reflection on *wundur* ('wonder', line 3062), the mystery that has led Beowulf to this death:

> Swa hit oð domes dæg   diope benemdon
> þeodnas mære,   þa ðæt þær dydon,
> þæt se secg wære   synnum scildig
> hergum geheaðerod   hellbendum fæst
> wommum gewitnad   se ðone wong strude;
> næs he goldhwæte   gearwor hæfde
> agendes est   ær gesceawod. (*Beo* 3069–75)

[So the renowned princes who put it there solemnly declared that until the Day of Judgement the man who plundered that place would be guilty of crimes, closed up in heathen shrines, firmly bound in the bonds of hell, punished with defilements; never before this time had he been more ready to see an owner's gold-bestowing favour.]

The first five lines here specifically tell us of a heathen curse which aims to send the robber of this hoard to hell. By virtue of his rank, Beowulf is the man who has robbed it. Jack Niles is surely right to stress reciprocity as a key element in the poet's understanding of gold in this poem, but he hardly gives this curse its due.[57] One does not have to share Boniface's views on treasure, or attribute these to the poet of *Beowulf*, to note the risk of this hoard to Beowulf's soul.

This risk is qualified by the last two lines of the passage above, even though these contain three major textual problems. One is MS *næs he*, which gives its line such sense as 'not all all, before then, had he more readily seen'. Another is the meaning of *agend*, which might denote God, or an 'owner' of the hoard rather

---

[56] On these lines, see Stanley, 'Hæthenra Hyht in *Beowulf*', 146–51.
[57] Niles, *Beowulf*, 220–3.

than God, either the dragon or one of the princes who stowed the treasure. A third difficulty, the meaning of the unique adjective *goldhwæt*, was resolved by G. V. Smithers, who translates this word as 'gold-bestowing'.[58] Eric Stanley, whose first reading I follow, reads *næs he* here but also acknowledges the divine sense of *agend*, in this case translating 'By no means had he previously seen more clearly the gold-bestowing favour of the Lord'.[59] Alan Bliss aims to confirm this reading with parallels for the divine rather than temporal meaning of *agend*.[60] But the 'Lord's gold' makes no sense if it describes gold which is cursed. The calibre of the scholars who support the retention of MS *næs he* is formidable.[61] It is possible, however, to emend MS *næs he* to *næfne he*, like *nefne* ('unless') on line 3054, with the assumption that the second scribe used *æ* for *e* (cf. his *earna næs*, line 3031), read *s* for *f* (cf. MS *fela ða* for *se laða*, line 2305), and lost the letters *he* through eyeskip. Orchard follows Klaeber in emending thus. He shows also that the poet presents a similar clause with *nefne god sylfa . . . sealde* not long before (lines 3054–5) and that he has already used this construction in *nefne him witig god* (line 1056) and *nemne . . . halig god* (lines 1052–3).[62] After all, lines 3074–5, with *næs he*, give Beowulf the full impact of the curse, putting him fully at the mercy of the divine remission indicated on lines 3055–7.

This dark reading of Beowulf's destiny may be confirmed, however, with a cross-reference to his command to Wiglaf to bring him some of the treasure, *þæt ic ærwelan, goldæht ongite, gearo sceawige swegle searogimmas* ('so that I may readily perceive the ancient wealth, the treasure of gold, behold the brilliant, cunning jewels', lines 2747–9). The words *gold-* and *agend* and the phrase *gearwor . . . hæfde gesceawod* at the end of the anathema are probably intended to incriminate Beowulf with his words *goldæht* and *gearo sceawige* in these lines.[63] Moreover, Beowulf contradicts himself here. The focus of his last desire, the dragon's *swegle searogimmas* on line 2749, nearly repeats the *searoniðas* which he said he avoided on line 2738. The limits of Beowulf's understanding are also to be seen in his verbs *ongitan* and *sceawian*, which denote only sensory awareness, not the cognition with which Hama saw an eternal reward.[64] Beowulf's desire to live on in the good opinion of his nation is seen not only in the lines above, but also in the equivocal word *lofgeornost*. The Geats appear to hail the fallen Beowulf with this word in its literal sense ('most eager for praise') here on line 3182, the last line of *Beowulf*. Yet it is disturbing that *lofgeorn* is elsewhere found as a gloss

---

[58] G. V. Smithers, 'Five Notes on Old English Texts', *English and Germanic Studies*, 4 (1951–2), 65–85, at 75–80.

[59] Stanley, 'Hæthenra Hyht in *Beowulf*', 143–6, at 145; *Beowulf*, ed. Mitchell and Robinson, 157.

[60] Bliss, '*Beowulf* Lines 3074–3075', 53–4.

[61] *Beowulf: A Student Edition*, ed. Jack, 204.

[62] Orchard, *Companion*, 153–5.

[63] Cf. Stanley, 'Hæthenra Hyht in *Beowulf*', 145–6.

[64] On *ongitan*, Lapidge, '*Beowulf* and Perception', 90–1. On the limits of Beowulf's *sapientia*, see Greenfield, 'Beowulf and the Judgement of the Righteous', 404.

for Latin *prodigus* ('wasteful').[65] In the light of the poet's three uses of *bealonið* in this poem, a secondary, Christian, meaning such as 'most wasteful' for *lofgeornost* shows how prodigally Beowulf may have spent his hope of the *ece rædas*, one which is held out to him at the heart of the poem.

To sum up, the poet of *Beowulf* supplements his heroic legends of Danes, Heathobards, Geats, and Swedes with three stories: Hama and the *Brosinga mene*; Hrethel and Herebeald; and Beowulf's last combat with the dragon. The Norse analogues of these tales give reason to believe that the poet euhemerized his versions from contemporary Danish mythology. Given the religious currency of this material in its homeland, and the other verbal parallels between the Old English and Norse (*gomel ceorl* and *karl*; *bealonið* and *nið*), it seems most likely that its mediators were pre-Christian Danes, rather than Frisians to whom I have attributed the transmission of Danish history. The poet's aim with this inclusion was probably to draw a moral from the religion of his hero, who dies the victim of a curse to which this religion exposed him. Although the question of Beowulf's salvation is left open, wisely unanswered, there is no mistaking the pathos. The poet's abiding sympathy reveals his interest in heathens: one more indication that he has met some for himself.

789: THE FIRST DANES IN ENGLAND

As we have seen, it has been shown that Mercians and Danes could understand each other's speech in the ninth and tenth centuries.[66] Before the Danes came here, their long-distance trade with England was run by Frisians, between centres in Sussex and East Anglia and marts in Denmark and Sweden.[67] Yet in England some of the artefacts in the Sutton Hoo grave, of *c*.625, point to an Anglian idealization of Scandinavia as a cultural homeland.[68] Bede probably reflects this idea when he cites, in *c*.732, a Northumbrian belief that some of the English could trace their ancestry to Danes (as well as Frisians, Huns, and Boructuari: *HE* V. 9). There can be no doubt that this belief was one reason why the English first attempted to convert Frisians and other heathens in the nearer parts of Germania. Willibrord is said to have tried to convert the Danes (of south-west Jutland) when he bought some slaves from King Ongendus of Denmark in *c*.710.[69]

[65] Two uses, of a butler eager to please: Gretsch, *Intellectual Foundations of the English Benedictine Reform*, 418–19.

[66] Townend, *Language and History*, esp. 43–87.

[67] Näsman, 'Vendel Period Glass from Eketorp II', 75–85; 'Om fjärrhandel i Sydskandinaviens yngre järnålder', 112–13. Hines, 'The Scandinavian Character of Anglian England: An Update', 328 n. 3. See my Ch. 1.

[68] Hines, *The Scandinavian Character of Anglian England*, 13–14; 'The Scandinavian Character of Anglian England: An Update', 327–8.

[69] *Passiones vitaeque sanctorum*, ed. Krusch and Levison, 113–14. *EHD*, 775–7, at 756 (no. 157). Bencard and Jørgensen, 'Excavation and Stratigraphy', 147–8.

In time, however, Scandinavians paid their own visits to the markets of western Europe.[70] From about 789 onwards the sails of their warships began to appear off the English coast. In the reign of King Beorhtric of Wessex (784–800), a group of strangers killed the king's reeve who had come to talk to them in the harbour of Portland, Dorset. This incident is reported in the *Anglo-Saxon Chronicle* for 789; in five versions the murderers are called 'Northmen' (BCDEF), three of them adding that they were from *Hæreðaland* (Hordaland, in Norway, DEF); in all versions of the *Chronicle*, the final sentence in this entry adds that these were the first Viking ships to seek out the land of the English.[71] This additional sentence calls all Scandinavians *Dene*, in line with the general linguistic perception.[72] It also concurs with Alcuin's remark to an English archbishop in *c*.797, probably Æthelheard, that the heathens *antecedentibus non temptaverunt temporibus mare nostrum navigare et maritima patrie nostre devastare* ('in previous times did not try to sail our seas nor devastate the coasts of our homeland').[73] If we take the *Chronicle's* statement to be written with this or with the hindsight of a later source, we can date the Portland incident to before 792, when a charter issued at *Clofesho* grants King Offa's immunities to Kentish minsters with the exception of the building of earthworks against *paganos maritimos* ('heathen seamen').[74] There is Frankish evidence to show that Charlemagne was by then fortifying his coast also.[75] On 8 June 793, according to the *Anglo-Saxon Chronicle* and Alcuin's letters, raiders plundered Lindisfarne in Northumbria.[76] Alcuin proffered his sympathy in two letters to Abbot Higbald of Lindisfarne, offering also to try for the return of any monks whom the Vikings enslaved; and in the same year he reminded the newly restored King Æthelred of Northumbria of this raid when he raised a matter of Norse fashion:

Considerate habitum, tonsuram, et mores principum et populi luxoriosos. Ecce tonsura, quam in barbis et in capillis paganis adsimilari voluistis. Nonne illorum terror imminet,

---

[70] Roesdahl, *The Vikings*, 187–90.

[71] For instance, *ASC* D, *s.a.* 787 [789] (p. 16). *The Anglo-Saxon Chronicle*, trans. and ed. Swanton, 54–5 n. 4. On elaborations of this incident in the twelfth-century Chronicles, see R. I. Page, ' "A Most Vile People": Early English Historians on the Vikings', *The Dorothea Coke Memorial Lecture in Northern Studies*, University College London, 19 March 1986 (London, 1987), 21–5. Page omits the *Vita duorum Offarum*, in whose grandiose account the reeve is tranformed into two people, an *oppidanus* and *villicus*, who *fuerunt primi, qui per Danicam tyrannidem in Britannia ceciderunt*; and in which Offa repels the Danish invasion, taking prisoners whom he sends back to Denmark with instructions never to attack the Mercian empire again; see *Vitae duorum Offarum*, ed. Wats, 22. This version looks so different that it appears to have led Haslam to claim that Offa took Danish prisoners in his reign: see his 'Market and Fortress in England in the Reign of Offa', 77–8.

[72] Townend, *Language and History*, 139.

[73] So Townend, ibid. 28–31. *Epistolae*, ed. Dümmler, ii. 193 (no. 130).

[74] S 134 (BCS 848). Russo, *Town Origins and Development in Early England*, 197.

[75] *Annales regni Francorum*, ed. Pertz, *s.a.* 800. P. H. Sawyer, *Kings and Vikings: Scandinavia and Europe A.D. 700–1100* (London, 1982), 78–91.

[76] *ASC* (E), 55–7 (*s.a.* 793, 794 (E)). *Epistolae*, ed. Dümmler, ii. 58–9 (no. 21: after 8 June 793); and 65 (no. 24: ?794).

quorum tonsuram habere voluistis? Quid quoque immoderatus vestimentorum usus ultra humane necessitatem nature, ultra antecessorem nostrorum consuetudinem?

[Consider the dress, hair-cut, and luxurious customs of the princes and the people. Look at the hair-cut with which you have wished to imitate heathen beards and hair-styles. Isn't there a terror looming from precisely the people whose hair-cut you have wished to have? Why, too, the immoderate consumption of clothing beyond the need of human nature, beyond the use of our forebears?][77]

In this letter Alcuin invokes Amos 2: 6, in order to shock Æthelred into good behaviour by reminding him that the Lord gave the Israelites into the hands of pagans.[78] The only pagans in the North Sea in the 790s were Danes or Norwegians. Our first deduction could be that in 792–3 a few highborn Danes arrived in York on their own ships. Charlemagne's outburst in 796, on hearing of Æthelred's assassination on 18 April of that year, that the Northumbrians were a race *peiorem . . . paganis* ('worse than pagans'), shows how easily the two groups could be linked.[79] It is tempting to speculate that Æthelred lived with King Sigfred of Denmark while in exile from Ælfwald, his main predecessor, in *c.*779 × *c.*788 (Widukind of the Old Saxons sought refuge there with Sigfred in 777). Whether or not this was so, it is likely that the 790s saw Danes beginning to sail to England, some as enemies, some as friends.

The year 789 is known for the dramatic rift in relations between Kings Offa and Charlemagne, when Charlemagne closed Frankish markets to English trade, having taken offence at Offa's request to marry Ecgfrith, his son, to Bertha, Charlemagne's daughter.[80] Neither the year in which this embargo was lifted, nor the reason why, is recorded in either of the two groups of sources for this story, in the *Gesta abbatum Fontanellensium* or in Alcuin's two letters of 790.[81] But trade had been restored for a while by the time Charlemagne and Alcuin wrote separately to Offa in 796.[82] One outcome of the English loss of export markets for half a decade was that the client kingdoms around Mercia grew restless, with King Æthelberht of East Anglia issuing his own coinage in 794 and perhaps thereby causing Offa to put him to death. There is the coincidence that the closure of Frankish markets to English shipping in 789 was soon followed by the appearance of longships off Wessex, Northumbria, and Kent. Charlemagne was in any case negotiating with Danish leaders at this very time. His withdrawal of protection for English merchants for three or four years after 789 would have have meant that, during this time, he let the Danes sail past Frisia to England unchallenged.

---

[77] *Epistolae*, ed. Dümmler, ii. 42–4, at 43 (no. 16).

[78] It is of interest that Amos 2: 4 condemns the Israelites because 'they have been deceived by the idols to which their fathers strayed' (*Deceperunt enim eos idola sua, post quae abierant patres eorum*).

[79] *Epistolae*, ed. Dümmler, ii. 146–8 (no. 101); *EHD*, 849–51 (no. 198).

[80] *Gesta abbatum Fontanellensium*, ed. Loewenfeld, 46 (ch. 16).

[81] Ibid. 46. *EHD*, 341 (no. 20). *Epistolae*, ed. Dümmler, ii. 31–3 (no. 7); 34–5, at 35 (no. 9).

[82] *Epistolae*, ed. Dümmler, ii. 144–6 (no. 100). Nelson, 'Carolingian Contacts', 141–3, esp. 141. See Hodges, *The Anglo-Saxon Achievement*, 136–9.

809: DANES AT BREEDON? ALDWULF'S RANSOM

In the summer of 789 Alcuin wrote to a friend near Bremen, asking, among other things, for news *si spes ulla de Danorum conversione* ('if there is any hope of the conversion of Denmark').[83] The following sections suppose that the community of Breedon was one that shared Alcuin's *hæþenra hyht*. This chapter will continue with a speculation that Breedon is where the poet of *Beowulf* later met some Danes for himself (see Ill. 2).

In England no Danish raids are recorded after Lindisfarne and Portland until *c.*835, in the second reign of Wiglaf (*c.*829–839). On the other hand, a meeting of some kind between Danes and Mercians took place in Mercia as early as 809. This came at the end of a story which began in 806, when King Eardwulf was driven out of Northumbria by Archbishop Eanbald (II) of York.[84] In the *Annales regni Francorum* it is said that the deposed Eardwulf met Charlemagne in Nijmegen around 16 April 808.[85] More on Eardwulf's expulsion, and on Charlemagne's desire to restore him, survives in three letters which Pope Leo wrote to the emperor in 808–9.[86] In the first, written after April in 808, Leo rejoices in Eardwulf's safety, telling Charlemagne that he has ordered Eanbald to explain his actions either to himself in Rome or to the emperor.[87] However, he adds that this order will have greater effect if backed up by an envoy from Charlemagne. He also suspects that Cenwulf of Mercia has conspired against Eardwulf with both Archbishop Eanbald II and Ealdorman Wada, whom Cenwulf sheltered after his failed uprising in 798.[88] Leo's second letter is dated to 31 December 808. This letter is an apology for the impulsive conduct of one Aldwulf, a 'Saxon' from Britain whom Leo, much earlier that year, had sent to meet Eanbald's envoy in York. Having been treated well by Charlemagne in Aachen, Aldwulf caused offence on his return from York by taking Eanbald's envoy on to Rome without waiting for an escort to bring them both to Aachen.[89] Leo says that he has sent the emperor all relevant correspondence.[90]

By the time of Leo's third letter, dated to 809, Eardwulf had been restored by Aldwulf and two envoys from Charlemagne. The fly in the ointment was Aldwulf, whom Charlemagne, having agreed to restore Eardwulf in April 808,

---

[83] *Epistolae*, ed. Dümmler, ii. 31 (no. 6). Allott, *Alcuin of York*, 71–2 (no. 55).

[84] Story, *Carolingian Connections*, 145–64. See also Nelson, 'England and the Continent in the Ninth Century', 17–20; Kirby, *Earliest English Kings*, 156–7.

[85] *Annales regni Francorum*, ed. Pertz, 126 (*s.a.* 808).

[86] Nelson, 'England and the Continent in the Ninth Century', 17.

[87] *Councils and Ecclesiastical Documents*, ed. Haddan and Stubbs, iii. 563. *Epistolae*, ed. Dümmler, iii. 90 (no. 2).

[88] *Epistolae*, ed. Dümmler, iii. 90: 'repperimus eorum [of Eanbald, Cenwulf and Ealdorman Wada] dolositatem, quam inter se habent.' Noted by Rollason, in 'The Cults of Murdered Royal Saints', 20. Story, *Carolingian Connections*, 202.

[89] *Epistolae*, ed. Dümmler, iii. 91 (no. 3).

[90] Nelson, 'England and the Continent in the Ninth Century', 19.

had sent back to England with his imperial envoys. The two latter men are named in the *Annales, s.a.* 808, as Abbots Hruotfridus (of Saint-Amand), who was the *notarius* ('secretary'), and Nantharius of Saint-Omer (near Boulogne, the shortest Channel crossing).[91] Working together, it appears that all three of them restored Eardwulf in 808. The *Annales* give an impression of what happened next:

Postquam Ardulfus rex Nordanhumbrorum reductus est in regnum suum et legati imperatoris atque pontificis reversi sunt, unus ex eis, Aldulfus diaconus, a piratis captus est, ceteris sine periculo traicientibus, ductus ab eis in Brittaniam a quodam Coenulfi regis homine redemptus est Romamque reversus.[92]

[After King Eardwulf of Northumbria was brought back into his kingdom and the emperor's and pope's legates had returned, one of them, Deacon Aldwulf, was captured by pirates, while the others got across without danger; having been brought by them into Britain, he was bought out by one of King Cenwulf's men and returned to Rome.]

This tells us that Charlemagne's men sailed back to Francia by themselves; the provenance of Nantharius makes Boulogne their likely way back home. In his third letter Leo looks forward to seeing the ransomed Aldwulf in Rome after his debriefing with Charlemagne.[93] In any event Aldwulf was probably arrested as soon he berthed in Francia, for Charlemagne may have suspected a collusion between Pope Leo and Eanbald.[94] News of the rescue had just been brought to Leo from the Frankish court by Bishop Sabinus, an envoy whom the pope had sent to England, vainly as it turned out, to collect Aldwulf before he went to Charlemagne.[95]

The entry in the *Annales* is all too brief, but in conjunction with Pope Leo's third letter to Charlemagne, it points to how and where Aldwulf was ransomed. As to how he was, we might ask where the pirates, clearly Vikings, captured him. His colleagues had sailed earlier, so it seems that neither London nor Kent, on the southern edge of Mercia, had to be Aldwulf's transit point to Francia. The fact that Bishop Sabinus, sent to get him after his release, returned empty-handed in 809 also suggests that Aldwulf was ransomed in a corner of Mercia far from either Canterbury or London. Aldwulf's separate sailing, together with his part in the restoration of King Eardwulf, might tell us that he stayed on in Northumbria (perhaps to conciliate Archbishop Eanbald's supporters)[96] and then sailed back to Francia out of the river Humber downstream from York.

[91] *Annales regni Francorum*, ed. Pertz, 126–7. McKitterick, *The Frankish Kingdoms under the Carolingians*, 386 (map 14).
[92] *Annales regni Francorum*, ed. Pertz, 128 (*s.a.* 809).
[93] *Epistolae*, ed. Dümmler, iii. 93 (no. 4).
[94] Nelson, 'England and the Continent in the Ninth Century', 19–20. J. Story, 'Charlemagne and the Anglo-Saxons', in Story (ed.), *Charlemagne: Empire and Society*, 195–210, esp. 207–8.
[95] *Epistolae*, ed. Dümmler, iii. 93 (no. 4). A monk named 'Savinus' attests in nineteenth place (out of forty-two) in a letter to Charlemagne from Pope Hadrian I in May or June of 781, in *Epistolae Merovingici et Karolini aevi I*, ed. Societas Aperiendis Fontibus, MGH, Epistolae 3 (Berlin, 1892), 597 (no. 67).
[96] Story, *Carolingian Connnections*, 148–9.

If this were so, Aldwulf's captors probably caught him near the Humber mouth. Thereafter they went into Mercia, in that the *Annales* states that they sold him to *quidam Coenulfi regis homo*. Mercia, as Janet Nelson points out, was 'in origin, if not a landlocked kingdom, then one less coastally orientated than its neighbours'.[97] From the Humber, their most plausible route into this enclosed country would have been up its principal eastern river, the Trent. However the sale with Cenwulf's ealdorman was arranged, from the Vikings' point of view there could have been no other way: Frisia was closed off, due to the tension between Charlemagne and King Godfred of Denmark in 808–9 (on which more below); given Eardwulf's power, Northumbria was the lion's mouth; in Mercia, on the other hand, they were applying to the trading network of a relatively disinterested region. Trade between Danes and Christians probably lay behind Alcuin's reference to King Æthelred's heathen coiffure in 790. Further south, there is the mid-ninth-century case of an ealdorman (named Aelfred) redeeming ecclesiastical property from the Vikings, before passing this on into the keeping of Christ Church, Canterbury.[98] Between these two regions, in the Trent valley, there is the later dynastic pretension, fuelled by local knowledge, which led four Danish kings (Healfdene, Guthrum, Oscytel, and Anwend) to bury a fifth (Inguar?) at the Mercian royal mausoleum at Repton in the midst of the first Danish invasion, in the winter of 873–4.[99] Indeed the intensity of Scandinavian settlement in Leicestershire in 877, after the third phase of Viking wars in 872–3, suggests that the Danes had long been aiming for the best farmland. From the North Sea, the Trent is the most suitable way into Mercia, for it is the gateway not only to Leicester, which the Danes made into a base, but also to the other boroughs of Derby, Nottingham, Torksey, and Lincoln.[100] On the basis of the Danish pattern of occupation three generations later, it can be surmised that the Trent was becoming familiar to Danish captains at the beginning of the ninth century.

The Trent valley is thus the most suitable region in Mercia for these Vikings to have sold Aldwulf to Cenwulf's man. That Cenwulf took an interest in saving Pope Leo's man was probably due to the recent mission from Charlemagne and the pope, which would have crossed his kingdom on the way to York. Not only had Cenwulf helped to expel Eardwulf from Northumbria in the first place, but he also aided Eardwulf's enemies after his restoration in 808.[101] However, as

[97] Nelson, 'Carolingian Contacts', 131.
[98] The Codex Aureus gospel book (now of Stockholm): D. Whitelock, *Sweet's Anglo-Saxon Reader in Prose and Verse*, 15th edn. (Oxford, 1967), 205. Townend, *Language and History*, 4–5.
[99] Haslam ('Market and Fortress in England in the Reign of Offa', 79–86) believes that Repton was already fortified before 873–4. On the mauling of Repton, see Biddle and Kjølbye-Biddle, 'Repton and the "Great Heathen Army", 873–4', 81–4. The authors believe that the great chieftain was Ívarr *beinlausi* ('the boneless'), better known from *Ragnars saga Loðbrókar*.
[100] On the paucity of literary and archaeological evidence, however, see Hall, 'Anglo-Scandinavian Urban Development in the East Midlands', 147–9.
[101] Kirby, *Earliest English Kings*, 197.

Joanna Story suggests, the papal and imperial envoys probably restored some equilibrium between him and Archbishop Wulfred; not without reason did Cenwulf later, in 821, believe that the pope and emperor might intervene on Wulfred's behalf (see Chapter 9).[102] Because the papal and imperial mission of 808 makes it clear that Cenwulf directed an ealdorman, rather than himself, to arrange for Aldwulf's ransom, it is unlikely that he was then in Mercia. A royal Mercian charter for 809, issued at Croydon, shows Cenwulf to have been in southern England mostly busy with Kentish affairs to do with Canterbury and Wulfred.[103] The name of Cenwulf's ealdorman cannot be known, but if we follow the territorial surmise above, it seems that his purchase of Aldwulf was negotiated in the Trent valley, near the Mercian heartland.

Among the sites that are known from this region that might host a delicate conference involving Mercians, Danes, and Northumbrians, the minster at Breedon on the Hill, deep in Mercian territory at more than 100 miles south of the Humber, stands out as the best. Years later, the grants by King Berhtwulf and his leading *princeps* Humberht in favour of this minster in 848, issued at Repton and excusing the abbot from feeding passing officials, shows how habituated Breedon was to the demands of both the local Tame valley ealdorman and international envoys of various kinds:[104]

Præcones si trans mare venirent ad regem venturi vel nuntii de gente Occidentalium Saxonum vel de gente Norþanhymbrorum. si venirent ad horam tertiam diei vel ad medium diem dabatur illis prandium. si venirent supra nonam horam tunc dabatur eis noctis pastum. et iterum de mane pergent in viam suam.

[Envoys, if they come from overseas on their way to meet the king, or messengers from the people of the West Saxons or from the people of the Northumbrians, if they come at terce [9 a.m.], or at midday [12 noon], breakfast will [still] be given to them; if they come after the nones [3 p.m.], then food and shelter for the night will [still] be given to them, so that they may go on their way again the next morning.]

Keynes suspects that the reception of these and other foreigners at Breedon, as 'one of perhaps a number of religious houses', fell within 'routine operations of royal government'.[105] That Breedon had this official role is clearest in the record of its seeing not only Northumbrians but also West Saxons, whose own country lay far to the south. The overseas origin of other *praecones* points to Breedon's reputation for hosting Carolingian and papal envoys as well.

It might be said that other minsters in north-eastern Mercia performed this role. Yet one thing that singles out the minster of Breedon from the others on this

---

[102] Story, *Carolingian Connections*, 203. *Councils and Ecclesiastical Documents*, ed. Haddan and Stubbs, iii. 597.

[103] S 164 (BCS 328). This charter and its background are discussed by Keynes, 'The Control of Kent in the Ninth Century', 114. See further my Chapter 9.

[104] S 197 (BCS 454). Discussed in Keynes, 'Councils of *Clofesho*', 39–40.

[105] Ibid. 40.

occasion, at least, is the near certainty that it was personally acquainted with King Eardwulf. Namely in its second element, the present dedication of the church at Breedon, SS Mary and Hardulph, refers to a tradition in which a 'St Hardulph' lies buried there. The twelfth-century *Chronicon* of Hugh Candidus of Peterborough, who relies on a lost Anglo-Saxon saints' list for this part of his information, says that the remains of one *sanctus Ærdulfus rex* ('saint Ærdulf, a king') lie at *Bredun*, along with those of other saints.[106] The two other surviving references are of a later date. The *Vita s. Modwennae* was written in the 1120s by Abbot Geoffrey of Burton (ruled 1114–51) in honour of the eponymous half-imaginary Irish saint who lived on the Trent isle of Andresey. Adapting the Conchubranus' Irish *Vita* of St Modwenna as his source, Geoffrey says that *In loco autem qui nunc Bredunia dicitur habitabat illo in tempore uir quidam uenerabilis ac religiosissimus heremita* ('at that time time there lived in the place now called Breedon a certain venerable man, a most devout hermit'), who would often visit Modwenna in her cell.[107] One day he forgets to bring the holy books which they like to read; a pair of girls go downstream to fetch them; a miracle occurs when they survive at the bottom of the Trent in an upturned boat (ch. 35). This tale might be held as baseless, were it not that the Norman-French author of a verse translation of Geoffrey's work, writing later in the twelfth century, names the hermit 'Erdulf'. The fact that he regularly calls this man a *prud(h)ume* ('man of worth'), but not a king, shows that he had not read Hugh Candidus, to whom 'Ærdulfus' is *rex*; and that he probably drew the Erdulf-name either from an annotated copy of the *Vita*, or from his own knowledge.[108] In this case we have a genuine tradition of a Breedon hermit named Eardwulf. Ann Dornier cites a seventh-century Heardwulf, king of Kent, but the gap of time here is too great; she refers also to three bishops Heardwulf, but the hermit's title *rex* makes it even less likely that 'Hardulph' refers to any of them.[109] Nor is this man likely to have been the lesser-known Eardwulf who was the king's Deiran father. Frances Arnold-Forster was in no doubt that St Hardulph referred to Eardwulf of Northumbria, thinking that this might be due to Breedon's twelfth-century incarnation as an Augustinian priory belonging to St Nostell's church near Wakefield in the West Riding.[110] Although there is no evidence of Eardwulf's association with Wakefield, rather than Ripon, Arnold-Forster seems to be right in concluding that Breedon was rededicated to this Northumbrian king.

[106] SS Cotta, Benna, and Frethoricus. *Peterborough Chronicle of Hugh Candidus*, ed. Mellows, 60. On his sources, see Rollason, 'Lists of Saints' Resting-Places', 71 and n. ('possibly' this is King Eardwulf of Northumbria). Dornier suggests that Hardulf was a lay patron otherwise unknown, in her 'The Anglo-Saxon Monastery at Breedon-on-the-Hill', 161.

[107] *Geoffrey of Burton: Life and Miracles of St Modwenna*, ed. and trans. R. Bartlett (Oxford, 2002), pp. xiv–xxvi, esp. xix (on sources) and 144–5 (text).

[108] *St. Modwenna*, ed. A. T. Baker and A. Bell, Anglo-Norman Texts 7 (Oxford, 1947), pp. xxii–xxiv (sources) and 201–5 (lines 5833, 5837, 5849, 5853, 5859, and 5963).

[109] Dornier, 'Breedon on the Hill', 161.

[110] *Church Dedications* ii. 325–7.

To find a place for Breedon in Eardwulf's story, we must study his movements in and out of exile. According to the *Northumbrian Annals*, his story begins when, as a nobleman, he was captured by King Æthelred's men in 790 and taken to Ripon for execution outside the minster gates. The king's men left and the monks carried Eardwulf inside, laying him in a tent outside the church, where they found him alive at midnight. From here Eardwulf escaped into a six years' exile, waiting while Æthelred murdered other contenders, in 791 the sons of King Ælfwald (779–88) and in 792 Osred, son of King Alhred (765–74).[111] Eardwulf was recalled when Æthelred's enemies caught him out on 18 April 796. Arriving in York in just over three weeks, he unseated Osbald, a rival ruler, then had himself proclaimed king on 14 May in a ceremony of Carolingian-papal style which was led by the first Archbishop Eanbald and three bishops.[112] Now facing his own rivals, Eardwulf crushed a conspiracy in 798, had Ealdorman Moll killed in 799 and Ealhmund, probably another son of King Alhred, killed in 800. Ealhmund was a friend of Cenwulf's who had probably sheltered him in or around Derby in north Mercia, where, as St Alkmund, he was later venerated as a saint.[113] To take care of any more pretenders lurking near the border, Eardwulf invaded northern Mercia in 801. Cenwulf made peace with him in the same year. But in the next few years Eardwulf fell out with his new archbishop, also named Eanbald, who deposed him probably in 806.[114] Following restoration two years later, Eardwulf ruled a second time until, in 811 or 812, he was succeeded by his son Eanred, who is thought to have ruled peacefully for more than thirty years.[115]

It seems that Eardwulf abdicated into the monastic life, 'chose God's light' one might say, in preference to another round of executions. A number of observations may be made about Eardwulf's movements to and from Northumbria. First, it has recently been suggested that in the eighteen months between his 806 deposition and arrival in Nijmegen in April 808, he was sheltered by Archbishop Wulfred in or around Canterbury.[116] His journey from York to Kent and Francia, if across Mercia, would have taken him up the Trent valley. On analogy with Ealhmund's hide-out and later legendary resting place, it is possible, therefore, that wealthy minsters of the adjoining east Midlands sheltered Eardwulf in his first exile in 790–6. The position of this region relative to Northumbria, at 100–150 miles south, matches the relative speed with which he arrived in York less than a month after Æthelred's death. It is also in keeping with the connection established a century earlier by Wilfrid between Ripon, which Kirby regards as Eardwulf's family heartland, and Brixworth, Wing, and Oundle.[117] In his own

---

[111] Kirby, *Earliest English Kings*, 154–5. Yorke, *Kings and Kingdoms*, 90 and 95–6.
[112] *ASC* D, *s.a.* 796 (p. 18). Story, *Carolingian Connections*, 129–30.
[113] Kirby, *Earliest English Kings*, 156–7. Hall, 'Anglo-Scandinavian Urban Development in the East Midlands', 145.
[114] Story, *Carolingian Connections*, 151–2.
[115] Kirby, *Earliest English Kings*, 157 and 196. Yorke, *Kings and Kingdoms*, 97–99.
[116] Story, *Carolingian Connections*, 202.
[117] Mayr-Harting, *The Coming of Christianity*, 156–9. Kirby, *Earliest English Kings*, 154.

Vita, written by Stephen of Ripon, Wilfrid is said to have spent his own exile in eastern Mercia (666–9 and 692–703), performing episcopal duties there and founding many monasteries.[118] Here it is said that he died *ad monasterium eius, quod in Undolum positum est* ('at his minster, which is situated in Oundle').[119] Bede says that he died in 709 *in monasterio suo, quod habebat in prouincia Undalum sub regimine Cudbaldi abbatis* ('in his minster, which he used to hold in the province of Oundle under the rule of Cuthbald').[120] Although it is uncertain which monastery this was, Wilfrid's erstwhile adherence to the rule of Cuthbald, who was abbot of *Medeshamstede* in 675–*c*.687, suggests that he helped to found the monastic 'empire' to which Breedon belonged.[121] His is the well-worn path which Eardwulf could have followed, first in 790–6, then for a while in the eighteen months after his deposition in 806, and finally at Breedon in or after 811/12.[122]

There are other links between Breedon and Northumbria. The only English parallel for the type represented by Breedon's narrow frieze (*c*.800 × *c*.810) is a projecting square-moulded band surrounding the south doorway of Ledsham church, near Leeds.[123] Sphinx-like beasts are found both in Breedon's broad frieze and in a Northumbrian cross-head at Hoddom; the animals and foliage of the broad frieze also have parallels in the Rothbury cross-shaft and Ormside bowl.[124] A vertical set of two panels (with images of Abraham and Isaac and below that Adam and Eve at the Fall) on a cross-shaft fragment in the church at Breedon, possibly of the eighth or ninth century, is paralleled by the same combination of scenes in Cumbria on a shaft from Dacre (with the addition of a beast in the upper scene).[125] These ties, together with the long history of Wilfrid's involvement in Middle Anglia, make an association between Ripon and Breedon plausible in the case of King Eardwulf.[126]

[118] *Life of Bishop Wilfrid*, ed. Colgrave, 30 (ch. 14). D. H. Farmer, 'Saint Wilfrid', in D. P. Kirby (ed.), *Saint Wilfrid at Hexham* (Newcastle, 1974), 35–59, esp. 52.

[119] *Life of Bishop Wilfrid*, ed. Colgrave, 80 (ch. 40).

[120] *HE* V. 19.

[121] This word is of Simon Keynes, in his 'Councils of *Clofesho*', 37–40, at 40. For Brixworth as Wilfrid's last stopping place, see the discussion in Hart, *The Danelaw*, 142–4. On 'period resemblances' between the Breedon inhabited vinescroll and early ninth-century Northumbrian sculpture (the Easby and Hoddom crosses), see Jewell, 'Classicism of Southumbrian Sculpture', 248–9.

[122] Like Kings Æthelred of Mercia in 704 (Bardney), Coenred of Mercia in 706 (Rome), Ceolwulf of Northumbria in 737 (Lindisfarne). See Kirby, *Earliest English Kings*, 126, 128, 149. This is not to include the kings whose tonsure was forced on them.

[123] Jewell, 'The Anglo-Saxon Friezes at Breedon on the Hill', 99 (pl. XLIV.b).

[124] Ibid. 101 and 108–9.

[125] Bailey, 'The Meaning of Mercian Sculpture', 10–11 and fig. 5.

[126] In 1144 Earl Robert Ferrers of Nottingham granted Breedon church with its lands to the priory of St Oswald at Nosthell, also in the West Riding. See T. Tanner, *Noticia Monastica, or An Account of all the Abbies, Priories and Houses of Friers heretofore in England and Wales* (London, 1744), 238. Ferrers 'fixed a cell of Black canons subordinate to that monastery [Breedon]', with a prior and five religious; two canons lived there at the time of the Reformation.

Whatever the truth of Eardwulf's movements, we have these reasons to believe that he was associated with Breedon; and that in 809 he was the wretched Aldwulf's best hope for a speedy return to (Charlemagne and) Pope Leo. If we connect one association with the other, it becomes plausible to treat Breedon as the place where Cenwulf's ealdorman bought Aldwulf off the Danes while men from Northumbria waited to escort him back to King Eardwulf. We can thus speculate that Breedon in 809 is where Aldwulf's Danish captors talked to the poet who is so concerned for the souls of Danish ancestors in *Beowulf.*

826: KING HERIOLD'S BAPTISM

No Christian could entertain heathens without receiving their undertaking to undergo *prima signatio* or some basic training in the creed. In Francia, attempts were made to convert Danish leaders as early as the 780s. When Alcuin, in 789, asked about the chances of a Danish conversion, he was reflecting policy. Charlemagne had been dealing intermittently with King Sigfred of the Danes since July 782 and began to negotiate with him again in 789.[127] To become the Franks' new friend in 782, Sigfred and others had agreed to become Christians. This stipulation attracted surreal humour in the Frankish court: there is a verse exchange from a year later in which Peter of Pisa, apparently echoing a jest of Charlemagne's, asks Paul the Deacon if he would prefer baptizing Sigfred to a spell in jail; Paul replies that the hairy Sigfred would not understand his (Lombardic) language, but neither would the Dane thank 'Thonar' or 'Waten' if he were taken bound to the font.[128] The West Germanic forms of these names show that Charlemagne's courtiers, Alcuin among them, were not dismayed by the thought of Danish gods in the 780s.[129] Indeed, a Frankish interest in them seems to have continued for in 826, in his eulogy for Louis the Pious, *In honorem Hludovici Pii*, Ermoldus Nigellus devotes many lines to Heriold and aims to show knowledge of his gods by saying that the Dane worshipped 'Iuppiter' and 'Neptunus'.[130] There is no reason why the same interest, in the same period, could not be attributed to the poet of *Beowulf.*

Indeed Charlemagne's court circles can probably be regarded as the English poet's second source of information about Denmark, given that Anglo-Saxon kings had no reason to talk to Danish leaders until the second half of the ninth century. Until then the gossip about Denmark probably crossed the sea to English minsters on Frisian trade routes. The Franks were anxious about King

---

[127] *Epistolae*, ed. Dümmler, ii. 31 (no. 6). *Die Gedichte des Paulus Diaconus*, ed. Neff, 100.

[128] Ibid. 98–105 (nos. 21 and 22).

[129] Ibid. 104 n. 2. *Waten* as opposed to *Godan*, Paul's native Lombardic form, in his *Historia Langobardorum*, ed. Waitz, 52–6.

[130] *Poetae Latini aevi Carolini*, ed. Dümmler, ii. 1–79 (*In honorem Hludovici Pii*), esp. 59 (IV. 9–10) and 60 (IV. 69).

Sigfred because he had sheltered Widukind in the late 770s; in the 780s Charlemagne needed to secure the borders in the event of future Saxon rebellions, of which there were plenty; also he needed to contain the threat of Danish piracy. In Francia this problem grew, until the Vikings terrorized the rivers of Gaul in the second half of the ninth century, laid siege to Paris, campaigned in Brittany, and got land in northern France.[131] In the early days, however, Charlemagne tried to staunch the flow by backing one Dane against another.[132]

Thus, while the Vikings began to sail to England from the time of his embargo on English trade in 789, Charlemagne began to deal with Danish kings. One of his legates, Godescalc, was slain by the Saxons on his return from Denmark in 798; and in 804 a Danish king named Godfred sailed to meet the emperor in Sliesthorp, in north Saxony, concerning the issue of fugitives, but had to make do with Charlemagne's envoys.[133] In 808, around the time of Eardwulf's troubles in Northumbria, Godfred attacked and defeated his Slav neighbours to the southeast.[134] In order to placate Charlemagne he claimed a year later that they had attacked him. When Charlemagne built a fort on the Danish border and planned an expedition, Godfred broke with him and raided Frisia in 810; he was killed by one of his followers and replaced by a certain Hemming, a brother's son, who made peace with the emperor at Heilingen in 811.[135] This turbulent state of Franco-Danish relations in 808–11 probably explains why, in 809, Aldwulf's vendors made their sale in Mercia, rather than in Frisia.

Notwithstanding this turbulence, it was Charlemagne's policy with Danish kings that led to the triumph of King Heriold's baptism in 826. He knew that 'Danish royal power was personal: it was vested in the individual, not the office of king.'[136] When Hemming died in 812, Sigfred Godfredsson and one Anulo killed each other in a fight for succession, before the kingship fell to two brothers, Heriold and Reginfrid, whose names (cognate with *Haraldr* and *Ragnarr*) identify them with Denmark's leading royals of the tenth century as they are known in Icelandic sources. Heriold later enjoyed the support of Louis, son of Charlemagne, and shared the rule of Denmark with the sons of Sigfred Godfredsson from 821 to 827. When they finally drove him out, he retired to his base in Rüstringen in Frisia, which Louis had granted him in exchange for his baptism. Later he became a pirate and sacked Dorestad at least four times, every year from 834 to 837; his brother Rorik appears to have held Frisian lands near Dorestad.[137] Louis had started to help Heriold against his rivals as early as 815.

[131] Roesdahl, *The Vikings*, 195–209.
[132] The sources are discussed in Maund, '"A Turmoil of Warring Princes"', 29–33.
[133] Ibid. 33–4.
[134] Ibid. 35. Näsman, 'Om fjärrhandel i Sydskandinaviens yngre järnålder', 110.
[135] Maund, '"A Turmoil of Warring Princes"', 34. Roesdahl, *The Vikings*, 195–6.
[136] Maund, '"A Turmoil of Warring Princes"', 34–5.
[137] Ibid. 36–9. Roesdahl, *The Vikings*, 196.

Although Heriold was an unfortunate choice of protégé, it seems that this help must have come in response to his agreement to convert. Nearly a decade after 815, Archbishop Ebo is recorded as having spent a year in Denmark when Louis' legates brought him back from a meeting with the sons of Godfred in 823.[138]

Heriold was finally baptized with his family and followers near Mainz in 826.[139] It was Corbie's daughter minster in Saxony, Corvey, that enabled this conversion to take place.[140] As we have seen, the post-baptismal ceremony in Ingelheim was given fulsome coverage by Ermoldus.[141] For Heriold's progress to the emperor's splendid palace, this poet based his scene on the *Aeneid*, casting Heriold in the role of Aeneas as he salutes King Evander of the Pallantines (*Aen.* VIII. 126).[142] Ermoldus and Louis' biographers Thegan and the 'Astronomer' show that 826 was a year in which Louis won renown for converting the Danes.[143] For the first time anywhere, the prospect of converting Danish princes was real. It would have been odd if the east Mercian minsters were without their own *spes de Danorum conversione* in the period 815–26. As English minsters lived in fear of Danish attack, so it seems likely that each twist in the saga of Heriold's imminent baptism was relayed to those minsters in Mercia, such as Breedon, with ties to the Frankish Church.

CONCLUSION

Given the ubiquity of Frisian traders, the poet of *Beowulf* would not have had to consult Danish visitors for legends about the kings of Zealand, Götland, and Sweden which he adapts to such effect in *Beowulf*. These could have been carried by Frisian ships and passengers together with news from Francia, as we have seen in my Chapters 1 and 6. On the other hand, the Frisians are unlikely to have mediated the essentials of Norse mythology which appear in the *Beowulf*-poet's adaptations of Freyja's necklace, Baldr's death, and Þórr's duel with the World Serpent. The poet's use of this working paganism shows a deeper level of experience. This could have come about, I suggest, through his talking to

---

[138] On Ebo in Denmark, see the speech imagined for King Heriold in *In honorem Hludowici Pii*, written by Ermoldus Nigellus in the late 820s: *Poetae Latini aevi Carolini*, ed. Dümmler, ii. 67 (IV. 317–26).

[139] *Thegani Vita Hluowici imperatoris*, ed. G. H. Pertz, MGH, SS 2 (Hanover, 1829), 597 (ch. 33).

[140] McKitterick, *The Frankish Kingdoms under the Carolingians*, 117–18.

[141] *Poetae Latini aevi Carolini*, ed. Dümmler, ii. 1–79, esp. 59–67 (IV. 65–377).

[142] Ibid. 66 (IV. 303). See my Chapter 4, where I argue that Beowulf is modelled on Aeneas from the same part of the *Aeneid*.

[143] Godman, *Poetry of the Carolingian Renaissance*, 46 (introduction) and 250–5 (text and trans.); *Poets and Emperors*, 123–5. *Vitae Hludowici imperatoris*, ed. G. H. Pertz, MGH, SS 2 (Hanover, 1829), 586–604 (*Thegani Vita Hludowici imperatoris*), esp. 597 (ch. 33) and 604–48 (*Vita Hludowici imperatoris*), esp. 619 (ch. 24).

Aldwulf's Danish vendors at Breedon in 809. A relationship seems to have existed between Breedon and King Eardwulf, Aldwulf's Northumbrian contact, just as there was another between Aldwulf and the Vatican. Later, the Frisian–Frankish trade networks would have allowed hopes of the Danish conversion to spread to England in the years leading up to the baptism of King Heriold in Mainz in 826. There are other reasons to believe that *Beowulf* was conceived in this year, but none so close to the pathos of King Beowulf's soul.

8

'Thryth' and the Reign of Offa

With this chapter begins my attempt to place *Beowulf* at a moment in Mercian history. *Beowulf* has already been housed in various periods from the seventh century to the eleventh; so far, in Chapters 2–7, on the strength of claiming certain narrative innovations in *Beowulf*, I have proposed that it was composed for King Wiglaf in the famous minster of Breedon on the Hill, some time after the death of King Beornwulf, so in 826 × 839. From now on until the end of this book, I shall try to determine more exactly when the poem was written.

The first step is Offa and the so-called 'Thryth digression' of *Beowulf*, lines 1925–62. Because the poet praises Offa of Angeln at the close of this passage, many have thought that *Beowulf* was composed in the late eighth century for King Offa of Mercia, given that Offa of Angeln, who is praised in this digression as the wise tamer of a suitor-slaying princess named 'Thryth', is given as Offa's ancestor in royal Anglo-Saxon genealogies.[1] So far Offa's historical parallel has been counted as the strongest of any latent in the poem. Even those scholars who date *Beowulf* in the early eighth century, before the Mercian Offa's time, are compelled to consider lines 1925–62 as an interpolation later made in his court. Others, who favour the tenth or eleventh centuries, have explained the Thryth-digression by suggesting that various West Saxon patrons of *Beowulf*, from King Alfred onwards, took both Offas for their forebears. What I propose is no less conjectural, but has the advantage of arguing a place for lines 1925–61 in the conception of the poem. Starting with the plentiful analogues for Offa and 'Thryth', I shall see how, if at all, this digression is related to the rest of *Beowulf*. Until a wider aim has been found which is plausible for these wayward lines, they will continue to be dismissed as opportunistic or interpolated.[2] For my part, I conclude that Offa is placed deliberately at the outset of the Geatish part of the poem: before we hear from Hygelac, see the last of Beowulf, and meet Wiglaf in the last 580 lines. Allegorically, in this way, I shall suggest that Offa and the others are there to represent a sequence of great Mercian kings: Offa (757–96), Cenwulf (796–821), Beornwulf (823–6), Wiglaf (827–8 and 829–39).

---

[1] Whitelock, *The Audience of Beowulf*, 58.
[2] Discussed in Murray, '*Beowulf*, the Danish Invasions, and Royal Genealogy' 103.

OFFA OF ANGELN IN *BEOWULF*

The poet of *Beowulf* honours his Offa chiefly as the man who tames a murderous princess. We meet him in *Beo* 1925–62, within a larger bridging section between the poet's portraits of Beowulf first in youth and second in age.[3] Beowulf has just returned to his uncle Hygelac's hall in Geatland, following his defeat of Grendel and Grendel's Mother in Denmark. The poet first elaborates on Hygd, Hygelac's queen; then suddenly on another woman who becomes a queen when she is wedded to Offa. If we begin with Hygd, introduced next after Hygelac, we see only gradually that she is his wife, thus the Geatish queen:

> Bold wæs betlic, bregorof cyning,
> heah healle, Hygd swiðe geong,
> wis welþungen, þeah ðe wintra lyt
> under burhlocan gebiden hæbbe,
> Hæreþes dohtor; næs hio hnah swa þeah,
> ne to gneað gifa Geata leodum,
> maþmgestreona. (*Beo* 1925–31)

[The building was magnificent, the king brave as a lord should be, the hall was high, Hygd was very young, wise, accomplished, although she had experienced few winters in the royal residence, she, the daughter of Hæreth; for all that she was not mean, nor too frugal in gifts, in treasures, to the princes of the Geats.]

In these lines Hygd's qualities match her name, which, as it is unattested elsewhere, is to be read as the poet's allegorical adaptation of *gehygd* ('thoughts, disposition'). To this image of a queen in tranquility, the following lines offer a sharp contrast. Hygd gives treasures, the next woman trouble:

> Modþryþe [MS *mod þryþo*] wæg,
> fremu folces cwen, firen' ondrysne;
> nænig þæt dorste deor geneþan
> swæsra gesiða, nefne sinfrea,
> þæt hire an dæges eagum starede;
> ac him wælbende weotode tealde
> handgewriþene; hraþe seoþðan wæs
> æfter mundgripe mece geþinged,
> þæt hit sceadenmæl scyran moste,
> cwealmbealu cyðan. Ne bið swylc cwenlic þeaw
> idese to efnanne, þeah ðe hio ænlicu sy,
> þætte freoðuwebbe feores onsæce
> æfter ligetorne leofne mannan. (*Beo* 1931–43)

---

[3] On the themes of youth and age as a guide to *Beowulf*, see J. R. R. Tolkien, '*Beowulf*: The Monsters and the Critics', *PBA* 22 (1936), 245–95.

[Passion of mind an excellent queen of the people had, monstrous crimes she committed; no man but a permanent lord among the dear companions was brave enough to dare risk gazing upon her in the open light of day, but he might count deadly bonds, ones woven by hand, destined for him; swiftly, after that, once hands had seized him, a sword was so appointed that the damascened blade was allowed to settle this, to perform his death-bale. No queenly virtue is it for a lady to carry out such a thing, though she be without peer, that she, a peace-weaver, in keeping with a pretended grief, should exact the life-blood from a beloved man.]

Lines 1931b–2 are veiled in their expression, while it is possible some more lines are missing, but here it is generally believed that a new woman is introduced whose epithet *cwen* ('queen') on line 1932 belies her pre-marital status at this point as a princess.

Almost all scholars call this woman 'Thryth' or 'Modthryth', despite two awkward facts. One is the lack of another simplex name OE *Þryþ*.[4] Another is the existence of a phrase *higeþryðe wæg*, which describes Hagar's pride against Sarah in *Gen* A 2240 ('she had passion of mind'; Bolton and Wrenn: 'showed insolence of character'). This would appear to be a traditional expression for which 'modþryþe wæg' in *Beowulf* is a variant.[5] Other words and phrases uniquely common to these poems have led Klaeber and Orchard to wonder whether or not the poet of *Beowulf* borrowed from *Genesis* A.[6] Certainly in this case, the words *higeþryðe wæg* offer the most straightforward solution to the problem of reading MS *mod þryþo wæg*: Hygd bears gifts, tokens of good will, whereas another queen once bore nothing but malice; the second woman's passions, in *modþryþe*, run counter to the good sense of OE *gehygd* on which Hygd's name seems allegorically founded.[7] Norman Eliason read 'modþryþe wæg' in order to suggest that the death-dealing princess, whoever she was, was an (even) younger version of Hygd once tamed by Offa and now married to Hygelac, a second husband.[8] This idea, however, has not swayed the critics. Nearly all commentators read *(Mod-)Þryþ(-o)* as a name with no great anxiety.[9] In this there is a kind of moral imperative. Few women are named in *Beowulf* as it

---

[4] Searle, *Onomasticon Anglo-Saxonicum, s.v.* 'Thryth' (p. 447).

[5] *Beowulf*, ed. Wrenn, 1st edn., 144. This idea was later dropped, in favour of 'Modthryth', in *Beowulf*, ed. Wrenn and Bolton, 170; it is not discussed in Stanley, '"A Very Land-Fish"', 88 n. 25.

[6] *Beowulf*, ed. Klaeber, p. cx. Orchard, *Companion*, 167–8.

[7] On the rational import of *hyge* and associated words, as against the emotional aspects of *mod* and *modsefa*, see North, *Pagan Words*, 63–98, at 79–93.

[8] N. Eliason, 'The "Thryth–Offa Digression" in *Beowulf*', in J. B. Bessinger and R. P. Creed (eds.), *Franciplegius: Medieval and Linguistic Studies in Honor of Francis Peabody Magoun, Jr.* (New York, 1965), 124–36.

[9] See *Beowulf*, ed. Wrenn and Bolton, 170 (Modthrytho); and *Beowulf: A Student Edition*, ed. Jack, 140 (Modthryth). In more recent times, this passage is discussed by J. Chance, *Woman as Hero in Old English Literature* (Syracuse, NY, 1986), 105–6; Overing, *Language, Sign, and Gender in Beowulf*, 101–7; Irving, *Rereading Beowulf*, 73. Magennis (*Images of Community in Old English Poetry*, 105 n.) is willing to accept the name Thryth 'without going into the fraught question of what the correct reading of line 1931b (MS *mod þryþo wæg*) should be'.

is; and Gillian Overing, without citing the parallel in *Gen* A 2240, takes a familiar high ground when she complains that those who read the queen's 'name' as an abstract noun 'have explained her away completely'.[10]

The morphological problem with 'Modthryth' arises in the ending of MS *þryþo*. Strenuous efforts have been made to emend this word in order to keep a proper noun as subject or object of its clause. So, to account for the awkward MS form, Klaeber emended the half-line to 'Mod Þryþe [ne] wæg'.[11] He did not translate this line, but the reading *-e* for *-o* is acceptable palaeographically. Mitchell and Robinson, in their turn, take *þryþo* to have an archaic ending in final *-ol-u* and leave the final letter unchanged; they translate as 'the excellent queen of the people (Hygd) weighed the arrogance of Thryth', and take Thryth 'as a model to avoid'.[12] Their retention of MS *þryþo* is clever, with MS *-o* as an accusative ending for f. *Þryþ*, but their figurative reading of *wæg* (as 'weighed', from *wegan*) is forced: two other constructions in *Beowulf* show that the verb *wegan* ('to carry; endure') is used of emotional states.[13] For these reasons, even before the admission of a parallel from *Gen A* 2240, the phrase 'modþryþe wæg' emerges as the simplest way to take line 1931b.

From these words it is still clear that the poet wishes to set one queen off against another. Indeed he has already compared Beowulf with the bad king Heremod (*Beo* 901–15, at 913–15 and 1707–23). The motif in this case is that of Kate and Petruchio:

> Huru þæt onhohsnod[e]   Hem*m*inges [MS -*n*-] mæg:
> ealodrincende   oðer sædan,
> þæt hio leodbealewa   læs gefremede
> inwitniða   syððan ærest wearð
> gyfen goldhroden   geongum cempan
> æðelum diore   syððan hio Offan flet
> ofer fealone flod   be fæder lare
> siðe gesohte,   ðær hio syððan well
> in gumstole   gode mære
> lifgesceafta   lifigende breac,
> hiold heahlufan   wið hæleþa brego,
> ealles moncynnes   mine gefræge
> þæs selestan   bi sæm tweonum,
> eormencynnes;   forðam Offa wæs
> geofum ond guðum,   garcene man,

---

[10] Overing, *Language, Sign and Gender in Beowulf*, 101.

[11] *Beowulf*, ed. Klaeber, 72, 187–90, and 409. He appears to mean '[Hygd] did not carry out pride, excellent queen of the people, [did not carry out] awful sins'.

[12] *Beowulf*, ed. Mitchell and Robinson, 112 n. For a general discussion of these lines, see C. L. Wrenn, in Chambers, *Beowulf*, 539–43.

[13] See *wæg modceare micle* ('I suffered great griefs of mind', lines 1777–8); *he lust wigeð* ('he takes pleasure', line 599). On the figurative use of *wegan* with emotional states, see Clemoes, *Interactions of Thought and Language*, 80.

wide geweorðod,   wisdome heold
eðel sinne,   þonon *Eomœr* [MS *geomor*] woc
hæleðum to helpe,   Hem[m]inges mæg,
nefa Garmundes,   niða cræftig. (*Beo* 1944–62)

[It was Hemming's kinsman, indeed, who checked this: drinking ale, men told another story, that she carried out fewer harms against the people, fewer malicious acts of hostility, when first she had been given, gold-adorned, to a young brave high-born champion, when, at her father's instruction, she sought Offa's hall on a voyage over the fallow flood; then, in that place, famous for generosity on her groom's throne, did she well employ in living what had been ordained for her in life, she did keep to an exalted love with that chieftain of heroes who was, according to what I have heard, the best of all mankind between the seas, of the vast human race; for Offa was widely honoured in his gifts and battles, a spear-keen man, guarded his inherited land with wisdom; from whom arose Eomer in aid of men, kinsman of Hemming, a nephew [or: grandson] of Garmund, skilled in hostilities.]

The textual problems in this passage will need a discussion of their own before I consider the identity of Offa here.

The first of these arises in the name of Offa's kinsman, MS *hem ninges* (line 1944) or *hem inges* (line 1961). Here it seems best to keep the vowel short and double the *m*, given the *hem ninges*, which is probably miscopied for *hem minges*. Kiernan posits a *Heming*, with a long first syllable and single consonant, on the basis of MS *hem inges* on line 1961; since he ignores the *n* in the first form, however, his reading cannot be sustained.[14] 'Hemming', then, whose name is unattested elsewhere, would appear to be Offa's father-in-law, to whom the poet has already referred with the words *be fæder lare* on line 1950 (if this father is not Offa's).[15] Another problem with the lineage in these lines is provoked by comparison with Offa's line in two other groups of royal genealogies, that of *Historia Brittonum* and the Anglian collection.[16] If we set these out father to son:

Beo 1944–62	*Historia B.*	*Vespasian B.vi, fo. 109ᵛ*
(Garmund)	Guerdmund	Uermund Uihtlaeging
Offa	Offa	Offa Uærmunding
		[..]gengeot Offing
Eomœr	Eamer	Eamer Angengeoting
		Icil Eamering

The genealogies in these groups give an *Eamer* as the son or grandson of Offa son of Wærmund. Thus it has long been customary to emend MS *geomor* on *Beo* 1960 to *Eomer* and take this man to be Offa's son in *Beowulf*.[17] Kiernan, on the other hand, followed by Newton, claims that the presence of Angengeot as Offa

---

[14] Kiernan, *Beowulf and the Beowulf Manuscript*, 184.

[15] Klaeber inclines to this idea in *Beowulf*, ed., 190 n.

[16] *L'Historia Brittonum*, ed. Lot, 198 (ch. 60). Dumville, 'The Anglian Collection', 30, 33, and 36. Dumville, 'The Anglian Collection', 24–5 and 33–6 (date) and 30 (text). The oldest text to quote from in this collection is Vespasian B.vi, fo. 109ʳ⁻ᵛ, whose writing Dumville dates to 805 × 814.

[17] *Beowulf*, ed. Klaeber, 73; *Beowulf*, ed. Mitchell and Robinson, 114.

I's son in the Anglian genealogy gives reason to discount the existence of an (emended) *Eomer* in *Beo* 1962, who would thus have to be Offa I's grandson.[18] He thus keeps the MS form and reads *Beo* 1960 as *eðel sinne. Þonon [on]geomor woc*, rendering the off-line as 'then, exceeding sad, he arose'.[19] Kiernan thus removes Offa's son, making Offa 'a help to his men' in putting an end to his queen's crimes (albeit these go on after he marries her). There are three arguments against Kiernan's reading. First, it contradicts the poet's story, in which the woman's crimes stop after marriage. Second, the words *Þonon [on]geomor* on line 1960 would give a metrically anomalous line: Kendall prefers the line in emended form.[20] Third, four constructions elsewhere in *Beowulf* with *(on-) wæcnan* ('awaken, arise') show that we should expect Offa to have a son at line 1960.[21] Given the poet's choice of the word *eðel* on line 1960a, the name of Offa's son has to alliterate with an open vowel. So it seems best to keep the emended *Eomer* and to make further comparison with the other royal genealogies.

According to the genealogies of *Historia Brittonum* and the Anglian collection, as above, Offa the grandfather of Eamer was Offa of Angeln: the ancestor of Offa of Mercia. The name *Garmund* in *Beo* 1962 is usually taken to be adapted from forms such as *Uærmund*. By this name is the continental Offa's father known not only in the Anglian collection but also in the *Vitae duorum Offarum* and in Danish analogues concerning Uffo. There are several possibilities. One is that 'Garmund' need not be the same as 'Uærmund', if the *Beowulf*-poet's *nefa* means 'nephew' on line 1962 as it does on lines 881, 2206, 2170, and probably 1203 (Hygelac being the *nefa* of an otherwise unknown Swerting). In this case, Garmund could be taken to be Offa's brother. Or perhaps the scribe miscopied *garmundes* from *wærmundes* because he was thinking of the form *gar* in MS *gar cene* in the middle of the folio three lines up.[22] A third possibility is that the poet of *Beowulf* consulted a genealogy which was also used in the *Historia*, in which the *Wærmund*-name was turned into something like *G(u)ærmund* through the influence of Welsh morphology.[23] The form of Garmund's name, at any rate, shows that the genealogy of Offa I at the heart of this passage in *Beowulf* lies closer to the older list in *Historia Brittonum* than to the early ninth-century Anglian collection.

As Sisam and Dumville have both shown, royal genealogies could be extended according to local political circumstance throughout the Anglo-Saxon period.[24] Both scholars point out that the Anglian pedigrees, numbering fourteen

---

[18] Kiernan, *Beowulf and the Beowulf Manuscript*, 184.

[19] Ibid. 184–5; Newton, *The Origins of Beowulf*, 66–8.

[20] Kendall, *The Metrical Grammar of Beowulf*, 148.

[21] *Þanon woc fela geosceaftgasta*, of Cain's progeny on lines 1265–6; *Ðæm feower bearn . . . wocun*, of Healfdene's sons one lines 59–60; *him eft onwoc heah Healfdene*, of the Danish Beow(ulf)'s son in lines 56–7; and *Þanon untydras ealle onwocon*, of the monsters spawned by Cain on line 111.

[22] *Beowulf*, ed. Zupitza, 90–1.

[23] G. Sarrazin, 'Neue Beowulf-Studien', *EStn* 42 (1910), 1–37, at 17.

[24] Sisam, 'Anglo-Saxon Royal Genealogies', 308–14; Dumville, 'Kingship, Genealogies and Regnal Lists', 72.

generations, appear to be constructed in emulation of the fourteen generations from Abraham to David in St Matthew (Matt. 1: 17).[25] In this case, Angengeot's name was probably interpolated between Offa of Angeln and his then alleged son Eamer, in order to bring the number of Mercian kings up to fourteen and into line with the others. The fact of this extension answers Kiernan's use of the Anglian collection to cast doubt on the existence of *'Eomer'* in *Beo* 1962.[26] Given Sisam's observation that a shorter genealogy is probably older than a longer one, it would appear that the Offa-genealogy in *Beowulf* belongs to a tradition separate from the Anglian collection. Dumville has argued that the Anglian collection originated in Deira in the 760s, and that its Vespasian version, the oldest extant, was copied not long before 814 for King Cenwulf of Mercia (796–821).[27]

As we have seen, the pressing question is whether or not the poet in these lines of *Beowulf* intends to flatter King Offa of Mercia (757–96). To what end does he celebrate Offa and his son, if their ancestor's renown is to tame a wicked princess? The poet's following panegyric goes beyond requirements for a wife-taming husband: *hælepa brego, alles moncynnes mine gefræge þæs selestan bi sæm tweonum eormencynnes* ('that chieftain of heroes who was, according to what I have heard, the best of all mankind between the seas, of the vast human race', lines 1955–7). These words recall the hyperbole with which the young Danes hail Beowulf: *suð ne norð be sæm tweonum ofer eormengrund oper nænig . . . selra* ('neither south nor north between the seas or across the earth's vast terrain was there any better man', lines 858–9). This praise is stronger than in the poet's description of Onela later in *Beowulf: þone selestan sæcyninga þara ðe in Swiorice sinc brytnade* ('the best sea-king who [ever] broke up treasure in Sweden', lines 2382–3). Moreover, the Danes' thoughts resemble an epitaph for Guthlac, erstwhile Mercian prince of the first half of the eighth century, in *Guthlac B*:

> se selesta   bi sæm tweonum
> þara þe we on Engle   æfre gefrunen
> acennedne   þurh cildes had
> gumena cynnes   to Godes dome (*Guth* 1359–62)[28]

[The best man between the seas of those whom we have ever heard created through childhood from the tribe of men among the Angles in the Judgement of God]

Offa of Angeln is not the main subject of *Beowulf*, nor even an actor in its story whether in present narrative or past. Nor is he needed for the moral contrast

---

[25] Sisam, 'Anglo-Saxon Royal Genealogies', 326–8; Dumville, 'Kingship, Genealogies and Regnal Lists', 89–90.

[26] Kiernan, *Beowulf and the Beowulf Manuscript*, 184.

[27] Dumville, 'The Anglian Collection', 45–50. The fact that the Lindsey list extends further back than the others, beyond 'Frealaf' to a certain 'Geot' or 'Geat' (ibid. 31 (Vespasian B.vi), 34 (CCCC 183), 36 (Tiberius B.v: Frealaf, Freoðowulf, Finn, Godwulf, Eat)), might indicate that this collection was copied in Lindsey.

[28] *The Guthlac Poems of the Exeter Book*, ed. J. Roberts, with introd. and commentary (Oxford, 1979), 123.

between Hygd and the princess in *Beo* 1926–43. So it is a mystery why the poet should laud him at least as much as Beowulf, hero of his poem.

As a solution, following the suggestion of John Earle, Dorothy Whitelock attributed *Beowulf* to Offa's court on the basis of its poet's allusion to Offa of Angeln.[29] Their reasoning has been accepted in recent times by Peter Clemoes; and the case has weathered half a century of debate on the dating of *Beowulf*.[30] While questions remain concerning the precise meaning of *Beo* 1925–62, it is clear that Offa of Angeln, with whom the passage culminates, is important to the poet beyond the confines of his main narrative. His need to praise Offa of Mercia is still the most plausible guess. Why he should need to do so, however, is a question which only Offa's analogues may answer.

OFFA OF ANGELN IN *WIDSITH* AND LATER ANALOGUES

Offa of Angeln is the subject of an allusion early on within the versified king-list of *Widsith*. He is also the first king in this poem to have his own story:

> Offa weold Ongle,   Alewih Denum;
> se wæs þara manna   modgast ealra,
> no hwæþre he ofer Offan   eorlscype fremede
> ac Offa geslog   ærest monna
> cnihtwesende   cynerica mæst;
> nænig efeneald him   eorlscipe maran
> on orette;   ane sweorde
> merce gemærde   wið Myrgingum
> bi Fifeldore.   Heoldon forð siþþan
> Engle ond Swæfe   swa hit Offa geslog. (*Wid* 35–44)[31]

[Offa ruled the Angles, Alewih the Danes; he was of all these men [i.e. the foregoing list of kings, of Goths and southern Germanic tribes, Franks, Frisians, Swedes, and others] the bravest, yet he did not perform deeds of courage greater than Offa did. But Offa, first among men, fought for and won the greatest of kingdoms even while he was a youth; no one of the same age was warrior enough to achieve greater deeds of courage; with one special sword he fixed a boundary against the Myrgings [whose king is Meaca on *Wid* 23] at Fifeldor [the river Eider]. From that time forth Angles and Swabians kept to it just as Offa, by fighting, had established it.]

Already it will be clear that the poet of *Beowulf* knows of this duel, for he refers to Offa as a 'champion' in the epithet *geongum cempan* on line 1948.

---

[29] Whitelock, *The Audience of Beowulf*, 58. Earle, *The Deeds of Beowulf*, p. lxxxiv. Bolton (*Alcuin and Beowulf*, 100–3, at 102) considers Offa of Mercia so pervasive in Alcuin's letters 'that there seems little reason to suppose an additional "continental" Offa to account for the character in *Beowulf*'.

[30] P. Clemoes, 'Style as the Criterion for Dating the Composition of *Beowulf*', in Chase (ed.), *The Dating of Beowulf*, 173–85; and *Interactions of Thought and Language*, 3–67, at 53–8.

[31] Text from *Beowulf*, ed. Mitchell and Robinson, 196–202, at 198; see *Old English Minor Heroic Poems*, ed. Hill, 30 (text) and 12–14 (discussion).

The other analogues on Offa nearly all date from the late twelfth century or after. There is a well-proportioned account in Sven Aggesen's *Brevis historia regum Dacie* (c.1188), in which Uffi, a coal-biter son of Wermundus, fixes the Danish border at the river Eider by slaying two big opponents.[32] Saxo writes an anti-German version of the same story in his *Gesta Danorum* (c.1200–16; of Lund); this story is condensed in the twelfth-century Danish *Annales Ryenses* (c.1290); and the continental Offa is also celebrated in the opening chapters of the English early thirteenth-century *Vitae duorum Offarum*, which commemorate Offa as the founder of St Albans (in c.794).[33]

In this work, Offa or Offanus, son of Uarmundus of Warwick ('Uarmundus' homestead') in the kingdom of the West Angles, is blind until the age of 7 and dumb until 30. When Uarmundus admits that he must cede his kingdom to a usurper named Riganus, Offa bursts into tears and calls God to witness that he will not leave Riganus and his henchman Mitunnus unpunished. Both sides prepare for battle, on either side of a river, with Riganus' army distinguished by two champions named Otta and Milio; Uarmundus arms his son with a sword; Offa wades across and kills not the two champions, but Riganus' two sons, putting the rest of their army to flight. He takes the throne from his father and marries a princess from York who has fled to the west Midlands to escape her incestuous father. Through her father's plotting, in a motif of the Constance type, this queen is later left with her children in the forest to die; but Offa finds them again.

There is no clear connection between *Widsith* and this clearly composite English version of Offa's story from the twelfth or thirteenth century. The author of the *Vitae* has Anglicized his tale of Offa I to match the early career of Offa II; and if his source can be guessed at for this part of Offa I's career, it is not likely to be directly *Widsith*, but rather a work which descends from *Widsith* or its source. There are things in common: the age of 30, at which Offa first speaks; the great stature of the hero; the king's council to debate a challenge; his sword as Offa's weapon; the two opponents whom Offa kills. The *Annales Ryenses* are even closer, in which Offa's age in the duel, though not his relevant infirmity, concurs with that of the *Vitae*. Chambers thus believed that the *Annales* were influenced by a legend from Britain related to the *Vitae*.[34] It has been suggested, however, that the loan went the other way, from Denmark to England in the eleventh or twelfth

---

[32] *Scriptores minores historiae Danicae*, ed. Gertz, i. 98 (*Svenonis Aggonis filii brevis historia*, ch. 3). *Works of Sven Aggesen*, trans. and comm. Christiansen, 51–4.

[33] *Gesta Danorum*, ed. Olrik and Ræder, pp. 92, 97–100, and 334; see *Saxo Grammaticus*, trans. Fisher, i. 101 and 106–9; *Scriptores minores historiae Danicae*, ed. Gertz, i. 161 (*Series ac brevis historia regum Danie*), 168 (*Series et genealogiae regum Danorum*), 175 (*Nomina regum Danorum*), 187 (*Incerti auctoris genealogiae regum Danorum*). *Danmarks middelalderlige Annaler*, ed. E. Kroman (Copenhagen, 1980). *Vitae duorum Offarum*, ed. Wats, 1–8; see Chambers, *Beowulf*, 217–28. The tale of Vermundr and Óláfr inn lítilláti, in the fourteenth-century *Flateyjarbók*, is also distantly related. See *Flat*, i. 27.

[34] *Beowulf*, 539.

century.[35] Whichever way it travelled, it seems likely that the tale from which the author of the *Vitae* at St Albans derived his tale of Offanus was also a source for the story of Uffo, prince of the Danes.

The treatment of Offa in *Widsith* is briefer but more complex than the opportunistic Dane-Saxon simplifications of Sven and the other Danish historians. In *Widsith* the continental Angles, sitting between the Danes and the Swabians, resemble the *Mierce* ('Mercians', lit. 'boundary dwellers', i.e. Angles living between Northumbrians and Saxons) to whom the poet probably alludes with the words *merce gemærde* ('he fixed a boundary', line 42).[36] It has also been suggested that Offa I's Fifeldor boundary on *Wid* 42–3 alludes to 'Offa's Dyke', the massive earth-wall rampart which Offa II constructed from south to north, perhaps at intervals throughout his long reign (757–96), in order to protect the English from the Welsh.[37] It might be noted that King Offa is given to refer to himself as an erstwhile *puer indolis* ('inactive boy') in a Worcester charter of c.757.[38] So it seems that the poet of *Widsith* intends to glorify Offa of Mercia with this reference to his alleged ancestor in these lines. Both from *Widsith* and the *Vitae duorum Offarum* of St Albans, we can deduce the existence of an Old English poem once written as a political allegory for Offa.

ANALOGUES FOR 'THRYTH'

Offa's wife in *Beowulf* has two surviving analogues: Queen Herminthrutha of Scotland, in Saxo's *Gesta Danorum* (IV. i. 12–20); and Quendrida, the wife of Offa II in the *Vitae duorum Offarum* and also in other sources. The first of these analogues is probably related to the *Beowulf*-poet's source. In his tale of Herminthrutha, Saxo says that the Danish prince Amlethus, having killed his usurping uncle Fengo, sails to Britain to visit the wife which Fengo has earlier betrothed to him. When Amlethus arrives his father-in-law, a king of low birth, sends Amlethus to Scotland on an errand to Queen Herminthrutha, whom he says he wishes to marry. Secretly, however, Amlethus' father-in-law hopes to have the young Dane killed. For Herminthrutha is no ordinary woman:

Sciebat namque eam non modo pudicitia cælibem, sed etiam insolentia atrocem, proprios semper exosam procos amatoribus suis ultimum irrogasse supplicium, adeo ut ne unus quidem e multis exstaret, qui procationis eius pœnas capite non luisset.[39]

[He knew that she was not only a spinster in virtue, but also savage in her insolence, in that she always hated the wooers who came to her and inflicted the extreme sanction on

---

[35] *Works of Sven Aggesen*, trans. and comm. Christiansen, 107 n. 16; *Saxo Grammaticus*, trans. Fisher, comm. Ellis Davidson, ii. 67–9.

[36] On the etymology of *Mierce*, see Brooks, 'The Formation of the Mercian Kingdom', 160.

[37] Wormald, 'The Age of Offa and Alcuin', 120–1, at 120.

[38] S 55 (BCS 183).

[39] *Gesta Danorum*, ed. Olrik and Ræder, 88–92, at 88 (IV. i. 12).

her would-be lovers, to the extent that there was not one of that multitude who had not paid the penalty of his boldness with his head.]

But Herminthrutha is so impressed by Amlethus' killing of Fengo that she begs him to marry her. Amlethus takes her back to Denmark as a concubine, along with his British wife, whose death shortly follows. Amlethus loses his life to Wiglecus, who marries Herminthrutha. Their son is Wermundus.

Uffo, the son of Wermundus, does not make a marriage with a narrative outline such as this. Saxo says that Wermundus summons the unnamed daughter of Frowinus, governor of Schleswig, as Uffo's bride; there is no mention of her name; nor, unlike the fact that Amlethus sails to Scotland, is there a suggestion that Uffo and his bride meet after a sea-crossing.[40] Yet the stories in *Beowulf* and Saxo (Book IV. i. 12–20) look essentially the same; and the English poet, with 'modþrype wæg' on line 1931, appears to hint at a nominal compound based on *þruð-* ('strength'), rather like 'Hermin*thruthá*'. In other words, the poet of *Beowulf* would appear to have known a story about Offa I's bride which was also an early analogue of Saxo's Danish tales of Amlethus and Herminthrutha.

The *Vitae duarum Offarum* provide *Beowulf*'s closest analogue for a story about Offa I's courtship and marriage. Here it is said that Offa I is a king of Warwick in England. After driving out his father's usurpers, Offa I saves a princess who had been cast adrift by her father the king of York. In later life he decides to marry her, but his letter to her father in York is switched for one which orders her execution and it is only through the miraculous intervention of a hermit, who revives her and the children after this takes place, that she marries Offa I at all. The life of Offa II echoes that of his namesake. Offa, son of Tuinfredus (i.e. Thingfrith) and 'Marcellina', and deaf and blind since child-hood, is initially named Winefredus and misspends his youth. Yet he is miracu-lously cured through his parents' prayers and defeats the usurper of his father's kingdom, Beornredus. Upon this deed he is renamed 'Offa' in memory of the great Offa I. But then he makes an unwise marriage with a Frankish princess, a kinswoman of Karolus (i.e. Carloman, Charlemagne's father):

quædam puella, faciæ venusta, sed mente nimis inhonesta, ipsi regi [Karolo] consangui-nea, pro quodam quod patraverat crimine flagitiosissimo, addicta est judicialiter morti ignominiose; verum, ob regiæ dignitatis reverentiam, igni vel ferro tradenda non judatur, sed in navicula armamentio carente, apposito victu tenui, ventis et mari, eorumque ambiguis casibus exponitur condempnata.[41]

[A certain girl of beautiful appearance but with a mind all too dishonourable, of the same blood as this king [Karolus], was judicially sentenced to an ignominious death on account of the most heinous crime which she had engendered; indeed, in reverence of her royal rank, she is not judged to be given to fire or sword, but is put out into a little ship lacking

---

40 Ibid. 92 (IV. iii. 1).
41 *Mathæi Paris Historia major*, ed. Wats, 12. See Chambers, *Beowulf*, 238–40.

its rigging and supplied with meagre provisions, condemned to the uncertain incidents of wind and sea.]

The princess comes before King Offa and reveals her kinship with Karolus, saying that her name is 'Drida'; adding, with tears, that she was put out to sea *per tirannidem quorundam ignobilium quorum nuptias, ne degeneraret, sprevit* ('through the tyranny of certain low-born men whose marriage proposals she had spurned, lest she disparage her lineage'). Offa falls in love with the girl and gives her into the keeping of his mother, Lady Marcellina. After a few days, Drida regains her colour and French garrulity, the author says, and begins to despise the kindly countess, who, nonetheless, suffers Drida's words of discord for the sake of her son. Offa falls in love with Drida and quickly marries her without the knowledge of his parents, for they already suspect that she was exiled for reasons other than those given. Old Tuinfredus dies of grief, followed by Marcellina a year later.

So far in the *Vitae*, the second Offa has led a life similar to that of the first: both are handicapped and cured, both overthrow usurpers, and both marry foreign princesses who meet them on the run from vindictive kinsmen. After other incidents in the life of Offa II, we meet Drida again. Her name in this story is now *Quendrida, id est regina Drida* ('Queen-Drida'), but her character has not changed.[42] She has a scheming disposition, turning her hatred now on the king's noble counsellors Humbertus, archbishop of Lichfield, and Unwona, bishop of Leicester. The time comes for Offa and Quendrida to marry off their daughters. But whereas Quendrida would prefer her daughters to marry kinsmen of Charlemagne, in order to bring about Mercia's downfall, Humbertus and Unwona persuade the king to make peace with his newly conquered enemies in England (in this case, the kings of Wessex, Northumbria, and East Anglia), by joining them in marriage with his daughters. Quendrida plots against the bishops, but loses her first two daughters to their schemes. So she is even more bitterly opposed to their plan to marry off the third, Ælflæda, to King Ælbertus of East Anglia. But King Offa agrees:

Vocatus igitur rex Ælbertus, a rege Offa, ut filium suam desponsaret, affuit festivus et gaudens, ob honorem sibi a tanto rege oblatum. Cui amicabiliter rex occurrens adventante, recepit ipsum in osculo et paterno amplexu, dicens: 'Prospere veneris fili et gener, ex hoc, juvenis amantissime, te in filium adopto specialem.'[43]

[So King Ælbertus, called by King Offa to marry his daughter, arrived with festivity and rejoicing on account of the honour conferred upon him by so great a king as this. As he approached, the king came forward and welcomed him with a kiss and fatherly embrace, saying to him, in friendly fashion: 'Prosper from this, O son and offspring of love, most loving young man, for I adopt you as my special son.']

---

[42] *Mathæi Paris Historia major*, ed. Wats, 24–5.   [43] Ibid. 25.

Drida fails to sow the seeds of discord, but in another way *in Ælbertum regem virus sue malitiæ truculenter evomuit* ('she sullenly spewed forth the virus of her evil against King Ælbertus'). When Offa confers with her about the time and place of their daughter's wedding, she urges him to kill the East Anglian king, saying that God has put him in Offa's power: it is clear, she says, that Ælbertus wishes to overthrow him, to invade and thereby *posterum suorum, immo et multorum, ut jactitat, quos regnis et possessionibus violenter et injuste spoliasti, injurias vindicare* ('to avenge the injuries of his forebears, indeed of his many forebears, whom, he claims, you violently and unjustly despoiled of their kingdoms and possessions').[44] Moreover Ælbertus, she says, has been in secret communication with Charlemagne, promising him tribute in exchange for support. She urges Offa to put the East Anglian king to death. Offa refuses and leaves in a fury against his wife. But his anger cools, and later, treating Ælbertus to a day's feasting and drinking, Offa *nil mali formidabat* ('had no thought of any evil') when Quendrida invites the young man to meet his future bride in the next room. The trap is sprung: Ælbertus sits on a throne which falls through a hole in the floor into the pit which Quendrida has prepared. The queen's servants suffocate him with cushions and curtains from the room above, so that no one hears him cry out:

Et sic elegantissimus iuvenis rex et martir Ælbertus, innocenter et sine noxa extinctus, accepit coronam vitæ [quam] ad instar Iohannis Baptistæ mulieris laqueis irretitus, meruit optinere.[45]

[And so the most handsome young man, king and martyr Ælbertus, extinguished without having done any harm or sin, received the crown of life which, trapped like John the Baptist by womanly wiles, he deserved to win.]

This narrative is based on a true event, Offa's murder of King Æthelberht of East Anglia in 794. Æthelberht was made into a saint, and there are several other sources for the story of his martyrdom. For now the most striking feature of Quendrida's story in the *Vitae* is its resemblance to the tale of the wicked princess in *Beo* 1931–44. Not only is the murdered suitor a point of comparison, but the female instigators both appear to have the same name: *Drida* in the *Vitae*; and many readers of *Beowulf* believe that on line 1931b Offa I's bride is named *Þryþ(o)* or 'Thryth'. Is it possible, then, that the author of the *Vitae* got part of this story from a version of *Beowulf*?

It may or may not be true that the author of the *Vitae* made use of a text or adaptation of *Beowulf*. Klaeber, for his part, appears to believe that lines 1931–44 of *Beowulf* had an influence on the *Vitae*, but notes a problem in the construction of Quendrida's tale, namely in 'the shifting of the story from the legendary Offa I to the historical Offa II'.[46] So the author of the *Vitae* could have read

---

[44] See Wright, *Cultivation of Saga*, 100–3 and 261–3.
[45] Chambers, *Beowulf*, 241.   [46] *Beowulf*, ed. Klaeber, 189.

the Offa-passage in *Beowulf* or in an intermediary source, seen a good story in the wicked princess, and given her suitor-slaying tale to Offa II's queen in the *Vitae* (who also, by coincidence, was credited with the murder of her daughter's suitor (St) Æthelberht). This author would then have christened Offa II's queen, while she was still a princess, 'Drida' on the basis of MS *þrypo*. Both Drida's name and her tale of drifting through the seas in a boat could thus be taken as evidence that the author of the *Vitae* had read a version of *Beowulf*.

On the other hand, the author of the *Vitae* gives no tale of murdered suitors to the wife of Offa I, and the lack of this motif in her case suggests that he did not know *Beowulf*. It is true that he names his anti-heroine 'Drida' before and '*Quen-drida*' after her marriage with Offa, as if responding to something like **'mod þrypo wæg fremu folces cwen'* in a text of *Beowulf* (line 1931). It is also true that in the *Vitae* the princess makes a journey to her new husband over water, unlike the story in Saxo's tale of Uffo's wife from Schleswig. Yet these two points can be explained in ways other than treating *Beowulf* as a source for the *Vitae*. First, the resemblance between Drida and an alleged *þrypo* is a red herring. The name 'Quendrida' in the *Vitae* appears to be derived from *Quendritha*, a name for Cynethryth in the immediate source, the *Chronica maiora* of Roger of Wendover. Roger, relating the queen's role in the martyrdom of St Æthelberht, had probably seen the form *Kynedritha* in his source, but confused this with a new form *Quænthrytha*, the villainness of another story, who martyrs her brother (St) Cynehelm (Cœnhelm, Kenelm), the son of Cenwulf of Mercia, 796–821) in two texts of a *Vita et miracula*.[47] The reason for Roger's confusion was no doubt that in this *Vita*, Quœnthrytha kills her own brother.[48] For the short name 'Drida', the author of the *Vitae duorum Offarum* needed no acquaintance with *Beowulf*. He likes to rename his characters to fit them to new roles, as the transformation *Wine(f)redus* to *Offa* shows. He is also fond of etymology, as in the link between the names *Uarmundus* and *Warwick* in the early part of the *Vitae*. Moreover, the name *Bertus*, Offa's name for *Humbertus* (this author's name for the bishop of Lichfield), shows that he likes his names in shortened forms.[49] The author of the *Vitae*, taking the name *Quen-dritha* from Roger of Wendover, could thus have identified its first element with ME *quene* and removed it from this woman's name earlier in the story, before she becomes queen.

Second, Drida's story, as Klaeber says, appears to be based on that of the seaborne princess in *Beowulf* (in a shift of motif from Offa I to Offa II).[50] But the likeness between these women is superficial. Not only is the Drida–Thryth(o)

---

[47] One the 'original', the other an adaptation by William of Malmesbury. See *Vita et miracula S. Kenelmi*, ed. Love, pp. cxxxvi–cxxxviii. These texts are also discussed in Hayward, 'The Idea of Innocent Martyrdom', 144–7. See Wright, *Cultivation of Saga*, 103–4. For Roger's text, see below.

[48] Bond ('Links between *Beowulf* and Mercian History', 486) treats 'Modðryðo' as the poet's representation of Cwenthryth.

[49] *Vitae duorum Offarum*, ed. Wats, 22.

[50] *Beowulf*, ed. Klaeber, 189.

connection probably illusory, but there is another disparity, in that Offa's wicked princess in *Beowulf* sails to his land as part of an agreement between him and her father: her journey to Offa's country, expressed in the phrase *Offan flet be fæder lare gesohte* ('at her father's instruction, she sought Offa's hall', lines 1949–51), is deliberate, unlike the *casus ambigui* ('uncertain events') of wind and sea with which Drida's French kinsman intends to kill her in the *Vitae*. The tale of Offa I's bride in the *Vitae*, as Klaeber notes, probably represents a version of the Constance legend, in which an injured heroine flees her father, marries a foreign prince, is banished with her offspring, but then rejoins her husband.[51] The author of the *Vitae* may have supplied this story for his Offa I in order to replace one of a seaborne bride which he has shifted to Offa II. If he has not, in other words, given Offa II the bride of Offa I whom he saw in *Beowulf*, he has arrived at a castaway motif for Drida, later Quendrida. The author makes Quendrida into a kinswoman of Charlemagne, Offa's enemy, in order to turn the murder of St Ælbertus, the dramatic climax of the second *Vita*, into a Carolingian plot, thereby to unburden Offa II of his guilt. As a Frank, Quendrida must be brought to Offa II from over the sea. The Constance legend in his first *Vita* helps the author to prefigure Drida's arrival in his second, if he is to keep the parallelism inherent in his *Vitae duorum Offarum*. These arguments allow that the author of the *Vitae* would not have had to read the Offa-passage in *Beowulf* in order to write his story of Quendrida. This author would have needed no source for Quendrida other than a life of St Æthelberht.

SOURCES FOR THE DEATH OF ST ÆTHELBERHT

The death of St Æthelberht is first recorded in the *Anglo-Saxon Chronicle* for 794: *Her Offa Miercna cyning het Eþelbryhte rex þæt heafod ofaslean.*[52] Even as early as here, however, the hagiographical method of his execution suggests that his death was converted into a martyrdom by the time this annal was written, or revised, in the late ninth century.[53] His death is recorded in all versions of the *Chronicle*; and according to *The Annals of St Neots*, the chronicle of Æthelberht's home country: *sanctus AETHELBRIHTUS Orientalium Anglorum rex innocenter sub pacis federe occisus est ab Offa rege Merciorum perfidissimo* ('St Æthelberht, king of the East Angles, without doing harm was killed under treaty of peace by the most treacherous Offa, king of the Mercians').[54] As the editors say, the language, 'with its violent anti-Mercian bias, shows the East Anglian concern very

---

[51] Ibid. 188 n. 7 and 189.

[52] *ASC* A, *s.a.* 792 [794] (p. 40): 'in this year King Offa of the Mercians ordered King Æthelberht's head to be struck off.'

[53] Wright, *Cultivation of Saga*, 103–6, at 103 n. 2 (a suggestion of B. Colgrave). The Latin word *rex* in the Chronicle entry may indicate that the annalist's source was a ninth-century Latin Life.

[54] *Annals of St Neots*, ed. Dumville and Lapidge, 39.

clearly'.[55] In these *Annals* Offa is again called *perfidus* in his own obit for the
year 796.[56]

These records may be taken as factual, relative to the prolixity of the author of
Vitae duorum Offarum, whose varied sources derive partly from them. This
author's immediate source, Roger of Wendover, was the special scribe of
St Albans until his death in 1236.[57] Roger's account of 'Quendritha' is briefer
than that in the *Vitae*, and closer to that in his own chief sources, which were a
version of the *Anglo-Saxon Chronicle*, such as those texts above, and a life of
St Æthelberht related to the early twelfth-century Hereford *Passio s. Athelberti*,
which is preserved in Corpus Christi College, 308.[58] I shall take Roger's text first,
in order to show its main discrepancies with the account in the *Vitae*, for these
show that it has a closer relationship with the Hereford tradition.

In Roger's account, Athelberhtus goes to Offa not by invitation, but of his own
accord, *petens ab eo ut filiam suam ei daret matrimonio copulandam* ('seeking from
Offa the right to join himself in marriage to his daughter').[59] Here, unlike in the
Vitae, Offa appears to covet East Anglia, for Quendritha in her altogether shorter
speech says that God has put Athelberhtus into his power, *cujus regnum tam
diuturno adoptastis desiderio* ('whose kingdom you have for so long singled out
as your own'). Roger gives Quendritha no words touching Athelberhtus' belief in
his wronged ancestors. Her trap is sprung in the same way as in the *Vitae*, however,
although with the difference that in Roger's account Athelberhtus' East Anglian
bodyguards flee the hall before dawn.[60] Roger says that Offa, when he hears the
news, retires to mourn for three days, then sends a force to join East Anglia to his
empire. That Roger drew his version from a saint's life becomes clear in that
Athelberhtus' body is discovered *caelesti lumine declaratum* ('revealed by a heavenly light').[61] It is clear that Matthew Paris or another author has shifted the blame

---

[55] *Annals of St Neots*, ed. Dumville and Lapidge, p. lxii.   [56] Ibid. 39.
[57] 'Paris, Matthew (d. 1259)', in E. Williams and H. M. Palmer (eds.), *The Dictionary of
National Biography: Compact Edition*, 2 vols. (Oxford, 1975), ii. 1585. For Matthew's dependence
on Roger, see *Vita et miracula S. Kenelmi*, ed. Love, p. xci.
[58] *Rogeri de Wendover Chronica*, ed. Coxe, i. 249–51. James, 'Two Lives of St Ethelbert', 239–40.
Roger's relevant text is also quoted alongside that of that of the *Vitae*, in Wright, *Cultivation of Saga*,
100–3. The two other main Lives of St Ethelbert which James considers, by Osbert of Stoke by
Clare and Giraldus Cambrensis, are derived from the Hereford version and need not concern us
here. For an up-to-date discussion of all sources for this story, see Hayward, 'The Idea of Innocent
Martyrdom', 124–8.
[59] *Rogeri de Wendover Chronica*, ed. Coxe, i. 249.
[60] Ibid. 250–1: 'Hoc tandem detestabile factum, quod regina malefica in procum filiae operata
fuerat, cum ad commilitones occisi regis pervenisset, ante lucem recesserunt ab aula, ne de ipsis
simile fieret judicium metuentes' ('At length, when the news of this hateful deed, which the cursed
queen had committed against her daughter's suitor, reached the fellow warriors of the king who had
been killed, they fled the hall before first light, fearing a like judgement would take place concerning
them'). The morning news formula occurs also in the dawn reaction of Cynewulf's men in the
Anglo-Saxon Chronicle: *ASC* A, s.a. 755 [recording an event of 786] (pp. 36–8, esp. 37).
[61] *Rogeri de Wendover Chronica*, ed. Core, i. 251. The hagiographic motifs in this story are
discussed by Hayward, 'The Idea of Innocent Martyrdom', 132–43.

from Offa, the founder of his house, partly by enlarging Quendrida's evil, as Wright points out in his comparison of Roger's version with the *Vitae*; and partly by removing the more hagiographical elements of his source.[62] However, the St Albans *Vitae* are unique in attaching Humbertus and Unwona as advisers to Offa in his daughter's East Anglian match. The inclusion of these names in the *Vitae*, one which cannot be attributed to the author's love of Offa, raises a new question. Unless these bishops are there as a foil for Quendrida, their relation to this affair here, whatever it was, may be based on an older record. Unwona was the diocesan bishop of St Albans when Offa founded this minster in 793, and his physical connection with St Albans becomes clear when it is said in the *Vitae* that he was present at the invention of the minster's patron saint, with Archbishop 'Humbertus' (i.e. Hygeberht), whose presence was vouched for *ad audientium informationem* ('according to the information of those who heard him').[63] With Unwona there is a link of some kind to the abbots of Leicestershire, among them Wigmund, whom I have placed in Breedon on the Hill (in Chapter 5).

The twelfth-century Hereford *Passio* is the oldest extended narrative of Æthelberht's death. M. R. James, followed by Wright, takes this story to descend from either a homily or a poem in the Old English vernacular, from the eleventh century either before or just after the Conquest.[64] Paul Hayward shows that this story is also preserved in two other contexts.[65] In the Hereford *Passio*, Athelberhtus is presented as a king of fourteen years, with the date of his accession given as 779.[66] There is much that is doubtful about this story. For example, a claim in the twelfth-century Durham *Chronicle*, that the East Anglian kingdom was partitioned on the death of Ælfwald in 749, between Hun, Beonna, and Æthelberht, would make Æthelberht about 65 in 794.[67] Kirby, however, makes a good case that the Durham entry was based on a misreading of a regnal list by which three successive kings were read as contemporaries.[68] Alan Thacker regards the story as based on a true incident which the *Magonsæte* of Herefordshire commemorated in sympathy with the East Angles in their common oppression by Offa of Mercia; yet Hayward goes so far as dismissing the story as a Hereford invention.[69]

Here I shall argue mostly for the story's authenticity. At the beginning of the Hereford *Passio*, Athelberhtus is advised to seek the hand of Offa's daughter by an

[62] Wright, *Cultivation of Saga*, 104–6, at 105.

[63] *Vitae duorum Offarum*, ed. Wats, 22.

[64] James, 'Two Lives of St Ethelbert', 219; Wright, *Cultivation of Saga*, 96–7.

[65] A collectar on pp. 227–78 of Cambridge, Corpus Christi College, MS 391, an assemblage of materials for the performance of the daily offices made for Bishop Wulfstan II of Worcester (1062–95); and in a metrical prayer in British Library, Cotton Nero A.II, fo. 13ᵛ (*Æthelberhte tiro die per quem fraudem secarat*). See Hayward, 'The Idea of Innocent Martyrdom', 126.

[66] James, 'Two Lives of St Ethelbert', 241.

[67] *Symeonis Monachi Opera omnia*, ed. Arnold, ii. 39.

[68] Kirby, *Earliest English Kings*, 135. Hart disputes this account for other reasons, in *The Danelaw*, 38–40. Barbara Yorke is more equivocal, in *Kings and Kingdoms*, 65 and 69.

[69] Thacker, 'Kings, Saints, and Monasteries', 18. Hayward, 'The Idea of Innocent Martyrdom', 129–30.

East Anglian counsellor, Oswaldus.[70] The name of this princess, *Alfthrutha*, is other than Roger's *Alflæda*, who was the daughter of Offa who married King Æthelred of Northumbria in 792. The *Passio's* form *Kynedritha* is also closer than *Quendrida* to *Cyneþryþ*. Against the wishes of his widowed mother Leofruna, Athelberhtus sets off across Mercia with a band of men. He has a dream presaging his martyrdom, the night before he arrives at Sutton St Michael where Offa can be found. Nonetheless, Athelberhtus hastens towards Offa, *rex in innocentia sua cum omnibus pacem gestans* ('a king in his innocence making peace with everyone'); but Offa is already plotting his downfall.[71] Alfthrutha catches sight of the East Anglian king and confides to her mother Kynedritha her impression that Athelberhtus is a better man than her father. Kynedritha finds this *non modice stimulatio ire* ('a provocation of an anger not modest in its size'). These words, and the explosive speech she makes to Offa, show that in the Hereford *Passio*, the oldest extended version of this story, Kynedritha has not yet planned Athelberhtus' downfall. She points out to Offa that he now stands to lose his kingdom to a more aggressive man: '*quem, O rex, olim auribus hausisti rumor nunc extat uerus*' ('My king, what you once drank up with your ears as a rumour now proves to be true'). Offa takes her advice, to offer half the kingdom to any man who will kill Athelberhtus.

He is answered by a certain Winberhtus, who tells Offa secretly that he held office at the East Anglian court in Athelberhtus' father's day, fifteen years earlier, until expelled for a murder; the visiting king will trust him. Athelberhtus never meets the king. Winberhtus greets him, like a wolf to the lamb, or Judas to Jesus; Athelberhtus asks for an appointment, referring to his plan for *pacificum cum eo consortium* ('a peaceful alliance with him'). Winberhtus puts him off, saying that Offa is being bled. When Athelberhtus insists, however, Winberhtus allows him into the hall, provided he remove his sword:

Cum paucis nobilibus rex sanctus ad regem in maligno positum ingreditur. Regia clauditur porta. Ilico hinc et inde insidie prorumpunt. Rex innocens capitur, uinculis artatur, grauissima afflictione affligitur. Demum proprio gladio a Winberhto plectitur.[72]

[With a few noblemen the king-saint goes in to meet the king steeped in evil. The royal door is shut. Instantly they burst forth in ambush from all sides. The king is taken without striking a blow, bound with chains and tortured with the heaviest torment. At length he is beheaded by Winberhtus with his own sword.]

Hayward discounts this tale, but its authenticity, relative to that of the others shown so far, seems clear in the criminal's name.[73] A certain *Wynberht* witnesses three extant Mercian charters, all issued at church councils:[74]

---

[70] James, 'Two Lives of St Ethelbert', 219.
[71] Ibid. 239.   [72] Ibid. 240.
[73] Hayward, 'The Idea of Innocent Martyrdom', 130: 'its account is not supported by any other records and is unacceptable without qualification.'
[74] Keynes, *Atlas of Attestations*, table X. Unfortunately no E. Anglian charters survive in which to look for his name in the 770s.

Date	Sawyer no.	BCS no.	place of issue	lay ranking
c.794	139	274	Clofesho	8
796	150	281	Chelsea	9 dux
796	151	280	Chelsea	4 dux

Charter S 139, of land at Westbury on Trym (Gloucs.) to Offa's *minister* Æthelmund, survives in a contemporary form and is datable first to 793 × 796, but then more narrowly to 794 on the basis of the similarity of its witness list to that of S 137 (BCS 269).[75] Although this evidence for the Mercian Wynberht is sparse, it seems to confirm the outcome of the twelfth-century *Passio* that Winberhtus achieved a special status with Offa in 794 by which he was granted land.

As regards Priest Abbot Wigmund, probably appointed by his teacher, Bishop Unwona of Leicester, the larger patterns may be seen in Fig. 5. Here it can be shown that Priest Abbot Wigmund was in council with Offa, Hygeberht, Unwona, and Wynberht in about 794, the year in which Offa had Æthelberht murdered. This was as part of a group which included Ealdorman Æthelmund, son of Ingeld, the other two Leicestershire priest abbots Beonna and Alhmund (and, of course, many other men).[76] It is not clear what can be made of Wynberht's disappearance from the record after 796, but the most likely reason for his absence is the accession of Cenwulf. A further link with Wigmund may appear in the fact that within two years of this date, in 798, an ealdorman named Wigberht, apparently Wigmund's kinsman, takes Wynberht's place in the ranking.

Offa is made almost fully guilty of Æthelberht's death in the *Passio*, for he is planning treachery even while this king arrives, and he needs little bidding to arrange for his death. Even the mourning, with which Roger softens his Offa's nature after the deed, seems to rework Offa's being bled at the time the young king called. The *Passio*'s anti-Offan version of events may reflect the feelings of St Æthelberht's eleventh-century cultists in Hereford, but its unwavering focus on Offa's guilt is also in line with the older record in the *Anglo-Saxon Chronicle*. Offa is in charge in the *Passio*, yet detaches himself from the murder, leaving this detail to an East Anglian traitor. He has long had ideas about Æthelberht, but allows Kynedritha to appear to initiate the murder herself. Kynedritha is thus important in the *Passio*, but she has a more limited role in this tale than the *Vitae*'s Quendrida in hers. Kynedritha's role is both to react and to encourage. There is her angry reaction to an insult that she imagines her daughter to have made on Æthelberht's behalf; and her encouragement of Offa to put his own malice aforethought into action. A late twelfth-century record from the Worcester *Chronicle*, s.a. 793, allots their guilt in the same manner:

---

[75] Cubitt, *Anglo-Saxon Church Councils*, 274; Scharer, *Die angelsächsische Königsurkunde*, 278. See Keynes, *Atlas of Attestations*, table X.
[76] S 139 (BCS 274).

S:	138	139	149	150	151	153	155	106	1260	
BCS:	264	274	279	281	280	289	293	201	308	312
Archive:	StAlb	Wor	Malm	StAlb	StAlb	CCC	CCC	CCC	Wor	CCC
Place of issue:	?Barford	*Clof*	[chc?]	Chel	Chel	[ ]	Tam	Chel	*Clof*	*Clof*
Year:	c.792	?794	796	796	796	798	799	c.800	803	803
KINGS										
Offa	+	+								
Ecgfrith			+	+	+					
Cenwulf						+	+	+	+	+
BISHOPS										
Hygeberht	1 ab	1 ab				2 ab	1 ab			
Unwona	4	5		2	2	4	3	2		
Werenberht								3		
ABBOTS										
Alhmund	1	1				1	1			1 Lei
Beonna	2	2		1	1	2	2	2		2 Lei
Forthred	4			2	2	4	3	3?		3 Lei
Wigmund	3	3				3	4			4 Lei
LAYMEN										
Brorda (1)	1 *pat*	1	1 *pre*	1 *dux*	1 *dux*	1 *pri*	1 *pri*			
Æthelmund	6 *d*	5	2 *pre*			5 *dux*	3 *dux*	2		
Wynberht		8		9 *dux*	4 *dux*					
Beornnoth						9 *dux*	9 *dux*	10	2 *pri*	
Cynehelm								11	4 *pri*	
Wigberht	5 *dux*	6 *dux*		2 *dux*	.*dux*	4 *dux*	4 *dux*			
Wigferth		6								
Wigheard								6 *p'*		

Figure 5. Kindred of Priest Abbot Wigmund (in c.792–803)

Source: Keynes, *Atlas of Attestations*, VIII–X, XIII, XV, XVII.

Gloriosissimus ac sanctissimus rex Orientalium Anglorum Ægelberhtus, uero regi Christo bonarum uirtutum merito acceptabilis, omnibus blando aloquio affabilis, Offe prepotentis regis Merciorum detestanda iussione sueque coniugis Cyneðrythe regine nefaria persuasione regno uitaque priuatus est capitis abscissione.[77]

[Ægelberhtus, most glorious and sainted king of the East Angles, acceptable in his practice of good virtues to Christ the True King, agreeable to all in his charming manner of speaking, by a detestable order of Offa, the very powerful king of the Mercians, and through the criminal persuading of Offa's wife the queen Cynethryth, was robbed of his kingdom and life by the cutting off of his head.]

Here and in the Hereford *Passio*, the earliest *vita* of St Æthelberht available to us, Kynedritha's role is secondary to that of her husband. In this respect, the Worcester and Hereford sources are more in line with the *Anglo-Saxon Chronicle* and *The Annals of St Neots*. In each of these works only Offa is blamed for Æthelberht's death. Thus for history, rather than legend, the account in the St Albans *Vitae* can be of no use to us. Instead, the climax of the Hereford *Passio* reads sufficiently like lines 1931–44 of *Beowulf* to be worth comparing with these lines on its own.

CYNETHRYTH GETS THE BLAME

Few have followed John Earle in interpreting 'Thryth' as an allegorical reference to Cynethryth, Offa's queen.[78] Yet this is what I shall attempt to do, suggesting that the poet blamed her for the murder of St Æthelberht, king of East Anglia, in 794. The transition from Hygd to the wicked princess in *Beo* 1931–2 is swift, but perhaps because the poet wants us to see Hygd's foil as a queen of the same rank as herself. In their first impact, these and the following twelve lines deliver a story about a queen who brings about the death of one man only. Not until line 1944 does it become unambiguously clear that this is an allusion to a legend of Offa's tamed queen, one which the audience of *Beowulf* might be presumed to know (if we take Saxo's tale of Herminthrutha as an analogue). A traditional narrative of this kind is no doubt implicit in the epithet *fremu folces cwen* ('an excellent queen of the people', line 1932), which appears to anticipate Offa's success. To begin with, however, the audience might be forgiven for taking the poet's meaning differently. His construction is ambiguous, for the words *firen[e] ondrysne* can refer to one crime (acc. f. sg.) rather than several (acc. f. pl.); and the subjunctive mood of the verb *tealde* on lines 1936, if not of *stared* on line 1935, is not distinct from an indicative mood by which the poet's story would be regarded as specific rather than general. If we translate *Beo* 1931–43 before making the

---

[77] *The Chronicle of John of Worcester*, ed. Darlington and McGurk, trans. Bray and McGurk, 224–5 (my translation).
[78] Earle, *The Deeds of Beowulf*, pp. lxxxiv–lxxxvi.

readjustment required by *Beo* 1944–62, this vivid story may be rendered as follows:

Passion of mind an excellent queen of the people had, a monstrous crime she committed; no man but a permanent lord among the dear companions was brave enough to dare risk gazing upon her in the open light of day, but he counted deadly bonds, ones woven by hand, destined for him; swiftly, after that, once hands had seized him, a sword was appointed in such a way that the damascened blade was allowed to settle this, to perform his death-bale.

There are at least four parallels between *Beo* 1931–43 and the Hereford *Passio s. Æthelberhti*. In *Beo* 1943, the *cwen* acts upon a *ligetorn*; in the *Passio*, the *regina* Kynedritha finds *non modice stimulatio ire* in the young prince. In *Beo* 1935, the young man sees the queen *an dæges*, which is also the time when the king meets Kynedritha in Sutton St Michael. With the words *wælbende weotode handge-wripene* in *Beo* 1936–7, the man is bloodily bound with chains, just as Æthel-berhtus *uinculis artatur, grauissima afflictione affligitur* in the *Passio*. And in *Beo* 1938, the suitor's death comes about through a *mece* which has been *æfter mundgripe gepinged*, as if appointed for this purpose earlier after the executioner had taken the sword from its owner; in the *Passio*, the king is killed with his own sword, *proprio gladio*, which he has been persuaded to hand to Winberhtus.

    In these four ways, the poet of *Beowulf* appears to accuse Cynethryth of Æthelberht's murder, in language barely veiled by his legendary setting. How vehement his accusation is, and how close in memory to the murder of 794, may be seen in the outcry of 'the authenticating voice':

> Ne bið swylc cwenlic þeaw
> idese to efnanne,   þeah ðe hio ænlicu sy,
> þætte freoðuwebbe   feores onsæce
> æfter ligetorne   leofne mannan. (*Beo* 1940–3)

[No queenly virtue is it for a lady to carry out such a thing, though she be without peer, that she, a peace-weaver, in keeping with a pretended grief, should exact the life-blood from a beloved man.]

Once again, there is a parallel: between the implication of *freoðuwebbe*, that the man is killed under truce, and the statement in *The Annals of St Neots*, Æthelberht's native chronicle, that *sub pacis federe occisus est* ('he was killed under treaty of peace').[79] One can see why Earle based his late eighth-century dating of *Beowulf* on its Offa-passage, believing that the poet (in his view, Archbishop Hygeberht of Lichfield) meant to admonish Cynethryth of this crime against Æthelberht.[80] Chambers, but without canvassing this theory, turned the poet's denunciation into a caption for two plates illustrating the chastisement of

[79] *Annals of St Neots*, ed. Dumville and Lapidge, 39.
[80] Earle, *The Deeds of Beowulf*, pp. lxxxiv–lxxxvi.

Cynethryth on pages of the *Vita duorum Offarum*.[81] There are other present-day moralizations in *Beowulf*, but none so unusual as one against a queen's murder of a man protected by treaty.[82] For about thirteen lines, until the legendary setting is established on line 1944, the poet could just as well be blaming Cynethryth for the murder of Æthelberht.

It is unknown whether Cynethryth was truly involved in this crime. Kirby is right when he says that the Lives of St Æthelberht, with their focus on Cynethryth's plotting, 'do not inspire great confidence in their historical details'.[83] The author of the Hereford *Passio* is relatively close to the event, spells names authentically, and may know who was involved, as we have seen with Winberhtus. But his scene with Kynedritha and Alfthrutha has the air of fiction; the purpose of Offa's planned alliance with Æthelberht appears to have been military, if we accept the site of their meeting as being near Hereford, not far from the border with Wales; the betrothal with Ælfthryth, given her impression of Æthelberht not as her husband but as Offa's rival, seems added on; and although Kynedritha's speech to Offa is a catalyst for action, the author gives her a secondary role. Yet over time the part of Offa's queen in this story grew.[84] Roger of Wendover, who adapts a source close to the Hereford *Passio*, seems already to confuse Cynethryth with Cwenthryth, a daughter of King Cenwulf who was alleged to have killed her brother Cynehelm. By the same token his *Quendritha* now takes the leading role. Roger is followed by the author of the *Vitae duorum Offarum*, whose rhetoric and romantic fictions increase the villainy of *Quendrida* further, in order to expunge the complicity of Offa, patron of St Albans. In each case the pattern is accentuated and more anger about Æthelberht's murder is deflected from Offa towards his queen.

From the following evidence it can be argued that this deflection began in Offa's lifetime. Of course misogyny was a popular standby for the writers of saints' lives.[85] To find out if the treatment of Cynethryth in these sources has a basis in older fact, it is first necessary to gather what is known about her.[86] In the late eighth century, at the height of her career, Cynethryth was stylized as a devout Christian. She became abbess of Cookham in Berkshire, possibly after the deaths of Offa and Ecgfrith in 796, if she is the same Cynethryth who exchanged lands with Archbishop Æthelheard of Canterbury, in settlement of a long-running dispute, in a charter issued at *Clofesho* in 798.[87] Alcuin,

---

[81] Chambers, *Beowulf*, plates I (frontispiece) and VI.

[82] The present tense appears in the poet's comment on Beowulf's assault on the dragon, *ne bið swylc earges sið* ('such is not the expedition of a coward', line 2541); but the word *swylc*, rather than *þæt*, the focus is on Beowulf's courage rather than his unusual opponent. For the poet's comments in general, see Greenfield, 'The Authenticating Voice in *Beowulf*', 58.

[83] Kirby, *Earliest English Kings*, 177.

[84] Hayward, 'The Idea of Innocent Martyrdom', 141–4 and 241.

[85] Ibid. 237–58.

[86] Stafford, 'Political Women in Mercia', 37–42, esp. 40–1.

[87] S 1258 (BCS 291). See *EHD*, 508–10 (no. 79).

Charlemagne's courtier theologian, seems to have written her epistles of moral exhortation, although none survives. However, in a letter to her son Ecgfrith, possibly not long after his coronation in 787, Alcuin urges the young king to follow his parents' example, learning:

a patre auctoritatem, a matre pietatem; ab illo regere populum per iustitiam, ab ista conpati miseris per misericordiam; ab utroque christianae relegionis devotionem, orationum instantium, elymosinarum largitatem et totius vitae sobrietatem.[88]

[authority from your father, piety from your mother; from him, how to rule the people with justice, from her to have compassion with pity for the poor; from both, learn devotion to the Christian religion, perseverance in prayers, generosity in alms and sobriety in each aspect of your life.]

About twenty silver coins have been found with a woman's portrait and Cynethryth's name, which were probably minted from the late 780s to c.792.[89] C. E. Blunt believes that Offa, by ordering this issue, was imitating imperial Roman coins with empress figures.[90] In Cynethryth's features on some of her coins, Anna Gannon finds evidence of eastern Mediterranean facial styles, 'in the context of an ongoing dialogue with the Carolingian court'; also that the name of Cynethryth, carefully inscribed on her coins, may have mattered more to Offa's authority than the depiction of her countenance.[91] So it is clear that Offa involved Cynethryth in government, at least until Ecgfrith's coronation: she witnessed at least nineteen charters after Offa, not only at Tamworth and other centres but also at church councils, throughout his reign from 770 to 787.[92] It seems unlikely that she was excluded from the planning of their daughters' marriages, whether of Eadburh's (to Beorhtric of Wessex, 789) or Ælfflæd's (to Æthelred of Northumbria, 792).[93] Thereafter the evidence suggests that Offa was powerful enough without Cynethryth, who still enjoyed respect at court and privileges in land, some of which she kept after Offa's death.[94]

[88] *Epistolae*, ed. Dümmler, ii. 104–5 (no. 61). Translated also in Allott, *Alcuin of York*, 48 (no. 35). Allott dates the letter to 786/7. Bullough ('What has Ingeld to do with Lindisfarne?', 116) dates it to Offa's last years.

[89] For an image of one of these, D. M. Metcalf, 'Anglo-Saxon Coins I: Seventh to Ninth Centuries', in J. Campbell (ed.), *The Anglo-Saxons* (London, 1982), 62–3.

[90] Blunt, 'The Coinage of Offa', 46–7.

[91] Gannon, *Iconography of Early Anglo-Saxon Coinage*, 40–1, esp. 41.

[92] Stafford, 'Political Women in Mercia', 38. Keynes, *Atlas of Attestations*, table X (2); in 770, S 60 (BCS 204); in '758', S 104 (BCS 206); in 774, S 110 (BCS 213) and S 111 (BCS 214); in 777, S 112 (BCS 222); in 780, S 116 (BCS 236), S 117 (BCS 234) and S 118 (BCS 235); in 781, S 120 (BCS 239) and S 121 (BCS 240); in 784, S 122 (BCS 244); in 785, S 124 (BCS 245); in 786, S 125 (BCS 248); in 787, S 127 (BCS 251); in 788, S 129 (BCS 253); in 790, S 133 (BCS 259); in 765 × 792, S 140 (BCS 207); date unknown, S 50 (BCS 197).

[93] For the dates, Kirby, *Earliest English Kings*, 174 and 177.

[94] On the importance of royal women in Mercia in the eighth and ninth centuries, see Stafford, 'Political Women in Mercia', 37–41.

In another letter, however, Alcuin gives reason to suppose that Cynethryth could be blamed for misfortunes which petitioners shrank from charging to Offa. Writing an elegant but conventional letter of thanks and exhortation to the Mercian nun Hundruda (probably while he was back at York in 790 × 793), Alcuin asks for his greetings to be passed on to the queen. In Alcuin's words, Hundruda lives *in palatio regis* ('in the king's palace', thus at Tamworth), where she has the opportunity to approach the queen. In this letter Alcuin reveals a matter of concern:

Saluta, obsecro, domnam reginam ex mee parvitatis nomine. Scripsissem exhortarias illi litteras, si illi propter occupationes regis meos apices legere licuisset. Sciat tamen certissime me sibi quoque domino, quantum valeo, fidelem esse. Tamen gestum est de monasterio In-mercum sicut de illorum non speravi bonitate. Faciant de me, sicut illis placeat. Nam fides mea apud illos non violabitur; credem tanto meliores habere illos, quanto meliores sunt meritis et dignitate.[95]

[Greet, I beseech you, your lady the queen in the name of my humble self. I would have written her a letter of exhortation, if the king's business had permitted her to read it. Yet let her know most surely that I am loyal to her, as well as to your lord, for what I am worth. Something has been done, however, concerning the monastery 'in Mercia', something which I did not expect from their good selves. With me let them do as they please, for my loyalty towards them will not be injured; believing, as I do, that they are so much my betters in merit as in rank.]

In these lines Alcuin's protest is deflected from Offa to Cynethryth, yet at such an angle that his anger disappears. Turning on Cynethryth while citing no one by name, he implicates Offa only within a plural pronoun (*illi*, 'they'), which includes Cynethryth.[96] Alcuin also adds enough humility to neutralize his protest to all but the trained eye. Presumably Hundruda would know what had happened without being told. But Alcuin's wording is even less direct than usual, as may be seen in his use of the passive voice (*gestum est*). He is full of the honorifics, only hinting at stressful things, the knowledge of which is thus lost. His circumspection resembles the awe in which the poet of *Beowulf* holds Offa's princess, even while he attacks her: *þeah ðe hio ænlicu sy* ('though she be without peer', line 1943). Had he chosen, Alcuin could have penned an exhortation to the queen, whose piety followed her title. But he lets Hundruda believe, and through her the queen, that he is too displeased with Cynethryth to write to her. Whatever her part, he blames Cynethryth for an injustice which is Offa's.

It seems that this pattern of proxy incrimination might have been convenient also when Æthelberht died in 794. Only the non-Mercian sources (the *Anglo-Saxon Chronicle*, of Wessex, and the *Annals of St Neots*, of East Anglia)

---

[95] *Epistolae*, ed. Dümmler, ii. 105–6, at 106 (no. 62). My translation is based on that of Allott, *Alcuin of York*, 49 (no. 36). Dümmler dates this letter to *c*.786 × 796.

[96] Story, in *Carolingian Connections*, 181, suggests that Cynethryth had previously asked Alcuin for advice.

record this event with a clear attribution of blame to Offa (the second source later calling him *perfidus*).[97] The Mercian chronicles have perished in a contemporary form. Here, however, where the death of King Æthelberht is concerned, the Hereford *Passio* (and the related *Vitae* of this saint), the *Chronica* of John of Worcester and of Roger of Wendover and the *Vitae duorum Offarum* of St Albans, all from formerly Mercian areas, give Cynethryth some of the blame. In Mercia, therefore, it is possible that Cynethryth was blamed for the murder within a generation of its taking place.

BEO 1944–1962: IN PRAISE OF OFFA

No letters from this period survive in which Æthelberht's murder is cited, despite the fact that Offa, by killing an anointed king, had broken canon 12 of the decrees of the Council of the Legates in 786: *In necem regis nemo communicare audeat, quia christus Domini est* ('in the murder of a king let no man conspire, for this is the Lord's representative').[98] Offa himself chaired this council at which this canon along with the others was read out to all both in Latin and in English. Alcuin was then present, having been sent by King Ælfwald from Northumbria; yet Alcuin is silent about Æthelberht in his extant correspondence. He makes no allusion to Æthelberht, for example, in a letter to two East Anglian men even when Offa and Ecgfrith were safely dead. Alcuin wrote to the bishops of East Anglia in *c.*797, Alhheard of Elmham and Tidfrith of Dunwich, without alluding to the murder of their king three or four years earlier.[99] Perhaps his and other men's silence may be attributed to the line against slandering a king which precedes the clause on regicide in the same canon 12.[100] That Alcuin feared Offa is clear from an anxious letter to a Mercian priest named Beornwine in which he is keen to underline his loyalty.[101] Alcuin knew of Offa's purges in his last years.[102] Alcuin also knew of exiles such as Eadberht Præn and Ecgberht, son of King Ealhmund of Kent. So is not surprising that his letter to Offa in 796, probably not long after Charlemagne replied to Offa about Anglo-Frankish trade, reads like a panegyric.[103] In the surviving correspondence, neither Charlemagne nor Alcuin connects Offa with Æthelberht, nor could Mercian noblemen have

---

[97] *ASC* A, *s.a.* 792 [794] (p. 40). *Annals of St Neots*, ed. Dumville and Lapidge, 39.
[98] *Epistolae*, ed. Dümmler, ii. 19–29, at 24. See *EHD*, 836–40 (no. 191), and Cubitt, *Anglo-Saxon Church Councils*, 164–6.
[99] *Epistolae*, ed. Dümmler, ii. 459–60 (no. 301).
[100] Ibid. ii. 24: 'Nullus regi detrahat, dicente Salamone: "in ore tuo ne detraxeris regi, et in corde tuo ne male dixeris principi, quia aves caeli portant illud, et qui habet pennas annunciabit verbum".'
[101] Ibid. 124–5 (no. 82); see Allott, *Alcuin of York*, 51 (no. 39). Allott dates the letter to 790.
[102] *Epistolae*, ed. Dümmler, ii. 178–80, at 179 (no. 122). Dumville, 'The Ætheling', 19–20. Kirby, *Earliest English Kings*, 176–7.
[103] *Epistolae*, ed. Dümmler, ii. 146–8 (no. 101), 144–6 (no. 100).

been advised to do so if they lived in Mercia from 794 to 796. In these years the country lived in fear of its king. This may be the implication in *Beowulf*, in the words *ealodrincende oþer sædan* ('drinking ale, men told another story', line 1945).

To paraphrase Offa of Angeln in this passage once more, he is *geongum cempan*, *æðelum diore* ('a young brave high-born champion', lines 1948–9); under his benign influence the queen stops her crimes and begins the life for which she was destined (*lifgesceafta lifigende breac*, line 1953); the love between her and Offa, a *hæleþa brego* ('chieftain of heroes', line 1954), is something exalted (*heahlufan*, line 1954); and Offa is *ealles moncynnes . . . þæs selestan bi sæm tweonum* ('the best of all mankind between the seas', lines 1954–5). He is widely honoured, *garcene man* ('a spear-keen man', line 1958) who rules wisely and begets Eomer as an heir. In this context the opening words *mine gefræge* ('according to what I have heard', line 1955) might reveal knowledge of more substantial eulogies. This poet's other formulae are typical of heroic eulogy in verse. But they also resemble some words of Alcuin, in a confident letter that he wrote to Offa from Francia apparently in a happier time, probably in 787–8 not too long after Ecgfrith's coronation:

Et valde mihi placet, quod tantam habetis intentionem lectionis, ut lumen sapientiae luceat in regno vestro, quod multus modo extinguitur in locis. Vos estis decus Brittaniae, tuba praedicationis, gladius contra hostes, scutum contra inimicos. Habete Deum semper ante oculos, facite iustitiam, amate misericordiam, quia, qui ignoscit, ignoscitur ei. Discite et diligite mandata Dei Christi, ut benedictio illius in omni bonitate et prosper-itate te tuosque nepotes consequatur in aeternum. Divina te tuumque regnum caelesti benedictione comitetur gratia, Domine excellentissime.[104]

[And it pleases me very much that you [pl.] have so great a programme for education that the light of wisdom that is now extinguished in many places may shine in your [pl.] kingdom. You [pl.] are the splendour of Britain, a trumpet of Christian teaching, a sword against enemies, a shield against foes. Always have [pl.] God before your eyes, do justice, love mercy; for whosoever knows not mercy, is unknown by it. Learn and teach the commands of Christ our God, that his blessing may follow you [sg.] and your descend-ants in all goodness and prosperity for all eternity. May the divine grace accompany you [sg.] and your [sg.] kingdom with a heavenly blessing, O most excellent lord.]

Military success is a component both of Alcuin's eulogy and in the praise of Offa of Angeln contained in *Beo* 1954–62. From Alcuin's words it also appears that in the late 780s Offa of Mercia wished to be known as a patron of learning, just like Charlemagne.[105] Alcuin sent Offa one of his students and planned to visit Offa himself.[106] That there was a library at Tamworth by 793 is clear from another

---

[104] *Epistolae*, ed. Dümmler, ii. 107 (no. 64). See Allott, *Alcuin of York*, 53–4 (no. 41). Dümmler's date for this letter is 787 × 796; Bullough's ('What has Ingeld to do with Lindisfarne?', 116), in Offa's last years.

[105] See McKitterick, *The Frankish Kingdoms under the Carolingians*, 145–52; *The Carolingians and the Written Word*, 165–78 and 211–44.

[106] *Epistolae*, ed. Dümmler, ii. 107.

letter to Offa in which Alcuin refers the king to his copy of Bede's *Historia ecclesiastica*.[107] There evidence of other sorts, archaeological, palaeographical, and numismatic, to show that Offa and his subjects had the wealth from 786 to 790 to make Mercian learning a rival to that of the cathedral school in Canterbury.[108] The designs on his coinage, 'the richly endowed legacy of a visually alert society', have recently been been praised as superior to those of Charlemagne, with whom Offa was also in competition.[109] Offa's triple triumph of 786–7 (the Council of the Legates, the new archdiocese at Lichfield, and Ecgfrith's coronation), may have given Alcuin a genuine reason to praise him. So it can be no coincidence that the formulation in *Beo* 1959–60, in which Offa of Angeln *wisdome heold eðel sinne* ('guarded his inherited land with wisdom'), echoes Alcuin's praise of Offa with respect to *lumen sapientiae in vestro regno* ('the light of wisdom in your kingdom').[110]

Offa's son Eomer in *Beowulf* suggests Ecgfrith, Offa's short-lived heir who was nonetheless the key to most of his actions: to the dogged consolidation of power in Mercia, the Welsh marches, East Anglia, Sussex, and Kent in the years leading up to 785; to his joyful welcome for the papal legates and chairing of their meeting in 786; to his creation of a Mercian archdiocese at Lichfield in the same year; to the coronation of Ecgfrith by Hygeberht, the new archbishop, at Lichfield in 787; to Offa's dynastic alliances with the major kingdoms north and south, with Beorhtric of Wessex in 789 and Æthelred of Northumbria in 792; to his liquidation of the rivals to Ecgfrith's succession; lastly, to the murder of King Æthelberht of East Anglia in 794, whom Offa probably saw as a threat to Ecgfrith.[111] How the East Angles avenged their king will become clear at the end of the following chapter.

CONCLUSION

This chapter begins with Offa of Angeln, first considering his place in *Beo* 1925–61 in which he tames a princess who kills all her suitors. These lines are usually known as the 'Thryth digression' after the princess, whom most critics still call 'Thryth' or 'Modthryth' on the basis of a misreading which can be

[107] P. Lehmann, 'Ein neuer Alchvinebrief', *Holländische Reisefrüchte I–III*, Sitzungsberichte der Bayerischen Akademie der Wissenschaften, Philosophisch-philologisch-historische Klasse, 13 (Munich, 1920), 29–34, esp. 32 (date: 790 × 793).

[108] See M. P. Brown, 'Mercian Manuscripts? The "Tiberius" Group and its Historical Context', in Brown and Farr (eds.), *Mercia*, 278–90. See also Wormald, 'The Age of Offa and Alcuin', 101–26, at 110–17, 122, 125. Russo, *Town Origins and Development in Early England*, 203–4. Blunt, 'The Coinage of Offa', 39–62. Stewart, 'Anglo-Saxon Gold Coins', 143–55. Hodges, *The Anglo-Saxon Achievement*, 126–32.

[109] Gannon, *Iconography of Early Anglo-Saxon Coinage*, 186–93, esp. 193.

[110] *Epistolae*, ed. Dümmler, ii. 107.

[111] Kirby, *Earliest English Kings*, 163–77.

defended on moral grounds. Yet the words *modþryþe wæg* (line 1931) may be read as the description of a new woman's mental state. This reading asks us to accept that the poet left Offa's princess unnamed and used her allegorically in order to blame Cynethryth, the queen of Offa of Mercia, for the murder of King Æthelberht of East Anglia. The risk of such a personal reference, if John Earle's old idea is true, makes it unlikely that *Beowulf* was written in Offa's reign or in that of his son. No one, at least, has sought to test lines 1925–62 as an expression of Offa's patronage. In short, we can leave that idea behind us. Instead, I suggest that the poet of *Beowulf* places King Offa of Angeln before Kings Hygelac and Beowulf as the first in a sequence of great Mercian kings: Offa, Cenwulf, Beornwulf—and Wiglaf?

9

Hygelac and Beowulf: Cenwulf and Beornwulf

This chapter offers nine parallels between Hygelac and Beowulf in *Beowulf* and the reigns of Cenwulf and Beornwulf in Mercian history. These parallels will complement Chapters 3–7, in which I argue that *Beowulf* was composed in the minster of Breedon on the Hill in Leicestershire; and build on Chapter 8, in which I support John Earle's suggestion that Cynethryth's alleged role in the death of (St) Æthelberht, king of East Anglia, in 794 was the poet's basis for his tale of Offa's queen in *Beo* 1925–61. Much of the textual basis in *Beowulf* for its following parallels in Mercian history has been discussed in earlier chapters. From the outset it has been my premiss that Wiglaf's lieutenancy to Beowulf is comparable with a dynastic sequence from Beornwulf to Wiglaf at an unstable moment in Mercian history. Chapter 2 seeks to define the poet's innovations to heroic legend, establishing that he probably moves Beowulf into Hrothgar's court, out of Hrothulf's, and connects him with Hygelac, all so that he may become a king. Chapter 4 attempts to show how the poet prepares his champion archetype for a kingship of his own, by creating a new rivalry between him and Ingeld over the hand of Freawaru; on the basis of three episodic parallels with Vergil's *Aeneid*, given in Chapter 3, I suggest on this basis that the poet authenticates Beowulf's new juxtaposition with Ingeld by recasting Vergil's initial tale of Aeneas, Turnus, and Lavinia in *Aeneid* VII and XI. In Chapter 7, where I attempt to show that the poet knew tales from Scandinavian mythology, I conclude that he uses three of them to foreground the moral question of Beowulf's salvation as a heathen. In short, it can be said that the poet works hard to separate Beowulf from Hrothulf, make him King Ingeld's rival and King Hrothgar's pupil, then turn him into a king himself, all while keeping an eye on the question of his spiritual suitability for this role. Politically these changes amount to a programme, particularly in relation to the Geatish part of *Beowulf*, in which the poet places Offa of Angeln before Hygelac, before King Beowulf, before the young Wiglaf. If we match Offa with the Mercian Offa (757–96), Wiglaf with the Mercian Wiglaf (827–39), as their names invite, then we may as well see how far Hygelac and Beowulf work as an allegory for Kings Cenwulf and Beornwulf in the intervening history of Mercia (796–826).

BEOWULF AS MERCIAN ALLEGORY: NINE MORE PARALLELS

After the poet cites murder by a princess who became the queen of Offa of Angeln, he introduces King Hygelac. Piecing together allusions in the remainder of *Beowulf*, we learn that Hygelac saves the Geatish kingdom from the Swedes, but then appears to reward his new men, one of whom becomes his son-in-law, with the lands of older retainers. Beowulf, the sister's son of Hygelac and also his close friend, is eventually endowed with land and hearth, though he is a lesser kinsman with a weak claim to the throne. Later Hygelac dies in pursuit of treasure: this is the only story of Hygelac we can call traditional. In the sequel, Beowulf avenges Hygelac and becomes regent to his son. When Heardred's reign fails, Beowulf is made king by Onela. He restores the robbed land to its rightful owners, but then dies unmarried and without an heir, in pursuit of treasure. The following offers nine ways in which this Geatish history of *Beowulf* could be said to reflect the progress of Cenwulf and Beornwulf in the thirty years after Offa's death in 796.

Hygelac saves his people, but robs them of land

Hygelac's entry into the history of *Beowulf* is not related until near the end of this poem, when after Beowulf's death the Geatish Messenger assesses future challenges by delving into the Geatish past. In this he presents Hygelac's death in Frisia, of which we have heard some three times already, as a failure to make good on the promise of his youth: *nalles frætwe geaf ealdor dugoðe* ('not at all did the chief give treasures to his retinue', lines 2919–20). In particular, the Messenger repeats the word *frætwe* in order to show the omens of Hygelac's prodigality further back in time.[1] At first the situation is dire, with the Geatish army besieged in *Hrefnawudu* ('Ravens' Wood', line 2925). King Hæthcyn is dead, Hygelac's elder brother, having failed to kidnap the Swedish queen; now the last remnants of his army spend the night listening to Ongentheow, the lady's husband:

> 'wean oft gehet
> earmre teohhe   ondlonge niht,
> cwæð, he on mergenne   meces ecgum
> getan wolde,   sume on gealgtreowum
> [fuglum] to gamene.' (*Beo* 2937–41)

[he often promised woe to the wretched company the livelong night, said he would cut them open with the edges of a sword in the morning, some on gallows-trees as fun [for the birds].][2]

---

[1] *Beowulf*, ed. Mitchell and Robinson, 150.
[2] On OE *getan* and human sacrifice see North, *Heathen Gods*, 116–17 and 140–2.

However, this dreadful moment is a turning point for the Geats:

> 'Frofor eft gelamp
> sarigmodum   somod ærdæge
> syððan hie Hygelaces   horn ond byman
> gealdor ongeaton   þa se goda com
> leoda dugoðe   on last faran.' (*Beo* 2941–5)

[Comfort once more befell those men of grieving heart gathered in the early day, when they made out the refrain of Hygelac's horn and trumpets, when that man of generosity came marching up in the rear of the company of men.]

Deadly charisma is the quality implicit in the poet's equation of Hygelac's trumpets with *gealdor*, probably referring to drums here but primarily 'a heathen spell' or 'charm'. After revealing Hygelac's trumpeted entrance into history in the relief of the Geats, the savage duel between Hygelac's champions Wulf and Eofor and the Swedish terror Ongentheow and finally Hygelac's triumphal homecoming, the Geatish Messenger tells his people, here reusing the word *frætwe*, that Eofor presents Ongentheow's weapons and armour to Hygelac. This homage the young king finds liberating:

> 'He (ðæm) frætwum feng   ond him fægre gehet
> leana (mid) leodum   ond gelæste swa,
> geald þone guðræs   Geata dryhten
> Hreðles eafora,   þa he to ham becom,
> Iofore ond Wulfe   mid ofermaðmum,
> sealde hiora gehwæðrum   hund þusenda
> landes ond locenra beaga   —ne ðorfte him ða lean oðwitan
> mon on middangearde   syðða[n] hie ða mærða geslogon—
> ond ða Iofore forgeaf   angan dohtor
> hamweorðunge,   hyldo to wedde.' (*Beo* 2989–98)

['He received those treasures and in fair language promised them rewards among his people and carried it out in this way: the lord of Geats, Hrethel's offspring, when he came to his home-seat, paid Eofor and Wulf for that battle-charge with an excess of treasure, gave each of them 120,000 in land and linked rings—there needed no one in the middle world begrudge them that reward, since they had won those glories by fighting for them—and then he gave Eofor his only daughter as an ennobler of his estate, as a pledge of his loyalty.']

This passage contains the third and final group of hypermetric lines in *Beowulf*. It seems unwise to reject it as an anomaly, a later interpolation, as Lapidge does, especially since he does not treat the first of the two earlier examples this way (at lines 1163–8 and 1705–7).[3] Not only the metre here, but also the climactic position of this passage before the Messenger's grand summation on lines 2999–3027, should broadcast Hygelac's act as significant. As Mitchell and

---

[3] Lapidge, 'The Archetype of *Beowulf*', 37–8.

Robinson note, there is an ambiguity in the dative pronoun *him* on line 2995 ('him' or 'them'?), one which might lessen Hygelac's blame.[4] Yet either way the litotes points to an excess for which Hygelac will be blamed.

If we look at Hygelac's generosity after the victory against Ongentheow, we find that the 'Wolf'-'Boar' names of Hygelac's beneficiaries show them to be brutes of no dynastic account. Yet they receive a quantity of land and treasure which is awesome, *ofermaðmas* as the poet says (line 2983: a hapax legomenon). With this expression the poet shows Hygelac's generosity going too far. It becomes prodigality to some, meanness to others, a combination for which we have seen Hugleikr, Hygelac's Norse analogue, lavishly condemned in Saxo's *Gesta Danorum* and Snorri's *Ynglinga saga*.[5] In *Beowulf* it seems that Hygelac's prodigality must be replenished by ever more risky ventures abroad, until *for wlenco* (line 1206), rather like his brother's *for onmedlan* (line 2926), he leads the Geatish army into a disaster. His first act as ruler sets the acquisitive pattern for his reign. The estates which he gives Wulf and Eofor are so vast, the poet's hint of resentment so strong, that it looks as if he funds his generosity with the wealth of older retainers. As I have tried to show in Chapter 2, Weohstan comes from Geatland, but is known as a resident in Sweden, with his son apparently born there; and yet he seems to die on a Geatish estate which is his and which Beowulf earns merit for restoring to Wiglaf. In the light of all this, we can see Weohstan as one of Hygelac's early victims. It is Weohstan's dispossession that might explain why he becomes an enemy to Heardred and why his son Wiglaf appears to be born in Sweden.

In Mercian history we see a similar pattern. On his accession Cenwulf likewise saved his people from crisis but then despoiled some of them of lands. First, when Cenwulf succeeded on Ecgfrith's death in 796 he found Wessex estranged, East Anglia seceding, the Welsh border open, and Kent fallen into the hands of Eadberht Præn, an apostate priest formerly exiled in Francia.[6] However, Cenwulf's response was swift. He seems to have crushed the East Angles, who had lost their king, St Æthelberht, to Offa two years before. The rebellion of East Anglia is implicit in the fact that in 796 a moneyer from this kingdom named LUL issued a new series for a King 'Eadwald', a short issue which he then replaced with another for King Cenwulf a year later.[7] After this, while Cenwulf waited for Pope Leo III to approve an invasion of Kent, he campaigned in Wales,

---

[4] *Beowulf*, ed. Mitchell and Robinson, 154: 'Wulf and Eofor are beyond reproach in accepting the reward since they had successfully carried out their mission; Hygelac is beyond reproach in conferring it since it is fitting for a king to reward loyal service by his subjects. It is not clear which meaning the poet intends.'

[5] See Ch. 2. *Gesta Danorum*, ed. Olrik and Ræder, 154–5 (vi. v. 11–13). *Heimskringla I*, ed. Bjarni, 42–3 (*Ynglinga saga*, ch. 22). *Beowulf and its Analogues*, trans. Garmonsway, Simpson, and Ellis Davidson, 114–15.

[6] Kirby, *Earliest English Kings*, 178–9.

[7] Blunt, 'The Coinage of Offa', 47–50, at 50. Mercia had no mints of her own at this time: Story, *Carolingian Connections*, 175.

killing King Caradog of Gwynedd in 798.[8] Later that year he marched into
Canterbury. Not quite as hard as Hygelac with Ongentheow, Cenwulf had
Eadberht captured, blinded, mutilated, and taken to Winchcombe in chains.

Cenwulf's Kentish campaign in particular brought him and his family
personal wealth as well as added political power. In Kent, there was a history of
minsters in royal ownership since the seventh century. Offa had seized Kentish
lands including some minsters, possibly Minster-in-Thanet and Lyminge; and
after c.800 these places continued to be ruled by two former beneficiaries of Offa,
Abbess Selethryth and her brother Ealdberht, in collusion with Cenwulf.[9] But
Cenwulf went further and by 801 he had put his brother Cuthred on the Kentish
throne; Cunred, who became abbot of St Augustine's in Canterbury in 802 (died
823), was another kinsman of Cenwulf;[10] and Keynes suggests that in a charter of
811 two other abbesses, Cwoenburg and Seleburg, may have 'both represented
further Mercian interests in Kent'.[11] In these cases, and perhaps in others of
which records have not survived, it appears that Cenwulf built on Offa's example
by acquiring lands which belonged to the church in Canterbury.

A year after Cenwulf's accession, a letter from Alcuin reveals his true position,
that he had started without money.[12] *Illum semper habeas in mente*, wrote Alcuin
to Cenwulf in 797, *qui te egenum exaltavit et posuit super principes populi sui
rectorem* ('Always have him in mind who raised you up from poverty and made
you ruler over the princes of his people').[13] Whether or not Alcuin alludes to Offa
as Cenwulf's erstwhile patron, his words echo those of Ps. 122; 7–8, in which it is
the Lord who raises the poor man from the earth to place him among the princes
of his people.[14] If this is the same Cenwulf who witnessed Offa's grant to
St Peter's, Westminster, in 785, he was probably in his late twenties when he
followed the short-lived Ecgfrith on the throne.[15] Cenwulf's cure for his poverty
was to enlarge the house at Winchcombe, which Offa had founded as a convent
of nuns in 787, with a community of monks. Later he transformed Offa's minster
into his own family fortress with an archive under the control of his daughter
Cwenthryth.[16]

What Kentish estates Cenwulf acquired he later seems to have used partly as
currency in transactions with Wulfred, the new archbishop of Canterbury

---

[8] Kirby, *Earliest English Kings*, 187. T. M. Charles-Edwards, 'Wales and Mercia, 613–918', in
Brown and Farr (eds.), *Mercia*, 89–105, esp. 100.

[9] Brooks, *Early History of the Church of Canterbury*, 111–15 and 183–5. Keynes, 'The Control
of Kent in the Ninth Century', 117.

[10] Brooks, *Early History of the Church of Canterbury*, 184. Yorke, *Kings and Kingdoms*, 118.

[11] S 168 (BCS 335). Keynes, 'The Control of Kent in the Ninth Century', 117.

[12] Kirby, *Earliest English Kings*, 177.

[13] *Epistolae*, ed. Dümmler, ii. 181 (no. 123).

[14] '[7] Suscitans a terra inopem, Et de stercore erigens pauperem: [8] Ut collocet eum cum
principibus, Cum principibus populi sui.'

[15] In fifth place, *minister*, S 124 (BCS 245).

[16] Levison, *England and the Continent in the Eighth Century*, 249–52.

S:	153	155	106	1260	1187	40	161	41	163
BCS:	289	293	201	308	313	322	321	318	326
Archive:	CCC	CCC	CCC	Wor	Wor	CCC	CCC	CCC	CCC
Place of issue:	*?Clof*	*Tam*	*Chel*	*Clof*	*Aclea*	*Aclea*	*Aclea*		*Tam*
Year:	798	799	c.800	803	804	805	805	805x7	808
ROYALS									
Cenwulf	+	+	+	+	+	+	+	+	+
Ælfthryth									+
ARCHBISHOPS OF CANTERBURY									
Æthelheard	1	2	1	1	1				
Wulfred							*ben*	1 *el*	1
BISHOPS OF LEICESTER									
Unwona	4	3	2						
Werenberht				3	3	2	2	3	
RELEVANT EALDORMEN									
Brorda		1 *pri*	1 *pri*						
Cynehelm	11	4 *pri*	1 *dux*	4 *dux*	4 *dux*	3 *dux*	1 *dux*		4 *dux*
Æthelmund	5 *dux*	3 *dux*	2						
Beornnoth	9 *dux*	9 *dux*	10	2 *pri*	2 *dux*	2 *dux*	6 *dux*		2 *dux*
Wigberht	4 *dux*	4 *dux*							
Wigheard				6 *p'*	6 *dux*	9 *dux*	9 *dux*		

Figure 6. Elevation of Beornnoth (798–808)

Source: Keynes, *Atlas of Attestations*, XIII, XVII.

in 805.[17] Wulfred had his own territorial policy; and after the likely intercession of the papal and imperial envoys who accompanied Eardwulf back to Northumbria in 808, from 809 to about 815, Wulfred exchanged lands with Cenwulf in order to consolidate and enlarge the estates belonging to Canterbury.[18] Wulfred was wealthy, spending a total of 590 mancuses buying the estates that eventually went to Christ Church Canterbury.[19] Seven charters of this kind survive between

[17] Brooks, *Early History of the Church of Canterbury*, 132–42.
[18] Story, *Carolingian Connections*, 203. Kirby, *Earliest English Kings*, 186–7. Brooks, *Early History of the Church of Canterbury*, 155–60.
[19] Keynes, 'The Control of Kent in the Ninth Century', 112 and 114.

him and Cenwulf; and there are others in which Wulfred purchases adjoining estates so as to enlarge the Canterbury endowments.[20] In return, Cenwulf got lands from Archbishop Wulfred with which to increase his territory nearer to Winchcombe.

Throughout this period Cenwulf acquired these and other church possessions for himself and members of his family.[21] Susan Kelly has argued that Cenwulf obtained 'an important Mercian royal minster in the Abingdon area', possibly for a daughter of his named Burhhild, if not also for his daughter Abbess Cwenthryth as well.[22] A 'Burgenhylda' is presented as Cenwulf's daughter in St Kenelm's *Vita et miracula*;[23] and a 'Burgenhilde' appears in that role also in an inspeximus charter issued for the abbot of Abingdon by King Edward III.[24] In the inspeximus, whose name-list seems based on a separate and genuine list of Cenwulf's family members, Cenwulf gives the monks of Abingdon 15 hides at Culham and a pasture at Otney, at the request of *Kenefwwit*' and *Burgenhilde*.[25] Susan Kelly believes that these forms represent the names of Cwenthryth and Burhhild, daughters of Cenwulf.[26] Some 8 miles south of Culham, near Hagborne, is a certain *Burgildetreow* ('Burhhild's tree') in a charter of *c*.891.[27] This name would not only appear to confirm the story about Burhhild's holdings there, but would also show how large they were. Thus Abingdon was probably Cenwulf's propietary monastery at this time. Rethhun, abbot of Abingdon at the start of the ninth century, was appointed bishop of Leicester in 814 while Werenberht, the previous bishop, was still in post (803–14). In the same year he signed two of Cenwulf's diplomas, the second as the only abbot (S 173, 177).[28] To this extent Rethhun was Cenwulf's man, whereas Werenberht, the bishop he replaced, has a name which Brooks identifies with the Middle Saxon family of Cenwulf's enemy, Archbishop Wulfred.[29]

---

[20] Keynes, 'The Control of Kent in the Ninth Century', 114: S 164 (BCS 328), 168 (335), 169 (341), 170 (340), 176 (344), 177 (348), 178 (353). Brooks, *Early History of the Church of Canterbury*, 135.

[21] Cubitt, *Anglo-Saxon Church Councils*, 224–9, at 226; and Kelly (ed.), *Charters of Abingdon Abbey, Part I*, p. cciv.

[22] *Charters of Abingdon Abbey, Part I*, ed. Kelly, p. ccvi.

[23] Subsequently in *Ricardi de Cirencestria Speculum historiale*, ed. Mayor, i. 295 (ch. lxv) and ii. 24 (iii. 2): 'Kenulphus, Kenelmus, Ceolwlphus'.

[24] On 3 June 1336. *Charters of Abingdon Abbey, Part I*, ed. Kelly, 45–9, at 46 (no. 10). See also *Chronicon monasterii de Abingdon*, ed. Stevenson, i. 18–20 (ch. 21).

[25] *Charters of Abingdon Abbey, Part I*, ed. Kelly, 45 (no. 10). Also discussed in Gelling, *The Early Charters of the Thames Valley*, 125–6 (no. 263).

[26] *Charters of Abingdon Abbey, Part I*, ed. Kelly, 46. Gelling (*The Early Charters of the Thames Valley*, 126) presumes that the scribe miscopied *Coensuið* or a similar form.

[27] S 354 (BCS 565), in which King Alfred gets this and other land from Bishop Denewulf of Winchester, in exchange for two estates in Wiltshire and Hampshire. *Vita et miracula s. Kenelmi*, ed. Love, 54–5.

[28] *Charters of Abingdon Abbey, Part I*, ed. Kelly, pp. cciv–ccvi, esp. ccv.

[29] Brooks, *Early History of the Church of Canterbury*, 141–2. Rethhun may show embarrassment in a profession of loyalty to Wulfred in *c*.816: 'quando alicujus provinciæ episcopus aut de sæculo migraret. aut alia qualicumque conditione Deus voluisset ut eo vivente ad illam parochiam novus institueretur episcopus' (BCS 355).

These half-forgotten land deals around Abingdon were small in comparison with Cenwulf's attempts on Glastonbury in Somerset. Two documents in series, allegedly of 798–9 (S 152), claim that Cenwulf settled this huge estate on his son Cynehelm. These are two charters preserved by William of Malmesbury in his *De antiquitate Glastonie ecclesie*, written in the late 1120s, in a Latin translation by him of versions which he says he found in the vernacular.[30] If William's text is genuine, it 'must be at least two removes from the original'.[31] One charter is a privilege allegedly of Pope Leo III in 798, confirming Glastonbury *Kinelmo Regi et eius ministris et cognatis et successoribus* ('to King Cynehelm, his thegns, kinsmen, and successors'), all *octingentas hidas* ('800 hides').[32] The other is an alleged confirmation of this privilege in 799 by Cenwulf, his two archbishops, nine bishops, thirteen abbots, six *principes*, and last, but not least, Abbess Cynethryth and her *congnatae* ('dearest kin'), Æthelburh and Ælfflæd, probably her daughters (emended from *Etheburh* and *Celfred*). The two twelfth-century *vitae* of St Kenelm tell us that 'Kenelm' or Cynehelm was the name of Cenwulf's son.[33] As Leo's privilege stands, however, it is open to suspicion, partly through some evidence of confusion, partly because of the 800 hides, which are more or less equal to Glastonbury's endowment in the Domesday Book.[34] Yet Levison considered this charter to be based on an authentic papal privilege.[35] Lesley Abrams also, though she questions the validity of both documents, treats Cenwulf's interest in Glastonbury as genuine.[36] Mercian kings were interested in ecclesiastical estates in this part of Wessex, especially in Glastonbury in Somerset, even before Offa acquired the minster at Bath at the Council of Brentford in 781.[37] In this alleged privilege of Pope Leo in 798, as well as in Cenwulf's confirmation following, it is said that Leo confirmed Glastonbury to Ecgfrith, son of Offa, in agreement with King Beorhtric of Wessex and the Mercian magnates and then that this was later confirmed in writing for Cenwulf of Mercia.[38] This claim tells us that Cenwulf was close to Offa and Ecgfrith during their reigns (how close, we shall see on pp. 268–70 below). Now, with

---

[30] S 152 (BCS (284) 285). *The Early History of Glastonbury*, ed. and trans. Scott, 106–10, esp. 107 (ch. 49). Levison, *England and the Continent in the Eighth Century*, 32 and 250–1. Abrams, *Anglo-Saxon Glastonbury*, 336.

[31] Cubitt, *Anglo-Saxon Church Councils*, 277.

[32] *The Early History of Glastonbury*, ed. and trans. Scott, 108–9 (ch. 50).

[33] *Vita et miracula s. Kenelmi*, ed. Love, pp. cxxxvi–cxxxviii.

[34] Cubitt, *Anglo-Saxon Church Councils*, 267 and 276–7. Abrams, *Anglo-Saxon Glastonbury*, 336. Hayward considers both the privilege and confirmation to be later forgeries produced in Glastonbury. See his 'The Idea of Innocent Martyrdom', 150.

[35] Levison, *England and the Continent in the Eighth Century*, 32.

[36] Abrams, *Anglo-Saxon Glastonbury*, 336.

[37] S 265 (BCS 327). Yorke, *Wessex in the Early Middle Ages*, 61–4, at 63. Sims-Williams, *Religion and Literature*, 159–61.

[38] *The Early History of Glastonbury*, ed. and trans. Scott, 109: 'cum iudicio et licencia Brithrici regis et cum licencis et testimonio Merciorum episcoporum et principum et sicut postea Kenulfo regi Merciorum omnes ille terre scripto confirmate sunt.'

both men dead, Cenwulf probably used a Mercian translation of a papal privilege and a confirmation to wrest Glastonbury from Cynethryth, Offa's widow.[39] If Heather Edwards is right, and William of Malmesbury found the Old English exemplar not at Glastonbury, but in Winchcombe, Cenwulf kept this confirmation in Cwenthryth's archive.[40] For Cenwulf, as for other kings, asset-stripping was a family business.

Yet Archbishop Wulfred took exception to Cenwulf's intervention in Kent even while he and the king exchanged lands. Wulfred's was the reaction on which I suggest the *Beowulf*-poet based his hypermetric lines on Hygelac's excessive land-gifts and implied despoliations in lines 2993–6. There had always been grounds for friction between Cenwulf and Wulfred: in 797, while Wulfred was still a deacon in Canterbury, Cenwulf had petitioned Pope Leo to establish London, not Canterbury, as the metropolitan see of southern England;[41] in 798 Cenwulf refounded the double monastery of Winchcombe and in *c*.811 he worked to get the papal privilege which ensured his and Cwenthryth's rights to this minster; the witness-list includes Cynehelm, his last appearance.[42] Cenwulf would doubtless have angered Wulfred if he asked him to anoint Cynehelm as a king of Kent in his father's lifetime, as Offa may have intended with Ecgfrith.[43] Canon 12 of the Council of the Legates in 786 condemns the abuse of anointed kingship as if this were already established.[44] If Cenwulf was grooming Cynehelm for the Kentish kingship, much of his discord with Wulfred is explained.

Alcuin may describe Cynehelm as a tyrant in a letter to Abbess Æthelburh of Fladbury, who was probably King Offa's daughter. In this letter he alludes to *reges vobiscum* who *tyranni facti sunt, non rectores; nec ut olim reges a regendo, sed a rapiendo dicuntur*.[45] One of these kings is no doubt Cenwulf; the other is identified by Ernst Dümmler with King Eardwulf of Northumbria (796–806, 809–10). Cenwulf's robbing of Æthelburh's estates could be nowhere better illustrated than in the Glastonbury document which we have seen, in which Abbess Cynethryth appears to refer to her daughters Æthelburh and Ælfflæd. If Cenwulf had recently acquired Glastonbury, however, in which Æthelburh had

---

[39] Cubitt, *Anglo-Saxon Church Councils*, 227. See Finberg, *The Early Charters of Wessex*, 120–1 (nos. 399 and 400).

[40] Edwards, *The Charters of the Early West Saxon Kingdoms*, 52–5.

[41] *Councils and Ecclesiastical Documents*, ed. Haddan and Stubbs, iii. 521–3. *Epistolae*, ed. Dümmler, ii. 187–9 (no. 127). See *EHD*, 861–2 (no. 205).

[42] Levison, *England and the Continent in the Eighth Century*, 249–59, esp. 257.

[43] Kirby, *Earliest English Kings*, 156, 172–3, and 188–9. For a suggestion that Offa wanted Bertha, Charlemagne's daughter, for his son so that both could rule Kent, see Story, *Carolingian Connections*, 186.

[44] *Epistolae*, ed. Dümmler, ii. 19–29, at 24. Hayward, 'The Idea of Innocent Martyrdom', 274.

[45] *Epistolae*, ed. Dümmler, ii. 458 (no. 300: 'Eugenia', *s.a.* 797 × 804): 'the kings where you are' who 'have become tyrants, not rulers; nor are they once called kings by ruling, but rather by robbing'. Against the identification with Offa's daughter, see Sims-Williams, *Religion and Literature*, 38.

an interest, the other tyrant is better identified with his son. Cynehelm is called *filius regis* ('the king's son') in the witness-list of another charter, S 156.[46] Cynehelm also appears in S 167, supposedly a foundation charter for Cenwulf's minster in Winchcombe in 811.[47] Although the basis on which the draftsman of S 152 named Cynehelm as a king has not been established, ten other charters from Cenwulf's reign with 'Cynehelm' show that he was probably being groomed as Cenwulf's successor.[48] According to Keynes, Cynehelm is ranked no. 1 (in S 161) after Brorda's death in 805, but thereafter falls back to stabilize as *dux* at no. 3 or 4 (Figs. 6 and 7). Because Cynehelm was titled solely as *dux* in the 'genuine' charters, rather than *filius regis*, some scholars do not believe that this Cynehelm was Cenwulf's son.[49] On the other hand, both Cynehelm's lesser title and his wavering position must be seen in the context of Kent, in which many of these charters were issued.[50] Kent was a foreign territory on which Cenwulf needed to impose a new kinsman as a king even before his brother Cuthred died there in 807. Any attempt by Cenwulf to impose his son there (this is while his 'man' was buying Aldwulf back from the Vikings) may have pushed the men of Kent beyond endurance. From 812 onwards Cynehelm's witness is no longer to be found: by the end of 811 it appears that he was dead.

At this critical moment it seems that Cenwulf tried to keep hold of the lands he had secured from Offa's family and the Church. This was now difficult, for under the terms given in Leo's privilege, Cynehelm's lack of heirs would ensure that Glastonbury reverted to the Church. It looks as if Wulfred took an interest in Glastonbury. In 814, two years after the disappearance of Cynehelm, Wulfred and Bishop Wigberht of Sherborne went together to Rome. In the *Anglo-Saxon Chronicle*, which records their journey without giving cause (812 [814]), Wigberht is known as the bishop of West Saxons.[51] Before Wulfred only three archbishops of Canterbury had gone to Rome: Wighard in 667/8, Berhtwald in 692, and Æthelheard in 801–2. So it is likely, as Brooks says, that Wulfred was there in 814–15 through 'some major crisis of policy decision' for which he

---

[46] This is supposedly of 799, although the text may have been forged in *c.*825 when Wulfred forced Cwenthryth to surrender estates which he considered to be his. See Edwards, *The Charters of the Early West Saxon Kingdoms*, 249 n. 3; and Scharer, *Die angelsächsische Königsurkunde*, 87–9.

[47] *Vita et miracula s. Kenelmi*, ed. Love, p. lxxxix. Hayward, 'The Idea of Innocent Martyrdom', 150. Wilhelm Levison showed the witness list of S 167 to be based on a genuine charter from 803 × 807: see his *England and the Continent in the Eighth Century*, 253–4.

[48] No. 11 in S 106 (BCS 201) in *c.*800; 4 *princeps* in S 1260 (BCS 308) in 803; 4 *dux* in S 1187 (BCS 313) in 804; 3 *dux* in S 40 (BCS 322) in 805; 1 *dux* in S 161 (BCS 321) in 805; *dux* in S 159 (BCS 316) in '804'; 4 *dux* S 163 (BCS 326) in 808; 4 *dux* in S 164 (BCS 328) in 809; 3 *princeps* in S 168 (BCS 335) in 811; 3 *dux* in S 165 (BCS 339) in 811.

[49] Sims-Williams, *Religion and Literature*, 167 n. 111. Keynes, for whom Cynehelm may conceivably be Cenwulf's kinsman, in 'Mercia and Wessex in the Ninth Century', 316 and n. 25. *Vita et miracula s. Kenelmi*, ed. Love, pp. lxxxix–xc.

[50] On Aclea (Cynehelm attests there in S 1187, 40, and 161) as a site in Kent, see Keynes, 'Councils of *Clofesho*', 28–30.

[51] *ASC* A, *s.a.* 812 [for 814] (p. 41). *The Anglo-Saxon Chronicle*, trans. Swanton, 58–9.

needed the pope; and that his journey was a suit connected with the same 'burning issue of the lordship of English monasteries'. From 793 × 801 to 816 × 824, over a period lasting anything between fifteen and thirty-one years, Wigberht was the bishop of Sherborne, in whose diocese Glastonbury lay; in addition, an interpolator later in the *De antiquitate*, probably using an eleventh-century necrology, says that 'Wibertus episcopus' had been a monk at this foundation.[52] Bishop Wigberht would be the immediate, Wulfred the political, beneficiary of a reversion of Glastonbury to the Church. In the event, Pope Leo gave them his blessing, the nature of which is not specified. Lesley Abrams believes that this minster remained in Mercian hands after 812, for there are no West Saxon royal charters in favour of Glastonbury until Edward the Elder (899–924).[53] Yet it is possible that after 814 Glastonbury passed back to the diocese of Sherborne. Cenwulf does seem to have lost that round.

On his return, Wulfred went further and tried to recover Reculver and Minster-in-Thanet which Cenwulf's family owned. Convening a landmark council in Chelsea in 816, he faced Cenwulf and asserted the right of bishops to elect abbots and abbesses over the minsters in their dioceses.[54] For Wulfred the two Kentish minsters were a test case. Minster-in-Thanet, in particular, belonged to Abbess Selethryth, an associate of Cenwulf. The dispute which started here with Cenwulf's family dragged on from 817 to 827.[55] The Canterbury record of 816 already shows that Wulfred attacked Cenwulf's lay lordship of monasteries in *ad hominem* terms:

ni si causa penuriae pro rapacitate secularium ita inviolabiles stare non possunt, judicabimus Episcopo cum suo auctoritate magis licuisse ovilem Christi defendere, quam in luporum faucibus invasione dimittere.[56]

[if [the monastic rules] cannot remain thus inviolate on account of the penury caused by the rapacity of secular men, we will adjudicate a right for the Bishop with his authority to defend the flock of Christ, rather than abandon it to the ravening jaws of wolves.]

The *lupi* ('wolves') in this case must be Cenwulf and his brother Ceolwulf, as the king's name, OE *cœn wulf* ('keen wolf'), and the *wulf*-suffix of Ceolwulf's name, both show. The form of Wulfred's denunciation, moreover, resembles the fact that in *Beowulf*, lines 2993–6, *Wulf* and *Eofor* ('wolf' and 'boar') receive lands which Hygelac appears to have despoiled from higher-born retainers.

---

[52] *The Early History of Glastonbury*, ed. and trans. Scott, 136–7 (ch. 67) and 206 (note).

[53] Abrams, *Anglo-Saxon Glastonbury*, 337.

[54] Brooks, *Early History of the Church of Canterbury*, 134. *Councils and Ecclesiastical Documents*, ed. Haddan and Stubbs, iii. 579–85, at 581 (cap. 4): 'Abbates et Abbatissae probi eligantur per Episcopum et conventum.'

[55] Gelling, *The Early Charters of the Thames Valley*, 102–4 (no. 206). Wormald, 'A Handlist of Anglo-Saxon Lawsuits', no. 14 (cf. no. 13). Brooks, *Early History of the Church of Canterbury*, 182–3.

[56] *Councils and Ecclesiastical Documents*, ed. Haddan and Stubbs, iii. 582. Brooks, *Early History of the Church of Canterbury*, 176–7.

Wulfred's dispute over Reculver and Minster-in-Thanet, which Cwenthryth went on to inherit from Selethryth, is known from a retrospective account written in Canterbury in 826. This records that in the council of *Clofesho* a year before, in 825, King Beornwulf of Mercia had helped to reconcile Wulfred with Abbess Cwenthryth.[57] By this time Mercian royal power was weaker, due to what Wormald describes as 'the determination of England's Carolingian prelates to challenge proprietary rights in religious communities by taking them under episcopal control'.[58] Other bishops had followed Wulfred's example: in the 820s, for example, Bishop Heahberht of Worcester pleaded a successful case for possession of the minster at Westbury on Trym (see Ill. 1), against the community at Berkeley, who were the maternal family of Æthelric, son of Ealdorman Æthelmund of the Hwicce.[59] In short, if *Beowulf* was written in 826 × 839, as I have suggested in Chapter 2, its image of Hygelac was formed at a time when the diocesan churches reviled Cenwulf's memory.

At the *Clofesho* council of 825, Wulfred asked Cwenthryth to abide by the terms of an agreement reached between him and her father, in London in 821. In retrospect, the author of S 1436, the longer of the two surviving records of the *Clofesho* council of 825, characterizes Cenwulf's family from the Kentish point of view, as predators who had ravaged Canterbury for ten years. In a fine hand, but with inadequate Latin, he explains that Wulfred was deprived of the two Kentish minsters:

per inimicitiam et violentiam avaritiamque Coenwulfi regis, sive quae hic in nostra propria gente peracta sunt, seu etiam ultra mare ad illam apostolicam sedem per ejus jussionem et inmissionem adlata sunt.[60]

[through the enmity and violence and avarice of King Cenwulf, both by his actions in this our own nation, but also overseas by his embassies and instructions at the Apostolic See.]

Looking back to 821, therefore, the record claims that Wulfred was dishonoured by Cenwulf and so were the English, whom the king, *per eadem supradictas accusationes et discordias* ('through the same aforesaid accusations and discords'), deprived of Wulfred's metropolitan authority and ministry of baptism for six years. In particular, Cenwulf threatened the archbishop with destitution and exile, regardless of mediation from either emperor or pope or any other ruler:

nisi hoc consentire voluisset. hoc est quod illam terram æt Iognes homme .ccc. manentium reddidisset. istamque pecuniam tradidisset .cxx. librarum.[61]

[unless he wished to agree that he would give back the estate at *Iognes homme* [Eynsham], 300 hides, and hand over this sum of money, 120 pounds.]

---

[57] S 1436 (BCS 384).

[58] Wormald, 'Charters, Law and the Settlement of Disputes', 157.

[59] Ibid. 152–3 and 154–8.

[60] *Councils and Ecclesiastical Documents*, ed. Haddan and Stubbs, iii. 596–601, at 597. My translations from this document are base on that of Brooks, *Early History of the Church of Canterbury*, 181.

[61] *Councils and Ecclesiastical Documents*, ed. Haddan and Stubbs, iii. 597.

Eventually Wulfred was persuaded to accept Cenwulf's terms, provided that Cenwulf cleared him of all charges in Rome.[62] If Cenwulf failed to do this, then he was to give Wulfred back the fine. If he cleared Wulfred's name publicly, on the other hand, he was to keep the money. In either case Cenwulf kept Wulfred's huge Eynsham estate, perhaps as his compensation for Glastonbury. In all this Cenwulf thus considered the fine to be equivalent to Wulfred's loss of income without his ministry. To judge by this document, it seems that Cenwulf never dropped his charges against Wulfred, whatever they were.[63] Of interest to *Beowulf* here is the fact that Cenwulf's final gain from Wulfred was £120: this figure resembles the *hund þusenda* ('120,000') in land and rings which Hygelac is said to grant to each of his low-born champions Wulf and Eofor implicitly after having robbed these sums from Weohstan and other landed men.

King Hygelac's friendship with Beowulf

The hero of *Beowulf* is defined as Hygelac's man long before he is named. The poet first introduces Beowulf as *Higelaces þegn* ('Hygelac's thegn', line 194). Beowulf then introduces himself and his men to the Danish coastguard as *Higelaces heorðgeneatas* ('Hygelac's hearth-companions', line 261) and to Wulfgar, Heorot's door-keeper, as *Higelaces beodgeneatas* ('Hygelac's table-companions', lines 342–3), before he gives his own name for the first time (line 343). With Beowulf waiting outside, the poet reveals his kinship with Hygelac through the words of Hrothgar, who recalls to Wulfgar that King Hrethel of the Geats gave his only daughter to Ecgtheow, Beowulf's father (lines 373–5): Beowulf is thus Hygelac's sister's son. The importance of this relationship to the Anglo-Saxons is well known.[64] As if to confirm it, Beowulf introduces himself to Hrothgar as *Higelaces mæg ond magoþegn* ('Hygelac's kinsman and young thegn', lines 407–8). In his offer to fight Grendel, Beowulf disdains the use of weapons so as to save Hygelac's good opinion (lines 435–6) and asks the king to send Hygelac his body armour, an heirloom of Hrethel, Hygelac's father, should he not survive (lines 452–5). Typical of Beowulf is the epithet *þryðswyð mæg Higelaces* ('the mighty strong kinsman of Hygelac', lines 736–7) as he follows Grendel's movements before the fight starts.[65]

Beowulf receives treasures from Hygelac. Many years later, before joining battle for the last time, Beowulf recalls his devotion to Hygelac in battle:

> 'Ic him þa maðmas   þe he me sealde
> geald æt guðe   swa me gifeðe wæs
> leohtan sweorde;   he me lond forgeaf

---

[62] *Councils and Ecclesiastical Documents*, ed. Haddan and Stubbs, iii. 597: 'ut omnium supradictarum sucggillationum discordiarumque insontem et securum contra domne papan fecisset. aut si hoc facere non potuisset illam pecuniam quod ei dedisset iterum episcopo omnia reddidisset.'

[63] For the suggestion that Cenwulf charged Wulfred with the death of Cynehelm, see North (forthcoming).

[64] R. H. Bremmer, Jr., 'The Importance of Kinship: Uncle and Nephew in "Beowulf"', *ABäG* 15 (1980), 21–38.

[65] See *mæg Higelaces* on lines 758, 813, 914, and onwards.

> eard eðelwyn.   Næs him ænig þearf
> þæt he to Gifðum   oððe to Gar-Denum
> oððe in Swiorice   secean þurfe
> wyrsan wigfrecan   weorðe gecypan.
> Symle ic him on feðan   beforan wolde
> ana on orde' (*Beo* 2490–8)

['Those treasures which he gave me, I repaid in battle as was granted me, with a gleaming sword: he gave me lands, a homeland and the joy of inheriting an estate. Nor was there any need for him to have to seek lower-ranking war-braves among the Gifthas, or the Spear-Danes, or in Sweden, to buy these for a price. Ever would I go before him in the foot-troop, alone in the vanguard']

If this reciprocal friendship precludes Hygelac hiring mercenaries, as the lines show, it also puts Beowulf in the role of protecting his uncle in battle.

Beowulf's homecoming centres on Hygelac for more than 300 lines (1888–2199). The poet thus looks forward to an emotional reunion. When they do meet, Hygelac welcomes Beowulf with a jealous reproach:

> 'Ac ðu Hroðgare
> widcuðne wean   wihte gebettest
> mærum ðeodne?   Ic ðæs modceare
> sorhwylmum seað,   siðe ne truwode
> leofes mannes,   ic ðe lange bæd
> þæt ðu þone wælgæst   wihte ne grette,
> lete Suð-Dene   sylfe geweorðan
> guðe wið Grendel.' (*Beo* 1990–7)

['But did you provide any remedy for the widely heard woe of Hrothgar the famous lord? I was brooding over that with grief of mind, with surging sorrows, I put no trust in the journey of a beloved man, I long asked you not to approach that slaughtering spirit in any way, but to let the Danes in the south settle with Grendel in their own battle.']

Earlier the poet tells us that *Ðone siðfæt him snotere ceorlas lythwon logon* ('wise churls little begrudged him that expedition', lines 202–3).[66] So we know that first, Hygelac may not be wise, and secondly, Beowulf left Geatland against his wishes. Now Beowulf answers by softening Hygelac with the offer, probably customary, of Hrothgar's treasure (lines 2000–151). As if aware that his honour is Hygelac's, he tells him, perhaps falsely, that all these treasures were granted *on minne sylfes dom* ('on my own terms', line 2147):[67]

> 'ða ic ðe, beorncyning,   bringan wylle,
> estum geywan.   Gen is eall æt ðe
> lissa gelong;   ic lyt hafo
> heafodmaga   nefne, Hygelac, ðec.' (*Beo* 2148–51)

---

[66] Niles (*Beowulf*, 169) takes this anomaly to be 'a product of the barbaric style'.
[67] *Pace* Mitchell and Robinson, in *Beowulf*, ed., 121 n. line 2147: 'This is a new piece of information.'

['These, O warrior- (/bear-) king, I wish to bring you, to bestow on you with good will. All happiness still depends on you; I have no close kinsman, Hygelac, but you.']

Hygelac is thus the emotional core of Beowulf's life, and, in a different way, of this poem.[68] His climactic designation as '*beorn*-cyning' appears to bind him to Beowulf in a specifically allegorical way.

When Beornwulf, whom I take to be the poet's contemporary model for Beowulf, first appears in the surviving Mercian records in 812 it is probably to safeguard the power of King Cenwulf. The adjoining table (Fig. 7) gives an impression of what might be termed the king's crisis years: the disappearance of his son Cynehelm late in 811, leading to the upheaval of the Chelsea council of 816, in which Archbishop Wulfred declared war on Cenwulf over the issue of the lay lordship of monasteries. In 812, in particular, shortly after Cynehelm's death, we see Beornwulf for the first time, together with Beornnoth, an old hand, and a third apparent kinsman by the name of Beornheard. Together they appear to be the king's show of force.

Cenwulf's need of Beornwulf and the others may be seen if we study his right to rule in relation to Offa's family. In William's retranslated Glastonbury charter of 798 King Cenwulf is alleged to say that Ecgfrith, his predecessor, conceded the liberty of Glastonbury to Cynehelm, just as he does now.[69] Thus he appears to show that Ecgfrith had once acknowledged Cenwulf's heir as his also. As Thacker says, this papal confirmation was 'an apparently authentic act which has all the appearance of a family settlement, ratifying arrangements made by Ecgfrith for the prince who was probably regarded as the heir of Cenwulf, his (Ecgfrith's) nearest surviving male relative'.[70] How far Cynehelm was related to Ecgfrith can be judged on the basis of Cenwulf's place in Cotton, Vespasian B.VI, 109ᵛ, which is the oldest list from the 'Anglian collection' of royal genealogies. Set out in sequence, this list goes as follows:[71]

Mercia I	Mercia II	Mercia III	Mercia IV
Pypba	Pybba	Pybba	Pybba
Penda	Eowa	Eowa	Coenwalh
Aeðilred	Alwih	Osmod	Cundwalh
	Aðelbald	Eanuulf	Centwine
		Ðincfrið	Cynreou
		Offa	Bassa
		Ecgfrith	Cuðberht
			Coenuulf

---

[68] A. G. Brodeur, *The Art of Beowulf* (Berkeley, 1971), 78–84, esp. 83.

[69] *Vita et miracula s. Kenelmi*, ed. Love, 110–11: *cum consilio et licentia terrenorum principum quorum inferius nomina cripta sunt et ei sine ullo mendacio aut dolo largior firmiter habendam* ('with the permission of the earthly leaders whose names are written below, and I bestow it upon him without deceit or trickery to be held forever').

[70] Thacker, 'Kings, Saints, and Monasteries', 8.

[71] Dumville, 'The Anglian Collection', 24–5 and 30–1.

S:	164	168	165	167	170	173	171	172	180
BCS:	328	335	339	338	340	343	351	350	357
Archive:	CCC	CCC	Roch	Winch	CCC	Wor	Wor	Wor	Wor
Place of issue:	Croy	Ldn	[Ldn?]	Winch	Ldn	[chc]	Tam	Tam	[chc]
Year:	809	811	811	'811'	812	814	814	814	816
ROYALS									
Cenwulf	+	+	+	+	+	+	+	+	+
Ælfthryth			+			+	+		+
ARCHBISHOPS OF CANTERBURY									
Wulfred	1	1	1	1	1	1		1	1
BISHOPS OF LEICESTER									
Werenberht				4		3	2	3	
Rethhun									3
ABBOTS OF BREEDON									
Wigmund?						2			
Eanmund									2
SOME *DUCES*									
Cynehelm	4 *dux*	3 *pri*	3 *dux*	4 *dux*					
Beornheard					1 *dux*				
Beornnoth	2 *dux*	2 *pri*	2 *dux*	3 *dux*	5 *dux*	2 *dux*	2 *dux*	2 *dux*	8 *dux*
Beornwulf					11 *dux*				
Beornheard (2?)							14 *dux*		
Wigheard	5 *dux*				8 *dux*				2 *dux*
Wigheard (2)	11 *pin*				19				

Figure 7. Cenwulf's crisis: the emergence of Beornwulf (809–816)

Source: Keynes, *Atlas of Attestations*, XIII, XV, XVII.

The genealogy tells us that Cenwulf was regarded as Ecgfrith's sixth cousin once removed. That he succeeded from Ecgfrith notwithstanding might be called a failure in Offa to liquidate all of his son's many cousins.[72]

---

[72] Dumville, 'The Ætheling', 19–20 and 26–8.

There is a trace, however, of a closer relationship between Cenwulf and
Ecgfrith which the dearth of Mercian records has all but obscured. Cenwulf
was already married when he succeeded Ecgfrith in 796. This is known from a
letter to 'Osbert', probably the Mercian patrician Brorda, in 797, in which
Alcuin reveals that Cenwulf had set his wife aside for a mistress.[73] A wife of
Cenwulf named 'Ælfthryth' is recorded witnessing charters for '804' (sc. 805),
808, and 811 (respectively S 159, 163, 165). Pauline Stafford suggests that
Ælfthryth was Cenwulf's second wife, after a certain Cynegyth, whose name
may be preserved in S 156; although this name may have been incorporated from
the earlier charter (S 15) on which this one was modelled.[74] Yet 'Alfthrutha' is
given as the name of a daughter of King Offa in the oldest Life of St Æthelberht,
the Hereford *Passio s. Æthelberhti*.[75] An 'Ælfthrytha' is also named in a genealogy
appended to John of Worcester's *Chronicon*, as the mother of 'Kenelmus' (and
'Quendrytha and Burgenilda').[76] That these two Ælfthryths were probably one
and the same might be seen in another charter, dated to 787, which is thought to
be forged on the basis of an original from *c.*780.[77] This charter gives, in the main
text at least, Offa's fourth daughter as 'Aethelþithe', which Birch rationalizes as
'Aethelswithe', Scharer and Keynes as 'Aethelfrithe'. But the *frið*-suffix of the
latter form is affixed to male not female names. As a reconstruction '*Aelþ*[r]*ithe*'
is more reasonable, given that there is a thorn, that *Aethel-* and *Ael-* were
interchangeable prefixes (namely *ASC* (E), *s.a.* 792 [794] 'Ælfled' for 'Æthelflæd'), and the letter -r- could have disappeared through haplography with the
-þ- before it. Moreover, Cynehelm's name-prefix is that of Cynethryth, Offa's
queen. From Anna Gannon's work on the iconography of Cynethryth's coins it
appears that the name of this woman in Offa's kingdom carried an authority all
of its own.[78] If Cenwulf was wise enough to marry Cynethryth's daughter,
much is explained both about his elevation from poverty to inherit Ecgfrith's
kingdom and the implication in S 152 that Ecgfrith treated Cynehelm as his
heir. Cynehelm could have been his sister's son, Offa's grandson through a
female line. If that is true, Cenwulf's initial claim to rule was that of a regent.
Consequently, Cynehelm's death in 811–12 would have ushered in a year in
which Cenwulf was threatened.

   With the Deiran-derived Cotton Vespasian B.VI, fo. 109^v, it seems that
Cenwulf set out to prove his blood-right to Mercia by a means other than

---

[73] *Epistolae*, ed. Dümmler, ii. 178–80, esp. 79 (no. 122). *EHD*, 854–6 (Osbert).

[74] Stafford, 'Political Women in Mercia', 42 n. 5.

[75] James, 'Two Lives of St Ethelbert', 238.

[76] *Florentii Wigorniensis monachi Chronicon ex chronicis*, ed. B. Thorpe, 2 vols. (London,
1848–9), i. 266. For the same, see *Ricardi de Circencestria Speculum historiale*, ed. Mayor, i. 295
(ch. lxv).

[77] S 127 (BCS 251), in BL Cotton Vitellius A.XIII, fo. 31. See S 125 and 129. Scharer, *Die
angelsächsische Königsurkunde*, 270–1.

[78] Gannon, *Iconography of Early Anglo-Saxon Coinage*, 41.

Cynehelm.[79] Dumville has argued that this manuscript, the oldest list in the Anglian collection of 805 × 814, was probably written nearer to 814.[80] Joanna Story, in whose view Anglo-Saxon kings would use Woden genealogies 'at moments of dynastic uncertainty to bolster the royal credentials of the ruling family', suggests that the date was *c.*812.[81] This approximation coincides even more neatly with the disappearance of Cynehelm in 811–12, which is also the time in which it is believed Cenwulf's family, including Cwenthryth, culted the dead Cynehelm as a martyred saint.[82] The above Anglian genealogy has no Cynehelm but does trace Cenwulf back to Coenwalh, apparently a son of Pybba. If we look at Bede's story in *HE* III. 7, we find that Cenwealh, king of the Gewisse, married Pybba's daughter (the sister of Penda of Mercia) only to repudiate her when Penda invaded Wessex. It can hardly be the case that King Pybba had a son named Coenwalh and a son-in-law named Cenwealh. It is tempting, therefore, to see Cenwulf's new genealogy as a statement that he was descended from Pybba through a failed marriage that was nonetheless consummated. Without contradicting Bede's *Historia*, supposing this was widely known, Cenwulf could leave it understood that his ancestor Coenwalh was Pybba's son (not his son-in-law). The base in Winchcombe lies closer to the Thames source than the Mercian heartland, and the C-names of Cenwulf's family better fit the pattern of Cenwealh son of Cynegils of the Gewisse.[83] In this way, Cenwulf appears to have claimed descent from Pybba at just the time when he could no longer rely on the royal blood of his son. In due course Mercian kingship came to be treated as legitimate through daughters as well as sons, but in Cenwulf's case it seems that the female line was still problematic. This is just the kind of difficulty which surrounds Beowulf's claim to royal blood in *Beowulf*, one which must be made through his mother (see below).

To sum up, it can be argued that the Cynehelm whom S 152 calls a *rex* ('king') was not only Cenwulf's heir and Cwenthryth's brother but also Offa's and Cynethryth's grandson. Cynehelm's disappearance from charter witnesses in *c.*812 would indicate that he died. Cwenthryth was later known as Cenwulf's heir, and this fact (in S 1436, of 826) probably shows that Cynehelm himself died without issue. The loss of Cynehelm probably threatened everything that

[79] On the likely Northumbrian origin of the collection, see Dumville, 'The Anglian Collection', 45–50. The greater length of the Lindsey list suggests that this genealogy, if Deiran, passed through this region before it reached south-west Mercia. Cuthberht *princeps*, possibly Cenwulf's father, had connections in Lincolnshire, given that there is land-lease in his favour for Swineshead (Lincs.) in S 1412 (BCS 271), *s.a.* 790. If this Cuthberht was Cenwulf's father, his father's name Bassa might indicate that Cuthberht was descended from a Lindsey family on his father's side, from Pybba on his mother's.

[80] Dumville, 'The Anglian Collection', 24. Keynes suggests *c.*810, in 'Mercia and Wessex in the Ninth Century', 311.

[81] Story, *Carolingian Connections*, 176–7.

[82] Thacker, 'Kings, Saints, and Monasteries', 8–12. Hayward, 'The Idea of Innocent Martyrdom', 180 and 283–4.

[83] Yorke, *Wessex in the Early Middle Ages*, 80–2. Keynes, 'Mercia and Wessex in the Ninth Century', 316.

Cenwulf had gained, by reopening the question of royal succession. Beornnoth's leap into Ealdorman Æthelmund's position in *c*.800, from tenth place to second, probably shows that Cenwulf elevated him because he was a friend (S 106, 1260: Figs. 6 and 7).[84] Not long after Cynehelm vanishes from the record in 811, Beornnoth's name is increased by those of Beornheard and Beornwulf (S 170). In this case it seems that Beornwulf rose to a position of trust with Cenwulf when the king needed his muscle to stay in power. In *Beowulf*, as we have seen, particularly in lines 2490–8, Beowulf commemorates a similarly protective relationship with Hygelac.

Hygelac gives Beowulf land and hearth

In *Beowulf*, Hygelac endows Beowulf in public in such a way that the young hero could be called *brego* ('a prince'). Signing off, as it were, that part of *Beowulf* which celebrates the hero's victories against Grendel and his Mother, the poet tells us that Beowulf suffered long ignominy as a child (*hean wæs lange*, line 2183). Then he was reckoned to be a slouch, but now things have changed:

> Edwenden cwom
> tireadigum menn   torna gehwylces.
> Het ða eorla hleo   in gefetian
> headorof cyning   Hreðles lafe
> golde gegyrede;   næs mid Geatum ða
> sincmaðþum selra   on sweordes had
> þæt he on Biowulfes   bearm alegde,
> ond him gesealde   seofon þusendo,
> bold ond bregostol. (*Beo* 2188–96)

[A change in fortune came to the glorious man for each of his griefs. It was then that [Hygelac] the protector of warriors, the king brave in battle, ordered Hrethel's heirloom, adorned with gold, to be fetched in; nor was there among the Geats at that time any higher-ranking precious treasure in the category of a sword than the one which he laid in Beowulf's bosom, granting him seven thousand hides, a hall, and princely throne.]

Thus Beowulf becomes a landed man. As we have seen, he recalls this moment later by saying that Hygelac *me lond forgeaf, eard eðelwyn* ('gave me lands, a homeland, and the joy of inheriting an estate', lines 2492–3). The poet uses this ritual to smooth Beowulf's path to kingship.

In Mercia, while Beornwulf was still a nobleman, it can be deduced that Cenwulf raised him to a position over the minster of St Peter's, Gloucester. This patronage is recorded in one grant made by Beornwulf as a royal companion (*Beornulphus comes*), in another by him as king (*rex Merciorum* in 821 [823]).[85] Whether or not its memory of Beornwulf was shaped by anti-clerical

---

[84] *The Anglo-Saxon Chronicle*, trans. and ed. Swanton, 58–9 (AE, *s.a.* 800 [802]).
[85] *Historia et cartularium Gloucestriæ*, ed. Hart, i. 111 and ii. 115.

developments in the tenth century or later, the St Peter's cartulary states that the grants of Frocester and Standish and Beornwulf's death in battle (in 826) took place *tempore clericorum ibidem degentium* ('at a time when degenerate clergy lived there').[86] The census-gatherer John Leland found a legend about King Beornwulf in the 1530s, among 'Things gatheryd out of certayne writyns in the wall of the worthe ile of the body of the church in Gloucester'.[87] Leland distilled one part of these as 'Bernulph kynge of the Merche bringethe in secular chanons and clerks [givinge possessions and liberties to them]'. He adds that these canons were expelled only by Cnut 'for yll lyvynge', to be replaced with monks by Bishop Wulfstan of Worcester. Late as it is, this record might confirm that Beornwulf turned Gloucester into his family's proprietary monastery.

The evidence also suggests that Beornwulf's family extended its domain northwards into Worcestershire. Beornnoth's great leap into Æthelmund's charter position in *c.*800 probably shows that he took his authority over this part of the Hwicce. The Tribal Hidage, a document dated variously in the seventh to ninth centuries, sets the domain of the *Hwinca* ('Hwicce') in Gloucestershire and Worcestershire at 7,000 hides.[88] It also appears that Beornnoth received land. A charter of *c.*972 refers to *vetusto . . . privilegio Beornotho duce optinente* ('ealdorman Beornnoth obtaining an ancient privilege') from Cenwulf in favour of the minster at Pershore in the vale of Evesham (see Ill. 1).[89] Pershore had been founded by Kings Osric and Oswald of the Hwicce in 679, so here, as well as in Gloucester, it seems that Beornnoth's family took over lands belonging to the old Hwiccean kings.[90] About 12 miles north-west of Pershore, in the sprawling Pershore Hundred west over the Severn near the river Teme, lies the village of Leigh (see Ill. 1).[91] In the same charter (which otherwise records a stream known as *Grindles becc*) this place is known as *Beornoðes leah*; north-east of Worcester below Bromsgrove, 'Barnsleyhall', formerly *Barndesley* (1255), has also been interpreted as *Beornnoðes leah*; S 786 names a *Beornwaldes sæte* in the same area.[92] These place names might indicate that Beornnoth's family purchased lands around Worcester in a policy of territorial enlargement. The area's existing landowning family is revealed through other sources. The dedication of the church in Leigh in part to St Eadburga, the fact that ealdorman Eadwulf is recorded as the owner of a swine-pasture in Sinton in Leigh in the Worcester

---

[86] Ibid. i. 77, and 111.

[87] *The Itinerary of John Leland*, ed. Toulmin Smith, ii. 59.

[88] Featherstone, 'The Tribal Hidage and the Ealdormen of Mercia', 23–34, esp. 24 (table 2.1) and 29–32. Hill, *Atlas of Anglo-Saxon England*, 76–7 (no. 136).

[89] S 786 (BCS 1282). On the authenticity, see Sims-Williams, *Religion and Literature*, 95.

[90] Ibid. 34–5. For the area, see D. Hooke, *The Landscape of Anglo-Saxon England* (Leicester, 1998), 13.

[91] O. S. Andersson, *The English Hundred-Names*, Lunds Universitets Årsskrift, N. f. avdeling I, Bd. 30, Nr. 1 (Lund, 1934), 140.

[92] A. Mawer and F. M. Stenton, with F. T. S. Houghton, *The Place-Names of Worcestershire* (Cambridge, 1927), 204–5 and 338 (the alternative is *Beornmodes*).

record of *Clofesho* in 825, and in the tenth century the name *Eadwoldincg leahe* at the southern edge of Leigh, may all show that in Beornwulf's reign most of this area was owned by the prolific kindred of Cenwulf's *duces* Eadberht (witnessed *c.*809–825) and his son Eadgar.[93] James Campbell has shown that real-estate transactions were probably more common among laymen in the seventh to ninth centuries than appears in the surviving charters, which are naturally concerned with the Church.[94] So there is a possibility that not only Wulfred but also Beornnoth transacted business in real estate with secular land-holders, perhaps including Æthelmund's and Eadberht's families and King Cenwulf himself. At any rate, the 7,000 hides of the Hwicce, over which it seems Cenwulf gave Beornnoth control, together with St Peter's, Gloucester, which Beornwulf endowed, may be seen as the model for the 7,000 hides plus hall and princely throne which Hygelac gives Beowulf in *Beo* 2195–6.

Beowulf's lesser royal blood

It is uncomfortable that following Beowulf's enrichment with sword, land, and hearth (lines 2190–6), the poet describes Hygelac as the better man:

> Him wæs bam samod
> on ðam leodscipe lond gecynde,
> eard eðelriht oðrum swiðor,
> side rice, þam ðær selra wæs. (*Beo* 2196–9)

[Both of them together had heritable land in that country, a homeland, ancestral rights and dues, but rather more so for one of them, a broad kingdom for the one who was higher-born.]

As I have attempted to show in Chapter 2, the poet has probably embellished his Beowulf-figure on an archetype which had hitherto never achieved or expected to achieve royal status. His statement in these lines acknowledges the difficulty of Beowulf's later transformation by suggesting that Hygelac is better because his father Hrethel was a Geatish royal, whereas Beowulf's father Ecgtheow was not. Yet the meaning of *god* is flexible: when Hrothgar begins his oration on Beowulf's achievements, saying that this man was *geboren betera* ('born better', line 1703), the context allows that it is Beowulf's deeds which have suddenly made him so. This is the opinion of the Danes on the ride back from the Mere, who declare that under the sun and across all the world there is no shield-bearing man *selra* or *rices wyrðra* ('better', 'worthier of a kingdom', lines 860–1) than Beowulf.

---

[93] S 1437 (BCS 386). Finberg, *The Early Charters of the West Midlands*, 100–1 (no. 246). D. Hooke, *Worcestershire Anglo-Saxon Charter-Bounds* (Woodbridge, 1990), 97, 189–90, 215–19 (esp. 218) and 216. The many *Ead*-names in Alfred's progeny probably stem from this west Hwiccean kindred.

[94] Campbell, 'The Sale of Land and the Economics of Power', 29–34. See also P. Wormald, in Campbell (ed.), *The Anglo-Saxons*, 139.

Hrothgar himself, now bidding farewell to his extraordinary guest, tells him that the Geats *selran næbben to geceosenne cyning ænigne* ('may not have any better man than you to elect as their king', lines 1850–1); but only if Hygelac should die, he says, and should Beowulf then want to become king. Despite room for personal merit within the meanings of *god* and *selra* or *betera*, it appears to be the maternal source of Beowulf's royal blood that makes Hygelac *selra* than Beowulf.

In Mercia there is no doubt that Beornwulf's claim to rule was weaker than that of Cenwulf, his forerunner but one. The first question with Beornwulf is what connection he had with Mercian royalty. The answer is 'not much'. Beornwulf is regarded as 'a man of unknown origins'.[95] This is possibly because of his portrait in Pseudo-Ingulph's *Historia Croylandensis*, a confabulation from the late twelfth to fifteenth centuries, which embodies some Anglo-Saxon material from the eleventh century or earlier.[96] The monks of this abbey saw Beornwulf as *in nulloque lineam regalem contingente* ('touched by no royal line').[97] Yet some guesses about Beornwulf's kindred may be made. At least we can exclude the possibility of his family relationship with King Berhtwulf (839–52) or with any other men with *Be(o)rht*-prefixes to their name. King Berhtwulf's genealogy shows us that in the early ninth century, the *Be(o)rn*- and *Be(o)rht*-prefixes serve to delineate kindreds that were established as distinct. In respect of Beornwulf's kindred, it may be noted that Beornnoth was promoted to first *dux* only on Beornwulf's accession in 824, despite a quarter-century of service to Cenwulf and Ceolwulf. This suggests that he was Beornwulf's father, for it seems less likely after his service he would stand aside from higher honours, namely the throne of Mercia, if he were Beornwulf's elder brother. Beornnoth's sudden appearance in charters in 798 and his promotion in *c.*800 probably show that he was Cenwulf's friend in 796 when this man became king (see Fig. 6).

It is possible that Cenwulf bound Beornnoth to him further, through marriage. There is a twelfth-century Abingdon tale of Cenwulf's grant to Abingdon of an estate in Culham, which begins by attributing two unnamed sisters to Cenwulf, whom *vero nonnulli proceres potentissimi, tum propter regiam dignitatem, tum propter earum famam memoria dignam, in copulam adoptaverunt sibi maritalem*.[98] The charters do show Beornnoth, usually ranked second, to have been one of Cenwulf's leading magnates such as Abingdon's *proceres potentissimi* ('most powerful princes'). In Wessex at this time, so it appears from a thirteenth-century verse chronicle, Weohstan, the Wiltshire ealdorman

---

[95] Thacker, 'Kings, Saints, and Monasteries', 10.

[96] Hill, 'Mercians: The Dwellers on the Boundary', 175. Roberts, 'Hagiography and Literature', 71.

[97] *Chronicle of Croyland Abbey*, ed. Birch, 12.

[98] *Chronicon monasterii de Abingdon*, ed. Stevenson, i. 18 (ch. 21): 'indeed some of the most powerful princes chose out for wedlock with themselves, partly through the royal honour, partly through their renown made worthy in memory.'

who was killed in battle with Æthelmund of the Hwicce in 802, was already married to Æthelburh, sister of the new king Ecgberht.[99] Yet there is no evidence that Beornnoth was his king's brother-in-law, tempting as it might be to see a sister's son relationship with Cenwulf as the ideology otherwise missing in Beornwulf's election as king.

In general, with Beornwulf's paternal family, the fact that he had a brother named Bynna suggest that he was a kinsman, perhaps nephew, of the Bynna who witnessed Offa's charters in high positions from 789 to *c*.794.[100] Further back he may have an ancestor in the usurper Beornred who ruled Mercia briefly before Offa in 757.[101] If names are anything to go by, a kindred with this prefix seems well established. Offa had a court chaplain named Beornwine who gave Alcuin reason to mistrust him in the late 780s.[102] An abbess named Beorngyth ruled at Bath (Wilts.) in *c*.680 and Offa had an ealdorman named Beornheard, listed as tenth *dux* in 757, to whom his sub-king Aldred of the Hwicce gave land at Huntingford (Gloucs.) in *c*.770.[103] Bynna may have fallen from grace, for in 794 Offa ruled that he had misappropriated an estate belonging to Worcester on the Severn at Aust (Gloucs.).[104] In the twelfth century Gloucester owned one charter allegedly of a grant by Beornwulf *comes* ('companion') of an estate at Standish, and another allegedly of a grant by his brother *Rabanus anglicus Revenswart* ('Raven') of an estate at Frocester, to St Peter's Church in Gloucester.[105] This had been the proprietary minster of the Hwiccean kings, passing out of their hands at the beginning of the eighth century;[106] Ealdorman Æthelmund, followed by King Beornwulf, are said to have enlarged it;[107] the *Beorn*-kindred seem to have acquired an interest there on Æthelmund's death in 802. Aust, Huntingford, Frocester, and Standish lie on a south–north line to the east of the ridge of the Cotswold Hills (see Ill. 1). They are grouped about the minster of Berkeley,

---

[99] *S. Editha sive Chronicon Vilodunense*, ed. Horstmann, 4 (lines 138–41): 'For Elburwys love . . . þat was þe erle of Wyltons wyf by-fore, And Kyng Egbertys sustre also he was').

[100] S 1437 (BCS 386). Keynes, *Atlas of Attestations*, table X (Laymen, 757–96): 8 *princeps* in S 1430 (BCS 256), 789; 2 *princeps* in S 138 (BCS 264), ?792 ('795'); 5 *dux* in S 136 (BCS 267), 793; 3 *dux* in S 137 (BCS 269), 794; 2 in S 139 (BCS 274), ?794; 2 *princeps* in S 132 (BCS 265), '790'; 2 *princeps* in S 146 (BCS 273), 793 × 796.

[101] *The Anglo-Saxon Chronicle*, trans. Swanton, 48–9 (AE, *s.a.* 755 [757]).

[102] *Epistolae*, ed. Dümmler, ii. 124–5 (no. 82). Allott, *Alcuin of York*, 51 (no. 39).

[103] Beorngyth: S 1167 (BCS 57). Sims-Williams, *Religion and Literature*, 111–12. Beornheard: S 55 (BCS 183); S 63 (BCS 218). For the identification with Huntingford, Finberg, *The Early Charters of the West Midlands*, 37–8. Ekwall's suggestion that this *Huntenatun* is Huntington near Hereford is founded on morphology alone: *Oxford Dictionary of Place-Names, s.v.* Huntingdon. It is worth adding that a certain Ealdred appears for the first time in 824 in Beornwulf's reign, kept on by Wiglaf (10 in S 188 and 11 in S 190).

[104] S 137 (BCS 269). Discussed in Abrams, *Anglo-Saxon Glastonbury*, 50–1.

[105] *Historia et cartularium Gloucestriæ*, ed. Hart, i. 9, 77 and 111; ii. 110–11 and 115. Finberg, *The Early Charters of the West Midlands*, 45 (no. 60).

[106] Sims-Williams, *Religion and Literature*, 123–6.

[107] *Historia et cartularium Gloucestriæ*, ed. Hart, ii. 110: '[ecclesia] quibusdam vero a quodam Ælmundo in geldinc et rege itidem Merciorum Bernulfo postmodum ampliata.'

which overlooks the river Severn and was a party to a famous lawsuit in the ninth century involving the son and widow of Ealdorman Æthelmund.[108] These possessions are so configured as to commend southern Gloucestershire and Wiltshire as the area in which the *Beorn*-kindred were landowners from the middle of the seventh century: landowners, yet never kings.

Although, in *Beowulf*, Beowulf's name differs from that of Ecgtheow, his foreign father, it seems that his family claims no royal blood except through his mother, Hrethel's (unnamed) daughter. This lower birth corresponds with the presumed folktale origins of the Beowulf-figure, which I have discussed in Chapter 2. Beowulf's rapport with the *snotere ceorlas* ('wise churls') is shown as effective in *Beo* 202–3. But Beowulf's humbler status in the Geatish court also matches the relatively obscure origins of King Beornwulf in Mercia. To this extent, it is possible that the poet of *Beowulf* selected the Beowulf-legend not only through the similarity of the name, but also because Beornwulf, like this folktale archetype, was 'touched by no royal line'.

Hygelac dies in pursuit of treasure; Beowulf avenges him

The poet of *Beowulf* alludes to Hygelac's death no fewer than five times (lines 1202–14, 2201, 2354–66, 2501–8, and 2913–21). The startling prolepsis with which Hygelac's death is initially foretold draws our attention not only to a contrast between the known present and unknown future, but also to the futile sense of the word *wlenco* by which he is remembered:

> hyne wyrd fornam
> syþðan he for wlenco   wean ahsode
> fæhðe to Frysum. (*Beo* 1205–7)

[fate seized him when through pride he asked for woe, a feud with Frisia.]

Later Beowulf himself recalls the Frisian raid in a fond memory of performing vengeance for Hygelac on his killer, Dæghrefn. Beowulf, so he proudly says, will always fight in the front line:

> 'þenden þis sweord þolað
> þæt mec ær ond sið   oft gelæste
> syððan ic for dugeðum   Dæghrefne wearð
> to handbonan,   Huga cempan;' (*Beo* 2499–502)

['as long as this sword endures which has always obeyed me then and now, since before the hosts I became the hand-to-hand slayer of Dæghrefn, champion of the Hugas.']

---

[108] OS Landranger Map 162, Gloucester & Forest of Dean, 575888 (Aust), 719937 (Huntingford), 785033 (Frocester), 801085 (Standish), and 685994 (Berkeley). Wormald, 'A Handlist of Anglo-Saxon Lawsuits', nos. 11 and 12; Wormald, 'Charters, Law and the Settlement of Disputes', 154–7.

After Beowulf killed him, he says, Dæghrefn could not bring Hygelac's gear in person *Frescyninge* ('to the king of Frisia', line 2503). However, Beowulf says that his *hildegrap* ('war-grip', line 2907) crushed Hygelac's killer to death. His speech thrills with this note of revenge.

The end of Cenwulf was no less sudden in Mercia. Although the sources give little information, it seems that Beornwulf avenged Cenwulf's death two years later. Cenwulf died near Basingwerk in Flintshire, according to a detail in *L'Estoire des Engleis*, of the late eleventh century, which freely adapts a lost version of the *Anglo-Saxon Chronicle*.[109] Basingwerk was on the north Welsh border. Cenwulf had raided Rhos in north Wales in 817, Snowdonia and Rhufuniog in 816/17, Anglesey in 817/18, Dyfed in south Wales in 818/19 and with his location in 821 he seems to have been planning a new campaign in Wales from the northern end of Wat's Dyke.[110] 'For the king to be killed', says one scholar of Cenwulf here, 'presumably a significant proportion of the Mercian military establishment would have fallen with him.'[111] Probably late in 823, the Mercians returned to north Wales to avenge Cenwulf by sacking the fortress of Degannwy in Gwynedd and by overrunning Powys. This attack has been attributed to Beornwulf at the outset of his reign, which went on until his defeat against Ecgberht of Wessex near Wroughton (Wilts.) in 825 and his death in battle in East Anglia in 826.[112]

So Beornwulf appears to have been a vigorous lord, loyal to Cenwulf. As we have seen, his coming of age in the charters coincides with the aftermath of Cynehelm's apparent death in 811 (Fig. 7). As eleventh *dux* in S 170, he emerges as a junior member of a kindred which is represented not only in Beornnoth but also by a certain Beornheard. Thereafter Beornwulf is absent until his witness in tenth position in 823 shortly before the deposition of Ceolwulf made him king (S 187). The one attestation of one Nothheard, recorded as King Beornwulf's *praefectus et comes regis in Magansetum* ('prefect and companion among the *Magonsæte*'), may show that Beornwulf had campaigned on the south Welsh border.[113] Given that Cenwulf had raided there from 817 to 821, it seems likely that Beornwulf witnessed so rarely until his accession because he served in Cenwulf's army. In all this it is plausible that Beornwulf avenged Cenwulf on the Welsh in late 823; and that the poet of *Beowulf*, for this reason, introduced Beowulf's vengeance into the well-known story of Hygelac's death on a raid. (See Fig. 8.)

[109] *L'Estoire des Engleis*, ed. Bell, 71 (lines 2235–6): 'Set anz aprés [after a campaign of Ecgberht in Wales] Kenulf de Merce | Transit el liu de Basewer[c]e.'

[110] Hill, 'Mercians: The Dwellers on the Boundary', 175 and 179 (map of Powys and Offa's Dyke). Yorke, *Kings and Kingdoms*, 121.

[111] Williams, 'Military Institutions and Royal Power', 304.

[112] Kirby, *Earliest English Kings*, 187–8.

[113] S 1782. See also Thacker, 'Some Terms for Noblemen', 213, and Sims-Williams, *Religion and Literature*, 51. *Historia et cartularium Gloucestriæ*, ed. Hart, i, p. lxxiii.

S:	179	181	182	186	187	1434	1433	1436	1437
BCS:	356	360	359	370	373	378	379	384	386
Archive:	Wor	Wor	Wor	CCC	CCC	CCC	Wor	CCC	Wor
Place of issue:				*Bydictun*	*Werb.wic*	*Clof*	*Clof*	*Clof*	*Clof*
Year:	816	817	817	822	823	824	824	825	825
KINGS									
Cenwulf	+	+	+						
Ceolwulf				+	+				
Beornwulf						+	+	+	+
ARCHBISHOP OF CANTERBURY									
Wulfred	1	1	1	1	1	1	1	1	1
BISHOP OF LEICESTER									
Rethhun	3		3	3		3	3	3	3
ABBOT OF BREEDON									
Eanmund	2				1	2	1	3	2
RELEVANT LAYMEN									
Cyneberht				8	13		11	6 *dux*	
Beornnoth	4*dux*	2 *dux*	3 *dux*		2 *dux*	1 *dux*	1 *dux*	1 *dux*	2 *dux*
Muca				4 *dux*	5 *dux*				
Beornwulf					10 *dux* [king				
Bynna (Beornwulf's brother)								11	
Wigheard	10								
Wighelm				9	12		13	14	12

Figure 8. Elevation of Beornwulf (816–825)

Source: Keynes, *Atlas of Attestations*, XIII, XV, XVII.

Hygelac's successor fails and Beowulf is made king

After Hygelac's death, a restless change of focus in *Beowulf* makes clear both the disarray in Geatland and the hero's enduring loyalty towards Hygelac's family, complete with a lack of ambition to succeed him. He swims from the beach in Frisia, carrying thirty coats of mail, back to Geatland:

> þær him Hygd gebead   hord ond rice
> beagas ond bregostol: bearne ne truwode
> þæt he wið ælfylcum   eþelstolas
> healdan cuðe   ða wæs Hygelac dead;
> no ðy ær feasceafte   findan meahton
> æt ðam æðelinge   ænige ðinga
> þæt he Heardrede   hlaford wære
> oððe þone cynedom   ciosan wolde.
> Hwæðre he him on folce   freondlarum heold
> estum mid are   oð ðæt he yldra wearð,
> Weder-Geatum weold. (*Beo* 2369–79)

[where Hygd offered him hoard and kingdom, treasures and royal throne: in her child she had no confidence, that he might be able to hold their ancestral thrones against foreign hosts, now that Hygelac was dead; no sooner for that could the destitute people find in that prince any conditions by which he might be a lord to Heardred or might wish to choose that kingship. But honourably for him instead Beowulf performed a gracious office of friend and counsellor, until Heardred came of age, ruled the Weder-Geats.]

Hereby the poet chronicles the death of Hygelac in relation to Beowulf's apparent lack of interest in becoming king of Geatland.

Later Beowulf is restored to the narrative (from a place unknown) in order to save his people. Heardred has namely lost his kingdom and life by giving shelter to Eanmund and Eadgils, two nephews of King Onela of Sweden who challenged their uncle's power. Onela comes after them, killing not only Eanmund but also Heardred:

> he þær *for* feorme   feorhwunde hleat,
> sweordes swengum,   sunu Hygelaces;
> ond him eft gewat   Ongenðioes bearn
> hames niosan   syððan Heardred læg,
> let ðone bregostol   Biowulf healdan,
> Geatum wealdan;   þæt wæs god cyning. (*Beo* 2385–90)

[He got a mortal wound for giving refuge, did the son of Hygelac, with the swipes of a sword; and back again went the son of Ongentheow to find his home, when Heardred lay dead, he let [or: made] Beowulf keep that princely throne, rule the Geats: that [: Onela] was a good king.]

It is implied that Beowulf is elsewhere when the young man dies. The poet has already praised Onela, Heardred's killer, as the best sea- or lake-king who ever broke up treasure in Sweden (lines 2382–4). Later, with the phrase *cealdum cearsiðum* ('with cold expeditions of care', line 2396), the poet mourns Beowulf's revenge-slaying of Onela as a duty, not a desire. Onela has namely done what the Geats were unable to, by removing a weak king and putting Beowulf on the *bregostol* in his place. In all this Beowulf remains oddly passive.

In Mercia, the charters show that King Ceolwulf, Cenwulf's successor, was supported by both Beornnoth and his younger kinsman Beornwulf. On pp. 275–6, I have speculated that Beornwulf may have been related to Cenwulf by blood, possibly as a sister's son; and his second charter appearance, as tenth ealdorman in 823, is during Ceolwulf's short reign; so it appears that Ceolwulf trusted in his support (see Fig. 8). In addition, the Canterbury record of *Clofesho* in 825 specifies *amicitia* ('a friendship') between Beornwulf and Cwenthryth, who was not only Cenwulf's but also Ceolwulf's heir (S 1436). In this light, the place of the *Beorn*-kindred in the southern and western Hwiccean kingdom, so close to that of Cenwulf's family around Winchcombe in the eastern Hwiccean domain, bears witness to a friendship which Ceolwulf invoked in order to keep power.

About Ceolwulf, however, no story survives other than his dates and the implication that after a short rapacious reign he was ousted by Archbishop Wulfred, with Beornwulf's help. The *Anglo-Saxon Chronicle* states that in 819 [821] 'Ceolwulf succeeded to the kingdom' and in 821 [823] 'Ceolwulf was deprived of his kingdom'.[114] The first record can be supplemented with charters, the second with coins; both with *L'Estoire des Engleis*. First, from the Canterbury record of the 825 Council of *Clofesho* (S 1436), it is clear that Ceolwulf let Cwenthryth withhold the rents from Reculver and Minster-in-Thanet, money which she was legally bound to return to Wulfred after his forced settlement with Cenwulf in 821. It is known from a West Mercian charter of 897 that Cenwulf's will made Ceolwulf's daughter, Ælfflæd, his other heir.[115] Doubtless this clause endeared Ceolwulf to his niece. A charter issued in 825 in favour of Selsey (S 1435) throws light on Ceolwulf's reign as a free-for-all:

Post mortem uero Coenulfi regis Merciorum multe discordie et innumerabiles dissonacie extollebantur contra uniuscuiusque principalium personarum, regum et episcoporum et pastorum ecclesiarum Dei erga plurima secularia negocia, ita ut multum dispoliate fuerant per loca diuersa ecclesie Christi in rebus internis, in tributo, in omnibus causis.[116]

[After the death of Cenwulf, king of the Mercians, many quarrels and innumerable disputes had arisen between important men of all kinds – kings, bishops, and ministers of God's churches – concerning a multitude of secular affairs, so that in various places the churches of Christ were much despoiled in property, in lands, and in payments of all kinds.]

This charter concerns the church estate at Denton (Sussex) which Cenwulf had inherited from Offa, promising to restore it to Selsey on his death. Yet when Cenwulf died it seems that Ceolwulf seized Denton for himself.[117] If this happened in Sussex, then it is likely that the situation within Mercia was worse. According to *L'Estoire des Engleis*:

---

[114] *The Anglo-Saxon Chronicle*, trans. Swanton, 60–1 (AE).
[115] S 1442 (BCS 575): 'de hereditate ipsius Cenuulfi…Cyneðryð patri suo…et Ælfflæd'. Finberg, *The Early Charters of the West Midlands*, 45 and 51 (no. 86).
[116] S 1435 (BCS 387). *Charters of Selsey*, ed. Kelly, 60 (no. 15). Trans. Keynes, 'The Control of Kent in the Ninth Century', 119.
[117] Wormald, 'A Handlist of Anglo-Saxon Lawsuits', no. 7.

Dous anz tint terre a grant ennui,
Al chef de dous anz la perdi;
N'est pas amé: pur ço fui;
Tant aveit feit, tuz le haeient,
Plusur oscire le voleient. (lines 2238–42)[118]

[['Ceawolf'] keeps the country in great wretchedness for two years, losing her when two years are up; he isn't loved, so he fled; so much had he done that all hated him, many wanted to kill him.]

Ceolwulf was not loved by Archbishop Wulfred either, who controlled Canterbury during his reign. Wulfred's moneyers in Canterbury struck coins in Cenwulf's last year without royal name or portrait, perhaps, as Brooks has suggested, to counteract the coins struck by Cenwulf's moneyers who left out Wulfred's name.[119] Now Ceolwulf was in power, it seems his writ ran eastwards barely beyond Rochester, close to the Mercian border, where he had three or four moneyers, in contrast with Cenwulf's two. In Canterbury only two moneyers struck coins for Ceolwulf, where for his brother there had been six; and they left out Ceolwulf's name, using a portrait type which is also found on coins of Baldred, the king who ruled Kent after Ceolwulf. It has thus been suggested that the Canterbury moneyers supported Baldred in Ceolwulf's reign, not declaring for him until Ceolwulf's death or exile in 823.[120] For his own part, Archbishop Wulfred held off from consecrating Ceolwulf as king until 17 September 822, a year after he took power.[121] Both this and Ceolwulf's other surviving charter were issued at meetings with Wulfred in Kent. After his consecration in 822, Ceolwulf sold Wulfred 5 sulungs at Milton in Otford in western Kent in exchange for 75 mancuses (S 186); on 26 May in 823 Ceolwulf sold the archbishop a house in Canterbury for a gold and silver dish worth 5 pounds and 10 shillings (S 187).[122] These transactions speak less of a rapprochement between Wulfred and Cenwulf's family than of an attempt by Ceolwulf to pay his followers. The Canterbury evidence could be read to suggest that Wulfred supported Baldred's unofficial kingship in Kent.

Further afield, there is reason to believe that Wulfred helped to crown Beornwulf as well. For Wulfred the incentive to remove Ceolwulf was to recover Reculver and Minster-in-Thanet, for him a test case.[123] At stake with the Kentish royal minsters in general was a revenue probably equal to a quarter of all the landed wealth of Kent.[124] No better incentive could be imagined for the

[118] *L'Estoire des Engleis*, ed. Bell, p. 71. Bond ('Links between *Beowulf* and Mercian History', 485) regards the bad king Heremod as the poet's portrait of Ceolwulf.
[119] Brooks, *Early History of the Church of Canterbury*, 134–6.
[120] Williams, 'Mercian Coinage and Authority', 222.
[121] Brooks, *Early History of the Church of Canterbury*, 135–6.
[122] Keynes, 'The Control of Kent in the Ninth Century', 119.
[123] Brooks, *Early History of the Church of Canterbury*, 155–60.
[124] Ibid. 178–206. Keynes, 'The Control of Kent in the Ninth Century', 117.

archbishop to bring Beornwulf to power. The Council of the Legates in 786 had ignored the issue of the lay lordship of monasteries, but later Wulfred based his reforms on Frankish ones and his journey to Rome in 814 followed Emperor Louis' accession in the same year.[125] Ten years later Louis would tighten his grip on the Vatican by imposing an oath of loyalty on the pope.[126] At this stage Beornwulf needed both papal and imperial support. As we have seen, Louis the Pious supported King Heriold of the Danes from *c.*815 to 826; so he would have done later with Beornwulf, with the pope's blessing: it is alleged that Beornwulf granted land to St Peter's in Gloucester as a *comes*, thus even before he became king.[127] In this Beornwulf resembles not only Cenwulf, who started by dedicating Winchcome to St Peter, but also Offa, who gave candles and 365 mancuses to St Peter's in Rome annually after the Council of the Legates in 786.[128] It is thus plausible that in 823 both the emperor Louis the Pious (814–40) and Paschal I, later followed by Eugenius II (824–7), helped Beornwulf to make himself king, with Wulfred as his archbishop.

Where *Beowulf* is concerned, we should note that Beowulf appears equally passive: having turned down the throne of Geatland on Hygelac's death, offered by the queen, he agrees only to support the next king; then, having stood by or off while the young king was killed, Beowulf still does not intervene but allows himself to be made king of the Geats by a benign foreign power. In Chapter 2 we have seen that Beowulf's assumption of kingship, as it is unparalleled in the analogues, was probably invented by the poet of *Beowulf.* In this case it seems that the poet has styled Beowulf's accession on the papal and imperial intervention in Mercia at the time of Ceolwulf's exile (and probably death) in 823.

King Beowulf restores land to its rightful owners

In *Beowulf,* the hero's restoration of familial land to Wiglaf, a distant kinsman, is given as the younger man's first reason for rushing in to help him:

> Gemunde ða ða are,   þe he him ær forgeaf,
> wicstede weligne   Wægmundinga,
> folcrihta gehwylc,   swa his fæder ahte. (*Beo* 2607–9)

[Then it was that he remembered the favours which Beowulf had formerly given him, a wealthy dwelling-place of the Wægmundings, each and every tribal entitlement just as his father had had.]

That Wiglaf son of Weohstan is both a Wægmunding and a Swede, *leod Scylfinga* ('prince of the Scylfings', line 2604), suggests that he was born in Sweden, the

[125] Brooks, *Early History of the Church of Canterbury,* 175–8 and 188–90.
[126] McKitterick, *The Frankish Kingdoms under the Carolingians,* 132–3 (the *Constitutio Romana*).
[127] *Historia et cartularium Gloucestriæ,* ed. Hart, i. 111.
[128] *Epistolae,* ed. Dümmler, ii. 187–9, at 188–9 (no. 127); *EHD,* 861–2 (no. 205). Levison, *England and the Continent in the Eighth Century,* 30–1.

country of his mother, where his father, as the holder of a Geatish estate, must therefore have been living in exile. Weohstan has killed Eanmund in the same battle in which Heardred also died. In this light, as we have seen in Chapter 2, Beowulf's decision to give Wiglaf the sword of Eanmund, which his father had kept, rather than kill him in vengeance for Heardred, is tantamount to his recognition that Hygelac was in the wrong.

In Mercia, likewise, there is evidence that Beornwulf at least tried to restore lands which Cenwulf and Ceolwulf had purloined from the Church. This process was no doubt begun by Archbishop Wulfred, who jointly presided with King Beornwulf over the Councils of *Clofesho* in 824 and 825. Each council survives in two records, that of Canterbury and Worcester. The first council was grand enough to be cited in the *Anglo-Saxon Chronicle* (*s.a.* 822 [824]) and the Worcester record of this council cites a papal envoy named Nothhelm, who is proof that the Carolingians were playing a role, as they had with Eardwulf in York, even if for different reasons.[129] Whereas the Canterbury version of this council says that king and archbishop presided jointly at *Clofesho* (S 1434), that of Worcester specifies that while Beornwulf presided (*præsidente ibi rege præfato*), Wulfred directed and guided (*Wulfredo archiepiscopo illo conventu regente ac moderante*, S 1433). In this light it looks as if Beornwulf's power depended on Wulfred.

Probably having used Wulfred to secure his Mercian kingdom, the new king almost certainly needed his archdiocesan infrastructure to hold it together. Outside Beornwulf's tribal area there were other ealdormen whose claims to rule may have matched his, nor is there reliable evidence that he controlled King Baldred in Kent or minted coins in Canterbury or in London.[130] The attestations of Cyneberht, apparently Cenwulf's nephew, after Beornwulf's accession probably show that Cenwulf's family still ruled their Winchcombe heartland, east of the Hwiccean regions which I have suggested were Beornwulf's expanded family domain.[131] Cwenthryth appears to have drawn Beornwulf into her orbit after her father's death, which is probably why Wulfred failed to recoup his property from her before Wiglaf's accession.

The whole case was summarized in the Canterbury record of the Council of *Clofesho* in 825, written in 827 (S 1436). Confused as the Latin is, it conveys an impression of Beornwulf as a man torn between piety towards Wulfred and an old obligation to Cenwulf's family. Although Cwenthryth had flouted her side of the 824 agreement, Wulfred forced Beornwulf to reopen the case:

Postea autem placuit Beornwulfo regi pro amicitia hereditatis Coenwulfi regis heredesque illius cum suis sapientibus illo prenominato archiepiscopo istarum supradictum rerum

    [129] Story, *Carolingian Connections*, 210–11. Cubitt, *Anglo-Saxon Church Councils*, 221.
    [130] Williams, 'Mercian Coinage and Authority', 223. Keynes, 'Mercia and Wessex in the Ninth Century', 320–2.
    [131] Keynes, 'Mercia and Wessex in the Ninth Century', 315–16 (S 1433, 1436).

reconciliationem et emendationem diligentissime facere decrevisset. humilique præce deposcebat ut huic reconciliatione pro amore Dei et amicitia illius adnueret. quia hereditas et heres ejus ad intercessorem et ad patronem eum expetivit.[132]

[And afterwards it pleased King Beornwulf, with his advisers and for the sake of his friendship with King Cenwulf's estate and his heir [Cwenthryth], to decree that a reconciliation and amendment be most diligently made concerning the above-named matters with the aforesaid archbishop [Wulfred]. With humble prayer he [Beornwulf] requested that he [Wulfred] assent to this reconciliation for the sake of his love of God and friendship with him [Beornwulf], in that the estate and heir of this man [Cwenthryth, Cenwulf's daughter] had desired him to be their go-between and advocate.]

Hereafter Cwenthryth paid Wulfred 100 hides of land around London, with all the pertaining charters and some new liberties, but continued to withhold Reculver and Minster-in-Thanet in Kent. Only at the beginning of King Wiglaf's reign (827–39) did Wulfred get these minsters back, together with other land in Harrow and in Kent.[133] On this score Beornwulf had failed, yet in his short reign he carried out at least some of what Wulfred expected of him with Cwenthryth; the Selsey charter shows that he restored Denton to Bishop Cynred of Sussex as well.[134] By 825 Beornwulf had won this much recognition for restoring stolen minsters to their owners.[135] Just so does the poet of *Beowulf* present Beowulf as a wise king who ignores his connection with Hygelac's family in order to restore Weohstan's land to Wiglaf, Weohstan's son (see further in Chapter 10).

Beowulf dies unmarried, childless, guiltless of intrigue

In Chapter 4 I have argued that Beowulf shows an interest in acquiring Freawaru, whom Hrothgar and Wealhtheow betroth to King Ingeld of the Heathobards. Nor does the poet give Beowulf a queen in later years when he becomes king, just at the time when he should consider begetting an heir. This omission is strange, unless we attribute to the poet some difficulty in the literary task of elevating a champion into a king. Stranger still is the Geatish lady by his funeral pyre who publicly laments both Beowulf and the fate of the Geats (lines 3150–5). She may be Beowulf's concubine, but the poet leaves this question open as well.

In his first dying speech, made to Wiglaf when he knows his time is up, Beowulf draws attention to his lack of offspring:

> 'Nu ic suna minum   syllan wolde
> guðgewædu   þær me gifeðe swa
> ænig yrfeweard   æfter wurde
> lice gelenge.' (*Beo* 2729–32)

---

[132] S 1436 (BCS 384). *Councils and Ecclesiastical Documents*, ed. Haddan and Stubbs, iii. 600–1.
[133] Gelling, *The Early Charters of the Thames Valley*, 102–4 (no. 206): Harrow, *Herefreðing lond*, Wembley and Yeading; 4 hides at Harrow, 30 *æt cumbe*.
[134] S 1435 (BCS 387). *Charters of Selsey*, ed. Kelly, 59–65.
[135] Cubitt, *Anglo-Saxon Church Councils*, 222.

['Now I would give battle raiment to my son, were it so granted to me that any heir related to my person should come after me.']

He goes on to proclaim his fifty-year monarchic record, the fear he instilled in royal neighbours, his continence as a ruler on earth, his disdain for *searoniðas* ('cunning enmities', contradicted by the poet on line 3067) and adherence to oaths. In all this he can take pleasure:

> 'for ðam me witan ne ðearf   waldend fira
> morðorbealo maga,   þonne min sceaceð
> lif of lice.' (*Beo* 2741–3)

['for this the Ruler of Men will have no need to blame me for the violent murder of kinsmen, when my life moves out of my body.']

Hereby, perhaps, Beowulf shuns the example set by the Frisians in Finnsburh, whose own *morþorbealo maga* consisted of Finn's slaying of his brother-in-law and the death of his son (line 1079). In the immediate context, however, Beowulf could be referring to his aid of kinsman Wiglaf despite the fact that Wiglaf's father deserved to die for his role in the battle in which Heardred, Beowulf's maternal cousin, died.

Neither is any queen, son, or internecine killing of Beornwulf's recorded in Mercia. Like Æthelbald, he may have found it expedient to take mistresses rather than a wife.[136] Gaimar, in *L'Estoire des Engleis*, says that Beornwulf ruled Mercia jointly with another king called *Lutecan* ('Ludeca'), *primi inter pares* among the seven ealdormen of Mercia.[137] According to the Worcester *Chronicle*, Ludeca was Beornwulf's *propinquus* ('cousin on the male side').[138] When Beornwulf died in 826, Ludeca lasted for about a year.

On the matter of intrigue, however, early in Beornwulf's reign, in the same year as the great *Clofesho* council of 824, or even at this council, two Mercian ealdormen were killed whose names were Burhhelm and Muca.[139] John of Worcester calls them *duces robustissimi* ('the most vigorous ealdormen').[140] Muca is not found in charters until Ceolwulf's reign, in which he attests both of this king's surviving charters as Ceolwulf's fourth *dux* in 822 and his

---

[136] Kirby, *Earliest English Kings*, 134.

[137] *L'Estoire des Engleis*, ed. Bell, 73 (lines 2277–81, esp. 2281); *entr'els aveit set reietels* ('there were seven earls among them').

[138] *The Chronicle of John of Worcester*, ed. Darlington and McGurk, trans. Bray and McGurk, 242–3.

[139] *The Anglo-Saxon Chronicle*, trans. Swanton, 60–1 (AE, *s.a.* 822 [824]). With the addition of *ibidem* ('in that place' rather than 'at the same time', Æthelweard may indicate that he thought these men were killed at the Council of *Clofesho*: *Chronicle of Æthelweard*, ed. and trans. Campbell, 28: 'Anno igitur transacto facta est synodus magna in loco qui Clofesho nuncupatur, et duo ibidem duces interimuntur, Burghelm et Muca'; see ibid., p. xxiv, where Campbell suggests that his 'at the same time' for *ibidem* is 'slightly mistranslated'.

[140] *The Chronicle of John of Worcester*, ed. Darlington and McGurk and trans. Bray and McGurk, 240–1.

fifth in 823.[141] Five places behind him on the latter occasion was Beornwulf. The fact that Muca had no visible standing in Cenwulf's reign probably tells us that he was Ceolwulf's man and had supported his claim to the throne on Cenwulf's death. The fact that he outlasted Ceolwulf suggests that Beornwulf needed Muca to secure power. Muca's death may show that by 824 Beornwulf had achieved this.

Muca's doomed associate Burhhelm has a name which suggests a relation between him and Burgred, later king of Mercia (852–74). In itself Burhhelm's name shows that he belonged to a kindred which later believed itself to be royal. The name can be linked with that of Burhhild, who, as we have seen, appears to have been a daughter of King Cenwulf with an estate at Culham, south of Abingdon. This name, which appears in St Kenelm's *Vita et miracula*, has been regarded as a fiction because her name does not alliterate with the C-prefixes of Cenwulf's family, also because she is produced as Cwenthryth's moral foil.[142] The more serious objection can be overturned in that Pybba and Penda, for example, both had sons with non-alliterating names (Penda, Eowa; Wulfhere, Æthelred, Merewalh; though not Coenwalh: see above). The implication in the case of these children, probably in Burhhild's also, is that they were born of different mothers with names chosen by or after maternal grandfathers. Despite Abingdon's implication to the contrary, it seems that Queen Ælfthryth was not Burhhild's mother.

Cenwulf's other woman fits with Alcuin's intimation to 'Osberht', probably Brorda, in 797 that both Cenwulf and Eardwulf were slighting their wives by adulteries with noblewomen.[143] A *Burg*-kindred on the southern border of the old Hwiccean kingdom seems likely in respect of Bishop Burghard of Würzburg (742–55), friend of Abbess Cyneburh (of Bradley near Inkberrow). Burghard may have counted as a West Saxon.[144] Burhhild's existence points to an affair between Cenwulf and a lady of this family which had become public knowledge before 797. If they had one child, why not two? The names of Burhhild and Burhhelm alliterate both in their prefix and in the *hild* and *helm* suffixes. Burhhelm also has the same name-suffix as Cynehelm, Cenwulf's legitimate son. This putative relation between Cenwulf and Burhhelm may be supported by a statement in Asser's late ninth-century *Vita Ælfredi*.[145] When Asser says that Eadburh, Alfred's mother-in-law, was *de regali genere Merciorum regis* ('of the royal family of the king of Mercia'), he probably refers to Burgred, who ruled

---

[141] S 186 (BCS 370) and 187 (BCS 373). Keynes, *Atlas of Attestations*, table XVII. Muca's 4th-*dux* position in S 186 may be explained by the fact that Beornnoth is not there.

[142] *Vita et miracula s. Kenelmi*, ed. Love, 54–5 n. 1.

[143] *Epistolae*, ed. Dümmler, ii. 179 (no. 122): 'nec despiciant uxores priores propter adulteria feminarum nobilium.'

[144] Sims-Williams, *Religion and Literature*, 192–3. Wallace-Hadrill, *The Frankish Church*, 155.

[145] I presume this is Asser's work, in line with S. D. Keynes, 'On the Authenticity of Asser's *Life of King Alfred*', *Journal of English History*, 47 (1996), 529–51; contrary to the case argued in A. P. Smyth, *Alfred the Great* (Oxford, 1995).

Mercia when Alfred married Eadburh's daughter (Ealhswith) in the late 860s.[146] Indeed Burgred, having fled the Vikings some twenty years before Asser was writing, could be called the last true king of Mercia. But where did Burgred's claim to royalty lie? Clearly not in antecedents such as Bishop Burghard; and the *Burg*-prefix is not found in the Anglian collection of royal genealogies. Asser's meaning is that Eadburh was of royal blood because like the king of Mercia, Burgred, she was descended from Offa or Cenwulf.

Both Offa and Cenwulf had a claim to royal blood through a genealogy. Eadburh's connection is clearer with Cenwulf, the more recent, if we take him to have fathered an illegitimate daughter named Burhhild. In this case there is reason to suppose that Burgred was a kinsman of Burhhild and that, like her, he could trace himself to Cenwulf, scion of Cenwalh. So Burgred was either Cenwulf's son or his grandson. If the latter, he was the son of Burhhild, or of the Burhhelm who was killed in 824. Either way, it seems Burhhelm was killed because he had a claim to the throne.[147] The *Anglo-Saxon Chronicle* makes no connection between Beornwulf and Burhhelm's untimely death. On the other hand, the fact that Beornwulf was then king, one without queen or heirs, makes it likely that it was he who had Burhhelm killed. Just as resolute as the *Chronicle*'s reserve in laying blame here is the hero's claim in *Beowulf* that the Lord will not reproach him for any *morðorbealo maga* of his own.

Beowulf dies in pursuit of treasure

As we have seen in my Chapters 2 and 7, Hygelac's is the example Beowulf should have reason to avoid. Dying on the Rhine far from home in pursuit of treasure, Hygelac embodies a negative *wlenco*, pride born of lust for gold. This disaster of his making is meant to stand in sharp contrast to the *ece rædas* ('eternal rewards', line 1760) to which Hrothgar directs Beowulf. That is to say, Hygelac becomes the devil to Hrothgar's angel: at the end of his own life Beowulf must choose between them. In various ways it seems that Beowulf might fail this moral test. When the barrow-thief hands him the cup that started the dragon's fire-raids over Geatland, the treasure comes physically close to Beowulf's heart:

> him to bearme cwom
> maðþumfæt mære   þurh ðæs meldan hond. (*Beo* 2404–5)

[towards his bosom came the renowned treasure cup from the hand of the informer.]

At the end of his speech to the bodyguard before facing the dragon, Beowulf might surprise us by announcing the motive of gain:

---

[146] *Asser's Life of King Alfred*, ed. Stevenson, 24 (ch. 29).
[147] Keynes, 'The Control of Kent in the Ninth Century', 119: 'it would appear that Mercia was beginning to come apart at the seams.'

> 'Ic mid elne sceall
> gold gegangan,   oððe guð nimeð,
> feorhbealu frecne,   frean eowerne.' (*Beo* 2535–7)

['With courage I shall get the gold, or battle, savage life-harm, will take your lord.']

It is startling to think of gold as the motive for Beowulf's combat with the dragon, yet once again, when he orders Wiglaf to enter the mound, he asks to see the ancient treasures:

> 'þæt ic þy seft mæge
> æfter maððumwelan   min alætan
> lif ond leodscipe   þone ic longe heold.' (*Beo* 2749–51)

['so that I may the more easily, in keeping with the wealth of this treasure, leave behind both my life and the nation which I have long ruled.']

Thus ends Fitt XXXVII, with proof, in Beowulf's own words, that he desires to plunder the dragon's hoard. As Eric Stanley has shown, Beowulf's words for the treasure in this speech anticipate the words *gold-* and *agend* and the phrase *gearwor...hæfde gesceawod* in the anathema of the cursed hoard in lines 3074–5.[148] In these vexed lines towards the end of the poem, the poet prepares us for the possibility that Beowulf will fail to attain heaven.[149] The question of riches and their temptation to heathens, Beowulf included, has in any case been introduced with the *Brosinga mene* early in lines 1197–201. Beowulf is a heathen king, whose ears may have been deaf to Hrothgar's words on eternal reward in lines 1758–61, in the textual heart of *Beowulf*.

Like Beowulf after Hygelac, in Christian Mercia of the early ninth century there is evidence that Beornwulf was killed as suddenly as Cenwulf and for the same reason: on a raid in pursuit of treasure. Beornwulf died this way in East Anglia in 826. Initially without the lineage to rule Mercia, as we have seen, he had to shore up his power. The later testimony hints at extravagance: Gaimar says that Beornwulf *menot boban* ('behaved with arrogance').[150] Neither this nor his statement that Beornwulf shared the kingdom with his cousin Ludeca gives the impression that he had the same hold over Mercia as Cenwulf.[151] An idea of Beornwulf as a big spender of no background appears also in the *Historia Croylandensis*, which says that King Ceolwulf *a Barnulpho quodam fatuoso, et diuitiis ac potentia pollenti, in nulloque lineam regalem contingente expulsus est* ('was driven out by a foolish man named Beornwulf, mighty in riches and power but touched by no royal line').[152]

---

[148] Stanley, 'Hæthenra Hyht in *Beowulf*', 145–6.
[149] Ibid. 148–51. See my Ch. 7.
[150] *L'Estoire des Engleis*, ed. Bell, 73 (line 2279).
[151] For *primus inter pares* as the style of ninth-century Mercian kingship, see Keynes, 'Mercia and Wessex in the Ninth Century', 319.
[152] *Chronicle of Croyland Abbey*, ed. Birch, 12.

As he was without an heir, it was probably the wealth for which Beornwulf strove to become king of Mercia. Fifty years before him, Offa's income had increased through his acquisition of monastic lands, as had that of Cenwulf later with Winchcombe.[153] Both Offa and Cenwulf secured the rights to minsters in West Saxon regions, Offa in Bath in 781 and Cenwulf in Glastonbury in 797; and both took advantage of victories to secure the rights to Kentish minsters, Offa in 785 and Cenwulf in 798.[154] There is no corresponding evidence of Beornwulf's affiliation, either by treaty or conquest, with a minster south of Mercia. Yet an ambition in Beornwulf to secure foreign revenues better than annual plunder can be read into the entry in the *Anglo-Saxon Chronicle* which leads up to his defeat at *Ellendun*, modern Elcombe near an ancient hill-fort by Wroughton, south of Swindon, at the foot of the Wiltshire Downs.[155] Kirby treats *Ellendun* as Beornwulf's attempted invasion of Wessex, timed to coincide with a presumption of Ecgberht's absence on campaign in Devon and Cornwall.[156] There is nothing unexpected in such a move. It had almost certainly been for territorial gain in 802 that Æthelmund of the Hwicce rode across the border south to Kempsford on the day of Ecgberht's coronation, only to die in battle against Ealdorman Weohstan of the Wiltshiremen.[157] Thereafter the frontier was fixed further north in favour of the West Saxons.[158] Later King Ecgberht seems to have responded, for in a tale recorded by Leland it was said that he defeated Cenwulf at a place called *Cherren hul*.[159] John Blair identifies this with Cherbury Hill, an ancient tumulus between Pusey and Southmoor south-west of Oxford.[160] This site also lies 6 or 7 miles south-south-east of Cenwulf's new Eynsham estate and some 9 miles west of Cenwulf's grant of land allegedly to Burhhild at Culham. Yet the name seems close to Churn Knob or Churn Hill, names for another tumulus which lies 11 miles south-south-east of Culham, a little to the west of the old Roman road from Silchester to Dorchester.[161] Whichever site it is, the legend of *Cherren hul*, if genuine, looks based on an attempt by Ecgberht to seize an estate belonging to Cenwulf's (second) family around Abingdon.

The position of Roman roads around Wroughton gives an impression of Beornwulf's starting point and aims. An old Roman highway may be seen leading north-west to south-east from Gloucester (*Glevum*) through Cirencester (*Corinium*) to Swindon (*Durocornovium?*), before a new road forks off almost due

[153] *The Anglo-Saxons*, ed. Campbell, 111–17.

[154] Cubitt, *Anglo-Saxon Church Councils*, 224–9, esp. 225–6. *Charters of Abingdon Abbey, Part I*, ed. Kelly, pp. cciii–ccvi, esp. cciv. Yorke, *Wessex in the Early Middle Ages*, 61–4.

[155] Trans. based on *The Anglo-Saxon Chronicle*, trans. Swanton, 60–1 (AE).

[156] Kirby, *Earliest English Kings*, 189.

[157] *The Anglo-Saxon Chronicle*, trans. Swanton, 58–9 (*s.a.* 800 [802]).

[158] Yorke, *Wessex in the Early Middle Ages*, 64.

[159] *The Itinerary of John Leland*, ed. Toulmin Smith, ii. 151–2.

[160] Blair, *Anglo-Saxon Oxfordshire*, 5–6 and 190 n. 60. OS Landranger Map 164, Oxford, 374963 (Cherbury).

[161] OS Explorer Map 170, Abingdon, Wantage & Vale of White Horse, 523845 (Charn Hill). OS, *Roman Britain*.

south up over the Downs to Marlborough (*Cunetio*), then south-east through East Anton (*Leucomagus?*) to Winchester in the West Saxon royal heartland (*Venta Bulgarum*).[162] Beornwulf, according to my speculation, may have mustered his troops around his base in Gloucester, marched them through West Saxon territory in north Wiltshire, then left the road before Swindon, in order to make the Marlborough highway further south at Chiseldon. Halfway on this cross-country detour along the foot of the Downs lies Wroughton, which is presumably where Ecgberht ambushed him from higher ground.[163]

Henry of Huntingdon, in the early twelfth century, embroidered his description of this battle with a Latin rendering of an otherwise unknown Old English battle poem.[164] Set out according to the alliterative rules of Old English poetry, it looks like this:

> Vnde dicitur: Ællendune riuus
>   cruore rubuit,   ruina restitit,
>   fetore tabuit.

[Whence it is said: Ællendune's stream was reddened with blood, was stopped up with the fallen, was filled with stench.][165]

This focus is on battle as a gory tableau in which a quiet aftermath is set off against the recall of earlier violence. The same is a feature of *The Battle of Brunanburh* (*s.a.* 937). In *Brunanburh* the Vikings flee in disarray; in Henry's lost poem, a similar flight for Beornwulf might be imagined consistent with his odd notice about Beornwulf later, that *ab Ecgbricto rege bello uictus demarcuit*.[166] Roger of Wendover records a victor's homecoming for Ecgberht not too unlike that of Æthelstan and Eadmund in *Brunanburh*:

Egbertus, rex occidentalium Saxonum, pugnavit contra Bernulfum, regem Merciorum, apud Hellendunam partes suas hostiliter petentem, ubi, maximo gentis utrorumque regum peracto exitio, Egbertus victor funestus ad propria remeavit.[167]

[King Ecgberht of the West Saxons fought at *Ellendun* (*Hellenduna*) against Beornwulf king of Mercia who was seeking out his regions with hostile intent, and here, the greatest destruction having been achieved among the people of both kings, Ecgberht, a victor in mourning, returned to his own lands.]

That *Brunanburh* survives in the *Anglo-Saxon Chronicle* gives reason to suppose that Henry read a version of the *Chronicle* with a West Saxon panegyric on *Ellendun*.[168]

---

[162] OS, Roman Britain. Hill, *Atlas of Anglo-Saxon England*, 116 (no. 199).

[163] OS Explorer Map 169, Cirencester & Swindon, 134183 (Elcombe).

[164] On his familiarity with Old English, see D. E. Greenaway, 'Henry of Huntingdon', in *EA-SE*, 232–3.

[165] *Historia Anglorum*, ed. and trans. Greenaway, 262–3 (iv. 29).

[166] Ibid. 270–1 (iv. 24): 'being defeated in war by King Ecgberht, he disappeared.'

[167] *Rogeri de Wendover Chronica*, ed. Coxe, i. 275.

[168] Bond ('Links between *Beowulf* and Mercian History', 492) sees an allusion to *Ellendun* in the word *ellensioc* ('with failing strength'), which describes the dying Beowulf on line 2787.

Notwithstanding the exaggeration of twelfth-century chroniclers, *Ellendun* seems to have been a turning point for King Beornwulf of Mercia. In the eighth and ninth centuries a king's power rested on his ability to keep followers; this derived from his means of paying them.[169] For Beornwulf after *Ellendun* this may have become difficult. The emporium in *Hamwih*, near Southampton, would already be in Ecgberht's hands.[170] Ecgberht now lost no time in sending his son Æthelwulf, Bishop Ealhstan of Sherborne, and Ealdorman Wulfheard with a force to invade Canterbury, drive out King Baldred and show no favour to Wulfred.[171] London may have been covered on the same march. If Beornwulf had had a stake in London's trade (it is not certain that he issued coins from there), London can hardly have been his city after 825. It was at this time that the East Angles made a request to Ecgberht, according to the *Anglo-Saxon Chronicle*, for his help against their *Miercna ege* ('fear of Mercians').[172] Evidently Cenwulf had tightened Offa's grip on East Anglia as a vassal province. Following Cenwulf, most extant coins of King Beornwulf and his successor Ludeca are known to have been minted in East Anglia.[173] Central to the East Anglian trading economy was Ipswich, a mart almost equal to London in importance.[174] Richard Hodges suggests that when Ipswich was enlarged in imitation of *Hamwih* (near Southampton) after 757, 'East Anglia may have had far more advanced production and distribution systems than its better-known and far grander neighbour Mercia.'[175] So it can be no coincidence that Offa, who shifted the balance of power towards Mercia in 780–5, reached his zenith in 786–9. In large measure the increased prosperity of his kingdom towards the end of the eighth century seems due to Ipswich. Charlemagne's embargo aimed to close continental ports to English shipping from 789 to at least 794 if not a year longer.[176] During this time it may well have suited the East Angles better to trade with the Franks on their own account; it is known that King Æthelberht began to mint coins independently of Offa, with a she-wolf motif that states the *romanitas* of his East Anglian kingdom;[177] hence, perhaps, his execution in 794 and a rebellion in East Anglia in 796. The decline in the Rhineland trade in the 820s would have provided an even greater incentive for Beornwulf to secure his control over the East Anglian economy in 826.[178]

---

[169] Williams, 'Military Institutions and Royal Power', 299–300 and 304–5.

[170] On *Hamwih* and *Lundenwic* see Welch, 'The Archaeology of Mercia', 157–8.

[171] Brooks, *Early History of the Church of Canterbury*, 197–8.

[172] *The Anglo-Saxon Chronicle*, trans. Swanton, 60–1 (*s.a.* 823 [825]).

[173] Williams, 'Mercian Coinage and Authority', 223.

[174] Hodges, *The Anglo-Saxon Achievement*, 115–49, at 119–20 and 135.

[175] Ibid. 142–3. For a view that Offa built *burhs* (as a second tier of Mercian trading sites further inland in Bedford, Cambridge, and Northampton; and on the western side of his kingdom, in Hereford and Worcester), see Haslam, 'Market and Fortress in England in the Reign of Offa', 87–92, esp. 89.

[176] *Gesta abbatum Fontanellensium*, ed. Loewenfeld, 46 (ch. 16). *Epistolae*, ed. Dümmler, ii. 31–3 (no. 7). *EHD*, 341 (no. 20).

[177] Gannon, *Iconography of Early Anglo-Saxon Coinage*, 145–7.

[178] R. Hodges, 'Trade and Market Origins in the Ninth Century: An Archaeological Perspective of Anglo-Carolingian Relations', in M. Gibson and J. L. Nelson (eds.), *Charles the Bald: Court and Kingdom*, British Archaeological reports, International Series 101 (London, 1981), 213–33.

Beornwulf was killed in a battle in East Anglia probably in the summer, the campaigning season, of this year. From 831 Beornnoth's absence in Wiglaf's charters may suggest that he died in the same battle. Beornwulf's successor and kinsman Ludeca is said to have died in 827: I shall study Ludeca in relation to Wiglaf in the following chapter. For now it is enough to consider Beornwulf in his last battle. For the West Saxons, this was small enough to be slipped into the *Chronicle*'s entry for 823 [825] as a sequel in which Ecgberht's clients mop up after the victory in *Ellendun*:

þy ilcan geare East Engla cyning ond seo þeod gesohte Ecgbryht cyning him to friþe ond mundboran for Miercna ege, ond þy geare slogon East Engle Beornwulf Miercna cyning.

[The same year the king and people of the East Angles petitioned king Ecgberht as a guarantor and protector for them for their fear of Mercians, and that year the East Angles slew King Beornwulf of the Mercians.]

But the twelfth-century *Chronicle* of John of Worcester presents a more detailed account:

Qui petitioni illorum adquieuit, et se libenter eos adiuturum in omnibus spopondit. Verum hec Beornuulfus rex Merciorum uilipendens exercitum collegit non modicum, illorumque fines hostiliter intrauit atque neci optimum quemque tradere festinauit. Contra quem rex eorum cum suis ascendit, initoque prelio, illum cum maxima parte sui exercitus interfecit.[179]

[Ecgberht agreed to their petition, and vouched safe that he would willingly help them in all matters. But Beornwulf, king of the Mercians, weighing this up cheaply, mustered no small army, invaded their territory with hostile intent, and hastened to deliver any man of standing to execution. Their king went up with his own men against Beornwulf, and with battle joined, killed him together with the greatest part of his army.]

This entry is found in the first part of the Worcester *Chronicle*, a work which was undertaken under Bishop Wulfstan (1062–95) by the monk John, partly with the help of a version of the *Anglo-Saxon Chronicle* which is now lost.[180] It is thus unlikely that Beornwulf's savagery in his last hours is a detail cooked up out of sympathy with East Anglia. New here is Ecgberht's offer of help, the success of this petition as Beornwulf's reason for invading East Anglia, his disdain for Ecgberht's generalship, his plan to exterminate the East Anglian bloodline, and the military role of the East Anglian king.

This man, if present, was probably 'Æthelstan' in whose honour a new series of coins appeared in East Anglia in the late 820s. As the new king of East Anglia, he has been identified with the Æthelstan who was Ecgberht's son, Æthelwulf's elder

---

[179] Trans. adapted from *The Chronicle of John of Worcester*, ed. Darlington and McGurk, trans. Bray and McGurk, 242–3.

[180] *The Chronicle of John of Worcester*, ed. Darlington and McGurk, pp. lxvii–lxxxi, esp. lxxix–lxxxi. S. Keynes, 'John, Monk of Worcester (d. *c*.1140)', in *EA-SE*, 262–3. Cyril Hart suggests a Ramsey provenance for this part of the Worcester *Chronicle*. See C. R. Hart, 'The Early Section of the *Worcester Chronicle*', *Journal of Medieval History*, 9 (1983), 251–315.

brother, and Alfred's uncle.[181] On the other hand, this *Æthel*-stan is more likely to have been a kinsman of *Æthel*-berht. When Ludeca died in 827, Mercia lost control of East Anglia for good. The coinage then tells us that Æthelstan, whoever he was, succeeded in wresting the East Anglian trade from Beornwulf's family. It may have been the prospect of this that drove Beornwulf to invade East Anglia. There is irony in John's expression of Beornwulf's pride. The word *uilipendens*, a financial metaphor with which John says he weighed up Ecgberht's intervention cheaply, reminds us that Beornwulf paid the ultimate price. The East Angles, Ecgberht's instrument for exacting this, were reminding Beornwulf of their own king whom Offa had killed thirty-two years before. It may be this East Anglian vengeance which explains why the poet of *Beowulf*, in lines 1925–61, appears to charge Offa's queen at such length for the death of St Æthelberht, *leofne mannan* that he was ('beloved man', line 1943). So I suggest that Beornwulf's apparently financial motive for invading East Anglia was why the poet of *Beowulf*, who had probably removed Beowulf from the battle with Heoroweard in order to make him king, gave his hero the poisoned chalice of fighting a *hordweard* instead ('hoard-guardian', lines 2293, 2302).

CONCLUSION

How much of this historical analysis can be laid alongside *Beowulf* might be a matter for debate. It should be obvious that this is a legendary poem, not a Mercian chronicle. Defining *Beowulf* as an 'allegory' has always run the risk of seeming to impose a critical straitjacket on the manifold approaches to this poem. Just as there is far more going on in *Beowulf* than would ever seem likely in an Anglo-Saxon *roman à clef*, so any history reflected in *Beowulf* is likely to have been vastly more complicated than any of the great narrative contortions or moral themes of the poem. There are more than a few differences between Beowulf and Beornwulf. There will be many discordant notes in the ten claims of harmony below.

Nonetheless, I add these to the findings of earlier chapters (2, 4, 7, and 8) in which I have attempted to show that the poet's tale of Offa, Hygelac, Beowulf, and Wiglaf is a confection of four or five legends without interaction in a previous source. Why this poet digressed on Offa of Angeln, added Hygelac's story to Beowulf's, made Beowulf a king, brave yet spiritually compromised, then introduced 'Wiglaf' in the Hjalti-role may now become clearer if we line up ten parallels between *Beowulf* on one hand and thirty-two years of Mercian history on the other (794–826):

---

[181] H. E. Pagan, 'The Coinage of the East Anglian Kingdom from 825–870', *British Numismatic Journal*, 52 (1982), 41–83, esp. 57–67.

1. **Murder by Offa's queen (see Chapter 8).**

   In *Beo* 1925–61 the poet digresses on a princess who later became the queen of Offa of Angeln. He charges this young woman with the killing of suitors, illustrating this in one scene with the murder of a *leofne mannan* (line 1943). In Mercia, after Offa martyred King Æthelberht of East Anglia in 794, there was a legend that Offa's queen, Cynethryth, contrived this murder so that Offa could invade and conquer East Anglia.

2. **Hygelac saves his people, but robs them of land.**

   In retrospect in *Beowulf*, it is hypermetrically implied that Hygelac, having saved the Geats from the Swedes, strips estates from men such as Weohstan of the Wægmundings in order to reward Wulf and Eofor, two made men of lower rank. While Eofor marries Hygelac's daughter, each man wins from this king one hundred and twenty thousand in rings and land (120,000). Cenwulf, after saving Mercia from shrinkage and disintegration, despoiled the community at Canterbury to the extent that they later described him and his family as wolves. In his last eight years he abused Archbishop Wulfred with seizure of church property, suspension from office, and a fine of £120, which he commuted to the forfeit of Wulfred's massive Eynsham estate (300 hides).

3. **Beowulf is a close friend of Hygelac,**

   Hygelac is the best friend of Beowulf, who later supports his son Heardred. Cenwulf promoted an ealdorman named Beornnoth and later Beornwulf himself, who may have been Beornnoth's son. A charter suggests that Beornwulf, Beornnoth, and a certain Beornheard appeared in 812 to support Cenwulf's kingship when it may have been in crisis, not long after the death of his son Cynehelm. For a while Beornnoth and Beornwulf also became the men of Ceolwulf, Cenwulf's brother.

4. **who gives him land and hearth.**

   In *Beowulf*, Hygelac settles 7,000 hides of land on Beowulf. In Mercia Cenwulf helped Beornwulf's family to dominate Gloucestershire and Worcestershire, the old lands of the Hwicce, which the Tribal Hidage sets at 7,000 hides. Moreover, Hygelac gives Beowulf a royal hall. It was with Cenwulf's approval that Beornnoth obtained a privilege for Pershore; it cannot have been otherwise that Beornwulf acquired what seems to have been his own proprietary monastery in Gloucester.

5. **Beowulf's lesser royal blood.**

   Beowulf's father was not a Geat. Beowulf thus has a status lower than that of Hygelac, who raises him to high office. This seems matched by the near certainty that Beornwulf's kindred had no royal blood. In another regard it may be guessed that Beornwulf was Cenwulf's sister's son, as in the case of Beowulf and Hygelac. But it must be emphasized that there is no record of Beornwulf's kinship with Cenwulf or with Mercian or other kings.

6. **Hygelac dies in pursuit of treasure; Beowulf avenges him.**

It has been noted that Hygelac's death in pursuit of Merovingian treasure is a recurring motif in *Beowulf*. So it is worth adding that in 821 Cenwulf, but not Beornwulf, met a similarly swift end on the Welsh frontier. Beowulf avenges Hygelac on the Frankish champion who killed him; it is thought to have been Beornwulf who sacked Degannwy and Powys in revenge for the death of Cenwulf.

7. **Heardred fails and Beowulf, his former regent, is made king.**

Upon Hygelac's death in *Beowulf* the land of the Geats becomes prey to weak kingship and invasion. At length, however, Beowulf becomes their saviour just as his mentor King Hrothgar predicts, when the good King Onela of Sweden, having killed Heardred, puts Beowulf on the Geatish throne. In Mercia, the anarchy engendered by King Ceolwulf, Cenwulf's brother, laid the country open to papal and imperial Frankish interference, which was realized when Archbishop Wulfred, with later papal and imperial aid, helped Beornwulf exercise power.

8. **Beowulf restores land to its rightful owners,**

It emerges in *Beowulf* that King Beowulf has the wisdom to restore Weohstan's family land to his son Wiglaf. In Mercia, there again, it was Beornwulf's royal mission to restore some stolen lands to the Church while he at least tried to win back others.

9. **dies unmarried, childless, and guiltless of intrigue,**

Neither Beowulf and Beornwulf appears to be married. Neither leaves an heir to rule after him. Beowulf claims that the Lord cannot reproach him for the murder of kinsmen; nor is Beornwulf associated with the killing of Ealdorman Burhhelm in 824, despite the fact that he was then king and despite the possibility that Burhhelm, who just may have been his cousin, had a stronger title to rule.

10. **but in pursuit of treasure.**

Beowulf is partly moved to slay the dragon for the treasure which it keeps in its hoard. This action costs him his life. Spiritually it may cost him his soul as well. Beornwulf died in an expedition against East Anglia while attempting to make himself sole heir to its economy.

How this disaster was regarded by Wiglaf, the next great king of Mercia, may tell us why the poem *Beowulf* was composed.

10

King Wiglaf and *Eanmundes laf*

This chapter will argue that *Beowulf* was composed for Wiglaf, an ealdorman of the northern Midlands, to help him win the throne of Mercia. Wiglaf ruled this kingdom from 827 to 828 and again from 830 to *c*.839. In the course of giving reasons for Wiglaf's patronage of *Beowulf*, I shall study his place in Mercian history. This is to continue the work of Chapters 8–9, in which I argue that the poet presented the kings Offa of Angeln, Hygelac, and Beowulf in sequence in the Geatish half of *Beowulf* in order to put his audience in mind, respectively, of the great Mercian kings Offa (757–96), Cenwulf (796–821), and Beornwulf (823–6). With Wiglaf it appears to be the poet's aim to complete the sequence; to show his audience that Wiglaf the Swede, who could be king of Geatland, has an English descendant, named Wiglaf, who should be king of Mercia. Thereafter I posit a date, speculate on how *Beowulf* reached Wessex, and make a case for the poet's aural signature.

WIGLAF IN *BEOWULF* AND MERCIA

The case for Wiglaf's patronage of *Beowulf* is supported by no reliable evidence outside the text. However, from studying the narrative common to Norse analogues for *Beowulf* in Chapters 2 and 4, I have concluded that the poet remodelled his legendary sources in order to develop his Beowulf-archetype from a champion into a king. The poet's novel integration of Hygelac into Beowulf's story may be added to the supposition, in Chapters 8–9, that the poet politicized his Beowulf-legend against a bitter vision of Cenwulf's reign. His delay, moreover, in imposing Wiglaf in the Hjalti-role towards the end in Geatland, rather than in the Danish court at the beginning of *Beowulf*, suggests that he wished to present the modern Wiglaf as King Beornwulf's kinsman and heir.

Wiglaf's lineages

The poet of *Beowulf* presents Wiglaf by name at the head of Fitt XXXVI, having introduced him at the end of the previous fitt as a man related to Beowulf by blood. Towards the end of Fitt XXXV the dragon fights back and Beowulf falters. Throughout the poet emphasizes Beowulf's new status as a king. He says that Beowulf's shield protected the *mærum þeodne* ('famed lord', line 2572) for less time than sought by his desire, that fate had decreed otherwise for the *Geata dryhten* ('Geats' warlord', line 2576), and that the sword of the *ðiodcyning* ('nation-king', line 2579) bit less sharply than required. He says that the *goldwine Geata* ('gold-giving friend of Geats', line 2584) did not boast of victory, but unwillingly was obliged to dwell in that otherworldly abode for which each man must give up his borrowed days.[1] Before the two combatants clash again, the dragon takes heart and for the first time reveals his voice; so Beowulf *nearo ðrowode fyre befongen se ðe ær folce weold* ('suffered harsh straits, engulfed in fire, he who had once ruled a people', lines 2594–5). At this moment Beowulf's retinue, the *æðelinga bearn* ('sons of princes', line 2597), leave him and run for their lives, all except one:

> Hiora in anum weoll
> sefa wið sorgum;   sibb' æfre ne mæg
> wiht onwendan   þam ðe wel þenceð.
>
> XXXVI   Wiglaf wæs haten,   Weoxstanes sunu
> leoflic lindwiga   leod Scylfinga
> mæg Ælfheres. (*Beo* 2599–604)

[In one of them the mind welled up with sorrows; nothing can ever turn kinship aside for the man who thinks what is right. XXXVI. Wiglaf he was called, son of Weohstan, an admirable shield-warrior, prince of the Scylfings, kinsman of Ælfhere.]

The poet in one fitt leaves an audience in suspense as to the young ætheling's identity, but in the next he leaves no doubt that Wiglaf and Beowulf come from the same stock. When it comes, Wiglaf's named introduction is the most formal in the poem, with appellation, patronymic, rank, tribal affiliation, and probably the name of his Swedish mother's brother as well.[2] Hereafter it is striking that Wiglaf is likewise foregrounded at the head of Fitts XXXVII, XXXVIII, [XXXVIIII], and XL: in total a concentration of five. With the opening details of Fitt XXXVI it is possible to connect him to Beowulf remotely through the Swedish mother of Beowulf's father Ecgtheow.[3] As deduced in Chapter 2, their relation may look like this:

---

[1] Mitchell and Robinson (*Beowulf*, ed., 139) make a bizarrely secular reading of these lines in which Beowulf is excused for retreating against his earlier vow not to (lines 2524–7).

[2] As noted by Orchard (*Companion*, 73), who, however, regards the poet's information on Ælfhere as 'variation being used for purely rhetorical effect' (p. 74).

[3] The simpler relationship posited by Norman Eliason ('Beowulf, Wiglaf and the Wægmundings', 98–105), with Wiglaf as Beowulf's (unknown) sister's son, cuts Beowulf out of the Wægmunding line in defiance of his claim to belong to it on lines 2813–14.

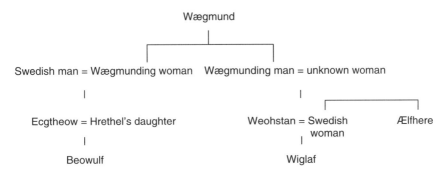

Yet the poet leaves the details vague. The most that can be said about his construct for the heritage of Beowulf and Wiglaf is that Wiglaf's claim to descend from the Wægmundings through his father is stronger than Beowulf's, which must proceed through Ecgtheow's mother. The poet makes it clear in this way that Beowulf belongs to a younger, less important, branch.

The poet continues to press home the connection between Beowulf and his young lieutenant. First he lets us know that Beowulf gave Wiglaf his father's estates (lines 2606–8). Then, through Wiglaf's Swedish sword, the poet reveals what might have been a different story: the risk to which Wiglaf was exposed in Beowulf's court as the son of the man who killed Beowulf's maternal cousin Heardred, Hygelac's son (lines 2610–25). The aim is probably to show their kinship reinvigorated. In his assumption of the Hjalti-role, Wiglaf's unnatural courage is justified as the most natural response to his kinship with Beowulf and to Beowulf's wisdom as a king. Alone of his friends, therefore, Wiglaf wades in to fight the dragon *under his mæges scyld* ('beneath his kinsman's shield', line 2675). When Beowulf revives but breaks his own sword with the strength of the blow, the dragon fatally bites him around the neck.[4]

> XXXVII Ða ic æt þearfe [gefrægn] þeodcyninges
> andlongne eorl ellen cyðan
> cræft ond cenðu swa him gecynde wæs. (*Beo* 2694–6)

[Then, I have heard, in the great king's hour of need did his upright nobleman make known his courage, his strength and bravery, as was fitting for the kin they had in common.]

Although he is not named at the head of this fitt, Wiglaf is praised through a powerful combination of three qualities, *ellen, cræft, cenðu*, which proceed in a chain of cause and effect.[5] Here they all come from a state of *gecynde*: both

[4] This is also the manner in which the serpent holds on to two unfortunates on the Repton cross-shaft, datable to the reign of Offa. See Clemoes, *Interactions of Thought and Language*, 59–65, esp. 63 (fig. 2).
[5] Ibid. 151: '"fighting spirit *and so* ability and boldness in action"'.

Wiglaf's courage and Beowulf's are drawn from the same Wægmunding well. So Wiglaf's hand burns, forcing him to help *his mæges* ('his kinsman', line 2698) by striking *þone niðgæst* ('that demon of enmity', line 2699) lower than the head. There is a divine guidance at work which tells Beowulf where to aim.[6] When Beowulf rallies, draws a knife and cuts through the dragon's middle, the poet gives credit for the slaying both to him and to Wiglaf as *sibæðelingas* ('nobles of a family', line 2708). Beowulf falls back and Wiglaf studies the dragon's megalithic chamber from inside the doorway, before laving his king's wounds.

Beowulf, recalling the poet's expression for Weohstan's legacy to his son on line 2623 (*geaf him... guðgewæda*), next says that he would give his *guðgewædu* ('battle-raiment', line 2730) to his son, if he had had one. This declaration leaves a strong hint that Wiglaf should be treated as Beowulf's adoptive son, now that the lack of a begotten one is clear. When Beowulf's speech ends with directions to bring back some of the hoard:

> XXXVIII   Ða ic snude gefrægn   sunu Wihstanes
> æfter wordcwydum   wundum dryhtne
> hyran headosiocum (*Beo* 2752–4)

[Then straightaway, I have heard, did the son of Weohstan, following these pronouncements, obey his wounded lord who was sick from the struggle.]

There follows an extended description of the hoard, one delivered as if passed down from ancestral memory, with a sardonic aside that *sinc eaðe mæg... gumcynnes gehwone oferhigian* ('treasure can easily outwit any man', lines 2764–6).[7] Yet Wiglaf is more eager to find out whether or not Beowulf is still alive. Hurrying back with some treasures, he finds him at the point of death and revives him so that he can sight the gold. Beowulf thanks the Lord for things which will accomplish his people's needs, now that he has bought them with his life. Now *in extremis*, he wants the treasure for his people, even if, in the end, the Geats choose to equip their king for his great hereafter by re-interring it all alongside him.[8] This hoard still intends to send its despoiler to hell (lines 3069–73) and Wiglaf ends up with none of it.

The only treasure Wiglaf accepts comes from around Beowulf's neck, when the *þeoden þristhydig* ('stouthearted king', line 2810), having ordered his tomb, gives Wiglaf a golden necklace, his gold-plated helmet, and coat of mail. This is just the giving of *guðgewædu* of which Beowulf spoke earlier, a father's to his son. So he makes Wiglaf his heir:[9]

> 'Þu eart endelaf   usses cynnes
> Wægmundinga;   ealle wyrd forsweop

---

[6] *Beowulf*, ed. Mitchell and Robinson, 142–3, n. to lines 2697–9.
[7] See Niles, *Beowulf*, 299 n. 6 (to ch. 10).
[8] Ibid. 222–3.
[9] *Pace* F. M. Biggs, who argues that patrilinear inheritance is the only royal model the poet endorses, in '*Beowulf* and Some Fictions of the Geatish Succession', *ASE* 32 (2003), 55–77, esp. 72–3.

> mine magas   to metodsceafte
> eorlas on elne;   ic him æfter sceal.' (*Beo* 2813–16)

['You are the last remnant of our tribe, the Wægmundings; all my kinsmen have been swept away by fate to their destiny, noblemen in their valour; I must go after them.']

Now that the Geats have run away, the Wægmundings are the only kindred who matter. In the light of this, it is of no consequence whether or not the Geats make Wiglaf their king. All the poet needs to prove in these lines is Wiglaf's right to become one.

How Wiglaf became king of Mercia is a matter for deduction rather than record. Following the death of Beornwulf in East Anglia in 826, Mercia was ruled for a year by a king named Ludeca, of whom little is known. Ludeca's name is listed ninth among laymen in King Beornwulf's surviving charters from *Clofesho* in 824 (S 1434, 1433), whereas no charters have come down from his own reign. John of Worcester refers to him as Beornwulf's *propinquus*, a word which probably denotes a 'cousin' on the paternal side.[10] But rule Mercia he did. A list of land-grants to Worcester refers to Ludeca's gift of an unknown estate at *Ludintun* to this western see.[11] Furthermore, a series of coins with Ludeca's name which was minted in East Anglia shows that he aimed to control the economy of this eastern kingdom as well.[12] He goes unmentioned in Æthelweard's version of the *Chronicle*, which derives from the earliest, but in versions of the *Chronicle* after 892, there are no fewer than four documented versions of his death. In the Alfredian version of the *Anglo-Saxon Chronicle* there is a tactful notice for '825' [827] that Ludeca was killed together with 'his five ealdormen'.[13] According to the Anglo-Norman *Estoire des Engleis*, based partly on another (now-lost) version of the *Chronicle*, Ludeca was killed by the Welsh, after having ruled Mercia jointly with Beornwulf.[14] There is a more fulsome account in the Worcester *Chronicle* in which Ludeca, his five earls, and many others were killed by the East Angles when he attacked them in a bid to avenge Beornwulf.[15] Roger of Wendover, without citing the ealdormen, says that Ludeca was killed by King Ecgberht of Wessex.[16]

This plenitude of diverse causes for Ludeca's death suggests that each later chronicler found his own way of giving meaning to an almost bare obit in the *Anglo-Saxon Chronicle*. Gaimar blames the Welsh for Ludeca's death with as little

---

[10] *The Chronicle of John of Worcester*, ed. Darlington and McGurk, trans. Bray and McGurk, 242–3.

[11] *Hemingi chartularii ecclesiae Wigorniensis*, ed. T. Hearne, 2 vols. (Oxford, 1723), ii. 369.

[12] Williams, 'Mercian Coinage and Authority', 223.

[13] *The Anglo-Saxon Chronicle*, trans. Swanton, 60–1 (AE).

[14] *L'Estoire des Engleis*, ed. Bell, 73 (lines 2279–90, esp. 2287–8): 'Cil [Lutecan] dunt dis anceis | [Il] fud ocis par les Gualeis.'

[15] *The Chronicle of John of Worcester*, ed. Darlington and McGurk, trans. Bray and McGurk, 224–5 ([825] (xii) 847): 'Cui prouinciales illi cum rege suo festinato occurrerunt, consertoque graui prelio, illum et quinque duces eius exercitus cum aliis quampluribus occiderunt, reliquos uero fugauerunt.' Followed in Kirby, *Earliest English Kings*, 191.

[16] *Rogeri de Wendover Chronica*, ed. Coxe, i. 276: 'Ludecanno, rege Merciorum, a rege Egberto interfecto.'

reason as he produces them for the deaths of Æthelmund and Weohstan in 802, having failed to understand that those ealdormen were fighting each other.[17] More plausibly, John of Worcester appears to have chosen the East Angles, Roger the West Saxons, to fill the same kind of gap. If we turn to the question of Ludeca's five ealdormen, we find this number to be equivalent to a Mercian king's permanent 'core'.[18] The names of eight men in the four extant charters of Beornwulf's reign are missing in those of Wiglaf's reign and after: roughly in order of rank, these are Beornnoth, Eadberht, Cuthred, Uhtred, Ealhheard, Bola, Eadwulf, and Wighelm.[19] Whereas Bola is styled as *pedisequus* ('footman') and Wighelm not at all, the other six are *duces*. In one way, their number is comparable with the *set reietels* ('seven earls') which, according to Gaimar, include Beornwulf and Ludeca; in another, with the five who are said to have died with Ludeca. It seems unlikely that six ealdormen died with Beornwulf in East Anglia in 826, to be replaced by five who fell with Ludeca in the same country a year later. It is more plausible that some of these six ealdormen died with Beornwulf while others got away. Ludeca's poor showing in the surviving records, therefore, cannot be treated as evidence that he was a weak king. Rather it appears that he took over Beornwulf's following on his cousin's death. The contradictions about Ludeca's own passing in 827 look like responses to a silence that was imposed because Wiglaf, the man who succeeded Ludeca, was also the man who killed him.[20] We can speculate that Wiglaf refers to the deaths of Ludeca and his men in the wording of his charter in the Council of Croft, in 836, when he sold a liberty to Hanbury Minster (Worcs.) *pro absolutione criminum nostrorum* ('for the absolution of our crimes').[21]

Of all historicizing accounts the most partial towards Wiglaf is the tradition within the *Historia Croylandensis*. Using earlier materials, some clearly from the twelfth century, the fifteenth-century compiler of this work gives no word on Ludeca or his reign, but moves straight to Wiglaf, alleged to be a benefactor of his abbey, after describing both Ceolwulf and Beornwulf as tyrants *qui contra fas purpuram induerent* ('who took the purple against divine law'), oppressed the kingdom, and destroyed the once proud army of Mercia. Then, he says:

omnium consensu Witlafius dux Merciorum, cujus filius Wimundus Alfledam filiam Celwolphi quondam regis, et fratris Kenulphi regis nobilissimi, duxerat in vxorem, in regem levatus est.

[a duke Wiglaf of the Mercians, whose son Wigmund had married Ælfflæd the daughter of Ceolwulf (who was once king and brother of the most noble king Cenwulf), was raised up as king by consent of all.][22]

---

[17] *L'Estoire des Engleis*, ed. Bell, 235 (note to lines 2217–22).
[18] Featherstone, 'The Tribal Hidage and the Ealdormen of Mercia', 32–3.
[19] Keynes, *Atlas of Attestations*, table XVII.
[20] Walker, *Mercia and the Making of England*, 34.
[21] S 190 (BCS 416). Cubitt, *Anglo-Saxon Church Councils*, 287.
[22] *Chronicle of Croyland Abbey*, ed. Birch, 13: but with *Mercioru[m]*. The form *Wicciorum* ('of the Hwicce') is read in *Ingulph's Chronicle*, trans. Riley, 15.

	1437	188	190	1438	192	195	1271	198	197
S:	1437	188	190	1438	192	195	1271	198	197
BCS:	386	400	416	421	430	433	443	450	454
Archive:	Wor	CCC	Wor	CCC	Wor	Wor	Abn	Wor	Pet
Place of issue:	*Clof*	*Wychbold*	Croft	*Æt Ast.*	Tam	Tam		Tam	Rept
Year:	825	831	836	839	840	841	844	'845'	848
KINGS									
Beornwulf	+								
Wiglaf		+	+	+					
Berhtwulf					+	+	+	+	+
ARCHBISHOPS OF CANTERBURY									
Wulfred	1	1							
Ceolnoth			1	1					
ABBOTS									
Eanmund	2		1		1	[2]	1	1	1 ben
Beornhelm			3						
LAYMEN									
Eadberht	1 *dux*								
Beornnoth	2 *dux*								
Bynna	11								
Wighelm	12								
Tidwulf		1 *dux*	2 *dux*						
Wigmund		6 *f.r.*							
Mucel (1)			1 *dux*		3 *dux*		1 *dux*	1 *dux*	1 *pri*
Humberht			7 *dux*		1 *dux*	2 *dux*	2 *dux*	2 *dux*	2 *pri*
Mucel (2)			9 *dux*		8 *dux*			6 *dux*	8 *pri*
Wiglaf			17					14	7 *pri*
Berhtwulf			20 [king						

Figure 9. Wiglaf's kindred takes power (825–848)

Source: Keynes, *Atlas of Attestations*, XIII–XVII.

This pleading statement is one of several in *Historia Croylandensis* with a concern for the ideology of Mercian kingship. If its snobbery rests on reliable sources, it would appear that Wiglaf was an ealdorman before he became king of Mercia.

Wiglaf, on this evidence, cleared his path to the Mercian kingship in a deliberate way. The surviving charters do not show him at Beornwulf's councils, whether ealdorman or not. But probably in the later 820s, no doubt after he was made *dux*, he married his son Wigmund to Ælfflæd, Ceolwulf's daughter and Cenwulf's niece. Thacker suggests he did this 'to legitimate his house', but it seems just as likely that he sought to enrich himself.[23] Through Ælfflæd, Wigmund's heir could expect to inherit the Winchcombe rights of Cenwulf's sole heir upon the death of his daughter Cwenthryth, a childless abbess. In due course Ælfflæd produced a son whom either Wigmund or Wiglaf, doubtless the latter, named Wigstan (after a figure whom we can identify as a Swedish fighter from legend later known as 'Vésteinn': see my Chapter 2).

Wigmund, father of Wigstan, was probably newly adult, aged between 15 and 18, in 831 when he appeared as sixth layman and *filius regis*, but not *dux*, in his father's council at the royal estate in Wychbold (S 188).[24] Within these limits, he would have been born *c*.813 × *c*.816. As this period coincides with the two years within which Priest Abbot Wigmund seems to have died (814 × 816), it is reasonable to suppose that Wiglaf named his son after the abbot.[25] On this reasoning, the young Wigmund was a boy in his teens on his father's accession in 827. Furthermore, the date of St Wigstan's martyrdom gives us the means to work out some approximate dates for his mother. The fullest account of Ælfflæd's life is preserved in her son's story in the thirteenth-century Evesham Abbey *Chronicle*, which has been judged to be based on fact, with his obit established as 1 June 849.[26] According to the Evesham story, Wigstan was murdered before his majority by his cousin Berhtfrith because he tried to prevent this man from marrying his widowed mother Ælfflæd.[27] Berhtfrith was the son of King Berhtwulf of Mercia (*c*.839–851). If Wigstan's mother was then still young enough to bear more children at a time when her son was old enough to play a political role, she would have been born in *c*.810 × *c*.820, roughly the birth-time of her husband Wigmund. This means that her betrothal or marriage to Wigmund would have taken place in the later 820s, around the time Wiglaf became king.

[23] Thacker, 'Kings, Saints, and Monasteries', 12–13, esp. 12. On Ælfflæd's royal property rights, see S 1442 (BCS 575), *s.a.* 897.

[24] Stafford, 'Political Women in Mercia', 38 and n. 1. Compare, however, the witness of Alfred and possibly Æthelbeald at six years at councils of their father Æthelwulf, in Abels, *Alfred the Great*, 50.

[25] S 173, 180: see Figs. 3 and 7. It seems likely that Wiglaf was the nephew of Priest Abbot Wigmund.

[26] Rollason, 'The Search for Saint Wigstan', 8–15, esp. 8. Hayward, 'The Idea of Innocent Martyrdom', 180–200.

[27] *Chronicon abbatiae de Evesham*, ed. Macray, 325–37.

Until his martyrdom in 849, Ælfflæd's son Wigstan was a fortunate man, blessed with money and ancestry both. There is a claim in the Evesham *Chronicle* that he was descended from King Cenred of Mercia: Evesham kept the bones of St Wigstan after King Cnut moved them there from Repton in the eleventh century in honour of Cenred, who was held to be the abbey's founder.[28] It is interesting that Thomas of Marlborough, author of the Evesham *Chronicle*, gives a descent from Cenred to St Wigstan but not to Wiglaf his grandfather. This probably means that Wigstan was descended from Cenred through his father's mother, Wiglaf's queen, whose name is given as Cynethryth.[29] So, despite Wigmund's alleged descent from one branch of Pybba's family (Cenred), Wigstan's from two (Cenred and Cenwalh), it does not appear that Wiglaf himself was descended from any Mercian kings. If, on the other hand, Cynethryth was of Evesham stock, it appears that Wiglaf had made himself connections with Cenwulf's family through his own marriage, even before he found a more prestigious match in Winchcombe for his son. Kirby believes that Wiglaf's Repton burial shows that he claimed descent from King Æthelbald (*c.*725–757), but this claim, if he made it, must have been pressed later.[30] If Thomas's unique description of Wigmund as *rex* ('king') is treated as genuinely based,[31] it would appear that Wiglaf initially came to power as a joint king with Wigmund before the birth of Wigstan. Wigmund's title to rule could scarcely have been stronger than his father's. Precariously enough, with the claim of full royal blood possible only in Wigstan, the evidence suggests that both Wiglaf and Wigmund staked their positions on this boy in order to be recognized as kings of Mercia.

To sum up the flow of two arguments, I deduce that the poet of *Beowulf* ends by presenting Wiglaf the Wægmunding, son of Weohstan, as Beowulf's remote kinsman, adoptive son, and natural successor; and that the Mercian Wiglaf, having no claim to descend from Beornwulf or any other Mercian king, came to power in 827 as a co-regent with his ailing son after killing Ludeca, Beornwulf's cousin, along with his ealdormen. To become king in these troubled times, the Mercian Wiglaf needed any ideology he could get. Perhaps a proclamation of ancient kinship with Beornwulf, through the poem we now know as *Beowulf*, was the way he began to acquire this.

Wiglaf's cross-border family

In Chapter 9 I have followed an implication in *Beowulf*, lines 2989–98, that Hygelac dispossessed Weohstan and other noblemen, presenting this as a literary parallel to Cenwulf's notorious seizures of land from the Church. Here it is appropriate to connect these events with Wiglaf's family. Before his third and

---

[28] Son of Wulfhere son of Penda. *Chronicon abbatiae de Evesham*, ed. Macray, 325–6: 'de prosapia (immo hæres et successor licet non proximus) fuerit regis Kenredi.'
[29] Kirby, *Earliest English Kings*, 191.
[30] Ibid. 191.
[31] Accepted in Rollason, 'The Search for Saint Wigstan', 7–11.

final group of hypermetric lines, the poet of *Beowulf* says that Hygelac rewarded each of his champions Wulf and Eofor, the physical killers of Ongentheow, with *ofermaðmum* ('excessive treasures', line 2993), which he then goes on to specify:

> hund þusenda
> landes ond locenra beaga   —ne ðorfte him ða lean oðwitan
> mon on middangearde   syðða[n] hie ða mærða geslogon. (*Beo* 2994–6)

[120,000 in land and linked rings—there needed no one in the middle world begrudge them that reward, since they had won those glories by fighting for them.]

Before God and man, however, the grants of land in these totals appear to come at the expense of other noblemen whom Hygelac despoils. Weohstan appears to be one of them, forced to leave Geatland to take service in Sweden, where his son Wiglaf is born to a Swedish mother.

In Mercia, similarly, there were *Wig*-names in common with Wessex. In the case of Wessex, I have already attempted to show that Cenwulf's retention of Glastonbury, after his son Cynehelm's death in 811 or 812, explains why Archbishop Wulfred and Bishop Wigberht set out from England to Rome in 814. Wigberht should have had an interest in Glastonbury. He had been trained there, he ruled the diocese in which it lay, and he would have wanted it back from King Cenwulf.[32] Wigberht's name-prefix was fairly prestigious in Wessex. The bishop of Winchester from about 813 to 825 was named Wigthegn.[33] As we have seen, Ealdorman Weohstan, who died in battle against the Hwicce in 802, was probably married to Ecgberht's sister, later abbess of Wilton.[34] The West Saxon charters from about 757 to 801, a time contemporary with Offa and a few years after, show Weohstan once as sixth *princeps* a year before his death, in 801.[35] Behind him on that occasion was Wigfrith, a *prefectus* or *princeps*, who steadily rose from seventeenth to seventh and then possibly third place over the period as a whole.[36] There is a second Wigfrith, who witnesses as ninth *prefectus* in 786 × 793; following him and the first Wigfrith on that occasion, a Wingbald, possibly for *Wigbald*, is listed as tenth *prefectus* as well.[37] It looks probable that Wigberht, bishop of Sherborne (793 × 801–816 × 824), was a younger member of the same family.

We have seen the *Wig*-kindred in Mercia in Chapter 5 (Fig. 2). The reason for this cross-border coincidence in eighth- and ninth-century nomenclature, as

[32] *The Early History of Glastonbury*, ed. and trans. Scott, 136–7 (ch. 67) and 206 (note).
[33] Keynes, *Atlas of Attestations*, table XIII, 12th bishop in S 173 (BCS 343), *s.a.* 814; 4th, *s.a.* 814 [Chelsea: no Sawyer/BCS no.]; 5th in S 1434 (BCS 378), *s.a.* 824; 7th in S 1433 (BCS 379), *s.a.* 824; 8th in S 1436 (BCS 384), *s.a.* 825; 8th in S 1437 (BCS 386), *s.a.* 825.
[34] *S. Editha sive Chronicon Vilodunense*, ed. Horstmann, 4 (lines 138–41).
[35] Keynes, *Atlas of Attestations*, table XII (Attestations in West Saxon Charters, 688–802), S 268 (BCS 282), *s.a.* 801 ('Wiohstan').
[36] Ibid. 17 in S 96 (BCS 181), *s.a.* ?757; 10 *pre* in S 261, *s.a.* 762; 9 *pre* in S 262 (BCS 200), *s.a.* 766; 8 in S 263 (BCS 224), *s.a.* 774; 7 in S 269 (BCS 258), *s.a.* 786 × 793; 7 *pri* in S 268 (BCS 282), *s.a.* 801; and ?3 in S 270a (BCS 300), *s.a.* 801.
[37] Ibid., S 269 (BCS 258).

Barbara Yorke has hinted, may be that Penda, nearly two centuries earlier, had
settled Mercian chieftains in the West and South Saxon areas under his control.[38]
It is always an approximate business to locate names in regions, but Cenwulf, as
we have seen, belonged to a kindred with *Cen-*, *Cyne-*, *Ceol-*, and *Cuth-*prefixes
which characterize both his family around Winchcombe and the Gewisse not far
to the south-east in the upper Thames valley. Beornwulf's family, moreover, in
their ownership of land in south-west Gloucestershire in the mid-eighth century,
might be regarded as West Saxon besides Mercian; until we see similar names in a
Selsey charter of 780, whose 'Beornnoth' and 'Beornheard', listed respectively
sixth and twelfth, may be South Saxon noblemen of Mercian descent.[39] Given
that this list also includes a 'Wiohstan' in eighth and a 'Beorhtnoth' in thirteenth
position, it seems likely that Penda planted other Mercian kindreds in southern
England as well. The names of each of these and others turn up among the West
Saxon missionaries associated with Bishop Boniface in the first half of the eighth
century.[40] Against the background of Penda's dominance of Sussex in the late
seventh century, the expansion of the *Wig-* and *Beorn-*kindreds in Saxon areas
may have been something for ninth-century Mercians to celebrate.

If we assemble the *Wig-*names in Mercia over the same period and later, we see
a dearth of attestations during the early reign of Offa, with a certain Wigheard
listed ninth out of ten laymen in 774.[41] However, after Ecgfrith's coronation in
789, things begin to improve (see Figs. 2 and 5–9): a Wigcga, if related, rises
from ninth to about fifth position, latterly as *dux*, across three reigns from 789 to
about 805;[42] Wigberht appears later, but does even better, rising from fifth *dux*
in ?792 to second *dux* in Ecgfrith's reign in 796, stopping as fourth *dux* in the
early reign of Cenwulf in 799;[43] there is a Wigferth who attests once, in Ecgfrith's
short reign;[44] and a second Wigheard appears as fourth *dux* in Cenwulf's early
reign in 798, witnessing steadily until 816, but falling equally steadily to the
position of tenth untitled layman in this turbulent year.[45] A third Wigheard is

[38] Yorke, *Kings and Kingdoms*, 120.

[39] S 118 (BCS 1334).

[40] *The Letters of Saint Boniface*, trans. Emerton, 17 (VI [14], *s.a.* 719–22): 'Berhthere'; and 67–8
(XXX [40], *s.a.* 737–8): 'To his most dear sons, the priests Tatwine and Wigberht, and to Bernhard,
Hiedde, Hunfrid, and Sturm.'

[41] Ibid., table X, S 110 (BCS 213). Keynes, 'Mercia and Wessex in the Ninth Century', 319.

[42] Keynes, *Atlas of Attestations*, 9th in S 130 (BCS 257), *s.a.* 789; 4th in S 131 (BCS 255), *s.a.*
789; 1 *dux* in S 136 (BCS 267), *s.a.* 793; 7 *pri* in S 132 (BCS 265), *s.a.* '790'; 3 *dux* in S 150 (BCS
281), *s.a.* 796 (Ecgfrith); 3 *dux* in S 151 (BCS 280), *s.a.* 796 (Ecgfrith); 7 *dux* in S 153 (BCS 289),
s.a. 798 (Cenwulf); 8 *dux* in S 155 (BCS 293), *s.a.* 799; 6 in S 106 (BCS 201), *s.a. c.*800; 5 *p*' in S
1260 (BCS 308), *s.a.* 803; 5 *dux* in S 1187 (BCS 313), *s.a.* 804; 5 *dux* in S 40 (BCS 322), *s.a.* 805; 8
dux in S 161 (BCS 321), *s.a.* 805.

[43] Ibid., 5 *dux* in S 138 (BCS 264), *s.a.* ?792; 4 *dux* in S 137 (BCS 269), *s.a.* 794; 6th in S 139
(BCS 274), *s.a.* ?794; 2 *dux* in S 150 (BCS 281), *s.a.* 796 (Ecgfrith); 4 *dux* in S 153 (BCS 289), *s.a.*
798 (Cenwulf); 4 *dux* in S 155 (BCS 293), *s.a.* 799.

[44] Ibid., 6th in S 149 (BCS 279), *s.a.* 796.

[45] Ibid., 4 *dux* in S 154 (BCS 295), *s.a.* 798; 6 *p*' in S 1260 (BCS 308), *s.a.* 803; 6 *dux* in S 1187
(BCS 313), *s.a.* 804; 9 *dux* in S 40 (BCS 322), *s.a.* 805; 9 *dux* in S 161 (BCS 321), *s.a.* 805; 5 *dux* in

listed as 11 *pincerna* ('servant') in 809 and nineteenth in Cenwulf's big council of 812;[46] and Wighelm, listed ninth and twelfth in Ceolwulf's two extant charters of 822–3, maintains the latter untitled position through Beornwulf's reign and then disappears, probably in Beornwulf's wars, before King Wiglaf's first extant charter in 831.[47] Thus the overall picture for the *Wig*-kindred in Cenwulf's Mercia, at least until Wiglaf, is one of decline: first a prosperity, in line also with Bishop Unwona, friend of Priest Abbot Wigmund (see Fig. 1); then special favour in the short reign of Ecgfrith in 796; finally, after about 805, a slump in the reigns of Cenwulf and Beornwulf, in which the *Wig*-kindred falls back to untitled positions at around 11 or 12. From this point of view, Wiglaf's family may have benefited from Offa's creation of the Mercian archdiocese at Lichfield; but after Ecgfrith's death it seems that they fell out of favour, not only with Cenwulf, but also with Beornwulf.

The relative instability of Cenwulf's reign in the years 814–16 seems matched in the anomalous way Wigheard is listed second *dux* in (the Worcester record of) Wulfred's Council of Chelsea in 816, as opposed to Beornnoth's position of eighth *dux* in the same record. If not due to the vagaries of copying and transcription, this transposition of rankings could be read as evidence that Wigheard favoured the party of Archbishop Wulfred against Cenwulf, his own king. In this he would have been aligned with the West Saxon Bishop Wigberht of Sherborne, whose rule possibly continued until 824. In this respect, it is worth speculating that the fall in the Mercian *Wig*-kindred's prestige, starting as it does in *c*.805, might be related to Æthelmund's death in battle against Ealdorman Weohstan of the West Saxons in 802. If this is true, the event that turned into the main chance for Beornwulf's kindred spelled the decline of Wiglaf's.

Indeed, the slump of Wiglaf's kindred in the charter rankings makes it look as if Cenwulf was inclined to treat the *Wigs* of Mercia and Wessex as branches of the same family. Through Penda's plantations, both Weohstan of Wiltshire and Wigberht of Glastonbury and Sherborne may have been regarded as men of Mercian descent, relatives of Wiglaf's kindred up in the Midlands. By the same token, Wigberht's quarrel with Cenwulf over his retention of Glastonbury, if that is what it was in 814, would have been a grievance shared by Wiglaf's family. King Hygelac's apparent dispossession of Weohstan in *Beowulf*, in this light, appears to reflect Cenwulf's quarrel with Wulfred and with Wiglaf's relatives south of the border.

S 164 (BCS 328), *s.a.* 809; 8 *dux* in S 170 (BCS 340), *s.a.* 812; 2 *dux*, however, in S 180 (BCS 357), *s.a.* 816; but 10 in S 179 (BCS 356), *s.a.* 816.

[46] Ibid., 11 *pin* in S 164 (BCS 328), *s.a.* 809; 19 in S 173 (BCS 343), *s.a.* 812.

[47] Ibid. 9 in S 186 (BCS 370), *s.a.* 822; 12 in S 187 (BCS 373), *s.a.* 823; 13 in S 1434 (BCS 378), *s.a.* 824; 14 in S 1433 (BCS 379), *s.a.* 824; 12 in S 1436 (BCS 384), *s.a.* 825; 12 in S 1437 (BCS 825), *s.a.* 825.

The Lord speaks through Wiglaf

The poet of *Beowulf* gives Wiglaf a moral insight more advanced than Beowulf's. Whereas we have seen Beowulf's purity of spirit compromised by an interest in gold, Wiglaf's moral authority seems clear in that he enters the poem not only to save Beowulf and help kill the dragon, but also to criticize Beowulf in saying that he joined others in advising him not to go (lines 3079–84). It is then that he makes Beowulf's epitaph, with a speech charged with theology (lines 3114–19).

So far I have suggested that the poet of *Beowulf* drew eclectically upon a mixture of heroic legends, Vergil's *Aeneid*, and biblical and homiletic typology in order to fashion a new narrative for the deeds of his older hero. Yet in all this he keeps back his Danish mythology for the greatest task, that of asking whether or not Beowulf is saved. His three great adaptations of Norse material serve to focus our minds on Beowulf's religion with the aim of reminding us of his moral choice ever more insistently towards the end. Beowulf, a heathen, is a king without the knowledge which would enable a Christian to help his own soul. The poet, having highlighted this ignorance as the hopeless condition for heathens in lines 175–88, obscures this so that we put Beowulf's day of reckoning to one side. For most readers this reprieve from damnation is a welcome distraction. It will last as long as the poet bathes his hero in sunshine and the monsters in darkness, keeps other people's feuds in the background, and lets Beowulf's youth, wit, and strength occupy the foreground. Only surreptitiously does the poet reveal the moral dimension to Beowulf's success. As soon as Wealhtheow speaks, we realize that Beowulf will not become Hrothgar's son; and when her necklace appears we learn that one day it will accompany, or perhaps lead, Beowulf and his uncle into an expeditionary disaster. The *Brosinga mene*, with which this necklace is compared, is probably the poet's first direct borrowing from a Danish source. It is also his first intimation of a moral choice: one day Beowulf will go the way of either Hama, who flees *searoniðas* ('cunning enmities', line 1200), or Hygelac, who dies in pursuit of them. In his own way, one day later, Hrothgar articulates this choice to Beowulf, referring to the historical effects of Heremod's avarice before calling this type of sin, the failure to redistribute wealth, a *bealoð* ('a grievous enmity', line 1758), from which Beowulf must protect himself.

Fifty years on, the mood darkens and we see Beowulf questioning his own conduct, apparently for the first time, after the initial dragon-fire; suspecting:

> þæt he wealdende
> ofer ealde riht   ecean drihtne
> bitre gebulge;   breost innan weoll
> þeostrum geþoncum,   swa him geþywe ne wæs. (*Beo* 2329–32)

[that he might have bitterly enraged the Ruler, the eternal Lord, against the old law; his breast welled up from within with dark thoughts, which with him was not usual.]

In Beowulf, therefore, there is a desire to distinguish right from wrong, but not until now has he examined his conscience. Not long after this moment, however, we see him holding a symbol of *bealonið* (line 2404) to his bosom, a cup which leads him to a hoard of cursed gold.

Before he joins battle with the dragon, latest owner of this hoard, Beowulf begins a speech which appears to be adapted from a West Germanic version of the *Bjarkamál* (see Chapter 2). Into this speech the poet now adds his story of Herebeald, with an allusion which may count as his second borrowing from a Danish mythological source. The effect is to highlight the heathen vulnerability to damnation: that of Hrethel, who may avoid it by rejecting an Odinic precedent of revenge; and Beowulf's own, in that for him a different choice still waits. The poet's third borrowing from mythology appears in Beowulf's final combat with the dragon. Although this scene seems largely based on a homily from a saint's life about St Michael and the dragon, the poet makes it heathen with the arresting imagery of Þórr's duel with the World Serpent. With this presumably living Danish influence he lets a heroic grandeur, doomed outcome for the world, and above all the Serpent's poisonous *níð* (as in *Vsp* 53, 'vile act') give a terrible dignity to Beowulf's end. However, this is a moral adaptation of heathen myths. The poison that kills Beowulf as if he were Þórr is of a spiritual kind, laced with *bealonið*. Later the poet will contradict Beowulf's dying claim that he did not seek *searoniðas* (line 2738), by saying that he did (line 3067). When the poet tells the story of a heathen curse which Beowulf has now incurred, he puts us in a position to ask whether the *nið* that kills Beowulf will also take his soul. It is against this threat of damnation that the poet hands Beowulf's obsequies to Wiglaf at the end of the poem (lines 3076–182).

In Chapter 3 of this book I have attempted to show that Wiglaf is type-cast in Beowulf's dragon-fight as the strong Simon Peter to Beowulf's Jesus in the confrontation in the garden near Cedron (John 18: 10). Now, after Beowulf's death, Wiglaf's first epitaph begins on a note of dissent. He hints that he will soon be moving on: events have proved that *oft sceal eorl monig anes willan wræc adreogan* ('Often through the will of one man shall many a nobleman endure exile [or: misery]', lines 3077–8). This line points to the idea of Wiglaf's migration to Britain, rather as the poet suggests Hengest is mindful of sailing to a new homeland before winter in the Finnsburh episode (*eard gemunde*, line 1129).[48] There was no way, Wiglaf says, that he and the other soldiers could give the advice to Beowulf which would stop him from meeting *goldweard þone* ('that gold-guardian', line 3081) or make him leave the dragon alone. This statement is heavily critical of Beowulf, for it is news to us that he proceeded against the wishes of his advisers. Without his knowing it, however, Wiglaf's idea of their leaving the dragon till the end of the world (*oð woruldende*, line 3083) makes Beowulf prefigure St Michael against the dragon in the Book of Revelation

---

[48] 'He was mindful of a homeland'. North, 'Tribal Loyalties', 26–7.

(see my Chapter 7). This typology seems contrived to palliate Beowulf's interest in the gold.

By pronouncing the 'hoard seen' (*hord ys gesceawod*, line 3084), Wiglaf unwittingly echoes the language of the poet's questioning of Beowulf's fate in the hereafter. His word *gesceawod* recalls the poet's vexed phrase *næs gearwor... hæfde gesceawod* nine lines earlier, which itself cites Beowulf's words *gearo sceawige* still earlier on line 2748.[49] Without knowing its dangers, Wiglaf claims to have seen the treasure, conveys Beowulf's last greeting to his people, and orders them on Beowulf's behalf to construct the king's great funeral pyre, to which he and they may then bring their beloved lord, *þær he longe sceal on ðæs waldendes wære geþolian* ('to a place where he shall long endure in the keeping of the Lord', lines 3108–8). This language recalls *The Dream of the Rood*, of the early eighth century, in which Christ releases noble pagans from their captivity in hell:

> Hiht wæs geniwad
> mid bledum and mid blisse,   þam þe þær bryne þolodan. (*Dream* 148–9)

[Hope was renewed, with blessings and rejoicings, for those who endured the burning in that place.]

So once again in *Beowulf*, Wiglaf reveals a Christian world-view without knowing it. With *geþolian* his words show Beowulf to be suffering in hell; on the other hand, with *waldendes wære* there is an inadvertent hope that Christ will descend to release him.[50]

Wiglaf reveals his fourth unwitting insight in a speech which he gives after ordering the pyre with the necessary practical commands. It is striking here that his words recall the biblical language of Hrothgar's sword-hilt speech, particularly its more homiletic section in lines 1740–57 (at the head of Fitt XX[V]). It seems Hrothgar was gifted with an intuitive grasp of the Christian scheme from which, as heathens, the people of *Beowulf* are all excluded. So is Wiglaf:

> 'Nu sceal gled fretan,
> weaxan wonna leg   wigena strengel
> þone ðe oft gebad   isernscure
> þonne stræla storm   strengum gebæded
> scoc ofer scildweall,   sceft nytte heold
> fæðergearwum fus,   flane fulleode'. (*Beo* 3114–19)

['Now the fire must consume, the dark flame engulf the ruler of men who often endured showers of iron when a storm of arrows, propelled by bowstrings, passed over the shieldwall, when the arrow-shaft hastening with its feather-gear made itself useful, assisted the arrow-head.']51

---

49 Stanley, 'Hæthenra Hyht in *Beowulf*', 145–6.
50 On the *adventus Christi*, see É. Ó. Carragáin, *Ritual and the Rood: Liturgical Images and the Old English Poems of the 'Dream of the Rood' Tradition* (London, 2005), 321–2.
51 Translation based on *Beowulf*, ed. Mitchell and Robinson, 159.

This epitaph on the dead Beowulf dwells, with an otherwise inexplicable obsession, on the flight of a stray arrow past the guard of Beowulf's *scildweall*. Whether appropriate formula or divinely inspired theology, its parting close-up of a dark flame, Beowulf under arrow-showers, and the flukes on the arrow-head begin to capture Hrothgar's warning about *bona swiðe neah, se þe of flanbogan fyrenum sceoteð* ('the slayer very close, who shoots wickedly from a fiery bow', lines 1743–4). Without knowing it, Hrothgar apparently took his image from St Paul's Ephesians 6: 15–16. With Wiglaf in turn, the poet lets another illiterate heathen deliver a message worthy of Christian theology, with the added disclosure that Beowulf has suffered many temptations and one spiritual failure. Visually Wiglaf's image suggests that one arrow got through. As a reflection on Beowulf's chances of entering heaven, this image confirms the import of *geþolian* on line 3108. That Wiglaf makes these statements shows that the poet regards him, not Beowulf, as Hrothgar's spiritual heir.

In my foregoing chapter I started by suggesting that the poet presented Hygelac as an embodiment of *wlenco* ('pride', line 1206). Hygelac is a bad moral influence on Beowulf which only Hrothgar can counteract by enjoining our hero not to heed *oferhydas* ('prideful thoughts', line 1760) but to think of *þæt selre, ece rædas* ('the better part, eternal rewards', lines 1759–60). Thereafter I showed that to a large extent Hygelac's acquisitive career resembles that of Cenwulf of Mercia. In this chapter I listed nine parallels to support the idea that the poet remodelled Hygelac's legend on Cenwulf's reign, as a prelude to offering Beowulf in some way as an allegory of Beornwulf, Cenwulf's erstwhile henchman and successor. The corollary is that Hrothgar, Hygelac's opponent in the matter of Beowulf's guidance, is in some way representative of Cenwulf's worst enemy: Archbishop Wulfred of Canterbury.

So far, through my Chapters 2–4 and 6–7, we have seen Hrothgar in various guises. He is first an empire builder on the strength of *heresped* ('success in expeditions', line 64) and then *se goda* who awaits Beowulf in Heorot ('the generous one', line 355). Yet he is intuitively Christian when, after Grendel's defeat, he proclaims Beowulf's destiny in Marian terms (lines 945–6). In his approach to Grendel's Mere, on the other hand, Hrothgar resembles the sibyl at the mouth of Avernus in Vergil's *Aeneid*, Book VI; yet he also recalls King Latinus wishing for a family union with the young stranger from overseas, in *Aeneid*, Book VII. There again, Hrothgar is the author of a *gid* ('song', line 1723) whose image of a man's defence against the devil alludes without knowing it both to St Michael and to Ephesians 6: 10–20. As Beowulf's conscience, with his injunction to choose *ece rædas* ('eternal rewards', line 1760), Hrothgar unwittingly presents Hama's moral choice to Beowulf in advance of his interest in the dragon-hoard at the end of the poem. In all this, Hrothgar is the self-proclaimed authority *se þe soð ond riht fremeð* ('who furthers truth and law', lines 1700–1). As he tries to exert some influence on the hero of *Beowulf*, so did Wulfred on King Beornwulf in Mercia. In each case there comes a Wiglaf who is truer to the wise old spiritual guide.

In Mercia, the love of Wiglaf for Wulfred was declared publicly in 831. In this year, the first of his second reign, King Wiglaf convened a council at Wychbold in northern Worcestershire in order to grant Wulfred five hides of land at Botwell (Middx.) which adjoined another property of the archbishop at Hayes. This Middle Saxon region is regarded as being Wulfred's homeland and Wiglaf's grant is unusual for being a true gift rather than a sale or exchange.[52] To that end the king makes it known that he grants Botwell *venerabili UULFREDO archiepiscopo pro ejus intimo spiritali sæcularique affectu et amore* ('to the venerable Archbishop Wulfred in return for his intimate spiritual and secular friendship and love').[53] This statement is strong: as Brooks has remarked, 'we would dearly love to know the nature of Wulfred's secular or spiritual *affectus* and *amor* towards Wiglaf at this critical time in Mercian fortunes'.[54] The most plausible answer is that Wiglaf settled once and for all the wrangle between Wulfred and Abbess Cwenthryth for the abbeys of Reculver and Minster-in-Thanet. Beornwulf had failed to resolve this dispute, despite making an effort on Wulfred's behalf; and if we trust the retrospective dating of the two *Clofesho* charters for 825, it appears that Wulfred did not recover his rights to these lucrative foundations, which controlled the trade in the Wantsum Channel, until the second year after 825: thus in 826–7.[55] It does not stretch the evidence to suggest that Wulfred's suit was granted by Wiglaf on his accession. By then, as we have seen, Wiglaf was probably the father-in-law of Cwenthryth's younger cousin Ælfflæd; the *Historia Croylandensis* refers to him as *dux Merciorum*;[56] so it is plausible that the new king compelled Cenwulf's daughter to settle with Archbishop Wulfred.

Some two years after his accession, Wiglaf's first reign came to an end in 829 when King Ecgberht invaded Mercia and pushed north as far as Dore on the border with Northumbria.[57] Of the latter, Roger of Wendover says that Ecgberht *provinciam illam gravi depopulatione contrivit* ('laid waste to that province with heavy ravaging'), until he took tribute from King Eanred, who was the son of Eardwulf.[58] Thereafter in 830 Ecgberht is said to have raided Welsh territory to take submission from kings over there. *Eodem anno*, says Roger, *West-Saxonum rex Egbertus, misericordia motus, Wilafo, regi Merciorum, concessit, ut regnum suum de eo teneret sub tributo* ('In the same year, moved by pity, King Ecgberht of the West Saxons granted to King Wiglaf of the Mercians that he might keep his kingdom from him under tribute').[59] In the meantime, if Roger is right, it

---

[52] Brooks, *Early History of the Church of Canterbury*, 132.

[53] Friday, 1 September 831, S 188 (BCS 400).

[54] Brooks, *Early History of the Church of Canterbury*, 137.

[55] S 1434 (BCS 378) and S 1436 (BCS 384). Kirby, *Earliest English Kings*, 187.

[56] *Chronicle of Croyland Abbey*, ed. Birch, 13.

[57] *ASC, s.a.* 827 [829]. *Rogeri de Wendover Chronica*, ed. Coxe, i. 276 (AD dcccxxviii; Wiglaf's exile lasts three years). *The Chronicle of John of Worcester*, ed. Darlington and McGurk, trans. Bray and McGurk, 244–5.

[58] *Rogeri de Wendover Chronica*, ed. Coxe, i. 277. Kirby, *Earliest English Kings*, 191 and 196.

[59] *Rogeri de Wendover Chronica*, ed. Coxe, i. 277 (AD dcccxxx). Wiglaf's tributary status is also claimed by Henry of Huntingdon, in *Historia Anglorum*, ed. and trans. Greenaway, 270–1 (iv. 34).

can hardly be thought that Ecgberht spared Mercia the treatment he gave Northumbria. The fact that the first Mercian royal and ecclesiastical council after Beornwulf's *Clofesho* in 825 took place on Croft Hill, Leicestershire, in 836, suggests that Ecgberht had rendered *Clofesho* inoperable.[60] There is no record of another council ever being held there. Here it is interesting to note that the fabric of the church at Brixworth, which some would identify with *Clofesho*, contains burnt stones which show that the roof was set ablaze.[61] It is unknown what happened in Mercia during Egberht's incursion, although a story in the *Historia Croylandensis* claims to fill the gap. According to this patchy source, Wiglaf was raised to the throne of Mercia with the agreement of all:

et 13 annis regnavit, sub ditione tamen et tributo Egberti regis West Saxonum. Mox enim ut rex factus est, et antequam exercitum poterat colligere, a ducibus Egberti per totam Merciam quesitus, industria domini Siwardi abbatis quattuor mensium spatio in cella sanctissime virginis Etheldrithe, ... nullo alio conscio abscondebatur, tutasque latebras illic agens, quousque mediante dicto Abbate venerabili Siwardo cum dicto rege West Saxonum concordatus est, et promissa tributi annualis pensione, ad regnum redire pacifice permissus.[62]

[but ruled for thirteen years under the authority and tribute of King Ecgberht of Wessex. For as soon as he had been made king, and before he could gather his army, he was sought by Ecgberht's earls across the whole of Mercia. By the diligence of lord abbot Sigeweard he was hidden for a period of four months in the cell of the most holy virgin Æthelthryth [*a parenthesis explains that she was Offa's daughter, St Æthelberht's wife who took the veil at Crowland*] with no other man knowing. More than once he found safe refuge in that place, until, through the mediation of the said venerable abbot Sigeweard, he was reconciled with the said king of the West Saxons and allowed, subject to his promising the payment of an annual tribute, to return to his kingdom in peace.]

With this story the author seeks to verify a twelfth-century forgery (which he then quotes) as a grant made by Wiglaf to the abbey of Crowland.[63] His tendency to collect royal names should make us wary of the story that Wiglaf hid out in Crowland, for earlier he produces a charter to show, for example, that Cenwulf undertook a pilgrimage to St Guthlac's shrine along with his queen and Archbishop Wulfred.[64] It is hard to believe this story, or the fiction that there

[60] Keynes, 'Councils of *Clofesho*', 48: 'significantly, perhaps, it was held at Croft.' W. G. Hoskins, 'Croft Hill', in his *Provincial England: Essays in Social and Economic History* (London, 1963), 170–80, esp. 172.

[61] D. Parsons, 'St. Boniface—Clofesho—Brixworth', in F. J. Much (ed.), *Baukunst des Mittelalters in Europa: Hans Erich Kubach zum 75. Geburtstag* (Stuttgart, 1988), 371–84, esp. 377. D. S. Sutherland, 'Burnt Stone in a Saxon Church and its Implications', in D. Parsons (ed.), *Stone: Quarrying and Building in England AD 43–1525* (London, 1990), 102–13, esp. 104–6. The clerestory of the present church was constructed 830 × 1015: D. Parsons, 'A Dated Timber Fragment from Brixworth Church, Northamptonshire', *Journal of the British Archaeological Association*, 133 (1980), 30–6.

[62] *Chronicle of Croyland Abbey*, ed. Birch, 13–14.

[63] S 189 (BCS 409).

[64] *Ingulph's Chronicle*, trans. Riley, 13.

was a minster in Crowland at this time, one whose abbot had the influence to mediate between kings. However, it remains plausible that Wiglaf took refuge in these fens, just as Æthelbald did a century before him.[65]

It is also tempting to believe that Archbishop Wulfred became involved. This part of the Crowland story accords with Roger's statement that Ecgberht was *misericordia motus*. The question is who could move him, for Ecgberht was no waverer. Ecgberht had fought his way to the West Saxon throne from a twenty-six-year Frankish exile starting in the reign of Offa. From 802 onwards his own reign was marked by campaigns, even before the years 825–9 when he routed Beornwulf's army at *Ellendun*, invaded Kent, sponsored an East Anglian revolt, invaded Mercia up to Northumbria, and pillaged in Wales. His treatment of Kentish possessions after *Ellendun* shows that he did not trust Archbishop Wulfred.[66] Yet he trusted the pope: it seems that Ecgberht planned for a pilgrimage to Rome towards the end of his life in 839.[67] As he could not have secured Beorhtric's throne in 802 without great sums of Frankish money, so it is likely that he respected the power of Charlemagne, Louis, and God. Kirby argues that Ecgberht faltered only when Louis withdrew his support in 830.[68] This idea at least explains the speed with which Wiglaf got back his kingdom in the same year.[69] Louis' problems were to do with a filial rebellion at home which broke out in February 830.[70] While fighting Lothar, his son, he cannot have been hoping that Ecgberht would become the master of four kingdoms in England. At the same time the southern English economy depended on trade with the Franks.[71] There is no record of Archbishop Wulfred's mediation between Ecgberht and Wiglaf, but the Council of Chelsea in 816 shows that he had kept pace with Frankish ecclesiastical reforms since Louis' coronation in 814. Broadly Wulfred based his policy on that of the Carolingian papacy. Of all the people high enough to influence Ecgberht at this time, only Wulfred could have made the emperor's influence felt.

In short, Wiglaf's declaration in 831 of the archbishop's love for him in secular and spiritual affairs is probably to be seen in terms of a history of mutual interest stretching back some five years. If it was he who finally restored Minster-in-Thanet and Reculver to the archbishop on his accession in 827, Wiglaf is likely to have won Wulfred's everlasting favour where Beornwulf had failed; and in 829–30, if Wulfred did mediate between Wiglaf, Ecgberht, and possibly Louis as well, much is explained about Wiglaf's generous grant to the Middle Saxon archbishop of Canterbury. Wulfred, devious as he was, might then be

[65] Roberts, 'Hagiography and Literature', 76. Kirby, *Earliest English Kings*, 129.
[66] Brooks, *Early History of the Church of Canterbury*, 197–8.
[67] Kirby, *Earliest English Kings*, 192.
[68] Ibid. 191–3. *Contra*, Story, *Carolingian Connections*, 219.
[69] *The Anglo-Saxon Chronicle*, trans. Swanton, 62–3 (*s.a.* 828 [830]).
[70] Reuter, *Germany in the Early Middle Ages*, 47–50.
[71] Hodges, *The Anglo-Saxon Achievement*, 147–9.

seen as a model for the Christian values with which the poet of *Beowulf* ennobles King Hrothgar.

Summary

These are the ways in which *Beowulf* may be seen to plead the case for a kingship not yet gained. My premiss has been to treat the Beowulf–Wiglaf sequence at the end of *Beowulf* as a reflection of Wiglaf's relation to King Beornwulf of Mercia. The poet becomes politically focused in the Geatish half of his poem, presenting Offa of Angeln as the first stage in a loose allegory of greater proportions, in which one progression (Offa–Hygelac–Beowulf–Wiglaf) suggests another (Offa–Cenwulf–Beornwulf–Wiglaf). In this chapter it has become even clearer that the poet of *Beowulf* makes Wiglaf the Wægmunding, son of Weohstan, exceptionally important. Namely he presents him as Beowulf's kinsman and natural heir. He does this as if both to compensate for the Mercian Wiglaf's lack of kinship with Beornwulf and to support his strategic use of Wigmund. There is also the likelihood that with Hygelac's apparent dispossession of Weohstan the poet alludes to King Cenwulf's withholding of Glastonbury from Bishop Wigberht of Sherborne, presumably regarded as Wiglaf's distant cousin, when the owner of this estate, his son Cynehelm, died without issue. If the piratical Hygelac conjures up the demon of Cenwulf, then the character of Hrothgar, who performs the role of Beowulf's good angel in the textual heart of the poem, was drawn with knowledge of Archbishop Wulfred, who, in his own way, did dispute with Cenwulf for the guidance of Beornwulf's soul.

A DATE FOR *BEOWULF*: THE WINTER OF 826–7

My Wiglaf-premiss places *Beowulf* within 826 × 839, a period which may now be narrowed down. In Chapter 7, I found that a date of late 826 for *Beowulf* is appropriate in another way, this being the year in which Louis the Pious baptized King Heriold of the Danes, his family, and his court. If Denmark was then brought into the fold of Christian nations subject to Louis and the pope in Rome, it is credible that during this time, the early to middle 820s, the old ways of its people were a talking point for the community from which *Beowulf* came. There could be no theme more tragic to a poet composing a requiem for King Beornwulf, nor any more useful for the patron who wished to succeed him. The length of the poet's concentration on Beowulf also suggests that the poem, if it did hail Beornwulf, was written when a requiem was still necessary. The fact that Wiglaf does not become king of the Geats in *Beowulf* allows us to date the poem, on the Wiglaf-premiss, before his accession in 827. Before this event, the most appropriate time for the start of *Beowulf*'s composition is the end of the campaigning season, thus the summer, in which Beornwulf was killed in East Anglia. All this points to the winter of 826–7.

HYPOTHESIS FOR A WEST SAXON *BEOWULF*

There is just one indication that a copy of *Beowulf* was held in the West Saxon court. This is in the names 'Scyld Scefing' and 'Beow' in *Beowulf*'s opening fitt (see my Chapters 1–2): earlier forms of these names crop up in the *Anglo-Saxon Chronicle* for the year 855, as part of the genealogy of King Æthelwulf (839–58). The rationalizations about Scef in Æthelweard's Latin version of this genealogy (*c*.975 × 983), together with the parallels in his Latin with the syntax of Scyld's ship-funeral in *Beo* 39–40, tend to show his source's dependency on *Beowulf*.[72] It seems more likely than not that a text of *Beowulf* was in Wessex where it could be quarried by King Æthelwulf or his bishops before 858.[73]

There is an additional hint of this in Asser's account of Alfred's prodigious childhood. Asser says that when Alfred was a boy his mother Osburh showed him and his brothers *quendam Saxonicum poematicae artis librum* ('a certain English book of poetic skill').[74] She offered to give the book to whichever boy could *discere citius istum codicem* ('learn this volume faster'): the comparative suggests she was talking to two brothers over Alfred's head. Impressed by the beauty of the book's initial letter, Alfred asked if she really would give it to whichever brother *citissime intelligere et recitare eum ante te possit* ('can understand it and recite it to you the fastest'). She assented and he took it to a *magistrum* ('tutor'), learned the contents, and recited them. Richard Abels credits Alfred with this feat when he was 6, presumably in Osburh's remaining lifetime in 854 or 855.[75] The nature of Alfred's book is not specified, but the story confirms that educated people had been trained to read their vernacular by the mid-ninth century.[76] Alfred's vocabulary in the *Metres of Boethius* later shows that he had mastered *Beowulf* or a warlike poem like it.[77] Clemoes has shown that Alfred is the only prose writer to elevate the word *ellen* ('active courage', then 'endurance') to the dignity of 'fortitude' as the third of four cardinal virtues in his translation of a version of *De consolatione Philosophiae*.[78] Otherwise it appears that this word was losing the

---

[72] Chambers, *Beowulf*, 68–86, esp. 76. North, *Heathen Gods*, 192–4. Townend, *Language and History*, 120–1.

[73] The present tense of Lat *trahit*, in Æthelweard's translation of a text which must therefore predate Æthelwulf's death. See North, *Heathen Gods*, 183–4.

[74] *Asser's Life of King Alfred*, ed. Stevenson, 20 (ch. 23).

[75] Abels, *Alfred the Great*, 55–6. For a longer discussion, see *Asser's Life of King Alfred*, ed. Stevenson, 221–5.

[76] P. Clemoes, 'Style as the Criterion for Dating the Composition of *Beowulf*', in Chase (ed.), *The Dating of Beowulf*, 173–85, esp. 184–5.

[77] Clemoes, 'King Alfred's Debt to Vernacular Poetry', 222–3.

[78] *King Alfred's Old English Boethius*, ed. Sedgefield, 62.

active meaning such as it has in *Beowulf*.[79] These are some additional reasons for believing that a copy of *Beowulf* was in Wessex in or before 855.[80]

If *Beowulf* was a Mercian poem, as I argue here, how did it cross into Wessex? Wiglaf was forced to pay an annual tribute to King Ecgberht, but this could not have included *Beowulf*.[81] There was a series of Mercian and West Saxon joint ventures which started in the 840s when moneyers minted coins in honour of both Berhtwulf and Æthelwulf.[82] But the most likely occasion for *Beowulf*'s transfer before 855, if it happened, was a marriage that took place between King Burgred and Alfred's sister Æthelswith, at Chippenham around Easter in 853.[83] Burgred and her father were military allies, for earlier that year Æthelwulf had helped the Mercians subjugate the Welsh. Asser adds that Æthelwulf gave his daughter to Burgred *nuptiis regaliter factis, ad reginam* ('as a queen at a wedding ceremony held in royal style').[84] Whatever gifts were exchanged, it might be thought that a book containing *Beowulf* was one of them. If Osburh showed her sons a text of *Beowulf*, we could speculate that she had obtained this as part of Burgred's payment for her daughter one or two years earlier.[85] For comparison, it is thought that a Frankish codex containing *The Later Genesis* (*Genesis* B) was brought to England with Judith, daughter of Charles the Bald, when Æthelwulf of Wessex married her in 856; there is also a Northumbrian Bible which Offa seems to have received from King Æthelred on the latter's marriage to Offa's daughter in 792.[86] Thus Burgred's marriage with Æthelwulf's daughter in 853 seems a likely occasion at which a volume containing *Beowulf*, a royal Mercian heirloom, crossed into Wessex.

How Burgred might have owned a copy of *Beowulf*, if he did, will take up the rest of this discussion. In the foregoing chapter I have argued that Burgred was Cenwulf's grandson: either through Burhhild, Cenwulf's probably illegitimate daughter; or through Ealdorman Burhhelm, possibly Cenwulf's illegitimate son, who was killed with Muca in 824. Burgred could have satisfied the demands of royal blood with the Anglian genealogy that traces him, if through Cenwulf, to Coenwalh, Penda's brother or brother-in-law. The deeper question is how a copy of *Beowulf* could have reached Burgred from Wiglaf's family.

---

[79] Clemoes, *Interactions of Thought and Language*, 69–73, esp. 72.

[80] So Lapidge, '"Beowulf", Aldhelm, the "Liber monstrorum" and Wessex', 187.

[81] *Rogeri de Wendover Chronica*, ed. Coxe, i. 277. *Historia Anglorum*, ed. and trans. Greenaway, 270–1 (iv. 34). Ecgberht also stopped Wiglaf minting his own coins. See Williams, 'Mercian Coinage and Authority', 223–4; in conjunction with H. E. Pagan, 'Coinage in Southern England, 796–874', in M. A. S. Blackburn (ed.), *Anglo-Saxon Monetary History* (Leicester, 1986), 45–65, esp. 47.

[82] J. J. North, 'The Coinage of Berhtwulf of Mercia (840–52)', *Spinks Numismatic Circular*, 69 (1961), 213–15. Williams, 'Mercian Coinage and Authority', 224–5.

[83] *The Anglo-Saxon Chronicle*, trans. Swanton, 64–7, esp. 66–7 (*s.a.* 853).

[84] *Asser's Life of King Alfred*, ed. Stevenson, 8.

[85] On payments, see C. Hough, 'Marriage and Divorce', in *EA-SE*, 302–3.

[86] Gretsch, *Intellectual Foundations of the English Benedictine Reform*, 388. Marsden, *The Text of the Old Testament*, 95.

King Wiglaf died in about 839. His son Wigmund seems to have died a few years before him. Not long after Wiglaf became king for the second time, this time as Ecgberht's vassal, *Wimundum filium suum longa dysenteria defunctum ad latus virginis dextrum tumulavit* ('he entombed his son Wigmund, who had passed away after a long bout of dysentery, on the right-hand side of the virgin'): that is to the side of Æthelthryth in whose cell Wiglaf is said to have hidden.[87] This report in the *Historia Croylandensis* tallies with the fact that Wigmund attests just once after his father's restoration, in 831 (S 188, no. 6, *filius regis*), but is not to be seen in Wiglaf's charters of 836 (S 190) or 839 (S 1438). For what it is worth, in his story in the Evesham *Chronicle*, Wigstan says that his father died soon after his birth.[88] The Crowland report also fits with Wigmund's absence in St Wigstan's royal mausoleum in Repton, in which Wiglaf was laid to rest. The story adds that *infra unius anni spatium* ('within the space of one year') from this date, Wiglaf had to bury Wigmund's *uxorem* ('wife') Ælfflæd on the virgin's left-hand side. The relevant obit for Ælfflæd cannot be right, however, for Wigstan was probably murdered in 849, shortly after trying to prevent her from remarrying.[89] Thomas of Marlborough says that when Wigmund died, Wigstan *totius regni ac paternarum facultatum unicus et verus relictus est hæres* ('was left the one true heir of all the kingdom and his father's possessions'). The Mercian clergy and laymen then acclaim Wigstan with one voice as *dominum suum naturalem et regni hæredem legitimum* ('their lord by birth and the legitimate heir of the kingdom'). But Wigstan, thinking of his heavenly inheritance, leaves the reins of office to *reginæ matri et regni proceribus* ('the queen mother and the kingdom's princes'). Mercia is then at peace until the day when the devil rouses *inter magnates regni maximum, Brifardum videlicet consulem* ('the greatest of the magnates, Berhtfrith the *consul*'). With the term *consul* Thomas presents Berhtfrith as one of two caretaker rulers, of whom neither is king. Berhtfrith resolves to get this title by marrying Ælfflæd, *quia ad culmen tantæ dignitatis jure successionis, licet beati Wistani cognatus existeret, attingere non potuit* ('since, although he was the blessed Wigstan's cousin, he could not attain to the heights of so great a dignity by the law of succession'). Thomas says that Ælfflæd consents to his proposal because she is *canonicarum impedimentorum nescia* ('unaware of canonical impediments'). In protest, Wigstan tells her of these, describing Berhtfrith as his *cognatus et compater* ('cousin and godfather'). His martyrdom follows. Thomas's claim that Berhtfrith was both kinsman and godfather to the boy he murdered receives some support from the *Historia Croylandensis*, which refers to Wiglaf simply as Berhtwulf's *frater* ('brother').

With these sources we can speculate on the ideology of the next two Mercian successions. If we follow the Evesham and Crowland accounts, we can explain

[87] *Chronicle of Croyland Abbey*, ed. Birch, 19.
[88] *Chronicon abbatiae de Evesham*, ed. Macray, 328: 'pater meus carnalis rex Wimundus te uxorem habuit, qui me ad regnum terrenum ex te generavit et mortuus est.'
[89] Ibid. 327–8.

the difference in Wiglaf's and Berhtwulf's names by treating these men as half-brothers by different fathers. Certainly the two branches helped each other: Wiglaf incorporated Berhtwulf as twentieth lay witness in his council of 836, while Berhtwulf raised a second Wiglaf (from seventeenth untitled layman) to seventh *princeps* in a council of 848 (see Fig. 10 below). On Wiglaf's death in *c.*839 the *Berht*-kindred found the trappings of power too good to lose. Wigstan is not included in any of King Berhtwulf's charters, so perhaps Wigstan was, as Thomas says, *adolescens* ('a youth') when he died.[90] If he was just 18 in 849, his birth would have coincided with Wigmund's first and last charter witness in 831. Wigstan's death ten years after Wiglaf's is probably to be blamed on the risk he posed to Berhtwulf on reaching his majority, which itself suggests that King Berhtwulf came to power as a regent for Wigstan, his grand-nephew.

Thomas says that Berhtfrith was driven out of Mercia after Wigstan's death.[91] There is no record of his marrying Ælfflæd, so there the hopes of the *Berht*-kindred would have perished; with her went Wiglaf's and Berhtwulf's connection with Cenwulf. The charters of Berhtwulf's reign in the 840s have been read as evidence of his attempt to buy or seize monastic lands for followers in a process which gradually deprived him of rights to hospitality in minsters across Mercia.[92] The closer Wigstan came to his majority, in this way, the more Berhtwulf's power crumbled. Burgred attests once as third *dux* in *c.*845 and on Berhtwulf's death he was made king.[93] Doubtless this happened peacefully, given the number of attestations in his reign by likely members of Berhtwulf's family.[94] Yet it seems likely that Ælfflæd, supposing that she died before 851, bequeathed her wealth not to Berhtwulf's sons (of Wiglaf's presumed half-brother), but to her own family on her father Ceolwulf's side. Burgred would be the most suitable beneficiary, her first cousin once removed, if there is any truth in my argument, in Chapter 9, that he was descended from Cenwulf. In all, then, my hypothesis ends with an assumption that a copy of *Beowulf* was in Ælfflæd's legacy: given to her, perhaps, with Wigmund in the late 820s when Wiglaf negotiated their marriage. This is one way how both the Mercian kingship and a copy of *Beowulf* could have passed into Burgred's West Mercian hands in 849; and the

[90] *Chronicon abbatiae de Evesham*, ed. Macray, 327.
[91] A certain 'Beorhtferd' *filius regis* witnesses an Abingdon charter of *c.*868, possibly in exile, in S 539 (BCS 873). Gelling, *The Early Charters of the Thames Valley*, 29–30 (no. 27): 'The form of the charter and the witnesses are of the reign of Æthelred I of Wessex.'
[92] Wormald, 'The Ninth Century', 138–9. *Charters of Abingdon Abbey, Part I*, ed. Kelly, 54–9 (no. 12: S 1271), esp. 57–8. Sims-Williams, *Religion and Literature*, 154 (S 1257 (BCS 241)).
[93] S 204 (BCS 452).
[94] (1) Beornoth (3: probably for *Beorhtnoth*: see (2)): 3 *dux*, S 206 (BCS 487), *s.a.* 855; 3 *dux*, S 207 (BCS 488), *s.a.* 855; ?2 *dux*, S 208 (BCS 492), *s.a.* 857; 2 *dux*, S 209 (BCS 503), *s.a.* 862; 1 *dux*, BCS 515, 860s; 2 *dux*, S 212 (BCS 513), *s.a.* 866; 2 *dux*, S 211 (BCS 514), *s.a.* 866; ?1 *dux*, S 215 (BCS 540), *s.a.* 875; 1 *dux*, S 216 (BCS 541), *s.a.* 875; 3 *ealdorman*, S 219 (BCS 552), *s.a.* 884. (2) Beorhtnoth: 2 *dux*, S 208 (BCS 492), *s.a.* 857; 1 *dux* in S 215 (BCS 540), *s.a.* 875. (3) Beorhtric (Berhtwulf's son?): 9 untitled, S 209 (BCS 503), *s.a.* 862; 10 untitled, S 212 (BCS 513), *s.a.* 866. (4) Beorhthelm: 19 untitled, S 220 (BCS 557), *s.a.* 888.

same or another copy of *Beowulf*, on his marriage, into the keeping of Æthelwulf in 853.

THE POET: ABBOT EANMUND OF BREEDON?

In Chapter 2 I concluded that Eanmund's sword becomes a symbol of Wiglaf's obligation to a kinsman, a physical token of gratitude for Beowulf's restoration of land. It is just nine lines after the first appearance, at the head of Fitt XXXVI, of Wiglaf's name (line 2602) that we hear the name of 'Eanmund', a Swede whose sword passed down to Wiglaf. Eanmund is also the name of the abbot of Breedon, which is where I suggest *Beowulf* was written in 826–7.

The poet says that Wiglaf enters the dragon-fight because he remembers the favours Beowulf gave him, including his father's estate. In the following quotation there is a line which may itself, like the emergence of Wiglaf, have an allegorical meaning:

> ne mihte ða forhabban,   hond rond gefeng
> geolwe linde,   gomel swurd geteah;
> þæt wæs mid eldum   Eanmundes laf
> suna Ohtheres;   þam æt sæcce wearð
> wræccan wineleasum   Weohstan bana (*Beo* 2609–13)

[then Wiglaf could not hold himself back, his hand seized his shield, the yellow board, he drew his ancient sword; that was Eanmund's legacy among men, of the son of Ohthere; to that friendless outlaw in combat did Weohstan give death.]

This is the first and last time Eanmund is named in *Beowulf*. He is Eadgils' brother, Ohthere's son, whom Weohstan kills while taking part in Onela's raid into Geatland. As we have seen in Chapter 2, Vésteinn, Weohstan's analogue, shows that Weohstan's place in this battle may have no basis in legend. Vésteinn's king is known as Áli, however.[95] Eanmund's analogue is Aun, father of Egill (i.e. Ongentheow) and an old king of Uppsala in the Norse poem *Ynglingatal* (st. 16–17, *c.*890). According to Snorri's prose commentary to this poem, Aun was a peaceful king, an inveterate sacrificer who lived for 200 years on the strength of sending Óðinn one son at 60 and then eight more, one for each decade, from the age of 120.[96] Earlier in his career, however, he is said to have been chased into Väster-Götland (western Geatland) by a king named Áli *inn frækni* ('the bold'). As the formation *Ean-mund* is dithematic, we do not know how peculiar the *mund*-suffix was to the poet. But if his source for 'Eanmund' was anything like Aun's tale at the root of *Ynglinga saga*, this poet has transformed it, by making Eanmund into Eadgils' brother and by arranging

---

[95] *Skáldskaparmál*, ed. Faulkes, i. 89 (v. 329) and 211 (note).
[96] *Heimskringla I*, ed. Bjarni, 47–50 (*Ynglinga saga*, ch. 25).

for Weohstan to kill Eanmund, so that the dead man's sword can be inherited by Wiglaf (lines 2620–5).

The phrase *Eanmundes laf* in *Beowulf*, lines 2609–13, describes Wiglaf's sword. Yet it is possible to find other levels of meaning, for a sword may also stand for the *verbum Dei* ('word of God') with which a Christian king fights the devil. This is how Alcuin, in *c.*799, defined a *gladius* ('sword') to Charlemagne, when the emperor asked him to explain Jesus' words in Luke 22: 36: 'whoever has a purse had better take it with him, and his pack too; and if he has no sword, let him sell his cloak to buy one.'[97] In reply to Charlemagne, Alcuin says that the sword is the *verbum Dei* which we must buy, selling all baggage of the worldly life, and with which we must fight against *omnes antiqui serpentis insidias* ('all the plots of the old serpent').[98] With this gloss Alcuin refers to Ephesians 6: 17, a familiar text in which St Paul enjoins converts to fasten on the belt of truth, to put on the breastplate of integrity, to let their shoes be the gospel of peace, and:

[16] in omnibus sumentes scutum fidei, in quo possitis omnia tela nequissimi ignea exstinguere: [17] et galeam salutis assumite: et gladium spiritus (quod est verbum Dei).

[with all of these, to put up the shield of Faith, with which you can quench all the fiery arrows of the most wicked one; and put on the helmet of salvation; and the sword of the spirit, which is the word of God.]

This is the same text that appears to inform Hrothgar's sword-hilt speech when he speaks of the fiery arrows which the soul-slayer shoots at the unwary (*Beo* 1744).[99] In the present chapter, I have already suggested that Wiglaf unwittingly refers to this image in Ephesians 6 in his final epitaph on *Beowulf* (lines 3114–19). So, with the image of Wiglaf grabbing shield and sword, *Eanmundes laf* could be read spiritually, with the meaning that Wiglaf, not Beowulf, fulfils the Lord's purpose against the serpent. The third meaning of *Eanmundes laf* is allegorical: what Eanmund bequeaths to Wiglaf is the tool with which Wiglaf proves himself to be Beowulf's heir. Hereby Eanmund's *laf* ('legacy') may be read as the poem itself, the legacy of Abbot Eanmund of Breedon, which proves Wiglaf fit to be king.

The teachers at Breedon, where I have argued that *Beowulf* was composed, trained their monks to read scripture historically, morally, allegorically, and spiritually. This is clear from Tatwine's riddle entitled 'De historia et sensu et morali et allegoria'.[100] If *Eanmundes laf*, towards the end of *Beowulf* on line 2611,

---

[97] 'Sed nunc qui habet sacculum, tollat similiter et peram: et qui non habet, vendat tunicam suam et emat gladium.'

[98] *Epistolae*, ed. Dümmler, ii. 205–10, esp. 207 (no. 136). Cf. Allott, *Alcuin of York*, 80–2 (no. 66).

[99] Orchard, *Companion*, 161. See my Ch. 3.

[100] This is the rubric over Tatwine's riddle about the four custodians of a treasury who 'gladly admit our friends to these safes, but to the ungrateful justly deny ready entrance'. *Tatuini Opera*, ed. de Marco and trans. von Erhardt, 170 (no. 3): 'gaudentes nostris hec mox reseramus amicis. Ingratisque aditum sed iure negamus apertum.'

was read allegorically as the poet's signature, it differs from Cynewulf's signature which took the form of runic acrostics in the poems *Elene, The Fates of the Apostles, Juliana,* and *Christ* II. Cynewulf's signatures are written in a form suitable both for eye and ear.[101] He produces them in order to ask for readers' prayers, with his runic letters connoting the transience of earthly beauty and the world and the universal terror of Judgement.[102] Of a pious style, his signatures are runic emulations of the complex acrostics which were often written in Roman letters for authorial attributions and dedications from the sixth to the ninth century.[103] Yet Cynewulf's signatures differ from the Latin models in that they appeal to listeners as well as readers. The less obvious rune-names draw a listener's attention to a group of letters which spell out a name. As Kenneth Sisam argued, 'Cynewulf used runes because, while they were obvious to a reader, they made possible the communication of his name to an audience in a way at once memorable and sure.'[104]

Acrostic inscriptions were common in Anglo-Saxon England. For example, there is a Latin poem in the ninth-century Book of Cerne with an acrostic reading *Aedeluald episcopus,* which Michelle Brown would identify with the name of the Æthelwald who was bishop of Lichfield 824–5, thus in Beornwulf's reign.[105] Further to the north, in the Trent valley, in Breedon in the 720s, Tatwine composed a poem with an acrostic before his collection of *Aenigmata,* which begins: *Versibus intextis vatem nunc jure salutat* ('Now let the reader rightly salute the poet in the interwoven lines').[106] His name heads the collection. So I suggest that later in the same minster, with the phrase *Eanmundes laf,* the poet of *Beowulf* adopted the principle, if not the Latin acrostic technique, of a signature to be remembered by a predominantly lay audience whose interests lay with King Beornwulf and Ealdorman Wiglaf. Even Cynewulf, when he says at the end of one signature, *Nu ðu cunnon miht hwa on þam wordum wæs werum oncyðig* ('Now you can understand who was revealed to men in these words', *The Fates of the Apostles* 105–6), acknowledges that 'words' rather than letters give people the right clue. *Beowulf* is a metrically conservative poem in which there is without doubt the expectation of a tight bond between the audience and the

---

[101] *Elene* 1256–70, *Fates* 98–105, *Juliana* 703–9, *Christ* II 797–807. On the eye, see Clemoes, *Interactions of Thought and Language,* 245.

[102] By poets such as Venantius Fortunatus, Aldhelm, Boniface, Alcuin, and Ermoldus Nigellus. See Clemoes, *Interaction of Thought and Language,* 392–3. Clemoes ('King Alfred's Debt to Vernacular Poetry', 213–14) argues that Cynewulf composed Christian narrative verse in order to compensate for the growing scarcity of Latin originals.

[103] Orchard, *The Poetic Art of Aldhelm,* 165–6, 248–9, and 275–7. Godman, *Poets and Emperors,* 56–8.

[104] Sisam, *Studies,* 1–28, esp. 25; first published as 'Cynewulf and his Poetry', *PBA* 18 (1933), 303–24.

[105] Brown, *The Book of Cerne,* 181–2 (fo. 21ʳ). Traditionally, the identification is with Bishop Aediluald of Lindisfarne (721 × 724–742).

[106] *Tatuini Opera,* ed. de Marco, 167. Orchard, *The Poetic Art of Aldhelm,* 242.

values of aristocracy in the narrative.[107] Although there are no runes in *Beo* 2611, consistent with the Cynewulfian style, Abbot Eanmund could have left his name on this line for the laity who were primed to look for contemporaries in *Beowulf* in any case, but especially after hearing Wiglaf's name for the first time.

The adjoining table shows that Abbot Eanmund first witnessed in 816, at Wulfred's stormy council of Chelsea, on the same level as Wigmund's last attestation two years before him, the ranking being a product of Worcester in both cases (Fig. 10: S 173, 180). For this and two other reasons I have associated Wigmund with the minster of Breedon on the Hill, where I have suggested he could have brought Speratus', that is Unwona's, poem on Hinieldus home to fill the repertoire of a poet who seems to have used Ingeld as Beowulf's mark in the Danish part of *Beowulf* (see my Chapters 4–5). Unlike Wigmund, Eanmund was never designated 'priest abbot'. Since this means that he was not appointed abbot by the bishop of Leicester, it follows that he was elected by the community of Breedon itself. This, in turn, would mean that Eanmund had been educated there during the abbacy (first indicated by the Wymeswold place name) of the man who preceded him, Priest Abbot Wigmund (*c.*792–814 × 816). Eanmund's allegiance to Archbishop Wulfred also seems indicated by the presence at Croft in 836 of a certain Werenberht, a namesake of the former bishop of Leicester (803–814; see Fig. 7), whose name has been grouped with the archbishop's larger family.[108] On this quite tentative basis it may be assumed that when the *venerabilis* Abbot Eanmund died, not long after his last witness in 848 (S 197), he had lived in Breedon for some fifty years as a friend of Wiglaf's family. It is presumably they, in the early ninth century, who would have provided him with legends about the princes they held to be their ancestors in Sweden.

In the full range of charters Eanmund's rankings fluctuate more than in the selection of the adjoining table (Fig. 10), but broadly speaking they show that he kept his position among the top two Mercian abbots across the reigns of five kings. The potential confusion between him and the Eanmund who was priest abbot of Bredon, south Worcestershire, is a matter I have attempted to resolve in Chapter 5 (Fig. 4). The prestige of the Breedon Eanmund's position (which is mostly in the top two) could be taken to suggest that he was regarded either as highly talented, or as connected to the Mercian court, or both. The charters show that he convened with all the kings from Cenwulf to Berhtwulf and mingled with other influential people as well. In this light it is obvious that Eanmund saw thirty years of Mercian history at close hand, including the infamous *fauces luporum*: the seizure of ecclesiastical lands by Cenwulf, Ceolwulf, and Cwenthryth.

---

[107] On the listening audience, see Niles, *Beowulf*, 205–12, and Clemoes, *Interactions of Thought and Language*, 68–116.

[108] Brooks, *Early History of the Church of Canterbury*, 141–2.

	173	180	187	1437	190	192	193	1271	197
S:	173	180	187	1437	190	192	193	1271	197
BCS:	343	357	373	386	416	430	434	443	454
Archive:	Wor	Wor	CCC	Wor	Wor	Wor	Wor	Ab	Pet
Place of issue:	[chc]	[chc]	*Werb.wic*	*Clof*	*Croft*	Tam	Tam		Rept
Year:	814	816	823	825	836	840	841	844	848
KINGS									
Cenwulf	+	+							
Ceolwulf			+						
Beornwulf				+					
Wiglaf					+				
Berhtwulf						+	+	+	+
ABBOTS									
Wigmund	2								
Eanmund		2	1	2	1	1	1 ben	1	1 ben
Beornhelm					3				
LAYMEN									
Beornnoth	2 *dux*	8 *dux*	2 *dux*	2 *dux*					
Beornwulf			10 *dux*	[king					
Mucel (1)				6 *dux*	1 *dux*	3 *dux*		1 *dux*	1 *pri*
Wigheard		2 *dux*							
Humberht					7 *dux*	1 *dux*		2 *dux*	2 *pri*
Wighelm			12	12					
Mucel (2)					9 *dux*	8 *dux*			8 *pri*
Wigcga (2)					10				
Werenberht					15				
Wiglaf (2)					17				7 *pri*
Eanwulf						18			
Berhtwulf					20	[king			

Figure 10. A life in politics: Abbot Eanmund of Breedon (814–848)

Source: Keynes, *Atlas of Attestations*, XV–XVII.

Eanmund's name bears a prefix that is itself royal. Although *Ean-* is a fairly popular prefix in Anglo-Saxon England, it is most concentrated in Northumbria and in the upper Avon kindred of Eanwulf, Offa's grandfather. In the first case, according to Ædiluulf's *Carmen de abbatibus* (803–21), there was an Eanmund who gave up the military for the monastic life, founding a Northumbrian minster (possibly Crayke, north of York) in the period 704 × 716.[109] In the second case, the Bredon Eanmund of the mid-820s looks descended from Eanwulf, whose first cousin, King Æthelbald, granted him before 717 the land on Bredon (Worcs.) as his family's proprietary monastery.[110] Besides Eanwulf, there were some distinguished people with the *Ean*-prefix in the old north-east Hwiccean area from the seventh to the ninth century.[111] One of them, Abbess Eanburg of Hampton Lucy, near Stratford, was Offa's *propinqua* ('paternal cousin'). In 780 Bishop Heathored of Worcester leased her the land at Hampton (and also *Fæhha læg*) for her lifetime in the same area as Offa's family possessions near Alveston (*Eanwulfes tun*; see Ill. 1) on the upper Avon in Warwickshire. Patrick Sims-Williams believes that this lease was part of Offa's 'ecclesiastical self-aggrandizement' in the period before his triple triumph of 786–7 (the visit of the papal legates and creation of the Lichfield archdiocese in 786 and Ecgfrith's coronation in 787).[112] It seems likely that both the Eanmund in Bredon (Worcs.) and his namesake in Breedon (Leics.) were beneficiaries: relatives of Offa, of the same regional background, who became novices in the 780s, monks in the 790s, abbots ten or more years after that. An 'Eanred' witnesses as ninth priest from Leicester in *Clofesho* in 803 (BCS 312). There is an untitled lay witness (at no. 18) named 'Eanwulf' in Wiglaf's charter for 836 (S 190).

If Abbot Eanmund of Breedon did compose *Beowulf*, his putative origins within Offa's programme of family monastic expansion after Lichfield would explain why Offa of Angeln is praised so highly in lines 1954–60. Although there is no proof, it can be claimed that the charter rankings of both Unwona and the *Wig*-kindred, including Priest Abbot Wigmund, show a similar pattern of rising prosperity in the ten years after the Mercians got their own archbishop at Lichfield (Figs. 1–3 and 5). Yet Eanmund's success was greater, for he kept his high standing in the reigns of Cenwulf and Beornwulf, even as the *Wigs* lost theirs.

[109] *Æthelwulf De abbatibus*, ed. A. Campbell (Oxford, 1967), 6–7 (line 53) and 8–9 (lines 74–7). M. Lapidge, 'Ædiluulf', in *EA-SE*, 6. Witness also the Archbishops Eanbald of York (I and II).

[110] Sims-Williams, *Religion and Literature*, 152–4, 155, 161–3, 165, and 374.

[111] The brothers Eanfrith and Eanhere, two Mercian sub-kings in Sussex in the 680s, mentioned by Bede (*HE* IV. 23); Eanberht, a Hwiccean sub-king in the 750s; another Eanberht, fourth abbot of Malmesbury after Aldhelm in 755 × 757; Eanbald, a magnate to whom Bishop Milred of Worcester granted land for a minster at Sodbury in the mid-eighth century; Eanburg, an abbess at Hampton Lucy near Stratford in the late eighth century; and Abbess Eanswith, granted an estate near Hereford in *c*.802. See Sims-Williams, *Religion and Literature*, 34, 58 (*Eanfrith* and *Eanhere*), 36–8, 155 (sub-king *Eanberht*), 226–8 (abbot *Eanberht*), 156–7 (*Eanbald*), and 163–4 (*Eanburg*). BCS 307 (*Eanswith*).

[112] Sims-Williams, *Religion and Literature*, 164.

There is a rich Latin style in the privileges which Abbot Eanmund obtained from King Berhtwulf in 841 (S 193) and from Berhtwulf and Ealdorman Humberht of Tame in 848 (S 197). The first charter survived in the Worcester archive, where it is thought to have been misplaced following a confusion of Breedon with the minster of Bredon on the east bank of the lower Avon in Worcestershire.[113] It is an agreement drafted for a council in Tamworth on Christmas Day in which Berhtwulf liberates Breedon from *fæstingmenn* ('royal entourages') at the high price of 120 mancuses in pure gold and a year's supply of 1,200 psalms (at 100 a month), together with 120 masses for the king and his friends. Nine years later, the second privilege (S 197) exacts an even higher price: a liberty from royal itineration and the feeding of royal and foreign envoys, in exchange for 180 mancuses in pure gold and 25 hides of land in two places; and in Humberht's case, a smaller exemption from entertaining the local Tame valley gentry, *in uno vaso prætiosa potatoria. quod fuit de nobile genere pulchraliter factum. et ex parte cum auro ornatum* ('for a beaker, a precious drinking-vessel beautifully made in a noble style and partly decorated with gold').[114] To judge by these deals, Eanmund ruled a wealthy foundation.

From the principle that the beneficiary drafts the privilege, it follows that the writing of these charters of the 840s was done or supervised by Abbot Eanmund himself. It is interesting, therefore, that the flourishes of S 193 mark out the draftsman as a poet:

Ut janitor caelestis bibliothece et vas electionis predicatur egregius apostolus Paulus dixit.
   'preteriit enim figura hujus mundi'
quoniam in velocitate dies et anni deficiunt. Et iterum sagax sophista
   qui quondam Solymis dives regnavit in arvis
katolectico versu cecinit dicens.
   'Non semper licet gaudere fugit hora qua jocemur'

[As the caretaker of the heavenly library and the prophet of grace foretells, [as] the eminent apostle Paul has said: 'the world as we know it is passing away' [1 Cor. 7: 31], for the day begins to wane in its quickness, as do the years. And again, the sage philosopher 'who at one time ruled as a rich man in the pastures of Jerusalem' [Aldhelm, *In basilica beatae Mariae semper virginis*, line 19], sang in a verse (with its last foot incomplete): 'It is not always permitted to rejoice; the hour flies in which we may make merry' [emended from *jacemur*]]

The draftsman assigns his *fugit hora* quotation to Solomon, whose Song of Songs features in the context of the poem by Aldhelm from which he quotes.[115]

---

[113] *Charters of Abingdon Abbey, Part I*, ed. Kelly, 56–7. Sims-Williams, *Religion and Literature*, 137 n. 103. Keynes stands by Bredon (Worcs.), in 'Councils of *Clofesho*', 40, no. 171. On the Marian line from Aldhelm which suggests an identification with St Mary's in Breedon, see above, in my Ch. 5.

[114] S 197 (BCS 454).

[115] Song of Songs 4: 12 and 2: 14: see *Aldhelmi Opera*, ed. Ehwald, 13 (*In basilica beatae Mariae semper virginis*, respectively lines 21 and 22).

His *fugit hora* line is a metrically corrupt version of a line in *Carpe diem*, a fifth-century poem of author unknown: *non semper gaudere licet; fugit hora, iocemur* ('it is not always permitted to rejoice; the hour is fleeting, let us make merry').[116] Abbot Eanmund, if he drafted these words in 841, does not know their source, but knows at least that the line does not scan and is publicly mindful of hexameters as an ideal poetic form. He exhibits a reading which blends the most diverse material. Moreover, he gives three epithets for his subject, varying the first verb of speaking (*predicatur*) with a second (*dixit*): this use of variation and apposition is the technique of Old English poetry. In all these respects it appears that the draftsman, whether or not he was Eanmund, was a poet. His fussing over metre, in particular, is consistent with the regularity with which the poet of *Beowulf* observes the metrical rules since defined as 'Kaluza's Law'.[117]

The free intertextuality of both S 193 and 197 reflects the Mercian craze for novelty about which Alcuin so bitterly complained to Mercia's leading ealdorman (probably Brorda) in 797, after Offa's death.[118] Eanmund was then one of a younger generation of clergy. In the opening years of Cenwulf's reign, as if living through a restoration, Eanmund would have been witness to profuse imports of Carolingian, Italian, Byzantine, and Syrian imagery in the manuscript illumination, sculpture, and metalwork of Mercia. This is the period with which the eclectic reading of *Beowulf* (see my Chapters 3 and 6) may be matched, more comfortably than with any other.

The Latin style associated with King Wiglaf is rather more straightforward. After the meeting with Wulfred in Wychbold in 831 (S 188), his most public display of piety survives in the Worcester record of the Council of Croft in Leicestershire in 836 (S 190), in which he granted a liberty to the minster of Henbury in Gloucestershire. If what I have argued is accepted, this council took place some nine years after the first performance of *Beowulf.* Mercia was now a defeated country, beset with unstable kingship and tributary to Ecgberht of Wessex. *Clofesho* was probably a charred ruin and the council at Croft, nearly 30 miles to the north-west if *Clofesho* truly was Brixworth (see Ill. 1), was the last church council recorded under Mercian jurisdiction. Wiglaf's queen Cynethryth was there, but there is no record of their son Wigmund (presumed dead) or their grandson Wigstan (perhaps 5 years old). Wiglaf's ten bishops were led by Ceolnoth, the new archbishop of Canterbury, Cyneferth of Lichfield (2) and Rethhun of Leicester (3). Eanmund of Breedon witnessed as the first of three abbots, the others being Wihtred (2) and Beornhelm (3). Otherwise there is a set of noblemen with a West Saxon complexion never seen before. Of Wiglaf's nine *duces*, only two had seen service with previous kings: Cyneberht (4), Cenwulf's nephew (with Ceolwulf and Beornwulf); and the older Mucel, the

116 H. W. Garrod (ed.), *The Oxford Book of Latin Verse: From the Earliest Fragments to the End of the 5th Century A.D.* (Oxford, 1912), 408 (no. 359).

117 Fulk, *A History of Old English Meter*, 385–90 (§§ 413–19).

118 *Epistolae*, ed. Dümmler, ii. 178–80, at 179 (no. 122: to 'Osberht', probably Brorda).

first ealdorman (with Beornwulf alone). The other seven had been made ealdor-men by Wiglaf himself. Five of these, including Humberht of the Tame valley (7) and the younger Mucel (9), would continue in Berhtwulf's service. This Mucel was possibly Æthelred Mucel of the *Gaini* (perhaps Gynge, 2 miles north of Farnborough on the West Berkshire Downs), who became Alfred's father-in-law.[119] The name-prefixes of the remaining successful new men give them out to be likewise affiliated to Wessex.[120] At the back of the assembly, however, were Werenberht (15), Wiglaf (17), and Eanwulf (18), whose names give them as Mercians respectively kin to Archbishop Wulfred, King Wiglaf, and Abbot Eanmund. Berhtwulf (20) witnessed last of all, perhaps held in waiting by Wiglaf. Berhtwulf's lack of title suggests that he had no lands, but in 836 he was only three years from succeeding his half-brother as king.

Wiglaf's declaration of piety begins with a proem lacking in flourishes, written with quotations which he appears to have chosen for himself (*hanc libertatem scripsi 7 scribere precepi*). Wiglaf takes his text from SS Paul and Matthew:

Regnum Dei querendum est super universa lucra terrena Paulo testante apostolo 'quae enim videntur temporalia sunt Sed que non videntur aeterna sunt' quid prodest homini totum mundum lucrare si anima ejus detrimentum patietur, Quapropter ego UUIGLAF rex Merciorum cum meis episcopis et ducibus et magistratibus.[121]

[The Kingdom of God is to be sought above all earthly gains, for Paul the Apostle is witness that 'what is seen is transient, but what is not seen lives for ever' [2 Cor. 4: 18]. 'What does it serve a man to gain the whole world if his soul should suffer harm?' [Matt. 16: 26] Wherefore I, WIGLAF, king of the Mercians with my bishops and ealdormen and officials ...]

His first text is from an epistle in which Paul enjoins converts to disregard their mortal decay. Wigmund had probably died by this time and Wiglaf may have been in poor health. This text is combined with a standard contrast between earthly and heavenly reward. This theme is nonetheless apposite to the ending of *Beowulf*, in which the dying hero could be said to endanger his soul for the treasures he can *sceawian* ('see') in exchange for those he cannot. Beowulf asks to see the dragon's hoard (*gearo sceawian searogimmas*, lines 2748–9), the poet appears to say that Beowulf was never keener to see an owner's gold-bestowing favour (*goldhwæte agendes est gearwor sceawian*, lines 3074–5), and young Wiglaf, when he offers his first epitaph, pronounces the hoard seen (*hord ys gesceawod*, line 3084).

---

[119] S. D. Keynes, 'King Alfred and the Mercians', in M. A. S. Blackburn and D. N. Dumville (eds.), *Kings, Currency and Alliances: History and Coinage of Southern England in the Ninth Century* (Woodbridge, 1998), 1–45, esp. 9. OS Explorer Map 170, Abingdon, Wantage & Vale of White Horse, 445867 (West and East Ginge).

[120] Æthelheard (1), 3 *dux*; Æthelwulf (2), 5 *dux*; Ælfstan, 8 *dux* (cf. with Ælfred, 13).

[121] S 190 (BCS 416). The manuscript, BL, Cotton Augustus II.9, is 'apparently a contemporary copy of the text', whose authenticity cannot be doubted: see Cubitt, *Anglo-Saxon Church Councils*, 287.

King Wiglaf's second text is drawn from a chapter in Matthew's Gospel in which Christ foretells that not one among his disciples will taste death before Doomsday. He returns to the same verse a little later: *Aut quam dabit homo commutationem pro anima sua?* ('Or with what will a man commute his soul?', Matt. 16: 26). In his charter Wiglaf makes a show of renouncing earthly gains, hoping to be absolved for unspecified crimes. Thus he grants the liberty to the minster in Henbury *pro redemptione animae meae* ('for the redemption of my soul'). Commonplace as they are, his Latin formulae seem to echo Beowulf's dying words in Fitts XXXVII–XXXVIII. With the dragon dead, Beowulf thanks the Lord for being allowed to see some of the gold:

> 'Nu ic on maðma hord   mine bebohte
> frode feorhlege.' (*Beo* 2799–80)

['now that I have bought a hoard of treasures at the wise price of my life.']

But we know that he is ignorant of the true price, that the *feorhlege* might encompass his soul. From the Christian point of view, these lines contain an irony of which Beowulf can know nothing.

In Mercia in 836, King Wiglaf alludes to *meas iniquitates quas per ignorantiam feci* ('my offences which I committed through ignorance'). This statement towards the end of his valedictory charter appears to shun Beowulf's example: both his dying claim not to have sought out cunning enmities (*ne sohte searoniðas*, line 2738), which the poet contradicts (*sohte searoniðas*, line 3067); and the heathen ignorance with which Beowulf made his claim. The latter is the theme of the penultimate fitt of *Beowulf* (*seolfa ne cuðe þurh hwæt his worulde gedal weorðan sceolde*, lines 3067–8, Fitt XLII). In the final fitt the same type of ignorance allows the dragon's cursed treasure to be laid with Beowulf back in the earth. King Wiglaf, on the other hand, bequeaths his wealth to heaven. Evidently fearing some repossessions after his death, he prays to his successors:

ut elemosinam quam in altitudinem caeli culminis in manus domini datam habeo communiter pro me 7 pro totum gentem Merciorum tam benigniter stare dimittetis 7 multiplicare dignemini.

[that you should kindly allow to remain, as well as condescend to increase, the alms which I have given into the Lord's hand in the height of heaven's vault, for the sake of myself and all the people of Mercia.]

Thus he endows the minsters. Not only in western Mercia was Wiglaf gratefully remembered, if we trust the detail embedded in a twelfth-century forgery presented as his charter in Crowland, Middle Anglia (S 189/BCS 409). This text, which probably changes only the terms and setting of a real transaction, claims that Wiglaf offers its refectory, for remembrance in the old monks' prayers, a drinking vessel with a transverse cross on the inside, each arm of which features a protruding angel. Wiglaf calls this *ciphum meum deauratum et per totam partem exteriorem barbaris victoribus ad dracones pugnantibus celatum* ('my cup which is gilded and chased on its whole outer surface with heathen conquerors fighting dragons').[122]

CONCLUSION

The many and varied arguments of this book deal more in likelihood and possibility than in fact. With all claims of this kind there is a risk that one day the supporting links will be cut by variant readings or new observations or discoveries. Yet I started with the premiss that the parallel between Beowulf–Wiglaf and Beornwulf–Wiglaf is not a coincidence. Those who disagree must believe that it is. If we start to date the poem on the basis of this parallel, some old and new readings of *Beowulf* fall into place in a way that was quite unforeseen. The Norse analogues tell us that the poem's legends have been changed. These changes relate Beowulf to Hygelac, turn him into a king, kill him in battle with a dragon, and delay the arrival of his young companion whose name, Wiglaf, has no analogue. The period of history that best fits with this pattern of innovation is the aftermath of Beornwulf's death in battle in 826. Second, the poet's erudition is concealed, but wide and eclectic. He appears to recast episodes from the *Aeneid* for moments in the story when he either had no precedent or wished to improve on an existing type-scene. The greatest of these is Aeneas' threat to the marriage plans of Amata in Books VII and XI, which helps the poet of *Beowulf* to put his hero briefly in the race for the daughter of Wealhtheow. By the time Beowulf's resemblance to Aeneas ends, there is a case for an 'anxiety of influence' which argues that the poet of *Beowulf* was challenged by a great work on Ingeld before him. This lost source on Ingeld is identifiable with a *carmen* on 'Hinieldus' which caused a stir in Speratus' court in 797. 'Speratus' has been identified with Bishop Unwona of Leicester (*c.*785–*c.*800). Was this *carmen* transmitted to the poet of *Beowulf* by one of his pupils? The Wiglaf-premiss points to one of them whose name was Priest Abbot Wigmund, a man whose status in the Leicester diocese tells us he was Unwona's friend and appointee. Three arguments then connect Wigmund with the minster of Breedon on the Hill, some 20 miles north of Leicester. Now I ask how many of the poem's presumed Latin sources could have been in Breedon's library. Lost as this is, both the works of Tatwine, who lived there in the 720s, and the sculptures of Breedon tell a tale. They also connect Breedon to Corbie and other great minsters in Francia some of whose books and book catalogues do survive. *Beowulf*'s forays into Norse mythology, moreover, can be traced to a contact with Danes through the suspicion of a link between Breedon and some Vikings in eastern Mercia in 809. The poet's incentive to

---

[122] BCS 409 (S 189). *Chronicle of Croyland Abbey,* ed. Birch, pp. ix and 16; *vinitoribus* ('wine-dressers') is read for *victoribus* in *Ingulph's Chronicle*, trans. Riley, 17). Souter, *Glossary of Later Latin,* *s.v.* 'barbarus'.

adapt their heathen myths at a later time is explained through Breedon's connection with Francia, from where, through the early 820s, news would have come to England about King Heriold of Denmark up to his baptism in 826.

Thus the setting; the *terminus a quo*, 826, is confirmed by a political context for the Geatish half of *Beowulf* which I explore in my last three chapters. First an old suggestion is revived that the 'Thryth' digression blames Offa's queen Cynethryth for the martyrdom of St Æthelberht of East Anglia in 794. Then it is argued that Offa and his later successors Cenwulf and Beornwulf furnished the poet of *Beowulf* with models for Kings Offa, Hygelac, and Beowulf. Their sequence suggests that the poet traced the cause of Beornwulf's death in East Anglia to the murder of an East Anglian king by Offa's queen. The same sequence leads forward in time towards Wiglaf, a youth who stands all but crowned at the end. Far from becoming king of Geatland, however, in legend Wiglaf seems ready to migrate. Allegorically, through his descendant, it looks as if he has arrived in Mercia. The poet heralds Wiglaf as the fourth great king after Offa. So the poem *Beowulf,* a sword at the service of the king in waiting, is datable to the winter of 826–7 before Wiglaf did become king. As for the poet, I find his aural signature nine lines after Wiglaf's first naming, in the line *þæt wæs mid eldum Eanmundes laf* ('that was Eanmund's legacy among men'). If what I have claimed is true, *Beowulf* is the legacy of Abbot Eanmund of Breedon on the Hill.

Bibliography

Two or more references bring a cited author here. Icelandic authors or editors are entered by forename.

ABELS, R., *Alfred the Great: War, Kingship and Culture in Anglo-Saxon England* (London, 1998).

ABRAMS, L., *Anglo-Saxon Glastonbury: Church and Endowment*, Studies in Anglo-Saxon History 8 (Woodbridge, 1986).

—— 'The Conversion of the Danelaw', in Graham-Campbell, Hall, Jesch, and Parsons (eds.), *Vikings and the Danelaw*, 31–44.

ALLOTT, S. (trans.), *Alcuin of York c.A.D. 732–804: His Life and Letters* (York, 1974).

ANDERSSON, T. M., 'Sources and Analogues', in Bjork and Niles (eds.), *Beowulf Handbook*, 125–48.

ARNOLD, T. (ed.), *Symeonis monachi Opera omnia*, 2 vols., Rolls Series 75 (London, 1882–5).

ARNOLD-FORSTER, F., *Studies in Church Dedications, or England's Patron Saints*, 3 vols. (London, 1899).

BAILEY, R. N., 'The Meaning of Mercian Sculpture', Vaughan Paper No. 34 (Leicester, 1988), 1–16.

BASSETT, S. (ed.), *The Origins of Anglo-Saxon Kingdoms* (Leicester, 1989).

BATELY, J. (ed.), *The Anglo-Saxon Chronicle: MS A*, The Anglo-Saxon Chronicle: A Collaborative Edition 3 (Cambridge, 1986).

BELL, A. (ed.), *L'Estoire des Engleis*, Anglo-Norman Texts 14–16 (Oxford, 1960).

BENCARD, M. (ed.), *Ribe Excavations 1970–76*, 4 vols. (Esbjerg, 1981–91).

—— and JØRGENSEN, L. B., 'Excavation and Stratigraphy', in Bencard (ed.), *Ribe Excavations*, iv. 15–167.

BENDIXEN, K., 'Sceattas and Other Coin Finds', in Bencard (ed.), *Ribe Excavations*, i. 63–101.

BENSON, L. D., 'The Originality of Beowulf', in M. W. Bloomfield (ed.), *The Interpretation of Narrative: Theory and Practice*, Harvard English Studies 1 (Cambridge, Mass., 1970), 1–43.

BERENDSOHN, W. A., *Zur Vorgeschichte des 'Beowulf'*, with a foreword by O. Jespersen (Copenhagen, 1935).

BETHURUM, D. (ed.), *The Homilies of Wulfstan* (Oxford, 1957).

BIDDLE, M., 'Archaeology, Architecture, and the Cult of Saints in Anglo-Saxon England', in L. A. S. Butler and R. K. Morris (eds.), *The Anglo-Saxon Church* (London, 1986), 1–31.

—— and KJØLBYE-BIDDLE, B., 'Repton and the "Great Heathen Army", 873–4', in Graham-Campbell, Hall, Jesch, and Parsons (eds.), *Vikings and the Danelaw*, 45–96.

BIGGS, F. M., HILL, T. D., and SZARMACH, P. E., with HAMMOND, K. (eds.), *Sources of Anglo-Saxon Literary Culture: A Trial Version*, Medieval and Renaissance Texts and Studies 74 (Binghamton, NY, 1990).

Birch, W. de G. (ed.), *The Chronicle of Croyland Abbey by Ingulph* (Wisbech, 1883).

—— (ed.), *Cartularium Saxonicum: A Collection of Charters Relating to Anglo-Saxon History*, 3 vols. (London, 1885–93).

Bischoff, B., *Mittelalterliche Studien: Ausgewählte Aufsätze zur Schriftkunde und Litera- turgeschichte*, 3 vols. (Stuttgart, 1966–81).

—— 'Hadoard und die Klassikerhandschriften aus Corbie', in Bischoff, *Mittelalterliche Studien*, i. 46–63.

—— 'Die Hofbibliothek Karls des Grossen. Mit sechs Abbildungen (Tafel V bis X)', in Bischoff, *Mittelalterliche Studien*, iii. 149–69.

Bjarni Aðalbjarnarson (ed.), *Snorri Sturluson: Heimskringla* I, ÍF 26 (Reykjavík, 1941).

—— (ed.), *Snorri Sturluson: Heimskringla* II, ÍF 27 (Reykjavík, 1945).

Bjarni Einarsson (ed.), *Ágrip af Nóregskonunga Sǫgum: Fagrskinna – Nóregs Konunga Tal*, ÍF 29 (Reykjavik, 1985).

Bjarni Guðnason, *Um Skjöldungasögu* (Reykjavík, 1963).

—— 'The Icelandic Sources of Saxo Grammaticus', in K. Friis-Jensen (ed.), *Saxo Grammaticus: A Medieval Author between Norse and Latin Culture* (Copenhagen, 1981), 79–93.

—— (ed.), *Danakonunga Sögur: Skjǫldunga Saga, Knytlinga Saga, Ágrip af Sǫgu Dana- konunga*, ÍF 35 (Reykjavík, 1982).

Bjork, R. E., and Niles, J. D. (eds.), *A Beowulf Handbook* (Exeter, 1997).

Blair, J., *Anglo-Saxon Oxfordshire* (Oxford, 1994).

—— *The Church in Anglo-Saxon Society* (Oxford, 2005).

Blessington, F. C., *Paradise Lost and the Classical Epic* (Boston, 1979).

Bliss, A. J., '*Beowulf* Lines 3074–3075', in M. Salu and R. T. Farrell (eds.), *J. R. R. Tolkien, Scholar and Storyteller* (Ithaca, NY, 1979), 41–63.

Blunt, C. E., 'The Coinage of Offa', in R. H. M. Dolley (ed.), *Anglo-Saxon Coins: Studies Presented to F. M. Stenton on the Occasion of his 80th Birthday, 17 May 1960* (London, 1961), 39–62.

Boer, W. W. (ed.), *Epistola Alexandri ad Aristotelem* (The Hague, 1953).

Bolton, D. K., 'The Study of the *Consolation of Philosophy* in Anglo-Saxon England', *Archives d'histoire doctrinale et littéraire du Moyen Âge*, 44 (1977), 33–78.

Bolton, W. F., *Alcuin and Beowulf: An Eighth-Century View* (London, 1979).

—— 'Boethius and a Topos in *Beowulf* ', in M. H. King and W. M. Stevens (eds.), *Saints, Scholars and Heroes: Studies in Medieval Culture in Honour of Charles W. Jones*, 2 vols. (Collegeville, Minn., 1979), i. 15–43.

Bond, G., 'Links between *Beowulf* and Mercian History', *SP* 40 (1943), 481–93.

Boretius, A. and Krause, V. (eds.), *Capitularia regum Francorum*, MGH, Leges, 2 vols. (Hanover, 1883–97).

Boyle, L. O., OP, 'The Nowell Codex and the Poem of *Beowulf* ', in Chase (ed.), *The Dating of Beowulf*, 23–32.

Brandl, A., 'Beowulf-Epos und Aeneis in systematischer Vergleichung', *Archiv für des Studium der neueren Sprachen [und Literatur]*, 171 (1937), 161–73.

Bremmer, R. H., Jr., 'Frisians in Anglo-Saxon England: A Historical and Toponymical Investigation', *Fryske Nammen*, 3 (1980), 45–94.

Brooks, N., *The Early History of the Church of Canterbury: Christ Church from 597–1066* (Leicester, 1984).

—— 'The Formation of the Mercian Kingdom', in Bassett (ed.), *The Origins of Anglo-Saxon Kingdoms*, 159–70.

BROWN, M. P., *The Book of Cerne: Prayer, Patronage and Power in Ninth-Century England* (London, 1996).

—— 'Mercian Manuscripts? The "Tiberius" Group and its Historical Context', in Brown and Farr (eds.), *Mercia*, 278–90.

—— and FARR, C. A. (eds.), *Mercia: An Anglo-Saxon Kingdom in Europe* (Leicester, 2001).

BULLOUGH, D. A., 'What has Ingeld to do with Lindisfarne?', *ASE* 22 (1993), 93–125.

—— 'Charlemagne's "Men of God": Alcuin, Hildebald and Arn', in Story (ed.), *Charlemagne: Empire and Society*, 136–50.

CAMPBELL, A. (ed. and trans.), *The Chronicle of Æthelweard* (London, 1962).

CAMPBELL, J. (ed.), *The Anglo-Saxons* (Harmondsworth, 1982).

—— 'The Sale of Land and the Economics of Power in Early England: Problems and Possibilities', *HSJ* 1 (1989), 23–37; also published in Campbell, *The Anglo-Saxon State*, 227–68.

—— *The Anglo-Saxon State* (London, 2000).

CHAMBERS, R. W., *Beowulf: An Introduction to the Study of the Poem*, 3rd edn., with supplement by C. L. Wrenn (Cambridge, 1959).

CHASE, C. (ed.), *The Dating of Beowulf* (Toronto, 1981).

CHRISTIANSEN, E. (trans.), *The Works of Sven Aggesen: Twelfth-Century Danish Historian*, Viking Society for Northern Research (London, 1992).

CLAYTON, M., *The Cult of the Virgin Mary in Anglo-Saxon England*, CSASE 2 (Cambridge, 1990).

CLEMOES, P., 'King Alfred's Debt to Vernacular Poetry: The Evidence of *ellen* and *cræft*', in Korhammer, Reichl, and Sauer (eds.), *Words, Texts and Manuscripts*, 213–38.

—— *Interactions of Thought and Language in Old English Literature*, CSASE 12 (Cambridge, 1995).

COLGRAVE, B. (ed.), *Eddius Stephanus: Life of Bishop Wilfrid* (Cambridge, 1927).

—— and MYNORS, R. A. B. (ed. and trans.), *Bede's Ecclesiastical History of the English People* (Oxford, 1969; repr. w. corrections, 1991).

CONDEE, R. W., *Structure in Milton's Poetry: From the Foundation to the Pinnacles* (Philadelphia, 1974).

COXE, H. O. (ed.), *Rogeri de Wendover Chronica sive Flores historiarum*, 4 vols. (London, 1841–2).

CRAMP, R. 'Schools of Mercian Sculpture', in Dornier (ed.), *Mercian Studies*, 191–233.

CROSS, J. E. (ed.), *Cambridge Pembroke College MS. 25: A Carolingian Sermonary Used by Anglo-Saxon Preachers* (London, 1987).

CUBBIN, G. P. (ed.), *The Anglo-Saxon Chronicle: MS D*, The Anglo-Saxon Chronicle: A Collaborative Edition 6 (Cambridge, 1996).

CUBITT, C., *Anglo-Saxon Church Councils c.650–c.850* (London, 1995).

DAMICO, H., *Beowulf's Wealhtheow and the Valkyrie Tradition* (Madison, 1984).

—— and OLSEN, A. H. (ed.), *New Readings on Women in Old English Literature* (Bloomington, Ind., 1990).

DARLINGTON, R. R., and MCGURK, P. (ed.), and BRAY, J., and MCGURK, P. (trans.), *The Chronicle of John of Worcester*, ii: *The Annals from 450 to 1066* (Oxford, 1995).

DORNIER, A., 'The Anglo-Saxon Monastery at Breedon on the Hill, Leicestershire', in Dornier (ed.), *Mercian Studies*, 155–68.

—— (ed.), *Mercian Studies* (Leicester, 1977).

DRONKE, U., '*Beowulf* and Ragnarǫk', *Saga-Book*, 17 (1968), 302–25.

—— (ed., trans., and comm.), *The Poetic Edda, ii: Mythological Poems* (Oxford, 1997).

DÜMMLER, E. (ed.), *Poetae Latini aevi Carolini*, MGH, Poetae Latini Medii Aevi I (Berlin, 1881).

—— (ed.), *Poetae Latini aevi Carolini*, MGH, Poetae Latini Medii Aevi II (Berlin, 1884).

—— (ed.), *Epistolae Karolini aevi*, II, MGH, Epist. IV (Berlin, 1895).

—— (ed.), *Epistolae Karolini aevi*, III, MGH, Epist. IV (Berlin, 1896).

DUMVILLE, D. N., 'The Anglian Collection of Royal Genealogies and Regnal Lists', *ASE* 5 (1976), 23–50.

—— 'Kingship, Genealogies and Regnal Lists', in P. H. Sawyer and I. N. Woods (eds.), *Early Medieval Kingship* (Leeds, 1977), 72–104.

—— 'The Ætheling: A Study in Anglo-Saxon Constitutional History', *ASE* 8 (1979), 1–33.

—— and LAPIDGE, M. (ed.), *The Annals of St Neots, with Vita prima sancti Neoti* (Cambridge, 1984).

EARLE, J. (trans. and comm.), *The Deeds of Beowulf* (Oxford, 1892).

EDWARDS, H., *The Charters of the Early West Saxon Kingdoms* (Oxford, 1988).

EHWALD, R., *Aldhelmi Opera*, MGH, Auct. Antiq. 15 (Berlin, 1919).

EKWALL, E., *The Concise Oxford Dictionary of Place-Names*, 4th edn. (Oxford, 1960).

ELIASON, N. E., 'Beowulf, Wiglaf and the Wægmundings', *ASE* 7 (1978), 95–105.

EMERTON, E. (trans.), *The Letters of Saint Boniface*, introd. T. F. X. Noble (New York, 2000).

FARRELL, R. T., '*Beowulf*, Swedes and Geats', *Saga-Book*, 18/3 (1972), 227–86.

FAULKES, A. (ed.), *Snorri Sturluson: Edda: Prologue and Gylfaginning* (Oxford, 1982).

—— (ed.), *Snorri Sturluson: Edda: Háttatal* (Oxford, 1991).

—— (ed.), *Snorri Sturluson: Edda: Skáldskaparmál*, 2 vols., Viking Society for Northern Research (London, 1998).

FEATHERSTONE, P., 'The Tribal Hidage and the Ealdormen of Mercia', in Brown and Farr (eds.), *Mercia*, 23–34.

FINBERG, H. P. R., *The Early Charters of Wessex*, Studies in English History 3 (Leicester, 1964).

—— *The Early Charters of the West Midlands*, 2nd edn. (Leicester, 1972).

FINNUR JÓNSSON (ed.), *Hrólfs Saga Kraka og Bjarkarímur*, Samfund til udgivelse af gammel nordisk litteratur 35 (Copenhagen, 1904).

FISHER, P. (trans.), and ELLIS DAVIDSON, H. R. (comm.), *Saxo Grammaticus: The History of the Danes: Books I–IX*, 2 vols. (Cambridge, 1979–80).

FRANK, R., 'Skaldic Verse and the Date of *Beowulf*', in Chase (ed.), *The Dating of Beowulf*, 123–39.

—— 'The *Beowulf*-Poet's Sense of History', in Howe (ed.), *Beowulf: Backgrounds and Contexts Criticism*, 98–111. Also published in L. D. Benson and S. Wenzel (eds.), *The Wisdom of Poetry: Essays in Early English Literature in Honor of Morton W. Bloomfield* (Kalamazoo, Mich., 1982), 53–65 and 271–7.

FRIIS-JENSEN, K., *Saxo Grammaticus as Latin Poet: Studies in the Verse Passages of the Gesta Danorum*, Analecta Romana Instituti Danici, Supplementum 14 (Rome, 1987).

—— 'Saxo Grammaticus' Study of the Roman Historiographers and his Vision of History', in Santini (ed.), *Saxo Grammaticus*, 61–81.

FULK, R. D., *A History of Old English Meter* (Philadelphia, 1992).

GANNON, A., *The Iconography of Early Anglo-Saxon Coinage: Sixth to Eighth Centuries* (Oxford, 2003).

GANZ, D., *Corbie in the Carolingian Renaissance*, Beihefte der Francia 20 (Sigmaringen, 1990).

GARMONSWAY, G. N., and SIMPSON, J. (trans.), and ELLIS DAVIDSON, H. R., *Beowulf and its Analogues* (London, 1968).

GELLING, M., *The Early Charters of the Thames Valley*, Early English History 7 (Leicester, 1979).

—— *Place-Names in the Landscape* (London, 1984).

—— *The West Midlands in the Early Middle Ages* (Leicester, 1992).

GERRETS, D., 'The Anglo-Frisian Relationship from an Archaeological Point of View', in V. F. Faltings, A. G. H. Walker, and O. Wilts (eds.), *Friesische Studien II: Beiträge des Föhrer Symposiums zur Friesischen Philologie vom 7.–8. April 1994* (Odense, 1995), 119–28.

GERTZ, M. C. (ed.), *Scriptores minores historiae Danicae Medii Aevi*, 2 vols. (Copenhagen, 1918–20; repr. 1970).

GODMAN, P., *Poetry of the Carolingian Renaissance* (London, 1985).

—— *Poets and Emperors: Frankish Politics and Carolingian Poetry* (Oxford, 1987).

GOFFART, W., '*Hetware* and *Hugas*: Datable Anachronisms in *Beowulf*', in Chase (ed.), *The Dating of Beowulf*, 83–100.

GRAHAM-CAMPBELL, J., HALL, R., JESCH, J., and PARSONS, D. N. (eds.), *Vikings and the Danelaw: Select Papers from the Proceedings of the Thirteenth Viking Congress, Nottingham and York, 21–30 August 1997* (Oxford, 2001).

GREEN, W. M. (ed.), *Sancti Augustini Contra academicos*, CCSL 29 (Turnhout, 1970).

GREENAWAY, D. (ed. and trans.), *Historia Anglorum: The History of the English*, by Henry, Archdeacon of Huntingdon (Oxford, 1996).

GREENFIELD, S. B., 'The Authenticating Voice in *Beowulf*', *ASE* 5 (1976), 51–62.

—— 'Beowulf and the Judgement of the Righteous', in Lapidge and Gneuss (eds.), *Learning and Literature in Anglo-Saxon England*, 393–407.

GRETSCH, M., *The Intellectual Foundations of the English Benedictine Reform*, CSASE 25 (Cambridge, 1999).

GUÐNI JÓNSSON and BJARNI VILHJÁLMSSON (eds.), *Fornaldarsögur Norðurlanda*, 3 vols. (Reykjavík, 1944–50).

HABER, T. B., *A Comparative Study of the Beowulf and the Aeneid* (Princeton, 1931).

HADDAN, A. W., and STUBBS, W. (ed.), *Councils and Ecclesiastical Documents Relating to Great Britain and Ireland*, 3 vols. (Oxford, 1869–71).

HALBERTSMA, H., 'Frieslands Oudheid', unpublished Ph.D. dissertation, 2 vols. (pages numbered sequentially), University of Groningen, 1982.

HALL, R., 'Anglo-Scandinavian Urban Development in the East Midlands', in Graham-Campbell, Hall, Jesch, and Parsons (eds.), *Vikings and the Danelaw*, 143–55.

HALSALL, G., *Warfare and Society in the Barbarian West, 450–900* (London, 2003).

HART, C., *The Danelaw* (London, 1992).

HART, W. H. (ed.), *Historia et cartularium monasterii Gloucestriæ*, 3 vols., Rolls Series 33 (London, 1863–7).

HASLAM, J., 'Market and Fortress in England in the Reign of Offa', *World Archaeology*, 19 (1987–8), 76–93.

HAYWARD, P. A., 'The Idea of Innocent Martyrdom in Medieval England ca. 700 to 1150 AD', unpublished Ph.D. dissertation, University of Cambridge, 1994.

HILL, D., *An Atlas of Anglo-Saxon England* (Oxford, 1981).

—— 'Mercians: The Dwellers on the Boundary', in Brown and Farr (eds.), *Mercia*, 173–82.

HILL, J. (ed.), *Old English Minor Heroic Poems*, Durham and St Andrews Medieval Texts 4 (Durham, 1983).

HINES, J., *The Scandinavian Character of Anglian England in the Pre-Viking Period*, British Archaeological Reports 124 (Oxford, 1984).

—— 'The Scandinavian Character of Anglian England: An Update', in M. O. H. Carver (ed.), *The Age of Sutton Hoo: The Seventh Century in North Western Europe* (Woodbridge, 1982), 315–29.

HODGES, R., *The Anglo-Saxon Achievement: Archaeology and the Beginnings of English Society* (London, 1989).

HOFSTRA, T., 'Ier-Aldfrysk neist Aldingelsk en Aldsaksysk', in De Fryske Akademy (ed.), '*2000 Jier Friezen': It Âlfte Frysk Filologekongres* (Leeuwarden, 1989), 38–49.

HØILUND-NIELSEN, K., 'Centrum og periferi i 6.–8. årh. Territoriale studier af dyrestil og kvindesmykker i yngre germansk jernalder i Syd- og Østskandinavien', in P. Mortensen and B. M. Rasmussen (eds.), *Fra Stamme til Stat i Danmark* (Århus, 1991), 127–54.

HORSTMANN, C. (ed.), *S. Editha sive Chronicon Vilodunense im Wiltshire Dialekt aus MS. Cotton. Faustina B.III* (Heilbronn, 1883).

HOWE, N. (ed.), *Beowulf: A Prose Translation: Backgrounds and Contexts Criticism*, trans. E. Talbot Donaldson, 2nd edn. (New York, 2002).

IRVING, E. B., Jr., *Rereading Beowulf* (Philadelphia, 1989).

JACK, G. (ed.), *Beowulf: A Student Edition* (Oxford, 1994).

JACOBS, N., 'Anglo-Danish Relations, Poetic Archaism, and the Date of *Beowulf*', *Poetica* (Tokyo), 8 (1978), 23–43.

JAKOB BENEDIKTSSON, 'Icelandic Traditions of the Scyldings', *Saga-Book*, 15 (1957), 48–66.

—— (ed.), *Íslendingabók – Landnámabók*, ÍF 1 (2 vols. in 1) (Reykjavík, 1986).

JAMES, M. R., 'Two Lives of St Ethelbert, King and Martyr', *EHR* 32 (1917), 214–44.

JESCH, J., 'Skaldic Verse in Scandinavian England', in Graham-Campbell, Hall, Jesch, and Parsons (eds.), *Vikings and the Danelaw*, 313–25.

JEWELL, R. H. I., 'The Pre-Conquest Sculpture at Breedon on the Hill, Leicestershire', unpublished Ph.D. dissertation, University of London, 1982.

—— 'The Anglo-Saxon Friezes at Breedon on the Hill, Leicestershire', *Archaeologia*, 108 (1986), 95–115.

—— 'Classicism of Southumbrian Sculpture', in Brown and Farr (eds.), *Mercia*, 247–62.

JOHNSON, R. F. 'Archangel in the Margins: St Michael in the Homilies of Cambridge, Corpus Christi College 41', *Traditio: Studies in Ancient and Medieval History, Thought and Religion*, 53 (1998), 63–91.

—— *Saint Michael the Archangel in Medieval English Legend* (Woodbridge, 2005).

KASKE, R. E., '*Sapientia et Fortitudo* as the Controlling Theme of *Beowulf*', in Nicholson (ed.), *An Anthology*, 269–310. First printed in *SP* 55 (1958), 423–56.

KELLY, R. J. (ed. and trans.), *The Blickling Homilies (with General Introduction, Textual Notes, Tables and Appendices, and Select Bibliography)* (London, 2003).

KELLY, S. E. (ed.), *Charters of Selsey*, Anglo-Saxon Charters 6 (Oxford, 1998).

—— (ed.), *Charters of Abingdon Abbey, Part I*, Anglo-Saxon Charters 7 (Oxford, 2000).

—— (ed.), *Charters of Abingdon Abbey, Part II*, Anglo-Saxon Charters 8 (Oxford, 2001).

KENDALL, C. B., *The Metrical Grammar of Beowulf*, CSASE 5 (Cambridge, 1991).

KEYNES, S. D., 'The Control of Kent in the Ninth Century', *EME* 2/2 (1993), 111–31.

—— 'The Councils of *Clofesho*', Vaughan Paper No. 38 (Leicester, 1993), 1–52.

—— *An Atlas of Attestations in Anglo-Saxon Charters, c.670–1066*, Department of Anglo-Saxon, Norse, and Celtic (Cambridge, 1995).

—— 'Mercia and Wessex in the Ninth Century', in Brown and Farr (eds.), *Mercia*, 310–28.

—— and LAPIDGE, M. (trans.), *Alfred the Great: Asser's Life of King Alfred and Other Contemporary Sources* (Harmondsworth, 1983).

KIERNAN, K., 'The Eleventh-Century Origin of *Beowulf* and the *Beowulf* Manuscript', in Chase (ed.), *The Dating of Beowulf*, 9–21.

—— *Beowulf and the Beowulf Manuscript*, 2nd edn. (Ann Arbor, 1996).

KIRBY, D. P. *The Earliest English Kings* (London, 1991).

KLAEBER, F., 'Aeneis und Beowulf', *Archiv*, 126 (1911), 40–8 and 339–59.

—— (ed.), *Beowulf and The Fight at Finnsburg*, 3rd edn. (New York, 1950).

KORHAMMER, M., REICHL, K., and SAUER, H. (ed.), *Words, Texts and Manuscripts: Studies in Anglo-Saxon Culture Presented to Helmut Gneuss on the Occasion of his Sixty-Fifth Birthday* (Woodbridge, 1992).

KRUSCH, B., and LEVISON, W. (eds.), *Passiones vitaeque sanctorum aevi Merovingici*, MGH, SRM 7 (Hanover, 1920).

—— —— (eds.), *Gregorii episcopi Turonensis libri historiarum X*, MGH, SRM 1.1 (Hanover, 1951).

LAPIDGE, M., '"Beowulf", Aldhelm, the "Liber monstrorum" and Wessex', *Studi medievali*, 3rd series, 23 (1982), 151–92.

—— 'Abbot Germanus, Winchcombe, Ramsey and the Cambridge Psalter', in Korhammer, Reichl, and Sauer (eds.), *Words, Texts and Manuscripts*, 99–129.

—— 'Surviving Booklists from Anglo-Saxon England', in M. P. Richards (ed.), *Anglo-Saxon Manuscripts: Basic Readings* (New York, 2001), 87–167 (with corrections); previously published in Lapidge and Gneuss (eds.), *Learning and Literature in Anglo-Saxon England*, 33–89.

—— 'The Archetype of *Beowulf*', *ASE* 29 (2000), 5–41.

—— '*Beowulf* and Perception', *PBA* 111 (2001), 61–97.

—— *The Anglo-Saxon Library* (Oxford, 2006).

—— and GNEUSS, H., *Learning and Literature in Anglo-Saxon England: Studies Presented to Peter Clemoes on the Occasion of his 65th Birthday* (Cambridge, 1985).

—— BLAIR, J., KEYNES, S. D., and SCRAGG, D. (eds.), *The Blackwell Encyclopedia of Anglo-Saxon England* (Oxford, 1999).

LAW, V., *The Insular Latin Grammarians*, Studies in Celtic History 3 (Woodbridge, 1982).

—— 'The Study of Latin Grammar in Eighth-Century Southumbria', *ASE* 12 (1983), 43–71.

LAWRENCE, W. W., *Beowulf and Epic Tradition* (Cambridge, Mass., 1928).

LEBECQ, S., 'On the Use of the Word "Frisian" in the 6th–10th Centuries' Written Sources: Some Interpretations', in McGrail (ed.), *Maritime Celts*, 85–90.

LEE, DONG-ILL, 'Character from Archetype: A Study of the Characterization of Beowulf with Reference to the Diction of Direct Speech in *Beowulf*', unpublished Ph.D. dissertation, University of London, 1995.

LEVISON, W., *England and the Continent in the Eighth Century: The Ford Lectures Delivered in the University of Oxford in the Hilary Term 1943* (Oxford, 1946).

LIEBERMANN, F. (ed. and comm.), *Die Gesetze der Angelsachsen*, 3 vols. (Halle a.S., 1903–16).

LOEWENFELD, S. (ed.), *Gesta abbatum Fontanellensium*, MGH, SRG 28 (Hanover, 1886).

LOT, F. (ed.), *Nennius et l'Historia Brittonum* (Paris, 1934).

LOVE, R. C. (ed. and trans.), *Three Eleventh-Century Anglo-Latin Saints' Lives: Vita s. Birini, Vita et miracula s. Kenelmi and Vita s. Rumwoldi* (Oxford, 1996).

McGRAIL, S. (ed.), *Maritime Celts, Frisians and Saxons: Papers Presented to a Conference in Oxford in November 1988*, Council for British Archaeology 71 (London, 1991).

McKITTERICK, R., *The Frankish Kingdoms under the Carolingians: 751–987* (London, 1983).

—— *The Carolingians and the Written Word* (Cambridge, 1989).

MACRAY, W. D. (ed.), *Chronicon abbatiae de Evesham ad annum 1418*, Rolls Series 29 (London, 1863).

MAGENNIS, H., *Images of Community in Old English Poetry*, CSASE 18 (Cambridge, 1996).

MALONE, K., *The Literary History of Hamlet: The Early Tradition* (New York, 1923).

MARCO, M. DE (ed.), and VON EBERHARDT, E. (trans.), *Tatuini Opera omnia*, CCSL 133 (Turnhout, 1968).

MARSDEN, R., *The Text of the Old Testament in Anglo-Saxon England*, CSASE 15 (Cambridge, 1995).

MAUND, K. L., ' "A Turmoil of Warring Princes": Political Leadership in Ninth-Century Denmark', *HSJ* 6 (1994), 29–47.

MAYOR, J. E. B. (ed.), *Ricardi de Cirencestria Speculum historiale de gestis regum Angliae*, 2 vols. (London 1863–9).

MAYR-HARTING, H., *The Coming of Christianity to Anglo-Saxon England*, 3rd edn. (London, 1991).

MEANEY, A., 'Scyld Scefing and the Dating of *Beowulf*—Again', *Bulletin of the John Rylands University Library of Manchester*, 71 (1989), 1–40.

MELLINKOFF, R., 'Cain's Monstrous Progeny in "Beowulf": Part I, Noachic Tradition', *ASE* 8 (1979), 143–62.

MELLOWS, W. T. (ed.), *The Peterborough Chronicle of Hugh Candidus* (London, 1949).

MITCHELL, B., and ROBINSON, F. C. (ed.), *Beowulf: An Edition with Relevant Shorter Texts*, including 'Archaeology and *Beowulf*', by L. Webster (Oxford, 1998).

MURRAY, A. C., '*Beowulf*, the Danish Invasions, and Royal Genealogy', in Chase (ed.), *The Dating of Beowulf*, 101–11.

MYNORS, R. A. B. (ed.), *P. Vergili Maronis Opera* (Oxford, 1969).

—— THOMSON, R. M., and WINTERBOTTOM, M. (eds. and trans.), *Gesta regum Anglorum: The History of the English Kings*, by William of Malmesbury, 2 vols. (Oxford, 1998–9).

NÄSMAN, U., 'Vendel Period Glass from Eketorp II, Öland, Sweden: On Glass and Trade from the Late 6th to the Late 8th Centuries AD', *Acta Archaeologica*, 55 (1984), 55–116.

—— 'Om fjärrhandel i Sydskandinaviens yngre järnålder: Handel med glas under germansk järnålder och vikingetid', *Hikuin*, 16 (1990), 89–118.

NEFF, K. (ed.), *Die Gedichte des Paulus Diaconus: Kritische und erklärende Ausgabe*, Quellen und Untersuchungen zur lateinischen Philologie des Mittelalters 3.4 (Munich, 1908).

NELSON, J. L., 'Carolingian Contacts', in Brown and Farr (eds.), *Mercia*, 126–43.

—— 'England and the Continent in the Ninth Century: Ends and Beginnings', *TRHS*, 6th ser. 12 (2002), 1–21.

NEWTON, S., *The Origins of Beowulf and the Pre-Viking Kingdom of East Anglia* (Cambridge, 1993).

NICHOLSON, L. E. (ed.), *An Anthology of Beowulf Criticism* (Notre Dame, Ind., 1963).

NILES, J. D., *Beowulf: The Poem and its Tradition* (Cambridge, Mass., 1983).

—— 'Reconceiving *Beowulf*: Poetry as Social Praxis', in Howe (ed.), *Beowulf: Backgrounds and Contexts Criticism*, 111–34. Also published in *College English*, 61/2 (1998), 143–66.

NORTH, R., 'The Pagan Inheritance of Egill's *Sonatorrek*', in T. Pàroli (ed.), *Poetry in the Scandinavian Middle Ages: Atti del 12. congresso internazionale di studi sull'alto medioevo*, (Rome, 1990), 147–67.

—— 'Tribal Loyalties in the *Finnsburh Fragment* and Episode', *LSE* NS 21 (1990), 13–43.

—— *Pagan Words and Christian Meanings*, Costerus NS 81 (Amsterdam, 1991).

—— 'Saxo and the Swedish Wars in *Beowulf*', in Santini (ed.), *Saxo Grammaticus*, 175–88.

—— 'Metre and Meaning in *Wulf and Eadwacer*: Signý Reconsidered', in L. A. J. R. Houwen and A. A. MacDonald (eds.), *Loyal Letters: Studies on Mediaeval Alliterative Poetry & Prose*, Mediaevalia Groningana 15 (Groningen, 1994), 29–54.

—— ' "Wyrd" and "weard ealuscerwen" in *Beowulf*', *LSE* NS 25 (1994), 69–82.

—— 'Boethius and the Mercenary in *The Wanderer*', in T. Hofstra, L. A. J. R. Houwen, and A. A. MacDonald (eds.), *Pagans and Christians: The Interplay between Christian Latin and Traditional Germanic Cultures in Early Medieval Europe*, Germania Latina II (Groningen, 1995), 71–98.

—— *Heathen Gods in Old English Literature*, CSASE 22 (Cambridge, 1997).

—— (ed.), *The 'Haustlǫng' of Þjóðólfr of Hvinir* (Enfield Lock, 1997).

O'BRIEN O'KEEFFE, K. (ed.), *The Anglo-Saxon Chronicle: MS C*, The Anglo-Saxon Chronicle: A Collaborative Edition 5 (Cambridge, 2001).

O'DALY, G., 'The Response to Skepticism and the Mechanisms of Cognition', in E. Stump and N. Kretzmann (eds.), *The Cambridge Companion to Augustine* (Cambridge, 2001), 159–70.

OLRIK, J., and RÆDER, H. (eds.), *Saxonis Gesta Danorum* (Copenhagen, 1931).

OLSEN, K. E., and HOUWEN, L. A. J. R. (eds.), *Monsters and the Monstrous in Medieval Northwest Europe*, Mediaevalia Groningana, NS 3 (Leuven/Louvain, 2001).

ORCHARD, A., *The Poetic Art of Aldhelm*, CSASE 8 (Cambridge, 1994).

—— *Pride and Prodigies: Studies in the Monsters of the Beowulf-Manuscript* (Woodbridge, 1995).

ORCHARD, A., 'Wish You Were Here: Alcuin's Courtly Poetry and the Boys Back Home', in S. Rees Jones, R. Marks, and A. J. Minnis (eds.), *Courts and Regions in Medieval Europe* (York, 2000), 21–43.

—— *A Critical Companion to Beowulf* (Woodbridge, 2003).

OVERING, G. R., *Language, Sign, and Gender in Beowulf* (Carbondale, Ill., 1990).

PAGE, R. I., 'The Audience of *Beowulf* and the Vikings', in Chase (ed.), *The Dating of Beowulf*, 113–22.

PERTZ, G. H. (ed.), *Vita s. Liudgeri*, MGH, SS 1 (Hanover, 1829; repr. 1925).

—— (ed.), and KURZE, F. (rev.), *Annales regni Francorum et Annales Einhardi*, MGH, SRM 6 (Hanover, 1895).

PHEIFER, J. D. (ed.), *Old English Glosses in the Épinal-Erfurt Glossary* (Oxford, 1974).

PLUMMER, C., and EARLE, J. (ed.), *Two of the Saxon Chronicles Parallel: With Supplementary Extracts from the Others*, 3rd edn., 2 vols. (Oxford, 1965).

POPE, J. C. (ed.), *Homilies of Ælfric: A Supplementary Collection*, EETS os 259–60 (Oxford, 1967–8).

PULSIANO, P., and WOLF, K. (eds.), *Medieval Scandinavia: An Encyclopedia* (New York, 1993).

RAUER, C., *Beowulf and the Dragon: Parallels and Analogues* (Cambridge, 2000).

RENOIR, A., 'The Terror of the Dark Waters: A Note on Virgilian and Beowulfian Techniques', in L. D. Benson (ed.), *The Learned and the Lewed: Studies in Chaucer and Medieval Literature*, Harvard English Studies 5 (Cambridge, Mass., 1974), 147–60.

REUTER, T., *Germany in the Early Middle Ages c.800–1056* (London, 1991).

REYNOLDS, L. D. (ed.), *Texts and Transmission: A Survey of the Latin Classics* (Oxford, 1983).

RILEY, H. T. (trans.), *Ingulph's Chronicle of the Abbey of Croyland* (London, 1854).

—— (ed.), *Gesta abbatum monasterii sancti Albani*, 3 vols. (London, 1867–9).

ROBERTS, J., 'Hagiography and Literature: The Case of Guthlac of Crowland', in Brown and Farr (eds.), *Mercia*, 69–86.

ROESDAHL, E., *The Vikings*, trans. S. M. Margesson and K. Williams, 2nd edn. (Harmondsworth, 1998).

ROLLASON, D., 'Lists of Saints' Resting-Places in Anglo-Saxon England', *ASE* 7 (1978), 61–93.

—— 'The Search for Saint Wigstan', Vaughan Paper No. 27 (Leicester, 1981), 1–19.

—— 'The Cults of Murdered Royal Saints in Anglo-Saxon England', *ASE* 11 (1983), 1–22.

RUGGERINI, M. E., 'St Michael and the Dragon: From Scripture to Hagiography', in Olsen and Houwen (eds.), *Monsters and the Monstrous in Medieval Northwest Europe*, 23–58.

RUMBLE, A. R. (ed.), *The Reign of Cnut: King of England, Denmark and Norway* (London, 1994).

RUSSO, D. G., *Town Origins and Development in Early England, c.400–950 A.D.*, Contributions to the Study of World History 58 (Westport, Conn., 1998).

SANTINI, C. (ed.), *Saxo Grammaticus: Tra storiografia e letteratura: Bevagna, 27–29 Settembre 1990* (Rome, 1992).

SAWYER, P. H., *Anglo-Saxon Charters: An Annotated List and Bibliography*, Royal Historical Society Guides and Handbooks 8 (London, 1968).

SCHARER, A., *Die angelsächsische Königsurkunde im 7. und 8. Jahrhundert*, Veröffentlichungen des Instituts für Österreichische Geschichtsforschung 27 (Vienna, 1982).

SCOTT, J. (ed. and trans.), *The Early History of Glastonbury: An Edition, Translation and Study of William of Malmesbury's De antiquitate Glastonie ecclesie* (Woodbridge, 1981).

SEARLE, W. G., *Onomasticon Anglo-Saxonicum: A List of Anglo-Saxon Proper Names from the Time of Beda to that of King John* (Cambridge, 1897).

SEDGEFIELD, W. J. (ed.), *King Alfred's Old English Version of Boethius' De consolatione Philosophiae* (Oxford, 1899).

SHIPPEY, T. A., *Beowulf,* Studies in English Literature 70 (London, 1978).

SIGURÐUR NORDAL (ed.), *Egils saga Skalla-Grímssonar,* ÍF 2 (Reykjavík, 1933).

SIMS-WILLIAMS, P., *Religion and Literature in Western England 600–800,* CSASE 3 (Cambridge, 1990).

SISAM, K., 'Anglo-Saxon Royal Genealogies', *PBA* 39 (1953), 287–348.

—— *Studies in the History of Old English Literature* (Oxford, 1953).

SKLUTE, L. J., '*Freoðuwebbe* in Old English Poetry', in Damico and Olsen (eds.), *New Readings on Women in Old English Literature,* 204–10.

SKOVGAARD-PETERSEN, I., *Da Tidernes Herre var nær: Studier i Saxos Historiesyn* (Copenhagen, 1987).

SLAY, D. (ed.), *Hrólfs saga kraka,* Editiones Arnamagnæanæ, Series B, 1 (Copenhagen, 1960).

SOUTER, A. (ed.), *A Glossary of Later Latin to 600 A.D.* (Oxford, 1949).

STAFFORD, P., *The East Midlands in the Early Middle Ages* (Leicester, 1985).

—— 'Political Women in Mercia, Eighth to Early Tenth Centuries', in Brown and Farr (eds.), *Mercia,* 35–49.

STANLEY, E. G., 'Hæthenra Hyht in *Beowulf*', in S. B. Greenfield (ed.), *Studies in Old English Literature in Honour of Arthur G. Brodeur* (New York, 1963), 136–51; repr. in his *A Collection of Papers,* 192–208.

—— 'The Date of *Beowulf*: Some Doubts and No Conclusions', in Chase (ed.), *The Dating of Beowulf,* 197–211; repr. in his *A Collection of Papers,* 209–31.

—— *A Collection of Papers with Emphasis on Old English Literature* (Toronto, 1987).

—— *In the Foreground: Beowulf* (Cambridge, 1994).

—— '"A Very Land-Fish, Languagelesse, a Monster": Grendel and the Like in Old English', in Olsen and Houwen (eds.), *Monsters and the Monstrous in Medieval Northwest Europe,* 79–92.

STENTON, F. M., *Anglo-Saxon England,* 3rd edn. (Oxford, 1971).

STEVENSON, J. (ed.), *Chronicon monasterii de Abingdon,* 2 vols. (London, 1858).

STEVENSON, W. H. (ed.), *Asser's Life of King Alfred Together with the Annals of Saint Neots Erroneously Ascribed to Asser,* with an introductory article by D. Whitelock (Oxford, 1904).

STEWART, I., 'Anglo-Saxon Gold Coins', in R. A. G. Carson and C. M. Kraay (eds.), *Scripta nummaria Romana: Essays Presented to Humphrey Sutherland* (London, 1978), 143–72.

STORY, J., *Carolingian Connections: Anglo-Saxon England and Carolingian Francia, c.750–870* (Aldershot, 2003).

—— (ed.), *Charlemagne: Empire and Society* (Manchester, 2005).

SWANTON, M. J. (trans.), *The Anglo-Saxon Chronicle* (London, 1996).

TESTER, S. J. (ed. and trans.), *Consolation of Philosophy*, 2nd edn. (Cambridge, Mass., 1973).

THACKER, A. T., 'Some Terms for Noblemen in Anglo-Saxon England c.650–900', *Anglo-Saxon Studies in Archaeology and History*, 2 (1981), 201–36.

—— 'Kings, Saints, and Monasteries in Pre-Viking Mercia', *Midland History*, 10 (1985), 1–25.

TOLKIEN, J. R. R., *Finn and Hengest: The Fragment and the Episode*, ed. A. Bliss (London, 1982).

TOLLEY, C., '*Beowulf*'s Scyld Scefing Episode: Some Norse and Finnish Analogues', *Arv*, 52 (1996), 7–48.

TOULMIN SMITH, L. (ed.), *The Itinerary of John Leland in or about the Years 1535–1543*, foreword by T. Kendrick, 5 vols. (London, 1964).

TOWNEND, M., *Language and History in Viking Age England: Linguistic Relations between Speakers of Old Norse and Old English*, Studies in the Early Middle Ages 6 (Turnhout, 2002).

TURVILLE-PETRE, E. O. G., *Scaldic Poetry* (Oxford, 1976).

UNGER, C. R. (ed.), *Flateyjarbók*, 3 vols. (Christiania [Oslo], 1860–8).

VENEZKY, R. L., and DIPAOLO HEALEY, A. (eds.), *A Microfiche Concordance to Old English* (Newark, Del., 1980).

WAITZ, G. (ed.), *Pauli diaconi Historia Langobardorum*, MGH, SRLI (Hanover, 1878).

WALKER, I. W., *Mercia and the Making of England* (Thrupp, 2000).

WALLACE-HADRILL, J. M., *The Frankish Church* (Oxford, 1983).

WAT[T]S, W. (ed.), *Matthæi Paris monachi Albanensis Angli Historia major*, containing *Vitae duorum Offarum* (London, 1640 [from an edition of 1571]).

WELCH, M., 'The Archaeology of Mercia', in Brown and Farr (eds.), *Mercia*, 147–59.

WHITELOCK, D., *The Audience of Beowulf* (Oxford, 1951).

—— (ed.), *English Historical Documents*, i: *c. 500–1042* (London, 1955).

WILLIAMS, G., 'Mercian Coinage and Authority', in Brown and Farr (eds.), *Mercia*, 210–28.

—— 'Military Institutions and Royal Power', in Brown and Farr (eds.), *Mercia*, 295–309.

WORMALD, C. P., 'Bede, *Beowulf*, and the Conversion of the Anglo-Saxon Aristocracy', in R. T. Farrell (ed.), *Bede and Anglo-Saxon England*, BAR, British Series, 46 (Oxford, 1978).

—— 'The Age of Offa and Alcuin', in Campbell (ed.), *The Anglo-Saxons*, 101–31.

—— 'The Ninth Century', in Campbell (ed.), *The Anglo-Saxons*, 132–59.

—— 'Charters, Law and the Settlement of Disputes in Anglo-Saxon England', in W. Davies and P. Fouracre (eds.), *The Settlement of Disputes in Early Medieval Europe* (Cambridge, 1986), 146–68.

—— 'A Handlist of Anglo-Saxon Lawsuits', *ASE* 17 (1988), 247–81.

—— 'In Search of Offa's "Law-Code"', in I. N. Wood and N. Lund (eds.), *People and Places in Northern Europe 500–1600: Essays in Honour of Peter Hayes Sawyer* (London, 1991), 25–45.

WRENN, C. L. (ed.), *Beowulf with the Finnesburg Fragment*, 1st edn. (London, 1953).

—— and BOLTON, W. F. (eds.), *Beowulf with the Finnesburg Fragment*, 4th edn. (Exeter, 1988).

WRIGHT, C. D., *The Irish Tradition in Old English Literature*, CSASE 6 (Cambridge, 1993).

WRIGHT, C. E., *The Cultivation of Saga in Anglo-Saxon England* (Edinburgh, 1939).

WRIGHT, T. and WÜLCKER, R. P. (eds.), *Anglo-Saxon and Old English Vocabularies*, 2 vols. (London, 1884).

YORKE, B., *Kings and Kingdoms of Early Anglo-Saxon England* (London, 1990).

—— *Wessex in the Early Middle Ages* (Leicester, 1995).

ZUPITZA, J. (ed.), *Beowulf: Reproduced in Facsimile from the Unique Manuscript British Museum Ms. Cotton Vitellius A.XV*, 2nd edn., EETS os 245 (Oxford, 1959 [for 1958]).

Index

Abel 67

Abraham 196, 231

Absalon, archbishop of Lund (1178–1201) 122–3

Academica priora, see Cicero

Achaemenides, Greek not eaten by Cyclops 86

Aco, see Haki Hámundarson

Adalhard, cousin of Charlemagne and abbot of Corbie (780–814 and 821–6) 180

Adam 10–11, 26

Ad Cuimnanum 151

Aðils, king of Uppsala and Norse analogue of Eadgils 46, 51, 59, 61

Aelfred, redeemer of Codex Aureus 216

Aeneas, progenitor of Rome 3, 10–13, 14, 15, 84, 90; as Turnus' rival, 124–30; see also Beowulf the Geat

Aeneid, see Vergil

Aethelþithe 270

Ædiluulf, *Carmen de abbatibus* of 326

Ælbertus, see St Æthelberht

Ælfflæd, daughter of Offa king of Mercia 236–7 (Ælflæda), 248, 261, 262, 263

Ælfflæd, Ceolwulf's daughter viii; made Cenwulf's heir, 281, 304 n. 23; married to Wigmund son of Wiglaf, 304, 313; allegedly buried alongside him, 319; hypothesis that she bequeaths copy of *Beowulf* to (first cousin once removed) Burgred, 320

Ælfhere, as mother's brother of Wiglaf the Wægmunding 58, 299

Ælfhere, king of Aquitaine and Waldere's father 58

Ælfhun 138 n. 34, 139 (fig. 1)

Ælflæda, see Ælfflæd, daughter of Offa

Ælfric, abbot of Eynsham (d. *c.*1010) 34, 94; *De falsis diis* of, 34; *The Life of St Martin* of, 34

Ælfthryth, daughter of Offa and Cynethryth 247, 259 (fig. 6), 269 (fig. 7); Cenwulf's queen, 270, 287

Ælfwald, king of East Anglia (d. 749) 159, 241

Ælfwald, king of Northumbria (779–88) 219, 250

Ærdulfus, saint and king at Breedon 218; see also Breedon on the Hill, King Eardwulf

Æschere, Hrothgar's best friend 91, 106

Æthelbald, king of Mercia (716–56/7) 150, 268, 305, 326

Æthelbeald, as Alfred's older brother 304 n. 24

Æthelberht, saint and king of East Anglia (779–94) vii, ix, 3, 239, 241, 245, 249, 292, 294; in *The Anglo-Saxon Chronicle*, 239, 249; in the Worcester *Chronicle* (Ægelberhtus), 243, 245; in *Annals of St Neots* (Aethelbrihtus), 239, 240, 249; in *Vitae duorum Offarum* (Ælbertus), 236–7, 239, 250; in Hereford *Passio s. Æthelberti*, 145, 240, 250; in Roger's *Chronica maiora*, 240–2, 250

Æthelburh, Offa's daughter 261, 262, 263

Æthelburh, sister of King Ecgberht and wife of Ealdorman Weohstan 276

Æthelflæd, Alfred's daughter and Lady of the Mercians 28, 29

Æthelheah, abbot of Canterbury 152 (fig. 3)

Æthelheard, abbot of Louth and archbishop of Canterbury (793–805) 133, 138 n. 34, 139 (fig. 1), 141, 143, 259 (fig. 6), 263

Æthelmod, bishop 138 n. 34, 139 (fig. 1)

Æthelmund Ingelding, ealdorman of the Hwicce (d. 802) vii, 144 (fig. 2), 243, 244 (fig. 5), 259 (fig. 6), 274; endowed by Offa, 145–6; enlarges St Peter's

Æthelmund Ingelding (*cont.*)
Gloucester, 276; as dedicatee of poem
on 'Hinieldus', 145, 155; killed in battle
with Ealdorman Weohstan, 275–6, 290
Æthelred, king of Mercia (675–704) 158,
220 n. 122
Æthelred, king of Northumbria
(d. 796) 133; orders execution of
Eardwulf, 219; murders other rivals,
219; alliance of with Offa, 252; Danish
haircut of, 212–13, 216
Æthelred Mucel of the *Gaini*,
see Mucel (2)
Æthelstan, king of East Anglia
(827–c.848) 293–4; kills King
Beornwulf 293
Æthelstan, son of Ecgberht
(d. 851) 293–4; see also Æthelstan of
East Anglia
Æthelstan, king of Wessex (924–39) 1,
25, 26, 29, 33, 165
Æthelswith, Alfred's sister and Burgred's
queen 318
Æthelthryth, daughter of Offa, cited in
Historia Croylandensis 314
Æthelwald, bishop of Lichfield
(824–5) 323; see also Book of Cerne
Æthelweard, West Saxon ealdorman
(d. 998), *Chronicon* of 26, 34, 286 n.
138, 317
Æthelwold, bishop of Winchester
(963–84) 177, 191
Æthelwulf, king of Wessex
(839–58) 26–7, 28, 292, 293, 317–18
Agnarr (Agnarus, Agner), king of the
Swedes 51, 56, 114
Alcuin (d. 804), courtier theologian of
Charlemagne 3, 140, 168; view of
Cicero of, 175; as lover of Vergil, 14, 15;
as reader of St Jerome, 136 n. 21, 137;
poem of refers to Boethius, 177 and n.
103; trips to Italy of, 177; denounces
post-Offan fashions, 183–4 (to Brorda);
denounces 'Hinieldus' (to Speratus), 17,
100, 133–4; *Carmina* of, 23 and n. 113
(IV), 24 (LIX); *Sequentia de s. Michaele*

of, 191–2; letters of to: **Adalhard:** 180;
Æthelheard: 133, (?)212; **Æthelred:**
133, 212–13 (on Danish *frisører*);
Alhheard and Tidfrith: 250; **an
archbishop:** 136; **a friend near Bremen:**
214, 221; **Beornwine:** 250, 276;
bishops of England: 136; **Brorda**
('Osberht'): 138, 183 and n. 135, 270,
287, 328; **Cenwulf:** 258; **Charlemagne:**
14, 322; **Eanwulf:** 145 n. 66; **Ecgfrith:**
248; **Eugenia (Æthelburh):** 262–3;
Higbald: 133, 137, 212; **Hundruda:**
249; **Offa:** 213, 250, 251, 252;
Speratus: 132–3, 134, 135–9, 140; **To
whom it may concern:** 142 (on
Fordradus); **Wulfheard:** 136 n. 24; see
also Bible
Aldhelm, bishop of Sherborne (d. 709/
710) 94; *Carmen de virginitate* of 98,
99, 160; *In basilica beatae Mariae semper
virginis* of, 154, 160 n. 18, 163, 188,
326 (in S 193); *Aenigmata* of, 160
Aldred, king of the Hwicce 276
Aldwulf, bishop of Lichfield 138 n. 34,
139 (fig. 1)
Aldwulf, deacon and feckless papal
envoy vii, 214–17, 221, 222, 263
Alexander the Great, see Beowulf
the Geat
Alfred, king of Wessex (871–99) 25, 33;
young charter witness of, 304 n. 24;
prodigious childhood of, 317–18; wars
of with the Danes, 25, 27–8; hospitality
to Ohthere, 27; Preface to translation of
Cura pastoralis of, 25; translation of
Orosius' *Historia adversus paganos* of,
27; translations of Boethius' *De
consolatione Philosophiae* of, 32–3, 38,
172–3 and n. 82, 317–18
Álfr (Alfus), Hugleikr's uncle 44
Álfr (Elfsi), king of the Swedes 58
Alfthrutha, daughter of Offa and
Kynedritha 242, 247, 270; see also
Ælfthryth
Alhheard, bishop of Elmham 138 n. 34,
139 (fig. 1), 250

Alhmund, priest abbot of Unwona
(786–805) 141, 142, 144 (fig. 2), 145,
146, 148, 151, 152 (fig. 3), 154, 243,
244 (fig. 5)
Alkmund, St, see Ealhmund son of Alhred
Alhred, king of Northumbria
(765–74) 219
Áli, king of Norwegian Uppland and
Norse analogue of Onela 46, 59
Alo, a king of the Swedes 118
Alsvinnsmál 59
Amata, queen of the Laurentines 3, 100,
124–30
Amlethus 234–5
Anchises, father of Aeneas 14, 90
Andreas, Old English religious
romance 206
Angengeot, son of Offa of Angeln (Anglian
Collection) 229, 231
Anglo-Saxon Chronicle, 25–6, 28, 33 (*On
the Capture of the Five Boroughs*), 37,
133 n. 4, 142 n. 56, 157, 212, 219,
239, 263, 270, 276, 281, 286, 290, 291,
292, 293, 301, 313, 315
Annales Quedlinburgenses 165
Annales regni Francorum 214–17
Annales Ryenses 233
Annals of St Neots 239, 240, 245, 246
Ansgar, missionary and saint 180
Anwend, Danish invader 216
Apollo 15
Aristotle, tutor to Alexander 78; see also
Epistola Alexandri ad Aristotelem
Arngrímur Jónsson, *Rerum Danicarum
fragmenta* of (1596) 46, 50, 60, 118;
see also *Skjǫldunga saga*
Arundel Psalter 5
Ascanius, son of Aeneas 13
Asser, bishop, *Vita Ælfredi* of 287–8,
317–18
Astronomer, The, biographer of Louis the
Pious 223
Athelney 27
Athene 11, 127
Atlakviða (stanza 9) 82
Attoari, see Hetware

Augustine, St, bishop of Hippo 14, 72,
96, 106, 175; *Contra academicos* of, 176
Augustine, St, missionary bishop of
Canterbury 140
Aun, Norse analogue of Eanmund the
Swede 59, 321

Bacchus 13, 78
Baldr (Balderus); in OE genealogy, 34
(Balder); as Herebeald, 47, 199–202, 310
Baldred, king of Kent 282, 284, 292
Barberini Gospels 178
Battle of Maldon, The 112
Beaw, see Beow
Bede (d. 735) 68; *Libri IV in principium
Genesis* of, 69; *Historia ecclesiastica
Anglorum* of, 22, 160, 211, 220, 252
(copy held by Offa), 271, 326 n. 111
Behemoth 68
Beigaðr (Beiguðr), one of Hrólfr's men 51
Benedictine Reform, English 33, 34
Benna, saint at Breedon 218 n. 106
Beonna, East Anglian king 241
Beonna, priest abbot of Unwona (late 780s
– c. 805) 142, 144, 145, 146, 148, 151,
152 (fig. 3), 154, 243, 244 (fig. 5)
Beorhtric, king of Wessex
(784–802) 212, 252, 261, 315
Beorngyth, abbess of Bath 276
Beornheard, ealdorman of King Offa of
Mercia 276
Beornheard, ealdorman, as muscle for
Cenwulf 268, 269 (fig. 7), 295
Beornhelm, Mercian abbot 152 (fig. 3),
153 (fig. 4), 303 (fig. 9), 328
Beornnoth, ealdorman (of the
Hwicce?) xiii, 244 (fig. 5), 259 (fig. 6),
269 (fig. 7), 279 (fig. 8), 303 (fig. 9),
325 (fig. 10); early career profile of, 259
(fig. 6); as Beornwulf's father by
Cenwulf's sister, 275–6; elevated to
ealdorman (of the Hwicce?) by
Cenwulf, 272–5; with interests in
Pershore and neighbouring lands,
273–4; as killed with King Beornwulf in
East Anglia, 293, 302

Beornoðes leah (Sinton in Leigh,
    Worcs.) 147 (ill. 1), 273
Beornwine, Mercian priest 250
Beornwulf, king of Mercia
    (823–6) vii–viii, xiii, 1, 4, 15, 65, 132,
    154, 225, 254–5, 269 (fig. 7), 295, 303
    (fig. 9), 325 (fig. 10), 328; family
    origins, 276–7; presumed distant West
    Saxon relatives of, 306–7; early career
    profile of, 269 (fig. 7); elevated to help
    Cenwulf, 275–6, 279 (fig. 8); given St
    Peter's, Gloucester, 272–3, 274, 295;
    ousts King Ceolwulf with help of
    Wulfred and Louis the Pious, 282–3;
    avenges Cenwulf on the Welsh, 278–9;
    restores some ecclesiastical lands,
    though a friend of Cwenthryth, 284–5;
    his (cousin?) Ealdorman Burhhelm
    killed with Muca (at *Clofesho*?), 286–8,
    296; no wife nor heir of, 286; alleged
    arrogance of, 289; routed by Ecgberht
    in attempt to invade Wessex, 290–1;
    later career profile of, 279 (fig. 8); killed
    in East Anglia (in bid to secure trade
    economy), vii–viii, 1, 225, 278, 291–4;
    as a model for Beowulf, 266–94
Beow (Beaw, Beo) 26, 27; as 'Beowulf' the
    Dane, 37; as constituent of Beowulf's
    name, 48
Beowulf, other theories of the origins of 1,
    2, 3, 24–34, 165, 205 n. 44, 225, 232,
    246; manuscript of, 2, 4–6; foliation of,
    4 n. 7; metre of, 2, 6–7, 323–4;
    hypermetric lines in, 107, 256–7,
    305–6; dialect of, 2, 6–7; a case of Latin
    syntax in, 66; word-play in, 108, 125;
    poet's use of fitts in, 1, 4, 58, 63, 103,
    104, 105, 112, 130, 172–3 and n. 81,
    176, 201, 289, 298, 310; fate in,
    169–73; perception in, 173–4 and n.
    86; 'Finnsburh Episode' in, 20–21, 60,
    129, 170, 205, 286, 310; **moral trail in**,
    42, **206–9**; Scandinavian heroic
    analogues of, 2, 17–19, 43–64; Danish
    mythology in, 2, 3, 32, 101, 194, 195–8
    (*Brísingamen*), 199–202 (Baldr and

Hǫðr), 202–205 (Þórr and the World
    Serpent), 309; biblical and patristic
    sources for, 67–74; and Saints' Lives,
    70, 186; *Epistola Alexandri ad
    Aristotelem* as a source for, 74–9, 99;
    Liber monstrorum as a source for,
    79–80, 99; Cassian's *Conlationes* as a
    source for, 68–9, 99, 181, 192; *Vita s.
    Guthlaci* as a source for, 159; *Liber
    historiae Francorum* as a source for, 21,
    42–3, 192; Boethius' *De consolatione
    Philosophiae* as a source for, 171–3, 192;
    St Augustine's *Contra academicos* as a
    source for, 176, 192; and *Blickling
    Homily* XVI, 76, 94–8, 99, 186; and
    Visio s. Pauli, 3, 90, 92, 95–6
    (Redaction XI), 99, 185; *Homiliary of
    St.-Père* (item 55) as a source for, 70, 71,
    99, 185–6, 202; and *Ragnarsdrápa*,
    30–32, 203–4; and *Aeneid* 2, 3, 7–14,
    39, 80–94, 99, 100, 110, 124–30;
    parallels of with *Aeneid*: 12, 80–4
    (building of Heorot); 84–7 (Grendel's
    table manners); 8, 10, 87–94 (Grendel's
    Mere); 124–31 (rivalry with Ingeld over
    Freawaru); lay of 'Hinieldus' as source
    for, 131, 155–6; suggested date of,
    316–17; suggested West Saxon
    acquisition of, 317–21
Beowulf the Dane, see Beow
Beowulf the Geat, viii, 1, 3, 16, 45, 49
    (*beadwe heard*), 225; and Hrothulf,
    46 n. 40; name of, 48–9; inferior birth,
    266, 274; miserable childhood, 272; as
    monster-slayer general, 49, 75, 202;
    men of, 51–2; hears of Grendel, 20;
    against Grendel, 84–7, 101, 111, 169,
    266; as king-material, 102–3, 125;
    promised kinship by Hrothgar, 100,
    101–110; against Grendel's Mother, 79,
    106; promises Hygelac's aid to
    Hrothgar, 108; interest in Freawaru,
    110–11, 285; as Ingeld's rival, 124–30;
    speaks to Hygelac, 53; receives hall and
    7, 000 hides, 47, 272, 274; avenges
    Hygelac's death, 277–8; avenges

Heardred's on Onela, 46, 280; restores Wiglaf's family land, 283; remembers Hygelac, 55; examines his conscience, 309–10; against the Dragon, 41, 46, 52, 53–4, 73, 170, 186, 199, 297–8; poisoned by the Dragon, 206–7, 310; with the Dragon's hoard, 69, 170, 209–10, 288–9, 300; and Wiglaf, 54–7; funeral of, 78–80; **prospects for soul of**, ix, 32, 98, 170–1, 205–11, **309–12**, 329–30; lineage of, 61–2; Scandinavian analogues for, 45–57; characterized with aid of: Aeneas, 67, 90; Alexander, 67, 78–80; David, 67, 72 and n. 38, 74; Hercules, 67, 78, 80; Jesus, 67, 73–4, 134; St Michael, 67; Samson 67, 72

Bera, Bǫðvarr bjarki's mother 47, 48

Berhtfrith, son of King Berhtwulf 304–5, 319–20

Berhtwald, archbishop of Canterbury 263

Berhtwulf, king of Mercia (839–49) 153; as half-brother of King Wiglaf, 319; elevation of, 303 (fig. 9), 325 (fig. 10), 329; as regent for Wigstan, 320; immunities of to Abbot Eanmund of Breedon, 160, 169, 217 (text), 327

Bernlef, Frisian poet 23–4

Bertha, daughter of Charlemagne 213

Biarco, see Bǫðvarr bjarki

Bible 3, 67, 70, 99, 231; possible instances of in *Beowulf*: **Genesis 6**: pp. 67–8; **Genesis 9**: p. 69; **Judges 14**: p. 72; **1 Samuel (1 Kings) 16–17**: p. 72; **2 Samuel (2 Kings) 9**: p. 85; **1 Maccabees 8, 2 Maccabees 15**: p. 69; **Matthew 1**: p. 73; **Matthew 26**: p. 74; **Matthew 27**: p. 66, 73; **Mark 14**: p. 74; **Mark 15**: pp. 66, 73; **Luke 11**: p. 73; **Luke 22**: p. 74; **John 18**: pp. 74, 310; **Ephesians 6**: pp. 98, 312, 322; **Revelation**: pp. 310–11; **1 Enoch 7**: pp. 67–8; in Alcuin's relevant letters: **Psalm 39 (40)**: pp. 134, 137; **Psalm 112 (113)**: p. 258; **Isaiah 5**: pp. 133–4, 137; **Isaiah 58**: p. 136; **Jeremiah 52**: p. 133;

Amos 2: pp. 213; **John 18**: p. 310; **1 Timothy 3**: p. 137 n. 28; **2 Timothy 4**: p. 135; **Ephesians 6**: p. 322; in King Wiglaf's charter S 190: **Matthew 16**: pp. 329, 330; **2 Corinthians 4**: p. 329

Biornhelm, see Beornhelm

Birka, Swedish emporium 22

Bjarkamál in fornu 17, 46, 49–51, 54, 56, 70, 199, 310; text of, 57; named *Húskarlahvǫt*, 50; prose renderings of, 54–6

Bjarkarímur, Icelandic ballad 17, 48, 60, 89, 115, 118

Bjarkaþáttr 51

Bjarki, see Bǫðvarr bjarki

Bjǫrn, Bǫðvarr's father 47

Blickling Homilies 72 (III), 94–5 (XVI), 188 (XIII); see also *Beowulf*

Bodvarus, see Bǫðvarr bjarki

Boethius, *De consolatione Philosophiae* of, 33, 171, 177; translations of Aristotle of, 177 and n. 103; as known in Alcuin's time, 177–8; see also Alfred, *Beowulf*

Bola, Mercian man of Beornwulf 302

Boniface (*c.*675–754), missionary and saint, 180, 209, 307; *Ars grammatica* of, 180

Book of Cerne 155, 178, 323 (Æthelwald)

Botwine, abbot of *Medeshamstede* 141, 148

Bragi Boddason, poet, *Ragnarsdrápa* of, 30–32, 203–4

Breca, Beowulf's swimming rival 173

Breedon on the Hill (NW Leics., now Derbys.) vii–ix, 3, 132, 147 (ill. 1), 158 (ill. 2); foundation of, 157–8; royal use of, 159, 160–1; finds at, 159 n. 13; sculptures of, 155, 161–3 and ill. 3, 178–9, 181–4 (and *Epistola Alexandri ad Aristotelem*, *Liber monstrorum*), 193, 220; Mary panel of, 157, 178 and ill. 4; Angel of and *Homiliary of St.-Père* (item 55), 187–92 and 189 (ill. 5), 193; dedications of, 188, 193, 218; Corbie connections of, 168–9, 177–81;

Breedon on the Hill (*cont.*)
  ranking in relation to Bredon (Worcs.),
  153 (fig. 4); as minster of Priest Abbot
  Wigmund, 148–55; and King Eardwulf
  (as St Ærdulfus, Erdulf, St Hardulph),
  218–21, 224; as host to Deacon
  Aldwulf's ransom, 101, 217–18; grants
  to from Berhtwulf and Humberht
  during abbacy of Eanmund, 160,
  327–8; lost library of, 3, 157–64; as
  home to composition of *Beowulf,*
  100, 225
Brevis historia regum Dacie, see Sven
  Aggesen
Brísingamen, see *Brosingamene*
Brorda, Mercian ealdorman (d. 805) 138
  and n. 30, 144, 183 n. 135 ('Osberht'),
  244 (fig. 5), 259 (fig. 6), 263, 270,
  287, 328
Brosingamene 40, 69, 98, 135;
  Brísingamen as a source for, 194,
  195–8, 208
Brunanburh (Bromborough?) 29; poem
  of, 291
Burghard, bishop of Würzburg
  (742–55) 287, 288
Burgildetreow 147 (ill. 1), 260
Burgred, king of Mercia (*c.*840–*c.*874), as
  Cenwulf's grandson 287–8; as
  presenting copy of *Beowulf* to Æthelwulf
  as bride-price, 318
Burhhelm, Mercian ealdorman (d. 825),
  286–8, 296, 318
Burhhild (Burgenhylda, Burgenhilde),
  Cenwulf's daughter 260, 270, 287,
  290, 318
Bynna, ealdorman of King Offa of Mercia
  (789–*c.*794) 276
Bynna, brother of King Beornwulf 276
  and n. 100, 279 (fig. 8)
Bǫðvarr bjarki (Bjarki, Biarco,
  Bodvarus) 18, 36, 45–57, 64, 75; kills
  Agnarr, 56, 114; gets Danish princess as
  bride, 114–15; in Hrólfr's last stand,
  51–4; name of, 49; lineage of, 47
Bǫðvarr Egilsson 199

Cædmon, late bloomer 6; *Hymn* of, 13
Cain, son of Adam 67–9, 98, 230 n. 21;
  see also Grendel
Calypso 11
Canute, see Cnut
Caradog, king of Gwynedd (d. 798) 258
Carloman, Charlemagne's father 235
Carmen de abbatibus, see Ædiluulf
Carmen de virginitate, see Aldhelm
Cassian (John Cassian), *Conlationes*
  of 68–9, 99, 181; *Institutae* of, 68, 163;
  see also *Beowulf*
Cassiodorus and Jordanes, *Getica* of 38
Cathwulf, English aide to
  Charlemagne 191
Cenred, king of Mercia, see Coenred
Cenwealh, son of Cynegils and son-in-law
  of Pybba 271
Cenwulf (Coenuulf, Coenwulf), king of
  Mercia (796–821) vii–ix, 4, 132, 138,
  143, 144, 225, 244 (fig. 5), 254–5, 259
  (fig. 6), 269 (fig. 7), 325 (fig. 10); name-
  prefixes of kindred of, 307; possible
  Lindsey origins of, 271 n. 79; initial
  poverty of, 258; as married to Ælfthryth
  Offa's daughter, 270; succeeds (brother-
  in-law?) Ecgfrith to throne, 257; deals
  with Eadberht Præn, 258; as starting
  second family (children Burhhild,
  Burhhelm?), 260; acquires estates from
  the church, 258–66; settles Glastonbury
  on son Cynehelm, 261–3; elevates
  Beornnoth, 272–5, 279 (fig. 8); Welsh
  campaigns of, 278; shelters
  Northumbrian rebel Wada, 214; makes
  peace with King Eardwulf, 219;
  suspected of conniving in Eardwulf's
  expulsion, 216; as a goodwill gesture,
  has Deacon Aldwulf ransomed, 215,
  263; feud of with Archbishop Wulfred,
  261–6; crisis years of, 269 (fig. 7), 308;
  creates new royal genealogy (to cover for
  Cynehelm's death?), 268, 270–1;
  elevates Beornwulf, 275–6; closes down
  Wulfred's office for six years, 265–6,
  295; he and Ceolwulf as 'the ravening

jaws of wolves', 264, 295, 324; falls on North Welsh frontier, 278, 296; as a model for Hygelac, 255–83

Ceolmund, bishop 138 n. 34, 139 (fig. 1)

Ceolnoth, archbishop of Canterbury 303 (fig. 9), 328

Ceolwulf, bishop 138 n. 34, 139 (fig. 1)

Ceolwulf, bishop of Lindsey 140 n. 43

Ceolwulf, Cenwulf's greedier brother, king of Mercia (821–2) 275, 279 (fig. 8), 296, 325 (fig. 10), 328; said to usurp power, 302; supported by Beornnoth and Beornwulf, 280–1; and by Muca, 286–7; seizes ecclesiastical lands, 281, 324; not a popular king, 282; sells off Kentish properties to Wulfred, 282; driven out by Beornwulf, 278, 283, 289

Cham, son of Noah 68; confused with Cain, 69

Charlemagne, emperor of the Franks (768–814) 14, 25, 140, 163; capitularies of, 167; *Admonitio generalis* of, 191; army of, 168; conquest of Lombardy of, 191; deals with Danish kings, 221–2; fortifies against Vikings, 212; trade embargo of against English, 213, 292; badmouths Northumbrians, 213; restores Eardwulf, 214–16; palace library in Aachen of, 175, 177, 178; in *Vitae duorum Offarum*, 236, 237; see also Offa king of Mercia

Charles the Bald, king of W. Francia (*c*.840–66) 26, 318

Charters: BCS 310: 152; BCS 312: 144, 150, 152; S 15: 270; S 40: 143 n. 58, 152, 259, 263 n. 48, 307; S 41: 152, 259; S 50: 248 n. 92; S 55: 234, 276; S 60: 248 n. 92; S 63: 276; S 96: 306; S 104: 248 n. 92; S 106: 139, 144, 146 n. 70, 244, 259, 263 n. 48, 307; S 110: 248 n. 92, 307; S 111: 248 n. 92; S 112: 248 n. 92; S 116: 248 n. 92; S 117: 248 n. 92; S 118: 248 n. 92, 307; S 120: 248 n. 92; S 121: 248 n. 92; S 122: 248 n. 92; S 123: 139; S 124: 248 n. 92; S 125: 248 n. 92, 270 n. 77;

S 127: 248 n. 92, 270; S 128: 139; S 129: 248 n. 92, 270 n. 77; S 130: 307; S 131: 307; S 132: 139, 276 n. 100, 307; S 133: 248 n. 92; S 134: 212; S 135: 139, 276 n. 100, 307; S 136: 243, 276 and n. 100, 307; S 137: 144, 244, 276 n. 100, 307; S 138: 139, 144, 145 n. 64, 146 n. 70, 243, 244, 276 n. 100, 307; S 139: 248 n. 92; S 145: 276 n. 100; S 148: 144, 244, 307; S 150: 139, 144, 243, 244, 307; S 151: 144, 243, 244, 307; S 152: 261, 263, 270, 271; S 153: 139, 144, 146 n. 70, 244, 259, 307; S 154: 307; S 155: 139, 144, 146 n. 70, 244, 259, 307; S 156: 263, 270; S 159: 263 n. 48, 270; S 161: 143 n. 58, 152, 259, 263, 307; S 163: 259, 263 n. 48, 270; S 164: 143 n. 58, 217, 263 n. 48, 269, 307–8; S 165: 263 n. 48, 269, 270; S 167: 263 and n. 47, 269; S 168: 263 n. 48, 269; S 170: 143 n. 58, 269, 307–8; S 171: 269: S 172: 269: S 173: 152, 260, 269, 304, 306, 308, 325; S 177: 260; S 179: 143 n. 58, 152, 279, 307–8; S 180: 143 n. 58, 152, 153, 154, 269, 304, 325; S 181: 279; S 182: 279; S 186: 143 n. 59, 279, 308; S 187: 143 n. 59, 152, 153, 154, 278, 279, 308, 325; S 188: 276 n. 105, 303, 304, 313, 328; S 189: 314, 330; S 190: 153, 276 n. 105, 302, 303, 325, 326, 328, 329; S 192: 303, 325; S 193: 153–4, 163–4, 325, 326–7; S 195: 303; S 197: 154, 155, 160, 163–4, 169 n. 68, 217, 303, 325, 326, 328; S 198: 303; S 204: 320; S 206: 320; S 207: 320; S 208: 320; S 209: 320; S 211: 320; S 212: 320; S 215: 320; S 216: 320; S 219: 320; S 220: 320; S 261: 306; S 262: 306; S 263: 306; S 265: 261; S 268: 306; S 269: 306; S 270a: 306; S 354: 260; S 539: 320 n. 91; S 749: 154 n. 101, 161 n. 27, 191; S 786: 273; S 1167: 276; S 1187: 143 n. 58, 259, 263 n. 48 and n. 50, 307; S 1257: 320; S 1258: 247;

Charters (*cont.*)
  S 1260: 144, 244, 259, 263 n. 48, 307;
    S 1271: 303, 320, 325; S 1412: 271 n.
    79; S 1430: 139, 276 n. 100; S 1433:
    153, 279, 284, 301, 306, 308; S 1434:
    153, 154, 279, 284, 301, 306, 308, 313;
    S 1435: 281, 285; S 1436: 154, 279,
    281, 284–5, 306, 308; S 1437: 153,
    154, 274, 276 n. 100, 279, 303, 306,
    308, 325; S 1438: 303; S 1442: 281,
    304; S 1782: 278; S 1803: 159 n. 5; S
    1804: 159 n. 6; S 1805: 159 and n. 6
Chaucer, Geoffrey 6
Chauci 165
Christ II, see Cynewulf
Chronicon abbatiae de Evesham, see
  Thomas of Marlborough
Chronicon Lethrense 36, 37, 61, 80–2, 87,
  88, 117
Chronicon monasterii de Abingdon 38–9,
  275
Chronicon Roskildense 117
Cicero, Roman lawyer, *Academica priora*
  of, 175–6, 192
Circe, sorceress 33, 39, 183
Clofesho 139 (fig. 1), 143, 144 (fig. 2),
  146, 147 (ill. 1), 152 (fig. 3), 153, 212,
  244 (fig. 5), 247, 274, 279 (fig. 8), 281,
  284; as Brixworth, 147 (ill. 1), 314,
  326, 328
Cnut (Canute, Knútr Sveinsson), king of
  Denmark and England (1016–35) 1, 5,
  34, 88, 273; translates St Wigstan, 305
Coenred, king of Mercia (d. 737) 220 n.
  122, 305
Coenwalh, allegedly son of Pybba 268,
  271, 287, 305; see also Cenwealh
Coenwalh, bishop 138 n. 34, 139 (fig. 1)
Coenuulf, Coenwulf, see Cenwulf
Coins 22–3 (*sceattas*), 180 (English *sceatta*
  at Corbie), 159 n. 13 (*sceatta* at
  Breedon), 183, 248, 252, 270, 282,
  284, 292, 293, 294, 301, 318
Conchubranus, *Vita s. Modwennae* of 218
Conlationes, see Cassian
Constantius, St 60

Contra academicos, see St Augustine of
  Hippo
Corbie, Francia 158 (ill. 2), 192–3;
  abbots of, 180–1; library of, 175,
  177–80; Psalter of, 178; Breedon
  connections of, 168–9, 177–81; founds
  Corvey, 180
Corvey, Saxony 180, 223; see also Corbie
Cotta, saint at Breedon 218 n. 106
Cotton Library 4
Cotton Vespasian B.VI, creation of 270–1
  and n. 79
Council of the Legates (786) 138–42,
  283; Canon 12 of, 250
Cunred, kinsman of Cenwulf 258
Cupid 13
Curtius, *Historiae* of 77
Cuthbald, abbot of *Medeshamstede* 220
Cuthberht, son of Bassa and father of
  Cenwulf 271 n. 79
Cuthbert, St 25
Cuthred, Cenwulf's brother 258
Cuthred, Mercian ealdorman of
  Beornwulf 302
Cuthwulf, abbot 152 (fig. 3), 153 (fig. 4)
Cwenthryth, daughter of Cenwulf 238,
  324; abbess of Winchcombe, 258, 260;
  keeps Cenwulf's archive, 260–1;
  childless heir of Cenwulf, 304;
  friendship (*amicitia*) of with Beornwulf,
  281; in *Vita et miracula s. Kenelmi*, 238,
  287 (Quoenthrytha)
Cwoenburg, abbess in Kent 258
Cyclops 84–7
Cyneberht, bishop of Winchester 138 n.
  34, 139 (fig. 1)
Cyneberht, nephew of Cenwulf 279
  (fig. 8), 284, 328
Cyneburh, abbess of Bradley 287
Cynegils, king of the Gewisse 271
Cynegyth, thought to be Cenwulf's first
  wife 270
Cynehelm (Kenelm, d. *c.*812), son of
  Cenwulf 238, 244 (fig. 5), 247, 259
  (fig. 6), 269 (fig. 7); as son of Offa's and
  Cynethryth's daughter, 271–2; endowed

with Glastonbury, 261–6; as groomed for kingship of Kent, 262, 263; disappearance of, 263–4, 271, 295; culted as saint, 271; career profile of, 263 n. 48; in *Vita et miracula s. Kenelmi*, 238 and n. 47, 287

Cynethryth, Offa's queen ix, 238; in charters, 248 and n. 92; becomes abbess of Cookham (Berks.), 247; portrait of on coins, 248; marriages of daughters of, 248; nagged by Alcuin, 249; blamed for the death of King Æthelberht, 245–50, 254, 295; dispossessed of Glastonbury by Cenwulf, 261–2; in the Worcester *Chronicle* (Cyneðryth), 245; in Hereford *Passio s. Æthelberti* (Kynedritha), 241–5, 246, 247; in Roger's *Chronica maiora* (Quendritha), 240–2, 247; in *Vitae duorum Offarum* (Quendrida, Drida), 235–9 (name of, 238), 247

Cynethryth, Wiglaf's queen 305, 328

Cynewulf, probably later ninth-century Mercian poet, poems of: *Elene*: 97, 165, 323; *The Fates of the Apostles, Juliana, Christ* II: 323; runic signatures of, 323–4

Cynred, bishop of Selsey 285

Dacre cross-shaft 220

Dæghrefn, Hygelac's killer 41, 48, 56, 72, 165; name of, 164–5

Dagaramnus 165

Dagobert (I, II, III), kings of Merovingians 164

Dagulf Psalter 178

Daigramnus 165

Dan, founder of Denmark 45, 80

Danes, in *Beowulf*, 2, 13, 16, 25, 53, 93; theories of influence of on *Beowulf*, 24–34; religious status of in *Beowulf*, 28, 32, 34, 94, 172, 195; in heroic legend, 24; in Skaldic poetry, 36–7; in Bishop Gregory's *Historiae*, 42–3; in *Liber historiae Francorum*, 21, 42–3; in *Historia de sancto Cuthberto*, 37

(Scaldingi); in Scandinavian prose literature, 17–19, 36–8; in Norway, 87; in England, vii, 2, 3, 19, 28–30, 32–4, 133 (Lindisfarne), 161 and 194 (East Midlands), 197, 211–17, 212–13 (Portland (Dorset) and Northumbria), 221; and the Franks, 213, 216, 221–3; mythology of in *Beowulf*, 2, 3, 32, 100, 101, 194–205

David, king of the Jews 73, 231; see also Beowulf the Geat

De antiquitate Glastonie ecclesie, see William of Malmesbury

Deneberht, bishop of Worcester 138 n. 34, 139 (fig. 1), 164, n. 37

Denefrith, bishop 138 n. 34, 139 (fig. 1)

Deor, Old English minor heroic poem 21, 196

Dido, queen of Carthage 10–13, 82, 84, 85, 124

Diseworth (Leics.) 191

Domburg 22, 23, 158 (ill. 2)

Donatus, grammarian 160

Dorestad (Wijk bij Duurstenden) 21, 22, 23, 158 (ill. 2), 222

Dream of the Rood, The 33, 311

Drida, see Cynethryth Offa's queen

Drífa, Drijfa, see Driva

Driva (Drífa, Drijfa), Rolfo's daughter (*Skjǫldunga saga*) 114–15

Dublin 44

Dud(em)an, abbot 152 (fig. 3)

Eadberht Præn, exiled in Francia 250; becomes king of Kent, 257; mutilated and imprisoned by Cenwulf, 258

Eadberht, West Mercian ealdorman of Cenwulf 274, 303 (fig. 9); as killed with Beornwulf, 302

Eadburga, St 273

Eadburh, daughter of Offa king of Mercia 248

Eadburh, King Alfred's mother-in-law 287–8

Eadgar, son of Ealdorman Eadberht 274

Eadgils, Swedish exile 46, 64, 280, 321; battle of against Onela, 60; king of the Swedes, viii, 59

Eadred, king of Wessex (946–54) 26

Eadwulf, short-lived king of East Anglia (796) 257

Eadwulf, bishop of Lindsey 138 n. 34, 139 (fig. 1)

Eadwulf, West Mercian ealdorman of King Beornwulf 273

Ealdberht, brother of Selethryth 258

Ealhheard, Mercian ealdorman of Beornwulf 302

Ealhmund (St Alkmund), son of Alhred 219

Ealhmund, king of Kent and father of Ecgberht 250

Ealhstan, bishop of Sherborne 292

Ealhswith, wife of King Alfred 288

ealuscerwen 169

Eamer, see Eomer

Eanbald, mid-eighth-century Hwiccean magnate 326 n. 111

Eanbald (I), archbishop of York (d. 801) 219

Eanbald (II), next archbishop of York, 214, 215, 219

Eanberht, mid-eighth-century abbot of Malmesbury 326 n. 111

Eanberht, mid-eighth-century Hwiccean sub-king 326 n. 111

Eanburg, abbess of Hampton Lucy and cousin of Offa 326 and n. 111

Eanfrith, Mercian sub-king in Sussex 326 n. 111

Eanhere, Eanfrith's brother 326 n. 111

Eanmund, Swedish exile viii, 59, 64, 280; name of, 321; killed by Weohstan the Wægmunding, 60; sword of given to Wiglaf (*Eanmundes laf*), 284, 299, 321–3

Eanmund, founding abbot of Crayke, Northumbria 326

Eanmund, abbot of Breedon (814 x 816-c. 848) vii–ix, xiii, 269 (fig. 7), 279 (fig. 8), 303 (fig. 9); career profile of, 152

(fig. 3), 153 (fig. 4), 324–5 and 325 (fig. 10); presumed family origins of, 326; present at Council of Chelsea (816), 324; receives grants (S 193, S 197) from Berhtwulf, 160, 327; as draftsman of S 193, 327–8; as poet of *Beowulf*, 321–4, 331–2

Eanmund, priest abbot of Bredon (Worcs.) ix, 152 (fig. 3), 153 (fig. 4); as descended from Eanwulf (Offa's grandfather), 326

Eanred, priest of Leicester 326

Eanred, son of King Eardwulf and king of Northumbria (811/12–840s) 219

Eanswith, abbess among *Magonsæte* 164, n. 37, 326 n. 111

Eanwulf, Offa's maternal grandfather 326

Eanwulf, Mercian layman 325 (fig. 10), 326, 329

Eardwulf, Northumbrian ealdorman and father of King Eardwulf 218

Eardwulf, king of Northumbria (796–806, 808–811/12) 214–221, 262; as St Ærdulfus, Erdulf, St Hardulph of Breedon, 218; escapes execution into (East Midlands?) exile, 219–20; crowned king in York the first time, 219; adulteries of, 287; invades North Mercia, 219; ousted from throne, 214, 219; restored by Charlemagne, 214; abdicates (to Breedon?), 218–20

Easby cross-head 183, 220 n. 121

Ebo, archbishop of Louis the Pious 223

Ecgberht, king of Wessex (802–39), outline of career of 315; in exile in Francia, 250; battles of with Cenwulf, 290; routs King Beornwulf at *Ellendun*, 290–1; backs East Angles against Beornwulf, 292–4; invades Mercia and Northumbria, 313–14; restores Wiglaf to his second reign, 313–15; overlord of Mercia, 328; plans for Roman pilgrimage of, 315

Ecgfrith, son of Offa and king of Mercia (796) 132, 137, 138, 140, 144, 244 (fig. 5), 268; consecrated king (787), 141; exhorted by Alcuin, 248; broken betrothal of to Charlemagne's daughter, 213; not long dead, 250; portrait of as likeness, 252

Ecgtheow, Beowulf's father 39, 54, 58, 61, 295, 298, 299; kills Heatholaf, 129

Edgar, king of England (959–75) 161 n. 27, 191

Eddic poetry, see Iceland

Edmund, king of Wessex (939–46) 26; in *On the Capture of the Five Boroughs*, 33

Edward the Elder, king of Wessex (899–24) 28, 29, 264

Edwin, king of Deira (d. 633) 137 n. 27

Egill Aunarson, Norse analogue of Ongentheow 59, 63, 321

Egill Skalla-Grímsson, Icelander 29; *Sonatorrek* of, 199

Einhard, biographer of Charlemagne 14; *Karolus Magnus et Leo Papa* of (?), 15

Elene, see Cynewulf

Elfsi, see Álfr of Sweden

Elg-Fróði, Bǫðvarr bjarki's brother 47

Ellendun, battle of 290–1; poem of, 291

Enoch, son of Cain 67; see also Bible

Eofor Wonreding, Geatish champion 63, 64, 256, 257, 264, 306

Eomer (Eamer), son of 'Thryth' and Offa of Angeln 228–31, 252

Eormanric, Gothic emperor 40, 135; as Erminríkr, 196

Epistola Alexandri, MSS of 77; as source for *Beowulf* 74–9; see also *Alexander's Letter to Aristotle*, Breedon on the Hill

Erdulf, 218; see also Breedon on the Hill, King Eardwulf

Erminríkr, see Eormanric

Ermoldus Nigellus, 23 n. 111; *In honorem Hludovici Pii* of, 15, 221, 223

Eugenius II, pope 283

Eve 10–11

Exeter Book, The 16

Eymundr, son-in-law of King Hálfdan 59

Eysteinn Valdason, poet 203 n. 37

Fabricius 33

Fáfnir, Sigurðr's dragon 70

Fáfnismál 70

Fates of the Apostles, The, see Cynewulf

Fates of the Teachers, The 135; see 2 Tim. 4:3–4

Faunus, father of Latinus 14, 126, 129

Felix, *Vita s. Guthlaci* of 88, 150, 151, 159; see also *Beowulf*

Fengo, 234–5

Fenrir, cosmic wolf 204

Feologeld, Kentish abbot 152 (fig. 3), 153 (fig. 4), 154

Ferrers, Earl Robert 220 n. 126

Finn Folcwalding, king of the Frisians 20, 286

'Finnsburh Episode', see *Beowulf*

Finnburh Fragment 15, 16, 20, 134

Fitela, sister's son of Sigemund 70

Fletton, St Michael of 186–8

Fordradus, travelling priest 142; see Priest Abbot Forthred

Forthred, priest abbot of Unwona (789–803) 142, 144, 145, 146, 148, 151, 152 (fig. 3), 244 (fig. 5)

Forthred, Northumbrian abbot 142 n. 36

Franks, vii, 3, 23, 213, 216, 221–3; in *Beowulf*, 40–2, 44, 164–9

Freawaru, Hrothgar's daughter 83, 99, 100, 101–111, 135; see under Beowulf

Fremu, name for queen of Offa of Angeln (R. D. Fulk, 'The Name of Offa's Queen: *Beowulf* 1931–2', *Anglia* (2004), 614–39; seen too late to be included other than here); see 'Thryth'

freoðe (*Beo* 1707) 107 n. 15

Frethoricus, saint at Breedon 218 n. 106; see also Friduricus

Freyja, goddess of love 194, 197–8,

Freyr (Ingvi-freyr), northern Dionysus 89, 197, 204

Friduricus *princeps* 157

Frisians, 2; in *Beowulf*, 15, 16, 20, 40–2, 164–9; in *Maxims* I: 22; as traders, 21–3, 223; language of, 23; as mediators of heroic lays, 2, 19, 21, 23–4, 34, 43, 45

Froda, king of the Heathobards 111–12
Frodo, see Fróði father of Ingjaldr
Fróði, a king of the Danes 51
Fróði (Frodo, Frothi, Frotho), king of the
   Danes and father of Ingjaldr 117, 118,
   123
Frothi, Frotho, see Fróði father of Ingjaldr
Frowinus, governor of Schleswig 235

Gabriel, saint and archangel 154, 187–8,
   193
Gaimar, *L'Estoire des Engleis* 278, 281,
   282, 286, 289, 301, 302
Gang of four, see Priest Abbots Alhmund,
   Beonna, Forthred and Wigmund
Gautreks saga 44, 45
Gawain-poet 6
Gargano, Monte 94, 185; St Michael's
   chapel at, 188, 191
Garganus, Epulian magnate 185
Garmund, kinsman of Eomer 229
Geatish lady at Beowulf's pyre 285
Geats, 20, 21, 28, 52, 77, 79, 108, 109
   ('Sea-Geats'), 110, 283; as an amalgam
   in *Beowulf*, 47–8
Gegatherus, Geigaðr 44
Genesis A, Old English biblical poem 94,
   196, 227–8; *Genesis B*, Old Saxon poem
   in English 318
Geoffrey of Burton, *Vita s. Modwennae*
   of 218
Geoffrey of Monmouth, *Historia regum
   Brittanniae* of 117
George, bishop of Ostia 140
Gervold, abbot of St.-Wandrille 21–2,
   169
Gesta abbatum Fontanellensium 169, 213
Gesta Danorum, see Saxo Grammaticus
Getica, see Cassiodorus and Jordanes
Glámr, a Swede 18, 19, 84
Glastonbury 261–6, 306
Godan, see Óðinn
Godescalc, envoy of Charlemagne 222
Godfred, king of Denmark 216, 222
Gospels 72 (Mt); see also Bible
Goths 21, 47–8 (*Hreðgotas*)

Granmarr, father of Hǫðbroddr 121
Gregory, bishop of Tours (s. vi) *Historiae*
   of 42, 43, 167; *Liber in gloria
   confessorum* of, 87
Gregory the Great, pope, *Dialogues* of 60
Grendel, Heorot's haunter 13, 16, 19, 49,
   226; descent from Cain, 67–8, 84;
   identified with Satan, 83, 84; eats
   Hondscio, 51–2, 85; fights Beowulf,
   85–7; arm nailed to gable, 69, 125;
   beheaded by Beowulf, 72, 272
Grendel's Mere 87–9, 91–2, 94–5, 312
Grendel's Mother 32, 49 (*brimwylf*), 76,
   226; descent from Cain, 68; raids
   Heorot, 106; sword of, 79, 96, 107;
   killed by Beowulf, 272
Grettir 18
Grettis saga Ásmundarsonar 84; and
   Beowulf 18–19
Grindles becc 273
Guðmundr, flyting of with Sinfjǫtli 30 n.
   159, 121
guðsceare 167–8
Gullinhjalti, Hrólfr's sword 52
Guthere, king of the Burgundians 57
Guthlac A 151 n. 92
Guthlac, saint of Crowland 88, 150–1,
   159, 314
Guthrum, Danish invader 27; in Repton,
   216; baptised as 'Æthelstan', 28
Gylfaginning, see Snorri Sturluson

Haco, king of the Danes 44
Hadoard, librarian of Corbie
   (*c*.850–70) 175
Hædda, first abbot of Breedon and bishop
   of Lichfield and Leicester 150–1, 158–9
Hæreth, father of Hygd 226
Hæthcyn, Hrethel's son 47, 54–5; pride
   of, 257; as Hǫðr, 199–202
Hagar 227
Hagena, friend of Waldere 57
Haldan, see Hálfdan
Haki the Bold, one of Hrólfr's men 51
Haki Hámundarson, pirate king 44, 61
   (Aco)

Haklangr, one of Hrólfr's men 51
Hákon Haraldsson, Æthelstan's foster-son and king of (parts of) Norway (*c*.947–*c*.960) 29
Háleygjatal, Skaldic dynastic poem (*c*.985) 117
Hálfdan (Haldan, Halfdanus), king of the Danes 59, 80, 118–19
Halga, Hrothgar's brother 37, 122
Hama 40, 69, 98, 135, 194, 196, 309
Hamwih 22, 292
Harley Gospels 178
Hár the Hard-Gripper, one of Hrólfr's men 51
Hárbarðsljoð 202
Hardulph, St, see Breedon on the Hill, King Eardwulf
Harðrefill, one of Hrólfr's men 51
Haustlǫng (*c*. 900), see Þjóðólfr of Hvinir
Heahberht, bishop of Worcester 154
Healfdene, father of Hrothgar 37, 82, 230 n. 21
Healfdene, Danish invader 216
Heardred, Hygelac's son 46 n. 40, 47, 64, 255, 280, 286, 296
Heardred, bishop 138 n. 34, 139 (fig. 1)
Heardwulf, king of Kent 218
Heathoberht, bishop of London 138 n. 34, 139 (fig. 1)
Heathored, bishop of Worcester 138 n. 34, 139 (fig. 1), 326
Hedda Stone 182
Hedeby, early Danish town 22
Heðinn, eternal enemy of Hǫgni 198
Heimdallr, mysterious Norse god 196–7
Heimir, good knight and German-Norse analogue for Hama 196
Heimskringla, see Snorri Sturluson
Helgakviða Hundingsbana (I, II; 'Helgi Lays') 30 n. 159, 116, 121–3
Helgi Sigmundarson 121
Helgo, killer of Hothbroddus 122
Helm, king of the Wulfings 129
Hemming, kinsman of Eomer 228–9
Hemming, brother's son of Godfred 222
Hengest, mercenary and settler 20, 310

Henry of Huntingdon, *Historia Anglorum* of 291
Heorogar, Hrothgar's brother 37, 53, 167
Heorot 12, 13, 16, 52, 69, 75, 110, 129, 155; name of, 89
Heoroweard, son of Heorogar 52, 53, 294
Hercules, see Beowulf the Geat
Herebeald, son of Hrethel 47, 54–5, 198, 310; see also Baldr
Heremod 27, 30 n. 159, 37–8, 103, 228
Heriold, king of Denmark (d. *c*.837) 3, 180, 194, 221–4, 283
Herminthrutha, Danish analogue for 'Thryth' 234–5
Hermóðr 199, 201
Hetware (Attoari) 41, 42, 164, 168; in *Widsith*, 42
Hialto, see Hjalti
Hiarwart, Hiarwarthus, see Hjǫrvarðr
Higbald, abbot of Lindisfarne 133, 137, 138
Hildeburh, queen of Finnsburh 66, 116
Hildegyth, Waldere's betrothed 57
Hilarius of Poitou, St 87
Hinieldus, see Ingeld
hippopotami 75, 77
Historia Anglorum, see Henry of Huntingdon
Historia Brittonum (formerly ascribed to 'Nennius') 229, 230
Historia Croylandensis, see Pseudo-Ingulph
Historia de sancto Cuthberto 37
Historia Langobardorum, see Paul the Deacon
Hjalti, Bǫðvarr's sidekick (Hialto) 48, 49–50, 65, 297, 299; renamed from Hǫttr, 48; delivers *Bjarkamál*, 49–51; threatens to burn Bǫðvarr inside the hall, 54
Hjǫrvarðr (Hiarwart, Hiarwarthus, Hiørvardus), Hrólfr's brother-in-law and analogue of Heoroweard 46, 49, 52, 53, 61, 110
Hnæf, son of Hoc 16
Hoddom cross-head 183, 220 and n. 121
'Homer' 11

Homiliary of St.-Père (item 55), see *Beowulf*

Hondscio, eaten by Grendel 51–2, 85; and Skrýmir's *hanzki*, 203

Horace, Roman poet, *Satires* of 120

Hothbroddus, see Hǫðbroddr

Hotherus, see Hǫðr

Hrethel, king of the Geats 39, 41, 198; name of, 47–8, 200; brings up Beowulf, 47, 54–5; grieves for Herebeald, 201; dies into God's light, 135, 201–2

Hrethric, son of Hrothgar 52, 53, 105, 106; invited to Geatland, 108

Hrodgar(i)us, scribe in Corvey 24

Hróarr (Ro, Roe, Roas), Norse analogue of Hrothgar 46, 135; as Ro: 80–2, 87, 89; as Roe: 121; as Roas: 118

Hrólfr kraki Helgason (Rolfo Krage, Rolvo, Hrólfur), king of the Danes and Norse analogue of Hroth(w)ulf 18, 45–57, 135; named by Vǫggr, 60; last stand of in Lejre, 49–51, 110

Hrólfr the Shooter, one of Hrólfr's men 51

Hrólfs saga kraka 17–19, 46–8, 51–2, 54–6, 60, 61, 89

Hrómundr, one of Hrólfr's men 51, 62

Hrothbert, abbot of Fontanelle 23

Hrothbert, merchant in Dorestad 23

Hrothgar, king of the Danes viii, 1, 16, 18, 25, 28, 36, 45, 64, 72, 75, 100, 123, 254; lineage of in *Beowulf*, 25–6, 167; builds Heorot, 82–4; detached by poet from paganism, 89; welcomes Beowulf, 46; promises Beowulf kinship, 101–110, 125; weakness of, 129–30 and n. 73; fails to deliver on promise, 275; as sermonic source of wisdom, 32, 68, 73, 96–8, 107–8, 135, 173, 176, 184–5, 207–8, 312; and Vergil's Sibyl of Cumae, 90–3, 96, 312; in *Widsith*, 16, 115–16; Scandinavian analogues for, 46, 80–2, 87, 89; sources for in bible, 73, 107, 126

Hrothmund, son of Hrothgar 52, 105, 106, 145

Hrothulf, Halga's son and Hrothgar's nephew viii, 3, 28, 36, 45, 64, 100, 123, 254; supported by Wealhtheow, 103–6; as a risk to her children, 108, 109, 116; treacherously attacked (by Heoroweard?), 53, 110, 202; in *Widsith* (Hrothwulf), 16, 115–16; role of supplanted in *Beowulf* by that of Hygelac, 46–8, 64

Hruotfridus, abbot of St.-Amand 215

Hugas 165–6, 168

Hugh Candidus, *Chronicon* of 159 n. 8, 218

Hugh the Great, Neustrian duke (923–56) 165

Huglecus, Hugleikr, Hugletus, see Hygelac

Humarcha (Humsterland) 166

Humberht *princeps*, Tame valley ealdorman, 160, 217, 303 (fig. 9), 325 (fig. 10)

Humbertus, see Hygeberht

Hun, East Anglian king 241

Hundingr, Hundingus 121

Hundruda, Mercian nun 249

Húsdrápa (c. 995), see Úlfr Uggason

Húskarlahvǫt, see *Bjarkamál in fornu*

Hvít, Bjǫrn's wicked stepmother 47

Hvítserkr, one of Hrólfr's men 51

Hygd, Hygelac's queen 47, 226, 227, 245; offers Beowulf throne, 280

Hygeberht, archbishop of Lichfield (788–803) 138 n. 34, 139 (fig. 1), 140, 142, 144, 243, 244 (fig. 5), 252; held to have composed *Beowulf* (by John Earle), 246; in *Vitae duorum Offarum* (Humbertus), 142, 236, 238, 241

Hygelac, king of the Geats viii, ix, 3, 17, 36, 39, 53, 108, 110, 114, 225, 254–5; as close friend of sister's son Beowulf, 266–8, 272, 277–8; rescues Hæthcyn's Geats, 62–3; destroys Ongentheow, 45, 63, 255, 306; charisma of, 256; rewards Eofor and Wulf (with other men's lands), 64, 256–7; speaks to Beowulf, 66; dies on a raid, 21, 39–42, 105, 166, 209, 255, 277; necklace of, 40, 42, 98,

105; remembered by Beowulf, 55; as a model to avoid, 198, 207, 288, 309; analogues of: in Gregory's *Historiae* (Chlochilaichus), 42; in *Liber monstrorum*, 21 (Huncglacus, Higlacus); in *Liber historiae Francorum* (Chochilaicus) 21, 42; in Snorri's *Ynglinga saga* (Hugleikr), 43–4, 47, 257; in Saxo's *Gesta Danorum* (Huglecus (or Hugletus)), 43, 44–5, 257

Hymiskviða 31

Hyndluljóð 17

Høgrimus and Hømothus, kings of the Swedes 45

Hǫðbroddr (Hothbroddus) 116, 121–3

Hǫðr (Hotherus), killer of Baldr 47

Hǫgni, eternal enemy of Heðinn 198

Hǫttr, see Hjalti

Iænberht, archbishop of Canterbury (d. 793) 138 n. 34, 139 (fig. 1), 140

Iceland, literature of (Old Norse) 3; Skaldic poetry of, 30 and n. 156, 32; Eddic poetry of, 30 and n. 159, 32; see also Danes

Iliad 11

i[n]cge gold, laf 20, 21

Ingeld, king of the Heathobards vii, 3, 16, 99; betrothal to Freawaru, 105, 110; imagined wedding party of, 110, 112–14; attacks Heorot, 83, 100, 108, 110–11, 116, 128, 155; in *Widsith*, 16–17, 115–16, 121, 122, 133–4; Scandinavian analogues for, 114–24; and 'Hinieldus', 3, 132–4, 144–6, 155–6

Ingellus, see Ingjaldr

Ingjaldr Fróðason (Ingellus, Ingialldus), Norse analogue of Ingeld 115–24

Inguar, Danish invader 216

Ing(ui), heathen god 20, 89, 205; in *Ingwine*, 39, 89

Ingvi-freyr, see Freyr

Ingwine, see Ing(ui)

Institutae, see Cassian

Iopas 12–13, 84

Iorundus, a king of the Swedes 118

Ipswich 22, 292

Isidore, bishop of Seville 160

Jerome, St 136 n. 21, 137

Jesus, see Beowulf the Geat

John of Worcester, *Chronicon* of 270, 286, 293–4, 301, 313

Jón Loptsson, father of Bishop Páll 118

Jonas, bishop of Orléans 177

Jonson, Ben, *Timber: Or, Discoveries* of, 9, 12, 13

Judas, later Bishop Cyriacus 97

Judas Maccabaeus 69

Judith, Old English poem 4

Judith, daughter of Charles the Bald 26, 318

Juliana, see Cynewulf

Juno 10, 13, 127

Jupiter 11, 13, 125, 221 (Iuppiter)

Jutes 20

'Kaluza's Law' 6; see also *Beowulf*

Kenelm, see Cynehelm

Knútr Sveinsson, see Cnut

Kynedritha, see Cynethryth Offa's queen

Lady Macbeth 129

Langfeðgatal 37, 117

Langland, William 6

Latinus, king of the Laurentines, 3, 36, 39, 100, 124–30, 312

Lavinia, Lavinus' daughter 14, 124

Leo III, pope (795–816) 141, 214–15, 257, 261

Lejre (Lethra) 80

Leland, John, *Itinerary* of 273, 290

L'Estoire des Engleis, see Gaimar

Letter of Alexander to Aristotle, The (Old English version) 4 and n. 7, 74–5, 78

Leviathan 68

Liber historiae Francorum 21; as source of *Beowulf*, 42–3, 45, 66, 164

Liber monstrorum 21, 43, 200; as source for *Beowulf*, 79–80, 87; see also Breedon on the Hill

Liudger, Frisian pupil of Alcuin 24
liturgical offices 66
lofgeornost 210–11
Loki, Norse god of mischief 197–201
Longobards 17, 38
Loptr Sæmundsson 37
Lot 196
Louis the Pious, emperor of the Franks
    (814–40) 15, 221, 222, 283, 315
Lucretius, *De rerum natura* of 13, 175
Lucullus, friend of Cicero 175
Ludeca, king of Mercia (826–7), viii, 286,
    289, 293, 294, 301–2, 305

Maganfrid, Charlemagne's military
    treasurer 168
Magnús berfœttr, king of Norway (d.
    1103) 37
Mainz 3, 224
Marcellina, mother of Offanus 235, 236
Mary, mother of God and saint, xiii, 126,
    154, 178, 179 (ill. 4), 312, 326 (in
    S 193); date of panel of in Breedon, 187
Matthew Paris 240
Maurdramn, abbot of Corbie
    (*c.*771–*c.*783) 181
Maxims I, Old English wisdom poem 22
Melbourne (Leics.) 191
Mercury 11, 33 (Mercurius)
Merewalh 287
Michael, archangel and saint, xiii; 70, 71,
    202; in *Blickling Homily* XVI, 94,
    185–7; as Breedon Angel, 184–92
    and 189 (ill. 5); in Fletton, 190 (ill. 6);
    and Þórr, 203, 310; see also Beowulf the
    Geat
Millio, champion 233
Milton, John, *Paradise Lost* of compared
    with *Aeneid* 10–13
Minster in Thanet and Reculver, minsters
    of 258, 264, 281, 282, 285, 313
Misenus, Trojan sailor 91
Mitunnus, henchman of Riganus 233
Moduinus, bishop of Auxerre 177
Modwenna, Irish saint 218
Moll, Northumbrian ealdorman 219

Muca, Mercian ealdorman 279 (fig. 8),
    286–7
Mucel (1), Mercian ealdorman 303 (fig.
    9), 325 (fig. 10), 328–9
Mucel (2), lesser Mercian ealdorman 303
    (fig. 9), 325 (fig. 10); as Ealdorman
    Æthelred Mucel of the *Gaini*, Alfred's
    father-in-law, 329

Nantharius, abbot of St.-Omer 215
Nennius, see *Historia Brittonum*
Neptune 221
Nicanor, persecutor of the Jews 69
Nijmegen 158 (ill. 2), 214, 216, 219
Nithad, Welund's captor 167
Noah, Alfred's ancestor 26; in Cassian's
    Conlationes, 68
nominetenus reges 132–3, 145 and n. 66
Northumbrian Annals 219
Nothheard, thegn of King Beornwulf 278
Nothhelm, papal envoy 284
Nowell Codex (Cotton Vitellius
    A.XV) 4–5, 74–5, 172–3

Oda, archbishop of Canterbury
    (941–58) 34
Oddi, Iceland 117–18
Odysseus 11
Odyssey 11
Óðinn 321; as Godan 221 n. 129; as
    Viðrir, 31; as Vuothen, 34, 114; as
    Waten, 221; vengeance of for Baldr,
    198–201; wolfed down by Fenrir, 204
oð þæt 97 n. 111
Offa (I), king of Angeln viii–ix, 145; in
    the 'Thryth' digression, 3, 225–32, 250;
    in *Widsith*, 16, 232, 234; in Anglian
    royal genealogy, 229–31; in the *Vitae
    duorum Offarum*, 233, 235; in
    Scandinavian analogues (Uffi, Uffo,
    Óláfr in lítilláti), 230, 233 and n. 33,
    234, 235; portrait of based on Offa king
    of Mercia, 251–2, 254–5
Offa (II), king of Mercia (757–96) vii–ix,
    1, 3–4, 25, 132, 144, 145, 243, 244
    (fig. 5); as *puer indolis*, 234; rise of, 143,

155, 252, 290, 292; acquires Bath minster, 261; builds Offa's Dyke, 234; chairs Council of the Legates, 140, 250, 252, 326; creates Lichfield archdiocese, 140–2, 252, 308, 326; gives annually to Rome, 283; crowns Ecgfrith, 141, 252, 326; praised by Alcuin, 251–2; would-be equal of Charlemagne, 22, 169, 180; quarrels with Charlemagne, 213; fortifies against Vikings, 212; founds St Albans minster, 241; receives bible from King Æthelred on daughter's marriage alliance with latter, 318; executes King Æthelberht, 239, 252, 294, 295; as rewarding Wynberht, 243; receives gifts from Charlemagne, 163, 250; purges of, vii, 250–2; libertine period after death of, 138; in the *Vitae duorum Offarum* (Offanus), 235–9, 240–1, 246–7, 250
Offanus, see Offa king of Mercia
Offa's Dyke 234
Olaf Guthfrithson, king of York 33
Óláfr in lítilláti, see Offa of Angeln
Óláfs saga Helga, see Snorri Sturluson
Old English Martyrology 88
On the Capture of the Five Boroughs, see *Anglo-Saxon Chronicle*
Old Norse, see Iceland
Onela, king of the Swedes viii, 46, 59, 255, 280, 296
Ongendus, Danish king 22, 195, 211
Ongentheow, king of the Swedes 45, 61; slayer of Hæthcyn, 55; destroyed by Hygelac, 63, 255–6, 258, 306
Origo gentis Langobardorum 38
Ormside Bowl 220
Osburh, mother of Alfred 317–18
Oscytel, Danish invader 216
Oskytel, archbishop of York (956–71) 34
Osric and Oswald, kings of the Hwicce 273
Oswald, bishop and saint (d. 992) 34
Orosius 27; see also Alfred
Osbald, rival of King Eardwulf 219
Osberht, see Brorda
Osred, son of Alhred 219
Oswaldus, East Anglian counsellor 242

Otta, champion 233
Óttarr Egilsson, king of Uppsala and analogue of Ohthere 51

Páll Jónsson, bishop of Skálholt (1195–1211) 36–7, 118
Paschal I, pope 283
Passio s. Æthelberti, 145, 240 n. 58; see also St Æthelberht, Cynethryth Offa's queen, Offa king of Mercia
Passion of St Christopher, The, 4 and n. 7, 5
Paul the Deacon 221; *Historia Langobardorum* of, 38
Paul, St 94, 96, 98, 135, 326, 329
Paulinus, saint and missionary 137 n. 27
Penda, king of Mercia (c.632–55) 268, 271, 287; plantations of, 307, 308
Pershore, minster of 273
Peter of Pisa 221
Picus, son of Saturn 39
Piot, abbot 152 (fig. 3), 153 (fig. 4)
Prudentius, *Psychomachia* of, 7
Psalms, see Bible
Pseudo-Ingulph, *Historia Croylandensis* of 275, 302, 304, 314, 319, 330–1
Psychomachia, see Prudentius
Pybba, king of Mercia 268, 271, 287

Quendrida, Quendritha, see Cynethryth Offa's queen
Quentovic (Étaples) 22, 169
Quoenthrytha, see Cwenthryth

Ragnarr Loðbrók, Danish invader 30
Ragnarsdrápa (c.850), see Bragi Boddason
Raphael, archangel and saint 11, 12
Reculver, minster of, see Minster in Thanet
Redaction XI, see *Visio s. Pauli*
Reference Bible 69
Regnerus, Swedish earl and father of Hothbroddus 121
Rerum Danicarum fragmenta, see Arngrímur Jónsson
Rethhun, abbot of Abingdon and bishop of Leicester 152 (fig. 3), 260, 269 (fig. 7), 279 (fig. 8)

Revenswart, bearlike name attributed to a brother of King Beornwulf 276

Ribe, possible mart of King Ongendus 22

Riganus, usurper 233

Ro, Roe, Roas, see Hróarr

Roger of Wendover, *Chronica maiora* of 291, 301, 313–14, 318; see also St Æthelberht, Cynethryth Offa's queen, Offa king of Mercia

Rolvo, king of the Danes, see Hrólfr

Rorik, brother of Heriold 222

Roskilde 80; foundation of 81

Rothbury cross shaft 220

Ruta, Rolvo's sister 51, 114–15

Sæmundr inn fróði Sigfússon 37, 81; as compiler of *Langfeðgatal*, 117; makes Ingjaldr a Dane, 123

Sabinus, papal envoy 213

Saints' Lives, dragon-fights in 70–1

Samson, see Beowulf the Geat

Samson of Dol, St 70; known in England (s. x), 71

Sarah, wife of Abraham 227

Satan 10, 11, 67, 83, 84

Saturn 39

Savinus, Italian monk 215 n. 95; see also Sabinus

Saxo Grammaticus, Danish historian 17; *Gesta Danorum* of, 18, 36, 43–5, 48, 49, 50, 51, 52, 54, 55–6, 57, 81, 116–23 (on Ingellus), 233–4 (on Uffo)

Scadana, Scadinavia, see Skåne

Scaldingi, see Danes

Scandzia, Scani, see Skåne

Sceaf(a) 17, 26–7, 36–9, 317

Sceattas, see coins

Scedenig, Scedelond, see Skåne

Scef, see Sceaf(a)

Sciol(l)dus, see Skjǫldr

Sconeg, see Skåne

Scura, see Skur

Scyld Scefing, progenitor of the Danes 16–17, 25, 26, 28, 37, 66; sources for in *Beowulf*, 36–9; and the *Aeneid*, 39

Scyldings, see Danes

Scyldwa (Sceldwea), son of Sceaf 25–7, 28, 37

Scylla, sea-monster 93–4

Seaxwulf, bishop of Lichfield (d. c.690) 159

Seleburg, abbess in Kent 258

Selethryth, abbess of Minster in Thanet 258, 281

Sibyl of Cumae, see Hrothgar

Sigemund Wælsing, dragon-slayer viii, 30 n. 159; as model for Beowulf, 70, 102–3, 202

Sigfred Godfredsson, king of Denmark 221, 222

Sighvatr Þórðarson, Icelandic poet 37

Sigmundr Vǫlsungsson, Norse analogue of Sigemund 70, 122

Sigrún, desirable valkyrie 121, 122

Sigurðr Fáfnisbani Sigmundarson 70

Simeon 73, 107, 134

Sinfjǫtli, ugly Norse analogue of Fitela, 30 n. 159, 121

Siward, legendary abbot of Crowland 314

Skaldic poetry, see Iceland

Skáldskaparmál, see Snorri Sturluson

Skjǫldr 36–9, 118; in *Chronicon Lethrense*, 36 (Scioldus); in Saxo's *Gesta Danorum*, 36 (Scioldus)

Skjǫldunga saga 17–19, 36, 44, 48, 49, 60, 61, 114–23 (on Ingialld); translated by Arngrímur Jónsson (*Rerum Danicarum fragmenta*, 1596) 46, 50, 60, 118

Skrýmir, Norse giant 203

Skuld, Hrólfr's half-sister 46

Skur (Scura, Skúr), Rolfo's daughter (*Skjǫldunga saga*) 114–15

Skåne (Scandzia, Scadana, Scadinavia, Scedenig, Scedelond, Sconeg, Scani) 38

Snorri Sturluson, Icelandic author (1178/9–1241) 30; upbringing in Oddi, 117–18; *Heimskringla* of, 50 (*Óláfs saga Helga*, 49–50, 56–7 (quotation of *Bjarkamál*); *Ynglinga saga*, 17, 21, 43–5, 118, 321); *Edda* of, 36, 46 (*Gylfaginning*, 199, 201, 205;

Skáldskaparmál, 17, 30, 50, 59, 60, 118, 202, 203, 206)

Sodom 196

Soissons Gospels 183

Sonatorrek (*c.*960), see Egill Skalla-Grímsson

Southampton, see *Hamwih*

Southwick Codex 4

Speratus, correspondent of Alcuin 3, 17, 100, 132–4, 135–9; see also Unwona

Starcatherus, see Starkaðr

Starkaðr Stórvirksson (Starcatherus, Starcardus) 114 and n. 26; as foster-father of Ingjaldr, 117–21; in *Skjǫldunga saga*, 118–19 (Starcardus); in Snorri's *Ynglinga saga*, 44; in Saxo's *Gesta Danorum* (Starcatherus), 44–5, 119–21; in *Gautreks saga*, 44; unnamed Old English analogue of, 112–14

Starólfr, one of Hrólfr's men 51

Stephen of Ripon, *Vita s. Wilfridi* of 219–20

St Modwenna, Norman French poem 218

St Nostell's Church 218

Suipdagerus, champion 44

Sutton Hoo 211

Sven Aggesen 17, 80–2, 117; *Brevis historia regum Dacie* of 233, 234

Sverrir, king of Norway (1177–1202) 123

Svertingus, Saxon father-in-law of Ingialldus 118–19

Svipdagr, one of Hrólfr's men 51

Swerting, Hygelac's uncle 40

Sǫrlapáttr 198

Tatwine, priest of Breedon and archbishop of Canterbury (731–4) 151, 160, 177; *Ars grammatica* of, 160; *Aenigmata* of, 160, 177, 322 and n. 100; acrostic signature of, 323

Thegan, biographer of Louis the Pious 223

Theoderic (Hug-Dietrich), son of Clovis 165–6

Theoderic, prefect of Italy (493–526) 166

Theodulf, bishop of Orléans 14, 146

Thingfrith, father of Offa king of Mercia 268; see also Tuinfredus

Thomas of Marlborough, *Chronicon abbatiae de Evesham* of 305, 319–20

Thonar, see Þórr

Thorkelin transcripts, 4 and n. 5,

'Thryth' ('Modthryth', Fremu) ix, 3, 226–9, 251, 295

Tidbald, abbot 152 (fig. 3)

Tidfrith, bishop of Dunwich 138 n. 34, 139 (fig. 1), 250

Tidwulf, Mercian ealdorman 303 (fig. 9)

Tilberht, abbot 152 (fig. 3), 153 (fig. 4)

Tribal Hidage, The 273, 295

Tuinfredus (Thingfrith), father of Offanus 235, 236

Turnus, king of the Rutuli 3, 14, 100, 124–30

Uffi, Uffo, see Offa of Angeln

Uhtred, Mercian ealdorman of Beornwulf 302

Úlfr Uggason, Icelandic poet, *Húsdrápa* of 197 and n. 10, 204, 206

Ulysses 33, 86; see also Odysseus

Unferth, 30 n. 159, 49, 52, 72, 75, 101, 116, 128, 173

Unwona (Unwana), bishop of Leicester (*c.*785–*c.*800) vii, xiii, 3, 132, 138–4, 157, 193, 243, 244 (fig. 5), 259 (fig. 6); career profile of, 139 (fig. 1), 155; priest abbots of, 144 (fig. 2); as 'Speratus', 3, 100, 138; in *Vitae duorum Offarum*, 142, 236, 241

Utel, bishop of Hereford 138 n. 34, 139 (fig. 1)

Vainglory, sententious Old English poem 208

Váli, born to avenge 199

Venus, mother of Aeneas 11, 13

Vercelli *Homilies* 98 (IV)

Vergil, 39; *Aeneid* of 7, 50, 124, 195; *Georgics* of, 160 n. 19; read by Tatwine, 160; read in York, 14; read in Francia, 14–15; *Aeneid* of and *Beowulf* 2, 3,

Vergil (*cont.*)
7–14, 39, 80–94, 124–30, 254, 309;
see also *Beowulf*
Véseti, one of Hrólfr's men 51
Vésteinn, 304, 321; Norse analogue of
Weohstan the Wægmunding 59; fights
for Aðils against Áli, 59
Viðrir, see Óðinn
Viggo, see Vǫggr
Víkarsbálkr, poem about Starkaðr, 45
Viking Age, see Danes
Virgil, see Vergil
Virgin, see St Mary
Visio s. Pauli 3, 90, 92, 95, 99; and
Redaction XI, 95–6
Vita Ælfredi, see Asser
Vita Alcuini 14
Vita et miracula s. Kenelmi, see Cynehelm
Vita s. Guthlaci, see Felix
Vita s. Liudgeri 22, 23–4
Vita s. Wilfridi, see Stephen of Ripon
Vita s. Willibrordi 195, 200 n. 22
Vita s. Wulframni 21
Vitae duorum Offarum 142, 212 n. 71; see
also Offa king of Mercia
Vitae s. Modwennae, see Conchubranus,
Geoffrey of Burton
Vitae s. Samsonis (I and II) 70–1, 185–6
Vǫggr, Hrólfr's avenger (V(W)iggo,
Woggerus) 58, 61, 65; etymology of
name of, 60
Vǫlsungr, father of Sigmundr and Norse
analogue of Wæls 122
Vǫlsunga saga 70
Vǫluspá, Icelandic sibylline poem
(*c*.1000) 199, 202, 204, 206, 310
Vǫttr, Danish earl and one of Hrólfr's
men 51–2, 203

Wada, Northumbrian ealdorman 214
Wægmundings 28, 60–1, 64–5; name of,
60–1, 143, 299–301; see also Weohstan
Wærmund, father of Offa of
Angeln 228–9
Wærmund, bishop of Rochester 138 n.
34, 139 (fig. 1)

Waldere, Old English minor heroic
poem 21 n. 89, 57, 196
Waltharius, German Latin poem 14 and
n. 58
Waten, see Óðinn
Wat's Dyke 278
Wealhtheow, queen of the Danes 3, 40,
72, 100; tribal origin of, 129; believes in
Beowulf, 101; but puts him down in
Heorot, speaking instead for Hrothulf,
83, 103 n. 7, 103–6, 127–8
(*hereri[n]c*), 131, 195, 309; gives
Beowulf a great necklace, 40, 105, 196,
207, 309
Weland the Smith 33, 167 (Welund)
Weohstan the Wægmunding viii, 59, 143;
(is dispossessed by Hygelac and) joins
up with Onela 64, 257, 295, 305; kills
Eanmund, 286; gives Wiglaf
Eanmund's sword, 59–60; as removed
by poet from Onela-Eadgils battle, 60
Weohstan, West Saxon ealdorman of
Wiltshire 290; married to Ecgberht's
sister, 275–6, 306
Werenberht, bishop of Leicester 144 (fig.
2), 244 (fig. 5), 259 (fig. 6), 260, 269
(fig. 7), 324
Werenberht, lay namesake of the
above 324, 325 (fig. 10), 329
Wermundus, king 45
Wernoth, abbot 152 (fig. 3), 153 (fig. 4)
West Tanfield cross-head 183
Widsith, Old English minor heroic
poem 15, 20, 42–3, 113, 115–16, 122,
134, 196; relation of to *Beowulf*, 16–17,
116; relation to of poem on 'Hinieldus',
134, 135
Widukind, Charlemagne's Saxon
rebel 213, 222
Wigbald, West Saxon ealdorman 306
Wigberht, Mercian ealdorman (d.
c.800?) 143–4, 244 (fig. 5), 259 (fig.
6), 307
Wigberht, bishop of Sherborne (*c*.793 ×
801–816 × 824) 138 n. 34, 139
(fig. 1); training of in Glastonbury, 264,

306; goes to Rome with Wulfred (over Glastonbury?), 263–4, 306

Wigcga, Mercian ealdorman 307, 325 (fig. 10)

Wigferth, Mercian layman 143–4, 244 (fig. 5), 307

Wigferth, priest of Lichfield 150, 151

Wigfrith, secretary of Bishop Hædda 150, 151

Wigfrith, West Saxon ealdorman 306

Wigfrith, lesser West Saxon ealdorman 306

Wiggo, see Vǫggr

Wighard, archbishop of Canterbury 263

Wigheard, Mercian ealdorman of Offa 307

Wigheard, younger Mercian ealdorman of Cenwulf 143–4, 244 (fig. 5), 259 (fig. 6), 269 (fig. 7), 279 (fig. 8), 307

Wigheard, even younger Mercian layman 269 (fig. 7), 307–8, 325 (fig. 10)

Wighelm, Mercian layman 143–4, 279 (fig. 8), 303 (fig. 9), 308, 325 (fig. 10); as killed with Beornwulf, 302

Wiglaf the Wægmunding, son of Weohstan viii, 1, 2, 3, 16, 52, 65, 225, 254, 296; introduced in *Beowulf*, 58, 298; family relationship to Beowulf of, 58–62, 297–301; grows up in Sweden, 257, 306; speaks before helping Beowulf, 54–5, 56, 57; comments critically upon Beowulf's death, 171, 310; prominence of in *Beowulf*, 1; creation of in *Beowulf*, 36; cast as Simon Peter, 74, 134, 310; as Beowulf's rightful royal heir, 299–301; as Hrothgar's spiritual heir, 309–12

Wiglaf, king of Mercia (827–8, 829–39), ix, 1, 2, 132, 143, 151, 225; family of, 143, 150, 244 (fig. 5), 303 (fig. 9), 307–8; presumed distant West Saxon relatives of, 306–7; slump in family fortunes of after Ecgfrith's reign, 307–8; as removing Ludeca, 301–2, 305; other machinations of to become king, 301–5; joint regency of with Wigmund,

305; as king of Mercia, 313–16, 328–31; entombed in Repton, 150; kindred of takes over in Mercia, 303 (fig. 9); death of, 319; association of with Abbot Eanmund, 325 (fig. 10); as patron of *Beowulf*, 1–4, 65, 225, 297–316, 330–1

Wiglaf, younger kinsman of King Wiglaf 303 (fig. 9), 325 (fig. 10), 329

Wiglecus, later husband of Herminthrutha 235

Wigmund, prince or king, son of Wiglaf viii, 143; as *filius regis*, 303 (fig. 9); dates of, 304; married to Ælfflæd, Ceolwulf's daughter, 304; early death of, 319 (dysentery), 328

Wigmund, priest abbot of Unwona (*c*.792–814 × 816) vii, 3, 142, 143–6, 152 (fig. 3); as abbot of Breedon, 100, 146–55, 194, 241, 269 (fig. 7); alternates rankings with Forthred, 145; Mercian kindred of, 143, 150, 244 (fig. 5), 303 (fig. 9), 307–8; presumed West Saxon relatives of, 306–7; Abbot Eanmund as successor of, 152 (fig. 3), 324

Wigstan Wigmunding, saint and grandson of King Wiglaf 150, 151, 304, 328; speaks out against mother's marriage with Berhtfrith, 319; killed by Berhtfrith, 304–5, 319–20; relics of translated from Repton to Evesham, 305

Wigthegn, bishop of Winchester (*c*.813–*c*.825) 306

Wihtred, abbot 152 (fig. 3), 153 (fig. 4)

Wijnaldum, W. Friesland 20

Wilferth, abbot 152 (fig. 3)

Wilfrid, bishop in Northumbria and Mercia (d. 709) 159, 219–20

Wilheard, abbot of Canterbury 151–2, 152 (fig. 3), 153 (fig. 4), 154

William of Jumièges, *Gesta Normannorum ducum* of 81

William of Malmesbury, *De antiquitate Glastonie ecclesie* of 261–2, 263, 268

Willibrord, saint and missionary 22, 195, 211

Winberhtus, Kynedritha's evil aide 242–3, 246; see also Wynberht

Wine(f)redus, birth-name of Offanus 235, 238

Wingbald, see Wigbald

Winnili, later the Longobards 38

Wiohthun, bishop of Selsey 138 n. 34, 139 (fig. 1)

Wistanstow (Shrops.), Wistow (Leics.) 150

Withergyld, imagined Heathobard 113

Witserchus, one of Rolvo's men 50, 51, 114

Woggerus, see Vǫggr

Wonders of the East, The, 4 and n. 7

World Serpent, 30–1; see also Þórr

Wulf Wonreding, Geatish champion 63, 64, 256, 257, 264, 306

Wulfheard, East Anglian abbot 136 n. 24, 152 (fig. 3)

Wulfheard, West Saxon ealdorman 292

Wulfhere, king of Mercia (658–74) 287

Wulfred, archbishop of Canterbury (805–836) viii, 258, 259 (fig. 6), 269 (fig. 7), 279 (fig. 8), 303 (fig. 9); feud of with Cenwulf over (Glastonbury and other) minsters, 261–6; as sheltering ex-King Eardwulf, 219; and Pope Leo's envoys, 217; territorial interests of, 259–60; goes to Rome with Bishop Wigberht, 263–4, 306; Council of Chelsea of, 264; office of closed down for six years, 264, 295; deal between and Ceolwulf, 282; patronage of Beornwulf of, 282–3, 296; mistrust of Ecgberht of, 315; friendship of with Wiglaf, 313–15;

gets back Minster in Thanet and Reculver from Cwenthryth, 285; as a model for Hrothgar, 312–16

Wulfstan, archbishop of Worcester and York (d. 1023) 34; *De falsis deis* of, 34; Law-Codes of, 88; cited by John Leland, 273

Wulfstan, bishop of Worcester (1062–95) 293

Wymeswold (Leics.) 148, 324

Wymondham (Leics., Norf.) 148

Wynberht, Mercian ealdorman (executioner of King Æthelberht?) 242–3, 244 (fig. 5)

wyrsan wigfrecan 41, 166–8

Ynglinga saga, see Snorri Sturluson

Ynglingatal (c. 890) see Þjóðólfr of Hvinir

Yngvo, king of the Swedes 44

Ypper, father of Dan 80

Yrsa, mother of Hrólfr Helgason 61

Þjóðólfr of Hvinir, *Ynglingatal* of 44, 46 n. 38, 51, 59, 117, 321; *Haustlǫng* of, 198 n. 12, 202

Þórir Hound's Foot, Bǫðvarr bjarki's brother 47

Þormóðr kolbrúnarskáld, reciter of *Bjarkamál* 50, 56

Þórr, son of Óðinn 30–31, 48, 114; as Thonar, 221; killed by the World Serpent, 206; and St Michael, 203, 205; and the World Serpent in *Beowulf*, 202–205, 310

Þórsdrápa (c.985) 202

Þrymskviða 202

Þǫkk, cave giantess 199–200

Zeus 11